Athene Series

An International Collection of Feminist Books

General Editors: Gloria Bowles, Renate Klein, Janice Raymond
Consulting Editor: Dale Spender

The Athene Series assumes that all those who are concerned with formulating explanations of the way the world works need to know and appreciate the significance of basic feminist principles.

The growth of feminist research internationally has called into question almost all aspects of social organization in our culture. The Athene Series focuses on the construction of knowledge and the exclusion of women from the process—both as theorists and as subjects of study—and offers innovative studies that challenge established theories and research.

Athene, the Olympian goddess of wisdom, was honored by the ancient Greeks as the patron of arts and sciences and guardian of cities. She represented both peace and the intellectual aspect of war. Her mother, Metis, was a Titan and presided over all knowledge. While pregnant with Athene, Metis was swallowed whole by Zeus. Some say this was his attempt to embody her supreme wisdom. The original Athene is thus twice born: once of her strong mother, Metis, and once more out of the head of Zeus. According to feminist myth, there is a "third birth" of Athene when she stops being an agent and mouthpiece of Zeus and male dominance, and returns to her original source: the wisdom of womankind.

Men's Studies Modified: *The Impact of Feminism on the Academic Disciplines*
Dale Spender, Editor

Woman's Nature:
Rationalizations of Inequality
Marian Lowe and **Ruth Hubbard,** Editors

Machina Ex Dea:
Feminist Perspectives on Technology
Joan Rothschild, Editor

Science and Gender: *A Critique of Biology and Its Theories on Women*
Ruth Bleier

Men's Ideas / Women's Realities:
Popular Science, 1870-1915
Louise Michele Newman, Editor

Black Feminist Criticism:
Perspectives on Black Women Writers
Barbara Christian

The Sister Bond:
A Feminist View of a Timeless Connection
Toni A. H. McNaron, Editor

Educating for Peace:
A Feminist Perspective
Birgit Brock-Utne

Stopping Rape:
Successful Survival Strategies
Pauline B. Bart and **Patricia H. O'Brien**

Teaching Technology from a Feminist Perspective: *A Practical Guide*
Joan Rothschild

THE
KNOWLEDGE
EXPLOSION

GENERATIONS OF FEMINIST SCHOLARSHIP

Edited by

CHERIS KRAMARAE
and
DALE SPENDER

ATHENE
SERIES

TEACHERS COLLEGE PRESS
Teachers College, Columbia University
New York and London

Published by Teachers College Press, 1234 Amsterdam Avenue, New York, New York

Library of Congress Cataloging-in-Publication Data

The Knowledge explosion : generations of feminist scholarship / edited
    by Cheris Kramarae and Dale Spender. — 1st ed.
        p.   cm. — (The Athene series)
    Includes bibliographical references and indexes.
    ISBN 0-8077-6258-X (alk. paper)—ISBN 0-8077-6257-1 (pbk.; alk. paper).
    1. Women scholars—United States. 2. Women's studies—United
States. 3. Feminism—United States.   I. Kramarae, Cheris.
  II. Spender, Dale.   III. Series.
HQ1397.K63   1992
305.42'0973—dc20   91-14334

Printed on acid-free paper

Manufactured in the United States of America

99 98 97 96 95 94 93 92   8 7 6 5 4 3 2 1

Contents

Contents   ix

PART II   DEBATES

Exploding Knowledge

Cheris Kramarae
Dale Spender

This volume is a testimony to the scholarship and successful achievements of Women's Studies over the last decades. While there are many areas in which the aims and explanations of Women's Studies have not been achieved (particularly in relation to our own personal/political pressures), it is also important to note that there are some areas of achievement (particularly in relation to the exposure of the construction of knowledge and the power of the academy) that go beyond even the wildest dreams of some of the early academic activists. Women's Studies has gone a long way, and the fact that it has not reached its desired destination should not stop us from appreciating the distances that have been travelled and the enormous gains that have been made. In many institutions, there is cause for commendation, and celebration.

Celebration because, as this volume makes clear, the development of Women's Studies, and its ways of knowing, constitute a challenge to some of the patterns of power and influence in academe. Women's Studies explodes the traditional knowledge-making practices, and their products.

CHRONOLOGY: PROMISE AND PROGRESS

The history of the challenges to established practices has sometimes seemed a simple—but significant—one. Until relatively recently, when women identified the limitations of their particular discipline (and the overwhelming absence of women) they believed that what was needed was for women to work together to remedy such omissions within the frameworks of their own disciplines. But as more women talked with each other *across* disciplines, there was the realization that this was not a problem only of an individual discipline: rather than the failure of the discipline, perhaps it was the process of knowledge making itself that was at issue?

With the recognition of a common problem came a critical change in focus. From the limitations of knowledge within each discipline there was a shift in attention to the knowledge makers. The way was open to move from the acceptance of disciplinary knowledge as objective, impartial, and neutrally discovered; the way was open for women to see that knowledge was constructed. Knowledge was constructed thus: that there was no knowledge without knowledge makers, and that those who were responsible for making the knowledge were almost exclusively male: that far from being objective, and impartial, disciplinary knowledge was the product of a particular group of men whose subjectivity,

1

partiality, priorities, and power base were deeply embedded in the knowledge-making process.

Analyses across disciplines revealed that little or nothing was known about women. What was "known" about women was invariably formulated by men who quite clearly didn't know or didn't care about women's lives and women's realities (see Mary Roth Walsh, this volume).

Confronted with the omissions, the indifference (or hostility) to women, and the resistance to change in the academic mind-set on what constituted legitimacy or "proof," women had to develop strategies for transforming the way knowledge was constructed in general and within their specific disciplines. Depending on the discipline, the training, the paradigm, and the perceived possibilities, different explanations about the particular causes for the problems, and different programs for action have been forthcoming. And while there has been both isolated and collective interdisciplinary corrective effort, there remains the belief (or keen hope) among many of us that the progress made in some other discipline is greater than our own.

Given all the differences in background and interpretation, the contributors to this volume have come to comparable conclusions; that after decades of feminist[1] activity and Women's Studies achievement—much of which is documented here—the patterns of power and privilege within the academy have been disturbed rather than dislodged. The contributions in this collection suggest that while the problem and possibilities differ in the various disciplines, and while some disciplines have recognized and valued some aspects of the feminist knowledge explosion, the malestream critics in all disciplines continue to actively resist feminist restructuring of knowledge even while incorporating some of the knowledges generated by feminist scholars.

So the success story is double edged. Some of the insights about the nature of knowledge, about multiple realities (of female experience), of difference, of dominance, and the politics of research, have been "appropriated" by the academy without necessarily advantaging women or leading to positive changes within the discipline.

FEMINIST FRAMEWORK

It is now almost 3 decades since women in numbers first started to voice their concerns and dissatisfaction with the knowledge that was made available in the academy; the difference between that early apprehension and the current established position of Women's Studies within the academy and across cultures is nothing short of a revolution.

The diversity and development of Women's Studies scholarship and programs is well documented within this collection, and while there are almost as many ways of introducing Women's Studies as there are courses, projects, and programs, there is generally a consensus about the nature of the feminist framework and the purpose of Women's Studies knowledge making within the academy.

Part of the rationale for working for a Women's Studies place within the knowledge-making institution of college/university was to provide a "safe house" for women. A space where women students and faculty, from different backgrounds with different experience, perspectives, and priorities, could explore their realities as women, and their own many explanations in a relatively safe environment. It was to be a safe space which provided the opportunities for a range of people to work together for change with enthusiasm and vigor; where they would learn to value other people in other places who could have different perspectives and priorities. And it was also be a place which afforded a measure of protection for women. (Joni Seager, this volume, points out that women's perceptions of "safe" or "unsafe" environments are markedly different from men's, with many fewer "safe" places for women.)

Given the hostility toward this naming of experience by women, in both the wider world and the academic institution (see Susan Arpad, this volume), the provision of a safe home base was a fundamental necessity and a monumental achievement.

From the outset in so-called western countries Women's Studies was referred to as "the academic arm of the women's *liberation* movement," a label with "political" overtones. The *ideology of knowledge construction* within Women's Studies stood in sharp contrast to the ideology of knowledge construction within the university. Whereas the model of the academy was one which proclaimed that knowledge was pursued for its own sake, and that those who "wrote it up" were merely impartial recorders, with no responsibility to the local or global community, the ideology of Women's Studies was one of a declaration of interest (see Shulamit Reinharz, this volume).

The purpose of Women's Studies was to enable women to become authorities on their own lives; to construct their own knowledge about women according to their criteria as women; to empower themselves through knowledge making. But even this was not sufficient to encompass the purpose of the exercise. Unlike the traditional ideology which disclaimed any responsibility for the knowledge that it generated, Women's Studies insisted on the ideology of accountability. Central to the practices of Women's Studies scholarship was the principle that the knowledges which were forged in its name should be subjected to rigorous scrutiny to ensure that the interests of women were being served and that a contribution was being made to the development of a better world. Women's Studies made its politics explicit; knowledge which exploited, oppressed, destroyed, should not be justified.

Such a departure from the conventional practices was understandably perceived as threatening to the established power bases within the university: this made the presences of a "safe house" even more desirable and necessary.

Some of the impetus for the accountability of Women's Studies knowledges came from the links between the academy and the community (see Pat Cramer and Ann Russo, this volume). Sometimes there was a partnership between academic women and community women. Sometimes women outside the university were making gains while women with similar training and concerns in the academy were having more difficulty (see Elizabeth Wood, this volume). But it is important to note that these states are not mutually exclusive as many of the authors in this volume can testify; sometimes the academic woman *is* also the activist in the community.

Structured on an exchange between the academy and the community, the avowed intentions of Women's Studies scholarship are often at odds with the prevailing values of the institution. On campuses, across cultures, feminists have struggled against the opposition to their activities and have searched for stable, funded, "safe houses" for Women's Studies programs. They have tried to provide places where women's knowledges can be constructed so that the work of transforming the curriculum, of building alliances and sharing resources, can be conducted without impediment.

And what must be taken into account when the extent to which Women's Studies has grown and multiplied is recognized, is that these radical developments were not the brain-child of the central administration. Many are the women (and in some places some men) who have fought long and hard to have these spaces made available. Behind most Women's Studies programs there is a struggle which persisted for years as feminists (or even one feminist) tried to convince the administrators of the need for the program. And although we are aware, usually we are not sufficiently explicit about the role played by women outside the academy in helping to get these programs established. But for the theory, activism, and courage of those in the grassroots communities, in national and global contexts, Women's Studies in its present proliferated form would assuredly not exist. (See Leslie Weisman, this volume, for reports of some out-of-school academic programs.)

Tribute must also be paid to the Women's Studies teachers who frequently laid the foundation stones with their unpaid, extra-curricular labor. (The editors of this volume met when they were conducting Women's Studies discussion groups outside their teaching hours, with students who had no safe place to voice their problems, protests, or perplexities.) This extra work remains a part of the lives of most Women's Studies teachers, as individually and in collective actions they work to maintain and strengthen Women's Studies programs.

So vast and varied have been the contributions made to the development of Women's Studies, by so many individuals, that it is not always easy to identify the common characteristics of these efforts. But if there is one quality which is indicative of the commitment to the growth and development of Women's Studies and feminist knowledges, it is that of the sheer energy which has gone into its achievement.

The amount of work which has been required is quite astonishing: the time and effort it has taken to challenge the process of knowledge making and to critique and "correct" disciplinary "bias": to do the necessary researching, teaching, and publishing (not to mention the applications for grants and funding); to support women, to support women students and women teachers, and to support women within the professional associations through everything from direct action to committee attendance, caucusing, and lobbying. This activity is all the more remarkable in the light of the many other responsibilities which women assume, and which are expected of them as part of the unequal division of labor (see Patricia Thompson; Marilyn Waring, this volume); and all the more admirable given the discouragement and hostility that women routinely encounter.

It was precisely because we wanted to document the achievements of feminist knowledge makers, and of Women's Studies, usually against the odds—and certainly "in defiance of the evidence" as Elaine Rueben (1978) declared at one of the early conferences on feminist scholarship—that the contributions in this book have been brought together. We wanted to set down for the record the work that women have done in all its many forms, and to assess the impact that this knowledge making has had upon the academy.[2] From the outset we recognized that we would also be documenting the resistance to women's initiatives, authority, and autonomy.

THE POLITICS OF LEGITIMACY

Changing the Models of Knowledge Making

The purpose of this volume is to assess the impact that Women's Studies has had on the theory and practice of knowledge making. It is clear that as the models of knowledge construction themselves change, partly as a response to feminist pressure, Women's Studies is both advantaged, and obstructed, by these shifts.

Virtually everyone has the capacity to "construct" knowledge; but traditionally only a few people have possessed the power to decree which knowledge will count for the culture, and which will not. Different societies have different privileged groups who have decided what is valid, and within western society there have been different arbiters at different times. Prior to the scientific revolution, for example, it was the priests of the church who were charged with the responsibility of determining what was true and what was false; so the world was made in six days and any alternate constructions of knowledge were not only "wrong," invalid, and heresy, they were likely to result in the punishment of the presumptuous knowledge-maker.

To some extent the conflict between Copernicus, Galileo (and later Darwin, of course) was the contest between the old belief system and the new. And with the triumph of the "scientific dogma" and its particular world view came a new breed of "priests"—the scientists—who could distinguish truth from error. Marion Lowe (this volume) points out that the world view presented by science is so prevasive that many people have come to believe it is the only possible or only correct view. Scientists set up the criteria of "scientific methodology" which, like that of its predecessor, "clerical dogma," asserted that there was only one truth. But whereas the church had claimed that their truth was revealed by divine inspiration, the scientists claimed that their truth was revealed by objectivity and proof.

Scientific method has been formulated from a linear view of the world in which there is a direct relationship between cause and effect. There can be no doubt that this has been a highly productive model in terms of the sophisticated technology that it has produced; the entire range of scientific and technological products from airplanes, microwaves, and computers to nuclear power, reproductive technology, and genetic engineering. But like all the earlier dogmas which decreed what was true and what was false the scientific dogma also has been exposed as having its own deficiencies (see Robyn Arianrhod, this volume; and see Autumn Stanley, this volume, for discussion of what has been considered valuable "technology.") There is much that is left out; there is much about the objects and events of the world which the linear, cause-effect model cannot explain.

And within the last decade it has been ecology, spirituality, and environmental studies and their "dogmas" which have constituted an increasing challenge to the capacity of scientific methodology to provide adequate analyses, answers, and accountability (see Carol Christ; Irene Diamond; H. Patricia Hynes, this volume).

Again the old belief system is often in conflict with the new as the ecologists assert that the world we are trying to explain is more complex and interconnected than the simple cause-effect model can suggest. For example, only with a linear model of cause and effect could the consequences of the pill be called "side effects." In a more interconnected context, it would be perfectly clear that these "side effects" are the products of pill taking, directly and indirectly.

But the emerging, credible ecological world view also has its precedents and interconnections. In the shift from objectivity and one truth, to a more value-laden and pluralistic world view, feminism has made a significant contribution. Along with the knowledge-making movements of other subordinated, invisible groups, including Afro-American Studies (see Rose Brewer, this volume), Women's Studies practitioners "defied the evidence"; and it wasn't always easy.

From One to Many Truths

Confronted with the massive bias—a singularly inappropriate term for the wholesale exclusion of women, from the knowledge on and about humanity—feminists insisted that meanings made in the name of objectivity simply were not good enough. (After all, this was the science which produced proof that women were not as intellectually competent, and that if educated, their brains would burst and their uteruses atrophy). A better, more comprehensive model was required. And Women's Studies as a discipline argued for its own style, its own dogma, its own validity, its own truths. The fact that the last 2 decades have witnessed the emergence of a plurality of truths within the academy is partly the result of feminist intervention.

When it was held that there was only *one* truth, the prized state promised by objectivity and the pursuit of a rigorous scientific methodology, the feminist insistence that there was *more than one truth*—more than one history (see Jane Lewis, this volume), more than one legal interpretation (see Jocelynne Scutt, this volume) and more than one sociological explanation (see Liz Stanley, this volume)—struck at the heart of scientific dogma.

How could there be more than one truth in a system that admits only one without the system being undermined? From the first ventures into the academic forum, the feminist insistence on the inclusion of women's experiences, on incorporating the views and values which were not encoded in the traditional system, was a constant and critical challenge to academic convention.

And, of course, within Women's Studies the concept of a single explanation was abandoned. Women's Studies, of necessity, moved away from the single, fixed truth, revealed by objectivity, and in declaring that the values of the knowledge maker are an integral part of the knowledge making, Women's Studies formulated its own dogma designed to account for its own origins.

Within Women's Studies the emphasis on—and the tolerance for—the plurality of shifting interpretations derived from different experience is still upheld. Whatever the approaches used most frequently these days—postmodernism, French feminisms, deconstructionism, ecofeminism (see Mary Ellen Capek, this volume)—we should not overlook the role that feminist scholarship has played in shifting the criteria of knowledge making. Feminist scholarship has helped to formulate a model which values plurality and commonality, which presupposes diversity as well as interconnectedness.

The move has not just been to plurality, to the possibility of many *fixed* truths; it has also been to a more *fluid* state of understanding. So that even the many truths are treated as transitory, as undergoing constant change. This is why it is inappropriate to envisage feminism as a state which can be achieved—and why the term *postfeminism* is even less appropriate! For feminism is not a single fixed state. It is an evolving and changing charter for a way of living—as illustrated by the Six Point Group, for example, which was formed in England after some women got the vote in 1919. (The women concerned were prepared to insist that there were six points which remained on their feminist agenda, the first one being the right of *all* women to vote. Over the years, as each point was achieved, another was automatically added to the list, on the grounds that there was always more work to be done in attaining a just and equitable society.)

The Six Point Group was disbanded in the 1960s; but despite the achievements since that time there would be no problem in finding Six Points for inclusion if the group were to be revived. There is no one feminist platform or feminist policy, such as traditional political parties have. Rather, many scholars and activists are involved in a global-variety of campaigns, programs, and research.

Including the Variables

It is this multilayered and ever-moving model which is central to the construction of feminist knowledges, which is gaining favor in a wider context, and which is making its mark (albeit unevenly) on the disciplines. Rather than a ritualistic incantation of an inventory of dimensions—such as gender, race, sexual orientation, etc.—there is a growing appreciation fostered by feminist scholarship that human experience is multidimensional and that the one individual can be a member of a particular dominant group (white, educated, able bodied, etc.), *and at the same time* a full member of another dominated, exploited group (sexual orientation, age, ability, etc.).

So instead of ordering and ranking a set of hierarchical oppressions, instead of fixing the boundaries between bands of experience and attempting to eliminate and control the variables, Women's Studies as a way of knowing has shifted toward tracing the many intersections and to noting the flow between the many sources of experience (see Maxine Baca Zinn, this volume). This movement beyond traditional divisions, this emphasis on continual exchange, has also had implications for the disciplines; interdisciplinary, cross-disciplinary, or multidisciplinary approaches are favored (for example, see Jane Jaquette; Carole Ogelsby and Christine Shelton, this volume).

Part of the art of feminist scholarship is keeping all these variables *in* (rather than keeping them out, which was the custom under the conventional model); feminist scholarship not only tries to include all the contradictions, it even tries to bring all the variables of the *researcher into the research*! And while it may be a more complex process and a more difficult exercise to develop an *inclusive* form of knowledge construction which looks for meaning in the wider context rather than in the smallest possible units, the establishment of such a goal is consistent with feminist ideology.

Breaking Set

Other pressures are also functioning to break the set and ordered patterns of many knowledge-making practices; with the ability to move from one source to another, to assess information from many different perspectives, and to identify some of the connections which can be generated, the new electronic media are making their own contributions to the process. There is an enormous qualitative difference between looking up a definition set in a print form, and in shifting in and out of the various possibilities of hypercard, for example (see Suzanne Damarin, this volume).

Set solutions have been replaced by processes, by evolving interconnected and cyclical explanations. While to some extent Women's Studies has been leading the way with the generation of new models of knowledge making, there are many disciplines, departments, even institutions, which are resistant or antagonistic to such fundamental changes and which continue to depend upon traditional forms of assessment. From within their conventional framework such disciplines can continue to claim the value-free and superior nature of their own knowledge making, and they can level accusations of partisanship, polemic, politics—and a lack of rigor, originality (see Berenice Carroll, this volume), and an absence of standards—at Women's Studies scholarship. Which is one reason Women's Studies does not always sit comfortably with institutionalized practices; and one way that its influence can be constrained.

The Value of "Value-free" Research

It could also be argued quite convincingly in Western societies that the traditional model of knowledge making which the university has advanced—that of the "apolitical," objective, impartial, and unaccountable pursuit of knowledge for its own sake—is a form which is fast losing credibility; and that the university as an institution could well lose some if its influence to other centers of knowledge making (e.g., electronic media, marketing and advertising agencies, which take more cognizance of the relationship between knowledge making and values, between information and presentation, and which are more inclined to explore rather than deny the possibilities of knowledge, manipulation, and exploitation.)

But to take a value stand, to declare itself for or against particular views, would demand an enormous shift in the ideology of the academy; to present itself as a "green" university which is concerned to produce information that is consistent with green politics, or to state its knowledge-making position in relation to peace studies, or third world development and exploitation (see Claudia Salazar, this volume), for example, would be to transform the theory, practice, and purpose of educational institutions. It would also make them places much more conducive to feminist knowledge construction, for in Women's Studies the politics of the personal are proclaimed.

Double Standard

Currently, however, the double standard of legitimation continues to prevail. So the established model of knowledge making—along with the sex associated with its making—are accorded more authority and more validity than the recently generated feminist models, and the women who created them. The word of a man counts for more than the word of a woman.

The male still holds the monopoly on intellectual authority. The male is still considered to be rational objective, superior; this appropriation of intellectuality is summed up in the phrase, a masculine mind. It remains a compliment "to think like a man" and an insult "to think like a woman." This double standard plays its part in the politics of legitimation and permeates the scholarly (and the wider) community.

It works to discourage feminist scholars from making links with groups, projects, institutions that are not suitably sanitized (or male sanctioned) for academic purposes. Yet it is vital that women in the academy make and maintain these alliances which help them go beyond their own biographical limitations. For unless women within the academy consciously look for what they do not know, they are likely to replicate the very values and vices of the institution they are trying to transform; white women, for example, are liable to miss some of the massive social issues which are part of racism if they confine their experiences and inspiration to the horizons of white-dominated universities.

Paradoxically, it can be the very strengths of Women's Studies knowledge making—the links which extend, challenge, and revise the process of construction—which render it most vulnerable, most different, and most dismissible in conventional academic circles.

Insider and Outsider

While Women's Studies may have made a major contribution to new ways of knowing, the hierarchy, which determines what counts, has not been dramatically modified. It is still mainly WHIMMs, the white, heterosexual, inside, middle-class men[3]—who have the power to pronounce on what will be validated and valued. In this politics of legitimation it is relatively easy for the insider to discount the reality and the research of the outsider (or "other") which originates in the experience of being female.

Scientific neutrality may be being threatened by some of the knowledges of Women's Studies (and other challenging intellectual movements) but it hasn't always lost its power and influence (indeed, it could even demand greater allegiance to its ideology in the face of such threat). Yet while it continues to predominate, the ideology of scientific neutrality (and its associated concepts of pure research, and hard data) can make institutions inhospitable places for women—precisely because the well-springs of women's experience and information can be the very outside and contaminating force which those in the powerful positions do not want to admit.

Even more alarming to the *insiders* can be the way in which the outsiders persist in emphasizing their difference by seeking to make their alliances *outside* the academy. Not surprisingly, the insiders can move to protect their priorities and practices with the result that women who are engaged in the work of critiquing established institutions or who are involved in activism can find themselves quickly, and categorically, discredited.

Only recently a woman academic in a prestigious U.S. university was criticized by a white member of the committee reviewing her application for tenure, for having given talks to the National Association for the Advancement of Colored People about her research on Black, urban politics when she should have been attending to her research.

Such stories of censure abound. From women who have been told that the classroom is no place for the discussion of women, to women who have been warned against bringing their politics into their teaching and research, there is ample evidence of the politics of legitimacy at work. And because there are so many ways in which the perspective and priorities of the outsider can be devalued and disqualified, numerous are the academic women who acknowledge the advisability of omitting, from their curriculum vita, their work with such groups as Lesbians Rising in Resistance, or with the local battered women's center or rape crisis counselling service. Even when their experience in these contexts is a major source of the knowledge they need and use in their research and classroom.

We note, again and again, that many men who do research on men's psychological, social, and political activities are labelled scholars; while women who focus their research on women's psychological, social, and political activities are often called political agitators or trouble makers.

These forms of discounting, discrediting, and invalidating the research and experience of women's lives are among some of the barriers which stand between Women's Studies and its impact upon the theory and practice of the academy. While there can be no doubt that Women's Studies has caused trouble across many disciplines there can be no doubt either that it has but "rocked the boat" rather than replaced the knowledge-making process with a more sea-worthy vessel. This, however, is all the more reason to continue the commitment to transformation, rather than to abandon it.

Those who are engaged in political activity outside the academy have a crucial contribution to make to the development of Women's Studies theorizing, curriculum extension, and teaching; they can provide the perspectives which allow for the necessary and more comprehensive forms of knowledge making. Yet the feminist scholar who quotes the relevant woman-activist/intellectual in most institutions can have the validity of the source questioned. (Or worse; the woman activist will be treated as an "unknown." The editors of this volume cannot be the only ones who have come up against male peers who roundly assert that they "have never heard of, never read of, never come across" the female authority we are quoting, and who then proceed to act as if this is our ignorance rather than theirs!)

Position and Perspective

Even supposedly scientifically neutral government statistics on health program recipients can assume qualitatively different dimensions when viewed through the perspective of Black activism, for example. U.S. government statistics do not state explicitly the complex oppressive interconnections between racism, poverty, and increased rates of heart disease, arthritis, diabetes, hypertensive cardiovascular, infant mortality, high blood pressure, and higher death rate from breast cancer. Angela Davis (1990), for example, does, placing these links, often unnoticed by whites, at the center of understanding. In addition, she points out that

The cycle of oppression is largely responsible for the fact that far too many Black women resort to drugs as a means—however ineffective it ultimately proves to be—of softening the blows of poverty. Because of intravenous drug use in the [U.S.] Black community a disproportionately large number of Black women have been infected with AIDS. Although the popular belief is that AIDS is a disease of gay, white men, the truth is that Afro-Americans and Latinos are far more likely to contract AIDS than whites. This is true among gays, among IV drug users, among heterosexual partners and among children . . . Latina women are nine times as likely as white women to contract AIDS . . . Black women . . . twelve times more likely. . . . (pp. 26–29)

This material and analysis, so vital for the generation of Women's Studies knowledges and for the construction of a better world, will become the substance of the research and theorizing *on* campus only if the women *off* campus are listened to. (See Joan Altekruse and Sue Rosser; Joan Mulligan, this volume, for reviews of many other health care issues.) Ruth Hubbard (1990) has stated that much of the energy, impetus, and agenda for change within the academy (and society) is more likely to be found within the women's groups which have focused on specific concerns and have produced their own knowledge, descriptions, explanations, and strategies for survival and transformation. The active theorizing of eco-feminism, reproductive technology, Australian Aboriginal Land Rights' movements, and the National Black Women's Health Project (and Our Bodies Our Selves Collective), as well as groups which have formed around the provision of clean water, the right of rural women to be counted in economic statistics, the women and AIDS crisis, women's refuges and counselling centers, are all a resourcing part of Women's Studies knowledge making, and academic women would be severed from these sources at their peril.

Yet the politics of legitimacy consistently question, undermine, and disqualify these essential inspiriting sources; much of the material in this volume documents the tension between the radical authority of women and the traditional authority of academic men.

CRITIQUE OF MALE POWER: THE ABSENCE OF AN ACCEPTABLE DISCOURSE

Another obstacle to the progress of Women's Studies knowledge making is that of the absence of an acceptable discourse for critiquing the dominance and power of males. It could be argued that men have been in charge of the language, and because they have not found their own status and privilege, vis à vis the female, problematic, they have not found it necessary to devise a code for conducting a "conversation" on this topic (see Lourdes Torres, this volume).

The absence of such a code allows individual males to respond personally and emotionally to critiques of the structure and dynamics of dominance. And while male is the norm, and as such is assumed to be unproblematic, it is those who are critical of this state who can be seen to constitute the problem. Hence the tendency to discredit feminists who critique male power (with all the names of embittered, uppity, strident, nags, even unattractive) rather than to discredit male power and its uses and abuses. By locating the problem in the women who protest, rather than in their own privilege, men can deny their own agency and further frustrate and exacerbate the position of women (see Barbara Pope, this volume).

The presence of men can also pose particular problems in the Women's Studies classroom and knowledge-making process (see Lillian Robinson, this volume). The dialogue across differences—especially hierarchical differences—can be fraught with misunderstanding and misrepresentations, not to mention penalties. Given that one of the goals behind the establishment of Women's Studies was to provide a "safe house" for women, where they could raise issues of specific concern with freedom and impunity, this "discourse difficulty" can be a deterrent and an obstruction to women's knowledge making.

The examples are numerous. Recently, at a prestigious U.S. university a group of academic women was discussing peer harassment in classrooms and the prevalence of date rape on campus. (*Date rape* is a term used to describe the rape of a woman by her date, by the male who is accompanying her. While a commonly used popular term, it does not connote the pain and anger women express when assaulted by someone who is known to them, and who in some cases has been considered a loving friend [see Jane Caputi, this volume].) From the discussions with the women who worked at the health center, who were counselling and treating the victims, it was known that many of those who had been raped were sorority members (that is, from select residential organizations). And they had almost all been raped by members of fraternities (select men's residential organizations), or by organized, popular, prestigious sports groups on campus. (This is consistent with a study carried out by staff and faculty at the University of Illinois, Urbana–Champaign 1989, where it was found that fraternity men, who comprised one quarter of the male student population, perpetrated 63% of the sexual assaults. See Ellen Sweet, 1985, and Peggy Reeves Sanday, 1990, for other studies.) This is not to say that fraternities, alone, are *the* problem. But, rather, that fraternities, like many other exclusive men's organizations, often help promote men's dominance, homophobia, and violence (Mary Anne Clawson, 1989).

This was a case where the behavior of some of the most privileged members of the student population was most problematic; but where could the criticism of the women faculty be expressed?

The women who had been raped refused to bring official charges for a variety of reasons, among them the fear that fraternity loyalty and united action might make their future life on campus miserable, even intolerable. Workers at the health center found this situation disturbing; they were working with women who knew the names of the men who had assaulted them but yet were unable to do anything officially to prevent future assaults. A further distressing issue was that they were working with women who were dealing with the aftermath of assault, who were experiencing serious difficulties with their studies, and who were, in some cases, leaving the university.

In this context the women academics felt the need to set up a series of seminars and discussions which addressed the problem of homophobia on campus, fraternity values, and the attitude they espouse toward women (Kathleen Hirsch, 1990; Patricia Yancey Martin & Robert Hummer, 1989; Peggy Reeves Sanday, 1990). They even talked about obtaining approval from the central administration for instituting such a project. And then the recognition struck; *they were assuming that they would have to get permission before they could publicly discuss the construction of masculinity, of the male rituals which condone sexual violence.*

They had assumed that they were not free to discuss fraternities, their politics and actions, and their impact on women's freedom and safety to move around the campus, without sanctions or fear of reprisals.

Every political system has its ways of discrediting and silencing its opponents and critics (witness the change in the population of political prisoners with a change in the political regime). That comparable dynamics can be seen at work in relation to political systems based on sex and race should not be surprising. But the absence of an acceptable discourse to critique male power is yet another factor which impedes the process of women's knowledge construction and which serves to contain its influence.

PENALTIES

Real penalties can be invoked against women who do break the boundaries and engage in feminist scholarship which can be perceived as threatening to the establishment. Apart from some of the penalties which have already been mentioned and which are associated with discrediting the individual, the nature of her sources, or the validity of her work, there can also be a price to be paid in terms of promotion and tenure. Feminists are not always considered the most desirable members of faculty.

Because a system of patronage still operates largely within the academy and because it is mainly men (WHIMMs) who function as "gatekeepers," determining what will be admitted to systems of knowledge—what will be funded, published, taught—there are many ways in which academic women are vulnerable. Directly and indirectly, many pressures can be brought to bear on women so that their speech and writing is constrained; and if they do persist in speaking and writing in a "subversive" manner then their appointments, promotions, or publications within the mainstream can be in jeopardy.

Of course, there is always sexual harassment. This is another factor which must be taken into account in relation to the establishment of Women's Studies teaching and research. From the time-consuming process of "female accountability" in a men's institution to the more crude attempts at intimidation, feminist scholars have their work load increased greatly in comparison to their nonfeminist peers; it would be interesting (and depressing) to study the time and energy Women's Studies practitioners expended in dealing with the male tactics of the academy and in providing reassurance to manage and preempt possible backlash.

PURPOSES OF THE UNIVERSITY

The campuses of western universities have not traditionally facilitated the aspirations of three particular groups which have been responsible for significant social change: the poor, women and men of color, and white women. The system is designed primarily to train young, middle-class white males to eventually take places of leadership in maintaining, not changing, a patriarchal system. As is pointed out in the article on education (see Dale Spender, this volume), while women have won the battle for equal education with men, they have not won the battle to change "men's education" so that it includes women's values. In her article "People of Color at White Elitist Colleges," Denise Tuggle (1990) states, "It's a common saying at Bryn Mawr that it teaches you to be a white man, which I always thought was funny"; but as she goes on to say, it's not funny if you are not white, or male, and if you don't want to be white or male, not even in an honorary capacity (p. 63).

People of color and poor women and men seldom manage to circumvent the many barriers to their entrance to universities, so their voices and values are seldom heard. This makes universities very peculiar communities where the standards of "merit," "rigor," and "impartiality" function to obstruct the encoding of knowledge from these points of view. Even where women, men of color, and the poor do gain entry, they can find that there is little authentic knowledge about their existence available on the library shelves, and that what is there is not necessarily considered appropriate curriculum material.

Many chapters in this volume focus on the way that woman has been treated as object in much of the research encoded by men; people of color have been objectified when studied by whites, and the poor when studied by the privileged. (Feminist scholars sometimes draw attention to the way those with resources study those without, whereas there is no established tradition of those without resources studying those with; so bureaucrats commission studies of the poor, judges call for reports on deviants, and sociologists study the workers at the coal face/mine—while the poor have little or no opportunity to study the bureaucrats, few studies have been commissioned on the values, life styles, and personalities of judges, and not many workers have had a chance to study sociologists at work, to name but a few. This one-way flow of information, whereby the insiders can construct knowledge about the outsiders, can become an increasingly important and inequitable factor in an information revolution.)

Feminist scholarship has also helped to expose the way those with power have encoded knowledge about those out of power in ways that rationalize differences in prestige and privilege, and maintain the status quo. The *differences* in the lives of women, men of color, and the poor are presented by many academic projects and publications as forms of deficiency which disqualify them from membership as part of the university meritocracy.

Race labels have historically been used to establish a hierarchy of intelligence and ability levels on the basis of such physical differences as skin color and facial features. But there is little research on the hierarchies themselves; on who made them up, whose knowledge they represent, and why to WHIMMs such hierarchies are not problematic.

We know from our histories of the academy, and from the history and philosophy of ideas, that it is possible to "prove" almost anything (which is one reason that a more reliable form of knowledge making is called for.) But given that almost anything can be "proven," it is necessary to ask why particular researchers are so keen to "prove" particular points. Putting the values of the researchers into the research provides a framework for asking questions about why the researchers seek the findings that they do; why studies to show that women have smaller brain capacity than men, why research to demonstrate that Blacks are better at physical than mental tasks? Because the way the question is asked helps to determine the answer that can be given, it is in order to question the researchers' questions; and even studies directed toward finding the *comparability* of sex brain size or the *intellectual achievements* of Blacks would produce fundamentally different results, in terms of research and in terms of social hierarchies!

PRIORITIES OF WOMEN'S STUDIES

Whether to form Women's Studies bases *within* individual disciplines, whether to form a Women's Studies base *outside* the existing disciplines—whether to do both, or neither: these questions about the location of Women's Studies have had to be addressed. In which context would Women's Studies be safest, strongest, the most influential? Is there a best place for the production of Women's Studies knowledge, or does this too change with changing circumstances?

And what about the different views and values of Women's Studies practitioners? How can they be best accommodated within the academy, and facilitate the construction of knowledge which empowers women?

As has been suggested, universities are open and affordable only to those who have the opportunity, encouragement, and willingness to learn how to "do" traditional education. This includes learning sufficient sexism, racism, classism, and homophobia—all integral elements of the meritocratic model of formal education—in order to come up to standard. Not surprisingly, many women in academe (students and teachers) have learnt well what they have been taught; they have come to accept the institutionalized biases of privilege and take these perspectives with them into the Women's Studies arena. These power configurations exist, in varying degrees, in the articulation of problems—at an individual, community, or country level.

How these issues are handled is often associated with how they are labelled; who does the naming, and defining, is as important a controversy inside Women's Studies as it is in relation to it. This is one reason for the focus on terminology, on metaphor and image in feminist scholarship. Whereas traditional work in most disciplines often treats language as an unproblematic tool, as a conduit which merely works to transfer ideas from one person to another, or to "neutrally" record the research findings which are consistent with established values and politics, feminists have developed new terminology and have formulated new woman-defined categories to more accurately reflect their own knowledge making. (*A Feminist Dictionary* documents some of this work by hundreds of linguistically creative scholars [Cheris Kramarae, Paula Treichler, with Ann Russo, 1985].) This search for authenticity is demanding in terms of time and conciliation.

Because thinking is enmeshed with the language we use, it is as critical to change the language as it is to change the thinking and the social/political organization. So, for example, the vocabulary of our relationship to nature has become problematic if we are to have a more interconnected and less hierarchical identification. Elizabeth Dodson Gray (1990) has pointed to some of these problems which are associated with images of ourselves as separate from nature, as having dominion over, and being above nature, which has virgin resources which can be exploited and raped. Conversely, the image of Mother Nature as bountiful and comforting (a concept not understood in some cultures) can be equally problematic. The terminology proposed by Gray is different from that which is suggested by Irene Diamond and Gloria Orenstein (1990), who seek to express different theoretical concerns. But far from distracting from the purpose, this debate about terminology is crucial to the construction of Women's Studies knowledge. Always, protesters need to use different symbols from those of the established order, and the more discussion—from the more perspectives—the more inclusive and accurate the terms can be.

Priorities about research within Women's Studies also need to be made explicit; does legitimacy and influence come from insisting on the validity of the feminist departure from the traditional model, or from "accommodating" the traditional within a feminist framework? And is legitimacy the purpose of the exercise—or ever likely to be forthcoming regardless of methods pursued?

Whereas within the traditional and positivist research model the priorities were often to reduce the area of study to the smallest possible (and controllable) unit, the intention in Women's Studies has more frequently been to bring in as many human variables as possible in the attempt to explain the human condition and to develop organizational patterns for a more humane, sane world. But how prescriptive is the Women's Studies research model to be? Can feminist research be positivist research; can it isolate the variables?

That participatory research is often favored within Women's Studies is understandable; it allows for a multiplicity of values to be expressed and for those who are the focus of research to have some say in the interpretation of the study. (So the coal mine workers can comment on the sociologists; the welfare recipients on the social workers.) But is there an obligation for feminist research to be participatory? And if this was an item on the agenda, who would decide within Women's Studies who has the proper feminist research and who does not?

There are many difficulties in the way of the development and distribution of Women's Studies within the academy, and some of the priorities of Women's Studies are aimed directly at circumventing or overcoming these obstacles. Women's Studies frequently has to organize to *resist* the pressures from outside, and to reconcile the differences inside, and this takes time, tolerance, ethics, and talent.

CONTENTS OF THIS VOLUME

Omissions

Despite the size and scope of this volume (and the time it has taken to compile), understandably there are some omissions. Some are the result of changes that have taken place while the work has been in progress so that what were faint murmerings when we began have now swelled to the dimensions of a debate. Some of the gaps are a product of our own conceptual limitations; it wasn't until we had the manuscript compiled in its entirety that we became conscious of the topics we had not taken into consideration. And some omissions are because writers who planned to contribute essays were unable to finish in time for inclusion in this volume. (The omissions which are more in the nature of the necessary limitations of logistics are discussed under the heading of "Organization.")

Recent Developments

Among the issues that have developed into debates since the outline of this volume was agreed on is that of an appropriate language for Women's Studies. Were we to begin now to request women to contribute, we would include a debate on desirable discourse and modes of feminist discussion (see Marilyn Frye, this volume). It does seem that in the last few years the role of language to inform or to intimidate has assumed increased importance. So too would we want to take into account the resistance to women's gains so impressively documented in Susan Faludi's *Backlash* (1991). She shows that the "trend" journalism purporting to *report* change is instead instrumental in *promoting* it via "scare stories"; despite this media campaign to convince women that feminism is bad for them (e.g., it causes depression, infertility, etc.), the benefits of feminism to women's physical and mental health, self-esteem, and life satisfaction are in fact much more readily established.

We would also include as a debate the recent analysis of beauty and the myth (see Naomi Wolf, 1990). That 150,000 women a year die of anorexia in the United States, that most women in the western world have a problematic relationship with food, that many see losing a few pounds as more important than success in work or love, and that there is evidence that many young women prefer to be thin rather than bright, puts the debate about women's bodies on a different plane. Add to this the huge increase in cosmetic surgery and the thesis that the closer women get to the top the more doubts can be planted about their physical appearance and the more their confidence can be eroded, and there is scope for presenting past research findings in a new framework. Is it that as women become more visible in the work place there is pressure on them to become more *invisible* as some suggest? Certainly there is evidence that western women are now being required to be thinner for longer and that there is now a powerful form of guilt associated with food intake.

Another issue we would want to pursue now is, where are all the young women? They are virtually invisible in these pages (see Jennifer Craik, this volume). What does this mean about ageism? About social movements and time frames? About the transmission of information to the next generation?

But perhaps the most significant change that we would make now is that we would put even more energy into trying to ensure the international nature of the research and reporting. As editors of this project, our consciousness has been changed; we have become acutely aware of our own ethnocentricity, and we think it is appropriate that we register and regret this bias.

Editorial Limitations

There are some areas we initially simply didn't think of: History and Philosophy of Science, for example. While it is treated in many contributions and underlies the volume as a whole, there is no article in which it is the focus of attention. And Women and Management probably warrants a chapter of its own, though to put it in would almost assuredly have meant that something else had to go out; and already we have been castigated for our poor coverage of the classics, including archeology. And still there are topics which are becoming increasingly important and which if not treated extensively within a discipline could well have done with individual treatment—such as personal chronicles, for example.

Biography (and Autobiography), Diaries, Journals and Letters are forms, along with Oral Histories, which are enjoying growing favor among Women's Studies scholars, partly because of the way they challenge prevailing boundaries and bridge the areas of much feminist interest—the links between the public and the private. In writing biography (and in some cases autobiography, diaries, journals, and letters) the author can be constantly making the connections between private consciousness and public persona, while at the same time the genre raises so many questions about the categorization of fact and fiction that it is a fertile area for investigation. (For further discussion see Teresa Iles, 1992.) Whose story is it, the reader can ask of a biography: the author's or the subject's?

And of course, in writing an autobiography, a diary, a letter, the author can choose which part of the self to make public, and the reader can question the authenticity—the qualification as fact and fiction. Because it generates so many issues about the nature of knowledge and authority, about veracity and validity—issues which have been a fundamental focus of feminist research—the genre of personal chronicles could well have called for discussion in its own right.

As could have debates about the causes of war, and the prevalence of war terminology in our daily lives. Is warring a part of human nature? A part of men's nature? Is war the activity that most basically and universally defines gender and the division of labor between women and men? Do we have so many wars because over the centuries warring cultures have destroyed those cultures which were not run by the warriors? What is the evidence for, and promise of, previous cultures that were not organized around preparations for war? (See Elise Boulding, this volume, for discussion of women's work in peace studies.)

And too there are the limitations of the divisions that we have created in this volume. While the collection includes analyses from many more disciplines than do most review volumes, we are aware that some are missing. In some cases we chose a research field (e.g., women and language) present in several disciplines (e.g., speech communication and linguistics), which means that many other areas of study in these disciplines have been omitted. We did not find these limitations satisfactory, but they were necessary if we were to avoid making this a multivolume work.

The omission of Social Work, however, is not an oversight; unfortunately it is one of the areas where the author was unable to complete the article by the last deadline. And while it is disappointing to go to press with such an omission, decisions which are fair to all contributors have to be made.

But perhaps the most significant omission from the pages of a volume devoted to the feminist knowledge explosion is the role in the process played by publishing.

Publishing

Publishing—or making public feminist scholarship—has been an integral part of Women's Studies success. When the first consciousness raising groups met in the western world in the late 1960s and early 1970s, one of their fundamental concerns was that women lacked a voice in the cultural and political discourse of society. One of the aims behind those early CR groups was to create the space for women to voice those concerns and to generate information and understandings about women's place. From this spoken word beginning the move to the printed word was a logical development. Women's publishing houses and presses were the next step in giving women a public voice and in extending the insights of women's consciousness and the fruits of women's scholarship to a wider community.

The feminist knowledge explosion has been inextricably linked with the emergence of women's publishing ventures, and what is surprising is that this fundamental feature of Women's Studies growth and achievement has attracted so little research attention within Women's Studies—which has such a commitment to examining its own processes.

One of the understandings which feminist research has given rise to over the last few decades is that women have little (or no) opportunity to determine the topic or define the terms in conversation with men. And this tenet can be extended from the spoken to the written word. In most media, including publishing, prior to the women's liberation movement it was men who were in charge and who set the priorities in relation to their own experience of the world. They served as "gatekeepers," defining the topic and the terms; in order to be *made public* women had to obtain the approval of the influential men, and the result was that the voices of women could be silenced or distorted.

This was the precise context in which Virago, the highly successful British feminist publishing house, made its appearance. It began by publishing reprints. Its aim was to put back into print, to give voice to, the many women who were out of print and to expose the fallacies of the insistence of mainstream publishers that there was no market for this work by women. (That the publishers' argument was the usual circular one familiar to women— damned if you do and damned if you don't—should be noted; the publishers decreed that there was no market for women's books; therefore they did not keep them in print, and of course without these women's books in print it was very easy for the publishers to prove that there was no market for women's books! The fact that Virago thrived on this *non- market* and was commercially so successful that mainstream publishers found it necessary to introduce women's lists is an indication of the way in which feminist theory and practice have undermined the rationale and responses of even the most entrenched patriarchal institutions.)

While Virago was the first major women's publishing house to emerge, it was soon followed by others which had similar agendas for the increased availability of women's writing. At the center of this remarkable expansion was the premise that women would be better served—more likely to get into print and more likely to stay there—if women were in charge of making the decisions, if women were the gatekeepers. That the nature of women's gatekeeping has not been systematically analyzed is another surprising gap in Women's Studies research; the ways in which different publishing houses and different journals and periodicals have developed their own particular politics often to the exclusion of any other view is in itself a matter of concern. The extent to which women serve as gatekeepers and silence the voices of other women should be a priority of research interest.

The establishment of a variety of publishing outlets in the 1970s helped to ensure that there was a diversity of views and voices. In Britain, the Women's Press was soon on the scene after Virago—followed by Pandora, Only Women, Sheba, and Attic, to name but a few. (The Feminist Book Fortnights in Britain and the extension to the regular and successful Feminist International Book Fairs give some idea of the astonishing expansion of the area internationally.) In the United States, the Feminist Press and Kitchen Table Press were among the first to publish new work by women as well as to bring back women of the past; and Kali for women pursued similar goals in India, while in Africa, South America, and Europe women also went into the business of publishing.

By putting back into the system many of the literary foremothers who had been lost to generations of women, women's publishing houses performed an invaluable service. They were instrumental in demonstrating that women had a rich heritage of dimensions often previously unsuspected; and they helped to make clear to millions of contemporary women that whatever the current issues, there were women who had been there before. With all the reprinting from the past, it became impossible for contemporary feminists to entertain the premise that feminism was a modern invention; publishing houses played a crucial role in educating the community to the idea that the women's movement did not start in the 1970s. And this understanding that feminism had a long and honorable history subtly transforms modern consciousness—yet another aspect of the influence of women's presses which has not been fully appreciated or explored.

There was much more to women's publishing, however, than reprinting lost women from the past. Pandora Press, for example, was founded with the precise aim of putting into popular form the findings of the research community that could be used by women. Concerned that much of the scholarship being undertaken might simply recirculate within the academic community and not get out to the women who could be empowered by the information, the initial aim of the press was to translate research dissertations and academic papers into more accessible and user friendly form.

The Athene Series (without which this book would not be published) also played a particular role in validating and distributing women's knowledge. It was one of the first lists where women were in charge of the decisions about the publication of women's scholarship and in itself deserves Women's Studies attention. We dedicate this book to Phyllis Hall, who has done so much to support feminist publications, including helping establish this series. As with academic journals (where women became the editors), these publishing ventures have not only ensured that women's voices reach a wider audience, but in providing some of the academic infrastructure (referred journals, professional notices, conference reports, etc.) they have also helped to legitimate Women's Studies as a discipline (see Susan Searing, this volume). Often taken for granted today, it is sometimes difficult to visualize what it was like not so long ago when there were no publications run by women—and when, as a result, women scholars were less likely to be published and less likely to gain editorial experience and less likely, therefore, to attain tenure or promotion.

There could also be a price to be paid for taking this achievement for granted. What must be taken into account is that it has really only been in the realm of books and magazine publishing that women have been able to gain a significant measure of control. It has been pointed out that women have not achieved anything like the same success in other media, for there is, as far as we know, only one women's daily newspaper (in Tokyo), and few if any television (or regular radio) stations (see Lana Rakow, this volume). It has also been pointed out that there could be a very disturbing explanation for this single achievement; it is that print is not the primary medium it used to be. Because the men have migrated to the electronic screen—the new information medium—the area of print is not being contested and protected in the way it has been for many years, with the result that some women have found their way in.[4]

If this were to be a permanent achievement, there would be no need for concern. But if it is the case that the information medium is moving from print to electronic transmission, what will this mean for the permanence of women's knowledge base? With a history of silences and interruptions, women are right to be wary about the changes taking place that pose a threat to the achievement of the past few decades. Yet if most of women's knowledge is encoded in print in books and does not make the transition to electronic storage, the greatest eclipse of women's meanings could currently be underway—while we are celebrating our success in print.

That this considerable publishing achievement so enmeshed with the knowledge explosion and so open to challenge has been the focus of so little attention within Women's Studies is one omission; that it has not been pursued in more detail as a debate in these pages is another. The fate of feminist publishing is changing rapidly as publishing houses have been bought or sold, with the disappearance of many small presses or imprints.

ORGANIZATION

While we were concerned to document the impact that Women's Studies has had across the disciplines, we were also aware that much of the powerful and influential knowledge of Women's Studies has been generated outside the traditional disciplinary framework. There are no **disciplines** of sexual violence (see Jane Caputi, this volume), or reproductive technology (see Renate Klein, this volume), or patriarchy (see Cheris Kramarae, this volume), or agency (see Barbara Pope, this volume), for example, and yet these areas are central to the feminist knowledge explosion. Hence the introduction of an additional form—**Debates**.

But **Debates** does cover more than one category; there are the areas that do not conveniently conform to discipline division but there are also areas where there is genuine feminist debate, such as in the area of pornography (see Susanne Kappeler, this volume), or men's studies (see Lillian Robinson, this volume), sexuality (see Jacqueline Zita, this volume), or sisterhood (Maria Lugones with Pat Alake Rosezelle, this volume). While this is a rough classification system with many limitations, it has allowed us to include a range of knowledge-generating bases and to make clear some of the different interpretations of feminisms.

Of course, this is not the only way in which the diversity is demonstrated. The chapters in this volume illustrate the many approaches, methodologies, and assumptions that inform feminist scholarship. But they also reveal the shared premises; about ethics, about the importance of knowledge making, about faith in the possibility of better societies and importance of resisting dominant ideology, about who can produce knowledge which counts. There is a shared interest in doing firsthand research, "indigenous" research that has significance in women's lives (see Micaela di Leonardo, this volume).

One of our expected tasks as editors was to standardize format spelling capitalization and terminology of all the chapters. We formulated the questions (see below) which we asked each author to keep in mind, and we recommended a citation form. But in some respects we were spectacularly unsuccessful in promoting uniformity, and as we much preferred the variety we did not change many of the authors' individual choices. For example, we did not alter an author's decision about whether or not to capitalize *Black*. That decision depends on what country she lives in and, within it, the current political history and terminology of race, ethnicity, and nationality, as well as her own political affiliations.

Many of the authors wrote to us about the problems they experienced with references to people living in the United States; there were those who followed the practice of some U.S. government agencies and used *Americans* to mean people living in the U.S. while some used it to mean North Americans, and others found the term too problematic (there being many cultures governments and histories in the Americas) to use the term at all.

We did ask all authors to follow the unconventional practice of including the first names of women (and men) for citations in the text and bibliography, and it is interesting to note just what difficulties this created. Our reasons for wishing to include women's names were clear.

1. *Authority*: It is important to know the authority of the researcher or writer; a woman writing about women's experience has a very different authority from a man writing about a woman's experience and vice versa. (There is a parallel with indigenous research here.) And while both may be perfectly valid, they are from very different perspectives. This is part of the process of putting the values of the researcher into the research, and while much use may be made of a man's research on women, it is not firsthand, but secondhand research he is conducting, research in which those being researched can be treated not as like subjects but as "other," as objects. So the gender/sex (or ethnicity, race) of the researcher can be a relevant factor in evaluating the research, and while by no means comprehensive or conclusive, first names of writers in the English-speaking world is a guide to gender/sex.

2. *Invisibility:* When gender is not signalled, there is a tendency for researchers and writers to be subsumed under the male-as-norm category. Just as the word *man* and *mankind* (purportedly standing for woman) gives primacy to male visibility at the expense of women, so too can the use of initials in references suggest male visibility at the expense of female. Because visibility (another debate that we might perhaps have included?) is such a significant issue in women's studies, it is helpful to integrate the theory and the practice and to show women as authorities in a text.

3. *Names*: As it is also the case in the English-speaking world that surnames are sire names, the names of men, it is important that women be given the names which are their own. To locate the names of women, however, proved to be extraordinarily difficult for many of the contributors and involved some of them in considerable delicate correspondence. The resistance to the proposal to signal women as authorities in the text, which has come from many quarters, is, however, even more fascinating and telling.

Original Research

By providing each author with 10 questions (one set for the debates and another for the disciplines), each contributor was engaged in a research exercise, and this in itself is another aspect of feminist influence. For this very volume breaks down some of the old compartments between research and writing, between questionnaire and essay; contributors have both conducted a survey and written an essay; they have engaged in empirical data gathering and written theoretical assessments. In bringing together all this information about the impact of feminism on the construction of knowledge in juxtaposing, connecting, and synthesizing data, a new path has been forged for future discussion and further exploration.

Once the basic format for the volume was agreed upon (and this in itself was no small exercise), we asked dozens of Women's Studies scholars to recommend authors for specific disciplines and debates. Because of space limitations, we could only ask one author to write on any one topic even though we were at times tempted to have two or more people (from different backgrounds) write on the same issue. We tried to ensure that there were viewpoints *across* disciplines and debates by using the recommendations we received to invite authors whom we knew to be able to express diverse perspectives. Readers will note the multiple approaches which are not necessarily in easy agreement.

Needless to say, the planning and editing of this volume required many hundreds of letters and cooperation from many people. During the time that the project has been underway, we have helped introduce contributors to each other, and a number of the authors have been able to meet at different conferences and discuss their essays, the interconnections, and overlaps. Which is why we are of the opinion that the whole is more than the sum of its parts. With all the difference there is still a unity.

General Guiding Statement for Essays on Disciplines and Debates

In order for readers to be able to make some comparisons across disciplines, we asked authors the to start with the same general guidelines (below) which we had gleaned from listening to and reading feminist scholars and activists.

We do not consider racism, classism, ageism, or homophobia as separate issues but as fundamental concerns in all debates and disciplines. In order to make some comparisons across disciplines and debates, we ask that you consider the following questions. We realize that these questions will not each be equally relevant to each discipline. Please use your own best judgment in determining where to put the focus, and where to add your own questions and answers. When possible, make reference to global issues and to Women's Studies research in several countries.

Guiding Questions for Essays on Disciplines

1. What was the position of women in your discipline about 20 years ago? Where were women as subjects? As practitioners? Are there any articles which document this particular period? Can you explain the significance (to discipline, to academy) of this status of women?

2. Considering what was happening about 20 years ago, is it possible to identify the first feminist protests and critiques of the organization and approaches of your discipline? What form did they take and what was the substance of the objection? Were they the responses of individuals or groups or both? Were they inside or outside the academy? What were the relationships with the larger women's movement? If applicable—what was your response or involvement?

3. Adrienne Rich wrote in early 1970s, "There is no discipline that does not obscure and devalue the history and experience of women as a group." What have been some of the basic tenets of your discipline that discriminate against/dismissed/denied the experience of women? With what consequences for women? Who have been the authorities? Are they being displaced? Are there well-recognized founding mothers in your field?

4. What new research priorities and directions emerged as a result of feminist activity? In her appraisal of sociology, Jessie Bernard has said that once women were aware of the discipline bias against them and determined to do their own thing it is fair to say, "To paraphrase Hamlet, 'There are more things in heaven and earth, gentlemen, than are dreamt of in your sociology.'" Is this also the case in your discipline—that women's concerns have taken it where men would never dream? (When we sent out our questionnaire we *thought* that Jessie Bernard had said this, but now we can't find it in her writings—Eds.)

5. Was it necessary to devise new methods to make this new knowledge? What

were the major methodological issues? Is the knowledge produced by feminists more trustworthy? More enduring?

6.   How did the mainstream respond (if at all)? What new tenets and authorities were welcomed? Which were "attacked"? Do you think that the new knowledge and methods challenged the mainstream leaders and promoted a backlash? Do you think that the new knowledge and methods were so "contained" that no backlash was necessary?

7.   Virginia Woolf said that the history of men's opposition to women's emancipation could be more interesting than the emancipation itself. To what extent have men protected their own power base and subverted the development of women's knowledge? What strategies have been used? How successful have women been in dealing with such male resistance? (Don't hesitate to use personal report and direct experience.)

8.   How extensive have the changes been in your discipline? How many male authorities have been challenged? Dislodged? How many female authorities have been recognized? How central are women in the discipline as subjects and practitioners? How accessible is this new knowledge to students—special courses? mainstream? extra-curricular? How satisfied are students? What demands do they make?

9.   What specific contribution does feminist knowledge in your discipline make to the enrichment of women's understandings and the enhancement of women's lives? What has been fundamental/superficial; transitory/enduring; embraced/resisted? What more could it do? Is there anything inherent in your discipline which makes it more resistant or open to change than are the other disciplines? What modifications of the discipline would you like to see? (Even an end to disciplines?)

10.   What is your assessment of the current situation? How far do you think feminist knowledge has made an impact? How secure do you think feminist gains are? What are your expectations of the future? What are the important questions? What is the relationship to the larger women's liberation movement?

Guiding Questions for Essays on Debates

1.   Can you define the issues of your debate and indicate the stage of development about 20 years ago? Are there any articles which help to account for its emergence and which can provide a historical perspective? What was the context in which the issues were raised, and how significant were they for women?

2.   How was the debate first introduced, and by whom? Was it the response of individuals or a group (or both)? Did it occur inside or outside the academy (or both)? What was the relationship between the debate and the larger women's movement? What form did it take and, if applicable, what was your own response or involvement?

3.   What were some of the social truths which prevailed then and which discriminated against/dismissed/denied the very experiences of women that the debate was trying to legitimate? Who were the male authorities that were being debated? Have they since been displaced? Who are the founding mothers in this area?

4.   What new research priorities and directions emerged as the result of this feminist activity? What new possibilities were glimpsed? In her appraisal of man-made knowledge in sociology, Jessie Bernard [?] suggests that once women have become aware of the bias against them and determined to do their own thing, it is fair to say (paraphrasing Hamlet), "There are more things in heaven and earth, gentlemen, than are dreamt of in your sociology." Is this also the case in your debate? That women's concerns have led it into areas men would never dream?

5.   Was it necessary to devise new methods to generate the new knowledge for the

debate? What were the major methodological issues? How far have these new methods provided more relevant/reliable/trustworthy knowledge? How much faith can you have in the knowledge generated? What attempts have been made to discredit it and with what success?

6. How have malestream institutions and disciplines responded (if at all)? What new tenets and authorities have been welcomed? Has the malestream engaged in debate, attacked, or ignored the issue?

7. Virginia Woolf said that the history of men's opposition to women's emancipation could be more interesting than the emancipation itself. To what extent have men protected their own power base and subverted the development of women's knowledge? What strategies have been used? How successful have women been in dealing with such male resistance? (Don't hesitate to use personal report and direct experience.)

8. To what extent has the debate been within feminism? Have any fundamental dimensions emerged? What is the current position, and where do you stand? Is the debate still the province of feminists, or has it been co-opted in any way? What traditional truths has it helped to discredit and what new insight has it helped produce? Does it provide a resource for particular disciplines—is it a regular item on their agendas—and how accessible is this new knowledge to students inside and outside the academy?

9. What specific contribution is your debate making to the enrichment of women's understanding and to the enhancement of their lives? What modification and/or resolutions would you like to see in the debate? What is the current relationship with the Women's Liberation Movement, and is this desirable?

10. What is your assessment of the current situation? How extensive an impact has feminist knowledge made? How secure do you think feminist gains are? What are your expectations of the future? What are the important questions to be asking now?

NOTES

We thank Elizabeth Kissling for her assistance in reading page proofs and composing the index for this volume.

1. We realize that the words *feminism* and *feminist* do not have common, universal (or even national) definitions. We use *feminist* in this chapter as a descriptive for people who work for women as a class and for the disappearance of this class (after Monique Wittig, 1981, p. 50), while recognizing the differing nature and conditions of women's oppression in differing cultures, societies, and economies (after Jill Lewis, 1981, p. 67). In general, we find useful the in-general statement by Rebecca West: "I myself have never been able to find out precisely what feminism is: I only know that people call me a feminist, whenever I express sentiments that differentiate me from a door-mat . . . " (1913).

2. It was when Dale Spender was asked to update *Men's Studies Modified: The Impact of Feminism on the Academic Disciplines* first published in 1981 (Athene) that the possibility and desirability of a contemporary "stock-taking" was mooted. This volume, however, is very different from the original survey.

3. This listing is used frequently in feminist writing. In order to better conceptualize this group as an entity, a social group which shares dominant political, economic, and social status in academe and many other "western" institutions, we propose giving the group a label such as WHIMMs: White Heterosexual Insider Middle-class Men. The H is aspirated (use a big puff of wind). We suggest the acronym WHIMM to be used in much the same way WASP (white, anglo-saxon protestant) has been used. This acronym allows us to recognize the individual components of the listing, but also to realize that, in the current system of separation and hierarchy, these are powerful components which,

combined, produce status and behavior different from any other combination. In proposing the acronym WHIMM we realize that we will be accused of inappropriate levity. This will be only a slight change from the usual charge of undue seriousness and requests to "lighten up" which feminists receive when we discuss social problems. The full message appears to be that we should take seriously what men say and make light of what women say.

4.   Here we talk about feminist-controlled publishing, since feminist influence in most media has hardly been spectacular. And, as Marjorie Ferguson (1990) writes, "given the worldwide trend to media concentration, vertical integration, and cross-media, cross-national corporate ownership . . . , it is reasonable to predict that ownership concentration will be matched by a tightening of masculine control over the corporate product and profit" (p. 226).

BIBLIOGRAPHY

Albrecht, Lisa, and Brewer, Rose M. (1990). *Bridges of power: Women's multicultural alliances.* Philadelphia: New Society Publishers, published in cooperation with the National Women's Studies Association.

Clawson, Mary Ann. (1989). *Constructing brotherhood: Class, gender and fraternalism.* Princeton, NJ: Princeton University Press.

Davis, Angela Y. (1990). Sick and tired of being sick and tired. *Woman of Power, 18* (Fall), 26–29.

Diamond, Irene, & Orenstein, Gloria. (Eds.). (1990). *Reweaving the world: The emergence of ecofeminism.* San Francisco: Sierra Club Press.

Faludi, Susan. (1991). *Backlash: The undeclared war against American women.* New York: Crown.

Ferguson, Marjorie Ferguson. (1990). Images of power and the feminist fallacy. *Critical Studies in Mass Communication, 7,* 215–230.

Gray, Elizabeth Dodson. (1990). The nature of our cultural assumptions. *Daughters of Sarah,* May/June, 7–10.

Hirsch, Kathleen. (1990). Fraternities of fear: Gang rape, male bonding, and the silencing of women. *Ms., 1*(2), 52–56.

Hubbard, Ruth. (1990, Fall). Women's bodies as battlegrounds. *Woman of Power, 18,* 10–14.

Iles, Teresa. (Ed.) (1992). *All sides of the subject: Women and biography.* New York: Teachers College Press.

Kramarae, Cheris, Treichler, Paula, & Russo, Ann. (1985). *A feminist dictionary.* London: Pandora Press.

Lewis, Jill. (1981). In Gloria I. Joseph & Jill Lewis (Eds.), *Common differences: Conflicts in black and white* (p. 67). New York: Anchor/Doubleday.

Martin, Patricia Yancey, & Hummer, Robert A. (1989). Fraternities and rape on campus. *Gender and Society, 3*(4), 457–473.

Rich, Adrienne. (1980). *On lies, secrets and silence: Selected prose 1966–1978* (pp. 134–135). London: Virago.

Reuben, Elaine. (1978). In defiance of the evidence: Notes on feminist scholarship. *Women's Studies International Quarterly, 1*(3), 215–218.

Sanday, Peggy Reeves. (1990). *Fraternity gang rape: Sex, brotherhood, and privilege on campus.* New York: New York University Press.

Sweet, Ellen. (1985). Date rape: The story of an epidemic and those who denied it. *Ms.,* October, 56–59, 84.

Tuggle, Denise. (1990). People of color at white elitist colleges. *Heresies, 25,* 7:1, 62–65.

West, Rebecca. (1913, Nov. 4). *The Clarion.*

Wittig, Monique. (1981). One is not born a woman. *Feminist Issues, 1*(2), 47–54.

Wolf, Naomi. (1990). *The beauty myth.* London: Chatto Windus.

Zandy, Janet. (1990). A conversation with Margaret Randall. *Room of One's Own, 13*(4), 35–49.

PART I

DISCIPLINES

Chapter 1

Feminism and Medicine
Co-optation or Cooperation?

Joan M. Altekruse
Sue V. Rosser

One force motivating the wave of feminism begun in the 1960s was women's health concerns. Women sought the right to control their own bodies, to have access to information about their physiology and anatomy, to define their own experiences as a valid aspect of their health needs, and to question the androcentric bias found in the hierarchy of the male-dominated health care system and its approach to research and practice.

Although feminism and women's health concerns are international, this chapter focuses on feminism and the debates within the discipline of medicine in the United States. The underlying problem of patriarchy, which endorses male control of women's bodies, is global and universal. However, the particular forms that control takes in women's health care vary considerably depending upon the country, its state of development, its form of government, and the details of its culture. For example, the Public Health Service in Great Britain poses different problems for women seeking access to health care (Mary Anna Elston, 1980) than does the diffuse, private health care system in the United States where health care coverage is strongly influenced by policies acceptable to employers. Using amniocentesis for sex selection in India and China may be different, but no less controlling than using amniocentesis in the United States to ensure that each woman can produce her own perfect biological child. Conversely, using a particular procedure, such as amniocentesis, may be motivated by diverse intentions in different locations. Whether for sex selection in India or to ensure a "biologically perfect" baby in the United States, its application has elements of societal control or strong outside influence on women's reproductive patterns. (Ruth Hubbard, 1983). To most westerners the increased incidence of infant clitoridectomy currently is noted among some ethnic/religious groups in America is abhorrent. Yet sophisticated examples of "reproductive fashions" translate to costly cultivated demands for various in vitro fertilization and embryo implantation techniques in our medical centers. (Gena Corea & S. Ince, 1987).

Because we felt constrained by not only the complexities, but also our limited knowledge of the many factors that interact in determining the precise nature of women's health care in diverse countries we have limited this discussion to the impact feminism has had on the medical field in the United States.

Twenty Years Ago. As in most disciplines prior to twenty years ago, the medical field tended to view the male subject as the norm, both experimentally and clinically. Only about

6% of medical school students were women. They were treated as intruders into the male sanctuary of medical practice. The book, *Why Would a Girl Go Into Medicine?* (Margaret Campbell, 1973), provides an insightful portrayal of the forms of discrimination female medical students endured during that period.

The dominance of the male physician within the profession led to androcentrism in research. Viewing the male as the norm resulted not only in exclusion of women as subjects in experimental and clinical trials, but also to the trivialization and denial of women's subjective symptoms by medical practitioners. Some examples from that era highlight the *adverse* consequences that the assumption of the male as norm has had on the health of the majority of the population, which is female. These examples include inappropriate dose determinations of pharmacologic agents, or even failure to suspect, detect, and properly manage conditions which were common and life threatening to women as coronary artery disease. Research agendas and clinical attention underemphasized a lengthy list of medical entities mediated by female hormones. This "scientific" bias occurred despite the consequences for women in terms of numbers of persons affected, morbidity/suffering or mortality/death as well as the resulting costs to society.

With the exception of a few studies in obstetrics and gynecology, women were virtually ignored as subjects in medical research. Traditionally, the rationale for using predominantly male primates and other male animal subjects for experimental drug testing was that the female's estrus cycle interfered with the collection of "clean data."

Testing of drugs on male subjects led to clinical problems of dosage regulation. Prescriptions were given to women without taking into account the wide variations in stature, weight, metabolic rates, and other physiological parameters that are sex distinctive. In addition, insufficient consideration was given to the special risks associated with drugs taken during pregnancy.

When a drug, such as a contraceptive pill, required testing on women because women were the targeted treatment group, dosage levels used in the testing processes were often so excessive as to induce serious secondary risks and overt clinical complications, including strokes and peripheral vascular damage. "Suitable populations" for high risk testing were often chosen from poor and minority women (B. Zimmerman et al., 1980). In the case of contraceptive pill studies, women in Puerto Rico were enrolled in the testing under conditions that did not satisfy the mandates of informed consent (Robert M. Veatch, 1971).

Little research was directed toward such problems as the risk factors for hip fracture in older women despite the enormous impact of that condition on personal and aggregate morbidity. Fracture of the hip was generally accepted as a "normal" concomitant of being old and female. Research to understand the underlying physiologic mechanisms and to establish active interventions were late in coming considering the magnitude of the problem in clinical, human, and financial terms.

The prevailing attitude towards women with various menstrual disorder complaints including PMS was, "It's hysterical until proven otherwise." Before the role of prostaglandins as a cause of constriction and ischemia of smooth muscles resulting in cramping was elaborated, the working assumption was that menstrual symptoms were psychological, not physiological, in origin (Ruth L. Kirschstein, 1985). Alternatively, symptoms perceived as physical were interpreted as the body's signal for the need to reduce the patient's physical activity to the "proper feminine level." Compliance with that advice justified exclusion of young women from demanding physical or mental exertion. [See Carol Ogelsby, this volume.] Vigorous sports, working in certain industries, and studying medicine fell into the category of excluded activites.

Feminist Critiques: Feminists (e.g., Elizabeth Fee, 1982; Hilde Hein, 1981; Evelyn Fox Keller, 1982) began to critique the notion of "objectivity" in basic science and clinical research. They suggested that the decisions, either conscious or unconscious, regarding what questions are asked, who is allowed to do the asking, what information is collected, who interprets that information, and how that information is used, all work to create a particular vantage point from which the knowledge or experimental results are perceived. Such particularity is neither neutral nor unbiased. They pointed out that frequently "objective" and so-called value-free medical research suffered from the biases of the gender, race, and class held by the researchers and practitioners who were overwhelmingly male, white, and upper-middle class. By including more holistic aspects such as importance of diet, exercise, and attitude in health practices, women revealed the contrasting attachment of traditional U.S. medical science to interventive therapies and its exclusion of data from what was labeled unscientific sources to investigate the etiology of disease. [See Joan Mulligan, this volume.]

Women sought to demystify roles and practices in the health field. They let physicians know that prescriptions written in Latin, obfuscating jargon, uninformative consultations, and the begrudging dialogue with patients all represented the need for reform in medicine. Women began knocking on the door of the medical establishment saying, "These are our bodies and we want to know more about them" (Boston Women's Health Book Collective, 1973).

Having sought and obtained new levels of information, women soon recognized the close kinship of that knowledge and their personal empowerment. Health had traditionally been a major focus of women's role—for themselves, the family, and community. Knowledge about health helped women to participate in choices about their care and caring for others; it aided them in expressing their autonomy both as women and as patients.

For professional women who were well acquainted with the exclusionary propensities of the medical establishment, the women's movement aided their claim to peer status. It converted overt discrimination from an accepted norm to a legal hazard. Women started to use legal means, including class action suits, to gain admittance to medical schools for women, Blacks, and other minorities. Medical malpractice actions were initiated against physicians and pharmaceutical houses (Mark Dowie & Tracy Johnston, 1977). In 1973 the U.S. Supreme Court ruled abortion legal. Thus the civil rights movement, litigation processes, and judicial findings were potent instruments of change in the behavior of the medical profession, and the self-assessment of women both as patients and health providers.

In retrospect it is apparent that male physicians have exerted strong professional influence to maintain control over the widest possible jurisdictions of health. However, changes rooted in women's consumer demands and the increase of women in medical schools are among the many factors working to decentralize and redistribute physician power. Women are engaged in these processes as providers and as collaborating recipients of health services.

Women in Medicine. One of the motives that quantitatively and qualitatively differentiates women in medicine from male physicians has been their interest in the community. They have promoted group-oriented preventive medicine and social hygiene activities, and have seen the link between medical problems, unhealthy living conditions, and behaviors of populations. Women physicians have tried to keep children well and have viewed older people in an interactive family context. Male physicians have tended to focus on autonomous practices or on leadership roles in institutional settings, on individual patients with acute medical and surgical problems, and on technological concerns even when the technology is primitive. [See Renate Klein, this volume.]

Regina Sanchez-Morantz (1988) tracks the historical record of U.S. physicians to detail the differing orientations of male and female health professionals. With women's roles channeled into community focused educational activities and collaborative work with nurses, early women doctors practiced in community schools, orphanages and what we now describe as voluntary health agencies. They initiated well-child clinics and mothers' milk banks, and urged humane laws to restrict child labor.

Women spent great efforts to establish their own educational and clinical institutions. In the late 1800s women medical doctors opened hospitals for women and for children. These hospitals gave them the opportunity to provide a full range of medical and surgical care not available to them in existing hospitals. Such stratification of the market was not done by choice; it was typically a last resort triggered by professional exclusion (M. R. Walsh, 1977).

Until recent decades the few women who entered medicine traditionally practiced in general medicine and pediatrics. Obstetrics/gynecology was virtually the only available channel open to those wishing to do surgery. In contrast, women now constitute about 40% of the students entering medical schools nationwide (up from the 6% quota held prior to the 1960s) and women are now represented in all specialties, although they remain unevenly distributed (Joan Altekruse & Suzanne McDermott, 1988). Surgical areas continue to be underrepresentative of women doctors.

Women in medicine have as a group typically placed a lower priority on the goal of high incomes than their male colleagues. The impact of their presence and the career characteristics they define as desirable, such as scheduled, salaried positions, are bound to have an effect on future medical practice.

New Directions. Most physicians, including many women doctors, have shown cautious restraint in response to the feminist health agenda. Adaptations by the medical profession to preferences experienced by feminists have occurred in limited contexts. One of these is the increased availability of health related information to women consumers, primarily due to the initiatives of women outside of professional circles (Sheryl Burt Ruzek, 1978). In contrast, consumers' complaints and suggestions have fostered only minor reforms in obstetrical care. The decor, ambiance, and regimens of birthing facilities, for example, now provide more personal and psychological support for the mother and promote infant-parent bonding. However, cosmetic features aside, efforts to increase knowledge, education and effective programs in maternal and child health remain inadequate.

Initiatives to use nurse-midwives as mainstream obstetric providers in the United States have met with effective and sometimes ruthless professional resistance. Many observers, in fact, suggest that the women's health movement has been co-opted by the medical profession (Nancy Worcester & Mariamne Whatley, 1988). When women started "voting with their feet" by consulting with midwives, choosing modified delivery services and hospitals with liberal labor room routines (such as admitting family members into the delivery room and not doing episiotomies or ritualistic elements of "prep"), physicians and institutions yielded to tangential demands for innovations. However, they retained firm control of the core of obstetrical care (Barbara Katz Rothman, 1981). Establishing "The Women's Hospital" as a precinct within larger, existing facilities provided an essentially nominal solution to women's more substantive concerns.

The backlash against nurse-midwives has been powerful and punitive. Significant numbers have been forced entirely out of the practices for which they are trained and licensed.

This action has proven again the exclusionary tendencies as well as the powerful and legal influence of the well financed ability of organized medicine to lobby in its own interests.

Patriarchal Paradigms. Much of the educational process of medicine is devoted to socializing the neophyte physician to the values inherent in the patriarchal paradigm. Three factors identify medical patriarchal modes: (1) the employment of hierarchical, pyramidal models of organization and authoritarianism in human relationships; (2) compartmentalization of knowledge into demarcated disciplines; (3) and the invocation of rationality and objectivity as driving forces behind the assumptions, criteria, and procedures that constitute accepted methodologies.

For centuries, hierarchical authority brought order to the endeavors of medical science and confidence to the providers of patient care. Unfortunately the patriarchal model is not only imperfect, but highly vulnerable to corruption and difficult to displace. For example, peer approval of "appropriate research, or approved treatment" can become stultified, as it did for radical mastectomy surgery. Changing the prescribed limits of authoritarian-derived habits is not easy, even when new data reveal the need for change. For example, in the surgical management of breast cancer strong advocacy for radical mastectomy procedures persisted even after modified excisional techniques showed favorable survival rates.

Current practices in medicine remind us that potent residuals of paternalism exist in the relationships between women and male physicians (Ben Barker-Benfield, 1977). Feminists of the previous generation are vividly aware of how recent is the emergence from the unquestionable authority of the physician. "Doctor knows best" was a prevalent professional stance at the bedside and in the laboratory. Women patients, nurses, or research assistants who questioned the doctor tended to be treated with disdain and/or dismissal.

Whereas compartmentalization of knowledge assists comparisons of methods, procedures, data, and experimental results, it also encourages isolation of one area of knowledge from others. It dissociates biomedical investigations from commonly occurring conditions that warrant study based on the extent of morbidity and death they cause. When faculty members are funded in a highly refined area of biomedical science, they tend to over-emphasize their area of specialized research when teaching medical students. That tendency reneges on their obligation to provide through the curriculum a valid sample of the overall field of knowledge and practice in medicine.

The historical record clearly reflects the inclination of women in medicine—as both scientists and practitioners—to function as generalists, often across disciplinary lines. Women physicians predominantly select the comprehensive primary care areas of practice such as general internal medicine, preventive medicine, pediatrics and family medicine (Joan Altekruse & Suzanne McDermott, 1988). They find it congenial to pursue multi-disciplinary and often inter-institutional activities although such ventures frequently evoke problems for attaining academic and professional recognition and reward.

Evidence refuting that objectivity is an inherent characteristic of physician behavior goes back to recorded attempts of nineteenth century male leadership in the United States medical community to restrict the entry of women into the profession (Barbara Ehrenreich & Deidre English, 1973, 1975; Mary Roth Walsh, 1977). Their resistance was publicly couched in terms of "objective scientific data" from anatomy, physiology (particularly reproductive) and psychology, not to mention theology and, indeed, phrenology. However, "objective arguments" did yield to monetary persuasion. This was plainly demonstrated by the historical record concerning the first entry of women to Johns Hopkins University. Faculty of the then financially ailing medical school had previously been stridently opposed to the admission of women. After much debate and poorly concealed chagrin they accepted the conditional gift of a female benefactor which stipulated that qualified women to be allowed to enroll.

Feminists in science have questioned the "objective" data that continue to be offered as a biological basis to maintain the status quo of entrenched interests. [See Marion Lowe, this volume.] Some (Elizabeth Fee, 1983) have suggested that more accurate information might be gleaned by alterations in methods that "shorten the distance between the observer and object of study." They point to the successful basic research of Barbara McClintock on genetic transposition in maize (Evelyn Fox Keller, 1983) as a model for new insights that may be obtained when the researcher follows intuitive "feelings" for organisms under study.

Women's presence in the sciences, and in medicine in particular, surely counts among those multifactorial influences which, with geologic-like gradualness, are reforming the patriarchal medical powerhouse and its "normal" way of doing business. Unfortunately some younger women in medicine feel disinterest and complacency about feminist issues in their profession. Optimism and inexperience assure them that the professional world has recovered from bias and exclusivity.

New Knowledge, Methods, Practice. The arrival of feminist thought and principles in medicine is beginning to be visible in three domains: research, education, and practice. Women in medicine have experienced circumscribed gains in recent years. However, the impact of feminism on mainstream medicine has derived more from the outside pressures of women consumers than from women researchers, educators, or practitioners.

Women have learned the important lesson that "Knowing our bodies and knowing ourselves creates both independence and responsibility (Boston Women's Health Book Collective, 1984). While most physicians continue to focus on acute medical interventions, women are seeking additional information and skills on how to promote and maintain health. Where the concerns they define fail to elicit physician response, they exercise initiatives outside of the conventional doctor-patient relationship. From preventive care to hospice sponsorship, the educated mothers of children and informed elderly widows express their keen desire for alternatives to painful, costly, and avoidable disease conditions. Often independent of their physician, they institute preventive measures to promote long-term health status and avoidance of the chronic diseases for which medicine has few cures. This evolution in consumer health consciousness recognizes that high-tech medical practices, which are the pride of American medicine, work best when the need for them is reduced by less dramatic disease evading tactics. So far, progress in adopting a unified preventive-curative model of health care is still so rare it cannot yet be properly assessed. It must be acknowledged that with important exceptions, the women's health movement has had only modest success in influencing physicians' clinical services (Sheryl Burt Ruzek, 1980).

Entrance into Medicine. We cannot deduce a quantitative estimate of the number of *potential* female candidates in earlier generations who may have had an interest in medicine. In contrast to today's relatively progressive admission policies for women, one can only conclude that until recent decades, the plans of most women who wanted to enter the field of medicine were effectively stifled (Ben Barker-Benfield, 1976). Moreover, most stories surrounding those failures of professional fulfillment remain untold. Far more examples of men's opposition to women's endeavors have survived, because as the scribes and spokesmen of their day, they had access to publications and public forums.

The celebrated women who made incursions into the nineteenth century world of American medicine had amazing strengths, paid a high price for conditional assimilation, and were frequently treated as if they were professionally expendable. Threatened with exclusionary tactics or, at best, limited career progress in mainstream medicine, women accepted assignments in entry level positions in academia or hospitals with virtually no possibility of advancement. They were forced to establish separate female-oriented educational and medical service institutions where they could secure a fuller range of activity, such as opportunities to perform surgical procedures or to serve in decision-making roles. Under threat of penalties by all-male medical societies, male physicians were dissuaded from joining and supporting women doctors as teachers and colleagues in the medical facilities the women established (Regina M. Sanchez-Morantz, 1988).

Reacting to the blatant hostility of potential male peers, many women relinquished hopes for medical pursuits. Those who did enter compromised both personal and career goals for the sake of limited participation. They became doctors, but also accepted spinsterhood, and limited expectations for advancement, leadership, scholarly and material rewards as compared to their male peers.

Today's situation differs in many respects. Women enter medicine in greater numbers than ever before, marry in the same proportion as do their non-doctor sisters, and fulfill roles as both doctors and mothers (C. U. Battle, 1983). Typically as committed to medicine as their male peers, women are unwilling to ransom social and family experiences for the sake of practicing medicine. About half of the spouses of women in medicine are doctors, too (M. F. Myers, 1984). This pattern may help create incentives for greater institutional empathy for obligations related to pregnancy, child-care, and other human endeavors.

Women's Studies and Medicine. The change in the numbers of women going into medicine has been followed by their expanded representation in specialty areas. The tendency for women doctors to practice pediatrics, preventive medicine, general medicine, and psychiatry remains. For the first time women practitioners are in every specialty of medicine, including urology, orthopedic surgery, as well as neurosurgery where women's fine motor skills should have been engaged long ago (J. Bowman & M. L. Gross, 1986).

However, Women's Studies is not very accessible in health profession curricula. A marked difference is apparent between the accessibility of such new knowledge in academic Nursing compared to Medicine. For example, nursing curricula often offer three or four courses that focus specifically on women's health and include feminist theory at levels appropriate for undergraduate students up through doctoral candidates. [See Joan Mulligan, this volume.]

Most medical schools have no Women's Studies in the curriculum. Scant information may be integrated into some traditional courses, but condescension toward feminist materials is far more common than requests for it. Along with other interrelated disciplines, like nutrition or community oriented primary care, Women's Studies is likely to be represented in the near future only in the curricula of exceptional medical schools.

Schools of Public Health often take an intermediate position in offering Women's Studies in their curricula. Despite the fact that the women's health movement is a community based activity strongly emphasizing health education and a focus on the health of the population, the amount of new feminist-related knowledge getting into the mainstream of health professional education can best be estimated as minimal. Extracurricular programs are, however, developing within progressive medical schools. Women in Medicine offices have been established at Harvard, Yale, Cornell, Case-Western Reserve, and the like, as well as in professional and voluntary health organizations such as the Association of American Medical Colleges and the American Heart Association. These efforts, if supported and sanctioned by senior administrators, hold much promise for effecting changes by working within the institutional structures of medical education.

Fundamental Contribution. A major contribution feminist knowledge in medicine makes is to the enrichment of understanding of women's lives derived from the idea that women are responsible for their bodies: that women need not and cannot blindly accept the authority of what the physician says and that the physician should accept the validity of women's experiences. Feminist knowledge has suggested the need for a more holistic approach to life and to health. It encourages a preventive orientation to avoid over-reliance on the "biological damage control" methods of late chronic disease management.

Some aspects of medicine may make it more resistant to feminist knowledge than other disciplines. Certainly the tradition of a male hierarchy, images of doctors who have power over matters of life and death, and the medical market may increase the profession's tendency to see feminist ideas in negative terms. The resurgence of the family physician and primary care practice does favor doctor-patient dialogue, allows critiques of providers, and works to improve patient understanding. Such a milieu should create a more favorable climate for future integration of attitudes and behaviors consistent with feminist concepts.

Rapid changes are currently visible throughout the health care professions and industry. The acute nursing shortage, absence of health insurance coverage for 37 million Americans, out-of-control costs, and the gradual recognition of false expectations of curative care all provide concrete illustrations of pervasive instabilities in the field.

As is the case with the practice portion of the health industry male leaders still set the priorities for medical research in the United States. This results in women and feminism being outside the central focus of research and funding, and allows androcentric bias to continue:

1. Two recent, widely publicized examples demonstrate that sex differences are *not* routinely considered in drug testing. In a longitudinal study of the effects of cholesterol lowering drugs, sex differences were not tested since the experiment was run on 3,806 men and no women (Jean Hamilton, 1985). In addition, a similar test of the effects of aspirin on cardiovascular disease, which is now used widely by the pharmaceutical industry to support "taking one aspirin each day to prevent heart attacks," also included no females. (Steering Committee of the Physicians' Health Study Research Group, 1988).

2. Some diseases that affect both sexes are defined as male diseases. Although it is the leading cause of death among older women heart disease has been so designated because heart disease occurs more frequently in men at younger ages. Therefore, most of the funding appropriated for epidemiologic research on heart disease has been for predisposing factors of the disease (e.g., cholesterol level, lack of exercise, stress, smoking, and weight) using white, middle-aged, middle-class males as the study population.

This "male disease" designation has resulted in very little research being directed towards high risk factors in women.

Recent data indicate that the designation of AIDS as a disease of male homosexuals and drug users has led researchers and health care practitioners to a delayed and flawed understanding of the etiology, diagnosis, and clinical treatment of AIDS in women (Chris Norwood, 1988).

3. Suggestions of fruitful questions for research based on the personal experience of women have also been ignored. Women have often had the experience of reporting symptoms which were rejected as clinically significant because they lay outside the scope of conventional scientific investigations or were not accepted as having credibility by researchers. For decades, dysmenorrhea was attributed by most health care researchers and practitioners to psychological or social factors despite the reports from an overwhelming number of women that these were monthly experiences in their lives. Only after the role of prostaglandins as a cause of constriction and ischemia of smooth muscles, resulting in

cramps, was elaborated did the male medical establishment accept the experiences reported by women as biologically valid (Ruth L. Kirschstein, 1985).

4. Research on conditions specific to females receives low priority, funding, and prestige. Some examples include dysmenorrhea, the effect of exercise on dysmenorrhea, incontinence in older women, nutrition in postmenopausal women, and the relationship between exposure to environmental and occupational toxins and the birth of deformed babies. Significant amounts of time and money are spent on clinical research on contraceptive processes for the use of which women must take full social and biological responsibility. Far fewer projects address the development of controls of male reproductive biology (Belita Cowan, 1980; Claudia Dreifus, 1977).

Thus, while the study of root causes of medical conditions in women are neglected, the medicalization of normal reproductive events has moved the locus of control for pregnancy and childbirth away from women and placed it within the domain of professionally institutionalized practices.

Feminists have critiqued the conversion of a normal, natural process controlled by women into a clinical, and often surgical, procedure controlled by men (Barbara Ehrenreich & Deidre English, 1978; Helen B. Holmes, 1981). More recently, new reproductive technologies such as amniocentesis, *in vitro* fertilization, and artificial insemination have become a major focus as means are sought to overcome infertility. Feminists (Rita Arditti, Renate Dueli Klein, & Shelley Minden, 1984; Gena Corea & S. Ince, 1987; Gena Corea et al., 1987; Renate Klein, this volume) have warned of the extent to which these technologies place pressure on women to produce the "perfect" child while placing expert consultation functions, that is control, in the hands of the male medical establishment.

Recognizing the gaps and inequities in government funded medical research from the women's perspective, the U.S. Congressional Women's Caucus sponsored hearings on the subject in late 1990. They called for changes in the design and review of research proposals submitted to the National Institutes of Medicine and mandated the inclusion of women subjects in research studies. Such efforts can begin to correct prejudicial practices that have effectively channelled public monies in the federal research budget away from issues concerning women's health.

The questions for feminists become: Will the presence of more women modify the patriarchal medical model? Can women in medicine effectively repair its persistent and blindsided weaknesses? Can women overcome the devaluation of their insights, perceptions and innovative approaches to problems? Can women prevent the new reproductive technologies from becoming another "option" which extends farther into the future male control over women's bodies? In brief, can women mend the serious deficiencies and inequities perennially manifested in research and practice that ignore their experiences and essential contributuions?

Medicine is, in a sense, more intrinsically connected to the future of women's roles in society than are other scholarly disciplines. By virtue of the pressure created by health consumers, women's health was one of the initial concerns of the women's liberation movement in the United States. Those efforts must continue because so much remains to be accomplished in attaining professional access and equity along with access to quality health care for women and, indeed, for all citizens. Women in medicine are now gaining ground that will enable them to influence the health care system for the greater advantage of the community. Such an effort is entirely consistent with their historical models and their own self-generated expectations.

BIBLIOGRAPHY

Abram, R. J. (1985). Send Us a Lady Physician: Women Doctors in America, 1835–1920. W. W. Norton and Company.

Adams, E. K., & Bazzoli, G. J. (1986). Career plans of women and minority physicians: Implications for health manpower policy. *Journal of the American Medical Women's Association, 41*(1), 17–20.

Altekruse, Joan, & McDermott, Suzanne (1988). Contemporary concerns of women in medicine. In Sue V. Rosser (Ed.), *Feminism within the science and health care professions: Overcoming resistance.* Elmsford, NY: Pergamon Press.

American Psychiatric Association. (1973). *Women in psychiatry.* Washington, DC: Author.

Angell, M. (1982). Juggling the personal and professional life. *Journal of the American Medical Women's Association, 37*(3), 64–68.

Arditti, Rita, Duelli Klein, Renate, & Minden, Shelley (1984). *Test-tube women: What future for motherhood?* London: Pandora Press.

Arnold, L., Willoughby, T. L., Calkins, V. & Jensen, T. (1981). The achievement of men and women in medical school. *Journal of the American Medical Women's Association, 36*(7), 213–221.

Ashley, JoAnne (1976). *Hospitals, Paternalism and the Role of the Nurse.* New York: Teachers College Press.

Barker-Benfield, Ben (1977). *The horrors of the half-known life.* New York: Harper & Row.

Barondess, J. A. (1981). Are women different: Some trends in the assimilation of women in medicine. *Journal of the American Medical Women's Association, 36*(3), 95–104.

Battle, C. U. (1981). The iatrogenic disease called burnout. *Journal of the American Medical Women's Association, 36*(12), 357–359.

Battle, C. U. (1983). Working and motherhood: A view of today's realities. *Journal of the American Medical Women's Association, 38*(4), 103–105.

Baucom-Copeland, S., Copeland, E. T., & Perry, L. L. (1983). The pregnant resident: Career conflict? *Journal of the American Medical Women's Association, 38*(4), 103–105.

Bernard, Jessie (1987). Re-Viewing the impact of women's studies on sociology. In Christie Farnham (Ed.), *The impact of feminist research in the academy.* Bloomington, IN: Indiana University Press.

Beshiri, Patricia H. (1964). *The woman doctor: Her career in modern medicine.* New York: Cowles Book.

Blout, M. (1984). Surpassing obstacles: black women in medicine. *Journal of the American Medical Women's Association, 39*(6), 192–195.

Bobula, J. D. (1980). Work patterns, practice characteristics, and income for male and female physicians. *Journal of Medical Education, 55,* 826–833.

Bonar, J. W., Watson, J. A., & Koester, K. S. (1982). Sex differences in career and family plans of medical students. *Journal of the American Medical Women's Association, 37*(11), 300–303.

Boston Women's Health Book Collective. (1973). *Our bodies, ourselves.* New York: Simon and Schuster.

Boston Women's Health Book Collective. (1984). *The new our bodies, ourselves.* New York: Simon and Schuster.

Bowman, J., & Gross, M. L. (1986). Overview of research on women in medicine—issue for public policymakers. *Public Health Reports, 101*(5), 513–521.

Braslow, J. B. (1981). Women in medical education. *New England Journal of Medicine, 304*(19), 1129–1135.

Brodkin, A. M., Shrier, D. K., & Buxton, M. (1982). Parenting and professionalism—a medical school elective. *Journal of the American Medical Women's Association, 37*(9), 227–230.

Brooke, K. L. (1982). Success—An historical perspective. *Journal of the American Medical Women's Association, 37*(12), 330–331.

Brooke, K. L. (1982). Drs. Carol and Ted Nadelson on dual-career marriage. *Journal of the American Medical Women's Association, 37*(11), 292–299.

Brown, Carol A. (1975). Women workers in the health service industry. *International Journal of Health Services, 5,* 173–184.

Brown, S. L., & Klein, R. H. (1982). Woman-power in the medical hierarchy. *Journal of the American Medical Women's Assocation, 37*(6), 155–164.

Brown, S. L., & Klein, R. H. (1986). Women physicians: casualties of organizational stress. *Journal of the American Medical Women's Association, 41*(3), 79–81.

Bullough, Bonnie. (1975). Barriers to the nurse practitioner movement. *International Journal of Health Services, 5,* 225–234.

Burnley, C. S. (1986). Specialization: are women in surgery different? *Journal of the American Medical Women's Association, 41*(5), 144–149.

Campbell, Margaret [Mary C. Howell]. (1973). *"Why would a girl go into medicine?" Medical education in the United States: A guide for women.* Old Westbury, N.Y: Feminist Press.

Chaff, S. L. (1977). *Women in medicine: A bibliography of the literature on women physicians.* Metuchen, NJ: Scarecrow Press.

Cole, Jonathan R. & Zuckerman, Harriet. (1987). Marriage, motherhood and research performance in science. *Scientific American, 256*(2), 119–125.

Conference on Meeting Medical Manpower Needs. (1968). *The fuller utilization of the woman physician report.* Washington, DC: American Medical Women's Association.

Corea, Gena. (1977). *The hidden malpractice: How American medicine treats women as patients and professionals.* New York: William Morrow.

Corea, Gena & Ince, S. (1987). Report of a survey of IVF clinics in the USA. In Patricia Spallone & Deborah L. Steinberg (Eds.), *Made to order: The myth of reproductive and genetic progress.* Oxford: Pergamon Press.

Corea, Gena, Hanmer, J., Hoskins, B., Raymond, J., Duelli Klein, R., Holmes, H. B., Keshwar, M., Rowland, R., & Steinbacker, R. (Eds.). (1987). *Man-made women: How new reproductive technologies affect women.* Bloomington, IN: Indiana University Press.

Cowan, Belita (1980). Ethical problems in government-funded contraceptive research. In Helen Holmes, Betty Hoskins, & Michael Gross (Eds.), *Birth control and controlling birth: Women-centered perspectives* (pp. 37–46). Clifton, NJ: Humana Press.

Cox, B. G., & Lewis, L. A. (1981). Responses of medical women to a survey on sexist language in medical publications. *Journal of the American Medical Women's Association, 36*(1), 15–18.

Curry, L. (1983). The effect of sex on physicians work patterns. *Research in Medicine,* Ed. 144.

Dowie, Mark, & Johnston, Tracy (1977). A case of corporate malpractice and the Dalkon Shield. In Claudia Dreifus (Ed.), *Seizing our bodies* (pp. 86–104). New York: Vintage Books.

Dreifus, Claudia (1977). *Seizing our bodies.* New York: Vintage Books.

Ducker, D. G. (1986). Role conflict in women physicians: a longitudinal study. *Journal of American Medical Women's Association, 41*(1), 14–16.

Ehrenreich, Barbara, & English, Deidre. (1973). *Witches, midwives, and nurses: A history of women healers.* Old Westbury, NY: Feminist Press.

Ehrenreich, Barbara, & English, Deidre. (1975). *Complaints and disorders: The sexual politics of sickness.* Old Westbury, NY: Feminist Press.

Ehrenreich, Barbara, & English, Deidre (1978). *For her own good.* New York: Anchor Press.

Eisenberg, K. (1981). The distaff of aesculapius—the married woman as physician. *Journal of the American Medical Women's Association, 36*(2), 1.

El Saadawi, Nawal (1980). *The hidden face of eve.* London: Zed Press.

Elliot, D. L. & Girard, D. E. (1986). Gender and the emotional impact of internship. *Journal of the American Medical Women's Association, 41*(2), 54–56.

Elston, Mary Anna (1980). Half our future doctors? In Rosahe Silverstone and Audrey M. Ward (Eds.), *The careers of professional women* (pp. 99–139). London Croom Helm:

Fee, Elizabeth. (1975). Women and health care: A comparison of theories. *International Journal of Health Services, 5,* 397–415.

Fee, Elizabeth. (1982). A feminist critique of scientific objectivity. *Science for the People, 14*(4), 8.

Fee, Elizabeth. (1983). Women's nature and scientific objectivity. In Marian Lowe & Ruth Hubbard
    (Eds.), *Woman's nature, rationalizations of inequality*. Elmsford, NY: Pergamon Press.

Fitzpatrick, M. Louise. (1977). Nursing. *Signs 2* (Summer), 818–834.

Gillespie, L., Cosgrove, M., Fourcroy, J., & Calmes, S. (1985). Women in Urology: A splash in the
    pan. *Urology, 25*(1), 93–97.

Gilligan, Carol. (1982). *In a different voice.* Cambridge, MA: Harvard University Press.

Goldstein, M. Z. (1981). Psychiatrists' life and work patterns: A statewide comparison of women and
    men. *American Journal of Psychology, 138*(7), 919–924.

Hamilton, Jean (1985). Avoiding methodological biases in gender-related research. In *Women's
    health report of the public health service, task force on women's health issues.* Washington, DC:
    U.S. Dept. of Health and Human Services Public Service.

Hamilton, J., & Parry, B. (1983). Sex-related differences in clinical drug response: implications for
    women's health. *Journal of the American Medical Women's Association, 38*(5), 126–132.

Hammond, J. M. (1981). Social support groups, women's programs, and research on gender differ-
    ences: The bad press for women in medical education literature. *Journal of the American Medical
    Women's Association, 36*(5), 162–165.

Harris, M. B., & Conley-Muth, M. A. (1981). Sex role stereotypes and medical specialty choice.
    Journal of the American Medical Women's Association, 36(8), 245–252.

Haseltine, Florence, & Yaw, Yvonne. (1976). *Woman doctor: The internship of a modern woman.*
    Boston, MA: Houghton Mifflin.

Hayes, M. D. (1981). The impact of women physicians on social change in medicine: The evolution
    of humane health care delivery system. *Journal of the American Medical Women's Association,
    36*(2), 82–84.

Haynes, S. G. (1984). Women and coronary heart disease. *Journal of the American Medical Women's
    Association, 39*(3), 102–105.

Hein, Hilde (1981). Women and science: Fitting men to think about nature. *International Journal of
    Women's Studies 4*, 369–377.

Heins, M. (1985). Update: women in medicine. *Journal of the American Medical Women's Associa-
    tion, 40*(2), 43–50.

Holmes, Helen B. (1981). Reproductive technologies: The birth of a women-centered analysis. In H.
    B. Holmes, B. B. Hoskins, & Michael Gross (Eds.), *The custom-made child? Women-centered
    perspectives*. Clifton, NJ: Humana Press.

Hubbard, Ruth (1983). Social effects of some contemporary myths about women. In Marion Lowe
    and Ruth Hubbard (Eds.), *Woman's nature: Rationalizations of inequality*. Elmsford,
    NY: Pergamon Press.

Introduction. (1983). *Women in pediatrics*. Pediatric Supplement, 679.

Jacobson, Arthur C. (1972, July). A medical view of women's lib. *Medical Times*, 180.

Jefferys, Margot. *Women in medicine: The results of an inquiry conducted by the medical practi-
    tioners' union in 1962–63.* London: Office of Health Economics.

Keller, Evelyn Fox. (1982). Feminism and science. *Signs: Journal of Women in Culture and Society,
    7*(3), 589–602.

Keller, Evelyn Fox. (1983). *A feeling for the organism.* San Francisco: W. H. Freeman.

Kinder, B. K. (1985). Women and men as surgeons: are the problems really different. *Current
    Surgery*, 100–104.

Kirschstein, Ruth L. (1985). *Women's health: Report of the public health service task force on
    women's health issues, 2.* Washington, DC: U.S. Department of Health and Human Services
    Public Health Service.

Lamphere, Louise. (1987). Feminism and anthropology: The struggle to reshape our thinking about
    gender. In Christie Farnham (Ed.), *The impact of feminist research in the academy*. Bloomington,
    IN: Indiana University Press.

Langwell, K. M. (1982). Differences by sex in economic returns associated with physician specializa-
    tion. *Journal of Health Policies, Policy and Law, 6*(4), 752–761.

Lanska, M. J., Lanska, D. J., & Rimm, A. A. (1984). Effect of rising percentage of female physicians on projections of physician supply. *Journal of Medical Education, 59,* 849–855.

Lerner, M. R. (1981). The women who, where, when and why? *Journal of the American Medical Women's Association, 36*(1), 5–12.

Levine, Robert J. (1978). The nature and definition of informed consent. *The Belmont Report: ethical principles and guidelines for the protection of human subjects of research.* Appendix *1.* (DHEW Publication No. OS 78-0013) pp. 3-1-91.

Longo, M. F. (1985). History of women surgeons. *Current Surgery,* 91–93.

Lopate, C. (1964). *Women in medicine.* Baltimore: Johns Hopkins Press.

Lorber, Judith. (1981). The limits of sponsorship for women physicians. *Journal of the American Medical Women's Association, 36*(11), 329–338.

Lorber, Judith. (1986). Sisterhood is synergistic. *Journal of the American Medical Women's Association, 41*(4), 116–119.

Lorber, Judith. (1975). Women and medical sociology: Invisible professionals and ubiquitous patients. In M. Millman & R. M. Kanter (Eds.), *Another Voice* (pp. 75–105) Garden City, NY: Anchor Books.

Lovelace, J. C. (1985). Career satisfaction and role harmony in Afro-American women physicians. *Journal of the American Medical Women's Association, 40*(4), 108–110.

Manley, Audrey, Lin-Fu, Jane, Miranda, Magdalena, Noonan, Alan, & Parker, Tanya (1985). Special health concerns of ethnic minority women. In *Women's health: Report of the public health service task force on women's health issues.* Washington, DC: U.S. Department of Health and Human Services.

Marieskind, H. I. (1984). Research in women's health problems and prospects. *Journal of the American Medical Women's Association, 39*(3), 91–105.

Martin, C. A. (1986). Attitudes towards women in radiology. *Journal of the American Medical Women's Association, 41*(2), 50–53.

McGoldrick, K. E. (1983). Humane approaches in the doctor-patient relationship. *Journal of the American Medical Women's Association, 38*(5), 133–135.

McNamara, M. F. (1985). Women surgeons: How much of an impact? *Current Surgery,* 94–99.

Melnick, Vijaya, & Hamilton, Franklin D. (1977). *Minorities in science: The challenge for change in biomedicine.* New York: Plenum Press.

Miller, J. B. (1984). Women and mental health. *Journal of the American Medical Women's Association, 39*(3), 97–111.

Mitchell, J. B. (1984). Why do women physician's work fewer hours than men physicians? *Inquiry, 21,* 361–368.

Morgan, B. C., Aplin, E. R., Garrison, L., Hilman, B. C., Howell, D. A., Navarro, A., O'Hare, D., Pittelli, A., Skansi, V., & Tanner, N. M. (1983). Report of the task force on opportunities for women in pediatrics. *Pediatric Supplement, 71*(4), 679–714.

Myers, M. F. (1984). Overview: the female physician and her marriage. *American Journal of Psychology, 141*(11), 1386–1391.

Norwood, Chris (1988, July). "Alarming rise in deaths." *Ms.,* 65–67.

Ory, M. G. (1984). Women and aging. *Journal of the American Medical Women's Association, 39*(3), 99–101.

Poirier, S. (1986). Role stress in medical education: A literary perspective. *Journal of the American Medical Women's Association, 41*(3), 82–86.

Porter, R. L. (1983). Resident, women, wife, mother: Issues for women in training. *Journal of the American Medical Women's Association, 38*(4), 98–102.

Rinke, C. (1981). The economic and academic status of women physicians. *Journal of the American Medical Women's Association, 245*(22), 2305–2306.

Rothman, Barbara Katz. (1981). Awake and aware, or false consciousness: The cooptation of childbirth reforms in America. In S. Romalis (Ed.), *Childbirth: Alternatives to medical control.* Austin, TX: University of Texas Press.

Ruzek, Sheryl Burt (1978). *The woman's health movement.* New York: Praeger.

Ruzek, Sheryl Burt (1980). Medical response to women's health activists: Conflict, accommodation, and cooptation. *Research in Sociology of Health Care, 1*, 335–354.

Sanchez-Morantz, Regina M. (1988). *Sympathy and science.* New York: Oxford University Press.

Sayres, M., Wyshak, G., Denterlein, G., Apfel, R., Shore, E., & Federman, D. (1986). Pregnancy during residency. *New England Journal of Medicine, 314*(7), 418–423.

Schermerhorn, G. R., Colliver, J. A., Verhulst, S. J., & Schmidt, E. L. (1986). Factors that influence career patterns of women physicians. *Journal of the American Medical Women's Association, 41*(3), 74–78.

Scully, Diane & Bart, Pauline. (1973). A funny thing happened on the way to the orifice: Women in gynecology textbooks. *American Journal of Sociology, 78*, 1045.

Shapiro, J. (1982). Pregnancy during residency: Attitudes and policies. *Journal of the American Medical Women's Association, 37*(4), 96–103.

Shore, E. G. (1984). Academia. *Journal of the American Medical Women's Association, 39*(3), 81–83.

Sirridge, M. S. (1985). The mentor system in medicine—How it works for women. *Journal of the American Medical Women's Association, 40*(2), 51–53.

Slade, Margot. (1975). The women in white. *The New Physician, 24*, 34–35.

Spieler, Carolyn (Ed.). (1977). *Women in medicine—1976.* New York: Independent Publishers Group.

Steering Committee of the Physicians' Health Study Research Group (1988). Special report: Preliminary report of findings from the aspirin component of the ongoing physician's health study. *New England Journal of Medicine, 318*(4), 262–264.

Tuohey, M. K. (1985). Working women, working lovers: The effect of our multiple roles on intimacy. *Journal of the American Medical Women's Association, 40*(3), 92–94.

Veatch, Robert M. (1971). Experimental pregnancy. *Hastings Center Report 1*, 2–3.

Wallis, L. A. (1981). Advancement of men and women in medical academia. *Journal of the American Medical Women's Association, 246*(20), 2350–2853.

Walsh, M. R. (1977). *Doctors wanted: No women need apply: Sexual barriers in the medical profession.* New Haven: Yale University Press.

Weisman, C. S., Levine, D. M., Steinwachs, D. M., & Chase, G. A. (1980). Male and female physician career patterns: Specialty choices and graduate training. *Journal of Medical Education, 55*, 813–825.

Worcester, Nancy, & Whatley, Mariamne (1988). The response of the health care system to the women's health movement: The selling of women's health centers. In Sue V. Rosser (Ed.), *Feminism within the science and health care profession* (pp. 117–130). Elmsford, NY: Pergamon Press.

Zimmerman, B. et al. (1980). People's science. In Rita Arditto, Pat Brenna, and Steven Cavrak (Eds.), *Science and liberation* (pp. 299–319). Boston: South End Press.

Chapter 2

Physics and Mathematics, Reality and Language
Dilemmas for Feminists

Robyn Arianrhod

My own experience helps illustrate the position of women in scientific disciplines 20 years ago; my high school physics teacher looked down at me and said, with bemused consternation, "You're so good at physics and you're a girl!" Ever since I'd first heard the word physics I had been enraptured by the power of the human mind to discover the secrets of nature's manifestations, from rainbows to motors.

My friends, however, thought I was showing off when I took science practical sessions seriously; by the time I reached my final year, there were 4 girls and 20 boys in the laboratory classes, and for the sake of peer group approval from both genders, I had to pretend to be like the other 3 girls and see these sessions as a chance to flirt with the boys and get them to do my practical work for me. That was the end of my career as a physicist—although whereas none of the other 3 girls even qualified for admission to a university, I am now working in mathematical physics.

My teachers could not decide whether to give the science prize for 1969 to me or to my male rival, with whom I had been academically equal all through our school careers. My chemistry teacher, a woman, said later that it had been unfair that the male-dominated science staff had finally chosen the boy for the prize, on the (totally false) assumption that I had to study to get my results whereas he did it "naturally"! This fit in with what I'd been told since primary school: girls had good memories rather than brains. I never forgave them for that arrogant piece of typecasting, and for not sharing the prize between us, which seemed to me to be the only logical and fair thing to do.

That is how I experienced the position of women in my discipline 20 years ago. There is a postscript to the story: Recently, there was a similar debate as to who should receive the undergraduate mathematical physics prize at a certain university. This time, and apparently partly for the sake of appearing not to be prejudiced, the male-dominated staff decided in favor of the female student. There was still no concept of *sharing* the prize, still a male-dominated staff, and although the gender of the winner was reversed, the really telling aspect of the story is that the young winner believed that her win was important for women. The fact that she felt this way says a great deal about how little improvement there has been over the past 20 years in this discipline.

I have not been able to obtain much statistical information about the quantitative representation of women in the fields of mathematics and physics 20 years ago, but I include the following information to give a glimpse of the situation, and for some sort of comparison with current figures.

1. In Australia women made up 26.9% of the number of undergraduates enrolled in the Science Faculty at Monash University in 1969 (Monash University Statistics, 1969). In 1976, 32.3% of gross enrollments in the Science Faculty were female. (Thanks to Gay Baldwin for these figures.)

2. In Great Britain in 1974, 22% of 'O' level physics and 19% of 'A' level physics passes were attained by women. (Janie Whyld, 1980).

3. In the United States in 1973, 8.7% of those with doctoral degrees in any of the sciences were women; the percentage of scientists with physics doctorates was 8.0, while the percentage of women scientists with physics doctorates was 2.6 (*National Science Foundation*, quoted in Margaret Gallard Kivelson, 1988).

FEMINIST CRITIQUES

There was a feminist reaction to the organization of the discipline even 20 years ago. I left academia (dropping out of Honors in math in 1973) for a period of about 10 years, because I wanted to *live* the feminist and counter-culture alternatives that challenged the academic structure that I found so damaging. (Speaking on *The Science Show*, ABC radio, 4.10.86, physicist Dr. Barbara Wilson, of the [American] Committee on the Status of Women in Science, commented on how women's self-esteem takes a drastic beating at the university level: in a study of top male and female high school graduates with high self-esteem, only 4% of the women still felt intelligent after one year at a university, while the boys' self-esteem was unaffected!) I did not believe that it was possible to be a feminist within academia, let alone within science, because I felt that to succeed in these institutions required all the qualities I despised as a feminist: aggressiveness, competitiveness, isolation, ambition, and so on. As for science, its pollution of the environment and erosion of culture was obvious. The dilemma for those trying to develop a critique of science, however, be they Marxists or feminists or black liberationists, is that Western, capitalist, white, male science has been, relatively speaking, enormously successful in improving many aspects of life; the recent dramatic changes in Eastern Europe and the USSR and the recent democratic movement in China (whose leaders included astrophysicist Fang Li Zhi) show that, ideology notwithstanding, a certain standard of living and freedom of thought—including the freedom to practice Western science and ideas—is essential to a meaningful life. From my ideologically sound life in the wilderness after I left academia, which minimally impacted the environment, I found that an ancient agrarian way of life was often counterproductive for women as its labor-intensiveness tended to reinforce gender stereotypes. (In a global context, such stereotypes, along with the need to produce more labor, have contributed to an environmentally disastrous population explosion among such agrarian peoples.) Hence, I have been forced to re-evaluate the philosophy of capitalism, and of the science which is clearly an integral part of it, at least insofar as it is practiced. This re-evaluation is still in progress, but the major change is that I am looking for a feminist solution within—or at least in conjunction with—the academy of science.

Because of my absence from academic science, my experience of the first (and subsequent) feminist protests or critiques of the organization and structure of my discipline may be somewhat fragmented. However, my absence was a criticism in itself, which also involved the practical exploration of a critique. In fact, I have found that most women who stayed on in the field of mathematics and physics were not feminists. Indeed, most early feminist criticism was general, criticizing the rigidity and competitiveness of academia in general rather than analyzing the problems of individual disciplines.

The first forums for feminist criticism of science that I am aware of came within the radical science movement, particularly "Science for the People," and the work of Steven and Hilary Rose. Whereas the old guard of radical scientists saw science itself as neutral and only its *applications* as problematic, younger radicals in the 1960s and 1970s began to suggest that science reflects not a dispassionate truth, but the values of the dominant culture. [See Marian Lowe, this volume.] For example, the reductionist nature of science was challenged and the concept of a holistic approach seemed to better reflect women's (and other radicals') concerns. Barbara McClintock's Nobel Prize gave a great boost to this idea of feminist science by, in effect, endorsing her methodology of gaining a feeling for the organisms she studied (Evelyn Fox Keller, 1983). But that is biology, not mathematics or physics. Long before the radical science movement, however, Einstein himself knew that physics was not objective:

> In the case of planets moving around the sun it is found that the system of [Newtonian] mechanics works splendidly. Nevertheless we can well imagine that another system, based on different assumptions, might work just as well.
>
> Physical concepts are free creations of the human mind, and are not, however it may seem, uniquely determined by the external world. In our endeavor to understand reality we are somewhat like a man trying to understand the mechanism of a closed watch. He sees the face and the moving hands, even hears its ticking, but he has no way of opening the case. If he is ingenious he may form some picture of a mechanism which could be responsible for all the things he observes, but he may never be quite sure his picture is the only one which could explain his observations. He will never be able to compare his picture with the real mechanism and he cannot even imagine the possibility or meaning of such a comparison. But he certainly believes that, as his knowledge increases, his picture of reality will become simpler and simpler and will explain a wider and wider range of his sensuous impressions. He may also believe in the existence of the ideal limit of knowledge and that it is approached by the human mind. He may call this ideal limit the objective truth. (Albert Einstein & Leopold Infeld, 1938 p. 33)

In the late 1970s, popular books such as physicist Fritjof Capra's *The Tao of Physics* popularized and extended the ideas of Bohr and Heisenberg that quantum physics, with its uncertainty principle, its acknowledgment of observer-affected observations, and its theory that light is both wavelike and particle-like, introduced a holistic way of thinking about physics, more akin to Chinese philosophy, with its all-embracing concept of "both-and," than to the dualistic "either-or" characteristic of traditional Western thought. Einstein's theory of General Relativity was holistic in that it conceived the nature of gravity as being not a separate force but rather the shape or curvature of spacetime itself (and, indeed, the concept of spacetime is a holistic way of looking at space and time): This flexible twentieth century mindset has continued with the development of such things as theories of chaos and superstrings. In fact, the major twentieth century metaphor for physics has been a holistic one: unity, the search for a unified field theory to describe all the forces of nature.

Thus, physics and its medium of expression, mathematics, are in some sense already compatible with feminist thought, and perhaps this is one reason—along with the apparent objectivity of the content of these disciplines—that not much progress has been made in developing a satisfactory feminist critique of the content of math and physics. But how could such a critique be formulated? What *is* feminist science?

Rita Arditti (1980) says that:

A feminist perspective in science would involve the creation of an environment that maximizes the development of minds and bodies and encourages positive attitudes towards one's own biological identity. . . . Science needs a soul which would show respect and love for its subjects of study and would stress harmony and communication with the rest of the universe. When science fulfills its potential and becomes a tool for human liberation, we will not have to worry about women "fitting" into it because we will probably be at the forefront of that "new" science. (p. 365).

This is inspiring rhetoric, but it is too general to be of much help to me as a feminist trying to become a mathematical physicist. I mean, it engenders a sort of complacency because, as mentioned above, mathematical physicists already have a paradigm of harmony and unity. In addition, one of our criteria for the success of a physical theory is beauty: the simplicity and elegance of its mathematical expression. This, of course, is clearly a cultural sensibility, not an objective one, and, indeed, it has already been challenged *within* the discipline by the (relatively) new theory of chaos, which will probably be a major research area in the 1990s. Thus there is a need to look beyond the rhetoric of harmony to fully explore questions such as whether or not a feminist aesthetic in this context would be any different from the current mainstream one, and what effect the scientific paradigms one works with has on the manner and application of one's work.

Janet Sayers (1986) is a bit more concrete when she describes a feminist science as "one that will equally serve women as well as men" (p. 178). But, as Elizabeth Fee (1983) says:

At this historical moment, what we are developing is not a feminist science, but a feminist critique of existing science. It follows from . . . the relationship of science to society that we can expect a sexist society to develop a sexist science; equally, we can expect a feminist society to produce a feminist science. For us to imagine a feminist science in a feminist society is rather like asking a mediaeval peasant to imagine the theory of genetics or the production of a space capsule; our images are at best likely to be sketchy and insubstantial.

However, as mentioned above, even a feminist critique of physics and mathematics has barely begun. Another reason for this is the lack of female, let alone feminist, physicists and mathematicians, for I believe that a feminist critique of intellectual content must clearly come from (at least a collaboration with) *within* these disciplines. The irony, of course, is that these small numbers of women in the field and the concomitant lack of feminist critique are in large part the result of a sexism that has systematically excluded women from these disciplines.

The only significant feminist critique of physics and math from a nonscientist that I am aware of is contained in Susan Griffin's powerful, original, but, for me, ultimately flawed *Woman and Nature* (1978). In its opening sections (on matter) this work is a lyrical condemnation of the way male scientists appropriate knowledge for themselves, to the utter detriment and degradation of women, through the arbitrary and dehumanizing definitions of mathematics and physics. Whereas her emphasis on the arbitrariness of these definitions is an important aspect of a critique of the content, the impact is undermined and the argument trivialized when Susan Griffin caricatures the physics she is describing, and indeed carries this parody over into a dualistic narrative structure in which male science is totally evil. This is not helpful to feminists within these disciplines, who are trying to understand the intellectual content before making judgments of it, and neither does it constitute an adequate critique of the material.

Critiques of science from feminist scientists in other disciplines (e.g., those by Women

In Science and Engineering [WISE], Women In Science and Technology in Australia [WISTA], Carolyn Merchant, Hilary Rose, Ruth Bleier, Elizabeth Fee) have been exciting and profound in discussing the way science in general excludes women because of its antifeminist applications and organization: its competitiveness; its "good old boys' network" for promotions; its sexist textbooks; the long, uninterrupted hours required for laboratory work; lack of childcare facilities; the unequal division of labor in the science structure itself, with women concentrated in the jobs of technician, tutor, cleaner, secretary, and almost absent in the upper echelons of most disciplines of science; its lack of positive female role models; its sexual metaphors in which nature (woman) is *penetrated* by the intellect (man); and the underconfidence of women as a result of the above metaphor and of years of being told they were biologically incapable of equalling men in mathematics and the hard sciences. [See Dale Spender, this volume.] But feminist analysis of the intellectual content of these disciplines has barely begun. Central to such a critique must be an exploration of the question: Does the content of these disciplines attract, or create, people with antifeminist mindsets? That is, is there anything about the content that is inherently antifeminist? And to what extent are my experiences—and my conclusions—which are in Applied Mathematics/Mathematical Physics, applicable to Pure Mathematics (but see, for example, Morris Kline, 1980) or Applied Physics (see Sharon Traweek, 1988; Paul Feyerabend, 1978)?

Certainly the intellectual core of physics and maths, for those who have not been sufficiently inspired by *The Tao of Physics* (Fritjof Capra, 1975) or *The Dancing Wu Li Masters* (Gary Zukav, 1979), appears to be inimical to feminist thought. Echoing Susan Griffin, Hilary Rose (1986b, p. 58) says, "Feminism also found that its reasoning differed from (science's) linear form of cognitive reasoning that took delight in dichotomies. Metaphors of spinning (Mary Daly, 1978) . . . are invoked as feminism speaks about its distinctive ways of thinking, feeling and acting in the world." The irony, however, is that despite the way mathematics and physics seem to like to present themselves to the public, and perhaps also to undergraduate and school students—as rational, dichotomous and true—in reality, they are built on a very intuitive and communal process to which, in my experience, women have difficulty adjusting. The problems for women with the communal part of the process are not surprising because of the masculine social interactions that are part of it: in my experience feelings are rarely discussed; the relationships formed between collaborating researchers are not explored as we feminists—and women in general—are used to doing. So that unacknowledged tensions and nuances, which don't appear to worry the men, do worry us; and the fact that men hold almost all the positions of power in the faculty make it difficult for women to interact socially or professionally without a sense of either inferiority or caution. Thus, although I have been encouraged by my (male) supervisor to join in the social life of our department, I have found this difficult to do. This has adversely affected my research because I have excluded myself from and, in turn, been excluded from much scientific discussion and networking.

The surprising problem that women seem to have in these disciplines is the intuitive part of the process. Perhaps because of our encultured lack of confidence, or because of our more down-to-earth attitudes born of our continual emotional responsibilities and interests, or perhaps because of our heretofore systematic exclusion from the scientific naming process (cf. Susan Griffin, 1978, Dale Spender, 1980) women tend to be mistrustful of the mathematical symbolism and formalism of science. Men, on the other hand, seem to just launch themselves into it, and then find that it has, to some extent, a life of its own that carries them on into the mainstream while we are lagging behind trying to convince ourselves that a particular piece of formalism is mathematically sound—and sometimes it isn't (although it can serve as a stepping stone or catalyst if one will just go with it), despite all the rhetoric about mathematics as an exact science!

Thus, there is a lot of work needed here in terms of a feminist analysis of how women perceive symbolic languages compared with men—or perhaps, on how women perceive symbolic languages developed by men—and there is a need to consider the inclusion of thought processes into the scholarly literature so that ideas are not lost or deliberately obscured in the formalism. On the other hand, it is important for mathematics to be seen as a language that engenders its own logic which may not be exactly expressible in other languages such as English. The problem is complex, and I can only say that on balance, the language of mathematics is enormously interesting and exciting, and I hope that more feminists become involved with it so that we can explore it in a feminist context and then, perhaps, contribute something entirely new to the discipline.

Nevertheless, the arcane nature of mathematics, like the experimental nature of physics, requires long, uninterrupted periods of work, and thus both mathematicians and physicists tend to require the services of a wife to handle their mundane matters. In fact, this separation between the mundane and the arcane has tended to produce, or attract, people with a lack of interest in, or time for, social issues, and hence with a conservative attitude. Funding pressures have further entrenched this conservatism, so that scientists have been generally very reluctant to speak out about the possible dangers to the community of their work. Younger scientists in all disciplines, however, are perhaps less conservative these days, particularly because of the environmental crisis. It should be noted, however, that 20 years ago, physicists were instrumental in establishing "Science for the People" (Kathy Greeley & Sue Tafler, 1980), and more recently, many physicists of all ages signed a resolution not to work on the Reagan administration's Star Wars program.

As a further example of the difficulty of establishing a feminist critique of mathematics and physics, consider the following opposing radical views: S. E. Anderson and Maurice Bazin (1980), in talking about "Science, Technology and Black Liberation," take the Marxist thesis of B. Hessen (1971) that Newton's *Principia* evolved out of the "needs of early capitalist development and its attendant technology. In short, *Principia* was not, and could not be, a work of 'pure science' by a value-free or 'neutral' science." On the other hand, Emilie de Breteuil, Marquise du Châtelet, translated Newton's *Principia* from Latin into French (adding her own mathematical commentaries) (Lynn Osen, 1974); the freedom of thought displayed in Newton's work (challenging the conventional notion of God's role in the nature of the universe) was an important intellectual influence on the conceptual development of the French Revolution.

These are aspects of a radical debate on the content of physics and mathematics that are of relevance to a feminist critique. Also (cf. Hilary Rose & Steven Rose, 1980, p. 26), there is always more possible science than there is funding, and so choices are made that will attract funding, and this is far from value-free; the effect on mathematics and science directions if the funding bodies were feminist is difficult to tell without further development of a feminist critique. Similarly, as discussed above, choices of metaphor or paradigm in the intellectual core of physics and mathematics are not value-free.

SOME OF THE BARRIERS

Adrienne Rich's 1973 comment, that "There is no discipline that does not obscure and devalue the history and experience of women as a group" (Adrienne Rich, 1980, pp.

134–135), is strikingly true of the mythology that has surrounded the supposed sex-differences in ability in math and the hard sciences such as physics (see, for example, R. E. Stafford, 1972). In the nineteenth century, one of the great debates was the effect of brain size on intelligence. The hope was of course, that women would be proven to be intellectually inferior to men. (See, for example, Eileen Byrne, 1986–1989). Finally, Elizabeth Fennema and Julia Sherman (1977) showed that environmental and cultural factors were more significant than any biological difference, and Gilah Leder (1980) suggested that fear of success, in a culture that views bright girls as unfeminine, was a major reason for girls' relative "failure" in mathematics and hard sciences. [See Dale Spender, this volume.] Ruth Bleier (1986) reports that differences in math ability *within* gender groups outweigh any differences *between* such groups.

Nevertheless, despite equal opportunity programs spawned in response to such research, the effects of these myths still linger. Certainly they still live in the psyches of women of my generation, and I do not believe that they have been eradicated entirely in today's generation of schoolgirls with their often-flaunted antifeminism.

In my experience, the main aspects of the disciplines themselves that have discriminated against women are the isolating (arcane) nature of their language and the time-consuming nature of their practice. Like all disciplines, these require long hours of uninterrupted concentration. A problem for women, however, who tend to take the most responsibility for the emotional maintenance and development of relationships, be they with partners, children, elderly parents, or co-workers, is that mathematics and physics have no bearing on everyday emotional life. The daily interruptions to work that can provide retrospective inspiration for arts and behavioral sciences play no such creative role in mathematics and physics (and other hard sciences). I have found that the emotional interruptions in my life (which enrich my life enormously, even if they are, at times, tumultous or difficult) have led me to be considered to be less "bright" (a word the boys love to use!) than my colleagues because I am choosing to take longer to do my Ph.D. than they expect a single-minded young man to take. (I have observed this to be true for other women, too.) I think it's still true that women's (much more than men's) emotional involvements are considered a sign of intellectual inferiority in these disciplines, whereas feminists value the intelligence displayed in living.

For me, the lack of visible positive role models for women has been a barrier to success. Though most current university science students have not heard of them, books such as *Women in Mathematics* (Lynn Osen, 1974) have been a wonderful inspiration to me, supplementing the official historical poster on many mathematics departments' walls: *Men of Mathematics*, which despite its title, includes one woman, Emmy Noether. As far as my own area of research goes, there is one well-recognized nineteenth century founding foremother, Sonia Kovalevsky, whose name is given to a fundamental theorem of applied mathematics (the Cauchy-Kovalevsky existence theorem for partial differential equations). Several years ago, when I mentioned to a male colleague that Kovalevsky was a woman, he was very surprised, and immediately began to suppose that her contribution was no doubt derivative of Cauchy's work. [See Bernice Carroll, this volume, on "originality."] Recently, however, I was present at an undergraduate lecture in which this theorem was introduced, and the lecturer make Kovalevsky's gender clear to his class. There are also two French women who are now about 60 years old and are still very active in research and whose respected, post-graduate-level text book is known in our department as "The Girls' Book." On balance, I like the appellation, as it makes women visible, and the book is too good to be put down.

NEW RESEARCH DIRECTIONS

No new research directions that I am aware of have emerged in these disciplines as a result of feminist activity, apart from the enormous amount of Girls and Math and Girls and Science research that has been done *about* these disciplines rather than *within* them. As Gilah Leder once said to me, it was easier as a woman to go into postgraduate study in mathematics education rather than in math itself; perhaps if women like Gilah had gone into math research, new directions would have emerged within the discipline, too! Nevertheless, the research about the disciplines has been fascinating. In 1984, Women Into Science and Engineering (WISE) was founded in England by the Equal Opportunity Commission (Hilary Rose, 1986a). During the same year in Australia, WISENET (Women In Science Enquiry Network) was established at the remarkably successful Women's Studies session of Australian and New Zealand Association for the Advancement of Science (ANZAAS) in Canberra. Groups such as these have generated research into the reasons for women's underrepresentation in most sciences. WISTA (Women In Science and Technology In Australia) was also initiated in 1984 by Dr. Elizabeth Hazel of the School of Microbiology at the University of New South Wales. It is a 4-year study (1985–1989) which looks "at factors which help or hinder women's access to and progression in, science and technology in higher education" (Eileen Byrne, 1988), in the context of institutional ecology (viz., the concept that institutions provide an environment subject to which organisms grow and develop. Note the creative choice of research paradigm given Dr. Hazel's discipline!)

Although such research about the disciplines is vital in providing clues for the development of a feminist critique of their content, it is still difficult to conceive of what a feminist direction within math or physics would be. Certainly in terms of applications of these disciplines, women's concerns for life and the environment could influence the direction of nuclear research. I would also expect women to be more interested than men in studying psychic phenomena (although the Russians have reputedly done a lot of research on these topics, so there are cultural as well as gender influences in such choices).

Physicist Roger Jones argues, in *Physics as Metaphor* (1982), that the philosophy of quantum mechanics and general relativity has been forgotten by physicists, and that "in fact, in the last fifty years, the trend in mainstream physical science has been away from consciousness and holism toward the mechanistic and divisible world of the nineteenth century," (p. 7) with its modern elementary particle theory. (This is not my area of study and so I know little about it. However, Sharon Traweek has done some anthropological studies of the particle physics community, which indicate that these physicists use particle physics imagery in their interpersonal communication that keeps them detached from each other and their environment [Elizabeth Fee, 1986; Sharon Traweek, 1988]. I would say that this is also true of the mathematical physics community, but that it reflects the general male culture rather than—or more than—the science which provides the imagery. I say this because the few women in the field don't appear to use the imagery in such a way, though further research on the subject would be essential to the development of a feminist critique.)

Jones says that the role of consciousness in early relativity and quantum physics was still a passive one, whereas our consciousness in fact *creates* reality; he argues that the basic constructs of physical science, space, time, matter, and number, are subjective metaphors. It is certainly true that different cultures see time and space differently, and I think that women in our culture see time differently from the way men do, as we have different priorities and demands on our time. (See also Frieda Johles Forman, 1989.) Indeed, in speaking of the metaphor of spacetime, which is a mathematical construct replacing the nineteenth century concept of a material ether, Jones says, "There's a serious question as to whether physics describes anything *physical* at all" (p. 139). Jones seems to think that he is exposing physics as a fraud. But for me, this is precisely what is so exciting and liberating about mathematics (as a language for physics): that it enables one to travel beyond one's physical preconceptions to a relatively (even if not an absolutely) high degree. Jones says, "In a world in which space, motion, and matter are distinct from mind and wisdom" (and although this is the way lay people in the West see it, in contrast to, say, the attitude expressed in the *I Ching*, I think that mathematicians and physicists do realize [though perhaps without any deep sense of philosophy] that they are creating notions of space and matter, which are thus not distinct from mind and wisdom), "perhaps the closest we can come to a spiritual realm is a mathematical one. The spirit/matter dichotomy slowly undermines itself . . . .(In) quantum theory and relativity . . . matter and substance are mathematical abstractions. Physics tells us that mind and body are one. (Causality) and spacetime are metaphors from different cultures that bespeak the unfathomable unity" (pp. 139–140).

Jones has touched on a very complex philosophical area that needs to be considered in a feminist critique of these disciplines. Such popular ideas as these, or those of Fritjof Capra or Gary Zukav, or even of the less popular academic philosophers of science, referring as they do to spiritual and philosophical matters, indicate possible starting points for feminist analysis or inspiration within these disciplines. In the foreword to Zukav (1979), physicist David Finkelstein refers to the two, usually mutually exclusive, ways of seeing quantum mechanics (pointed out by the great mathematician John von Neumann):

1. Quantum mechanics deals with propositions defined by processes of preparation and observation involving subject and object and obeying a new logic; not with objective properties of the object alone.
2. Quantum mechanics deals with objective properties of the object alone, obeying the old logic, but they jump in a random way when an observation is made.
    Most working physicists seem to see one of these ways (the second) and not the other. Perhaps personality can determine the direction of science. I think there are 'thing' minds and 'people' minds. Good parents, psychologists and writers have to be 'people' people, while mechanics, engineers and physicists tend to be 'thing' people. Physics has become very scary for such physicists because it is already so thingless. New evolutions, as profound as those of Einstein and Heisenberg, are waiting for a new generation of more daring and integrated thinkers. (p. xxii)

Such a generation of feminist mathematicians and physicists could, given enough spinning, sparking, and genius, lead to the discovery that there are more things in heaven and earth, gentlemen, than are dreamt of in your physics.

RESPONSE TO FEMINIST KNOWLEDGE

As yet there is no new feminist knowledge within these disciplines. The new knowledge about these disciplines (WISTA, Girls and Maths, etc.) has been relatively well received and financed by the mainstream. How lasting will be its effect on the mainstream—and on women—remains to be seen. I think the fact that this research about girls and science has been done within the existing male academy, and has accompanied a general Western political climate in which antidiscrimination laws have been passed at the same time as governments are seeking to increase the number of young people in science makes a backlash seem unlikely in the short-to-medium term, at least.

Robyn Arianrhod

HOW HAVE MEN PROTECTED THEIR POWER BASE?

Men have protected their power base in these disciplines by keeping women out! They've done this by perpetuating the myth that girls are inherently inferior to boys in their ability to do mathematics and hard sciences, but women have been successful in fighting this myth. It must be said, however, that we have only attained an unstable equilibrium with respect to this debate, and the effects of such myths are still felt by some girls and women, and believed by some male scientists. Of those (majority of) male scientists who do accept the dismantling of the myth, very few, I believe, have any concept of feminist concerns with the discipline such as I've touched on here, nor would they support such concerns at this stage.

Nevertheless, there has already been some improvement in women's participation in these disciplines in the last 20 years as the comparisons between the following figures and those at the beginning of the essay indicate:

1. In 1988 (Monash University Statistics, 1988), 41.7% of undergraduates in the science faculty at Monash University were women (cf. 26.9% in 1969), while 32.3% of postgraduates were women.

2. In 1984 (Gabrielle Baldwin, 1985) 34.8% of "other than higher degree" (essentially undergraduate) enrollments in mathematics were female, while 26.6% of Masters' Preliminary candidates, 29.4% of Masters' candidates and 0% of Ph.D. candidates were women. (Some of those women have subsequently changed their Masters' enrollment to Ph.D. status.) Women represented 5.4% of the mathematics lecturing staff, and 9.6% of the total academic staff (including tutors) were women.

The same year in physics, there were no women on the academic staff at Monash, though 2.9% of the sessional (causal) teachers were women (cf. 15.9% in math). Females represented 3.3% of postgraduate enrollment, while 13.7% of the "other than for higher degree" enrollments were female.

In 1986 at Monash (WISTA), 42% of math undergraduates were women, 28.6% of math Ph.D. students were women; 21.8% of physics undergraduates, and 3.6% of physics Ph.D. students were women.

Note that relative to the other Australian institutions surveyed by WISTA, Monash had the largest percentage of female undergraduate enrollments in math, and the second largest in physics.

In 1985 in the United States, 15.1% of those with doctoral degrees in science were women. The percentage of physicists has decreased since 1973: 5.9% of scientists with doctorates were physicists, and 1.5% of women scientists with doctorates were physicists.

THE CURRENT SITUATION

Feminist knowledge about the discipline increases women's self-esteem by counteracting destructive myths about their lack of ability or brain size! If this knowledge succeeds in encouraging more women into these disciplines, it will certainly enhance their intellectual opportunities and it may enhance their economic opportunities. Because (in Australia) the majority of physicists (63%) work in tertiary institutions (A. W. Pryor, 1989), which have never offered enviable salaries, choice of career path is important in this context.

As mentioned earlier, feminist knowledge within these disciplines has yet to be developed. These disciplines have been resistant to change because of their arcane language and the seeming objectivity of their content.

Many countries are entering an interesting time as far as science goes; changes in university structures with forced amalgamations of universities and institutes, the introduction of more business-oriented and business-funded science research, more accountability of researchers to funding bodies, both private and government, and the likelihood of a division between teaching institutions and staff and research institutions and staff, all have profound implications for women.

The traditionally male, competitive style of business could prove to be yet another hurdle for women entering science research, and if there is a demarcation between teaching and research, it is possible that women will be concentrated—by choice or otherwise—in their traditional domain of teaching, which may become devalued in comparison with (male) research. (On the other hand, the opposite may happen, that teaching institutions may provide unprecedented job opportunities for women in science because governments may decide to see teaching the younger generation of scientists as vital to the economy.)

This is an important time for women to consider entering these disciplines, especially as there are predictions that both Australia and the United States will suffer severe shortages of scientists in a few years' time. However, this shortage is due to lack of adequate career paths and funding (which may be one reason that girls are being encouraged into these fields, one can never be sure of governments' motives), and to the growing public perception that science has caused the global environmental crisis. It is true that chemistry is the discipline most associated with industrial pollution, and in fact in Australia 30% of chemistry Ph.D.'s work in industry compared with only 6% of physics Ph.D.'s (A. W. Pryor, 1989). These figures would be different in countries like the United States with a nuclear industry. The nuclear problem, in all its aspects, including uranium mining in Australia, is, indeed, physics' problem. (As noted earlier, physics is declining in popularity among United States science graduates, and I think similar trends are developing in other Western countries.) Science desperately needs an effective public relations program, for there are many popular misconceptions about science, particularly with respect to its compatability with feminism and other human issues. On the other hand, the question as to whether or not the answer to environmental problems, and even economic problems, is simply more science, is complex and its answer is unclear and needs a feminist and scientific analysis.

Thus women, with the support of the women's movement and a feminist analysis, now have the chance to play an unprecedented part in influencing the direction of science, and consequently, our way of life. Despite the current problems, I think that the potential and power of science for good and ill is too great for women to leave to men. I think that the growing conservatism of Western (not to mention other) societies requires vigorous feminist counteraction in all disciplines.

Besides, to glimpse the intellectual beauty of these disciplines is to experience a consummate joy that should not be denied to women. Unfortunately, for me at least, this joy is often diluted by a working environment in which interpersonal interactions are not the lively, time-consuming riches that I as a feminist need to do my best creative work. I need more feminist mathematicians and physicists—unfortunately, women without a feminist consciousness are not enough, as they tend to reinforce the status quo. Perhaps this is simply a reflection of the fact that women are not yet present in these disciplines at a "critical mass" level, and are struggling to survive as best they can. Perhaps, too, the women's movement needs to embrace those of us who are in these disciplines with more understanding than it has done heretofore.

BIBLIOGRAPHY

Anderson, S. E. & Bazin, Maurice. (1980). Science, technology and Black liberation. In Rita Arditti, Pat Breenan, & Steve Cavrak (Eds.), *Science and liberation*. Boston: South End Press.

Arditti, Rita. (1980). Feminism and science. In Rita Arditti, Pat Brennan & Steve Cavrak (Eds.), *Science and liberation*. Boston: South End Press.

Arditti, Rita, Brennan, Pat, & Cavrak, Steve. (Eds.). (1980). *Science and liberation*. Boston: South End Press.

Baldwin, Gabrielle. (1985). *Women at Monash University*. Clayton: Monash University.

Byrne, Eileen. (1986–1989). *Women in science and technology in Australia (WISTA)*. There are a number of interesting WISTA discussion papers with good bibliographies, for example, The image of science, Mathematics as critical filter. Correspondence to Professor Eileen Byrne, Professor of Education (Policy Studies), Department of Education, University of Queensland, St. Lucia, Queensland 4607, Australia. (Thanks to Margaret James for this information.)

Byrne, Eileen. (1988, July 11–12). *Educational policy: Institutional ecology and management directions*. Paper presented at the meeting of the International Forum on Women in Public Sector Administration, Queensland Institute of Technology, Queensland, Australia.

Bleier, Ruth. (Ed.). (1986). *Feminist approaches to science*. Elmsford, NY: Pergamon Press.

Bleier, Ruth. (1986). Sex differences research: Science or belief? In Ruth Bleier (Ed.), *Feminist approaches to science* (pp. 147–164). Elmsford, NY: Pergamon Press.

Capra, Fritjof. (1975). *The Tao of physics*. Berkeley, CA: Shambala.

Clements, M. A. (Ken). (1979). Sex differences in mathematical performance: An historical perspective. *Educational Studies in Mathematics, 10*, 305–322.

Daly, Mary. (1978). *Gyn/Ecology: The metaethics of radical feminism*. Boston: Beacon Press.

Einstein, Albert, & Infeld, Leopold. (1938). *The evolution of physics*. Cambridge: Cambridge University Press.

Feyerabend, Paul. (1978). *Against method*. London: Verso.

Fee, Elizabeth. (1983). Woman's nature and scientific objectivity. In Marian Lowe & Ruth Hubbard (Eds.), *Woman's nature: Rationalizations of inequality* (pp. 9–28). Elmsford, NY: Pergamon Press.

Fee, Elizabeth. (1986). Critiques of modern science: The relationship of feminism to other radical epistemologies. In Ruth Bleier (Ed.), *Feminist approaches to science* (pp. 42–56). Elmsford, NY: Pergamon Press.

Fennema, Elizabeth & Sherman, Julia. (1977). Sex-related differences in mathematics achievement, spatial visualization, and affective factors. *American Educational Research Journal, 14*, 51–71.

Forman, Frieda Johles. (Ed., with Sowton, Caoran). (1989). *Taking our time: Feminist perspectives on temporality*. Elmsford, NY: Pergamon Press.

Gleick, James. (1987). *Chaos: Making a new science*. New York: Viking Penguin.

Griffin, Susan. (1978). *Woman and nature: The roaring inside her*. New York: Harper & Row.

Greeley, Kathy & Tafler, Sue. (1980). History of science for the people. In Rita Arditti, Pat Brennan, & Steve Cavrak (Eds.), *Science and liberation*. Boston: South End Press.

Hessen, B. (1971). *The social and economic roots of Newton's Principia*. New York: Howard Furtig.

Jones, Roger. (1982). *Physics as a metaphor*. New York: Meridian.

Keller, Evelyn Fox. (1983). *A feeling for the organism: The life and work of Barbara McClintock*. San Francisco: W. H. Freeman.

Kivelson, Margaret Gallard. (1988, Sept.). Women in physics: Trends in U.S. higher education. *The Australian Physicist, 25*(8).

Kline, Morris. (1980). *The loss of certainty*. New York: Oxford University Press.

Leder, Gilah. (1980). Bright girls, mathematics, and fear of success. *Educational Studies in Mathematics, 11*, 411–422.

Merchant, Carolyn. (1980). *The death of nature: Women, ecology and the scientific revolution*. New York: Harper & Row.

Osen, Lynn. (1974). *Women in mathematics*. Cambridge, MA: MIT Press.

Pryor, A. W. (1989, May). Physics PhD's in Australia. *Australian Physicist, 26*, 113–119.

Rich, Adrienne. (1980). *On lies, secrets and silences: Selected prose 1966–1978.* London: Virago.

Rose, Hilary. (1986a). Nothing less than half the labs. In Steven Rose & Lisa Appignanesi (Eds.), *Science and beyond.* Oxford: Blackwell.

Rose, Hilary. (1986b). Beyond masculinist realities: A feminist epistemology for the sciences. In Ruth Bleier (Ed.), *Feminist approaches to science* (pp. 57–76). Elmsford, NY: Pergamon Press.

Rose, Hilary & Rose, Steven. (1980). The myth of the neutrality of science. In Rita Arditti, Pat Brennan, & Steve Cavrak (Eds.), *Science and liberation.* Boston: South End Press.

Rose, Steven & Appignanesi, Lisa. (Eds.). (1986). *Science and beyond.* Oxford: Blackwell.

Sayers, Janet. (1986). Feminism and science. In Steven Rose & Lisa Appignanesi (Eds.), *Science and beyond.* Oxford: Blackwell.

Spender, Dale. (1980). *Man-made language.* London: Routledge & Kegan Paul.

Stafford, R. E. (1972). Hereditary and environmental components of qualitative reasoning. *Review of Educational Research, 42*(2), 183–201.

Traweek, Sharon. (1988). *Beamtimes and lifetimes: The world of high energy physicists.* Cambridge, MA: Harvard University Press.

Whitrow, Gerald James. (1961). *The natural philosophy of time.* Melbourne: Thomas Nelson and Sons.

Whylde, Janie. (1980, summer). Girls and science education. *Science for the People, 46.*

Zukav, Gary. (1979). *The dancing Wu Li masters: An overview of the new physics.* New York: Bantam.

Chapter 3

Women's Experiential Approaches to Peace Studies

Elise Boulding

The Women's International League for Peace and Freedom, recognizing the urgency of mobilizing the intellectual as well as the moral and psychological forces of mankind for the making of peace, advocates international cooperation in peace research, preferably under the auspices of the United Nations.

It is important that the various institutes and organizations working in this field in different countries should be kept in contact and informed about each other's activities and findings. The Congress urges UNESCO as soon as possible to call an international conference of scholars working in this field, that scientists engaged in peace research may not only exchange ideas but also develop a new vision of their contribution to the building of world order. (WILPF, 1962)

This minute of the Fifteenth International Women's International League for Peace and Freedom (WILPF) Congress at Asilomar, California, in July 1962 was followed by the appointment of a WILPF Committee on Peace Research to nurture the new field. Thus it came about that the women appointed to that committee, Johanne Reutz Gjermoe, economist, and Ingrid Eide Galtung, sociologist, both of Norway; Sushila Nayar, Minister of Health, India; Fujiko Isono, anthropologist, Japan; Sheila Young, Canada; and myself, became midwives to what was to become, in 1965, the first international professional association for the diverse and interdisciplinary group of scholars on five continents who call themselves peace researchers. The committee did this by starting an International Newsletter for scholars (which soon became transformed into the official newsletter of the new professional association, with myself as editor), and getting the United Nations Educational, Scientific, and Cultural Organization (UNESCO) to help convene the gathering proposed in the 1962 WILPF Resolution. The International Peace Research Association (IPRA) was launched at a meeting in 1965 held in Groningen, The Netherlands. The Norwegian members were among the founders in the late 1950s of what became Peace Research Institute—Oslo (PRIO), the Oslo-based mother of the new breed of peace research institutes. During those years, I worked with Elizabeth Converse, managing editor of the first major academic peace research journal (*Journal of Conflict Resolution*) from 1957 to the early 1960s, and subsequently developed a seminar program for the first U.S. peace research institute (Center for Research on Conflict Resolution, 1957–1971), at the

---

I thank Berenice Carroll for her helpful comments on this essay.

University of Michigan. In Japan, WILPF educator Hisako Ukita was both a founder and first secretary for the new Japan Peace Research group, and by 1970 I was the first Executive Secretary for the new North American Consortium on Peace Research, Education, and Development (COPRED).

Probably in no other discipline have women been so actively involved in the founding process. This may be due in part to the scholar-activist tradition of WILPF, which came into being in 1915 to try to bring World War I to an end. Its founders, including Jane Addams and Emily Green Balch and scholars and professional women from Europe and Asia, served as exemplars of female intellectual innovation in the tired old field of international relations. In our own generation we had Alva Myrdal of Sweden, rapidly rising to a position of leadership in the disarmament field, and we had Betty Goetz Lall in the United States, serving as disarmament consultant to both governmental and nongovernmental bodies.

In spite of this midwife role, and the continuing activity of women scholars in the peace studies field, it appears today as a very male field. Although women have held leading positions in COPRED, other peace research associations and peace studies sections of mainstream professional organizations have had predominantly male officers. All the Secretaries General of IPRA were male until 1989, only male researchers are considered for chairs in peace research, and usually only male scholars are thought of when a "leading" peace researcher is required for speaking or writing engagements. That this could be true from such a beginning only underscores the pervasiveness of male dominance in academia.

FEMINIST CRITIQUE OF PEACE STUDIES

Only in recent years has a specific feminist critique of peace studies developed. The first feminist challenge to IPRA came in 1975, International Women's Year. Women scholars requested, and were given, a special program slot at the IPRA Biennial Conference held that year in Finland, on the subject of "Women and World Order." This was however a declaration of visibility rather than a critique of the discipline. Two years later, at the next IPRA Congress in Mexico City, there was a "women's rebellion." All-women's protest meetings were held to discuss the shortcomings of male-oriented peace research, and the Secretary General was prevailed upon to call a special plenary session for women to present their concerns about the maleness of peace studies. By the time the Women and Militarism Study Group was formally recognized at the IPRA Congress of Canada (1981) there was already a body of writing by women scholars on the relationship between militarism, male dominance, and exploitative development practices. [See Claudia Salazar, this volume.] Much of that writing came from women members of the Peace Education Commission, who began to identify the connections between sexism, militarism, and educational practice, both formal and nonformal. At the 1983 IPRA Congress women members read a formal declaration to the Plenary Business Session addressing both issues of women's participation in IPRA and the failure of male researchers to address critical issues of structural violence involving gender as a variable.

By and large, members of the Women and Militarism Study Group, and the overlapping Peace Education Commission, were inside the academy but peripheral to the mainstream. Some were more comfortable with conventional systems analysis than others, but the support group phenomenon was important to everyone. A major disappointment for women peace researchers has been the lack of interest in their work on the part of the women's liberation movement. The women's movement, understandably focused on the situation of women per se, has devoted little time to tracing the connections between women's problems and the war prone tendencies of the international system. Also the drive for equality has led many women to seek equality in existing power systems, including the military. This approach to equality is now under heavy criticism in the women's liberation movement, however.

On the whole, mainstream peace research has looked on feminist research as a special case rather than as contributing to the main body of peace theory. The work is seen as primarily of interest to women. This attitude has always characterized the mainstream attitude to peace education as well, which was also seen as "women's work."

THEORY AS EXPERIENCED REALITY

Model building as an intellectual exercise appears to devalue women's experience because of the level of abstraction inherent in the activity. Models of arms races, arms control systems, and economic conversion processes usually leave no place for women's abundant knowledge of the way militarism and its antithesis, nonviolence, operate at the concrete level of human experience in family and community. When I conducted a survey of women peace researchers (Elise Boulding, 1979) I was struck by the clarity of these women about the necessity for anchoring analysis in experienced reality. Also, the approach to theory building was different. Initially I tried to classify the researchers according to one of three different orientations: (1) mainstream traditions of international relations, (2) new conceptual frameworks, and (3) new social order. However even the "traditionalists" among the survey participants wanted new conceptual frameworks. The only significant distinction, then, was between those who focused primarily on a reconceptualization of national security, asking new questions about the conditions of peace, and those who based their work on a more radical rejection of the existing order [see Irene Diamond, this volume], seeking new models for a future world order based on a different approach to power.

The new methods women have introduced are all basically ways of linking the experiential and the theoretical modes. It is systems analysis anchored in human relations. It is a new form of critical peace research. The old form critiqued society as a set of structures that generated violence and injustice but was gender blind in its social analysis and drew sharp distinctions between public and private spaces. The new form of critical peace research, abolishing the distinction between public and private spaces, identifies the human behaviors of men and women, and the cultural patterns that underlie those behaviors, to demonstrate the continuous reproduction of systems of injustice. The new analysis is both more complete and more soundly empirical.

Few people realize that one of the first women writers on peace research was Jessie Bernard (1957), one of the mothers of women studies. Following her initial analysis of actors and issues, women scholars began to explore power, developing the feminist conception of power as power *to*, or empowerment, rather than power *over*. Margaret Mead's work (1967) was a useful starting point. Early scholars addressing this issue included Elizabeth Converse (1968, 1972), Inge Powell Bell (1968), Joan Bondurant (1965, 1971), Eva Senghaas-Knobloch (1969), Berenice Carroll (1970, 1972), Betty Reardon (1971), Judith Stiehm (1972), and Elise Boulding (1972, 1974 a,b). The concepts of these founding mothers of peace studies are only today gaining acceptance. However, with the exception of Bondurant (she would be thought of primarily as a specialist on Gandhian nonviolence) and Mead, they are not referenced in the mainstream peace research literature.

By the 1970s women peace researchers were reconceptualizing security as security with an adversary, or common security, rather than security against the adversary, also expanding the notion to mean security against want, security of human rights, the security of an empowered civilian society: Hanna Newcombe (1973), Ruth Silvard (1974), Alva Myrdal (1976), Judith Torney (1974), Betty Goetz Lall (1977), Mary Kaldor (1977), Pat Mische (1977), Elise Boulding (1976, 1977). By the 1980s they were analyzing the relationship between war and patriarchy (Betty Reardon, 1985; Birgit Brock-Utne, 1986, 1989; Riane Eisler, 1984, 1987; Sheila Tobias, 1985). While some of these names are well-known, they are not thought of by the mainstream as leading developers of the field of peace research. The fact is that they have managed to find their own audience, independently of the peace research community.

FEMINIST RECONCEPTUALIZATIONS

I have already indicated that two major contributions of women researchers have been toward the redefinition of power and of security. The very fact that these redefinitions are being increasingly accepted today (though without acknowledgment of their source) is all the more reason why it should be remembered that women have played and are still playing an important role in developing the reconceptualizations. Note for example the work of Randall Forsberg (1984) and Carolyn Stephenson (1982) on alternative security, Scilla McLean (1988) and Sheila Tobias (1985) on women and security decision making, Riitta Wahlstrom (1986) on enemy images, Eva Senghaas-Knobloch (1986, 1988), Corinne Kumar d'Souza (1986, 1988) and Diana Russell (1989) on feminist analysis of power and women's ways of knowing, and Carol Cohn (1988) on the role of male language in shaping security strategy divorced from experienced reality.

Women were among the early peace researchers to examine the interactive effects of militarism, development, and the environment. Interestingly enough, this development came through IPRA's Peace Education Commission, which from its beginning in 1972 provided a special niche for women scholars and teachers. The Commission pioneered a series of summer schools in Vasterhaningen in the mid-1970s with strong Third World participation, beginning the sensitization of the Western peace research community to Third World issues. The peace development nexus was introduced into peace studies curriculae along with community-based learning before these were "officially" research topics (Robin Burns, 1980, 1981, 1984). Gender studies that focused on male as well as female socialization also first appeared in this Commission (Celina Garcia, 1981).

Women have been more comfortable with the scholar-practitioner role than many of their male colleagues. It matches their preference for linking theories with experienced reality. Not only have they pioneered experiential approaches to peace learning (Birgit Brock-Utne, 1985; Barbara Roberts, 1989), but they have explored mediation at every level: family, local community, corporate, national, and international. They have particularly flourished in the field of community mediation as research practitioners (Susan Carpenter, 1977, 1988; Jennifer Beer, 1986).

The models that women have developed of more local, more resource-conserving, less hierarchical societies characterized both by greater diversity and greater interdependence in a gentler world free of power blocks and the domination of the West, are also commanding more attention in the context of the present ecological crisis. Note Pat Mische (1977), Joanna Macy (1983), Eva Senghaas-Knoblich (1969, 1986), Vandana Shiva (1988), Corinne Kumar d'Souza (1988), and Berenice Carroll (forthcoming). Cultural analyses of women's images of the future (Eleanora Masini, 1983; E. Boulding, 1983; Isaksson, 1988) have, however, yet to be taken seriously.

The most striking new thinking being introduced by feminist researchers today has to do with reconceptualizing militarism and war in terms of patriarchy and violence against women and minors (Elise Boulding, 1978; Cynthia Enloe, 1983, 1987; Birgit Brock-Utne, 1985, 1989; Betty Reardon, 1985; Andree Michel, 1985). This changes the concept of peace. As Birgit Brock-Utne emphasizes, no society can be characterized as peaceful in which women and children are battered and raped. The same patriarchal institutions that permit that kind of violence also permit war. This means that peace building is a far more complex task than arranging for adequate institutions of mediation between states.

Violence against women is of course widely written about outside the peace research community. [See Jane Caputi, this volume.] What women in the peace research field have contributed particularly to that literature is an in-depth analysis of how violence against women is linked not only to militarism and war but to economic and environmental exploitation. In relation to the latter, IPRA's Food Policy Study Group (another study group with a lot of leadership from women) did some groundbreaking work during its decade of activity on linking exploitative practices of the countries of the North and Third World hunger in an analysis of cycles of violence and disempowerment of women, basing much of its work on Ester Boserup's pioneering study, *Women's Role in Economic Development* (1970). Examples of this group's work can be found in Ursula Oswald (1979), and Elise Boulding (1979).

New research directions stemming from women's work: (1) Identifying linkages between interpersonal and familial violence, general cultural predispositions to violence, and war; (2) continuing analysis of the patriarchal system as an economic, political, social, and psychological system based on domination; (3) identifying the interrelationships among human and social development, economic development, environmental stewardship, and peace; (4) exploring the role of imaging alternative futures, alternative sources of security, in peace processes; (5) the study of enemy images and social perceptions of threat in maintaining cycles of violence; (6) study of the experiential basis of peace learning, development of peace studies curriculae that link the experiential and the theoretical.

MEN'S BELITTLING OF FEMINIST PARADIGMS

In the peace studies field it would be overstating to say that men have subverted the development of women's knowledge, unless ignoring something is equivalent to subverting it. It does appear that men frequently have a less multidimensional view of reality, and can also live more in their heads without checking the empirical "out there" for confirmation of their mental constructions. They tend to protect those constructions by belittling feminist paradigms, and staying within their own old boy's networks. The old saying about there being no competent women in a given field is continuously if spuriously confirmed in peace studies because men recommend each other all the time both for posts and interesting special assignments.

But, on second thought, one can argue that some significant part of the peace research tradition has indeed subverted women's knowledge by interpreting their skills as essentially service skills directed toward the maintenance of some level of peace in an otherwise violent society. "Gentling the military" and "gentling little boys" in family and school systems geared to producing aggressive achievers and defenders of the realm represent concepts that subvert feminist critique of existing institutions. Women's critiques of society are continuously being reframed in more traditional contexts, thus removing their critical edge. The fuzzy-minded stereotype of women as being innately more peaceable than men creates a blindness to the level of innovation and creativity required for peace, and reinforces a tendency to dismiss women's creative work in peacemaking, particularly their work as mediators, as biological destiny. [See Mary Roth Walsh, this volume.] Male peace researchers are hardly the worst offenders in this regard, and the growing number of male scholars who are supportive of feminist analysis needs to be recognized and celebrated (e.g., Ake Bjerstedt, Kenneth Boulding, Clinton Fink, Johan Galtung, Jan Oberg, & Ofer Zur).

I have already indicated that women scholars' work on redefining security and developing new conceptions of power is finding its way into the mainstream. In the process, unfortunately, the fact that women were among the pioneers in this work has been lost sight of. They have become invisible through cooptation. The one area where an open challenge remains is in the analysis of patriarchy and in the linkage of war to violence against women. [See Cheris Kramarae, this volume.] It is hard to get many men to take that question seriously.

In general, peace studies has not been very practitioner-oriented until quite recently. Therefore the rapid development of a set of careers in mediation for women has not affected the field very much. As international mediation and dispute settlement begin to take center stage for peace researchers as we move toward the 1990s, the role that women have played in developing the field is once again likely to be ignored.

One thing that may change the status of women in the field in the long run is that the next generation of researchers, both women and men, will have available for the first time a curriculum in feminist peace studies during their student years. The proposal developed by Alice Wiser (1987) of the University of London together with Doris Elbers, University of Dortmund, and Barbara Roberts, Universite Concordia, Montreal, for a graduate program in "Transnational Education from a Feminist Perspective" is a harbinger of things to come. The materials are all there, the books and articles have been written, but they have not been assembled in a comprehensive fashion for teaching. The next generation of peace researchers will begin professional life with a higher level of awareness than their predecessors, and eventually feminist peace studies will percolate into the general peace studies curriculum.

In my view the most basic contribution that feminist knowledge has made to the life and work of women in the field of peace research is an understanding of the interface of the public and the private. Old conceptions of public and private have gone forever, and women have a new freedom to move across the entire range of social spaces present in a society. This increased freedom of movement has made it possible for women to extend their models of how society operates from the interpersonal to international. The ability to see connections makes it easier for women to bring variables from socio-economic development and ecology together in a more complex model of peace processes. It also enables women to extend their traditional networking skills from the local to the global level. The concept of an ecology of peace is easy for women to understand, and ecofeminism will be an important new area in peace research. The women's peace studies community is a transnational community, and the feminist commitment to nonhierarchical relationships has fostered a nurturant colleagueship among women with very different backgrounds.

Women peace researchers bear the same burdens of excessive responsibilities, inadequate support systems, and financial hardship that women elsewhere bear. Another kind of burden they bear is separation from large parts of the women's movement. Historically, the academic part of the women's movement has focused on the problematique of the situation of women, whereas women peace researchers have focused on the problematics of a society at war with itself, seeing gender issues as a part of that problem. To take two extremes, Dorothy Dinnerstein (1977) and Sara Ruddick (1980), two prominent exponents of new theories of socialization for nurturance and peaceableness who are also part of the mainstream women's movement, have done their work entirely outside the formal discipline of peace studies. Alva Myrdal, Betty Lall, Mary Kaldor, and Randall Forsberg, major names in the field of peace studies, have worked inside the discipline on problems of disarmament but outside the framework of feminist studies. There is a strong tension between these two foci for many women researchers today. I believe it is a creative tension. In the long run its resolution will bring women peace researchers closer to the larger women's movement and vice versa.

There is no question but that feminist knowledge has made an impact on peace studies at the conceptual level, as I have amply illustrated. The impact however has been blunted through cooptation, and women have remained largely marginalized in the field. The sharpness of the present challenge by women researchers to their male colleagues to recognize the centrality for the continued reproduction of militarism and warfare, of patriarchal institutions, and the cultures and practices of violence they foster, defies co-optation. As more men become willing to enter into dialogue on this subject and to undertake their own analyses of male domination and warfare (as, for example, Ian Harris, 1988, and Ian Welch, 1989), peace research paradigms will evolve toward more inclusive representations of the processes of conflict, peace, and change.

The same challenge that will bring about a major shift in the conception of peace research will also narrow the gulf between women peace researchers and the women's liberation movement. The perception that a major transformation in gender relationships is necessary for humans to live more justly and more fully with one another and their environment will provide the common ground for a future rapprochement.

I am pessimistic in the short run and optimistic in the long run, both about gender-inclusive developments in the disciplinary substance of peace studies, and about a freer, more equal and more creative partnership between women and men professionals in the field. The threat of human-induced catastrophes can either slow down or speed up the desired changes, but the direction of change is clear.

BIBLIOGRAPHY

Beer, Jennifer. (1986). *Peacemaking in your neighborhood.* Philadelphia: New Society Publishers.

Bell, Inge Powell. (1968). *Care and the strategy of non-violence.* New York: Random House.

Bernard, Jessie. (1957). Parties and issues in conflict. *Journal of Conflict Resolution, 1*(2), 11–121.

Bondurant, Joan. (1965). *Conquest of violence: The Gandhian philosophy of conflict.* Berkeley: University of California Press.

Bondurant, Joan. (1971). *Conflict, violence and nonviolence.* New York: Atherton.

Boserup, Ester. (1970). *Women's Role in Economic Development.* New York: St. Martin's Press.

Boulding, Elise. (1972). The child as shaper of the future. *Peace and Change, 1*(1), 11–17.

Boulding, Elise. (1974a). The measurement of cultural potentials for transnationalism. *Journal of Peace Research, 7*(3), 190–202.

Boulding, Elise. (1974b). The child and nonviolent social change. In Christopher Wulf (Ed.), *Handbook on Peace Education* (pp. 101–132). Frankfurt: International Peace Research Association.

Boulding, Elise. (1976). *The underside of history, a view of women through time.* Boulder, CO: Westview Press.

Boulding, Elise. (1977). Women in the twentieth century world, (Part III). *Women and the International System.* New York: Sage Publications.

Boulding, Elise. (1978). The child and nonviolent social change. In Israel Charny (Ed.), *Strategies against violence* (pp. 68–100). Boulder, CO: Westview Press.

Boulding, Elise. (1978). Women and social violence. *International Journal of Social Science, 30*(4), 801–815.

Boulding, Elise. (1979). Women, peripheries, and food production. In Luis Herrera and Raimo Vayrynen (Eds.), *Peace, development, and new international order* (pp. 294–310). Tampere, Finland: International Peace Research Association.

Boulding, Elise. (1981). Perspectives of women researchers on disarmament, national security, and world order. *Women Studies International Quarterly, 4*(1), 27–40.

Boulding, Elise. (1983). Women's visions of the future. In Eleanora Masini (Ed.), *Visions of desirable societies* (pp. 9–24). Elmsford, NY: Pergamon Press.

Brock-Utne, Birgit. (1985). *Educating for peace: A feminist perspective.* Elmsford, NY: Pergamon Press.

Brock-Utne, Birgit. (1989). *Feminist perspectives on peace and peace education.* Elmsford, NY: Pergamon Press.

Burns, Robin. (1980). Peace education: Between research and action. *Peace Research, 12*(3), 131–136. Canadian Peace Research Institute.

Burns, Robin. (1981). Development education and disarmament education. *Prospects, 11*(2), 123–137.

Burns, Robin. (1984). Can educational change precede research and development? *Research and Education Futures, Vol. I, Technological Development and Educational Futures* (pp. 79–86). Perth: National Conference of Australian Association for Research in Education.

Carpenter, Susan. (1977). *A repertoire of peacemaking skills.* Kent, OH: COPRED.

Carpenter, Susan, with W. J. D. Kennedy. (1988). *Managing public disputes.* San Francisco: Jossey-Bass.

Carroll, Berenice. (1970, Nov.). War termination and conflict theory. *Annals of the American academy of political and social science, 392.*

Carroll, Berenice. (1972). Peace research: The cult of power. *Journal of Conflict Resolution, 14*(4), 585–615.

Carroll, Berenice. (forthcoming). *Minerva in the shadows: Social and political thought of women.* Urbana: University of Illinois Press.

Cohn, Carol. (1988). A feminist spy in the house of death. In Eva Isaksson (Ed.), *Women and the military system.* London: Harvester/Wheatsheaf.

Converse, Elizabeth. (1968). The war of all against all: A review of the journal of conflict resolution. *Journal of Conflict Resolution, 12*(4).

Converse, Elizabeth. (1972). A posteditorial. *Journal of Conflict Resolution, 16*(4), 616–619.

d'Souza, Corinne. (1986, April). *Research as re-vision: Towards a new feminist scholarship.* Paper presented at IPRA Conference, Sussex, U.K.

d'Souza, Corinne. (1988, August). *The South Wind.* Paper presented at International Peace Research Association Conference, Rio de Janeiro, Brazil.

Dinnerstein, Dorothy. (1977). *The mermaid and the minotaur.* New York: Harper & Row.

Eisler, Riane. (1984). Violence and male dominance: The ticking time bomb. *Humanities in Society, 7*(1/2), 3–18.

Eisler, Riane. (1987). *The chalice and the blade.* San Francisco: Harper & Row.

Enloe, Cynthia. (1981). *Ethnic soldiers: State security in divided societies.* London: Penguin.

Enloe, Cynthia. (1983). *Does khaki become you? The militarization of women's lives.* Boston: South End Press.

Enloe, Cynthia. (1987). Feminist thinking about war, militarism, and peace. In Beth Hess and Myra Ferree (Eds.), *Analyzing gender: Handbook of social science research.* Newbury Park, CA: Sage Publications.

Forsberg, Randy. (1984, Winter). Confining the military to defense as a route to disarmament. *World Policy Journal,* 285–318.

Garcia, Celina. (1981). Androgyny and peace education. *Bulletin of Peace Proposals, 2.*

Harris, Ian. (1988, August). The role of social conditioning in male violence. Paper presented at IPRA Conference, Rio de Janeiro, Brazil.

Isaksson, Eva. (Ed.). (1988). Visions of a peaceful future: War and peace in feminist utopias. *Women and the military system.* London: Harvester/Wheatsheaf.

Kaldor, Mary, with David Elliott. (1977). *Alternative work for military industries.* London: Richardson Institute for Conflict and Peace Research.

Kaldor, Mary. (1987). The world economy and militarization. In Saul Mendlovitz & R. B. J. Walker (Eds.), *Towards a just world peace.* London: Butterworth.

Lall, Betty Goetz. (1977). *Prosperity without guns: Economic impact of reduction in defense spending.* New York: Institute for World Order.

Macy, Joanna. (1983). *Despair and personal power in the nuclear age.* West Hartford, CT: Kumarian Press.

Masini, Eleanora. (Ed.). (1983). *Visions of desirable societies.* Oxford: Pergamon Press.

McLean, Scilla. (1988). Women and decisions on nuclear weapons. In Eva Isaksson (Ed.), *Women and the military system.* London: Harvester/Wheatsheaf.

Mead, Margaret. (1967). *Cooperation and conflict among primitive peoples.* New York: McGraw-Hill.

Michel, Andree, (issue Ed.) (1985). La militarisation et les violences a l'egard des femmes [Militarization and violence against women]. *Nouvelles Questions Feministes, 11/12.*

Mische, Patricia, with Gerald Mische. (1977). *Toward a human world order.* New York: Paulist Press.

Myrdal, Alva. (1976). *The game of disarmament: How the United States and Russia run the arms race.* New York: Pantheon.

Newcombe, Hanna, with Alan Newcombe. (1969). *Peace research around the world.* Ontario: Canadian Peace Research Institute.

Oswald, Ursula. (1979). Agribusiness, green revolution, and cooperation. In Luis Herrera and Raimo Vayrynen (Eds.), *Peace, development, and the new international order.* Tampere, Finland: IPRA.

Reardon, Betty, with Priscilla Griffith. (1971). *Let us examine our attitudes to peace.* Culver City, CA: Social Studies School Series.

Reardon, Betty. (1982). *Militarization, security, and peace education.* New York: United Ministries in Higher Education.

Reardon, Betty. (1985). *Sexism and the war system.* New York: Teachers College Press.

Roberts, Barbara. (1989). Reclaiming the discourse: Feminist perspectives in peace research. In Diana E. H. Russell (Ed.), *Exposing nuclear phallacies* (pp. 278–287). Elmsford, NY: Pergamon Press.

Ruddick, Sara. (1980). Preservative love and military destruction: Reflections on mothering and peace. In Joyce Tribilcot (Ed.), *Mothering and feminist theory.* Totowa, NJ: Littlefield, Adams.

Russell, Diane E. H. (Ed.). (1989). *Exposing nuclear phallacies.* Elmsford, NY: Pergamon Press.

Senghaas-Knobloch, Eva. (1969). *Integration und assoziation, literaturbericht und problemstudien* [Integration and association: Literature report and problem study]. Stuttgart: Klett.

Senghaas-Knobloch, Eva, with Birget Volmerg (1986). Zur sozialpsychologie des friedens [On the social psychology of peace]. *Erst der Frieden noch zu retten* (pp. 217–235). Frankfurt: Peace Research Institute Frankfurt.

Senghaas-Knobloch, Eva. (1988). Zu einer unterbelichteten problemstellung in der friedens- und konfliktforschung: Bewusstwerdung der frauen und politik gegen gewalt [On an underexposed problem in peace and conflict research: Building awareness of women and politicians against abuse]. In Bernhard Mollman, (Ed.), *Perspektiven der friedensforschung.* Baden-Baden: Nomos Verlag.

Sivard, Ruth (1974). *World military and social expenditures.* Leesberg, VA: UMSE Publications.

Shiva, Vandana. (1988). *Women, ecology and development.* London: Zed Books.

Stephenson, Carolyn. (Ed.). (1982). *Alternative methods for international security.* Washington, DC: University Press of America.

Stiehm, Judith. (1972). *Non violent power.* Washington, DC: Heath.

Stiehm, Judith. (1983). *Women and men's wars.* Elmsford, NY: Pergamon Press.

Tobias, Sheila. (1985). Toward a feminist analysis of defense spending. *Frontiers: A Journal of Women Studies, 8*(2), 65–68.

Torney, Judith V. (1974). Political socialization research in the United States. In Chris Wulf (Ed.), *Handbook on peace education* (pp. 369–374). Frankfurt: International Peace Research Association.

Wahlstrom, Riitta. (1986, April). *Enemy images and the development of moral judgment.* Paper presented at the IPRA Conference, Sussex, U.K.

Welch, Ian. (1989, April). *Men, masculinity, and the social construction of peace.* Paper presented at International Studies Association Conference, London, U.K.

Wiser, Alice. (1987). *Transnational education from a feminist perspective.* Program proposal. (Available from the author at 19 Elmfield Ave., Teddington, Middlesex, TW11 8BV, England.)

Chapter 4

Black Studies Transformed
A Consideration of Gender, Feminism, and Black Women's Studies

Rose M. Brewer

PROLOGUE

I have found writing this chapter quite difficult. I believe this reflects the troublesome nature of coming to terms with gender in the context of Black[1] Studies. Moreover, the reality is that Black women's experiences are still quite marginalized in the field (Beverly Guy-Sheftall & Patricia Bell-Scott, 1989; Gloria Hull, Patricia Bell-Scott, & Barbara Smith, 1982). Of course, quite promising is the burgeoning scholarship on Black women in a number of disciplines. Some examples include History (Elsa Barkley Brown, 1989); Sociology (Rose M. Brewer, 1989; Bonnie Thornton Dill, 1979; Patricia Hill Collins 1986a, 1986b; and Deborah King, 1988), Literature (Barbara Christian, 1985; Trudier Harris, 1981; Barbara Smith, 1982) and Economics (Margaret C. Simms & Julianne M. Malveaux, 1986). Moreover, many of these women are considered Black Studies scholars and have appointments in the field, so there is no absolute bifurcation. More important for this discussion is the emergence of Black Women's Studies (Patricia Hill Collins, 1986; Beverly Guy-Sheftall & Patricia Bell-Scott, 1989). Yet I resonate with Barbara Christian's (1989) observation of the continuing marginality of Black feminists and Black Women's Studies. Many Black women scholars find themselves between Black Studies, Women's Studies, and other disciplines. The issue of place is far from resolved. So, I am faced with the formidable task of coming to terms with gender in the context of Black Studies. This is true despite my scholarly immersion in explicating the "intersection of race, class, and gender." This is true because of my life.

Indeed, my rite of passage into the academy was shaped profoundly by the political struggles and tensions of the late 1960s and early 1970s. Just nine years before my entry into graduate school, Black students at North Carolina Agricultural and Technical State University (A&T) set the tone for the era by refusing to play by the old rules of white domination and Black "place." These students instigated what is known as the "student phase" of the Civil Rights movement. I was poised to graduate during what would become known as the second phase of the Black Liberation movement, the so-called Black Power phase. By then, 1969, the events of the decade before and the years after would send shock waves through colleges and universities. Black students pressed the struggle into the academy. Young Black militants insisted that the university be transformed. Academic decolonization was essential to Black liberation. In this context, the first Black Studies programs were established in white universities and colleges in the United States. In this context, I entered graduate school.

In this short chapter I ruminate about gender in the field of Black Studies. I examine the periods encompassing the late 1960s and the 1970s, the first phases of Black Studies institutionalization; and a second phase encompassing the 1980s into the 1990s when gender is more clearly relevant to Black Studies discourse, largely through an emerging Black Women's Studies. Three themes are emphasized in this chapter: (a) Black Studies as an oppositional practice and theory with racial struggle and Afrocentric philosophy at its center, (b) structural and political changes undergirding Black women's heightened interest in gender inequity and self-defined scholarship, and (c) Black Women's Studies as a third area encompassing Black Studies and Women's Studies, yet instantiated as a Black women's standpoint apart from the study of Black men and white women.

BLACK STUDIES AS OPPOSITIONAL PRACTICE AND THEORY: THE LATE 1960s AND THE 1970s

The formal study of the Black experience predates the 1960s (Nick Aaron Ford, 1973), yet the formal instantiation of the study of Black life through Black studies emerged out of the political struggles of the late 1960s. The first Black Studies program was established at San Francisco State University in 1968 (Nathan Huggins, 1985). The fact that Black studies and the scholarly delineation of the Black experience would be structured into a formal discipline as well as a formal philosophy is the earmark of this period.

Molefe Asante (1987) centers the theory and philosophy of Black studies in Afrocentricity. He delineates the Afrocentric philosophy:

The Afrocentric thinker understands that the interrelationship of knowledge with cosmology, society, religion, medicine, and traditions stands alongside the interactive metaphors of discourse as principal means of achieving a measure of knowledge about experience. The Afrocentrists insist on steering the minds of their readers and listeners in the direction of intellectual wholeness. (p. 164)

Johnella Butler (1981) describes the subject content of Afro-American studies as reflecting

a cultural sensibility which is simultaneously in accord with and diametrically opposed to American/Western values . . . The affective and effective must be employed equally to bring about the cognitive. (p. 122)

And finally, Floyd Hayes (1988) says,

Afrocentric critical practice is an interpretation of the world from a particular philosophical and ideological standpoint. The Afrocentric perspective finds its essential grounding in the history, culture and thought of African and African descended people. Hence, there is an assumption that there exists a distinct and valid African-Centered world view. (p. 81)

The Black studies paradigm was rooted in critique of Eurocentrism. The key actors were young Black men and women who would draw upon a powerful racial experience. Explicating academic racism was at the center of the student attempt to confront Eurocentric assumptions. These assumptions were universalized to all disciplines. Black studies was about retheorizing the Black experience through an Afrocentric analysis and preparing students to engage in social change. Indeed, it meant preparing Black students to go back to communities and struggle for social transformation.

This oppositional perspective in Black Studies affected nearly all the social science disciplines. For example, in the field of sociology, the Black Studies critique was embodied in the work of Joyce Ladner's *Death of White Sociology* (1973). Robert Staples, in that collection, defined "Black Sociology." He says that this sociology would be based on the premise that

> Black and white peoples have never shared, to any great degree, the same physical environment or social experiences. People in different positions relate to each other and to their physical environment differently. The result is a different behavior pattern, a configuration that should be analyzed from the view of the oppressed not the oppressor.

In short, the academy was a tool of domination. It provided the reproduction and information sharing of powerful elites for purposes of social control. Activists said this reality should be turned on its head. In this context, the first phase of Black Studies was forged.

The actual institutionalization of Black Studies represented a furious rite of passage in the annals of the American universities. The struggles at San Francisco State, Harvard University, Cornell, and the University of California at Berkeley, among others (see Nick Aaron Ford, 1973; Nathan Huggins, 1985), point to the severe difficulties of establishing a Black Studies presence. Despite the early struggles, by 1973 over 200 college campuses had some form of Black studies. These ranged from a few courses to formal departments and colleges.

However, in the first phase, little if any course content focused on African American women. Nick Aaron Ford (1973), in examining the course offerings of a cross-section of programs, delineated a range of topics. Of the seven programs he surveyed, two listed a single course on Black women's literature. Of course, without having access to syllabi and actually doing a systematic examination of all these courses, it is impossible to reach any firm conclusion about gender content. Yet cursory evidence suggests that in this first phase, Black women were not at the center of the Black Studies curriculum. If African American women were discussed, it was in the context of a single course or of "the great Black woman mode" in other courses. It would be another decade before the issue of gender was systematically debated and discussed in the context of Black studies.

The exclusion, however, was not simply in Black Studies. Women's Studies generally and the overall liberal arts curriculum had paid little, if any, attention to black women. Beverly Guy-Sheftall and Patricia Bell-Scott (1989) bring this point home in their examination of the Spelman curriculum. They note:

> A thorough examination of the Spelman curriculum revealed that despite the presence of Women's Studies courses (which far exceed such offerings in other Atlanta colleges and in most black colleges), the curriculum was still not "gender-balanced" or sufficiently sensitive to Black women's studies. Furthermore, most of these were electives in the major or minor. Relegating attention to women, and Black women specifically, to a set of elective offerings at the margin of the curriculum had not provided our students with a comprehensive understanding of the diverse experiences and contributions of women generally or an appreciation of the roles of Black women in society and as subjects of scholarly inquiry. (p. 212)

Indeed, despite the struggles and impact of Black Studies, the fight was not about gender inequality, and the fight in women's studies was not about race. At the center of Black

Studies paradigm was coming to terms with racism from a Black perspective. In the early phase of white feminism, white middle-class women were to represent all women: they were the universalized woman. Johnella Butler (1981) aptly notes:

> Black Studies and Women's Studies, despite many affinities and common agendas, do have their own biases and blind spots. Just as black studies as a discipline has too often focused on the contributions of black men, women's studies is marked by its early focus on white, middle class women. Although educators working in these two fields need each other's expertise . . . they often work in isolation from one another. (p. 75)

STRUCTURAL CHANGES AND THE INCREASING IMPORTANCE OF GENDER IN BLACK STUDIES: THE 1980s

Black women have not always been considered change agents in the social movements literature, yet Black women have always been change agents in their communities and nationally (Cheryl Gilkes, 1980, 1988). They have always linked themselves to racial struggle and, historically, have articulated a gender dimension in their resistance (Rosalyn Terborg-Penn, 1986). Yet, it is in the past 15 years that Black women's change energies have become more squarely focused on gender inequality in community struggle and as a subject of scholarly discourse.

By the early 1970s, Black feminist activist organizations such as the Combahee River Collective would give a significant boost to the notion of the simultaneity of oppressions. Black women's lives, according to their thinking, reflected the intersection of race, class, and gender. By 1977, Black feminist scholar Diane Lewis noted,

> The black liberation movement began to generate important structural changes in the relationship between blacks and whites. For black women, these changes serve to heighten their perception of sexism, since they experience deep-seated sex discrimination as they engage in increased participation in the public sphere. Middle class black women, in particular, are becoming sensitive to the obstacles of sexism as racial barriers began to fall and as the bulk of the higher status, authoritative positions reserved for blacks have gone to black men. (p. 358)

Despite such status tensions, Black feminists defined themselves in a resistive context. (Gloria Hull, Patricia Bell-Scott, & Barbara Smith, 1982). As noted, organizations such as the Combahee River Collective stressed race, class, and heterosexism as "isms" to overcome. Combahee was clearly a precursor to more systematic scholarly discourse on Black women and the emergence of contemporary Black Women's Studies.

Finally, in a broader political economic sense, given the new international division of labor, women globally were being brought into the center of capitalist world economy. Multinational corporations were increasingly using women workers, paying them exceedingly low wages. Within the United States, some Black women were losing work just as others were obtaining low-paid, secondary labor. Such occupational shifts sent shocks through the class and gender structures of the African American community, especially as more Black men were marginalized from work altogether. Indeed, it was increasingly apparent that Capitalist patriarchy worked differently for Black men and women (Rose M. Brewer, 1991). Black feminist scholars would call for a gendered analysis of race and class dynamics. This would be the conceptual bedrock of an emerging Black Women's Studies.

Black Studies Phase II: Gender and Black Women's Studies, the 1990s

Beverly Guy-Sheftall and Patricia Bell-Scott (1989) refer to Black Women's Studies as a new field of study. They go on to say:

> Black women's studies is the scholarly investigation of the history, cultures and experiences of Black women. This new field confronts the problem of gender bias in Black studies and racial bias in women's studies and analyzes the ways in which gender/race forms an "otherness" in relationship to Black men and in relationship to nonblack women. (p. 205)

Patricia Hill Collins (1986a), in explicating the conceptual underpinnings of Black Women's Studies, says such scholarship must be rooted in the "material and ideological underpinnings of racism, patriarchy, and class oppression, without assuming that any one of these paradigms is more fundamental than the others." Especially important to generating a Black women's standpoint is "accurate description and reinterpretation of Black women's experiences." Yet key to Black women's studies is the assumption of "triple oppression," says Hill Collins. The additive model is inadequate for explaining inequality in an oppressive social order. Thus, adding race + class + gender is not a satisfactory analytical tool.

In her most recent book, *Black Feminist Thought*, 1990, Patricia Hill Collins states:

> Because Black women have access to both the Afrocentric and the feminist standpoints, an alternative epistemology used to rearticulate a Black women's standpoint should reflect elements of both traditions. . . . While an Afrocentric feminist epistemology reflects elements of epistemologies used by African Americans and women as groups, it also paradoxically demonstrates features that may be unique to Black women. On certain dimensions Black women more closely resemble Black men; on others white women, and on still others Black women may stand apart from both groups. (pp. 206–207)

Black Studies is now being challenged to transform its curriculum to be gender inclusive. The forces for change have arisen most profoundly from the development of a Black feminist standpoint, articulated by Black feminists, and embodied in a new field of study, Black Women's Studies. Ideally, African American women are structurally situated to challenge, question, and overturn mainstream ways of viewing the world. The multiple disjunctures Black women bring to the study of the Black experience are the bedrock for gender analyses in the field. Black feminists have argued that it is not simply the issue of restoring the feminine and eliminating the masculinist bias in the field or solely about class conflict. It is about capturing what it means to exist between the lines as Black women in this society.

CONCLUSIONS

I came into the academy on the wings of the Black liberation struggle in the university. My location in the broader sociohistorical context was multiple: poor, Black, working class, young, female. This was a period of tremendous historical change: streets were afire; Black people were demanding justice. Yet a decade more would pass before I seriously confronted gender inequality. This personal journey is reflected in the very real changes which have occurred in the field of Black studies as Black feminists generate a Black women's standpoint culminating in Black Women's Studies. These scholars place gender, race, and class in intersection at the center of the discipline.

NOTE

1.   Black became a term of empowerment during the struggles of the 1960s. In nearly every case, I've chosen to use it rather than African American. In some selected instances I've used the term *African American* rather than *Black*, as currently African American is more and more the preferred term.

BIBLIOGRAPHY

Asante, Molefi. (1987). *The Afrocentric idea.* Philadelphia: Temple University Press.
Brewer, Rose M. (1989). Black women and feminist sociology: The emerging perspective. *American Sociologist, 20*(1), 57–70.
Brewer, Rose M. (1991). *African Americans and class formation: Theorizing race, gender, and labor.* Unpublished manuscript.
Brown, Elsa Barkley. (1989). African-American women's quilting: A framework for conceptualizing and teaching African-American women's history. *Signs, 14*(4), 921–929.
Butler, Johnella. (1981). *Black studies.* Washington, DC: University Press of America.
Christian, Barbara. (1985). *Black feminist criticism, perspectives on black women writers.* Elmsford, NY: Pergamon Press.
Christian, Barbara. (1989). But who do you really belong to—Black studies or women's studies? *Women's Studies, 17*(1–2); 17–23.
Collins, Patricia Hill. (1986a). The emerging theory and pedagogy of Black women's studies. *Feminist Issues, 6*(1), 3–17.
Collins, Patricia Hill. (1986b). Learning from the outsider within: The sociological significance of Black feminist thought. *Social Problems, 33,* 14–30.
Collins, Patricia Hill. (1990). *Black feminist thought: Knowledge, consciousness, and the politics of empowerment.* Boston: Unwin Hyman.
Dill, Bonnie Thornton. (1979). The dialectics of Black womanhood. *Signs, 4*(3), 543–555.
Ford, Nick Aaron. (1973). *Black studies: Threat-or-challenge.* Port Washington, NY: Kennikat Press.
Gilkes, Cheryl Townsend. (1980). Holding back the ocean with a broom: Black women and community work. In La Frances Rodgers-Rose (Ed.), *The Black woman* (pp. 217–232). Beverly Hills, CA: Sage.
Gilkes, Cheryl Townsend. (1988). Building in many places: Multiple commitments and ideologies in Black women's community work. In Ann Bookman and Sandra Morgen (Eds.), *Women and the politics of empowerment* (pp. 53–76). Philadelphia: Temple University Press.
Guy-Sheftall, Beverly, & Bell-Scott, Patricia. (1989). Black women's studies: A view from the margin. In Carol S. Pearson et al. (Eds.), *Educating the majority: Women challenge tradition in higher education* (pp. 205–218). New York: Macmillan
Harris, Trudier. (1981). Three Black women writers and humanism: A folk perspective. In R. Baxter Miller (Ed.), *Black American literature and humanism* (pp. 50–74). Lexington: University of Kentucky Press.
Hayes, Floyd. (1988). Politics and education in America's multicultural society: An African-American studies response to Allan Bloom. *The Journal of Ethnic Studies, 17*(2), 71–87.
Huggins, Nathan. (1985). *Afro-American studies: A report to the Ford Foundation.* New York: The Ford Foundation.
Hull, Gloria, Bell-Scott, Patricia, & Smith, Barbara. (1982). *All the women are white, all Blacks are men: But some of us are brave.* New York: The Feminist Press.
King, Deborah K. (1988). Multiple jeopardy, multiple consciousness: The context of a Black feminist ideology. *Signs, 14*(1), 42–72.
Ladner, Joyce. (1973). *The death of white sociology.* New York: Random House.
Lewis, Diane K. (1977). A response to inequality: Black women, racism, and sexism. *Signs, 3*(2), 339–360.

Simms, Margaret C., & Malveaux, Julianne M. (Eds.). 1986. *Slipping through the cracks: The status of Black women.* New Brunswick, NJ: Transaction Publishers.

Smith, Barbara. (1982). Racism and women's studies. In Gloria T. Hull, Patricia Bell Scott, & Barbara Smith (Eds.), *But some of us are brave* (pp. 48–51). Old Westbury, NY: Feminist Press.

Staples, Robert. (1973). Black sociology. In Joyce Ladern (Ed.), *The death of white sociology.* New York: Random House.

Terborg-Penn, Rosalyn. (1986). Black women in resistance: A cross-cultural perspective. In Gary Y. Okhiro (Ed.), *In Resistance: Studies in African, Caribbean and Afro-American history* (pp. 188–209). Amherst: University of Massachusetts Press.

Chapter 5

Post-Tweeds, Pipes, and Textosterone
Perspectives on Feminism, Literary Studies, and the Academy

Mary Ellen S. Capek

I studied contemporary American and English literature at a large Midwest graduate school in the mid-1960s. When I arrived, the department was one of the few in the country that had a small core of tenured women faculty, but they were all near retirement and being replaced with ambitious young men. The chair of the department was a woman, a noted scholar who had helped to build a department strong in her own field of specialization.

During my first year of study, I met other students—at least several from women's colleges—who had come specifically to study with these women. Yet despite hand-picked women students and their own formidable positions in the department, these scholar/teachers did not prompt special attention to women writers or critics in the curriculum. We read few women in departmental courses of seminars. (The poets I remember from my own course work included only Anne Bradstreet, Emily Dickinson, Elizabeth Barrett Browning, Christina Rossetti, and H.D.—each seldom represented by more than a few poems on a supplemental list.) As an undergraduate at a small Methodist college in 1962, I had been assigned a paper on Mary Wollstonecraft by a revered older male professor who was a Victorian specialist. But, with few exceptions, little of my graduate curriculum's required reading included women of any color or nationality. Women simply were not present in the literary canon 20 years ago. The few who were "proved the rule."

As budding scholars and critics who were female, we saw our models laced with rigid constraints, especially hard to emulate when our community in the mid-1960s was a hotbed of love-ins and "free" sex. To my knowledge, neither the chair nor her female colleagues had ever married, and in at least one instance, it was clear that marriage was seen as betrayal: when one friend, a promising Shakespearean, announced her impending marriage, she was "disinherited" by her spinster-scholar adviser. Such bias was objectionable and upsetting, but although we did recognize that it would be harder as women to marry, have children, and a career (lesbian life styles were never an openly discussed option), we also were living in the midst of a social revolution that challenged authority and arrogantly pronounced (at least some of us pronounced) that we could do anything we chose to do.

As a consequence, perhaps because we were empowered by rebellion all around us, much of what we experienced did not feel like discrimination, even from male professors. I argued at the time that I was being treated fairly. I thought I fit as well in that department as I saw myself fitting anywhere in a traditional institution. Again—this was 1965, 1966,

1967—I was caught up in the headiness of the beginning antiwar protests, the spirit of the free speech movement, and friendship with at least one articulate male radical who read Virginia Woolf.

In spite of dropping out for a semester, I was able to maintain my teaching assistantship, got scholarships and financial aid, and participated vigorously in my classes—after first-year intimidation, participated as freely as most of my male associates. There were few departmental favorites, and I was not among them, but neither were other students, men or women, whose minds I thought interesting. I knew I was not being mentored or professionally groomed, but in retrospect I think I did not expect it because I knew I was "difficult," not given to nodding sagaciously as tweedy, leather-patched and bearded young men, professors and graduate students, proceeded to fracture a male text with the latest trendy lit crit grid. We were probably more aware of affirmative action issues for women faculty than we were of any discrimination against ourselves.

After finishing course work and preliminary examinations close to schedule, I proceeded to start a dissertation on Sylvia Plath's poetry, which was odd for two reasons: she was a woman, and she was dead less than 20 years, the generation gap it usually took to be canonized and legitimized for study. Although I had an advisor (male) who had agreed to work with me, by the time I actually began to write, I was teaching at a community college in Newark, New Jersey, that had been started after the 1967 Newark race riots, and by then, I think, he had given up on me as an apprentice.

Feminist criticism had just begun, and with few exceptions like Mary Ellman's *Thinking About Women* (1968) and Kate Millett's *Sexual Politics* (1970), most of the analysis and commentary seemed simplistic, especially on Plath.[1] Writing in isolation, I struggled, not very effectively, for language I had only begun to piece together, to lay out what felt like a frivolous aesthetic vision. By 1973, when I finally finished my dissertation, I had nursed my mother through terminal cancer, married, and been teaching functionally illiterate Black and Hispanic adults for four years. I did not understand what I had been trying to write until several years later when poems that would be collected in Adrienne Rich's *The Dream of a Common Language* (1978) first began to appear. I had heard Rich on an MLA (Modern Language Association) Women's Caucus panel with Tillie Olsen and others in 1971—the first presentation of what would become "When We Dead Awaken"—but it was not until I read a reprinted version of that essay in 1976, along with the *Dream of a Common Language* poems, that I began to see where I had been trying to go and why I never got there on my own.[2] Some of "When We Dead Awaken" must have sifted through my consciousness at that 1971 conference, but I was not yet ripe enough to hear it.

In 1975, I moved into college administration, prompted by the urge to gain more control over the forces that had shaped my teaching experiences in Newark. Even though I worked with other committed teachers, we were often as trapped as our students in a corrupt educational system that had left adults with high school diplomas functionally illiterate. With a shift into administration came exposure to books like *Academic Women on the Move* (Alice Rossi, 1973); the 1973 Carnegie report, *Opportunities for Women in Higher Education; Women in Higher Education* (W. Todd Furniss & Patricia Albjerg Graham, 1974); and *Another Voice: Feminist Perspectives on Social Life and Social Science* (Marcia Millman & Rosabeth Moss Kanter, 1975). Taken together, these collections began to provide important institution-wide perspectives on the status and issues confronting women in higher education, and they highlighted some of the first thoughtful excursions of feminist analysis in and of the academy. Here too, I found Rich, who had managed to link literary consciousness with institutional politics—what might be possible if we could just get organized. Her essay "Toward a Women-Centered University" and the other essays in

Women and the Power to Change (Florence Howe, 1975) offered compelling alternative visions.

Contributions of Feminist Literary Theory

Theoretical frameworks shape literary studies as they do other disciplines, whether or not the theories are named and acknowledged. Any understanding of the dynamics of feminism in the academy and its relationships with a larger women's movement must grapple with the roles, for better or for worse, implicit or named, that theory plays in our work.

As an undergraduate, I grew up with New Criticism, a school of analysis that taught us to read a piece of literature apart from any intrusions from authorial or historical data. The words on the page were what mattered. Nothing more, nothing less. The limitations of such narrow frames for analysis have been critiqued and thoroughly "deconstructed" in recent years. But, at least for the naive and marginal student that I was in the early 1960s, the New Critics in their own formal, courtly way were comforting, grandfatherly subversives. The call of the text, the clarion call to read, to interpret what the words said, to play with the ambiguity and the patterns they made on the page, freed and empowered me as a graduate student. I was a stubborn reader. The newer critical grids we were being taught could occasionally produce breathtaking, daring syntheses that sewed up The Meaning, but more often than not, these rigorously applied lenses felt like distortions or reductions of the rich complexity that drew me to literature in the first place. There were still professors who stressed thorough and diligent readings in historical contexts, and structuralism occasionally wafted down the hall from the linguistics and anthropology departments, but most of the critical analyses I remember drew from what was then called the "Chicago School" and from Marxist, Freudian, and Jungian critics with occasional nods to the Russian Formalists.

For me, the kaleidoscope of language, continually shaping and reshaping itself in my imagination, was what poetry was all about. It was comforting to go back to a poem and savor the words in still another new dimension than I had seen a week before. This empowering to read was beyond much damage from pompous male critics. The real damage was that we seldom got to read women writers; the secondary damage was (and is) that we were trained to be analytical, trained to pull texts apart but not to put them together again. We were trained to critique, to judge, but not often to relish the ambiguity. We annotated and elucidated but were seldom taught to savor the discomfort of not understanding completely. Most discipline practitioners rarely thought to create, much less teach *how* to create, a safe space to share impressions, to weave free-floating connections that went beyond the text. Nor did they confront the cultural biases and contexts that preserved the canon and shaped aesthetic values and readings.

Confronting these experiences, feminist writers began to call into question fundamental assumptions about the canon, literary history, and aesthetic values. (See Barbara Smith, 1977; Marilyn R. Farwell, 1977; Blanche Wiesen Cook, 1979; Annette Kolodny, 1980; Elaine Showalter, 1981; and Myra Jehlen, 1981.) Women scholars and critics had to revise or invent new frames of reference to reread the texts of those few women who had made it into the canon, and they began systematically to expose how male writers had written about and stereotyped women in their characters, themes, narrative voices, symbols and metaphors—documenting sexism, heterosexism, and racism and giving us new lenses for re-visioning the texts we grew up on.

The emerging scholarship about women also prompted women critics to devise new criteria for reading and critiquing the wealth of resources we were finding in our grandmothers' attics. How were we to know it was "literature?" We probed and read—at first curious, then exhilarated, then outraged that so much fine writing had been excluded as literature because it did not fit traditional genre definitions. Diaries, letters, other personal writing, and oral narratives—much of it published by the alternative presses and periodicals or shared on blurred, purple-inked class handouts or dog-eared, photocopies of old publications—all poured into reading lists in women's studies programs, and women scholars began to piece together and reconstruct a history of writing women, laying claim to a "female imagination" that is celebrated, not chided as second-rate and marginal.

Women critics empowered women as writers. (See Hélène Cixous, 1976, and Carolyn Heilbrun, 1988.) And we began to take lessons from the other disciplines and learned from the experiences of women scholars tackling the embedded sexism, unquestioned "universals," and male norms that lard theory, methodologies, and the very structure and vocabulary of our language. (See Cheris Kramarae & Paula Treichler, 1985; Mary Ellen S. Capek, 1987.) As in other disciplines, feminist literary studies questioned the very structures that traditionally shaped the discipline itself: reading by historical periods (the "periodicity" itself challenged by feminist historians), genre classifications, the "ins" and the "outs" that canonization produced, and the styles and artificial constraints of often brittle analytical literary theory. Combined with the assumptions about language that were being cracked open [see Lourdes Torres, this volume] all these questions generated lively, rich, intellectual resources, curricula, and teaching strategies.

Beyond Textosterone: A Critical Juncture

Feminist literary criticism has come of age. From the fabrics of our daily experiences with language as writers and readers, feminist critics and scholars in the 1980s began to unravel fundamental questions that yielded theoretical strands like *gynocriticism* (focusing on the history and contexts of women's writing) and *gynesis* (probing the symbolic and textual representation of sexual difference). At least some feminist criticism is now a significant part of the "malestream" itself: the same influential currents that drive what is known as French feminist theory, for example, also drive some mainstreams of modern linguistic criticism, literary and historical theory in our most prestigious universities. Lacan, Derrida, Foucault, and other French male writers and those who work with and from them have forged useful tools for finding and unscrewing embedded norms and assumptions about language, texts, and the texts' contexts (even to the extent of naming certain inclinations *phallogocriticism*). And some of what is known as postmodern criticism has offered up strategies for holding onto discomfort, the ambiguity of sustaining conflicts of meaning (even the possibility of no meaning at all) without plunging into a convenient but often empty synthesis.

In puzzling over a discipline's evolution and shifts in theory, however,—especially the history of ideology within the disciplines—one cannot help but be struck with curiosity that so much literary theory (Freudianism, Marxism, structuralism, deconstruction, and poststructuralism, now postmodernism and the "new historicism") have been around in other sources, in other written forms, many of them more readable, yet not recognized until abstracted or translated. Freud, at least, drew from Dostoevsky and Sophocles and acknowledged his sources. Must we privilege abstraction? Alice Walker, Gloria Anzuldúa, Paula Gunn Allen, Adrienne Rich, other ethnic women writers, women of color writers, lesbian writers—writers writing "from the margin"—have imaged and woven many different shapes and selvages of these theories. But at least in some quarters, it is not until theories are abstracted and translated (lately from the French) that they are accorded the dignity of theory.

With few exceptions (e.g., bell hooks, 1984), writers cited in the current debates about feminist literary theory are white scholars writing from bases in prestigious institutions, often writing in traditional male academic writing styles. This is not to knock success. In the process of staking our claims in the academy, however, we need not abstract ourselves from our sources. We need to recognize the status, class, and race issues at the heart of the theories we practice and honor the vital contributions to theory made by writers experimenting with different styles of doing theory (e.g., Barbara Smith, 1983; and Cherríe Moraga & Gloria Anzuldúa, 1981). As we struggle for tenure and recognition in the academy, tools that have helped us deconstruct embedded sexism and heterosexism in texts too often fail to help us find the embedded racism and classism, those status needs that shape our own language and styles of discourse.[3] [See Maria Lugones, this volume.]

In my experience, it helps to view these narrower debates in broader contexts. To understand and build knowledge about areas of study like gender, we need cross-disciplinary theories, methodologies, and data collecting that no one disciplinary perspective can provide. Smaller interdisciplinary units within colleges and universities have been essential for the development of women's studies. [See Pat Cramer and Ann Russo, this volume.] Centers, institutes, women's studies programs—all have helped create imaginative ways of getting beyond the boundaries of the disciplines where knowledge can be gathered, integrated, created, shared, and taught (e.g., Dale Spender, 1981; Elizabeth Langland & Walter Gove, 1981; Ellen Carol DuBois et al., 1985; Paula A. Treichler, Cheris Kramarae, & Beth Stafford, 1985; Mariam K. Chamberlain, 1988; and American Council on Education's Office of Women in Higher Education, Carol Pearson et al., 1989). Scholar/activists like Charlotte Bunch (*Passionate Politics,* 1987), founding editor of *Quest* and the 1987-1989 holder of the Laurie Women's Studies Chair at Rutgers University, have shown us ways to bridge gaps and situate western feminism within global women's communities. Dorothy Smith's collection, *The Everyday World as Problematic* (1988), describes sociologists' efforts to build a methodology that attempts to go beyond the academy. Philosopher and curriculum transformation specialist Elizabeth Minnich (*Transforming Knowledge,* 1990) analyzes how conceptual errors in one discipline distort methodologies across the curriculum. As Bunch, Smith, and Minnich describe, discipline-based academic discourse too often narrows our range of vision and isolates us from the messiness—grappling with which has been essential for the insights that have informed and empowered so much of our best work in the last 20 years.

A fundamental strategy that has emerged from these struggles is the shift of women from the margin to the center of inquiry. This shift—especially as it has linked recognition of the social construction of gender with the social constructions of class, race, ethnicity, sexual preference, age, and other classifications traditionally used to marginalize—this shift of women from the margin to the center has exposed and dramatized the limits of objectivity and traditional "scientific," detached methodologies. [See Shulamit Reinharz, this volume.] This turnabout has been profound: it is *not* a substitution of one form of dominance for another (what Elizabeth Minnich calls a "palace coup") but has given us instead the metal to construct tools we can use to undermine fundamental assumptions and epistemologies of the distorted dialectics that posit "margin" and "center" as oppositions in the first place—false universals and faulty thinking that have defined nonwhite, nonwestern, non-male as "other" and hence marginal.

This shift is not so much a function of "women's concerns taking us where men would never dream" (the *Knowledge Explosion* question), as it is a Copernician revolution, a powerful confluence of insights into how discrimination functions—at all levels of social organization, in all disciplines and theories, in our very language itself. In literature, we have begun to reclaim our own histories and our power of naming, our rightful places in the histories and lexicons, but we have also called into question the dynamics, even the right to exist, of the canons, the lexicons, and the "-isms" themselves—at least to exist in the forms and with the authority they have traditionally been accorded.

Backlash and Subversion

Women's skill in "calling into question," in influencing and invigorating leadership within the discipline associations and on campuses, has had its effects. Caucus efforts have resulted, for example, in at least one discipline association, the American Anthropological Association, acting on its power to censure departments that do not meet its goals of hiring and promotion pegged to the proportion of women doctorates produced in the field. And at least some branches of the mainstream have come to accept, even to welcome the new critical energy: exhumed texts have taken their places in literature survey courses, and sensitivities to the need to include writing by women and men of color and diverse ethnicity and different sexual preferences have led to richer reading lists and transformed curricula at the undergraduate and graduate levels.

Predictably, however, those in power have struggled to protect their own bases of power, their own work, and their hegemony in the disciplines. A revised canon and course lists, for example, that attempt to balance Western cultural hegemonic traditions have met with considerable backlash. Witness the debates in the United States focusing on curriculum restructuring at Stanford; the "Great Books" debate sparked by former Secretary of Education William Bennett; books like Allen Bloom's *The Closing of the American Mind;* increasingly provocative right-wing student publications like *The Dartmouth Review* (published with significant conservative financial backing); and major news media coverage (and distortion) of "politically correct" pressures on campus. These forces came together in a new organization, The National Association of Scholars, that has begun what it calls a movement to "reclaim the academy" (Joseph Berger, 1988). The vituperation of these backlash agendas are a measure of the strength of success in recent years in opening up the traditional curriculum, but we are entering an even more dangerous period of challenge to the fragile gains won.

With the relaxing of federal affirmative action pressure and, in the United States at least, the increasing organization and funding of the New Right behind conservative scholar groups like The National Association of Scholars, the stakes are going to become higher, the instances of backlash and subversion more blatant and more tenacious. And in spite of gains at all levels and in all types of institutions, the proportions of women in the tenured ranks in most disciplines is still significantly lower than that of men. (The Committee on the Status of Women in Physics has dubbed their survey data distribution the "Zeros Table.") The proportions of women in tenured ranks is in inverse ratio to the prestige of the institution. The more elite the college or university, generally still, the fewer the women.

As dangerous as this backlash and feet-dragging toward equality is, the positions of women within institutions and the development of women's knowledge are themselves vulnerable to subversion. Feminist scholars have risen, numbers of them now, to the heads of their disciplines. They have been hired as full professors and administrators at prestigious institutions across the country. Although not in large numbers, there are now enough to constitute a significant subset, an elite of feminist scholars, that in both numbers and quality document the extent to which women's studies and women's knowledge have become a part of the mainstream. Many of them grew their roots in the women's movement and continue to be feminists first, supportive of and advocates for women and the principles of the women's movement in both their personal and professional lives.

The powers of tradition, however, the weights of our hierarchical institutions, and the pressures of status and recognition are such that vitality risks becoming trapped in convention, and "cutting edge" thinking risks building its own hegemony. Recognizing these concerns, naming them to myself, I am troubled. Am I distorting, unfairly characterizing, not seeing the pressures we all face balancing the dynamics of new thinking against the weight of what has gone before us and the responsibilities of managing complex institutions? Do theories, refined and codified, inevitably lose their muscle as working tools for understanding? Translated into "letter"—and "letters" into texts, literary movements, and English Departments—is "spirit" doomed to be lost? And especially ironic, does our increasingly sophisticated ability to reread the traditions, the language and texts we inherited, make us less able to see that we are building our own canon—different, perhaps, and more representative, but with its own "politically correct" schools, the "ins" and the "outs" that echo at times like a parody of our 1960s' graduate education?

To the extent that we can not avoid these traps, knowledge is subverted, taken in by perhaps the most insidious forms of domination: we work well within traditional governance structures and mimic traditional male styles of discourse and needs for status and recognition. Inevitably any discipline or area of work builds up a short-hand of discourse that users take for granted. But there is a fine line between code words that ease communication and those that operate to create and preserve "the purview of an elite cognoscenti"—use of which, however, facilely, makes us handmaidens of status. The early years of the women's movement are peppered with arguments about and tests of "politically correct" feminism [see Barbara Pope, this volume]—and we have certainly seen the term hurled back at us lately in the media—but I am not invoking these old—or new—ghosts here. One of the strengths of the women's movement as it has evolved over the last 20 years has been its recognition that truths have indeed come in different packages. Here I am here stressing the importance of clarity and the willingness to acknowledge difference, indeed celebrate it, in ways that allow us better to listen to each other, critique, and shape more vibrant models of public writing and speaking.

Feminist Futures

To the extent that we have attempted to clarify terms of the discussion and create meeting grounds for new ways of exchanging differences of opinion and perspectives, we have made significant contributions to the style of the academy. An essential task as feminist writers and critics is to continue to take apart our own privilege; to find ways to hold the tensions, sustain the ambiguities, ultimately celebrate the complex knowledge that truth is multifaceted, multicolored, and appears in many guises. An essential task is to create institutions that not merely tolerate difference and different perspectives but build curricula and teach teachers how to create safe spaces that encourage and support the discomfort of difference; institutions that teach us to build tools for taking apart our assumptions about each other and the ways we read. [See Dale Spender, this volume.]

Women's Studies needs to reach out and sustain stronger, more creative coalitions with ethnic and multicultural studies, lesbian and gay studies, environmental studies, ecology and peace studies, and other interdisciplinary perspectives. These communities of knowledge, many of which build on core understandings of experience as "other," are among the few options in higher education that seem able to struggle creatively with the messiness and link theory and research to complex social change agendas, incorporating into their organizational structures as well as their curricula the knowledge we have gained from more complex class, race, and gender analyses. Although difficult to sustain and frequently not resulting in immediate solutions—waxing and waning with energy levels, temperaments, and competing pressures—there have been ongoing, often imaginative and forthright attempts to find new ways of building both theory and organizations to hold our visions.

With the best of intentions, however, there is only so much that even interdisciplinary feminist knowledge, well-integrated into other coalitions on campus and the larger women's movement, can do to bring action on the critical questions facing our civilization. Feminist theory—and the larger women's movement—must continue to "work large" and find imaginative ways to work larger. Beyond campus coalitions, we also need to forge coalitions of scholars, policy makers, grassroots activists, funders, educators, and media experts working together to break problems into solvable portions and shape new meeting grounds and common agendas for solving them. Gender differences cannot be understood apart from racism, classism, ageism, homophobia, xenophobia, and other tenacious forms of discrimination. Discrimination cannot be understood apart from fear, greed, and arrogance. Fear, greed, and arrogance cannot be understood apart from political, economic, and class systems that privilege the few, most of the time blindly. Our organizational and corporate structures all too often strengthen and underpin the privileges of the few and place our next generation at risk.

Our work in the next decade needs more and better organizing, needs to build and sustain interdisciplinary and intercultural links among scholarly, policy, and activist communities. We need to use our skill at theory to help shape more inclusive questions and styles of working and communicating—wherever possible underpinned with technology—that move us closer to pragmatic agendas for change. We need to apply our knowledge—how language functions, for example, as both process and system to inhibit and distort communication. How do we clarify, in accessible metaphors, what our common agendas might be? How do we continue to find new ways to write women's lives and narrate our past? How can we shape images of the future, with narratives and projects to realize them?

At this stage in our history, after more than 20 years of feminist work, our knowledge is closer to the bone, more trustworthy, only to the extent that it has been consistently informed by our mistrust of objectivity, our skepticism, and our willingness to challenge our own comfort with insights and theories hard-won and honed. The extent to which we can validate diverse experiences—our own and others—the extent to which we can translate that awareness into our social, economic, and political structures and languages and continue to experiment with new forms of communication, to that extent will our knowledge endure.

NOTES

1.   For me, at least, the sense of being part of a community of women writing and thinking about these concerns did not jell until the mid-1970s, when other helpful overviews of feminist literary theory began to appear, documenting and synthesizing women's struggles as both subjects and practitioners within the discipline: Josephine Donovan's 1975 edition, *Feminist Literary Criticism;* Patricia Spacks' *The Female Imagination* (1975); the first *SIGNS* review essays by Elaine Showalter (1975) and Annette Kolodny (1976); and Ellen Moers' *Literary Women* (1976).

2.   As evidenced by the influence that caucus-sponsored conferences and publications had on many of us—articulating our experiences as the 1971 MLA Women's Caucus panel did mine—the women's caucuses and commissions of the disciplines and professional associations were clearly instrumental in organizing and broadening critiques and alternative visions for the disciplines in the late 1960s and early 1970s. Caucus newsletters like *Concerns: Newsletter of the Women's Caucus of the Modern Languages,* which began publication in 1971 and is still published three times a year, were among the first systematic means of communicating activities and scholarship among women who were beginning to challenge the structures, culture, and methodologies of the disciplines with

more concerted efforts. The MLA Commission on the Status of Women in the Profession formed in 1968 and helped create a strong tradition of women presidents of MLA: Florence Howe (1973), Germaine Brée (1975), Edith Kern (1977), Jean Perkins (1979), Helen Vendler (1980), Mary Ann Caws (1983), Carolyn Heilbrun (1984), Barbara Hernnstein Smith (1988), and Catharine Stimpson (1990).

3.   For historical perspectives on these debates, see Elaine Showalter's introduction to *The New Feminist Criticism* (1985) and other collections of essays like *Feminist Issues in Literary Scholarship* (Shari Benstock, 1987)—my favorite is Nina Baym's essay, "The Madwoman and her Languages: Why I Don't Do Feminist Literary Theory." See also Elizabeth Abel, 1982; Gayle Greene and Coppelia Kahn, 1985; Mary Eagleton, 1986; Maggie Humm, 1987; and Wendy Frost, 1988. Catharine Stimpson's recent collection, *Where the Meanings Are* (1988) is a chance to follow almost two decades of evolving understanding through a key shaper of the discipline. Other analyses like *Gynesis* (Alice Jardine, 1985); *Sexual/Textual Politics* (Toril Moi, 1985); *Feminist Practice and Poststructuralist Theory* (Chris Weedon, 1987); *Feminist Literary History* (Janet Todd, 1988); *No Man's Land: The Place of the Women Writer in the Twentieth Century* (Sandra M. Gilbert & Susan Gubar, 1988, 1989); *Beyond Feminist Aesthetics* (Rita Felski, 1989); and the Autumn 1989 *SIGNS* review essay (Betsy Draine, 1989) include overviews and syntheses as well as additional bibliographies.

BIBLIOGRAPHY

Abel, Elizabeth (Ed.). (1982). *Writing and sexual difference.* Chicago: University of Chicago Press.

Baym, Nina. (1987). The madwoman and her languages: Why I don't do feminist literary theory. In Shari Benstock (Ed.). *Feminist issues in literary scholarship.* Bloomington: Indiana University Press.

Benstock, Shari (Ed.). (1987). *Feminist issues in literary scholarship.* Bloomington, IN: Indiana University Press.

Berger, Joseph. (1988, November 15). Scholars attack campus "radicals." *The New York Times*, p. A22.

Bunch, Charlotte. (1987). *Passionate politics: Feminist theory in action.* New York: St. Martin's Press.

Capek, Mary Ellen S. (Ed.). (1987). *A women's thesaurus: An index of language used to describe and locate information by and about women.* New York: Harper & Row.

Carnegie Commission on Higher Education. (1973). *Opportunities for women in higher education: Their current participation, prospects for the future, and recommendation for action.* New York: McGraw-Hill.

Chamberlain, Mariam K. (Ed.). (1988). *Women in academe: Progress and prospects.* New York: Russell Sage Foundation.

Cixous, Hélène. (1976). The laugh of the medusa. (Keith Cohen & Paula Cohen Trans). *SIGNS, 1*(4), 875–893. (The *SIGNS* essay is a revised version of "Le Rire de la Médusa," first published in France in *L'Arc* in 1975.)

Cook, Blanche Wiesen. (1979). "Women alone stir my imagination": Lesbianism and the cultural tradition. *SIGNS, 4*(4), 718–39.

Draine, Betsy. (1989). .Refusing the wisdom of Solomon: Some recent feminist literary theory (review essay). *SIGNS, 15*(1), 144–70.

Donovan, Josephine (Ed.). (1975). *Feminist literary criticism: Explorations in theory.* Lexington: The University Press of Kentucky.

Donovan, Josephine. (1985). *Feminist theory: The intellectual traditions of American feminism.* New York: Frederick Unger.

DuBois, Ellen Carol, Kelly, Gail Paradise, Kennedy, Elizabeth Lapovsky, Korsmeyer, Carolyn W., & Robinson, Lillian S. (1985). *Feminist scholarship: Kindling in the groves of academe.* Urbana, IL: University of Illinois Press.

Eagleton, Mary. (1986). *Feminist literary theory: A reader.* Oxford: Basil Blackwell.

Ellman, Mary. (1968). *Thinking about women.* New York: Harcourt Brace Javanovich.

Farwell, Marilyn R. (1977). Adrienne Rich and an organic feminist criticism. *College English, 39*(2), 191–203.

Farwell, Marilyn R. (1988). Toward a definition of the lesbian literary imagination. *SIGNS, 14*(1), 100–118.

Felski, Rita. (1989). *Beyond feminist aesthetics: Feminist literature and social change.* Cambridge, MA: Harvard University Press.

Frost, Wendy & Valiquette, Michele. (1988). *Feminist literary criticism: A bibliography of journal articles 1975-1981.* New York: Garland.

Furniss, W. Todd & Graham, Patricia Albjerg. (1974). *Women in higher education.* Washington, DC: American Council on Higher Education.

Gilbert, Sandra M. & Gubar, Susan. (1979). *The madwoman in the attic: The woman writer and the nineteenth-century literary imagination.* New Haven: Yale University Press.

Gilbert, Sandra M. & Gubar, Susan. (1988). *No man's land: The place of the woman writer in the twentieth century. The war of the words,* Vol. 1. New Haven: Yale University Press.

Gilbert, Sandra M. & Gubar, Susan. (1989). *No man's land: The place of the woman writer in the twentieth century. Sexchanges,* Vol. 2. New Haven: Yale University Press.

Greene, Gayle & Kahn, Coppelia. (1985). *Making a difference: Feminist literary criticism.* London: Metheun.

Heilbrun, Carolyn G. (1988). *Writing a woman's life.* New York: W W Norton.

hooks, bell. (1981). *Ain't I a woman: Black women and feminism.* Boston: South End Press.

hooks, bell. (1984). *Feminist theory from margin to center.* Boston: South End Press.

Howe, Florence (Ed.). (1975). *Women and the power to change.* New York: McGraw-Hill.

Humm, Maggie. (1987). *An annotated critical bibliography of feminist criticism.* Boston: G. K. Hall.

Jardin, Alice. (1985). *Gynesis: Configurations of woman and modernity.* Ithaca, NY: Cornell University Press.

Jehlen, Myra. (1981). Archimedes and the paradox of feminist criticism. *SIGNS, 6*(4), 575–601.

Kaplan, Sydney Janet. (1979). Literary criticism (review essay). *SIGNS 4*(3), 514–27.

Kolodny, Annette. (1976). Literary criticism (review essay). *SIGNS, 2*(2), 404–421.

Kolodny, Annette. (1980). Dancing through the mine-field: Some observations on the theory, practice, and politics of a feminist literary criticism. *Feminist Studies, 6,* 1–25. (Reprinted in Dale Spender (Ed.). (1981). *Men's Studies Modified: The Impact of Feminism on the Academic Disciplines.* Elmsford, NY: Pergamon Press.)

Kramarae, Cheris & Treichler, Paula, with Ann Russo. (1985). *A feminist dictionary.* Boston: Pandora Press.

Langland, Elizabeth & Gove, Walter. (Eds.). (1981). *A feminist perspective in the academy: The difference it makes.* Chicago: The University of Chicago Press.

Millett, Kate. (1970). *Sexual politics.* Garden City, NY: Doubleday.

Millman, Marcia & Kanter, Rosabeth Moss. (1975). *Another voice: Feminist perspectives on social life and social science.* Garden City, NY: Anchor Books.

Minnich, Elizabeth Kammarack. (1990). *Transforming knowledge.* Philadelphia: Temple University Press.

Moers, Ellen. (1976). *Literary women: The great writers.* New York: Doubleday.

Moi, Toril. (1985). *Sexual/textual politics: Feminist literary theory.* London: Metheun.

Moraga, Cherríe & Anzuldúa, Gloria. (1981). *This bridge called my back.* Watertown, MA: Persephone Press.

Morris, Meaghan. (1988). *The pirate's fiancée: Feminism, reading, postmodernism.* London: Verso.

Pearson, Carol, Shavlik, Donna, & Touchton, Judith (Eds.). (1989). *Educating the majority: Women challenge tradition in higher education.* New York: American Council on Education and Macmillan.

Rich, Adrienne. (1972). When we dead awaken: Writing as re-vision. *College English, 34*(1). (Reprinted 1979 in *On Lies, Secrets, and Silence: Selected Prose 1966-1978.* New York: W W Norton.)

Rich, Adrienne. (1978). *The dream of a common language: Poems 1974–1977.* New York: W W Norton.

Robinson, Lillian S. (1983). Treason our text: Feminist challenges to the literary canon. *Tulsa Studies in Women's Literature, 2,* 83–98. (Reprinted in Elaine Showalter (Ed.). (1985). *The new feminist criticism: Essays on women, literature, & theory.* New York: Pantheon.)

Rossi, Alice & Calderwood, Anne. (1973). *Academic women on the move.* New York: Sage Publications.

Showalter, Elaine. (1975). Literary criticism (review essay). *SIGNS 1*(2).

Showalter, Elaine. (1981). Feminist criticism in the wilderness. *Critical Inquiry, 2*(2), 179–205. (Reprinted in Elaine Showalter (Ed.). (1985). *The new feminist criticism: Essays on women, literature, & theory.* New York: Pantheon.)

Showalter, Elaine (Ed.). (1985). *The new feminist criticism: Essays on women, literature, & theory.* New York: Pantheon Books.

Smith, Barbara. (1977). Toward a Black feminist criticism. *Conditions: 1*(2), 25–44. (Reprinted in *Women's Studies International Quarterly 2* (1979), 183–194 and in Elaine Showalter (Ed.), (1985). *The new feminist criticism: Essays on women, literature, & theory.* New York: Pantheon.)

Smith, Barbara (Ed.). (1983). *Home girls: A Black feminist anthology.* New York: Kitchen Table: Women of Color Press.

Smith, Dorothy. (1988). *The everyday world as problematic: A feminist sociology.* Boston: Northeastern University Press.

Spacks, Patricia Meyer. (1975). *The female imagination.* New York: Alfred A Knopf.

Spender, Dale. (1985). *For the record.* London: The Women's Press.

Spender, Dale (Ed.). (1981). *Men's studies modified: The impact of feminism on the academic disciplines.* Elmsford, NY: Pergamon Press.

Spender, Dale. (1989). *The writing or the sex? Or why you don't have to read women's writing to know it's no good.* Elmsford, NY: Pergamon Press.

Stimpson, Catharine R. (1988). *Where the meanings are.* New York: Methuen.

Todd, Janet. (1988). *Feminist literary history.* New York: Routledge.

Treichler, Paula A., Kramarae, Cheris, & Stafford, Beth. (Eds.). (1985). *For alma mater: Theory and practice in feminist scholarship.* Urbana, IL: University of Illinois Press.

Weedon, Chris. (1987). *Feminist practice and poststructural theory.* Oxford: Basil Blackwell.

Chapter 6

Feminists—Sojourners in the Field of Religious Studies

Carol P. Christ

The field of Religious Studies is still not well understood by many academics, including feminists. The field, in theory at least, takes as its subject matter the religious lives and expressions of all people in all places and times. Religious expressions include rituals, prayers, and laws, as well as spiritual, philosophical, theological, and other types of reflection. Evidence of religious ritual is found among the earliest human archaeological remains. Religious texts—mythological, ritual, and legal—are among the earliest written records. Religious reflection dates to the so-called classical periods of all the so-called higher cultures of the world, and continues up to the present day. (Here as elsewhere, the terms which follow the word "so-called" are standard, but questionable.) Indeed it has been argued that the separation of religion from other spheres of life is a particularly modern conception. Because of its diversity of subject matter, the field of Religious Studies is multidisciplinary of necessity. Scholars employ a variety of methods, including archeological and anthropological, literary and textual, philosophical and theological, sociological and historical, and others, to interpret this vast data. Many find close colleagues or hold joint appointment in departments such as History, Near Eastern or Oriental Languages, and others.

The idea of Religious Studies as an academic discipline has its roots in the enlightenment quest for universal understanding and objective pursuit of truth (two aims which themselves have been subjected to criticism of late, not only by women and other so-called minorities, but also by white male deconstructionists and postmodernists). In North America the academic field of Religious Studies was established in the 1960s when its largely white, male, and Protestant champions waged a campaign to separate the teaching "of" religion from teaching "about" religion. One could study "about" what Christians, Jews, Muslims, Hindus, and others believed and practiced, they argued, without being a believer or a practitioner. A second justification for the field was found in the notion of humanities as moral education. Students in the 1960s were concerned about ethical issues, and courses on religion would allow them to test their idealism against the moral teachings of the world's great religions. With these two arguments, the door was opened to the establishment of departments of Religious Studies in state and other nonreligiously affiliated institutions.

In fact the break between the teaching of religion and teaching about religion was never as sharp as the latter's advocates claimed. A large proportion of the scholars in Religious Studies (and members of the American Academy of Religion, the field's major professional association) are employed at seminaries and religiously affiliated institutions which did not fully adopt the notion of the objective study of religion. In addition, the majority of those trained to staff the newly created departments of Religious Studies were white and male, and educated in Protestant institutions in the fields of Old Testament (itself a Christian term), New Testament, Church History (sometimes renamed History of Christianity), Theology, and Philosophy of (Western) Religion. The Society of Biblical Literature which meets jointly with the American Academy of Religion still has almost as large a membership as the Academy, providing one indication of the specializations of a large number of scholars in the field.

There was no conspiracy to exclude women and others from the founding of Religious Studies. It was simply that white Protestantism had the longest history of freedom of inquiry in religious matters, and that Protestantism, Catholicism, and Judaism all associated the scholarly study of religion with the ministry, the priesthood, and the rabbinate, which at that time were almost exclusively male domains. In practice, most departments of Religious Studies began with a core of white male Protestant scholars and began to look for a Catholic and a Jew, sometimes hiring the campus priest and rabbi until new positions could be created. The Jewish community which was often called on to fund chairs in Judaism, usually insisted that a Jew, and preferably one with rabbinical training (i.e., a male) be found to fill the posts in Judaism. Most departments planned to teach non-Western religions as well. Hinduism and/or Buddhism usually came first (because of their romantic appeal to students and faculty) with Islam and possibly nonliterary religions (e.g., African, Native American, Australian, etc.) projected to follow.

The field of Religious Studies is highly patriarchal. It has no founding mothers such as Ruth Benedict and Margaret Mead in Anthropology, Jessie Bernard in Sociology. The classical texts of all the so-called higher religions (Judaism, Christianity, Islam, Hinduism, Buddhism, Confucianism) were written by men and reflect patriarchal worldviews. Many religious texts and traditions enshrine the notion that women are spiritually, morally, and mentally inferior to men. Religious texts and traditions have often been viewed as divinely ordained (and in the monotheistic traditions as written or created by God Himself), thus providing divine sanction for the patriarchal order. Throughout history, women who have challenged patriarchal religious traditions have been accused of blasphemy and heresy, some paying with their lives. Modern scholars wearing the cloak of objectivity often stifle women's questions by stating that the task of the student of religion is to interpret and understand religious history, not to ask contemporary (irrelevant) moral questions of it.

Because of the textual bias in Western religion and in the academy, the religious lives of both men and women are less frequently studied than the classical texts and later philosophical and theological reflections on them. As Rita M. Gross has pointed out, ordinary women have religious lives even in the most patriarchal of traditions (lighting candles, saying prayers, etc.), but the bias of the field toward text serves to obscure women's participation. Women, both educated and uneducated, have sometimes excelled in the spiritual realm, becoming revered as saints, within the patriarchal religious traditions of East and West. Some of these women have written their spiritual experiences and reflections. But such phenomena are labeled popular and have been less studied than the so-called mainstream traditions which flow from the classical texts through their medieval and modern male interpreters. Women have often been leaders in movements at the so-called fringes of so-called mainline traditions (e.g., in Shakerism, Christian Science, Haitian Vodou, new Japanese religions, etc.) but these movements, too, are infrequently studied. A great deal of evidence suggests that women have had equal or more equal roles in many tribal and clan-based nonliterary religious traditions in the so-called prehistory (defined as the absence of written records) of the areas where the so-called higher religions arose, and in at least some of the traditions where tribal and clan-based religions have survived (e.g., parts of Africa, Australia, America, etc.).

As the foregoing discussion makes clear, the terms "higher," "classical," "mainstream" "philosophical or reflective," and "historical," and their antitheses, "popular," "folk," "fringe," "practical or spiritual," and "prehistorical," which are used to set priorities and mark boundaries in the field, are not scientific and value free, but themselves connote and conceal biases against the history of women (and other nonelite groups). These biases are deeply ingrained in the structure of the field, and more than liberal expressions of openness to women and so-called minorities will be required to transform them.

At the time of the founding of the academic field of Religious Studies in North America, there were very few women among its ranks, not only because of the inherent patriarchalism of its subject matter, but also because the ordinary route to a doctorate in religious studies was through a Bachelor of Divinity (B.D.) degree (now Master at Divinity [M. Div.]), a ministerial degree requiring three years of graduate study, and few women were likely to pursue a degree which they were barred from using. When I entered the Yale University graduate program in religious studies in 1967, I was not only one of two women in a program which had close to one hundred students, but also one of a handful of students without a B.D. One black male entered the program the year I did, and several other white women were admitted the following year. Growing numbers of white women entered the field in the 1970s and 1980s, along with smaller numbers of black and other nonwhite women and men.

Women's Studies in religion entered this scene in 1971 with the founding of the Women's Caucus—Religious Studies (which I cochaired with Elizabeth Schüssler Fiorenza) at the annual meetings of the American Academy of Religion and Society of Biblical Literature in Atlanta, Georgia. This group of about 40 women—most of whom were white doctoral students—took advantage of the bylaws of the American Academy of Religion which allowed nominations of candidates who would become president of the Academy and the proposal of motions from the floor. (Both of these provisions have since been modified.) At the conclusion of the typically sparsely attended business meeting, the Women's Caucus had elected Christine Downing to become the first woman president of the Academy and had passed a proposal which led to the founding of the Women and Religion Working Group (chaired by Mary Daly) which was allotted program time for the presentation of research at the 1972 annual meetings of the Academy. The Women and Religion Working Group later became a regular "section" of the Academy, which along with a dozen or so other areas of study are given maximum program time (currently five 2½-hour sessions) at the annual meetings. Other Working Groups in feminist studies have been formed over the years, including one titled Lesbian Studies in Religion.

For a field which at the 1969 and 1970 annual meetings had only a handful of women in attendance, and in which women made up approximately 10% of the graduate students and far fewer of the tenured professors, this was an astonishing achievement. It can be attributed in part to the openness of the academy's bylaws, which had never before been tested, and in all fairness also to the willingness of a number of white men (their opposition was vocal and for its genre, eloquent) to support an issue which they perceived as ethical.

Sections in the American Academy of Religion are autonomously run, subject to periodic reviews by the Program Committee. The Women and Religion group and section, chaired over the years by Mary Daly, Judith Plaskow, Joan Arnold Romero, Rita M. Gross, Susan Setta, Carol P. Christ, Susan Brooks Thistlethwaite, Ellen Umansky, and Naomi

Goldenberg, has been unusually lively and innovative. Whereas many sessions of the academy are attended almost exclusively by white men, the Women and Religion sessions have always been well-integrated along gender lines, and often have the highest overall attendance among the sections of the academy.

Publishers in the field of religion discovered a much larger than expected audience for books on women and religion, both for those written by feminist scholars in the academy and for those written by scholars and thinkers without formal academic training. Many of the books published ten or more years ago still record high sales, and publishers eagerly seek new titles for their women and religion lists. Thus scholars in Women and Religion have not found it overly difficult to get their work published and read by scholars and nonscholars alike.

Feminist research in religious studies, like the field itself, spans all of human history. Feminist scholars write about Goddesses in Old Europe and the image of God the Father and King in Christianity and Judaism, about Buddhist nuns and Muslim saints, about Christian mystics and European witches, about women's rituals in Australian aboriginal and Native American religions, about women's leadership in Haitian Vodou and the early Christian communities. A sampling of these riches can be found in the collections: *Unspoken Worlds* (Nancy Auer Falk & Rita M. Gross, 1989), *Womanspirit Rising* (Carol P. Christ & Judith Plaskow, 1979), *The Politics of Women's Spirituality* (Charlene Spretnak, 1982), and *Weaving the Visions* (Judith Plaskow & Carol P. Christ, 1989).

Feminist research in religion is more than an academic subject. Because religion is one of the cornerstones of patriarchy, it is not surprising that movements for the liberation of women have attracted religious opposition. In the nineteenth century abolitionists Sarah and Angelina Grimke were forced to reflect on Biblical justifications for women's equality when they were told by Protestant ministers that the Pauline injunction for women to keep silent in church forbade all public speaking by women. Similar opposition prompted Matilda Joslyn Gage to write a scathing attack on organized religion called *Women, Church, and State,* Elizabeth Cady Stanton to edit *The Woman's Bible,* and Charlotte Perkins Gilman to pen *His Religion and Hers.* Black abolitionist and feminist Sojourner Truth viewed herself as called by God to be a sojourner (without a home) because of the truth she spoke about racism and sexism.

In the twentieth century, the resurgence of the women's movement in North America led not only to the founding of the Women's Caucus—Religious Studies, but also to the creating of task forces and study groups on women among Protestants, Catholics, and Jews, which led to movements for the ordination of women, pressure to remove sexist language from prayerbooks and hymnals, and even to a revision of the translation of the portions of the Bible read in Protestant worship services. Similar groups have more recently been formed by American Buddhist women. And at least one book on Muslim feminist theology is in the works. From the beginning women not affiliated with any institutional form of religion began forming womanspirit and Goddess study and ritual groups [see Irene Diamond, this volume].

These twentieth century feminists in religion have met strong opposition. As I write this essay, CNN International News reports on the Roman Catholic pope's statement on the occasion of his meeting with the leader of the Anglican Church, that the greatest "obstacle" to "religious unity" is the ordination of women. The same broadcast brings reports of what was "perhaps" the largest antiabortion demonstration in the United States, led by Protestant fundamentalists and Roman Catholic groups. A recent newspaper states that the appointment of a 72 year-old Orthodox woman to the Jewish Religious Council of Jerusalem threatened to "paralyze religious councils because rabbis would refuse to decide issues if they had to sit with women." (*Athens News,* Oct. 1–2, 1989, p. 13.) And it is no secret that opposition to women's liberation is one of the touchstones of the new Muslim fundamentalism.

Work in feminist theology and women's spirituality directly challenges the patriarchal worldview enshrined in religious texts and traditions. Traditional theologies have not only often assumed that women are less human than men, but also that the right relation between "God," "man," and "the world" is dualistic and hierarchical. Early work in feminist theology and women's spirituality named the misogyny in the traditions and sought out the history of women in the histories of Judaism, Christianity, Gnosticism, and Goddess religions. Feminists rewrote traditional Jewish and Christian liturgies, and created new rituals celebrating women's experience, connection to nature, and Goddesses. Feminists writing from various perspectives wrote of the centrality of relationship in human life and argued that our relationships to human and other beings need not be hierarchical.

As in all areas of Women's Studies, the early work on women and religion was done primarily by white women. The increasing chorus of diverse voices has been the most important development of the past ten years. Women of color and lesbians have argued that sexism is interstructured with racism, imperialism, heterosexism, and ethnocentrism in religious symbol systems. Alice Walker was pointing out the obvious when she wrote in *The Color Purple* (1982) that the God most of us picture is not only old and male, but white. But this obvious point had been infrequently remarked upon in feminist writing about God. Similarly lesbians have noted that while God may not be married, he certainly is not gay. It has been painful for black and other so-called minority women to recognize and for white heterosexual women to admit, that the "women's experience" which feminist theology took as its starting point was all too often the experience of white, middle-class, heterosexual women. Women who do not share the dominant white Christian heterosexual culture have had to assert (because it was not commonly assumed) that women's identities are positively shaped by race, class, ethnicity, religious tradition, and sexual preference. Whereas once the call was for all women to recognize a common identity in the struggle against patriarchy, there is now a growing recognition that women's experiences are not all the same, and that we may never share a single common religious vision. Women of color have also broadened the scope of women's history, expanding it from a North American, European, and Near Eastern (Biblical and related cultures) base to include the histories of Africa, Native and Latin America, and Asia.

These intrafeminist struggles have often taken place within an academic power structure which is not only male, but white, heterosexual, middle and upper class, for the most part Christian, and not particularly hospitable to feminism. Women's awareness of being overheard (and judged for hiring, promotion, and tenure) has made it difficult for us to hear and politically support one another. Yet the study of women and religion is slowly being transformed as its practitioners are being called to a deeper listening, greater inclusiveness, and humility in the creation of theory and vision.

But despite its success within a male-dominated field, the study of women and religion is far from integrated into the teaching and hiring priorities in the field. Because of budget cuts in the universities in the 1970s and 1980s, many departments were frozen with their original core of white male scholars in Christianity, Judaism, and often only one non-Western religion. Feminists who hoped that this situation might change with retirements in the 1990s have begun to notice that many traditional white male scholars are using every means at their disposal to ensure that their white male clones are firmly ensconced before they retire. (One story making the rounds speaks of a senior scholar who threatened to commit suicide if his replacement was a feminist, while another tells of a department chair who suffered mental stress and sought psychological help while leading a nasty battle to deny tenure to a highly qualified nonwhite woman.) Because the hiring committees are still dominated by white men who consider feminist studies peripheral to the field, women whose work is on so-called major male texts or thinkers find it easiest to be hired, followed by those whose work is on the history of women but does not radically challenge the foundations of religious and scholarly traditions. Radical feminist Christian theologians are sometimes hired by seminaries, but those who have openly left the church are barred from permanent employment in church-affiliated institutions. (Theologian Matthew Fox was censured and silenced by the Roman Catholic Church for, among other things, hiring the feminist witch Starhawk to teach Goddess religion at his Creation Spirituality Institute at the College of Holy Names in Oakland, California. Protestant and Jewish institutions have their own written and unwritten codes.) Many of the women whose work has been influential in shaping the study of women and religion languish at primarily undergraduate colleges with heavy course loads (mine was four a semester), little time for research, and few opportunities to pass their knowledge on to a new generation of scholars. Mary Daly, possibly the best known woman in the field, was denied tenure and promotion to associate professor at Boston College, decisions which were later reversed under pressure of student protests. In 1989 she lost her second attempt to win promotion to full professor. In the process, she garnered a long list of laudatory letters from prestigious scholars in the field, both female and male, but she has never been offered an opportunity to move to another academic position.

Many departments of religious studies now teach a course on women and religion, and many courses on traditional subjects such as the Bible or theology offer a week at the end on women. But feminist concerns have rarely had an impact on the curriculum as a whole. Graduate students often complain about being discouraged from pursuing research on women, if they want to get a "good" job. Those who wish to study the history of ancient Goddess traditions or modern Goddess spirituality usually cannot even find a place to begin their studies, as most of the feminist work on Goddesses continues to be done by independent scholars and thinkers without formal academic training and affiliations. On the positive side, Harvard Divinity School, which has sponsored research associateships and visiting lectureships in Women's Studies since 1971, has recently founded a graduate specialization in Gender, Culture, and Religion.

In summary, although research and reflection on women and religion is flourishing both inside and outside the academic world, a great deal of work remains to be done if feminist scholarship is to transform the teaching and study of religion. The challenges posed to the field of Religious Studies are profound and substantive. They cannot be addressed by the simple addition of a book here and a course there, nor by time at annual meetings, nor by the hiring of one or two women in departments. The study of women and religion questions the established priorities in the field, and foundations of the religious which are studied, and the notion that the study of religion is and should be objective and value free. The majority of those who hold power in the field have not changed their worldviews overnight, nor as we now have seen, over the course of the past 20 years. And they are not likely to do so while resources remain scarce and conservative forces gain greater power in the larger culture. I imagine that feminists in religion will be sojourners for a long time to come.

BIBLIOGRAPHY

(This list of references is limited to review essays, methodological reflections, and general anthologies, where students and scholars can find references to a wide variety of work in the field.)

Christ, Carol P. (1988). Toward a paradigm shift in the academy and religious studies. In Christie Farnham (Ed.), *The impact of feminist studies in the academy*. Bloomington, IN: Indiana University Press.

Christ, Carol P. (1979). The new scholarship on women and religion. *Bulletin/Council on the Study of Religion, 10*(1), 3–5.

Christ, Carol P. (1977). The new feminist theology: A review of the literature. *Religious Studies Review, 3/4*, 203–212.

Christ, Carol P. & Plaskow, Judith. (Eds.). (1979). *Womanspirit rising: A feminist reader on religion*. San Francisco: Harper & Row.

Driver, Anne Barstow. (1976). Review essay: Religion. *Signs: Journal of Women in Culture and Society, 2*(2), 434–442.

Falk, Nancy Auer & Gross, Rita M. (Eds.). (1989). *Unspoken worlds: Women's religious lives* (2nd ed.) Belmont, CA: Wadsworth Publishing Company.

Gross, Rita M. (1974). Methodological remarks on the study of women and religion: Review, criticism, and redefinition. In Judith Plaskow & Joan Arnold Romero (Eds.), *Women and religion*. Missoula, MT: AAR & Scholars' Press.

Plaskow, Judith. (1978). Christian feminism and anti-Judaism. *Cross Currents, 28*, 306–309.

Plaskow, Judith & Christ, Carol P. (Eds.). (1989). *Weaving the visions: New patterns in feminist spirituality*. San Francisco: Harper & Row.

Ruether, Rosemary Radford. (1985). Feminist theology in the academy. *Christianity & Crisis, 45*(3), (March 4, 1985), 55–62.

Ruether, Rosemary Radford. (1981). The feminist critique in religious studies. In Elizabeth Langland & Walter Gove (Eds.), *The feminist perspective in the academy*. Chicago: University of Chicago Press.

Spretnak, Charlene. (Ed.). (1982). *The politics of women's spirituality*. New York: Doubleday.

Walker, Alice. (1982). *The color purple*. New York: Harcourt Brace Jovanovich.

Yates, Gail Graham. (1983). Spirituality and the American feminist experience. *Signs: Journal of Women in Culture and Society, 9*(1), 59–72.

Chapter 7

Cooking Up Cultural Studies

Jennifer Craik

The title of this chapter is deliberately provocative. Can feminism transform the parameters of cultural studies? Can it revise its practices and agendas? Or is it doomed to be incorporated as a marginal or special interest? If the effectivity of feminism is measured by the number of publications about issues of women in cultural production and women's cultures, it would appear that feminism has had a significant impact on academic practice. The question remains as to whether feminism has succeeded in challenging the epistemological foundations of knowledge as it informs academic disciplines. Given the radical basis of feminist thought, feminists have three choices: to embark on the huge task of inventing a new academy; to retreat to a feminist coterie which "will eventually discover new paradigms and found a new normative science" (Coyner, cited by Marilyn Strathern, 1987, p. 283); or to set about reworking fields of enquiry from within.

The argument developed here is that the characteristics of cultural studies make it appropriate for reworking existing approaches to the analysis of gender (cf. Cathy Schwichtenberg, 1989). First, cultural studies is not a discipline in the traditional sense but a fragmented collage of paradigms, theories, methods and objects of analysis. Second, cultural studies has developed at a time when the disciplinary regime has been questioned and hence has been constructed in a manner which is more congenial to intervention. Third, cultural studies prioritizes the study of visual and oral forms in contrast to the modal and behavioral foci of many disciplines and to the origins of "scientific" method. If there is space for revision in the literal sense of the word, then cultural studies offers a suitable terrain. Feminism has already had a decisive impact on cultural studies in terms of its theory, reading practices, and production. There is further potential to review, resituate, and reconstruct the tools of cultural studies according to feminist maxims.

Cultural studies consists of an eclectic array of approaches and disciplinary legacies which have been applied to the analysis of the production, circulation, and consumption of different cultural forms. It is especially concerned with how and why certain forms and conventions are dominant, some are subordinate, whereas others are challenged and subverted. As a multifaceted and interdisciplinary forcefield, cultural studies has addressed many aspects of cultural production including youth, popular and mass culture, film and

The comments and suggestions of the editors and Tony Bennett are gratefully acknowledged.

media, literature, art, rituals and rites of passage. The importance of cultural forms lies in the production of meaning systems that underpin other areas of social life.

In Great Britain, Europe and Australia, cultural studies is a subset of film and media studies but some North Americans use the term interchangeably with communication studies (James Carey, 1977; 1983). Yet American communications studies developed in the main from positivist and empiricist traditions which focused on questions of intentions, effects (social change, persuasion) and the mass production basis of the culture industry. Cultural studies in the United States has grown up outside these dominant research approaches.

Although positivist and empiricist perspectives have underpinned some of the media and cultural studies work in Great Britain, other influences came from literary studies and historical studies of popular culture. British cultural studies address the expressive and ritualistic uses of cultural production, particularly of cultures (and subcultures) outside official, legitimated, aesthetically sanctioned arenas. The field has been focused over the past decade by the theoretical interventions of semiotics, Marxism, and feminism. Perhaps the most significant feature of British cultural studies is that it emerged in the late 1960s as part of those movements which advocated political and social upheaval. The struggles of the 1960s laid the foundations of its disciplinary concerns. Despite the persistence of the sociological model in American communication studies, elements of the British tradition are now being mapped onto those concerns. Generally, however, the American tradition has been less attuned to Marxism and feminism.

Whereas cultural studies has developed alongside the debates and struggles of feminism, feminist concerns have had to fight for their place in the field. For example, in a 1976 book on youth subcultures in Great Britain, only two chapters were devoted to girls and subcultures. Their authors noted the invisibility of female subcultures in earlier work on youth and teenage life. References to girls reproduced crude stereotypes as "dumb," passive or "painted" (Angela McRobbie & Jenny Garber, 1976, p. 209). Although occupying the same institutional spaces, men and women do so "in different relations and on different trajectories." Significant differences appear in the teenage years, a period which is constructed as one of danger for girls. The lives of girls are organized around family life and domestic space. Working class girls occupy a limited choice of roles—little mother, bedroom culture, steadies, disco groupies, career girl, or "slags/scrubbers" (a linguistic pairing that denotes a more fundamental role choice) (Rachel Powell & John Clarke, 1976, p. 226). This array of role models for girls is derived from wider rhetorics which are reinforced within those subcultures.

The problematic representation of teenage girls illustrates a fundamental issue for cultural studies, namely that many of the cultural forms that it studies exhibit oppressive and repressive representations of, attitudes to, practices concerning women. Redressing the sexism of cultural production has been a focus of feminist cultural studies, though with less success than feminists would like. Nonetheless, the study of gender has become a growth industry, especially for women students and researchers. The suitability of cultural studies as a topic of analysis by and for women (cf. Caroline Ramazanoglu, 1989, p. 428) is in part an effect of its concern with "womanly" things—personal, private, expressive, consumed, and noninstrumental—topics that are regarded as "suitable subjects" for women. Whereas this tendency has put many under-researched areas onto the academic agenda, there is a danger that feminist topics and feminist researchers can be marginalized as "women's studies" and separated from "mainstream" academic practice. In this connection, Angela McRobbie has questioned the emphasis in feminist research on oral histories as "parasitic on women's entrapment in the ghettos of gossip" (Angela McRobbie, 1982a, p. 57).

THE PLACE OF FEMINISM IN
CULTURAL STUDIES

The academy has traditionally referred to gender largely in terms of demographic categories (sex, class, age, race, marital status, income) that can be identified as components of communities, markets, institutions, and cultural practices. The category "woman" is defined in very different ways depending on the use-value of the information. For example, advertising has enthusiastically embraced some elements of new definitions of "woman" such as the "signs" of women's "liberation," career women and new codes of sexuality at the same time recuperating traditional (and objectionable) definitions (cf. Rosemary Betterton, 1987, pp. 1–17).

Yet elsewhere, cultural studies has included the analysis of gender alongside its central concerns—those of community, class, and populism. In North America, feminism has addressed the representation of gender, the intersection of ideology and economics, power relations in cultural production, the applicability of feminism to social theory, the importance of lived experience, and social change (Paula Treichler & Ellen Wartella, 1986, p. 1).

In Great Britain, a broadly marxist framework has emphasized the material conditions of cultural production. Historical, economic, class, and ideological factors were aligned with social histories of everyday life which featured the role of women in visible and invisible ways. This material focus was complemented by textual analyses concerning the way that meanings were produced within and by texts (whether written, visual, or social). Although produced within a specific historical context, the rules and boundaries of textual construction themselves determine the parameters of content by principles of inclusion, exclusion, and juxtaposition. Although texts appeared to be natural and neutral, textual analysts argued that cultural production was "cast" by ideology (Roland Barthes, 1973, p. 112).

Consequently, textual analysis was particularly suitable for examining the representation of gender. The first major feminist studies (e.g., Gaye Tuchman, Arlene Kaplan Daniels, & James Benet, 1978; Women's Studies Group, 1978) explored the conditions under which women were invisible and visible within culture, or in Tuchman's terms, the subject of "symbolic annihilation." Janice Radway has referred to the process of making women silent, constructing them as objects, and as the Other:

> ... patriarchal culture has done more than simply silence individual women. It has also managed, through its own speech, to construct a position for female subjectivity which is, in reality, that of an object.... (W)omen have been rendered as the silent Other, that is, as the focal point for male desire and as the means for its fulfillment. ... (Janice Radway, 1986, p. 97).

To complement the analysis of representation, other analysts looked at practices of consumption, especially the determinants of possible reading or viewing positions (spectatorship) (e.g., Angela McRobbie, 1978, 1984; Janice Radway, 1984; Janice Winship, 1980). Studies of spectatorship have argued that meanings are produced in the act of reading or taking up a text, and that readers may interpret and use texts in ways which resist or react against the inscribed meaning.

The significance of readings that go "against the grain" of the text lies in the potential "for challenging the material situation which gave rise to the particular form of the fantasy in the first place" (Janice Radway, 1986, p. 99). These studies examined "the class, gender and ethnic determinations of the social and cultural relations" of cultural production, prioritizing areas such as popular media, romance novels, and literature, as well as gender relations within institutions such as sport, the workplace, and politics (Stuart Hall, Dorothy Hobson, Andrew Lowe, & Paul Willis, 1980, pp. 246–268).

The semiotic approach was popularized as a tool of analysis because of its particular suitability for the analysis of visual material. The production of images relies heavily on the literal representation of the body by constructing notions of femininity within the site, and by the sight, of bodily space. In this process, almost any part of the body can be represented in terms of an association with the "essence" of femininity. Any bodily part may or may not be sexualized by rhetorical associations, as Ros Coward argued (Rosalind Coward, 1984, pp. 80–81). This process has been vastly extended by the representational practices within the mass media, especially advertising, which have multiplied the parts of the body which can be marketed as "sexual" (Rosalind Coward, 1978, p. 15).

Textual analyses were particularly sensitive to detecting the shifting codes and conventions of representation. Judith Williamson's *Decoding Advertisements* (1978) exposed the conflict between the processes of ideological construction in advertisements (producing women as the objects of the gaze) and the pleasures of women as spectators, looking at, and being attracted to, these images. Advertising constructs spectators in terms of the objects of consumption: "Material things that we need are made to represent other, non-material things we need" (Judith Williamson, 1978, p. 14). Consumers are made by what they consume and are valued in terms of their ability to consume, their buying power: "We are both product and consumer; we consume, buy the product, yet we *are* the product" (Judith Williamson, 1978, p. 70).

The appeal of textual analysis was its methodology. It inspired a "dizzying array" (Cathy Schwichtenberg, 1989, p. 205) of analyses, particularly the representation of women. The study of gendered texts was extended to a myriad of forms of cultural production in line with the argument that representation was informed by the idea of "woman" as a "problem"—as a lack, as an agent of disruption, as emotional, and as synonymous with domesticity. Gradually, studies have come to recognize a range of forms of representation and of contradictory concepts of "woman."

The trajectory of this work has been strengthened by Laura Mulvey's article, "Visual pleasure and narrative cinema." Mulvey problematized the magic of Hollywood film style in its "satisfying manipulation of visual pleasure" (Laura Mulvey, 1981a, p. 206). She argued that the pleasure of looking was derived from codes of representation that inscribed a masculine point of view as the ideal position of spectatorship.

Mulvey uses psychoanalytic terms to account for the conventions of cinematic practice in terms of how that produces points of identification, reading positions, and viewing pleasure: "The scopophilic instinct (pleasure in looking at another person as an erotic object), and, in contradistinction, ego libido (forming identification processes) act as formations, mechanisms, which this cinema has played on" (Laura Mulvey, 1981a, p. 213). In this, the image of woman functions as the passive object of the gaze from a masculine point of view; the dominant position of spectatorship is thus *as if* through male eyes, irrespective of the actual gender of a spectator.

The image of women thus works both to induce voyeurism and fetishism as well as a sign of the threat of castration. The uniqueness of film in achieving these contradictions lies in its ability to shift the emphasis of the look. All forms of media construct women as objects of display for men "to be looked at and gazed at and stared at by men" for male sexual fantasies. Mulvey argues that women must reclaim their bodies (or ownership of the image thereof): "The time has come for us to take over the show and exhibit our own fears and desires" (Laura Mulvey 1987, p. 131). [See also Laura Rakow, this volume.]

REVISING CULTURAL STUDIES—INCORPORATION, RECUPERATION, NEW PRIORITIES

There have been three main trends in the incorporation of feminist perspectives into cultural studies: first, adding feminism onto a materialist focus; second, privileging gender as the key determinant of cultural production; and third, exploring female pleasure and cultural production by women.

Sociological and class-based forms of cultural studies were revised under the impact of feminism. The more radical version argued that gender underpinned class relations and thus overdetermined the material conditions of cultural production. Other versions positioned gender as one of a number of subordinate factors (see Lucy Bland, Trisha McCabe, & Frank Mort, 1979, p. 80). The relative autonomy of gender as a determinant force in socialist feminism remains contested and produces an uneasy tension in its application to cultural studies. Nonetheless, many new areas of interest have been opened up by this recasting including social history, domestic architecture, fashion, feminist film, and art history.

Second, much work has focused on the cultural texts and forms which specifically represent gender or are addressed primarily to women. Much of this work has addressed the inferior status and invisibility of such phenomena as well as proposing female positions of spectatorship and pleasure, and investigating the possibility of alternative cultural forms. Studies have explored women's fiction such as romance (Janice Radway, 1984; Valerie Walkerdine, 1984), melodrama and soap opera (Ien Ang, 1985; Charlotte Brunsdon, 1983; Dorothy Hobson, 1982; Annette Kuhn, 1984, 1985; Tania Modelski, 1979, 1982), women's lived experience (Dorothy Hobson, 1980; Angela McRobbie, 1978), women's cultures (Elizabeth Dempster, 1988; Barbara Hudson, 1984; Angela McRobbie, 1982b, 1984; Janice Radway, 1986), and domesticity (Ann Douglas, 1977; Rozsika Parker, 1986; Gwendolyn Wright, 1981), fashion (Anne Hollander, 1978; Elizabeth Wilson, 1985), and consumerism (Erica Carter, 1984; Meaghan Morris, 1988).

These studies acknowledge the specificity of cultural forms which are produced for and by women, consumed in particular ways, and used to deal with the realities of women's lives "to resist dominant practices of patriarchal signification" (Janice Radway, 1986, p. 98). As Hobson (1978) discovered, women use women's fiction strategically, to temporarily escape the demands of domesticity and the unfulfilled promises of femininity. By clinging to the fantasy that, "Some day my prince will come" (Valerie Walkerdine, 1984), women can deal with their desires and problems. Surprisingly, feminist exposés of these practices did not lead to their abandonment; lifting "the veil of distortion" from women's eyes and replacing hopeless romanticism with progressive content would fail unless it took account of women's desires and fantasies (Valerie Walkerdine, 1984, p. 164, 182).

The third approach has shifted away from the emphasis on making women visible, indicating their specificity, theorizing reading and spectatorship, and critiquing ways of seeing. Possibly due to an impasse—the exposé of cultural production has not halted its relentless manufacture—feminist attention turned the pleasures of cultural consumption and possibilities for the construction of alternative pleasures and alternative texts. The pursuit of pleasure or suspect enjoyment of certain texts and activities rests on a sense of "complicity" between the apparently innocent pleasures of everyday life and structured regimes of looking and desire. Pleasure is produced around the sexualization of social life not just at the level of individual spectatorship (private pleasures) but as "part of a more generalized voyeurism of the social and political scene" (Colin Mercer, 1986, p. 56). In accounting for the diversity of pleasures and its audiences, the terms personal, body, and subversive readings have been employed in order to resist the polarization of pleasures as *"solidly* ideological/repressive or *solidly* liberatory" (Colin Mercer, 1986, p. 67).

The study of female pleasure has focused on family life and consumerism (Erica Carter, 1984, pp. 186, 197). In contrast to the public face of masculinity (heroism, aggression, demonstration), femininity is constructed around private endurance and the projection of fantasy (Valerie Walkerdine, 1984, 167). Female culture concerns the production of aids to achieve femininity (and later domesticity) through commodities (Erica Carter, 1984, pp. 196–197). Yet Carter suggest that consumer culture may not be a dupe to "seduce women into slavish submission to the authority of the market" but that women may use consumption to refuse "dominant codes of social taste" (Erica Carter, 1984, p. 213). She suggests that consumerism is not an adequate name for the problems of women but rather a facade that "itself 'speaks' the problems (and the delights) of the female condition" (p. 213). Consumerism both offers and partially fulfills "its promise of everyday solutions—albeit limited and partial ones—to problems whose origins may lie elsewhere" (p. 213). The exploration of the production of pleasure, especially of women's and feminist pleasure, is crucial to the development of feminist paradigms and forcefields (cf. Beverley Brown, 1981).

NEW METHODS

Feminist work in cultural studies has developed the concepts of female pleasure and desire (Rosalind Coward, 1984; Laura Mulvey, 1981b) especially in relation to film and the possibilities for alternative readings and cinema (Charlotte Brunsdon, 1986; Teresa de Lauretis, 1984, 1987; Mary Ann Doane & Linda Williams, 1984; E. Ann Kaplan, 1983a; Annette Kuhn, 1982, 1985; Diedre Pribram, 1988). Other visual media have also been addressed (Rosemary Betterton, 1987; E. Ann Kaplan, 1983b; Rozsika Parker & Griselda Pollock, 1987). Other work has applied ethnographic methods to women's cultures (Dorothy Hobson, 1978, 1980, 1982; Janice Radway, 1986). In a process of:

> Rejecting the conventional gratifications . . . and the voyeuristic spectacle feminism explores the pleasures of resistance, of deconstruction, of discovery, of defining, of fragmenting, of redefining, all of which is often still tentative and provisional. Feminism constantly questions the identifications of popular and high culture and their pleasures. . . . (Rozsika Parker & Griselda Pollock, 1987, p. 54)

These methods have entailed new forms of textual readings and the exploration of women's lives through ethnography, archival and spatial studies. These have included critiques and deconstructions as well as feminist constructions of cultural forms. For example, the idea of feminist art (and women's arts and crafts) has gradually been acknowledged by the art establishment, though this in turn raises questions about how to maintain the political edge of feminist work within institutional parameters.

THE IMPACT OF FEMINISM ON CULTURAL STUDIES

The role of women and feminism in the development of cultural studies has had a crucial impact on the practice, teaching, and fallout from the discipline. Gender has become at least as important as class and other structural conditions in pedagogic strategies (cf. Lawrence

Grossberg & Paula Treichler, 1987). As well as theoretical issues, substantive case studies of areas such as advertising, soap opera, fashion, women's magazines, and women's writing have lent themselves to teaching situations. Two themes recur: the role of gender in consumerism, especially for women; and the role of the "private" in women's lives.

However, gender has not remained an exclusively feminist concern. Not all the work on gender is feminist, nor are all analysts female. Indeed, some male analysts have become keen to explore misrepresentations of sexuality (e.g., John Fiske, Bob Hodge, & Graeme Turner, 1987; Stephen Heath, 1982). The most interesting work by men has applied the terms of feminist analysis to studies of homosexuality and male sexuality (e.g., Richard Dyer, 1982; Ian Green, 1984; Steve Neale, 1983). However, the relationship between this work and feminist work on female sexuality has been contested (Parveen Adams & Jeffrey Minson, 1978).

The rapid growth of cultural studies indicates its popularity but does not guarantee that it has successfully intervened in regimes of cultural production. This poses a problem for graduating students of cultural studies because the fundamental assumptions of their degree programs are frequently at odds with the conditions in the home or workplace. Institutions of advertising, film, media, culture industries, teaching, and bureaucracies have scarcely been touched by the critiques of cultural studies, let alone by feminist reforms.

CULTURAL STUDIES AND FEMINISM

The feminist framing of cultural studies has had a profound impact on the recognition of the "problem" of women generally. Techniques of textual analysis, including substitution of male in conventionally female scenarios, role reversals, and nonstereotypical representations (cf. Griselda Pollock, 1977) have become stock-in-trade of current affairs, schools, popular magazines, soap opera scripts, even in advertising itself.

Cultural studies has contributed to many areas of feminist debate including nonsexist language handbooks, codes for advertisers, and pornography and erotica. But the question remains as to how feminism should feed into policy formation and whether, once legitimated, the critical edge of feminism is necessarily blunted. As Rosemary Betterton has written:

> If the task of feminist criticism is to unpick the threads which bind women and men to certain representations of femininity, can it also enable them to reconstruct and redefine that femininity in different and more positive terms? (1987, p. 14).

CURRENT SITUATION

One of the successes of cultural studies has been its uptake in schools as well as in tertiary institutions. This is due to its interdisciplinary nature and its relevance to everyday life. Because of the centrality of feminism to the study of culture, there is perhaps more scope for its impact on curricula than other disciplines. Already cultural studies has shifted away from an overriding emphasis on textual forms to the study of cultural production, practice, and consumption. Elspeth Probyn has argued that the success of this broader project depends on prizing open the term "the feminine" to explore how the feminine is inscribed "across planes, and fragmented quite literally with our bodies and memories" (Elspeth Probyn, 1987, p. 358). She suggests that feminist research must acknowledge the political ramifications of feminist work by bringing studies of cultural texts into alignment with studies of more consequential feminine practices. By way of example, Elspeth Probyn suggests that the kinds of analyses offered for teenage dancing and dance films "might seem frivolous when applied to abortion, or even anorexia nervosa" (Elspeth Probyn, 1987, p. 358). Yet there are important connections between the froth and bubble of femininity and the images of the female body and motherhood that structure other social registers. How successfully feminism can intervene in cultural studies to revise, resituate and reconstruct the disciplinary foci remains a question. Nevertheless, the challenge for feminist cultural studies is to train women and men in new regimes of seeing, reading, and using cultural products as the basis for intervening in processes of cultural production. This feminist political agenda has the potential to rewrite culture as the precondition for reconstructing the academy.

BIBLIOGRAPHY

Adams, Parveen, & Minson, Jeffrey. (1978). The 'subject' of feminism. *m/f, 2,* 43–61.

Ang, Ien. (1985). *Watching Dallas: Soap opera and the melodramatic imagination.* London: Methuen.

Barthes, Roland. (1973). *Mythologies.* St Albans: Paladin.

Betterton, Rosemary (Ed.). (1987). *Looking on. Images of femininity in the visual arts and media.* London: Pandora.

Bland, Lucy, McCabe, Trisha, & Mort, Frank. (1979). Sexuality and reproduction: Three 'official' instances. In Michele Barrett, Philip Corrigan, Annette Kuhn, & Janet Wolff (Eds.), *Ideology and cultural production* (pp. 78–111). London: Croom Helm.

Brown, Beverley. (1981). A feminist interest in pornography—some modest proposals. *m/f, 5/6,* 5–18.

Brunsdon, Charlotte. (1983). Crossroads: Notes on soap opera. In E. Ann Kaplan (Ed.), *Regarding television* (pp. 76–83). Los Angeles: University Publications of America Inc.

Brunsdon, Charlotte (Ed.). (1986). *Films for women.* London: British Film Institute.

Carey, James. (1977). Mass communication research and cultural studies: An American view. In James Curran, Michael Gurevitch, & Janet Woollacott (Eds.), *Mass communication and society* (pp. 409–425). London: Edward Arnold.

Carey, James. (1983). The origins of the radical discourse on cultural studies in the United States. *Journal of Communication, 33*(3), 311–313.

Carter, Erica. (1984). Alice in consumer wonderland. In Angela McRobbie and Mica Nava (Eds.), *Gender and generation* (pp. 185–214). London: Macmillan.

Coward, Rosalind. (1978). Sexual liberation and the family. *m/f, 1,* 7–24.

Coward, Rosalind. (1984). *Female desire: Women's sexuality today.* London: Paladin.

de Lauretis, Teresa. (1984). *Alice doesn't: Feminism, semiotics, cinema.* Bloomington: Indiana University Press.

de Lauretis, Teresa. (1987). *Technologies of gender: Essays on theory, film, fiction.* Bloomington: Indiana University Press.

Dempster, Elizabeth. (1988). Women writing the body: Let's watch a little how she dances. In Susan Sheridan (Ed.), *Grafts. Feminist cultural criticism* (pp. 35–54). London: Verso.

Doane, Mary Ann, & Williams, Linda (Eds.). (1984). *Re-Vision: Essays in feminist film criticism.* Frederick, MD: University Publications of America and the American Film Institute.

Douglas, Ann. (1977). *The feminization of American culture.* New York: Avon Books.

Dyer, Richard. (1982). Don't look now: The male pin-up. *Screen, 23*(2–3), 61–73.

Fiske, John, Hodge, Bob, & Turner, Graeme. (1987). *Myths of Oz: Reading Australian popular culture.* Sydney: Allen & Unwin.

Green, Ian. (1984). Malefunction. *Screen, 25*(4–5), 36–48.

Grossberg, Lawrence, & Treichler, Paula. (1987). Intersections of power: Criticism, television, gender. *Communication, 9,* 273–287.

Hall, Stuart, Hobson, Dorothy, Lowe, Andrew, & Willis, Paul (Eds.). (1980). *Culture, media, language.* London: Hutchinson.

Heath, Stephen. (1982). *The sexual fix.* London: Macmillan.

Hobson, Dorothy. (1978). Housewives: Isolation as oppression. In Women's Studies Group (Eds.), *Women take issue: Aspects of women's subordination* (pp. 79–95). London: Hutchinson.

Hobson, Dorothy. (1980). Housewives and the mass media. In Stuart Hall, Dorothy Hobson, Andrew Lowe, & Paul Willis (Eds.), *Culture, Media, Language* (pp. 105–114). London: Hutchinson.

Hobson, Dorothy. (1982). *Crossroads: The drama of a soap opera.* London: Macmillan.

Hollander, Anne. (1978). *Seeing through clothes.* New York: Avon.

Hudson, Barbara. (1984). Femininity and adolescence. In Angela McRobbie & Mica Nava (Eds.), *Gender and generation* (pp. 31–53). London: Macmillan.

Kaplan, E. Ann. (1983a). *Regarding television.* Los Angeles: American Film Institute.

Kaplan, E. Ann. (1983b). *Woman and film: Both sides of the camera.* New York: Methuen.

Kuhn, Annette. (1982). *Women's pictures: Feminism and the cinema.* London: Routledge & Kegan Paul.

Kuhn, Annette. (1984). Women's genres. *Screen, 25*(1), 18–28.

Kuhn, Annette. (1985). *The power of the image: Essays on representation and sexuality.* London: Routledge & Kegan Paul.

McRobbie, Angela. (1978). Working class girls and the culture of femininity. In Women's Studies Group (Eds.), *Women take issue* (pp. 96–108). London: Hutchinson.

McRobbie, Angela. (1982a). The politics of feminist research: Between talk, text and action. *Feminist Review, 12,* 46–57.

McRobbie, Angela. (1982b). Settling accounts with subcultures: A feminist critique. *Screen Education, 34,* 37–49.

McRobbie, Angela. (1984). Dance and social fantasy. In Angela McRobbie and Mica Nava (Eds.), *Gender and generation* (pp. 130–161). London: Macmillan.

McRobbie, Angela, & Garber, Jenny. (1976). Girls and subcultures: An exploration. In Stuart Hall & Tony Jefferson (Eds.), *Resistance through rituals. Youth subcultures in post-war Britain* (pp. 209–222). London: Hutchinson.

Mercer, Colin. (1986). Complicit pleasures. In Tony Bennett, Colin Mercer, & Janet Woollacott (Eds.), *Popular culture and social relations* (pp. 50–68). Milton Keynes: Open University Press.

Modleski, Tania. (1979). The search for tomorrow in today's soap operas: Notes on a feminine narrative form. *Film Quarterly, 33*(1), 12–21.

Modleski, Tania. (1982). *Loving with a vengeance: Mass produced fantasies for women.* London: Methuen.

Morris, Meaghan. (1988). Things to do with shopping centres. In Susan Sheridan (Ed.), *Grafts. Feminist cultural criticism* (pp. 193–225). London: Verso.

Mulvey, Laura. (1981a). Visual pleasure and narrative cinema. In Tony Bennett, Susan Boyd Bowman, Colin Mercer & Janet Woollacott (Eds.), *Popular film and television* (pp. 206–215). London: Open University Press.

Mulvey, Laura. (1981b). On *Duel in the sun:* Afterthoughts on visual pleasure and narrative cinema. *Framework, 15*(17), 12–15.

Mulvey, Laura. (1987). You don't know what is happening, do you, Mr. Jones? In Rozsika Parker and Griselda Pollock (Eds.), *Framing feminism. Art and the women's movement 1970-85* (pp. 127–131). London: Pandora.

Neale, Steve. (1983). Masculinity as spectacle. *Screen, 24*(6), 2–16.

Parker, Rozsika. (1986). *The subversive stitch.* London: Verso.

Parker, Rozsika, & Pollock, Griselda (Eds.). (1987). *Framing feminism. Art and the women's movement 1970-85.* London: Pandora.

Pollock, Griselda. (1977). What's wrong with images of women? *Screen Education, 24,* 25–33.

Powell, Rachel, & Clarke, John. (1976). A note on marginality. In Stuart Hall & Tony Jefferson

(Eds.), *Resistance through rituals. Youth subcultures in post-war Britain* (pp. 223–229). London: Hutchinson.

Pribram, Diedre (Ed.). (1988). *Female spectators. Looking at film and television.* London: Verso.

Probyn, Elspeth. (1987). Bodies and anti-bodies: Feminism and the postmodern. *Cultural Studies, 1*(3), 349–360.

Radway, Janice. (1984). *Reading the romance: Women, patriarchy and popular literature.* Chapel Hill: University of North Carolina Press.

Radway, Janice. (1986). Identifying ideological seams: Mass culture, analytical method, and political practice. *Communication, 9,* 92–123.

Rakow, Lana. (1986). Rethinking gender research in communication. *Journal of Communication 36*(4), 11–26.

Ramazanoglu, Caroline. (1989). Improving on sociology: The problems of taking a feminist standpoint. *Sociology, 23*(3), 427–42.

Schwichtenberg, Cathy. (1989). Feminist cultural studies. *Critical Studies in Mass Communication, 6*(2), 202–208.

Strathern, Marilyn. (1987). An awkward relationship: The case of feminism and anthropology. *Signs, 12*(2), 176–92.

Treichler, Paula, & Wartella, Ellen. (1986). Intervention: Feminist theory and communication studies. *Communication, 9,* 1–18.

Tuchman, Gaye, Daniels, Arlene Kaplan, & Benet, James. (Eds.) (1978). *Hearth and Home: Images of women in the mass media.* New York: Oxford University Press.

Walkerdine, Valerie. (1984). Some day my prince will come. In Angela McRobbie & Mica Nava (Eds.), *Gender and generation* (pp. 162–184). London: Macmillan.

Williamson, Judith. (1978). *Decoding advertisements.* London: Marion Boyars.

Wilson, Elizabeth. (1985). *Adorned in dreams.* London: Virago.

Winship, Janice. (1980). Sexuality for sale. In Stuart Hall, Dorothy Hobson, Andrew Lowe, & Paul Willis (Eds.), *Culture, media, language* (pp. 217–223). London: Hutchinson.

Women's Studies Group (Eds.). (1978). *Women take issue: Aspects of women's subordination.* London: Hutchinson.

Wright, Gwendolyn. (1981). *Building the American dream: A social history of housing.* New York: Pantheon Books.

Chapter 8

Toward a Multicentered Women's Studies in the 1990s

Patricia Cramer
Ann Russo

FOUNDING GOALS

Like the feminist movement out of which it developed, Women's Studies in the United States began as a collective challenge to male domination in the early 1970s. Its origins can be traced to the civil rights movement, especially the Southern Freedom Schools; the anti-Vietnam War teach-ins; the Free Universities begun in 1965; and the frustrations of large numbers of women confronting discrimination in their private and public lives. (For discussion of the development of Women's Studies in the United States see Florence Howe, 1972 and Marilyn Boxer, 1982; for discussion of Women's Studies internationally, see Australia: Robyn Rowland, 1987; China: Wan Shanping, 1988; Eastern Africa: Marjorie Mbilinyi, 1984; England: Roisin Battel, Renate Duelli Klein, Catherine Moorhouse, & Christine Zmroczek, 1983; Germany: Tobe Levin, 1979; India: Maithreyi Krishna Raj, 1981; Japan: Junka Wada Kuninobu, 1984; Korea: Sei-wha Chung, 1986; Latin America: Fanny Tabak, 1985). U.S. Women's Studies' origins in social movements outside the university—especially women's struggles for equality—have shaped the goals, content, and theory of feminist scholars and teaching from the beginning. Early statements from Women's Studies programs reflect this political orientation. The organizers of a program in Buffalo, New York, wrote, "This education will not be an academic exercise; it will be an ongoing process to change the ways in which women think and behave. It must be part of the struggle to build a new and more complete society" (quoted in Florence Howe, 1984b, p. 106). Goddard College feminists wrote that women should "leave [the academy] . . . not only with a body of knowledge, but a reason for learning it, a context to fit it in, but most importantly, a strong sense of an inner core of self that most women never develop. We want to be able to act on the world, and in the world" (Florence Howe, 1984b, p. 106).

In ideals, at least, Women's Studies was never intended to be merely a struggle for equal rights, but a fundamental rethinking of male knowledge. Confronted with centuries of male erasure and distortion of women's achievement and experiences, we have generally rejected abstract universals, seeking truth in the concreteness of our daily lives. Florence Howe's definition of a feminist pursuit of knowledge typifies this position: "First, there is the matter of truth, of knowledge that is accurate and honest, which omits no essentials—like the history of half the human race in making a judgement about an age and civilization. Second, there is the purpose of truth and knowledge: to affect the lives we live, the opportunities we have. . . . "(1972, p. 219). Although not explicitly articulated often enough by white feminists, this commitment to historical truth and to empowering women has always meant—at least as an ideal—all women, not merely those who are white, heterosexual and/or middle class (see Patricia Bell Scott, Gloria Hull, & Barbara Smith, 1982; Alice Yun Chai, 1985; Marilyn Frye, 1985).

In evaluating U.S. Women's Studies in the 1980s, these founding goals—accountability to the women's movement, the formation of knowledge and theories which reflect and improve all women's lives, and a fundamental questioning of male traditions—are still central and can be a basis from which we can judge our progress as well as plan needed changes. For this reason, when Johnnella Butler reminds Women's Studies scholars to reflect the differences among women she does so on the basis of our shared commitments to truth-telling and to improving women lives: "The question is not: what will we give up in the canon and what will we include? Rather, the question is: how does the world really look—and what is there that was and is that can help us live better in it" (Johnnella Butler, 1989, p. 16). Our origins and continuing interaction with diverse social movements, especially Black, Latino, American Indian, third world, lesbian, Jewish, disabled, and peace movements as well as the movements against violence against women (battery, rape, child sexual abuse), pornography, and for economic justice and reproductive freedom have very much made Women's Studies what it is today. These social movements are a continuing source of strength and excitement reflected in the growth and popularity of Women's Studies courses, books, and conferences. However, Women's Studies courses and curriculum that ignore these political goals and do not acknowledge our diversity falsify our history and retreat from our commitment to all women (see Cruickshank, 1982; Merrill Harris, 1985; Maxine Baca Zinn, Lynn Weber Cannon, Elizabeth Higginbotham, & Thornton Dill, 1986). By remaining accountable for empowering women and committed to a pursuit of knowledge which is accurate and honest, we can resist assimilation and work toward reflecting, in structure and content, the multicultural, international women's movement that is needed if global changes are to be achieved.

Women's Studies programs in this country (as well as throughout the world) have grown dramatically since the early 1970s. In December 1970, Florence Howe counted two Women's Studies courses (one at San Diego College and the other at Cornell University), and in December 1971, 610 courses and 15 Women's Studies programs (Florence Howe, 1984b, p. 79). Today there are approximately 500 programs listed by the National Women's Studies Association (NWSA), and there is talk about better insuring the longevity and autonomy of Women's Studies by developing it as a discipline (see "Chronology" in Jo Baird, Shirley Frank, & Beth Stafford, 1982; Evelyn Torton Beck, 1989; and Gloria Bowles, 1983). There are more than 60 women's research centers in the United States alone, with the number growing annually. Most of these are university based.

NEW RESEARCH/PRIORITIES/DIRECTIONS

There has also been an unprecedented publication of writings by and about women, growth of feminist presses, and creation of knowledge about women unimaginable 20 years ago. Although so many areas of this tremendous expansion of scholarship are important, we want to highlight the emergence of the large body of writings by and about African-American, Jewish, Puerto Rican, Mexican-American, Native American, Asian-American, and/or third world women, as well as lesbians, working class women, self-identified fat women, disabled women, and old women. We choose this focus because the explosion of knowledge in this area is so unprecedented and because this is one area of the knowledge explosion that Women's Studies and feminist theory seems least successful in finding a language and structure for speaking and teaching about.

In 1971, designers of a course on Images of Women in Literature at a school with a sizeable minority population found so little writing about third world or working class women available in print that they had the students create a literature of their own by writing narratives, stories, and poems about themselves (Kathleen Chamberlain, 1971). Today, no teacher of Women's Studies should have difficulty finding materials of this kind. The following is a partial list suggesting the diversity and volume of theoretical and literary work that has evolved from the challenges within feminism to be for all women:

Jane B. Katz, *I am the Fire of Time—Voices of Native American Women* (1977)

Edna Acosta Belen, *The Puerto Rican Woman* (1979)

Nawal el Saadawi, *The Hidden Face of Eve* (1980)

Julia Penelope Stanley and Susan J. Wolfe, *The Coming Out Stories* (1980)

Cherrie Moraga and Gloria Anzaldua, *This Bridge Called My Back* (1981)

Angela Davis, *Women, Race, and Class* (1981)

bell hooks, *Ain't I a Woman* (1981)

Gloria Joseph and Jill Lewis, *Common Differences: Conflicts in Black and White Feminist Perspectives* (1981)

Margaret Cruikshank, *Lesbian Studies* (1982)

Patricia Bell Scott, Gloria Hull, and Barbara Smith, *All the Men are Black, All the Women are White, But Some of Us are Brave* (1982)

Evelyn Beck, *Nice Jewish Girls: A Lesbian Anthology*

Barbara Smith, *Home Girls* (1983)

Cherrie Moraga, *Loving in the War Years* (1983)

Barbara MacDonald with Cynthia Rich, *Look Me in the Eye: Old Women, Aging and Ageism* (1983)

Lisa Shoenfielder and Barb Wieser, *Shadow on a Tightrope: Writings by Women on Fat Oppression* (1983)

Miranda Davies, *Third World/Second Sex* (1983)

Beth Brant, *Gathering of Spirit: Writing and Art by North American Indian Women* (1984)

Elly Bulkin, Minnie Bruce Pratt and Barbara Smith, *Yours in Struggle: Three Feminist Perspectives on Anti-Semitism and Racism* (1984)

Paula Giddings, *When and Where I Enter: The Impact of Black Women on Race and Sex in America* (1984)

Susan E. Brown, Debra Connors, and Nanci Stern, *With the Power of Each Breath: A Disabled Women's Anthology* (1985)

Melanie Kaye/Kantrowitz and Irena Klepfisz, *The Tribe of Dina: A Jewish Women's Anthology* (1986)

Rochelle Lefkowitz and Ann Withorn, *For Crying Out Loud: Women and Poverty in the United States* (1986)

Juanita Ramos, *Compañeras: Latina Lesbians* (1987)

Asian Women United of California, *Making Waves: An Anthology of Writings By and About Asian American Women* (1989)

Lisa Albrecht and Rose M. Brewer, *Bridges of Power: Women's Multicultural Alliances* (1990).

New journals have also been formed—including among many others:

Lilith
Sage: A Scholarly Journal on Black Women
Connexions: An International Women's Quarterly
Manushi: A Journal about Women and Society (India)
Lesbian Ethics
Sinister Wisdom
Common Lives/Lesbian Lives
Third Woman

Although we have both heard even feminist academics publicly refer to the 1980s as the postfeminist phase (a tactic for killing off the movement when we've really just gotten started), even this glance at what has actually been happening suggests not a decline but an unprecedented expansion, diversification, and broadening of our experiential and knowledge base. This is especially true of black women's literature, as evidenced by the success of Alice Walker's *The Color Purple* (1982); Gloria Naylor's, *The Women of Brewster Place* (1982); Toni Cade Bambara's, *The Salt Eaters* (1980); Toni Morrison's, *Beloved* (1987)—to name but a few.

This trend toward diversification and self-identification is apparent in conference topics and panels as well. In 1977 NWSA was founded, and at the first convention in 1979, a Lesbian Caucus was formed. In 1981, at Storrs, Connecticut, the theme was "Women Respond to Racism" and Audre Lorde ("Women and Anger") and Adrienne Rich ("Disobedience is What Women's Studies is Potentially About") were the keynote speakers. In 1983, at the NWSA conference, an ad hoc coalition of women of color, third world women, Jewish women, lesbians, students, working class and poor women organized to gain a commitment from NWSA to better meet the demands of a more inclusive feminism; they organized an Autonomous Institute for the 1984 conference which highlighted the concerns of groups previously underrepresented at NWSA conferences; and at the next few conferences similar groups formed to plan further programming. Since then, plenary sessions by, for and about specific groups of women have been organized, for instance, the first Jewish plenary session was held at the NWSA conference in 1986 at the University of Illinois at Urbana-Champaign; the first African American plenary in 1987 at Spelman College, Atlanta; and the first lesbian plenary in 1988 at the University of Minnesota, Minneapolis.

Numerous conferences and meetings have also been organized around issues of difference, power, and feminism. At the University of Illinois, as part of a group of undergraduate and graduate students, we initiated and organized an international conference "Common Differences: Third World Women and Feminist Perspectives" which took place in April 1983. This conference was volatile and controversial, bringing together many women from different racial, ethnic, class, and political backgrounds. None of us left the conference unchanged. More recently, two conferences on race and gender were held, "Parallels and Intersections: A Conference on Racism and other Forms of Oppression," April 6–9, 1989, in Iowa City, Iowa; and "Women in America: Legacies of Race and Ethnicity," April 6–8, 1989, at Georgetown University in Washington, D.C. The Iowa conference was organized by the Women Against Racism Committee in Iowa City, Iowa, a group which has been working on these issues for quite a few years. The international growth of Women's Studies is further indicated by the United Nations Decade for Women Conferences (1975 in Mexico City, 1980 in Copenhagen, and 1985 in Nairobi) where meetings were held that focused on the research and study of women. Moreover, other national and international conferences have been held around the world, including the first feminist Latin American Conference at Bogota, Colombia, in 1981 where women from 11 Latin American countries met; a Women's Studies International Conference at the Free University of Berlin in 1981; a National Conference on Women's Studies held at the S.N.D.T. Women's University in Bombay in 1981; and an International Conference on Research and Teaching Related to Women held at Concordia University, Montreal, Canada (see *Women's Studies International Supplement* 1982, 1983, and 1984 for reports on Women's Studies internationally).

Organizations and conferences by, for, and about specific groups of women have also been initiated. For instance, in 1980, the first National Conference on Third World Women and Violence convened in Washington, D.C., as did the first National Asian/Pacific American Women's Conference; and in 1981, the Third World Women's Archives and Kitchen Table: Women of Color Press were founded in New York City. Each of these publications, conferences, and organizations exemplify the growth and expansion of Women's Studies in the 1980s—and this is only a sampling of the work being done throughout the world.

RESPONSES TO THE CHALLENGE OF DIVERSITY

To assess the impact of the challenges and developments in Women's Studies with respect to diversity, in the fall of 1988, we conducted a survey of introductory Women's Studies courses offered in the United States. We analyzed 100 syllabi taught in 1987–1988, looking at how issues of race, class, sexual orientation, religion, ethnicity, age, and disability were or were not incorporated into the course. The following is a brief assessment of some of our findings.

We found that although most of the syllabi had incorporated some material from women of color and lesbians, the majority did so in a limited and tokenizing fashion. Approximately two thirds had very little and 20% had nothing at all on women of color, and 50% of those who addressed issues of race used exclusively literature on black women. Happily, about one third of the courses had writings by and about women of color interspersed throughout the syllabus, under a number of categories, for instance, economics, sexuality, family, and violence against women. Jewish women were notably underrepresented—only nine syllabi included works by and about Jewish women or antisemitism, and only three syllabi dealt with disability issues. Among the twenty women writers who appear most often on syllabi, three are women of color: Audre Lorde, Cherrie Moraga (primarily as editor of *This Bridge Called My Back*), and Alice Walker.

Overall, we found that the syllabi indicated a need for more self-education about diverse groups of women and a more consistent effort to decenter white, middle-class, heterosexual women so that women of color do not only appear under discussions of racism, or lesbians only under discussions of sexuality, but throughout. Alternatively, the syllabi which addressed diversity throughout were by far more provocative and interesting in the questions they raised about the complexity of women's experience. For example, to address diversity within categories, one might include under the category of "Identity and Socialization," the following articles: Lenore J. Weitzman, "Sex-Role Socialization: A Focus on Women;" Barbara Smith, "Homophobia: Why Bring It Up;" Letty C. Pogrebin, "The Secret Fear that Keeps Us From Raising Free Children;" and Louise Derman-Sparks et al., "Children, Race and Racism: How Race Awareness Develops." Under reproductive rights, one might include Linda Gordon, "The Struggle for Reproductive Freedom;" Helen Rodriguez-Trias, "Sterilization Abuse," and Anne Finger, "Claiming All of Our Bodies: Reproductive Rights and Disability." Moreover, although white women are also clearly affected by race and racism, few syllabi include essays on white women thinking about what it means to be white; one might include, for example, Minnie Bruce Pratt's, "Identity: Skin Blood Heart" in *Yours in Struggle;* Adrienne Rich's, "Disloyal to Civilization" in *On Lies, Secrets, and Silences* and other essays from *Blood, Bread and Poetry;* Marilyn Frye's "On Being White" in *Politics of Reality;* and May Stevens, "Looking Backward in Order to Look Forward: Memoirs of a Racist Girlhood" in *Heresies.* For more discussion of strategies to create Women's Studies courses which address the commonality as well as diversity among women, see Nancy Bazin, 1983; Elly Bulkin, 1980; Laurie Crumpacker and Eleanor Vendor Haegen, 1987; Evelyn Glenn, 1988; Jean Griscom, 1987; Nancy Hoffman, 1977; Barbara Omolade, 1987; and Vicky Spelman, 1982.

This continuing failure to reflect diversity not only deprives all of us of the empowerment and self-knowledge which comes from working with women with different backgrounds and priorities, but also leaves Women's Studies repeating the pattern of selectivity and distortion which has characterized the patriarchal tradition we oppose. For example, as reflected in the syllabi, the most frequently taught feminist writer is Adrienne Rich. But how can we understand Rich's development as reflected in *Blood, Bread, and Poetry* and her recent poems where she identifies herself as Jewish and lesbian without reference to the works by Jewish and lesbian writers with whom she has been in dialogue (see, for example, Melanie Kaye/Kantrowitz and Irena Klepfisz, Eds., 1986, *The Tribe of Dina*)? How can we account for her repeated references to writings by women of color throughout *Bread, Blood, and Poetry* (but not in *On Lies, Secrets, and Silences*) without also teaching the women of color she has been in dialogue with over the past decades (see, for example, Audre Lorde and Adrienne Rich, "An Interview with Audre Lorde," 1981)? Like Rich, we have all been changed by these dialogues. Centralizing only certain types of women deprives us of a history of how our ideas and self-concepts have developed and deprives women in the future of models for bringing about this kind of growth and dialogue.

Many courses use first person narratives, poetry, short stories, or novels for experiences of Black women, Latinas, and Asians, while white, middle-class women's lives are more often analyzed by social scientific research or more abstract theoretical essays. The most frequently occurring articles by women of color on the syllabi we surveyed were the Combahee River Collective Statement and Sojourner Truth's, "Ain't I a Woman" speech; there are very few fully developed theoretical pieces on, for example, women of color's relationship to such issues as reproductive rights, employment, sexuality, and education. This recreates the same polarization men have imposed on us—equating "high" (i.e., abstract and allegedly objective) with the privileged class and "low" (i.e., personal and emotional) with the less privileged (for further discussion of these issues, see Scheman, 1985; and Stanley, 1984). Although we reject this patriarchal categorization, we do suggest using both types of essays—personal and abstract—for all types of women more often. There are many first person essays available by white women and there is now a great deal of research on women of color. A recent bibliography entitled *Women of Color and Southern Women: A Bibliography of Social Science Research, 1975–1988* (Eds. Andrea Timberlake, Lynn Weber Cannon, Rebecca F. Guy, and Elizabeth Higginbotham) is an excellent resource. There is also little movement material being used—material, for example, from *Conditions, Heresies, Off Our Backs, Calyx, Sinister Wisdom, Common Lives/Lesbian Lives, Aegis: A Magazine on Ending Violence Against Women,* or *Black/Out.* This perpetuates a dangerous split between movement and academic women and deprives Women's Studies students and faculty of the important work being done outside the university.

Interestingly, there is also a tendency to use abstract or more conceptual approaches to homophobia or lesbianism. Adrienne Rich's, "Compulsory Heterosexuality" is most often taught under the lesbian category, and while it is an excellent article, it seems to speak more to compulsory heterosexuality than to the complexity and richness of the lives of lesbians. Are first person narratives or studies on lesbian life being excluded because less comfortable to teach? We suggest the use of more specific and directed discussions of lesbian life in conjunction with this essay; or as stated above, integrate lesbian life throughout the syllabi (for excellent articles, see Darty and Potter, 1984; Julia Penelope Stanley and Susan J. Wolfe, 1980).

Women's Studies continues to demand our commitment to self-education, and we cannot rely on academic journals and conferences for the information we need. As even our partial listing of resources suggests, much of the most challenging work continues in nonacademic circles, journals, and presses. We must remember that in addition to reading *Signs, Feminist Review, Women's Studies, Sage: A Scholarly Journal on Black Women* among others, we can also be reading journals such as *Heresies, Conditions, Off Our Backs,* and *Black/Out* and *Sojourner.*

By making these suggestions, we hope to encourage the dialogue already going on in Women's Studies on these issues. We do so not in the spirit of guilt or accusation, but to ask how we can do better. How can we share the resources we all need for the self-education that feminist studies has always been about? How can we rethink our programs and courses to keep Women's Studies what it set out to be—a discipline devoted to discovering the truths of women's lives and to empowering all women on the basis of that knowledge?

RESISTANCE TO BACKLASH AND ASSIMILATION

When Women's Studies first evolved, opponents often accused feminists of being unscholarly, biased, subjective, and political (see Lora Robinson, "The Emergence of Women's Courses in Higher Education"). In many ways, we are today the same daughters facing the same hostility from the same fathers—although perhaps at times in more insidious, "friendly" forms. The outright attacks are too familiar to cause much confusion among us—the enemy is clear, and although unnerving, attacks usually inspire rather than undermine solidarity among us. A recent example is Michael Levin's article in *New Perspectives,* published in the U.S. Commission on Civil Rights (Summer 1985). Levin writes, "Feminists contend that they have been barred from the rigorous, prestigious disciplines by overt and covert pressures, yet, given a free hand, they have done little more than restate the doctrines of feminism itself in the classroom, which is transformed into a forum for consciousness/raising and advocacy of a political agenda." He describes *Our Bodies, Our Selves* (Boston Women's Health Book Collective, 1976) as "overly concerned with lesbianism, masturbation, venereal disease, and rape." In response to feminist claims for an inclusive history, he writes, "An equal-time doctrine is a useless principle for assessing historical significance; some periods, nations, and individuals have exercised a disproportionate influence over the rest of mankind." He concludes with, "Suffice it to say that feminism has contributed to the 'decline of standards' which is now so fashionable to deplore" (p. 10). While Levins' arguments are familiar, the fact that his essay appears in a publication of the U.S. Civil Rights Commission warns us of the continuing threat of such attitudes to Women's Studies.

Accusations that label feminists as manhaters, lesbian (intending insult rather than compliment) still thrive as a tactic to intimidate and isolate women scholars and students.

Recently, Peter Schaub, a student at the University of Washington in Seattle, led a campaign against their Women's Studies program after being dismissed from the class for disruptive and antagonistic behavior. In an interview, he claims that the instructor "ardently boasts of lesbianism and delivers shallow sermons on socialism, while making hate-breeding statements about men." Rather than investigate him, the administration investigated the Women's Studies program (see Caryn McTighe Musil & Carol Combs, 1988; "Can One Male Voice Silence Us?" 1988). Our students have frequently complained about receiving ridicule of this type from men for attending Women's Studies courses. Shaub epitomizes an attitude still prevalent on our campuses, a threat to all of us, but especially our women students.

A more insidious form of backlash, however, has arisen among the male "friends" of Women's Studies and it is this liberal attack which most effectively undermines women's confidence as well as the autonomy of women's studies. One instance is the creation of "men's studies." Men's Studies can be positive when truly feminist and committed to challenging male power, but too often it focuses on how sex differences limit all of us equally, rather than on sexual inequality and the social significance of men's subordination of women (see Harry Brod, 1987; Mary Libertin, 1987; Catharine A. MacKinnon, 1987). [See Lillian Robinson, this volume, for a discussion of Men's Studies.] The neutralization of Women's Studies to gender studies is a backlash phenomenon to watch very carefully in the upcoming decade.

The most effective source of this backlash strategy appears among the critical, psychoanalytic, and poststructuralist theory circles. On the surface their gestures of interest in feminism appear friendly, and although a significant group of women have embraced their theories, critical theory has, in fact, been used to delegitimize the majority of feminist theories—especially those which are radical, experiential, third world, and historically based. Its proselytizers commonly "valorize" theories derived from Freud, Lacan, and male philosophers and disparage feminist theories derived from women's experiences and writings as nontheoretical, essentialist, confessional, and reductive (see Liz Stanley, 1984). [See also Mary Ellen Capek, this volume.] Regardless of the conscious intentions of individuals working with theories of this type, our personal experiences and those of other women we have spoken with suggests that these theories are being used to intimidate, silence, and replace other forms of feminist theory and knowledge. In the four universities we have been associated with, we have observed how this happens: as graduate students we were reprimanded by male professors claiming friendship with feminists for not using so-called sophisticated sources from the psychoanalytic and deconstructive canon; we have seen men (and sometimes women) committed to male-derived feminist theories control hiring decisions so that more radical feminists were not hired; and we have seen feminists retreat from their early self-confidence into silence because they feel inadequate in the face of the obfuscating jargon of critical theory.

This use of "high" theory and mystification of knowledge to exclude the majority of women from scholarly traditions has been used against us before. For example, in the mid-nineteenth century male critics co-opted women's early domination of the novel by devising theories separating the "serious" (i.e., male) novels from the "popular" (i.e., female) (see Nina Baym, 1984; Dale Spender, 1986); in the 1930s American literature departments focused on the masterpiece and creation of periodizations like the Frontier Spirit which rationalized the exclusion of women, working class, and ethnic writers from the canon (see Paul Lauter, 1983); and in the early twentieth century the radical attacks by first-wave feminists on male sexuality were replaced by the misogynous theories of Havelock Ellis, Krafft-Ebing and Freud (see Lillian Faderman, 1978; Sheila Jeffreys, 1985).

Feminists are producing the most exciting and innovative scholarship today; our classes generate a great deal of excitement; our books often sell well. As Barbara Christian suggests in her excellent response to the critical theory phenomenon, "it is perhaps no accident that the language [of critical theory] surfaced, interestingly enough, just when the literature of peoples of color, black women, Latin Americans, and Africans began to move to 'the center'" (Barbara Christian, 1987, p. 71; see also Sandra M. Gilbert & Susan Gubar, 1988).

Clearly, critical theory is *not* the only way to theorize. As Barbara Christian notes, "people of color have always theorized—but in forms quite different from the Western form of abstract logic. And I am inclined to say our theorizing (and I intentionally use the verb rather than the noun) is often in narrative forms, in the stories we create, in riddles and proverbs, in the play with language, because dynamic rather than fixed ideas seem more to our liking" (p. 68). Feminists have created sophisticated theoretical analyses of male domination, of the connections between sexism and war, of race, of female aesthetics, ethics, incest, etc.—but our theories have tended to be inductive—derived from our experiences in the real world not deducted from pre-existing male models (see Liz Stanley, 1984). The increasing reliance on male formulated theoretical traditions poses a threat to the building of a tradition of radical writers and speakers. As it is, radical, lesbian, and feminists of color are continually accused of being nontheoretical, and thus not respected within the academy. This categorization influences feminist theory as well. As Naomi Scheman notes:

> What gets to count as theories at all are those works that bear some family resemblance to earlier, culturally accredited theories (in style if not in substance); and a traditionally central stylistic constraint has been the demand that particularities of authorial identity be invisible. Although being white and heterosexual are, of course, particulars of identity, racism and heterosexism provide the privilege of thinking they're not. They also encourage—as sexism does for men—the spurious universalizing of one's own experience. Lesbian women and women of color are writing searchingly theoretical books and articles, but, being less likely to claim to be theorizing universal womanhood, such works are less likely to be counted as articulating theory at all. (1985, p. 15)

Given the tremendous excitement and knowledge generated by feminist methods in the last 20 years, we should not be intimidated out of confidence in our own methods and ways of knowing now. It is because they've worked so well that we are again being relegated to the "lower" ranks by the patriarchal philosophical schools.

EXPECTATIONS FOR THE FUTURE

As the continuing emergence of new feminist voices and scholarship throughout the 1980s indicates, Women's Studies and feminist scholarship is thriving and growing in diversity and strength. Our most important challenges in the next decade will be to resist assimilation by strengthening our connections with the political and social movements which continue to be vital and important sources of new ideas and perspectives, and to integrate the experiences and knowledge of the diverse groups of women now writing. As Susan Koppelman reminds us, "If we ignore our early, extrainstitutional herstory, we lose our connections with that original passion, with the incredible courage and imagination it took us to begin, and with our analysis of the risks we run by being in the academy" (1989, p. 6). We need to reject the language of "incorporation" or "addition" which still perceives white, middle-class, and heterosexual as the center, and work toward a multicentered and multicultural women's studies. Not, of course, out of guilt or even "fairness" but because only a Women's Studies committed to all women can create the truth about women's lives that we all need. We can do this not in a spirit of obligation but because there is pleasure in the self-discovery and mutual exchange which occurs when we share our commonalities and differences with others. As Evelyn Nakano Glenn writes, "Perhaps the clearest reward of achieving some degree of incorporation is that we will attain a clearer sense of ourselves and our connections to others. We will find that our histories and experiences are not just diverse, they are intertwined and interdependent" (1988, p. 6).

BIBLIOGRAPHY

Abel, Emily K. & Nelson, Margaret K. (1985, January). Feminist studies: The scholarly is political. *The Women's Review of Books,* 10–12.

Abu Nasr, Julinda. (1982). Institute for women's studies in the Arab world. *Women's Studies International Supplement, 1,* 15–16.

Adamson, Nancy. (1985, March). Lesbian issues in women studies courses. *Resources for Feminist Research, 12,* 5–7.

Albrecht, Lisa & Brewer, Rose M. (1990). Bridges of power: Women's multicultural alliances. Philadelphia: New Society Publishers, in cooperation with NWSA.

Andersen, Margaret L. (1985). Women's studies/Black studies: Learning from our common pasts. In Marilyn Schuster et al. (Eds.), *Women's place in the academy* (pp. 62–72). Totowa, NJ: Rowman and Allenheld.

Aptheker, Bettina. (1981). Strong is what we make each other: Unlearning racism within women's studies. *Women's Studies Quarterly, 9*(Winter), 13–16. (Aptheker notes that because women's studies places women at the center, we have a unique perspective on racism. Because feminism requires action to empower all women, we have a mandate to struggle with all women on the basis of our common experiences while simultaneously recognizing and celebrating the diversities among us. She also outlines the psychological structures which create barriers between women of color and white women. First, women are socialized to feel guity for any deviation from female norms; to accommodate others through self-denial; and to assume responsibility for the emotional stability of relationships. One manifestation of this politically motivated socialization is that white women are afraid to speak honestly with women of color, particularly fearing that they will make incorrect, racist comments. Aptheker reminds us, "Communication requires equality and equality demands dignity, not patronization." Other barriers to coalitions that are women's friendships are generally devalued and that white women often think friendships can be merely personal rather than dependent on social relations and conditions. She urges white women in women's studies to risk making mistakes and losing status; do the hard emotional work required to confront their own and others' racism; and face women of color's and their own anger.)

Ås, Berit. (1984). The feminist university. Women's studies today: An assessment. *National Women's Studies Association Newsletter, 3*(Winter), 391–394.

Asian Women United of California. (1989). *Making waves: An anthology of writings by and about Asian American women.* Boston: Beacon Press.

Astin, Helen S. & Parelman, Allison. (1973). Women's studies in American colleges and universities. *International Social Science Journal, 25*(3), 389–400.

Baird, Jo, Frank, Shirley, & Stafford, Beth. (1982). *Index to the first ten years, 1972–1982.* Feminist Press.

Bambara, Toni Cade. (1980). *The Salt Eaters.* New York: Random House.

Bannerji, Himani. (1987, March). Introducing racism: Notes towards an anti-racist feminism. *Resources for Feminist Research, 16,*10–12.

Battel, Roisin, Duelli Klein, Renate, Moorhouse, Catherine, & Zmroczek, Christine (Eds.). (1983). Special issue: So far so good—So what? Women's studies in the U.K. *Women's Studies International Forum, 6*(3).

Baym, Nina. (1984). *Novels, readers, and reviewers: Response to fiction in antebellum America.* Ithaca, New York: Cornell University Press.

Bazin, Nancy Topping. (1983). Integrating third world women into the women's studies curriculum [at Old Dominion University]. *Frontiers, 7*(2), 13–17.

Beck, Evelyn Torton. (1983). 'No more masks': Anti-semitism as Jew-hating. *Women's Studies Quarterly, 11*(Fall), 11–14. (Evelyn Beck describes her fears in naming herself as Jewish-identified, and that like all Jews, she lives in fear of anti-semitism. She reminds her audience that Jewish identity is not homogenous. There is a wide range of religious observance; many Jews celebrate Jewish holidays for cultural not religious reasons; and although 97% of American Jews are Ashkenazi from Europe, 67% of Jews in Israel are Sephardic or Arab Jews. A basic commonality among Jews is a sense of self as a survivor of thousands of years of prejudice and persecution. She warns against the following examples of anti-semitism: the stereotype of Jews as "pushy, rich, materialistic" or "smarter" and of the Jewish American Princess; trivializing anti-semitism unless Jews are killed; remaining ignorant of Jewish oppression, for example, scheduling feminist events on Jewish holidays; omitting Jewish materials from courses and books; equating Jews with Israel. Bulkin criticizes NWSA's decision to define anti-semitism as directed against both Arabs and Jews as refusing to take Jew-hating seriously.)

Beck, Evelyn Torton. (1989, February). Asking for the future. *Women's Review of Books, 6.5.*

Beck, Evelyn Torton. (1982). *Nice Jewish girls: A lesbian anthology.* Watertown, MA: Persephone Press.

Belen, Edna Acosta (Ed.). (1979). *The Puerto Rican woman.* New York: Praeger.

Benson, Ruth C. (1972). Women's studies: Theory and practice. *AAUP Bulletin, 58*(3), 283–286.

Bolsterli, Margaret J. (1982). Teaching Women's Studies at the University of Arkansas. In P. Stringer & I. Thompson (Eds.), *Stepping off the pedestal: Academic women in the south* (pp. 71–75). New York: Modern Language Association.

Boxer, Marilyn. (1982). For and about women: The theory and practice of women's studies in the United States. *Signs, 7*(3), 61–95.

Bowles, Gloria. (1982). Review of textbooks in women's studies. *Women's Studies International Forum, 5*(1), 109–112.

Bowles, Gloria. (1983). Is women's studies an academic discipline? In Gloria Bowles, and Renate Duelli Klein (Eds.), *Theories of Women's Studies* (pp. 32–45). London: Routledge & Kegan Paul.

Bowles, Gloria & Klein, Renate Duelli (Eds.). (1983). *Theories of women's studies.* Boston: Routledge & Kegan Paul.

Brant, Beth (Ed.). (1984). A gathering of spirit: Writing and art by North American Indian Women. Special Issue. *Sinister Wisdom, 22/23.*

Brod, Harry. (1987, Summer). Does manning men's studies emasculate women's studies? *HYPATIA, 2,* 153–157.

Brooks, Betty Willis & Sievers, Sharon L. (1983). The new right challenges women's studies: The Long Beach women's studies program. In Charlotte Bunch & Sandra Pollack (Eds.), *Learning our way: Essays in feminist education* (pp. 78–88). Trumansburg, NY: Crossing Press.

Browne, Susan E., Connors, Debra, & Stern, Nanci (Eds.). (1985). *With the power of each breath: A disabled women's anthology.* San Francisco: Cleis Press.

Bulkin, Elly. (1980, Spring). Teaching lesbian poetry. *Women Studies Newsletter, 8,* 5–8.

Bulkin, Elly, Pratt, Minnie Bruce, & Smith, Barbara. (1984). *Yours in struggle: Three feminist perspectives on anti-semitism and racism.* New York: Long Haul Press.

Butler, Johnnella E. (1982, Summer). Toward a plural and equitable society. *Women's Studies Quarterly, 10*(2), 10–11.

Butler, Johnnella. (1989, February). Difficult dialogues. *The Women's Review of Books, 6*(5), 16.

"Can One Male Voice Silence Us?" (1988, Summer). *NWSAction, 1*(2), 1.

Chai, Alice Yun. (1985). Toward a holistic paradigm for Asian American women's studies: A synthesis of feminist scholarship and women of color's feminist politics. *Women's Studies International Forum, 8*(1), 59–66.

Chamberlain, Kathleen. (1971). Women students at Manhattan Community College. *ERIC* ED073761.

Chayat, Sherry. (1987, Fall). JAP baiting on the college scene. *LILITH, 17,* 6–7.

Childers, Mary. (1984). Women's studies: Sinking and swimming in the mainstream. *Women's Studies International Forum, 7*(3), 161–166.

Chow, Esther Ngan-Ling. (1987, September). The development of feminist consciousness among Asian-American women. *Gender and Society, 1,* 284–299.

Christian, Barbara. (1987, Spring). The race for theory. *Feminist Studies, 14,* 67–79.

Chung, Sei-wha [Chang-hyan Shin et al. Trans.]. (1986). *Challenges for women: Women's studies in Korea.* Seoul, Korea: Ewha Women's University Press.

Cole, Johnnetta B. (Ed.). (1986). *All American women: Lines that divide, ties that bind.* New York: Free Press. (This is an excellent introduction to women's studies. It is divided along the lines of many courses by having major sections on Work, Families, Sexuality and Reproduction, Religion, and Politics, and consists of a variety of articles by different groups of women. Johnetta Cole introduces each section with a discussion of the commonalities and differences between women. There are articles by Puerto Rican, elderly, Black, Jewish, upper middle-class, Asian-American, disabled, and Native American women.)

Collins, Patricia Hill. (1986, Spring). The emerging theory and pedagogy of Black women's studies. *Feminist Issues, 6*(1), 3–18.

Collins, Patricia Hill. (1990). *Black Feminist thought: Knowledge, consciousness, and the politics of empowerment.* Boston: Unwin Hyman.

Connors, Debra. (1985). Disability, sexism and the social order. In Susan E. Browne, Debra Connors, & Nanci Stern (Eds.), *With the power of each breath: A disabled women's anthology* (pp. 92–107). Pittsburgh: Cleis Press. (This article summarizes how the religious, corporate, and medical views toward the disabled as "abnormal," "defective" and "deviant" have lead to such abuses as mandatory sterilization, medical experimentation, and discrimination. Recalling the long history of disabled women's resistance to their "no-win societal position," she urges disabled women to work for more than participation in a political economy which oppresses all workers and to join in alliance with other disadvantaged groups to create fundamental social changes.)

Coss, Clare. (1988, May-June). Women against racism. *New Directions for Women, 17,* 1.

Cruikshank, Margaret. (1982). *Lesbian studies.* Old Westbury, NY: Feminist Press.

Cruikshank, Margaret. (1986). Looking back on Lesbian studies. *Frontiers, 8*(3), 107–109.

Crumpacker, Laurie & Haegan, Eleanor Vender. (1987). Pedagogy and prejudice: Strategies for confronting homophobia in the classroom. *Women's Studies Quarterly, 15*(3/4), 65–74.

Darty, Trudy & Potter, Sandy (Eds.). (1984). *Women-identified women.* Palo Alto, CA: Mayfield.

Davies, Miranda. (1983). *Third world/second sex.* London: Zed Press.

Davis, Angela. (1981). *Women, race, and class.* New York: Random House.

Davis, Angela. (1982, July-August). Women, race, and class: An activist perspective. (Keynote Address Fourth National NWSA Convention, Humboldt State University. Arcata California, June 17, 1982). *Women's Review of Books, 4,* 1. (Angela Davis calls for an international multiracial movement fighting sexism within the context of world liberation struggles—especially the struggles against racism and class oppression. Our educational system has omitted the history of all women, but especially black poor women, and Davis reminds us that we can only correct these gaps in our knowledge by actively seeking out the information we need. To illustrate how little we know, she talks about the accomplishments of little known black women who have made important contributions to black liberation. For example, Julia Wilder and Maggie Buzeman, longtime civil rights workers, were convicted in January 1982 for voter fraud, paroled, and banned from their home town. Lucy Taylor Prince, a freed slave and contemporary of Susan B. Anthony and Elizabeth Cady Stanton, was the first black woman to address the United States Supreme Court when she fought against whites seizing her land; and Catherine Ferguson opened the first sex and race integrated school in the United States. Like Sojourner Truth, black women like these are important models for all women and Davis reminds us that only an international feminist movement committed to the liberation of all women will have the power to make the changes we need.)

Davis, Angela. (1982, Winter). Women, race, and class: An activist perspective. *Women's Studies Quarterly, 10*(4), 5–9.

Derman-Sparks, Louise, Higa, Carol Tanaka, & Sparks, Bill. (1980). Children, race, and racism: How race awareness develops. *Interracial Books for Children Bulletin, 11*(3/4), 3–9.

Deutsch, Sarah. (1987, Summer). Women and intercultural relations: The case of Hispanic New Mexico-Colorado. *Signs, 12*(4), 719–739.

Douglas, Carole Anne. (1977, December). Can a radical feminist find happiness teaching women's studies? *Off Our Backs, 7,* 11.

Duelli-Klein, Renate. (1987). The dynamics of the women's studies classroom: A review essay of the teaching practices of women's studies in higher education. *Women's Studies International Forum, 10*(2), 187–206.

Duelli-Klein, Renate. (1983). The 'men problem' in women's studies: The expert, the ignoramous, and the poor dear. *Women's Studies International Forum, 6,* 413–421.

Duggan, Lisa. (1979). Lesbianism and American history: A brief source review. *Frontiers, 4*(3), 80–86.

Evans, Mary. (1986). Learning to love it: On teaching women's studies in Great Britain. *Women's Studies International Forum, 9*(2), 129–136.

Faderman, Lillian. (1978, Fall). The morbidification of love between women by 19th-century sexologists. *Journal of Homosexuality, 4*(1), 73–75.

Fields, Cheryl. (1983, October 2). Allegations of Lesbianism being used to intimidate, female academics say. *Chronicle of Higher Education, 27,* 1.

Finger, Anne. (1985). Claiming all of our bodies: Reproductive rights and disability. In Susan E. Browne et al. (Eds.), *With the power of each breath: A disabled women's anthology* (pp. 292–307). San Francisco: Cleis Press.

Fisher, Berenice M. (1982, Fall). Professing feminism: Feminist academics and the women's movement. *Psychology of Women Quarterly, 7*(1), 55–69.

Follet, R. J. & Larson, R. (1982, April). It is dishonest of English teachers to ignore the homosexuality of literary figures whose works they teach. *English Journal, 71,* 18–21.

Fox-Genovese, Elizabeth. (1984, Fall). Women studies in the 1980's: Now more than ever. *Women's Studies Quarterly, 12,* 25–28.

Freeman, Jo. (1971, December). Women's liberation and its impact on the campus. *Liberal Education, 57,* 468–478.

Froines, Ann. (1983, Summer). Readers' speakout: Staying the course: The necessity for remaining true to a radical vision. *Women's Studies Quarterly, 11,* 3.

Frye, Marilyn. (1985, October). A lesbian perspective on women's studies. *Lesbian Studies, 3*(1), 15–16.

Frye, Marilyn. (1983). On being white: Toward a feminist understanding of race and race supremacy. *Politics of reality: Essays in feminist theory* (pp. 110–127). Trumansburg, NY: Crossing Press.

Giddings, Paula. (1984). *When and where I enter: The impact of Black women on race and sex in America.* New York: Bantam Books.

Gilbert, Sandra M. & Gubar, Susan. (1988). *No man's land: The place of the woman writer in the twentieth century.* New Haven, CT: Yale University Press.

Glenn, Evelyn Nakano. (1988, March). Incorporating racial ethnic women into the curriculum. *Women's Studies Newsletter,* 2–6. University Center at Binghamton, New York.

Gordon, Linda. (1979). The struggle for reproductive freedom: Three stages of feminism. In Zillah Eisenstein (Ed.), *Capitalist patriarchy and the case for socialist feminism* (pp. 107–136). New York: Monthly Review Press.

Gould, Ketayun H. (1987, Fall). Feminist principles and minority concerns: Contributions, problems and solutions. *AFFILIA, 2,* 6–19.

Green, Rayna. (1979). American Indian women meet in Lawrence. *Women's Studies Quarterly, 7*(3), 6–7.

Grevatt, Margaret. (1987, Fall). Sisters to the dispossessed. *AFFILIA, 2,* 67–71. (On the need to link with poor women.)

Griffin, Jean Thomas & Hoffman, Nancy (Eds.). (1986). Special issue: Teaching about women, race and culture. *Women's Studies Quarterly, 14,* 1/2.

Griscom, Joan. (1987, Spring/Summer). Trying to teach the experiences of women of color to white students. The Women of Color Issue. *NWSA Perspectives,* 6–8.

Harris, Merril. (1985). Making our students aware of ableism. *Feminist Teacher, 1*(3), 8–10.

Heyniger, Line Robillard. (1985). The international conference on research and teaching related to women: Report of coordinator. *Women's Studies International Forum, 8*(2), 157–60.

Hillyer, Barbara. (1988). *Women with disabilities: Essays in psychology, culture and politics.* Philadelphia: Temple University Press.

Ho, Liang. (1982). Asian-American women: Identity and role in the women's movement. *Heresies: Racism is the Issue, 15,* 60–61. (Liang Ho points out how stereotypes about Asians [for example, the "inscrutable and exotic Oriental"] affect her work and interpersonal relationships in the United States. She also suggests that Asian-American women utilize the advantages of their bi-cultural background in their struggles against sexism and racism. Asian-American women should fight for economic and legal equality, placing race and community over feminist needs; remain skeptical of white feminists' commitment to Asian-American women's priorities; and make conscious choices about when to emphasize their Asain or American identities.)

Hoffman, Nancy. (1977, Winter/Spring). White woman, Black women: Inventing an adequate pedagogy. *Women's Studies Newsletter, 5*(1/2), 21–24.

hooks, bell. (1981). *Ain't I a woman: Black women and feminism.* Boston: South End Press.

hooks, bell. (1989). *Talking back: Thinking feminist—Thinking Black.* Boston: South End Press.

Howe, Florence. (1975). *Women and the power to change.* New York: McGraw-Hill.

Howe, Florence. (1984a). *Myths of coeducation: Selected essays, 1964–1983.* Bloomington: Indiana University Press.

Howe, Florence. (1984b). Women's studies and social change. In Florence Howe (Ed.), *Myths of coeducation: Selected essays, 1964–1983* (pp. 78–110). Bloomington: Indiana University Press.

Howe, Florence, Mazumdar, Vina, & Papanek, Hanna (Eds.). (1984, April). Special issue: Focus on India [women's studies]. *Women's Studies International Supplement, 3.*

Howe, Florence & Lauter, Paul. (1980). *The impact of women's studies on the campus & the disciplines.* National Instititute of Education. Mail Stop 7, 1200-19th St. NW Washington DC 20208.

Hull, Gloria T. (1982, Summer). Black studies and women's studies: Search for a long overdue partnership. *Women's Studies Quarterly, 10*(2), 12–13.

Jameson, Elizabeth. (1988, Summer). Toward a multicultural history of women in the western United States. *Signs, 13*(4), 761–791. (Elizabeth Jameson's article illustrates the type of multicultural approach to scholarship and teaching recommended by feminists calling for a women's studies accountable to the diversity of women's lives. Jameson provides a review of the literature which has been produced in response to Joan M. Jenson's and Darlis A. Miller's "The Gentle Tamers Revisited: New Approaches to the History of Women in the American West" which called for a multicultural history of women on the frontier. Jameson reviews work on Euro-American, American, Indian, Hispanic, Mexicana, Mexican-American, Black, Chinese-American, and Japanese-American women. She notes that past researchers have assumed that studying women on the frontier meant studying Euro-American women, although between 1860-1900 ¼ to ⅓ were foreign born. A multi-cultural approach provides a new comparative framework to study the ways gender, regional economics, and ethnicity affect women and provides information about diverse groups women needed before any generalizations can be made.)

Jeffreys, Sheila. (1985). *The spinster and her enemies: Feminism and sexuality 1880–1930.* Boston: Pandora.

Jorge, Angela. (1980, Fall/Winter). Issues of race and class in women's studies: A Puerto Rican woman's thoughts. *Women's Studies Newsletter, 8,* 17–18. (Angela Jorge urges the integration of all women into women's studies and offers some facts about the lives of Puerto Rican women in the United States to illustrate how we need to attend to the specifics of women's lives rather than making large generalizations. Most Puerto Rican women in the U.S. come from an uprooted peasant class and know very little white culture except through television. The urban renewal of the 1950s and 1960s destroyed the extended family system which they had relied on. Many have been victims of forced sterilization—in 1976, 35%.)

Joseph, Gloria & Lewis, Jill. (1981). *Common differences: Conflicts in Black and white feminist perspectives.* New York: Anchor Press.

Karcher, Carolyn L. (1983, Fall). Black studies/women's studies: An overdue partnership. *Feminist Studies, 9,* 605–610.

Katz, Jane B. (1977). *I am the fire of time—The voices of Native American women.* New York: E. P. Dutton.

Kaye/Kantrowitz, Melanie & Klepfisz, Irena (Eds.). (1986). The tribe of Dina: A Jewish women's anthology. [Special issue.] *Sinister Wisdom.* Vermont: Montpelier.

Klein, Kathleen Gregory, Mayhew, Paula Hooper, Silber, Ellen S., & Stitzel, Judith Gold (Eds.). (1986). Special issue: Women's studies administrators—Personal and professional intersections. *Women's Studies International Forum, 9*(2).

Klein, Renate Duelli. (1983). A brief overview of the development of women's studies in the UK. *Women's Studies International Forum, 6*(3), 255–260.

Koppelman, Susan. (1989, June). Letter to the Editor. *Women's Review of Books, 6*(9), 6.

Kuninobu, Junko Wada. (1984). Women's Studies in Japan. *Women's Studies International Forum, 7*(4), 301–306.

Lauter, Paul. (1983, Fall). Race and gender in the shaping of the American literary canon: A case study from the Twenties. *Feminist Studies, 9*(3), 435–463.

Lefkowitz, Rochelle & Withorn, Ann (Eds.). (1986). *For crying out loud: Women and poverty in the United States.* New York: Pilgrim Press.

Levin, Michael. (1985, Summer). Women's studies, Ersatz scholarship. *New Perspectives, 17*(3), 7–10.

Levin, Tobe. (1979). Women's studies in West Germany: Community v. academy. *Women's Studies Quarterly, 7*(1), 20–22.

Libertin, Mary. (1987, Summer). The politics of women's studies and men's studies. *HYPATIA, 2*(2), 143–152.

Loeb, Catherine. (1983). Black women's studies and Black feminist polotics: Selected sources. Available from: Women's Studies Librarian-At-Large, University of Wisconsin, 112A Memorial Library, Madison, Wisconsin, 53706.

Lorde, Audre. (1984). Uses of anger: Women responding to racism. In *Sister outsider* (pp. 124–33). Trumansberg, NY: Crossing Press.

Lorde, Audre & Rich, Adrienne. (1981). An interview with Audre Lorde. *Signs, 6*(4), 713–736.

MacDonald, Barbara with Rich, Cynthia. (1983). *Look me in the eye: Old women, aging and ageism.* San Francisco: Spinsters Ink.

MacKinnon, Catharine A. (1987). Difference and dominance: On sex discrimination. *Feminism unmodified: Discourses on life and law* (pp. 32–45). Cambridge: Harvard University Press.

Maglin, Nan Bauer. (1986, Fall/Winter). Gender balancing in the curriculum: Women, minorities, and the "American Dream." *Women's Studies Quarterly, 14,* 16–17.

Mahoney, Pat. (1988). Oppressive pedagogy: The importance of process in women's studies. *Women's Studies International Forum, 11*(2), 103–8.

Matute-Bianchi, Maria Eugenia. (1982, Spring). A Chicano in academe. *Women's Studies Quarterly, 10,* 14–15.

Mazumdar, Vina. (1980). Why women's studies? *Women's Studies International Supplement, 1,* 4–5.

Mazumdar, Vina & Howe, Florence. (1980). Women's studies international: Copenhagen to Montreal and beyond. *Women's Studies International Supplement, 2,* 2.

Mbilinyi, Marjorie. (1984). Research priorities in women's studies in Eastern Africa. *Women's Studies International Forum, 7*(4), 289–300.

Mohanty, Chandra Talpade, Russo, Ann, & Torres, Lourdes (Eds.). (1991). *Third world women and the politics of feminism.* Bloomington and Indianapolis: Indiana University Press.

Moraga, Cherrie. (1983). *Loving in the war years.* Boston: South End Press.

Moraga, Cherrie & Anzaldua, Gloria (Eds.). (1981). *This bridge called my back: Writings by radical women of color.* Watertown, MA: Persephone Press.

Morgan, Robin. (1984). *Sisterhood is global.* Garden City, NY: Anchor Press.

Morrison, Toni. (1987). *Beloved.* New York: Knopf.

Mudd, Karen. (1984, October 15). Black women's studies. *Off Our Backs, 14.*

Musil, Caryn McTighe & Combs, Carol. (1988, Fall). A cautionary tale: Women's studies programs under attack. *NWSAction, 1*(3), 1–3.

Naylor, Gloria. (1982). *The women of brewster place.* New York: Penguin Books.

Omolade, Barbara. (1987). A Black feminist pedagogy. *Women's Studies Quarterly, 15*(3/4), 40–46.

"An Open Letter from the Disabled Women's Network, D.A.W.N., Toronto to the Women's Movement." (1987, January). *Resources for Feminist Research, 15,* 80–81.

Philips, Susan U. (1987, Autumn). The new gender scholarship: Women's and men's studies. *Signs, 13,* 192–195.

Pogrebin, Letty Cottin. (1987, June-August). Going public as a Jew. *Ms., 16,* 76–77.

Pogrebin, Letty Cottin. (1983). The secret fear that keeps us from raising free children. *Interracial Books for Children Bulletin, 14*(3/4), 10–12.

Pogregin, Letty Cottin. (1982, June). Bitter fruit: Anti-semitism at the Copenhagen women's conference. *Ms., 10,* 48–49.

Pratt, Minnie Bruce. (1983, Fall). Identity: Skin blood heart. *Women's Studies Quarterly, 11,* 16. (Minnie Bruce Pratt speaks about how her socialization as a white southern woman raised Christian and middle class prevented her working on racism and anti-semitism until her painful losses after coming out as a lesbian opened her eyes to the conditions of her privilege. She urges that white women should not fight racism and anti-semitism out of guilt but from the "deep desire of women to be together" as "friends in this unjust world." She reminds us that confronting discrimination gives us a more truthful and multidimensional world view; frees us from the fear of difference and of people of color's anger; and can end the loneliness of ethnocentrism and build connections among diverse groups women. Rather than a guilt-motivated duty, fighting racism and anti-semitism is exciting as we shed the false values of racist capitalism and create a new self aimed at a multicultural, multiracial future. Complete essay of same title in Bulkin, Elly, Minnie Bruce Pratt, and Barbara Smith, *Yours in Struggle: Three Feminist Perspectives on Anti-Semitism and Racism.* Long Haul Press, New York, 1984.)

Reagon, Bernice Johnson. (1983). Coalition politics: Turning the century. In Barbara Smith (Ed.), *Home girls: A Black feminist anthology* (pp. 356–368). New York: Kitchen Table Press.

Raj, Maithreyi Krishna. (1981). International news: First national conference on women's studies in India. *Women's Studies Quarterly, 9*(2), 21–22.

Ramos, Juanita. (1987). *Compañeras: Latina lesbians.* New York: Latina Lesbian History Project.

Rich, Adrienne. (1986). *Blood, bread, and poetry: Selected prose 1979–1985.* New York: Norton. (Compared with Rich's earlier essay collection, *On Lies, Secrets, and Silences, Blood, Bread, and Poetry* illustrates the impact that challenges from women of color have had on the feminist movement. For example, teaching the title essay "Blood, Bread, and Poetry" (1984) in conjunction with "When We Dead Awaken: Writing as Re-Vision" (1971) can highlight the ways in which these challenges have altered the lives and theories of white as well as third world women. In the 1980s, Rich speaks more self-consciously from her identity as a Jew and lesbian and stresses the need for a less naive notion of sisterhood than she and other feminists had first imagined. She also consistently acknowledges her own race and class as determinants of her theories and perspective. In essays addressing women's studies, Rich warns against the dangers of assimilation; urges women's studies to remain accountable to the larger movement which created it and rooted in women's real histories and daily lives; and attempts to outline how feminist theories and studies can develop a decentered and multi-cultural movement responsible to all women. Rich also criticizes women in academia for frequently ignoring the work of women in non-academic feminist journals like *Conditions, Feminary,* and *Sinister Wisdom.* Throughout she stresses her commitment to and love of women as the foundation of feminist work—especially coalition work among diverse groups of women.)

Rich, Adrienne. (1981, Fall). Disobedience is what NWSA [National Women's Studies Association] is potentially about. *Women's Studies Quarterly, 9*(3), 4–6.

Rich, Adrienne. (1981) (1986). Compulsory heterosexuality and Lesbian existence. (Reprinted in *Blood, Bread and Poetry: Selected Prose 1979–1985.* Norton, New York.)

Rich, Adrienne. (1979). *On lies, secrets, and silences: Selected prose 1966–1978.* New York: Norton.

Robinson, Lora H. (1973, Winter). The emergence of women's courses in higher education. *Research currents from publication department,* American Association for Higher Education, One DuPont Circle, Suite 780, Washington, DC 20036, 2(1).

Rodriguez-Trias, Helen. (1982). Sterilization abuse. In M.S. Henifin (Ed.), *Biological woman—The convenient myth.* Cambridge, MA: Schenkman.

Rowland, Robyn. (1987). Women's studies in Australia: State and status, and What are the key questions which could be added in women's studies. *Women's Studies International Forum, 10*(5), 517–518.

Rubenstein, Judith Allen. (1987, Fall). The graffiti wars. *LILITH, 17,* 8–9. (On how to respond to JAP baiting on campus.)

Saadawi, Nawal el. (1980). *The hidden face of Eve.* London: Zed Press.

Sanchez, Carol Lee. (1983, Fall). Racism, profit, product—and patriarchy. *Women's Studies Quarterly, 9,* 14–15. (Carol Lee Sanchez speaks about the similarities between black and American Indian people's oppression in the United States. Unlike other ethnic groups, blacks and Indians did not choose to live under the Anglo-Saxon Protestant class which has dominated the U.S. since colonization. Both are victims of the racism in this country which guarantees a menial labor force for capitalist production. She calls attention to the distortion of scholars and teachers who continue to ignore the U.S. genocide of the American Indian as well as their significant cultural achievements. For example, she points out that teaching the truth that the U.S. Constitution and Bill of Rights borrowed its framework and structure from The Law of the Great Peace of the Iroqois, would challenge stereotypes of Indians as uncivilized. Sanchez links the destruction of the black and Indian tribal cultures with the European wars which destroyed Britain's, Ireland's and Europe's tribal gynarchies. She stresses the urgency of reclaiming these lost histories and restoring the ancient traditions.)

Shamping, Wan. (1988). The emergence of women's studies in China. *Women's Studies International Forum, 11*(5), 455–64.

Scheman, Naomi. (1985, October). The force of reason. *Women's Review of Books, 3.1,* 15–16.

Schoenfielder, Lisa & Wieser, Barb (Eds.). (1983). *Shadow on a tightrope: Writings by women on fat oppression.* Iowa City, IA: Aunt Lute Book Co.

Schnur, Susan. (1987, Fall). Blazes of truth. *LILITH, 17,* 10–11. (On JAP stereotyping on campus.)

Scott, Patricia Bell, Hull, Gloria, & Smith, Barbara (Eds.). (1982). *All the Blacks are men. All the women are white. But some of us are brave.* Old Westbury, NY: Feminist Press.

Smith, Barbara (Ed.). (1983). *Home girls: A Black feminist anthology.* New York: Kitchen Table: Women of Color Press.

Smith, Barbara. (1983a). Homophobia: Why bring it up? *Interracial Books for Children Bulletin, 14*(3/4), 7–8.

Smith, Barbara. (1983b, Fall). A rock and a hard place: Relationships between Black and Jewish women. *Women's Studies Quarterly, 11,* 7–9. (Barbara Smith looks at the barriers and potentialities for cooperation between Black and Jewish women. She warns black women not to equate all Jews with Israel, remembering that many Jewish feminists are active in the peace movement in Israel and in the New Jewish Agenda which supports Israel but also recognizes a Palestinean homeland. Jewish women should not assume Black women are more racist than other women or that Jews have confronted their racism more than Black women their anti-semitism. She warns both groups not to assume a homogeneity among the other and gives examples of her own coalition work with Jewish women to reenforce the possibility that Jewish and Black women can work together. Complete essay of same title in Bulkin, Elly, Minnie Bruce Pratt, and Barbara Smith, *Yours in Struggle: Three Feminist Perspectives on Anti-Semitism and Racism.* Long Haul Press, New York, 1984.)

Spelman, Vicky. (1982, Summer). Combatting the marginalization of Black women in the classroom. *Women's Studies Quarterly, 10*(3), 15–16.

Spender, Dale. (1986). *Mothers of the novel.* New York: Pandora.

Stanley, Julia Penelope & Wolfe, Susan J. (Eds.). (1980). *The coming out stories.* Watertown, MA: Persephone Press.

Stanley, Liz. (1984). Whales and minnows: Some sexual theorists and their followers and how they contribute to making feminism invisible. *Women's Studies International Forum, 7*(1), 53–62.

Stasiulis, Daiva K. (1987, December). A feminist anti-racism. *ISIS, 16,* 13–16.

Stasiulis, Daiva. (1987, March). Rainbow feminism: Perspectives on minority women in Canada. *Resources for Feminist Research, 16,* 5–9.

Stevens, May. (1982). Looking backward in order to look forward: Memories of a racist girlhood. *Heresies, 15,* 22–23.

Tabak, Fanny. (1985). UN decade and women's studies in Latin America. *Women's Studies International Forum, 8*(2), 103–106.

Tate, Claudia. (1988, Spring). Reshuffling the deck: or (Re) reading race and gender in Black women's writing. Review Essay. *Tulsa Studies, 7,* 119–132.

Thompson, Martha E. (1987). Diversity in the classroom: Creating opportunities for learning feminist theory. *Women's Studies Quarterly, 15*(3/4), 81–89.

Timberlake, Andrea, Cannon, Lynn Weber, Guy, Rebecca F., & Higginbotham, Elizabeth (Eds.). (1990). *Women of color and southern women: A bibliography of social science research, 1975–1988.* Memphis, TN: Research Clearinghouse and Curriculum Integration Project on Woman of Color and Southern Women, Center for Research on Women, Memphis State University.

Tobias, Sheila. (1978). Women's studies: Its origins, its organization and its prospects. *Women's Studies International Forum, 1*(1).

Van Daele, Christa. (1978). Women studies: Time for a grass roots revival. *Branching Out, 5*(1), 8–11.

Velayudhan, Meera & Hydari, Vidya. (1982, December). Women's studies in India: A national conference [held at Shreemati Nathibai Damodar Thackersey (SNDT) Women's University, April 20-24, 1981]. *Women's Studies International Supplement, 1,* 32–33.

Vipono, Mary. (1976, August). Women's studies comes of age. *Canadian Review of American Studies, 7,* 225–229.

Walker, Alice. (1982). *The Color Purple.* New York: Harcourt Brace Jovanovich.

Weitzman, Lenore J. (1984). Sex role socialization: A focus on women. In Jo Freeman (Ed.), *Women: A feminist perspective* (3rd ed.) (pp. 157–237). Palo Alto, CA: Mayfield Publishing.

Zinn, Maxine Baca, Cannon, Lynn Weber, Higginbotham, Elizabeth, & Dill, Bonnie Thornton. (1986, Winter). The costs of exclusionary practices in women's studies. *Signs, 11*(2), 290–303.

Special Issues

Heresies (1982). Racism is the issue. #15. Includes Rosario Morales. The Origins of Racism, May Stevens, Looking backward in order to look forward: Memories of a racist girlhood, Michelle Cliff, Object into subject: Some thoughts on the work of Black women artists, Liang Ho, Asian-American women: Identity and role in the women's movement, Audre Lorde, Sister outsiders, Keiko Kubo, Matsuda's wife, Alice Walker, If the present looks like the past, what does the future look like?

NWSA Perspectives. (1987, Spring/Summer). The women of color issue. 5.

Off Our Backs. (1982, May). Education issue. *12*(5). Includes Evelyn Torton Beck, Teaching about Jewish lesbians in literature: from Zeitel and Rickel to the Tree of Begats; Gloria T. Hull and

Barbara Smith, Keeping Black women at the center; Melanie Klein, Anti-semitism, homophobia, and the good white knight.

Off Our Backs. (1982, April 4). *12.* Special issue on third world women, includes Jewish women.

Women's Studies International Forum. (1984). Strategies for women's studies in the 80s, *7*(3). Ed. Gloria Bowles. Includes Johnnella E. Butler, Minority studies and women's studies: Do we want to kill a dream?; Marian Lowe and Margaret Lowe Benston, The uneasy alliance of feminism and academia.

Women's Studies Quarterly. (1982, Spring). Transforming the traditional curriculum, *10*(1). Includes articles by Myra Dinnerstein, Sheryl O'Donnell, and Patricia MacCorquodale; Kim Merrill; Peggy Brown; Florence Howe; Peggy McIntosh.

Women's Studies Quarterly. (1982, Summer). Black studies and women's studies. Search for a long overdue partnership: A panel presented at the sixth annual conference of the National Council for Black Studies. *10*(2). Includes Johnnella E. Butler, Toward a plural and equitable society; Gloria T. Hull, The 'bridge' between Black studies and women's studies: Black women's studies; Charles Henry, Afro-American studies and women's studies at Berkeley: A case of cooperation; Vicky Spelman, Combatting the marginalization of Black women in the classroom.

Women's Studies Quarterly. (1983, Fall). Racism and anti-semitism in the women's movement. *11*(3). Includes Barbara Smith, A rock and a hard place: Relationships between Black and Jewish women; Azizah al-Hibri, Unveiling the hidden face of racism: The plight of Arab American women; Evelyn Torton Beck, 'No more masks': Anti-semitism as Jew-hating; Carol Lee Sanchez, Racism: Power, profit, product—and patriarchy; and Minnie Bruce Pratt, Identity: Skin blood heart.

Women's Review of Books. (1989, February). Women's studies at twenty. *6*(5). Includes: Evelyn Torton Beck, Asking for the future; Johnnella Butler, Difficult dialogues; Myra Dinnerstein, Questions for the nineties; Linda Garber, Still coming out; Florence Howe, A symbiotic relationship; Paula Rothenberg, The hand that pushes the rock; Susan Searing, A quiet revolution; Catherine R. Stimpson, Setting agendas, defining challenges.

Chapter 9

Women, Culture, and Society Revisited
Feminist Anthropology for the 1990s

Micaela di Leonardo

Women—largely American, sometimes British, most rarely Continental—have been widely known as anthropologists over the course of the twentieth century. Margaret Mead in particular has been hailed by feminists as an early commentator on the variability of global gender arrangements. But Mead, as we shall see, was an unusually lucky woman in the field, and her emphasis on gender issues was equally unusual among her sister anthropologists—not to mention her brothers. As well, anthropology was instituted as a discipline in the full flood of late-nineteenth to early-twentieth century Euroamerican colonialism. Thus any consideration of women's status as anthropologists or as fieldwork subjects must reflect first of all the irony of a handful of largely white, bourgeois Euroamerican women developing professional identities through the exploitation of their privileged access to colonized Third World and Native American women. (Physical anthropology and archeology, leaving aside postwar primatology, were overwhelmingly male fields until the last two decades.)

Of course, not all female anthropologists specialized in studying women of other societies, but the overarching American pattern, despite the independent Mead and Ruth Benedict, was for a woman to accompany her husband to the field, working de jure or de facto as the secondary investigator, sometimes for female affairs. Many of these uncredentialed and unacknowledged (and therefore, of course, often unemployed) wives wrote female-focused ethnographies of great power and insight, as did Laura Bohannon (Nigeria), Margery Wolf (China) and Elizabeth Fernea (Iraq). A more common pattern for Great Britain was the spinster anthropologist who took her place side-by-side with male researchers—as did Elizabeth Colson (American but Manchester-trained). Oftentimes, of course, these women's work was accorded lower status—both because they were women and because they often documented the importance of women's activities—as did Daisy Bates, whose research on Australian aboriginal women was both unacknowledged and apparently plagiarized by British "great" Radcliffe-Brown (Ruby Rohrlich-Leavitt, Barbara Sykes, & Elizabeth Weatherford, 1975, p. 124ff.)

Theoretical and political-economic shifts combined to alter the American "women and anthropology" landscape in the post–World War II era. Burgeoning American imperial interests in the Pacific, Asia, and Latin America led to increased funding and growing academic departments. At the same time, prevailing scientism in popular and intellectual cultures influenced the rise of new schools of thought lauding "scientific" understandings of other cultures and deriding formerly dominant frameworks—most particularly the "culture and personality" school associated with Mead and Benedict. Thus the stage was set for a resurgence of the image of the heroic (but well funded) male ethnographer who, eschewing "soft" concerns, considered the failure of peasants to modernize; weighed and measured people, food-stuffs and the larger environment; scientifically elicited native taxonomies; and compared baboons to contemporary foragers, delineating the evolution of "man the hunter." From a different direction, Claude Levi-Strauss' linguistics-derived structuralism increasingly influenced the entire British and American academy, anthropology departments not the least. Both symbolic and cognitive anthropology took on its imprint—and Levi-Strauss' presumption that human culture is the product of male creative activity, females being relegated in this scheme to the status of the first human "goods" exchanged (in exogamy) between culture-creating males. Finally, the 1960s saw as well the renaissance of crosscutting radical and Marxist perspectives in both the social sciences and popular culture. This work, in its self-critical, anticolonial, anticapitalist and antistratification bent, would greatly influence feminist anthropologists of the 1970s.

CORRECTING MALE BIAS

In the United States, feminism moved from the streets to the university. As women in general (but particularly those who had been active in the antiwar and civil rights movements) organized, marched and seized the public stage, calling for transformed understandings and practices related to gender, female (and some male) faculty, graduate and undergraduate students began to scrutinize anthropological knowledge and practice for evidences of gender bias. The first anthropology of women courses were offered as a result of or concurrent with small reading groups in which students and faculty reconsidered available knowledge with reference to women's lives and statuses. The two mid-1970s "bibles" of American feminist anthropology, *Towards an Anthropology of Women* (Rayna Reiter, 1975) and *Women, Culture and Society* (Michelle Rosaldo & Louise Lamphere, 1974), were the fruits of this nationwide process. Considered together, they reflected the theoretical eclecticism of the period. Women made use of, criticized and transformed the work of Marx and Engels, Durkheim, Weber, and Levi-Strauss and the scientific tradition in order to document the varieties of human sexual asymmetry, to consider their meanings in social contexts, and to speculate on the origins of women's lower status. One particular concern in each anthology was to respond to popular feminist literature that claimed the existence of prior matriarchal societies (as opposed to relative sexual equality). Although sympathetic to the desires of many women to be inspired by the notion of past woman-ruled states, feminist anthropologists took pains to prove the irrelevance of past goddess-worship (which can coexist quite handily with extreme oppression of women) and the genuinely mythological status of myths of past female rule. [See Irene Diamond, this volume.] Unfortunately, this is one arena in which the efforts of well-intentioned scholars have been insufficient: belief in the Great Goddess and her prior reign remains strong in Western feminist popular culture.

The discipline as a whole, however, not the beliefs of some sister feminists outside the academy, was the true object of feminist anthropologists' dialogue in absentia in these two key books and in many other books and articles appearing in the ensuing decade. Feminists in anthropology set out to correct male bias—which simply reflected, after all, sexist presumptions in the larger society—in all four subfields (physical, archeology, linguistic and social-cultural). Early work pointed out that it was Woman the Gatherer, not Man the Hunter, who provided the bulk of daily food in contemporary foraging societies—and that

She rather than He might therefore be the prime mover of human evolution. Feminist primatologists began restudies of various monkey and ape populations, and documented the great range of gendered primate behaviors, including female group "leadership" and female-female bonding. Physical anthropologists and archaeologists corrected sexist presumptions—such as that slightly larger skeletons must inevitably be male and that all fossilized tools must have been for masculine use. Feminists severely criticized the social anthropological tendency to attend carefully only to men in ethnographic studies, providing only "thin descriptions," as Sylvia Yanagisako (1979) notes, of women's activities, organizations, and political disputes. They elaborated new theoretical frameworks that accounted for the political meanings of personal spheres for groups around the world. Feminists pointed out that the anthropological convention, "the X say or believe," translated, because of the history of male bias, to "the old male headmen of the X say or believe." They demanded, in concert with the Marxist demand for attention to working-class sentiments, that ethnographers attend to women's perceptions and analyses in the field. Finally, making use of Marxist frameworks and methodology, feminist anthropologists were able to unravel the effects of colonization and capital penetration in a wide variety of societies to uncover varying native gender arrangements—female land rights, female marital, kinship and political power—ended by the direct or indirect effects of Western contact. (The opposite case obtained as well, of course. But the notion that colonization and missionization had "saved" women's rights and dignity was part of hegemonic Western discourse until feminists began to consider the deleterious effects of enforced Western economic and political practices and ideologies. [See Claudia Salazar, this volume.])

The scholarly landscape changed very rapidly in physical anthropology and primate studies—so much so that today the early 1970s feminist criticisms look crude and unnecessary to younger scholars who were trained in more gender-neutral theories. As well, after a flurry of rewriting speculative histories of the evolution of women's lower status (often influenced by Engels' formulations) feminist anthropologists have left the field to this new generation. Feminist "just-so stories"—inferential narratives—were certainly as plausible as sexist ones, but in the absence of new data, they were precisely that.

The feminist reformulation of the field has been less successful in social/cultural anthropology, despite the high volume of excellent work published over the past 15 years. Specific concerns with gender have been ghettoized within anthropology departments, where feminist demands usually have been met by the hiring of one feminist anthropologist and the provision of one gender course. But the majority of social anthropology courses—and basic texts—simply fail to reflect two decades of feminist research and insight. Very prestigious schools of thought and associated departments—such as symbolic anthropology at the University of Chicago—remain largely innocent of feminist influence. Sexist recalcitrance was aided by an American job market crisis from the mid-1970s to the early 1980s. Many graduate students were discouraged from doing feminist research, were unable to find jobs after finishing their Ph.D.s, or dropped out of academics entirely. Now that job market prospects have improved, we are said to be in a "postfeminist" era (characterized by the claim that women have already secured equal rights) in which it is much more difficult to push for incremental feminist appointments and feminist curriculum revision.

NEW DIRECTIONS

Nevertheless, anthropological feminist research over the 1970s and 1980s has remained lively and has greatly influenced feminists in other fields. Gayle Rubin's (1975) important formulation, "the sex-gender system," rippled out across literary criticism, history and other social sciences, and stands now as an early herald of the now mature interdisciplinary scholarship on the social construction of sexuality. Michelle Rosaldo's contention that women's lower status derived from a universal devaluation of the "female" domestic sphere sparked feminist debates across history, sociology, political science and literature (Michelle Rosaldo & Louise Lamphere, 1974). Sherry Ortner's positing of a different universal dichotomization and differential cultural valuation—that between woman/nature and man/culture—which she derived from Levi-Strauss' schemata, washed across the disciplines (Michelle Rosaldo & Louise Lamphere, 1974). Its effects are still discernible, despite Carol MacCormack and Marilyn Strathern's 1980 anthology *Nature, Culture and Gender,* which documented the nonuniversality, even in the West, of Ortner's dichotomous associations.

In any event, most feminist anthropologists soon abandoned the search for universals and began digging into the heretofore less-represented lives and perceptions of women around the globe, and looking into female–male relations in context. One strong emphasis has been on women's roles in a variety of kinds of economies, from small-scale foraging to advanced capitalist or state socialist. Careful ethnographic work in "exotic" societies has inspired feminist labor studies at home, such as Patricia Zavella's (1987) monograph on Chicana cannery workers in northern California. A second emphasis has been on women's reproduction as part of total social systems, and again work abroad has come home to roost, as for example in Emily Martin's (1988) work on white and black American women's cultural perceptions of a fundamental female biological process—childbirth—versus the cultural framework of modern medicine. Finally, sociolinguists such as Susan Gal (1991) have contributed to larger feminist concerns with gender and language, tempering early notions of women's universally greater politeness, tentativeness and quietness (relative to male speakers) through the provision of abundant counterexamples. These researchers have shown how gender stratification is part of other, overlapping stratifications such as class and race that are expressed—and contested—in daily speech.

THEORETICAL FRAMEWORKS

As one can envision from this discussion, feminism in anthropology has made use of and transformed a variety of already available theoretical frameworks. In recent years, as theoretical Marxism has rid itself of antihistorical scientism—that is, as Marxists have eschewed the imposition of "laws of motion" and have respected and studied the varieties of actual human societal patterns—many feminist anthropologists have fruitfully used a Marxist framework in their research. The other major trend in recent academic life, poststructuralism, has had less effect to date on feminist anthropology than it has had, for example, on literary criticism. Theorists such as Ann Stoler (1991), however, are investigating the use of gender within historical colonialist discourse, while Rayna Rapp's multiracial, multiclass ethnography of amniocentesis use in New York City (1991) reflects polyvocal realities.

Nevertheless, despite the claims of some scholars (see Ann Oakley, 1981), there are no particularly feminist *methods* in anthropology. Attempts to undermine power differentials between fieldworker and informant stem from liberal, Marxist and especially phenomenological insights concerning power and interaction. The ethnomethologists of the 1960s, inspired by phenomenological insights concerning the social construction of knowledge, focused on power dynamics in the social processes of gaining information about ongoing societies—such as interviews and questionnaires. Recent feminist attention to the influence of the genders of researcher and subject is an extension of earlier ethnomethodological attention to other social characteristics—class, color, nationality. Feminism certainly brings transformative power to theoretical frameworks and methods: but it works within given intellectual inheritances.

RESISTANCE AND INFLUENCE

As I noted earlier, there has been considerable male (and female) resistance to feminist work in anthropology—most of it taking the form of benign neglect. One institutional example will suffice. In 1973, the American Anthropological Association passed a resolution abjuring the use of sexist language and the generic he in American anthropology departments. In the 1990s, The Yale University Department of Anthropology, among many others, continues to offer a course entitled "Man and Culture" in which students consider the "science of man."

A recent trend in cultural anthropology, however, is far more actively antifeminist. Many in the "ethnography as text" movement, a loose congregation of cultural anthropologists influenced by poststructuralism who focus on analyses of ethnographic texts, display overt hostility to feminism, either labeling it too little intellectually advanced to bother with, or claiming (counterfactually, because many men do feminist work in anthropology) that feminism excludes all men from its discourse (see Micaela di Leonardo, 1987, 1991). One need not, of course, belong to this school of thought to engage in antifeminist polemic. A former colleague, something of an old-fashioned Marxist-structuralist, invited me to lunch a few years ago in order to inform me, with a world-weary air, that feminist anthropology was after all simply "trivial me-tooism."

In sum, then, feminist anthropology to date has had more influence outside than inside anthropology. Feminists in North American anthropology departments (and these are more progressive than those in Great Britain or continental Europe) have not developed a power base sufficient to transform curricula, train graduate students, or hire new faculty for whom feminism is an automatic part of one's intellectual baggage. Women in the discipline still have significantly lower status than men and are sparsely represented at large research universities. At the same time, large numbers of women and men continue grassroots battles to alter departmental structures and curricula and continue to pursue exciting research at home and abroad. Much of this work falls increasingly into a "culture and political economy" vein: it makes use of Marxist perspectives while focusing heavily on varying human perceptions of social reality. Elizabeth Povinelli (1991), for example, in her ethnographic work with Australian aboriginal women, looks both at material life in a colonized economic context, and uses the tools of sociolinguistics to assess the meanings and effects of women's ordinary daily talk as political strategizing.

A HALT IN THE MUD

This situation for feminist anthropology, it seems to me, reflects the larger "postmodern" realities in the West. That is, while some continue to fight for the basic "modernist" goals for women (and racial minorities and the poor), others claim that we are beyond such fights, the goals are already won, and thus special attention to gender (or class, or race, or sexual preference) is old-fashioned, passé. This seemingly sophisticated perspective is given added fuel inside the academy by simplistic, easily disputed feminist work. Similar patterns obtain in public life where, for example, feminism is often associated with Andrea Dworkin's (1987) and Catherine MacKinnon's (1982) radically oversimplified vision of heterosexuality—which defines men's sexuality as innately demonic and all heterosexual intercourse as tantamount to rape. [See Barbara Pope, this volume.]

In addition, despite the institutionalization of many feminist organizations and the achievement of some feminist goals, in Western states, feminism is clearly in retreat rather than advance as an ideology mobilizing large numbers of individuals to political participation. Since this relative decline has occurred in tandem with the decline of the left in Europe and the United States, Western feminist organizations now respond more to challenges from the right than the left, and tend to engage in rearguard battles to secure feminist reforms largely affecting affluent white women, rather than focusing on the needs of the poor and of women of color. Thus American women—at least as of this writing—may still obtain abortions legally, although in many states, only if they can afford them. Thus women in the West may become high-paid professionals and administrators—if they have access as children to quality education. Feminist reforms in insurance and pension laws offer little to women living in welfare hotels and hostels.

Although many American radicals, as Russell Jacoby (1987) acidly notes in *The Last Intellectuals,* have established secure beachheads in universities, they have done so at the expense both of direct political involvement and the production of work meant to be of use to political activists. The same may be said of tendencies in feminist intellectual activities, which with the continuing maturation of feminist scholarship, have often become overspecialized, arcane, and unrelated to women's daily lives.

In many ways, the current situation may be characterized as Stendhal labeled the reactionary postrevolutionary Louis Phillippe regime in France—a "halt in the mud." As scholarly work and political climate are linked together, one can hope that feminist anthropology, and all feminist scholarship, will work to unpack current powerful Western antifeminist and bourgeois ideologies—blaming the poor for their fate, the mythology of the black welfare mother, continuing ahistorical, ethnocentric beliefs (from the right and the left) in women's special biological responsibility for children, notions that women are innately sexless and thus should be punished for sexual expression. Such intellectual work alone, however, will not pull the carriage out of the mud. A resurgence of class- and race-sensitive feminist political activism is needed to push the frozen wheels into motion.

BIBLIOGRAPHY AND SELECTED REFERENCES

Bohannon, Laura (Eleanor Smith Bowen, pseud.). (1954). *Return to laughter: An anthropological novel.* New York: Harper.

Caplan, Pat (Ed.). (1987). *The cultural construction of sexuality.* London: Tavistock. (The most recent collection of good ethnographic studies of global sexuality.)

Caplan, Pat & Bujra, Janet (Eds.). (1979). *Women united, women divided: Comparative studies of ten cultures.* Bloomington: Indiana University Press. (An excellent set of ethnographic essays focusing on the differing ways in which women worldwide experience solidarity with one another.)

di Leonardo, Micaela (Ed.). (1991). *Gender at the crossroads of knowledge: Feminist anthropology in the postmodern era.* Berkeley: University of California Press. (This collection encompasses all fields of anthropology and represents cutting edge work within a general "cultural and political economy" framework.)

Dworkin, Andrea. (1988). *Intercourse.* New York: Free Press.

Etienne, Mona & Leacock, Eleanor (Eds.). (1980). *Women and colonization: Anthropological perspectives.* New York: Praeger. (This classic collection is the first full-dress treatment of the claim that colonization destroyed native institutions assuring women's rights and status.)

124 Micaela di Leonardo

Fernea, Elizabeth. (1969). *Guests of the sheik: An ethnology of an Iraqi village.* New York: Doubleday.

Gal, Susan. (1991). Between speech and silence: The problematics of research on language and gender. In Micaela di Leonardo (Ed.), *Gender at the crossroads of knowledge: Feminist anthropology in the postmodern era.* Berkeley: University of California Press.

Golde, Peggy (Ed.). (1986). *Women in the field: Anthropological experiences* (2nd ed.). Berkeley: University of California Press. (Widely varying first-person accounts from Mead to the moderns.)

Jacoby, Russell. (1987). *The last intellectuals: American culture in the age of academe.* New York: Basic Books.

MacCormack, Carol & Strathern, Marilyn (Eds.). (1980). *Nature, culture and gender.* Cambridge: Cambridge University Press. (The anthology that rebuts Ortner's claims concerning the universality of women's status as "natural." Also excellent essays on late eighteenth-century intellectual history—the rise of "nature" and its connection to gender.)

Martin, Emily. (1988). *Woman and the body.* Boston: Beacon Press.

Moore, Henrietta L. (1989). *Feminism and anthropology.* Minneapolis: University of Minnesota Press. (New British synthesis of feminist insights—social anthropology only.)

Nash, June & Fernandez-Kelly, Patricia (Eds.). (1983). *Women, men and the international division of labor.* Albany, NY: State University of New York Press. (Good studies on the globalization of capital and labor and its meanings for women workers in the first and third worlds.)

Ortner, Sherry & Whitehead, Harriet (Eds.). (1981). *Sexual meanings: The cultural construction of gender and sexuality.* Cambridge: Cambridge University Press. (A follow-up collection. Reflects more complicated institutional vision on the meaning of gender worldwide, but continues the search for universals.)

Povinelli, Elizabeth. (1991). Organizing women: Changing language, economics and politics among Australian Aboriginal women. In Micaela di Leonardo (Ed.), *Gender at the crossroads of knowledge: Feminist anthropology in the postmodern era.* Berkeley: University of California Press.

Rapp, Rayna. (1991). Moral pioneers: Women, men and fetuses on a frontier of reproductive technology. In Micaela di Leonardo (Ed.), *Gender at the crossroads of knowledge: Feminist anthropology in the postmodern era.* Berkeley: University of California Press.

Reiter (Rapp), Rayna. (1975). *Towards an anthropology of women.* New York: Monthly Review Press. (One of the two classic texts in feminist anthropology. Most articles reflect Marxist perspectives. Strong emphasis on third world women and some reflection of work in physical anthropology, archeology and linguistic anthropology.)

Rohrlich-Leavitt, Ruby, Sykes, Barbara, & Weatherford, Elizabeth. (1975). In Rayna Rapp Reiter (Ed.), *Toward an anthropology of women.* New York: Monthly Review Press.

Rosaldo, Michelle & Lamphere, Louise (Eds.). (1974). *Women, culture and society.* Stanford, CA: Stanford University Press. (The second classic feminist anthropology text. More Weberian and Durkheimian in orientation, and no work outside social-cultural anthropology represented.)

Rubin, Gayle. (1975). The traffic in women: Notes on the "political economy" of sex. In Rayna Rapp Reiter (Ed.), *Toward an anthropology of women.* New York: Monthly Review Press.

Stoler, Ann. (1991). Carnal knowledge and imperial power: Gender, race and morality in colonial Asia. In Micaela di Leonardo (Ed.), *Gender at the crossroads of knowledge: Feminist anthropology in the postmodern era.* Berkeley: University of California Press.

Wolf, Margery. (1968). *House of Lim: A study of a Chinese farm family.* New York: Appleton-Century-Crofts.

Yanagisako, Sylvia. (1979). Family and household: The analysis of domestic groups. *Annual Review of Anthropology, 8,* 161–205.

Young, Kate, Wolkowitz, Carol, & McCullagh, Roslyn. (1981). *Of marriage and market: Women's subordination internationally and its lessons.* London: Routledge & Kegan Paul. (Excellent collection of Marxist-feminist studies around the world. Focusses on both women's economic and kinship lives—and the intersections between the two.)

Zavella, Patricia. (1987). *Women's work and Chicano families: Cannery workers of the Santa Clara Valley.* Ithaca, NY: Cornell University Press.

Chapter 10

The Body Philosophical

Marilyn Frye

I have not directly addressed most of the questions that guide the essays in this anthology. A direct address seemed to presuppose that the writer has participated in an ongoing debate or battle in which feminists have challenged mainstreamists both politically and by making novel knowledge claims and novel theories, and that we can chronicle the parries and responses and describe the outcome. I do not feel I have participated in such an encounter with traditional philosophy or the discipline as now institutionalized. My experience has been that of one who perched on the edge of the discipline and the academy, not displeased with my marginality; with other women both more and less pleased with living on the boundary, I undertook simply to do what I do, with integrity. Of course I have not always succeeded in the integrity department, but my noncombative orientation vis-a-vis the discipline has at least reduced to a dull roar the temptation to try to please men (or get their attention, or be recognized by them). But my reflections here do address most of the questions at least at a slant, a slant that mirrors the slant of my own relation to the discipline I am problematically and ambiguously a part of.

Everyone moves, but not everyone dances. Movement is universal, but dance is local—temporally, culturally and historically specific.

Within a cultural setting at any given time, there are or may be a wide variety of kinds of dancing, none of which are much like the dancing in distant cultures and times, all of which may have something about them that makes them "belong" to that particular time and place. Think of breakdancing, ballroom dancing, square dancing, ballet, tap, and disco.

Movement is natural to all humans (and other animals). Modes and styles of movement (one's gait, one's repertoire of gesture, etc.) are acquired, like regional and local speech mannerisms. Dance is studied.

In some kinds of dance, there are very specific steps and sequences of steps which one learns. (One trains oneself to do them; one does them over and over, and may have a teacher or coach critiquing the performance, until it comes easily and gracefully.) In some kinds of dance there are not specific steps, but if it is a *kind* of dance, there is a repertoire of distinctive kinds of movement and ways of combining them.

Philosophy is to thinking as dance is to moving.

Everyone thinks[1] but not everyone philosophizes. Thought is universal, but philosophy is local—temporally, culturally, and historically specific.

Within a cultural setting at a given time, there are or may be a wide variety of philosophies, none of which are much like the philosophies in distant cultures and times, all of which have something about them that makes them "belong" to that particular time and place. There are many kinds of philosophy done by people in the United States which retain marks and traces of different sources and histories, kinds as unlike as ballet and square dancing, which nonetheless would likely strike observers from other cultures as all quite "western." Even the kinds which derive from asian and other "nonwestern" philosophies have generally been transposed into some mixture of the languages of the euro-american philosophies in order to make them intelligible and appreciable within euro-american settings, and with that have also acquired a distinctly "western" cast.

Thought is natural to all humans (and some other animals, I suppose). Modes and styles of thought (like our gaits) are acquired like, and along with, regional and local styles of speech and gesture. Philosophy is studied.

To become a philosopher, one trains oneself in certain kinds and styles of thinking: ways of conceptualizing issues, uses of particular vocabularies, ways of paying attention and of selecting things to pay attention to, ways of organizing and understanding the structured flow and composition of argument. These are specific and peculiar to certain species and subspecies of philosophy.

Learning to philosophize, one studies and analyzes the philosophy of those who have gone before and have been canonized. One works at understanding and explaining their views and arguments; one imitates them (at best, not slavishly) to get the knack of how they go at setting up problems, how they work out the consequences of various suppositions or principles, how they construct arguments, how they mine the resources of the language they are using, what is the internal logic of their presuppositions and terminology. One becomes an interlocutor with the texts, engaging in a dialogue with the author, critiquing, extending, improving, refuting, and going off on tangents of one's own. One engages in critical dialogue with peers and teachers, and learns to anticipate responses and criticisms, and to explain, or hedge, in ways that incorporate them or dodge them. All the while, one works one's own views, shaping and articulating them, distinguishing them from those presented in the text. One moves by logic, metaphor, topical interest, the making and marking of different distinctions, and so on, to somewhat different terrain and different claims, perhaps to a quite different picture of the world. But one goes on, nonetheless, in movements of the mind that are habituated, become second nature, through the training pursued and/or suffered at a particular time and place and within particular institutions.

Suppose that you have studied and practiced a particular kind or school of ballet for many years. You then undergo a political awakening and you newly critique that school of dance and more generally the institutions that shape and promote dance in your culture and you willfully set out both to dance very differently and to make new contexts for and within dance. Your new dancing may be beautiful, exciting, and outrageous and may be gratefully appreciated by very different audiences, and you may do things which are found revolutionary and/or despicable by aficionados, critics, promoters, and other dancers. But I think that the movements of ballet will be in your bones still, in your ligaments, muscles, skin, and nerves, and they will have shaped your imagination. Perhaps over the years, the outlines of the ballet you studied will become more diffuse in your current kind of dance, some aspects of it will seem to disappear, but then will turn up again as a shadow in something you do. I think that you will bear ballet with you, bodily, to your grave.

Feminist philosophers are like dancers. We have studied and practiced certain quite specific kinds and ways of thinking. We do not simply stop thinking in the ways we learned to think as we studied and engaged with the teachers and texts of our formative years. We critique the institutions and practices of philosophy generally and the doctrines, styles, and methods of the particular schools of philosophy we were trained in. We strike off to philosophize new territories. Our new philosophizing is often beautiful, exciting, and outrageous and is gratefully appreciated by very different audiences than before, as we say things which are found revolutionary and/or irrational, irrelevant, or haggard by un-reconstructed philosophers and their usual audiences (who are usually only other philosophers). But the particular ways of thinking we acquired in our training are in our bones, ligaments, synapses, syntax and semantics.[2] They shape our attention, our curiosity, our intuitions for solutions of problems, our selection and understanding of problems and projects, our ways of constructing and moving through arguments and explanations, our imagination, our passion.

Rita Mae Brown published a paper in 1976 called "It's All Dixie Cups To Me." She says that Americans have a Dixie Cup mentality, that we think we can cast off and throw away anything we no longer need, want or like and replace it with something else, something new. She says we think we can do this even with ourselves, that we can throw away old selves we don't like and get new ones that are more satisfactory, fashionable, or politically correct.

> Mother called it, "Turning over a new leaf." Religious folks call it, "Rebirth." Madison Avenue sells it as a "New You." . . . It's all Dixie cups to me. (Brown, p. 193)

She argues that you cannot throw away your past and if you try, it will return like a boomerang; and that you cannot get a new self to replace an old one you don't like.

> A lover, a therapist, the Women's Movement will not make a "new" you. . . . For instance, suppose before you became a feminist you were a dogmatic Lutheran. Now after feminism you are a dogmatic Lesbian. You won't see this repeating pattern because you think you threw the Dixie-cup away. (p. 197)

There are people who can tell what county certain people came from by their accent and speech mannerisms. In a roughly similar way, if you know your way around the famous and influential philosophers from Plato to Richard Rorty or John Rawls, you often can tell what philosophers an individual philosopher studied by reading her work. Many of us aren't very comfortable with this; we might like to Dixie-cup our former selves and their models and mentors. But, just for example, shades of Aquinas and Heidegger infuse Mary Daly's philosophy; those of Wittgenstein, Sartre and Beauvoir play through Sarah Hoagland's *Lesbian Ethics;* and not just in the content, but in the style of thought and the way of constructing essays, the instincts for refutation and argument, Alison Jaggar's philosophy is Marxist. My own philosophy has marked echoes of Wittgenstein, J.L. Austin (a contemporary of Wittgenstein's), W.V.O. Quine—some of the leading figures of the "contemporary" anglo-American analytic school of 20 years ago when I was in graduate school. All but one, men. But that was the philosophy we studied, immersed ourselves in, engaged with, critiqued, rebelled against, imitated. Perhaps over the years, the influence of the philosophies we studied will become more diffuse; some of the habits of thought may seem to fade out altogether. But I think that if one was an existentialist or an analytic philosopher before feminism, one will be to a great extent an existentialist or an analytic feminist philosopher. It is in our bones, and we cannot jettison our bones and still keep walking and thinking.

A good deal of the work feminist philosophers have done is just philosophy, not a new kind of activity, not a novel kind of mental motion.

One thing feminist philosophers have done is to go into the works of the "great" philosophers and ferret out the sexism and misogyny in them, showing both that these evils are to be found in all of the greats and that misogyny and attempts to justify or "normalize" male dominance are not accidental or peripheral addenda to their philosophies but central to their main metaphysical, epistemological, ethical, and political projects. The philosophical work of showing the centrality of misogyny and justification of male dominance is, though, ordinary philosophical work: find the heretofore unarticulated structure of assumptions and motivations in a part of the work and show how those assumptions shape other parts and aspects of that work. Its the sort of thing workaday yeoman philosophy professors do for a living. What's "feminist" about the feminist work is that the worker is looking for structures of assumptions about women and things conceived as "feminine," is alert to the falsehoods and misogyny in those assumptions, as is able to be shocked by her findings and dismayed by how corrupt and self-serving all the lofty metaphysics is. Others, not feminists, are most unlikely to think a philosopher's views and assumptions about women could be of any "philosophical" importance. They expect you'd find views about women that are "obsolete" or quaint, and that there would be no interesting connections between what the philosopher says about women and what he says about knowledge, substance, or justice. So, as we have seen in the case of the sciences, a lot happens at the point of framing one's questions. But the framing of this *sort* of question (what is the structure of underlying assumptions about such-and-such and how do they affect the philosopher's thinking about so-and-so?) is just philosophy. We are all trained in graduate school to form and pursue such questions. And doing it, we use the skills we learned in graduate school So far, then, feminist philosophy is philosophy as usual, not some radically different activity.

Similarly, some feminist philosophy takes the western patriarchal worldview, as a whole or in particular aspects, as a sort of text, as the "philosophy" of a whole culture, and works the same sort of analysis on it—locating and articulating underlying assumptions and working out their implications, identifying justificatory motivations and the processes of their "naturalization" through enshrinement in fundamental assumptions about the nature of reality. It is a bit nonstandard in the contemporary professional philosophy scene to take on such a "text" and to do so with political motivations (though the "Critical Theory" people do something similar); but again, the *work,* what one *does,* sitting at the computer, taking notes, thinking it out, perceiving connections, articulating, arguing, explaining, is to a great extent what one was trained to do in graduate school and what one trains graduate students to do.

Feminist philosophers have come up with new approaches to old problems and have defined and/or discovered new problems. Putting women in the world as beings not defined in terms of men and children alters the shape of many philosophical problems and suggests different angles for their solution. Most feminist philosophers reject (or try to) the mind–body dualism which is embedded in and shapes almost all of western philosophy, and the problems in epistemology and ethics take on very different shapes without that dualism. Feminist philosophers revise and reject some of the very fundamental assumptions generally made in contemporary and modern philosophy, such as those involved in theories of politics and of the nature of consciousness which posit an original state of conflict and competition among people (or among "subjects"), and these deviations generate novelty in our philosophies.

Feminists have also generated philosophical novelty by blending and crossing the local varieties of philosophy more than is common in the academic mainstream. Feminist philosophers in the various schools and types of philosophy talk to each other, and listen to each other, brought together by woman-loving and by their political commitments both within and outside the academy and the discipline. We improvise with a larger palette, a more varied repertoire. (The "postmodern" influence in philosophy is tending to promote more work that is "cross-traditional" (within the discipline) and interdisciplinary, so feminists are not unique in this.)

In a recent article Adrian Piper (1989), who is a philosopher and an artist, compared anglo-american analytic philosophy with contemporary visual arts. She says that training in analytic philosophy inculcates a stringent intellectual conscience which holds one to certain standards of understanding and clarity, and that creativity in this sort of philosophy is a matter of coming up with new approaches to old problems or discovering and/or defining new problems, which includes extending philosophical analysis to areas of human experience and puzzlement that have not been included in the scope of previous philosophizing. In analytic philosophy, creativity is not, or is only very rarely, a matter of challenging or changing those standards of understanding and clarity; it is rarely a matter of breaking the rules. Summing up her comparison of analytic philosophy and contemporary visual art bluntly at one point, she says:

> Whereas a philosopher considered to be first-rate says something new in the same old way, an artist considered to be first-rate says the same old thing in a new way (breaking the rules, violating the standards of "good" art). (p. 29)

Are feminist philosophers, then, doing anything other than first-rate philosophy?

There is one difference which makes a difference. It is in the matter of *voice*. A change of voice may be the most fundamental kind of change in philosophy. By "voice" I mean (at least) the *implicit* presence, assertion and identification of the philosopher—of who or what it is that is philosophizing. To my ear, the voice of western philosophy has not changed in 2,600 years. It is the debut of that voice which is marked when philosophy's own "origins myth" cites Thales of Miletus (c. 580 B.C.E., credited with being the first to attempt to comprehend the world through reason alone) as the first philosopher. And to this day, a person who cannot animate this voice is not a philosopher (in the canonical sense of the word).

In a paper titled "Duelism in Philosophy," Janice Moulton (1980) described the Adversary Method in philosophy, and says that it taken by most philosophers as the paradigm of philosophical method, as *the* one best way of evaluating philosophy. According to this method, "a position ought to be defended from and subjected to, the criticism of the strongest opposition" from the most extreme contrary position. She is quite right. The art of philosophy in the western tradition is generally taken to be the art of argumentive dueling. A philosophical thesis or account must be admitted as true or right if no one can come up with an argument against it which its defenders cannot defeat, and you must give up your own thesis or account if you cannot defeat arguments brought against it. Moulton gives a number of very good arguments for the thesis that the Adversary Method is in fact in many cases a very poor method for getting at the truth in philosophy, and I myself cannot see how to construct any arguments which would defeat her arguments. The practice of the Adversary Method in philosophy is a matter of marshalling and applying force. When your argument is defeated, you are forced to abandon your claim; if you can defeat the other's arguments, they are forced to agree with your claim . . . on pain of being irrational; on pain of not being human (human beings, and philosophers in particular, are rational animals). Philosophy is the science of the a priori, the apodictic, the necessary; in this impersonal voice "one" says what it is that "one" *must believe.*

A few feminist philosophers have talked about their purposes in philosophizing in ways that I understand as indicating by contrast some of the meanings of philosophizing in this voice. For instance, Sarah Hoagland (1988) introduces her new book, *Lesbian Ethics,* with the suggestion that readers not read the book through, trying to understand and critique her claims and arguments, but that they read it in small parts and talk about it with their friends. Joyce Trebilcot (1988), trying to conceive philosophy which is not "persuasive," invites us to think of philosophers not as participating in a marketplace or a duel of ideas, but in a potluck supper to which we bring our most delicious dishes and offer them for the delectation and nutrition of those whose tastes they suit. Feminist philosophers also tend more than most academic philosophers to mingle expressive forms in our writing, writing in poetic or story-telling modes or personal narrative for instance, which add immediacy, expressive richness, and passion to philosophy, and change the character of the dialogue.

A "voice" can be identified in terms of what kind of listening it wants or dictates. A change of voice is a change of power relations. Feminist philosophers are moving to redefinition of philosophical power and its relations.

But the voice of philosophy in the academy in the United States has *not* changed, even though some mainstream philosophers are arguing for the abandonment of argument as its primary mode. For Richard Rorty (1986), for instance, the authority of argument is only replaced by the leadership of "strong poets" whose metaphors will strike us as "inevitable," poets made "geniuses" by the same social economy of privilege (he calls it "luck") that canonized the earlier kings of argument. The exercise of force is only gone more diffuse and more arbitrary.

Though some of the more postmodern trends in current practice may have some un-acknowledged feminist sources, most academic philosophical activity appears to me to be almost untouched by feminism, either the political movement or the philosophy. It appears that most of those with high status in the discipline have simply not noticed women or feminism beyond the moment of their contemptuous rejection of the suggestion that the use of the "generic he" is sexist. And in the profession, this ignorance is not perceived as a serious enough defect (when it is perceived at all, or perceived as a defect) to warrant any modification of the consensus that these individuals are the leading thinkers of our times. No amount of sexism, misogyny, or ignorance of feminism and feminist thinking on the part of a well-known contemporary philosopher is enough to stop philosophers generally, including feminists, from further empowering him by reading, discussing, and citing his work often and respectfully and by inviting him to give papers, be a visiting professor, teach at institutes and so on, for astronomical fees.

There are academic philosophers who have cleaned up their language to the extent of their understanding and have gender-mixed their illustrative examples so that some of the imaginary murderers, physicians, talking robots and so on that people the little scenarios by which philosophers make their points are now females. And just a few philosophers who are not doing feminist philosophy are more or less profeminist people and seem to have been reading feminist philosophy and taking it into account. Only 10 to 15% of the doctorates in philosophy are women, and even fewer have decent jobs in the academy. My sense is that most of them identify themselves as feminists (giving various meanings to that identification), though not necessarily as "feminist philosophers." (It almost seems that being a feminist and a philosopher is not as paradoxical as being a woman and a phil-osopher.) The current gossip is that one now can do a feminist dissertation in philosophy in most "good" graduate programs, but with very few exceptions one gets a faculty position only on the strength of one's expertise in mainstream modes and areas.

The power relations of philosophy in the academy—philosophy's voice—will not change significantly, I think, except as more philosophers who had feminist teachers and learned philosophy partly from feminist texts begin to come into their mature powers, bone and sinew differently schooled. The rational animal is an animal. She changes like an animal—by long exercise of new ways, and over generations.

NOTES

1.   By "thinking" I mean any or all of the following sorts of things: Recognizing, interpreting, figuring out, investigating, solving problems, designing something, doing sums or logic proofs, reading, writing, inventing, strategizing, meditating, constructing a musical composition, recollecting, storytelling, imagining. I'm thinking of human activity which mediates and/or is mediated by signs, symbols, concepts, language. I do not suppose there is an exclusive distinction between thinking and moving. Usually we are doing both and they are not separable. Some moving, though, may involve only subliminal flickers of thinking; some thinking involves no more than subliminal flickers of moving.

2.   One of our more outrageous claims has been that thinking is "located" as much in the body as in the "mind." (We are not, in this respect, unique; some other nonfeminist philosophers have also claimed something like this.)

REFERENCES

Brown, Rita Mae. (1976). *A plain brown rapper.* Oakland, California: Diana Press.
Hoagland, Sarah. (1988). *Lesbian ethics: Toward new value.* Palo Alto: Institute of Lesbian Studies.
Moulton, Janice. (1980). Duelism in philosophy. *Teaching Philosophy, 3*(4).
Piper, Adrian. (1989, April). A paradox of conscience: Analytic philosophy and the ethics of contemporary art practice, *New Art Examiner, 16*(8), 27–31.
Rorty, Richard. (1986, May 8). The contingency of selfhood. *London Review of Books, 8*(8), 11, 12, 14, 15.
Trebilcot, Joyce. (1988, Summer). Dyke methods. *HYPATIA: A Journal of Feminist Philosophy, 3*(2), 1–13.

BIBLIOGRAPHICAL NOTES ON SOURCES USEFUL FOR SURVEYING RECENT FEMINIST PHILOSOPHY

An anthology that is very good, especially in the breadth of its representation of the variety of feminist philosophy, and for inclusion of work that has been very influential within the development of feminist philosophy is *Women, Knowledge, and Reality,* edited by Ann Garry and Marilyn Pearsall (Boston: Unwin Hyman, 1989).

Another recent anthology with similar merits, and drawing more from the work of Canadian philosophers is *Feminist Perspectives: Philosophical Essays on Method and Morals,* which is edited by Lorraine Code, Christine Overall, and Sheila Mullet (Toronto: University of Toronto Press, 1988). Also useful is *Gender/Body/Knowledge: Feminist Reconstructions of Being and Knowing,* edited by Alison M. Jaggar and Susan R. Bordo (New Brunswick, N.J.: Rutgers University Press, 1989). Each of these anthologies contain a wealth of bibliographical information, usefully organized by topic and type by way of the organization of the anthology.

The only U.S. journal that is devoted exclusively to feminist philosophy is *Hypatia: A Journal of Feminist Philosophy,* published by Indiana University Press, 10th and Morton Streets, Bloomington, IN 47405. The first three issues of *Hypatia* were published as special issues of *Women's Studies International Forum* from 1983 through 1985. They are re-published together as *Hypatia Reborn,* edited by Azizah Y. al-Hibri and Margaret A. Simons (Bloomington: Indiana University Press, 1990).

In the last two or three years, more work has been done by feminist philosophers which deviates more markedly in method and voice than has been managed before. A prime example of this is Sarah Hoagland's *Lesbian Ethics: Toward New Value* (Palo Alto: Institute of Lesbian Studies, 1988). Hoagland writes primarily for an audience not presumed to have philosophical training, and focuses not on rights, virtues or "an ethic," but on a permanent project of "enhancing agency."

Chapter 11

Feminism and Engineering
The Inroads

H. Patricia Hynes

Engineering is not an academic discipline in the sense that humanities, social sciences and many of the sciences are—although it has plenty of intellectual mountains to climb. Thus, a few points about engineering may shed light on how feminism can affect this field. Engineering is more an applied profession than a theoretical discipline, in which women work largely in consulting firms, industry, and public agencies, not academia. The "knowledge explosion" in feminism is likely first to challenge and begin to change engineering at places other than the theoretical and academic.

Engineering encompasses such deeply dissociated activities as water development, purification, and distribution, and aerospace, military, and defense technology. I know no woman nuclear weapons engineers or military technologists and find it inconceivable that the carapace of overkill technology will be cracked by feminism from within that branch of engineering. Feminist critics of these phallic technologies are like small stonethrowers against men with oversized, deadly weapons. Most are not engineers nor scientists; some say they are "antitechnology" (whatever that means because they use typewriters, word processors, the telephone, subways, etc.). Stones are no match for the weapons, but stonethrowers do rouse a lethargic and unaware world, with their imagination and courage against such odds. I hope that as women move into engineering that feminist engineers would become courageous, credible critics of risk-laden technologies and designers of alternative ones.

Engineering is often put down as linear and slavish to rules. It can be surprisingly flexible and diverse and offer women "worldly" pursuits. As an environmental engineer, I used public health, geology, chemistry, and environmental science to solve hazardous waste problems. Women engineers can put their hands on the world, so to speak, and this is one major appeal of engineering for us. Where we do put our "hands on" is ultimately where feminist engineers must challenge the order of things.

The emergence of the feminist movement in the late 1960s and early 1970s in the United States is the most critical event in recent history that explains the entry of record numbers of women into science and engineering (MIT, where I teach, has 35% women students). Women's demands for admission into male fields have cracked the armor of male control. Those cracks are the fault lines through which we have entered fields resistant to us. The cracks are also vents for male backlash against women insisting on equality.

In December 1989, a man killed 14 women engineering students in the University of Montreal School of Engineering. He shot them, yelling, "You're women, you're going to be engineers. You're all a bunch of feminists. I hate feminists." Probably these students were not a bunch of feminists: engineering is typically conservative and less politically minded than other fields. But he correctly saw that women's resolute entry into engineering has broken the armor of male control. The act of killing 14 women students in engineering was not the act of a madman, but the act of a male terrorist, the result, said the mayor of Montreal, of men not willing to give up male dominance.

The massacre of 14 women engineering students expresses how threatening our presence in the world is to men, and how determined they are to keep us out. If we have dispelled the myths of our intellectual inferiority, then some men will replace them with the threat of violence. Male dominance is as rampant in engineering as anywhere.

With all of this in mind—including the caveat that I am a civil/environmental engineer casting my net more widely than the world in which I work, but no wider than the world in which I think—I will offer some insights into how feminism has shaken up engineering and where it has not.

TWO DECADES AGO

In 1970 the average engineering firm and engineering school in the United States had less than 1% women as practicing engineers, faculty, or students. By 1980, 4% of professional engineers were women; and women comprised 10% to 15% of the student body of some engineering schools. The rapid increase in women students through the 1970s has slowed; between 15% and 20% of engineering students in 1990 are women. Engineering in the United States has had and continues to have fewer women practitioners, faculty and students than any science field. A woman engineer can conduct a work meeting or attend a professional conference and still find herself the only women present. Women in engineering suffer the same mechanisms of male dominance as women in the sciences: the sheer bulk of men in them; erasure of women's achievements; discrepancy between women and men in hiring, salary, merit, evaluation, promotion, and mobility to management or tenure; and a rigid or not-so-rigid, but usually hierarchical organizational style. But, why engineering has fewer women than the other sciences—and thus retains a unique male odor—is a hard-shelled question. Is it because engineering studies have required an intermediate level of advanced mathematics, while girls have been universally discouraged from math? Those few women who resist the discouragement may go on to study mathematics. Is it because engineering has an aura of being practiced in the outside world, the public domain of men, while other sciences can be done in the "domestic privacy" of one's workbench or lab? Is it because engineering has traditionally been seen as conservative, unimaginative, and the starting point for boys of the lower middle class to begin their upward mobility? [See also Suzanne Damarin, this volume.] Whatever the reasons, one significance of so few women in engineering is that engineering remains a male microworld where men can evade the material issue of women's equality and can ignore the more difficultly articulated issue of feminist content in engineering.

THE QUESTIONS RAISED

The major impact of feminism on engineering has been in the realm of affirmative action and equity. Since the inception of academic and professional conferences on women and the scientific professions in the mid–1960s, one major concern has reigned: how to get more women into the profession. With the objective of increasing the number of women en-gineers, professional societies such as the Society of Women Engineers have developed multiple strategies: having women engineers speak to high school and junior high school girls to break down stereotypes (the issue is *which* stereotypes: that women aren't equally capable as men in science and engineering, or that a woman can be an engineer and feminine at the same time); developing networks for undergraduate and graduate women students to fortify them against faculty and peer prejudice and alienation; recognizing outstanding college women and women professionals with Women in Engineering Awards, supported by corporate sponsors; and restoring the history and credibility of former prom-inent women engineers. Most women engineers are not in universities; they are in corpora-tions, consulting firms, and public agencies. There many continue to work for affirmative action in their workplace and also to champion innovative working conditions, such as working at home, job sharing, and flex-time. A major preoccupation of many of these women is "How to combine marriage and career?" Or, more accurately, this is the life question mediated to working women by mainstream women's magazines and then picked up by professional women's support groups and organizations as their most important question. Feminism, in summary, has had an important, but limited impact on engineering, an impact which rarely steps away from the albeit substantive issues of justice, such as equal pay for equal work. Questions about the political uses of one's work (e.g., defense, space, nuclear power, biotechnology) or the sexual politics of one's work (e.g., why men and their institutions have shut women out and made it so hard for women who insist on entering; why it takes *women working* to raise the issues of childcare, job sharing, combining work and personal life; the penile nature of a lot of tools, machinery, and weapons; the presence of pornography in the workplace as a form of degradation and intimidation to women, etc.) are raised more by women in the sciences than by women engineers.

ERASURE IN EARLY HISTORY

Engineering and the history of engineering use two mechanisms to devalue our past and our possibilities. The first is to treat the inventions of women in early human history as so much irrelevant apocrypha. Cut off from remembering our possibilities, imagining them means inventing them. The second is to diminish the cutting edge, authoritative work of modern women by "feminizing" it as was done to Ellen Swallow, who originated en-vironmental engineering in the early twentieth century at Massachusetts Institute of Tech-nology (MIT) (H. Patricia Hynes, 1985); or subsuming it with their husband's work, as was done to Lilian Gilbreth, who with her husband and then for nearly *50 years* after his death, built the field of industrial engineering in the United States (Martha Trescott, 1984). In both cases, the women acquiesced. Because of this, restoring their stature is a mixed experience. Acquiescing, these women made it easy for the men around them and male historians to shrink their stature—to the "mother of home economics" in the case of Ellen Swallow; and to the assistant of Frank Gilbreth, in the case of Lilian Gilbreth. Acquiescing, they have made those of us who restore their stature easy targets for critics who assert that we appear to know better than the women themselves what happened to them.

Let us look at an example of erasure in early history. The history of the creation of agriculture and agricultural implements, of dwellings which naturally warm and cool, of transport and sanitary storage of water, in brief, of all vital systems, is the record in myth, in symbol, and in oral and written tradition of invention by women. Ancient Greeks and Romans recorded that the Assyrian queen Semiramis invented canals, causeways, and bridges over rivers. Diodoros the Sicilian historian wrote that she built a pedestrian tunnel under the Euphrates River at Babylon. And, most memorably, she adorned her city with legendary hanging gardens (H.J. Mozans, 1974). Typical of how men create a thick haze of improbability around women's early invention is a recent revisionist version of Semiramis. The "slender basis," writes a historian of engineering, for the city-building legends and the chimerical tunnel under the Euphrates must be the period in which an Assyrian dowager queen "acted as regent for her son." Whatever she accomplished, "she certainly never did any of the deeds credited to Semiramis." The hanging gardens of Babylon—the only element of the legend with "a foundation in fact"—were more likely built, he speculates with his thick lens of heteroreality, by an Assyrian king for his "favorite" wife, who was lonely and homesick for her native Media (L. Sprague de Camp, 1963).

The second wave of feminism has had a rippling effect rather than a dramatic, catalytic one in engineering in the United States, primarily raising consciousness around affirmative action. Many women engineers, who might not call themselves feminists, do feel that their personal success as an engineer is a success for women, because this is still somewhat uncharted territory for us. The first wave of feminism had a similar rippling effect, in my opinion, upon Ellen Swallow. She originated a wholistic application of engineering knowledge to urban and industrial problems, uncharacteristic of the men with whom she collaborated. Her fate, however, should make us vigilant. Ellen Swallow, the first woman to receive a degree from MIT, distinguished herself as a water chemist, an industrial chemist, a metallurgist, and mineralogist, an expert in food and nutrition, and an engineer. While a European contemporary, Ernst Haeckel, named and defined the science of ecology, it was Ellen Swallow who devised and taught the first interdisciplinary curriculum and scientific methods of ecology, leading students to test air, water, soil, and food. In 1890, she initiated and taught the world's first courses in sanitary engineering. Chemistry, bacteriology, and engineering formed the matrix of Ellen Swallow's curriculum, the forerunner of today's environmental science and engineering. The man who put into effect the recommendations of Ellen Swallow's statewide survey of water and sewage was named the "Father of Modern Sanitation." A man Ellen Swallow trained in bacteriology in her own laboratory was named the "Father of Public Health." Her science of ecology, which integrated the chemistry of soil, air, and water, as well as biology, sanitary engineering, and the human environment, was ultimately rejected at MIT as unpedigreed, not sufficiently specialized, and too much a field of women who were not sufficiently trained in the sciences. Ellen Swallow was canonized the "Mother of Home Economics." [See Patricia Thompson, this volume.]

WHAT WE HAVE, WHAT WE NEED

One must speak in future tense—not the past, not even the present—about new feminist methods and knowledge in engineering, for feminist insight and feminist paradigms have made little difference to mainstream engineering. Feminist scholarship has changed individual women, but not the profession itself. It is more fruitful, then, to show how feminist scholarship influences my own ideas, analysis and work as an environmental engineer.

Feminist scholarship has many methods, while not being a slave to method (Janice G. Raymond, 1988). Feminist scholarship deconstructs the male perspective that permeates traditional scholarship and knowledge about women. Feminist scholarship is context-creating: affirming race, class, sexuality as centers of focus. Feminism cuts through clichés like "environmentalism is the issue of the leisured class." It is the poor—the majority of whom are women and children—who are the victims of pollution. Environmentalism is not the privileged cause of the upper class; it is the necessary cause of women and the poor. Feminist scholarship is interdisciplinary, overcoming the limitations of fragmented, disciplinary knowledge. Cost-benefit analysis—at the center of most engineering decisions—is a limited, rationalistic tool which does not comprehend deeper values that are unquantifiable or that are generally not quantified. For example, the cost-benefit analysis of the Green Revolution and other industrial models of development introduced by western aid agencies and multinational governments to developing countries has not taken into account the effects of their programs on women of those countries. Women are seldom consulted or trained when water and agricultural systems are mechanized or their agricultural fields are turned into woodlots for village men to manage. Women have been left behind and impoverished by "development." The natural resources they depend on are being destroyed or made more remote in favor of models of development taught to local men.

Feminist scholarship is political knowledge that seeks to change the world as well as understand it. I founded the Institute on Women and Technology for the purposes of influencing technology assessment and public policy. The institute exists to analyze how technologies objectify, physically harm or marginalize women. The institute exists equally to advocate for technology that frees women from laborious work; that empowers women intellectually, financially, and politically; and that sustains the natural world (H. Patricia Hynes, 1988).

GIVEN CRUMBS, NOT CREDIT

In my experience, male authorities often like the initial debates and critique that come with feminist challenge to traditional thought and institutional structure. Sparks from passionate debate and the flash of anger enliven, warm, and excite people who've grown lethargic and passionless in bureaucracies and upper echelons of academia. Some men are savvy enough to see what's in it for them to champion women—grants or awards, perhaps because the topic is temporarily hot with the National Science Foundation, major foundations, or their respective agency. In the end, we are given crumbs: affirmative action is practiced at entry level only, not throughout the pyramid structure; a lot more corporate and institutional angst goes into soothing the bruised and threatened psyches of men, than the spirits of women who fought, change is made at the fringe, but never at the core of thought and institutional decision-making. The few men who would do more, rarely have the clout (or courage) to do so, because they aren't perceived as virile or dominant and haven't found alternative ways to express strength.

The following strategies are used by institutions to contain change demanded by feminists. Affirmative action is practiced at the entry level, so that the structure of power is relatively unchanged. Differences between men and women in salary, office space, merit awards, and position throughout the rest of the institution (which are also affirmative action issues) are left intact, trusting to some trickle up effect in time. Upper level opportunities for women may open up here and there; but women—no matter what age—are considered "young" for upper level, senior positions and awards, whereas men of the same age and younger are considered "wunderkind," promising, brilliant, and, by the way, responsible for supporting an existing or future family. Another strategy used in the face of woman-centered knowledge is to treat feminist analysis as domestic, limited, soft, and unpedigreed. One physicist who has worked both as a feminist and a critic of the almost exclusive defense-related research in her department at MIT, compared the reaction of male colleagues to her feminist and peace politics. They ignored her feminism, as if it were irrelevant and beneath their pinnacles of thought. They gave more respect to her more "substantive" critique of the priorities of science done in the department. A male-controlled nonprofit group with whom I have worked on issues of new reproductive technologies and their effect on women sees the Institute on Women and Technology as limited and less than wholistic. We look only at the effects of technologies on *women's* health and welfare, while they possess a broader, more comprehensive humanistic philosophy of assessing the impacts of such things as biotechnologies and genetic engineering on *human beings*.

PRE-EMINENCE OF THE QUANTITATIVE

Certainly there are more women studying, practicing, and teaching engineering than 20 years ago. A few women have been rescued from second sex status in the history of the discipline, such as Ellen Swallow and Lilian Gilbreth. And women are given awards in the field, usually in the women's chapters of engineering societies. Engineering has not yet been challenged from within the discipline or profession by feminist scholarship in the most critical of ways: to deconstruct the male perspective that permeates traditional scholarship and knowledge about women; to affirm race, class, and gender as centers of focus; to use the experience of other than white men to analyze reality; to seek knowledge to change the world, as well as to understand it; to overcome the limitations of fragmented, disciplinary knowledge; and to create alternative vision or to push critique beyond itself to reconstruct reality while not relinquishing the critique.

I have seen, for example, feminists in environmental engineering, whose area of expertise is risk analysis, call for more accessible and empathic presentation of risk by public agencies like the U.S. Environmental Protection Agency (E.P.A.), to people who live near hazardous waste sites. In other words, they have influenced that agency to humanize the process of risk communication. However, the more radical and far-reaching issue in risk-benefit analysis is the increasing use of risk analysis and risk communication by industry and government to convince people that they must live with risk. What are the roots of the concept of living with risk? The male game mentality, for one: life is a game; we sometimes win, we sometimes lose. If you want to play the game, you have to be willing to lose. In risk analysis, every factor must be able to be quantified or weighed numerically. Those that can't be quantified are soft and are dismissed. The pre-eminence of the quantitative is not surprising in a world where people still seriously try to prove that women and people of color have inferior quantitative skills. Risk analysis is locked in the quantitative arena where men are confident they are superior and where they are surer of the "truth." This type of feminist analysis—the roots of risk analysis in the male game mentality and in their dominance of the quantitative—would be ridiculed or ignored in engineering, as the MIT physicist found. Most women engineers won't lift above the already heavy weight of keeping quantitative and technical skills sharp and keeping parity with (which means outperforming) their male colleagues.

FEMINIST KNOWLEDGE WITHIN AND
OUTSIDE THE DISCIPLINE

Feminist knowledge outside the discipline has shaken the engineering field in ways it has resisted from within. Feminists have exposed the agenda of male theoretical and applied science to exclude women from their ranks: theories of biologically based differences in intelligence by sex and a complex fabric of socialization in which girls are discouraged in their science and engineering abilities (Ruth Bleier, 1984). Undoing the second sex status of women's ability for math and science—a prejudice that still lingers but with many cracks in the armor—is comparable to women in engineering to getting the vote. Once gotten, it is inconceivable that we could not have had it by way of being adults in our society. As with the vote, we can use our technical abilities to conform or radically to change things. From within the profession, women engineers have formed professional women's associations which have well-defined, strongly professional identities and radiate a sense of competence. However, as with the record of women's vote, women in engineering have not substantially separated themselves from the male way of doing things. Equality is defined as equality with men, that is proving themselves by becoming as good as men within a male-conceived system of engineering. To use a building analogy, women have gotten in the front door of the engineering establishment; but women have not yet challenged the load-bearing members of the discipline or institution. Feminist engineers could start with any member. But as with a building, you don't successfully eliminate rotten load-bearing structures without putting in place an alternative.

A brief example here. In December 1989 the National Academy of Engineering picked the top 10 engineering accomplishments of the past 25 years:

moon landing, application satellites, microprocessors, computer-aided design, CAT scan, advanced composite materials, the jumbo jet, lasers, fiber optics, genetic engineering.

Let us look at what could have been picked in the fields of energy, transportation, pollution, agriculture, and medical technology, were the social usefulness of technology a primary consideration:

photovoltaics; wind turbines; high-speed trains; safe, permanent disposal of hazardous waste; biodegradation of solid and hazardous waste; alternatives to chlorofluorocarbons (CFCs); widespread use of IPM and organic agriculture; an effective male birth control device.

How feminism can and should change engineering is complex. For one, some areas of engineering may only be challenged from without: nuclear engineering and genetic engineering, for example. Like Greenpeace activists in a rubber dinghy confronting a Japanese whaling ship (with media present, of course), feminists have been more effective as sophisticated activist critics than as nuclear engineers. But we cannot do without feminist mechanical engineers who could be credible critics, radical reformers, and visionaries by way of their expertise with alternative energy systems and conservation—if we are to replace rotten load-bearing members with alternatives. The first steps of demanding affirmative action, finding and restoring the foresisters of our field, and analyzing the mechanisms which have kept women invisible and inferior in the realms of science and engineering are being taken. Most women in engineering stop somewhere in between these steps. Feminist scholarship as political change, as alternative vision, as using our own experience to analyze reality: these are the more difficult inroads to make. We must understand technologies and technological development for their impacts on women: birth control technology, housing technology, development technology, even Star Wars. One tentacle of Star Wars, for example, siphons resources from health, housing and welfare for the dominance fantasies of white men and renders more women poor, homeless, illiterate, and prey to the drug and sex slave trade. The development of the suburbs after World War II and the design of the modern house which have so isolated women; the impacts of western industrial development on women in developing countries [see Claudia Salazar, this volume]; the ways women are displaced, underpaid, and then turn to prostitution when countries urbanize, industrialize, and militarize: these connections between technology and women's lives are fundamental to ask about and answer. Engineering is a world in which women could have so much control over the future of technology; in our absence, in the absence of feminist analysis, we have so little.

BIBLIOGRAPHY

Bleier, Ruth. (1984). *Science and gender: A critique of biology and its theories on women*. Elmsford, NY: Pergamon Press.

de Camp, L. Sprague. (1960). *The ancient engineers*. New York: Ballantine Books.

Haas, Violet B. & Perrucci, Carolyn (Eds.). (1984). *Women in scientific and engineering professions*. Ann Arbor: University of Michigan Press.

Hynes, H. Patricia. (1985). Ellen Swallow, Lois Gibbs, & Rachel Carson: Catalysts of the American environmental movement. *Women's Studies International Forum, 8*(4), 291–298.

Hynes, H. Patricia. (1988). Feminism and environmental engineering. In *Women and Planning Conference*. Urban Studies Department. MIT. Cambridge, Massachusetts.

Hynes, H. Patricia. (1989). *The recurring silent spring*. Elmsford, NY: Pergamon Press.

Mozans, H.J. (1974). *Woman in science*. Cambridge, MA: The MIT Press.

Raymond, Janice G. (1988). Course syllabus for women's studies 311 (Methods in women's studies). University of Massachusetts. Amherst, Massachusetts.

Trescott, Martha. (1984). Women engineers in history: Profiles in holism and persistence. In Violet B. Haas & Carolyn Perrucci (Eds.), *Women in scientific and engineering professions* (pp. 181–204). Ann Arbor, Michigan: University of Michigan Press.

Chapter 12

Political Science—Whose Common Good?

Jane S. Jaquette

Women throughout history have been marginalized from politics, both its practice and its study. When women are mobilized into revolutionary movements or organize themselves as feminists, their legal and economic status may improve, but their access to political power remains limited. That, in brief, is the historical pattern in country after country.

Deep seated prejudices against women in politics are found in a range of cultural settings. Since at least the 5th century BCE, Western political thought has had trouble reconciling the concepts of "woman" and "citizen." In general, women are not the primary actors nor even the subjects of political discourse; they are rarely seen as appropriate commentators on political topics or as having an adequate perspective from which to make political judgments or engage in political activities (Barbara J. Nelson, 1989, p. 2).

The purpose of this essay is to assess the impact of modern feminism on political science. It looks back 20 years to the status of women in the discipline and to early feminist efforts to introduce new data and new issues; discusses the directions and content of feminist research over the last two decades; and analyzes the response of both mainstream and radical political science to the challenges that research has raised. The conclusion examines postmodernist trends in feminist theory and their implications for the future of feminist theory and practice.

WOMEN IN POLITICAL SCIENCE:
20 YEARS AGO

Although women were nearly 25% of the undergraduate majors in political science in the late 1960s, they represented only 9% of the Ph.D.s and only 6.5% of the full-time political science faculty in U.S. colleges and universities (Jane S. Jaquette, 1971, p. 530). By 1989, these numbers had changed dramatically as women made up about a quarter of those receiving doctorates and the percentage of women faculty had more than doubled.

Special thanks to Kathy Staudt and Abe Lowenthal who provided thoughtful comments on an earlier draft of this essay, and to Dale Spender and Cheris Kramarae whose editorial comments helped clarify the arguments presented here.

With increased representation, women began to gain visibility and some leverage in the professional organizations of the discipline. By the late 1980s, women's caucuses had become part of the governing establishments of the national and regional political science associations and research on women had become a salient theme at professional meetings. The American Political Science Association (APSA) routinely monitored and published data on women's status in the profession and had taken a leading role in developing and promoting women's studies resource materials for teaching. Women's studies research merits it own journal, *Women & Politics*.

These gains, though impressive, are not yet fully consolidated. In a recent study of the top 400 most cited scholars in the field (Hans Dieter Klingemann, Bernard Grofman, & Janet Campagna, 1989), only eight are women, and only four of these do any gender-related research.[1] Much of the malestream core of the discipline operates as though gender is irrelevant, ignoring many of the new insights brought forth by the new wave of feminist research.

Twenty years ago, virtually no attention was given to the role of women in politics and, in retrospect, much of what was written seems patronizing and male-centric. In the 1920s there was a brief flurry of interest as scholars wondered whether the newly enfranchised female electorate would vote as a bloc and substantially alter the content of politics by pitting their moral and pacifist values against foreign expansionism and the "big interests."

Instead, studies showed that women tended to vote as their husbands voted. By the 1950s, with the threat of women's bloc voting a distant memory, women were seen as thoroughly domesticated. They provided the "affective" counterpart to the instrumental roles of males in the family and in the polity. The hard-fought battle for women's suffrage seemed a distant and slightly embarrassing memory, its vision of fundamental change largely forgotten. The classic study of political participation, *The Civic Culture,* widely used in classrooms in the 1960s and 1970s, reflects the perspective of those few studies that mentioned women at all:

> it would appear that women differ from men ... only in being somewhat more frequently apathetic, parochial, conservative, and sensitive to the personality, emotional and esthetic aspects of political life.... (Gabriel A. Almond & Sidney Verba, 1965, p. 325)

FEMINIST CRITIQUES OF THE DISCIPLINE

The first feminist challenge to this view was Kirsten Amundsen's *The Silenced Majority,* published in 1971. Amundsen attributed women's political invisibility to their profound economic dependency and drew attention to the unrecognized but coercive patterns of institutional sexism. She called for a broad-based women's political movement in which women would use the weapons of democratic politics to bring about the changes that, from her European perspective, seemed long overdue.

At the 1973 APSA convention, two papers directly attacked the male biases of the discipline. Bourque and Grossholtz (1974) identified four distortions of female experience: the assumption of male dominance; promotion of a masculine ideal of political behavior; evocation of the "eternal feminine" as the appropriate norm for women; and "fudging the footnotes"—that is, generalizing without adequate documentation. Such "recycling" of stale survey data had produced the received wisdom reflected in Almond and Verba's assessment, as well as other "truths"—such as the view that women were more intolerant than men, for example, and the notion that boys were "naturally" more political than girls. In a similar essay, Jaquette underlined the implications of a definition of politics bounded by male experience, pointing to a much-cited study of childhood political socialization in which it was argued that girls were less interested in politics than boys because they were less interested in war (Jane S. Jaquette, 1974; Lynne B. Iglitzin, 1974). Further, low rates of political participation and indicators of women's political "apathy"—data that would have provoked heated debates about causes and consequences had they been reported for men—were regarded as normal for women, a result of their choices and not a problem for democratic theory or practice.

Further, the newly authoritative behavioralists, who claimed to be creating a truly "value free" political science, quickly abandoned objectivity when the subject was women. Robert Lane's analysis of (male) voters, which he grandly titled *Political Life* (1959), strayed from the descriptive long enough to attack women for endangering family values by engaging in paid or volunteer work outside the home. Citing an earlier study, Lane wrote:

> [A]s Kardiner points out, the rise in juvenile delinquency [and, he says, homosexuality] is partly to be attributed to the feminist movement and what it did to the American mother. (Lane, 1959, p. 523)[2]

Both essays agreed that the discipline's approach to political institutions and issues was heavily biased against understanding women's participation in politics. Formal political institutions, both elected and administrative, had very few women in decision-making roles. Even when the definition of political participation was expanded to include participation in pressure groups and the study of public opinion, the primacy given to defense policy over domestic issues and the tendency to ignore local politics combined to keep women's political activities virtually invisible.[3]

Today one would surely add that anticommunism played a role by reinforcing the tendency of American political science to define politics so narrowly as to exclude political economy and Marxist frameworks as outside of the mainstream. To study politics was to study public "value allocating" institutions; little attention was given to the macroeconomic bases of politics or to the micro relations of power in the household or the workplace. By contrast, in Europe and the Third World, where Marxism was taken seriously and leftist parties and revolutionary movements were political forces, women's political participation and economic roles were, theoretically at least, significant issues.

Finally, in retrospect, it is interesting that the feminist challenge par excellence—"the personal is political"—was ignored by the discipline or rejected out of hand. It seemed that Aristotle's firm separation of the household from the world of politics had survived intact. [See Patricia Thompson, this volume.]

FEMINIST RESEARCH AND METHODOLOGICAL ISSUES

Feminist research emerged in three distinct streams in the 1970s: "behavioral" studies, institutional analysis, and political theory. These divisions were deepened by the battle that raged in the late 1950s and early 1960s between the "behavioralists," who were trying to take the study of politics along the scientific path already carved out by sociology, economics, and behavioral psychology, and those who were resisting this pressure. Behavioral research on women in politics grew rapidly as efforts were made to fill in the gaps of our knowledge of male–female differences in political participation.

Jeane Kirkpatrick's 1974 study of women state legislators, carried out under the auspices of the newly created Center for the American Woman in Politics at Rutgers University, was one of the first major projects in the field. Within a few years, two anthologies highlighted new findings (Jane S. Jaquette, 1974; Marianne Githens & Jewel L. Prestage, 1977), and at least 85 articles were published in more than 40 scholarly journals between 1976 and 1978. It is worth noting, however, that the *American Political Science Review,* published by the APSA and the "gatekeeper" journal of the discipline, did not publish one article on women during this period (Berenice A. Carroll, 1979, pp. 289–90).[4]

The women's movement itself provided the grist for institutional research on the implementation of a new women's agenda. A good example is Jo Freeman's analysis of how the triangular relationship between women's groups, key legislators and sympathetic bureaucrats working from inside the system had cooperated to produce a wave of women's rights legislation in the early 1970s (Jo Freeman, 1975). Later books would explore why this wave had broken by the mid-1970s and others would document the antifeminist backlash seen in the abortion issue and the failure to pass the Equal Rights Amendment (ERA) (e.g., Janet K. Boles, 1979; Jane J. Mansbridge, 1986).

The feminist empiricists did not see themselves as "value free" in the sense of disengaged; on the contrary many were convinced that the most effective way to bring about change was to document how the norm of political equality was being violated in the case of women in order to make women's underrepresentation an issue.

By the mid-1970s, the discipline had become sensitive to the more blatant forms of sexism, and it would have been considered a lapse in methodological etiquette to exclude women respondents from survey research. Yet most U.S. studies still took male political behavior as the norm against which women's participation should be measured, and few questioned the pluralist model of politics that underlay behavioral research (Berenice A. Carroll, 1979).

This left considerable room for the feminist theorists to attack the "fill in the gaps" approach of the empiricists. Allying themselves with the more radical critiques of quantitative methods and the pluralist paradigm, feminist political theorists argued that consciousness-raising, egalitarian socialization and feminist legislation by themselves were inadequate to explain or to change women's political status. They sought to understand how gender inequality reinforces and is reproduced by the fundamental economic and social structures of modern society. Many joined radical male colleagues in finding the high levels of violence, inequality, alienation, and environmental degradation clear evidence of the crisis of late twentieth century capitalism and elitist democracy. Unlike their male counterparts, however, feminist theorists sought the root causes of these phenomena in the politics of gender. They looked to women's life experiences as a new basis on which to redefine politics and revitalize political life.

From the beginning, feminist political theory in the United States was responsive to radical feminism and open to influences from other disciplines. Kate Millet, Shulamith Firestone, Mary Daly, and Juliet Mitchell were widely read and discussed. New feminist research in philosophy, literary criticism, feminist theology, and women's history were probed for their political implications. Nancy Chodorow's (1978) work on the psychodynamics of gender formation, which argues that girls' identities are more closely bound up with their mothers and that boys distance themselves not only from their mothers but from "feminine" characteristics during the Oedipal period, has been incorporated in feminist political thought to envision a more connected, more communitarian politics.[5] Carol Gilligan's (1982) discussion of male–female differences in moral reasoning is crucial to arguments that a new form of politics could be envisioned if "care" were substituted for "rights" (see Seyla Benhabib, 1987; Joan C. Tronto, 1987). And Evelyn Fox Keller's (1984) analysis of the gendered nature of the "scientific method" has been taken up by those who find behavioralist epistemologies antithetical to the feminist project (see Sandra Harding, 1986).

In an early attempt to ground political analysis on women's experience, Jean Elshtain (1981) traced the use of the public/private distinction in western political thought, building on work done by anthropologists Michele Rosaldo and Louise Lamphere (1974). Elshtain argued for the relevance of nurturance and moral engagement to the public world of politics, while emphasizing the need to preserve the family against the growing power of the state (see Sara Ruddick, 1980; and critiques in Mary G. Dietz, 1987; & Zillah R. Eisenstein, 1984).

Nancy Hartsock (1983) located women's oppression in the hegemony of the market model of exchange as the norm for human behavior in all spheres of life. The market assumption that exchange occurs between equals can be proven false by our experience, yet its widespread acceptance legitimizes relations of domination and submission by rendering them invisible in both the public and private spheres. (See Anna G. Jonasdottir, 1988; Catharine A. MacKinnon, 1983; Carole Pateman, 1983). Hartsock opposed a feminist standpoint grounded in women's work, which she called "feminist historical materialism" to the reigning model of "abstract masculinity":

> [T]he unity of mental and manual labor and the directly sensuous nature of much of women's work leads to a more profound unity of mental and manual labor, social and natural worlds, than is experienced by the male worker in capitalism. (Nancy C.M. Hartsock, 1983, p. 243; see Young, 1980)

Kathy Ferguson (1984) added to these ambitious critiques the "feminist case against bureaucracy," underlining the incompatibility between feminist values—equality, recognition of the other, connectedness—and the patterns of hierarchy, internal coercion, and external manipulation that characterize bureaucracies, public and private. Adding feminist content to Michel Foucault's analysis, Ferguson argued that women represent a "submerged discourse," and that "revealing the notions of personal identity and social interactions embedded in women's traditional experience can suggest a nonbureaucratic vision of collective life" (Kathy E. Ferguson, 1984, p. 5).

Through these developments, feminist theory in the United States has found itself in a strong position to influence critical theory, and thus to cast the latter's opposition to behavioralism, interest group pluralism, and capitalism in new terms (see Seyla Benhabib & Drucilla Cornell, 1987). At the same time, U.S. feminist theorists became increasingly critical of the earlier wave of liberal feminists whom they saw as reinforcing male definitions of participation and success and as promoting political and economic access for a privileged few without challenging the persistent structures of race and class.

The growing split between "liberal" and "difference" feminism, and the critiques of white, middle-class feminism by women of color, created new problems and opportunities for feminist theory and practice. The hope that a feminist framework would restructure the discipline and change the content of politics has given way to the recognition that there are deep divisions among feminists as to which framework should prevail.

THE DISCIPLINE RESPONDS TO THE NEW SCHOLARSHIP

The male, behavioralist core of the discipline responded to the political reality of the feminist movement and to the new wave of feminist scholarship by incorporating gender as a variable, but it did not take the feminist ideological challenge seriously. A study of introductory texts in American politics found that the most widely used texts culled bits and pieces of women's political history to provide illustrative material for "case studies" of key concepts. For example, the suffrage movement and the campaign for the ERA were used to illustrate the constitutional amendment process. Often there was a negative assessment of the effects of women's involvement, as when *Roe* v. *Wade* is used to show what can happen when the Supreme Court goes beyond its appropriate role and "legislates" social change (Jane S. Jaquette, 1985).

Further, these texts almost without exception characterized the women's movement as an "interest group" rather than as a social movement intent on making fundamental changes in society, and their treatment of women's interest reveals the ambivalence with which the women's movement, historically and today, is viewed. In the pluralist model of politics, interest groups, not voters, are the basic units of democratic politics. They develop issues in response to members' demands, and they lobby Congress and government agencies to assure attention to their needs. The competitive interaction among these groups produces new laws responsive to public needs; collectively they create the "common good."

In the model, interest groups are necessary and even positive factors in politics, although texts may differ in their degree of enthusiasm for pluralism's displacement of classical democratic politics and the principle of "one man, one vote." But when it comes to women, these same texts often portray the women's movement as a "special interest," that is as a group so narrowly focused on achieving its own goals that it threatens the common good. One popular introductory text (James MacGregor Burns, J.S. Peltason, & Thomas E. Cronin, 1981) actually describes the suffragettes as a "cohesive group bent on their own self interest." "What does this kind of factional struggle mean for the people?" the text asks, as though the fight for votes for women was at odds with the public interest, on a par with the activities of such groups as, say, the National Rifle Association.

Portraying the women's movement as a special interest rather than as a social movement, although its implications are probably not consciously thought out by the scholars who do so, provides an effective line of defense for the discipline's mainstream. Feminists can't complain that women are being ignored, yet the movement's goals are trivialized and its motives questioned. Even at the most superficial level these texts reveal their gender bias. "Self-interest" is a perfectly proper motivation for most interest groups but somehow inappropriate for women (see Kathleen B. Jones & Anna G. Jonasdottir, 1988; Virginia Sapiro, 1981).[6] Of course, both the interest group and social movement approaches assume the primacy of the public sphere, and thus overlook the possibilities of seeing everyday life as a political arena it its own right (e.g., Jane S. Jaquette, 1984; Carole Pateman, 1984; Dorothy E. Smith, 1987).

Although feminism has drawn on Marxist analysis and its concerns often parallel Marxist critiques of modern society, the relationship between feminism and the left has not been without conflict (see Heidi Hartmann, 1981; Batya Weinbaum, 1978). For those on the left who resist the idea that patriarchy cannot be subsumed under class, and that gender exploitation preceded capitalism, the women's movement seen as diversionary. A widely used Marxist text in American politics (Edward S. Greenberg, 1977) ignores women and fails to acknowledge feminist contributions to Marxist theory. The conflict between Marxism and feminism has had much more serious consequences in Europe and the Third World where leftist movements have set the terms of political debate or, in some cases, captured the state. (See Claire Duchen, 1986; Maxine Molyneaux, 1985; Judith Stacey, 1983). There are some important exceptions, such as Isaac Balbus' *Marxism and Domination* (1982) which argues that a "genuinely radical anticapitalist movement must be a movement against sexual, technological and political domination" (Isaac Balbus, 1982, p. 2) and which incorporates feminist theory throughout.

With the growing rapprochement between East and West and the declining appeal of the Marxist economic model, the international left has borrowed from Gramsci and others to make cultural resistance and "submerged discourses" the means to escape the hegemony of Western capitalism. In this new literature, women are often seen as a so-called "peripheral" group which, precisely because it is marginalized, has the ideological potential to resist domination. In a recent explication of "world systems theory," for example, Immanuel Wallerstein devotes an entire paragraph to "taking the women's movement seriously." After noting that the women's movement is "in many ways the hardest phenomenon for the left to handle, because it requires the most rethinking in the most different spheres of human activity," Wallerstein finds this its strength:

> Precisely because it opens up the question not merely of equal access to the workplace, but of the very structure of the workplace, of the very patterns of consumption, of the very workings of the family (which, the conservatives are right, is a fundamental institution of social life), of the very organization of the everyday reproduction of material life—precisely because it raises all these questions simultaneously, in what seems a torrent of questioning and protest, the women's movement forces us to face up to what will be the true content of a socialist world, one based on production for use, one egalitarian in reality. (Immanuel Wallerstein, 1987, p. 79)

Because it recognizes the breadth of the feminist challenge, Wallerstein's recognition seems closer to the spirit of the feminist project. This is elegant tokenism, but tokenism nonetheless.

Student responses provide grounds for both optimism and pessimism concerning the long-run impact of feminist research. To my knowledge, student opinions have not been systematically studied for political science, but impressionistic data indicates that students who are exposed to feminist research via mainstreaming find the accessibility of the material inversely related to its critical and theoretical content; consistent with the texts analyzed above, students more easily absorb feminist research when it is translated into the women as a "variable" or the women's movement as an illustrative "case study." However, faculty who persistently raise women's issues or emphasize women's studies scholarship may be vulnerable to student criticism for having an axe to grind or for stepping over the line between education and advocacy.

By contrast, students who choose to take women's studies courses, which continue to command strong enrollments in colleges and universities across the United States, are particularly interested in feminist theory which they see as relevant to the questions they are asking about their lives, questions about sexual liberation and the double standard, changing role relationships in the family, race and class differences in feminism, and ways to rethink their own views on abortion or date rape, or to heighten their awareness of women's exploitation in the economy and in the media.

For students and faculty alike, the process of internalizing feminist perspectives in the discipline is not yet well advanced. Although there is some evidence of a gender gap, which shows up in electoral results as well as in opinion polls, women have not changed their political behavior so dramatically as to force the behaviorists to adopt a new model of politics. Few male political scientists, even those who are not personally threatened by the prospect of restructuring the gender relations of power, see themselves as gaining status by becoming authorities on feminist issues. Thus, although Barbara Nelson's recent assessment of the discipline holds out the hope that political science is at last open to the realization that "interpretive, positivist and postmodernist ways of knowing are each *gendered* ways of knowing," (Barbara J. Nelson, 1989, p. 19), there is little evidence that this awareness has changed the ways in which most political scientists go about their scholarly business.

Further, the fragmentation of feminist theory over the last decade has made it difficult for women in the discipline to adopt a unified strategy. Nor can unified strategies work in a discipline that is increasingly becoming "postmodern"—that is, a political theory increasingly critical of any universalistic norms and resistant to the notion that political science must seek truth. Under such circumstances, no single framework can be expected— or allowed—to reorder our values or our perceptions. Yet relativism, as Nancy Hartsock (1983) observes, inevitably weakens feminism's claims.[7]

COMPETING FEMINIST FRAMEWORKS:
IMPLICATIONS FOR THEORY
AND PRACTICE

In a sense, the fragmentation of feminist theory has resulted from the successes of liberal egalitarianism as a feminist political strategy in the United States. The bad news is that the divisions among women seem to be widening. Of course, there has always been conflict within feminism. In the United States in the 1970s, for example, the opposition between radical Marxist and liberal feminists on the one hand, and between lesbian and straight feminists on the other, was reflected in women's organizations, on university campuses, and internationally in the UN (United Nations') Decade for Women. The conflict in the 1980s between "egalitarian" and "difference" feminisms has produced fundamental conflict about the content of the feminist agenda and competing interpretations of the meaning of women's political history (e.g., Wendy Sarvasy, 1990).

In the American political context, the assertion that women must be treated *differently* to achieve *equal results* (Mary Lou Kendrigan, 1984), or the more radical view that women must preserve or develop those qualities that differentiate them from (aggressive, technologically exploitative) men, as implied in the work of Gilligan and others, has aroused heated debate. (See Zillah R. Eisenstein, 1984; Catharine A. MacKinnon, 1987; Irene Diamond, 1983; Martha Minow, 1987; and David L. Kirp, Mark G. Yudof, & Marlene Strong Franks, 1986). Critics fear that any relaxation of the pressure for full equality will raise the specter of "separate but equal" so vividly illustrated by the history of African Americans in the United States. When difference translates into a positive benefit for women, like maternity leave or barring women but not men from jobs that expose them to hazardous chemicals or radiation, it is reasonable to expect (in the American context) that the costs of such benefits will be used as an excuse for not hiring women, thus repeating the earlier experience with "protective" legislation during the first half of this century.

Yet to argue for equality in a world where women's nurturing responsibilities still greatly exceed those of men is to put an unfair burden on women. Research, such as Lenore Weitzman's study of no fault divorce (1985), show that policies once supported by feminists in the name of equality can have very devastating effects on women's lives. Women rarely achieve a truly equal division of the fixed assets under no-fault, and their labor contributions to the marriage, their greater responsibility for child care after divorce, and their relatively weak position in the labor market are not adequately taken into account. Thus a policy that assumed men and women were equal accentuated women's powerlessness.

The division between equalitarian and difference feminism can also be seen in two much publicized legal cases. In the Cal Fed case (which involved deciding whether pregnancy leave involved sex discrimination because it applied only to women) the Ninth Circuit Court of California decided that it could not achieve equality of employment opportunity without treating men and women differently, though the prospect that distinctions between men and women would become further legitimized in the law had prompted some feminist groups to testify against that outcome. In a case involving Sears Roebuck and Company, feminist testimony was introduced to support a difference argument—that women's choices accounted for why so many more men were working in the higher-paid commission sales jobs. Those demanding that more women be hired argued that women did not choose to earn less, but that they had been discriminated against. The difference argument prevailed, reinforcing the fears of the liberal egalitarians and reducing the pressure on Sears to do affirmative action hiring in this job category (Ruth Milkman, 1986).

Both egalitarian and difference arguments can be defended on feminist grounds, but the policy dilemmas this poses cannot easily be resolved. Due to its legal and political history, the conflict between egalitarian and difference arguments is particularly sharp in the United States. Whether decisions are made on one ground or the other is not "academic" but has real consequences for women's choices and women's lives. Such conflicts are likely to become more important in other countries as the Decade of Women sets standards for gender equality (such as the UN Convention for the Elimination of All Forms of Discrimination Against Women, now ratified by over 100 countries, but not by the United States), and as women's organizations press for egalitarian change (see Margaret Schuler, 1986).

In this dynamic environment, American feminists should draw more heavily on the experiences of women who have tried to create feminist values within very different institutional and cultural settings—Third World women, European women, and women of color. [See Claudia Salazar, this volume.]

Some of the comparative work being done in political science may move us closer to this goal. Adams and Winston's pathbreaking study (1980) comparing public policies on women's issues (abortion, childcare, work) in Sweden, China, and the United States is an early example of the potential of this work, for its provides a much richer context for understanding the relationship between public opinion, women's groups, legislation, and bureaucratic response and puts American policy and the feminist movement in a much broader perspective. Recent work on gender and the state goes beyond the pluralist model with important implications for women's political strategies (see Sue Ellen Charlton, Everett Jana, & Kathleen Staudt, 1989). Some of the recent comparative studies speak directly to the issue of difference politics, including Claire Duchen's discussion of the influence of French feminism on French politics (1986) and the example of the *Madres* of the *Plaza de Mayo,* who gave the values of motherhood political resonance and helped bring down the military regime in Argentina (Maria del Carmen Feijoó, 1989).

As the women's movement in the United States becomes more representative of ethnic diversity and more open to international influences, there is a healthy tendency toward celebrating diversity. If it is the role of feminism to challenge the "hegemonic universals" of the Western tradition to give space to feminist subjects and recognition to feminist voices, it will fall to politics, and especially to feminist theory and practice, to insure that difference does not lead to inequity nor postmodernism to apathy.

NOTES

1.   Women listed (by Ph.D. cohort) are: Theda Skocpol and Valerie Bunce (1975–1979); Susan Welch (1970–1974); Jeane Kirkpatrick and Suzanne Berger (1965–1969); Frances Piven (1960–1964); Daisy Flory (1955–1959); and Doris Graber (1945–1949). Susan Welch's research has focused on women and politics; Jeane Kirkpatrick has a book on women political elites, and Fred Greenstein and M. Kent Jennings research sex differences in political participation. Theda Skocpol, who is credited with refocusing the discipline on the role of the state, is now turning her attention to issue of gender and the state.

2.   The most unsettling aspect of looking back at this material is that I and the other women scholars I knew read this material without feeling a sense of outrage and without even registering its overt hostility to women and, by extension, to ourselves.

3.   As drugs, migration, and environmental issues and the persistence of gross economic inequalities within and among nations blur the conventional distinctions between international and domestic issues, the classic division between "high" and "low" politics is also breaking down. In this context, it is especially important to note that international relations has been the least amenable to feminist analysis of any field in the discipline. This was the topic of a recent conference on gender and international relations held at the Center for International Studies at the University of Southern California in April, 1989. For a copy of the conference report, edited by Spike Peterson, contact the Center at USC, Los Angeles, CA 90089. The Winter, 1988, issue of *Millenium: A Journal of International Studies* was devoted to the topic of women and international relations. [See also Claudia Salazar, this volume.]

4.   For more recent examples, see Baxter and Lansing, 1983; Darcy, Welch and Clark, 1987; Poole and Zeigler, 1985; Mueller, 1988, to name a few of the many studies now available.

5.   Chodorow's work has also been incorporated by the ecofeminists as anticipated by Dinnerstein (1976).

6.   The distinction between a social movement and an interest group is not merely academic. When Walter Mondale named Geraldine Ferraro as his vice-presidential candidate, he made it easier for the opposition to argue that the Democrats had lost their claim to represent "the people" and had become the party of the "special interests," thus nailing the Democratic Party and the women's movement at the same time.

7.   On difference feminism and postmodernism, see also Jaggar, 1983; Lloyd, 1984; Cocks, 1984; Flax, 1987; Hekman, 1987; DiStefano, 1988.

BIBLIOGRAPHY

Adams, Carolyn Teich & Winston, Kathryn Teich. (1980). *Mothers at work: Public policies in the United States, Sweden, and China.* New York: Longman.

Almond, Gabriel A. & Verba, Sidney. (1965). *The civic culture.* Boston: Little Brown.

Amundsen, Kirsten. (1971). *The silenced majority: Women and American democracy.* Englewood Cliffs, NJ: Prentice-Hall.

Balbus, Isaac D. (1982). *Marxism and domination: A neo-Hegelian, feminist psychoanalytic theory of sexual, political and technological liberation.* Princeton, NJ: Princeton University Press.

Baxter, Sandra & Lansing, Marjorie. (1983). *Women and politics: The visible majority.* Ann Arbor: University of Michigan Press.

Benhabib, Seyla. (1987). The generalized and the concrete other: The Kohlberg—Gilligan controversy and feminist theory. In Seyla Benhabib & Drucilla Cornell (Eds.), *Feminism as Critique* (pp. 77–95). Minneapolis: University of Minnesota Press.

Benhabib, Seyla & Cornell, Drucilla (Eds.). (1987). *Feminism as critique.* Minneapolis: University of Minnesota Press.

Boles, Janet K. (1979). *The politics of the Equal Rights Amendment: Conflict and the decision process.* New York: Longman.

Bourque, Susan & Grossholtz, Jean. (1974, Winter). Politics as an unnatural practice: Political science looks at female participation. *Politics and Society 4*(1), 225–266.

Burns, James MacGregor, Peltason, J.S., & Cronin, Thomas E. (1981). *Government by the people.* Englewood Cliffs, NJ: Prentice-Hall.

Carroll, Berenice A. (1979). Review Essay Political Science Part I: American politics and political behavior. *Signs, 5*(2), 289–306.

Charlton, Sue Ellen, Everett, Jana, & Staudt, Kathleen (Eds.). (1989). *Women, the state and development.* Albany, NY: State University of New York Press.

Chodorow, Nancy. (1978). *The reproduction of mothering: Psychoanalysis and the sociology of gender.* Berkeley: University of California Press.

Cocks, Joan. (1984). Wordless emotions: Some critical reflections on radical feminism. *Politics and Society, 13*(1), 27–57.

Darcy, R., Welch, Susan, & Clark, Janet. (1987). *Women, elections and representation.* New York: Longman.

Diamond, Irene. (1983). *Families, politics and public policy: A feminist dialogue on women and the state.* New York: Longman.

Dietz, Mary G. (1987, Fall). Context is all: Feminism and theories of citizenship. *Daedalus,* 1–24.

Dinnerstein, Dorothy. (1976). *The mermaid and the minotaur.* New York: Harper Colophon.

DiStefano, Christine. (1988). Dilemmas of difference: Feminism, modernity, and postmodernism. *Women & Politics, 8*(3/4), 1–24.

Duchen, Claire. (1986). *Feminism in France.* London: Routledge & Kegan Paul.

Elshtain, Jean Bethke. (1981). *Public man, private woman: Women in social and political thought.* Princeton, NJ: Princeton University Press.

Elshtain, Jean Bethke. (1983). Antigone's daughters: Reflections on female identity and the state. In Irene Diamond (Ed.), *Families, politics and public policy.* New York: Longman.

Eisenstein, Zillah R. (1984). *Feminism and sexual equality: Crisis in liberal America.* New York: Monthly Review Press.

Feijoó, Maria del Carmen. (1989). The challenge of constructing civilian peace: Women and democracy in Argentina. In Jane S. Jaquette (Ed.), *The women's movement in Latin America: Feminism and the transition to democracy* (pp. 72–94). Winchester, MA: Unwin Hyman.

Ferguson, Kathy E. (1984). *The feminist case against bureaucracy.* Philadelphia: Temple University Press.

Flax, Jane. (1987). Postmodernism and gender relations in feminist theory. *Signs, 12*(4), 621–43.

Freeman, Jo. (1975). *The politics of women's liberation.* New York: David McKay.

Gilligan, Carol. (1982). *In a different voice.* Cambridge: Harvard University Press.

Githens, Marianne & Prestage, Jewel L. (1977). *A portrait of marginality: The political behavior of the American woman.* New York: David McKay.

Greenberg, Edward S. (1977). *The American political system: A radical approach.* Cambridge: Winthrop Publishers.

Greenstein, Fred I. (1961). Sex-related political differences in childhood. *Journal of Politics, 23,* 353–371.

Harding, Sandra. (1986). *The science question in feminism.* Ithaca, NY: Cornell University Press.

Hartmann, Heidi. (1981). The unhappy marriage of Marxism and feminism. In Lydia Sargent (Ed.), *A discussion of the unhappy marriage of Marxism and feminism.* Boston: South End Press.

Hartsock, Nancy C.M. (1983). *Money, sex, and power: Toward a feminist historical materialism.* New York: Longman.

Hekman, Susan. (1987). The feminization of epistemology: Gender and the social sciences. *Women & Politics, 7*(3), 65–83.

Iglitzin, Lynne B. (1974). The making of the apolitical woman: Femininity and sex stereotyping in girls. In Jane Jaquette (Ed.), *Women in politics* (pp. 25–36). New York: John Wiley & Sons.

Jaggar, Alison M. (1983). *Feminist politics and human nature.* Sussex: Rowman & Allenhead.

Jaquette, Jane S. (1971). The status of women in the profession: Tokenism. *P.S., 4*(4), 530–32.

Jaquette, Jane S. (1984). Power as ideology. In Judith Stiehm (Ed.), *Women's view of the political world of men* (pp. 7–30). New York: Transnational Press.

Jaquette, Jane S. (1985). Beyond the new orthodoxy: Teaching about women in introductory courses in American politics. *Feminist Teacher, 1*(2), 22–26.

Jaquette, Jane S. (1974). Introduction. In Jane S. Jaquette (Ed.), *Women in politics.* New York: John Wiley & Sons.

Jaquette, Jane S. (1989). *The women's movement in Latin America: Feminism and the transition to democracy.* Winchester, MA: Unwin Hyman.

Jonasdottir, Anna G. (1988). Does sex matter to democracy? *Scandinavian Political Studies, 11*(4), 299–322.

Jones, Kathleen B. & Jonasdottir, Anna G. (Eds.). (1988). *The political interests of gender.* London: Sage.

Keller, Evelyn Fox. (1984). *Reflections on gender and science.* New Haven, CT: Yale University Press.

Kendrigan, Mary Lou. (1984). *Political equality in a democratic society: Women in the United States.* Westport, CT: Greenwood Press.

Kirkpatrick, Jeane J. (1974). *Political woman.* New York: Basic Books.

Kirp, David L., Yudof, Mark G., & Franks, Marlene Strong. (1986). *Gender justice.* Chicago, IL: University of Chicago Press.

Klingemann, Hans Dieter, Grofman, Bernard, & Campagna, Janet. (1989). The political science 400. *P.S.: Political science and politics, 21*(2), 258–269.

Lane, Robert E. (1959). *Political life.* Glencoe, IL: The Free Press.

Lloyd, Genevieve. (1984). *The man of reason: "Male" and "Female" in Western philosophy.* Minneapolis: University of Minnesota Press.

MacKinnon, Catharine A. (1987). *Feminism unmodified.* Cambridge, MA: Harvard University Press.

Mansbridge, Jane J. (1986). *Why we lost the ERA.* Chicago, IL: University of Chicago Press.

Milkman, Ruth. (1986). Women's history and the Sears case. *Feminist Studies, 12*(2), 375–400.

Minow, Martha. (1987, September). Feminist reason: Getting it and losing it. Paper presented at the American Political Science Association Annual Meeting, Chicago, IL.

Molyneaux, Maxine. (1985). Mobilization without emancipation? Women's interests, the state and revolution in Nicaragua. *Feminist Studies, 11*(2).

Mueller, Carol M. (Ed.). (1988). *The politics of the gender gap: The social construction of political influence.* Sage Yearbooks in Women's Policy Studies #12. Beverly Hills: Sage Press.

Nelson, Barbara J. (1984). Women's poverty and women's citizenship: Some political consequences of economic marginality. *Signs, 10*(21), 209–231.

Nelson, Barbara J. (1989). Women and knowledge in political science: Texts, histories and epistemologies. *Women & Politics, 9*(2), 1–27.

Pateman, Carole. (1983). Feminism and democracy. In G. Duncan (Ed.), *Democratic theory and practice.* Cambridge: Cambridge University Press.

Pateman, Carole. (1984). The shame of the marriage contract. In Judith Steihm (Ed.), *Women's views of the political world of men* (pp. 67–98). New York: Transnational Press.

Poole, Keith T. & Zeigler, L. Harmon. (1985). *Women, public opinion and politics.* New York: Longman.

Rosaldo, Michelle & Lamphere, Louise (Eds.). (1974). *Women, culture and society.* Stanford, CA: Stanford University Press.

Ruddick, Sara. (1980). Maternal thinking. *Feminist Studies, 6*(3), 343–67.

Sapiro, Virginia. (1981). When are interests interesting? The problems of the political representation of women. *American Political Science Review, 75*(3), 701–16.

Sapiro, Virginia. (1983). *The political integration of women: Roles, socialization, and politics.* Urbana, IL: University of Illinois Press.

Sarvasy, Wendy. (1990). Beyond difference versus equality: Post suffrage feminist, citizenship and the quest for a welfare state. Berkeley, CA: Bain Research Group, University of California, Berkeley.

Schuler, Margaret (Ed.). (1986). *Empowerment and the law: strategies of third world women.* Washington, DC: OEF International.

Stacey, Judith. (1983). *Patriarchy and socialist revolution in China.* Berkeley, CA: University of California Press.

Smith, Dorothy E. (1987). *The everyday world as problematic: A feminist sociology.* Boston: Northeastern University Press.

Tong, Rosemarie. (1989). *Feminist thought: A comprehensive introduction.* Boulder, CO: Westview Press.

Tronto, Joan C. (1987). Beyond gender difference to a theory of care. *Signs, 12*(4), 644–663.

Wallerstein, Immanuel. (1987). *The politics of the world economy: The states, the movements and the civilizations.* Cambridge: Cambridge University Press.

Weinbaum, Batya. (1978). *The curious courtship of women's liberation and socialism.* Boston: South End Press.

Weitzman, Lenore. (1985). *Divorce revolution.* New York: Free Press.

Young, Iris. (1980). Socialist feminism and the limits of dual systems theory. *Socialist Review, 10*(2/3).

Chapter 13

Women's History, Gender History, and Feminist Politics

Jane Lewis

It was the Second Berkshire Conference on the History of Women, October 1974, that turned my historical world upside down. I listened to Natalie Zemon Davies setting the goal of understanding the significance of sex and gender in history and suggesting new questions to ask of traditional source materials, such as court records (Natalie Zemon Davies, 1975–1976), and to Linda Gordon's analysis of the nineteenth and twentieth century arguments about birth control (Linda Gordon, 1977). And I thought that to study for a Ph.D. in history might be all right after all.

The Berkshire Conference was a large North American event that continues to be held every 3 years. I learned there about Sheila Rowbotham's pioneering general history of women (Sheila Rowbotham, 1973). But whereas many of the speakers at the Berkshire Conference already had academic jobs and were to go on to develop women's history and Women's Studies courses in most universities in the United States, in Britain historians of women were found for the most part outside or on the margins of the academy and have largely remained so. We need to go back a considerable distance before we discover women occupying a prominent place in the profession. The Economic History Society, for example, had more prominent women members in the 1930s than it does in 1990.

This is not to gainsay the energy and excitement generated by the freestanding meeting of Feminist History Groups in London and other British cities during the 1970s. These meetings attracted mainly young women, but many women in established positions also made the discovery that history could never look quite the same once they had decided to think about women's place in it. In the United States, Joan Kelly described her own change of consciousness as dramatic. She was teaching history in 1971 when a feminist historian colleague, Gerda Lerner, asked her to participate in developing courses, programs, "or even a lecture" about women in relation to her field. Kelly remembers "dropping her a note, commending her for her interests but saying that since I was in Renaissance history, there was nothing much I could offer about women" (Joan Kelly, 1984, p. xii). After a 4-hour conversation with Lerner, she changed her mind. It took no fresh discovery of evidence, no new archival materials. Rather it was the sudden perception that Renaissance history to date was for the most part "partial, distorted, limited, and deeply flawed by those limitations" because questions about women had never been asked. Looking at women's Renaissance texts, she was forced to conclude, notwithstanding the universalist theme of the period and received wisdom as to the equality of Renaissance women with men, that there had been no Renaissance for women. In many respects, such new ways of seeing history were not dissimilar to the sudden understanding of particular aspects of women's position in the contemporary world achieved by women in the consciousness-raising groups of the early 1970s.

One of my own most formative experiences came as an undergraduate hearing Olwen Hufton deliver as a lecture her paper on women's experience of the French Revolution which she subsequently published in *Past and Present* (Olwen Hufton, 1971). But at the time it was difficult to integrate this lecture with the other material I was reading. This issue of integration has remained a problem for women's history. Although it has been exciting to have women's past discovered and to have discussed topics such as menstruation and birth control that did not make it into the usual run of textbooks, it has remained possible for the male professional historian to say, "My understanding of the French Revolution is not changed by knowing that women participated in it" (quoted in Joan Scott, 1988, p. 31).

NEW RESEARCH QUESTIONS

Most of the work on women's history published during the 1970s concentrated on the task of restoring women to history and history to women, albeit the interpretative frameworks used varied considerably. Merely charting women's contribution involved considerable rethinking. How useful was the periodization used hitherto: Did women's experience not demand more attention to, say, fluctuations in fertility rates than time periods bracketed by wars or particular government administrations? How possible was it to uncover the private familial worlds that comprised the experience of so many women? Much of the early work on women's history set about reconstructing "what happened to women" through prescriptive source materials of one kind or another. Medical literature, for example, revealed a series of horror stories about Victorian gynecologists who were prepared to resort to clitorectomy, and who regarded the uterus as little more than "a toybox." Some of this work made little attempt to fully understand nineteenth century practice and beliefs on their own terms, mirroring as it did contemporary feminist anger over women's lack of control over their bodies. Nevertheless, Victorian social and medical scientists' ideas about the nature of sexual difference seemed to support a "women as victims" interpretation. Women were held to be less perfectly evolved and their reproductive systems were held to dominate their physiology. Doctors were leaders in the opposition to the achievement of women's higher education (for fear that it would divert their energy from the development of their reproductive systems) and to the suffrage. There was plenty to be angry about. But this sort of research, while going beyond the "women and ... " contribution history, remained one-dimensional. Following one of the major strands in 1970s radical feminist theory, many feminist historians relied heavily on patriarchal oppression as an explanatory framework. But conspiracy is rarely simple and the last 10 years have seen more attention paid to the possibilities of resistance, negotiation, and mediation. In politics, women used ideas about separate spheres to argue that they should be applying their knowledge of housekeeping and childcare to the world of workhouses, hospitals, and schools beyond the home (Pat Hollis, 1987). In the politics of reproduction, when late-nineteenth century feminists opposed birth control, as many did, it was from an understanding of what the separation of sex from procreation might do to the middle-class woman who depended on marriage as a trade (Linda Gordon, 1977; Angus McLaren, 1978). In the case of childbirth, there is considerable evidence that while women resisted some aspects of medical intervention, they fought hard for others, such as anesthesia (Judith Walzer Leavitt, 1980; Jane Lewis, 1980).

Women's history of the 1970s also drew upon another major strand in feminist theory—socialist feminism, which insisted that property relations were the basic determinant of the sexual division of labor. Women's subordination was traced to capitalism rather than patriarchy and women's work of biological and social reproduction in the home was seen as supporting a male dominated economic, social and political public world, while serving as the major impediment to women's participation in that world. Socialist feminist explanations did point to the centrality of reproduction in women's lives and did attempt to incorporate the work of the private sphere. But just as in feminist theory the domestic labor debate rumbled on during the 1970s, as marxist feminists struggled to make room for the idea of housework as productive labor (Eva Kaluzynska, 1980), so in the world of social and labor history, where it was expected that women's history would most readily be accepted, the issues raised by feminist historians more often provoked a debate over sex versus class, rather than a constructive and theoretically sophisticated effort to see gender and class being constructed together. [See Cheris Kramarae, this volume.]

More recently, feminist labor historians have been much more successful in demonstrating the intersections between gender and class and the extent to which workplace conflict cannot be understood without consideration of sexuality and family. For example, Nancy Grey Osterud (1986) and Judy Lown (1989) have shown that the interests of men as husbands and as either employers or trade unionists have often conflicted. In one of the best recent explorations of the process of sexual segregation, Ruth Milkman (1987) has shown how variable male trade unionists' behavior could be. In the United States auto industry during World War II, the issue became job discrimination and the union colluded with management to oppose women's seniority rights, while in electrical manufacture, wages became the issue with the same male employment insecurity resulting in an equal pay campaign. Additonally, early twentieth century women may well have shared the male trade unionists' ideal of a family wage (which benefited men as wage earners and as husbands), accepting in large part the primacy of their responsibilities to husbands and children and the secondary nature of any wage-earning they engaged in, not least because of the arduous nature of housework combined with frequent pregnancy.

MAINSTREAM RESPONSE

In 1973 James Hinton found it possible to write the classic account of the rise of the shopstewards movement during World War I in Britain without ever mentioning that the struggles of the male engineering unions over the "dilution" and "substitution" of labor were about women workers replacing men. Most probably there is now a sufficient body of literature on the role of women in World War I to force any future labor historian to take it into account. But we return to Joan Scott's point that male historians, even on the left, where feminist history has made the largest contribution, have felt able to leave women's history to women. In 1980 Barbara Taylor and Angela Phillips were demonstrating the way in which skill has been gendered; for example, oxyacetylene welding was classified as skilled work prior to 1914, but as soon as women entered the trade during the war, employers reduced the pay by 50%. Also in 1980 a study of skill appeared in which the author felt able to begin with the disclaimer that he did not intend to consider "women workers" (Charles More, 1980). But can a history of skill be written without consideration of gender? It is arguable that the important part played by the voluntary sector in erecting the apparatus of the welfare state in the United Kingdom has been largely missed because its protagonists were mostly female. Similarly overlooked is the extent to which negotiation and mediation between working class families and the officials who either entered their homes or sat on bodies such as school management committees involved, in practice, negotiation between working and middle-class women. Historians considering the intellectual debates of the early twentieth century have concentrated their attention on the expanding role of the state and consequent struggle between individualism and collectivism and the alliance between liberalism and sociology, missing the way in which the social theory of the period laid far more emphasis on the relationship between the individual, the family and the state (Jane Lewis, 1991), and the way in which women and the family became in practice both the agents and objects of reform.

The insights of women's history have to a considerable extent been effectively ghettoized. Male historians do not read the feminist journals in which much of the most sophisticated new work appears, although they sometimes read the books. Indeed, in Great Britain, the reviewing of women's history has increasingly been colonized by the few men who have chosen to write on women themselves. In the September, 1988, issue of the *Historical Journal*, no fewer than 16 works on European women's history, many of them substantial and covering a wide range of topics and countries, were dismissed by a male reviewer in five pages. Male reviewers also clearly favor work that is firmly grounded in good empirical research, but which eschews theory. One of the best recently received works has been that of Pat Hollis (1987), who skillfully unravelled the complexity of the local government franchise and politics, mounting an impressive task of recovery involving the histories of some 300 women who were active in late nineteenth and early twentieth century local government. However, she did not choose to engage in the current vigorous debates about women's political culture and the sources of women's authority, or to use any of the recent thinking of feminist historians about the nature of the relationship between public and private and about gender as a category for historical analysis. In the view of a male reviewer in the *Times Literary Supplement* (Martin Pugh, 1989), the work of Hollis is to be regarded as real history, whereas the work of Scott, with which many feminists may disagree, but which all would regard as being of pathbreaking significance, is sidelined. Fortunately, this could not happen in the United States, where after all, Scott (1986) was accorded the lead article in the *American Historical Review* for a piece on gender as a category in historical analysis. But history in Britain is still a very establishment-dominated discipline and increasingly, in common with most social sciences and humanities, peopled by those trained traditionally and unwilling to change. Cuts in government funding to universities have seriously affected recruitment, with the result that the number of people under the age of 30 in university departments can literally be counted on the fingers of two hands. It is hard enough for women to get hired in any circumstances, virtually impossible in the ones that prevail today, and there are therefore very few within the academy to rattle the complacent view of the profession's male leadership. In Britain, there are only three university centers for Women's Studies, although the polytechnics do considerably better. It is relatively difficult for young feminist historians to find supervisors and even examiners for their dissertations.

CHANGING APPROACHES

It is in this context that the new emphasis within feminist history on the importance of gender becomes important. One of the reasons for the poor receptions by some male historians of Joan Scott's major theoretical contribution on the subject may be because it sets out to use gender as a tool for integrating the study of women into history. Once gender is recognized as a fundamental organizing principle, it becomes impossible to ghettoize the study of gender in the same way as work on women. Indeed, we have already seen an instance of this with Leonore Davidoff and Catherine Hall's study of the middle class (1986). Moving beyond the public–private divide in their focus on the gendered nature of class formation, they have shown that the career of the middle-class man who sought to be "someone" in the world of business cannot be understood without reference to the networks of private familial and female support in which he was socially embedded and which underpinned his rise in the public sphere.

The approach advocated by Scott also proposes a definition of gender—as knowledge about sexual difference—that is in sympathy with poststructuralist analysis. Such an approach raises additional issues in terms of first, a shift in women's history away from its most valued preoccupations during the 1970s with consciousness and experience, and second, the nature of feminist history's relationship with feminist politics. During the 1970s, whether prioritizing explanations based on patriarchy or capitalism, feminist historians were committed to reconstructing female experience. To this end, considerable use was made of oral history as a means of discovering the inarticulate world of women's lives as wives and mothers. Consciousness of women's lives in the past fed consciousness about women's position in the present. It may be argued that both methodologically and in terms of its (limited) effect on the writing of history more generally, this approach was no longer making waves by the 1980s. The perception was certainly that intellectual excitement now centered much more on the world of literary criticism and textual analysis. Scott's application of some of the methods now familiar in literary criticism to history has reinvigorated feminist debate. She insists that "the story is no longer about what has happened to men and women and how they responded, instead it is about how the subjective and collective meanings of women and men as categories of identity have been constructed" (1988, p. 6). It is not easy overnight to accept that history cannot document lived reality and that because experience enfolds cultural concepts, the meaning of these, rather than experience, must become the focus of analysis with the result that we can study only epistemological categories and not objective realities. In terms of writing history the need to answer the crucial question of how hierarchies such as gender are constructed and legitimized does much to justify Scott's approach. The benefits for feminist politics are less clear.

In a recent U.S. court case brought by the Equal Employment Opportunity Commission (EEOC) against Sears Roebuck and Company, in which the latter was charged with discriminating against women in the hiring of sales commission workers, two women's historians were called to give evidence, Alice Kessler Harris for the EEOC and Barbara Rosenberg for Sears. Rosenberg grounded her evidence firmly in the idea that women were equal-but-different. Kessler Harris tended towards a position that stressed equality-with-men, although her presentation was considerably more nuanced than this, emphasizing the degree to which historically there has been variety in the work which women have done. This did not find favor with the judge, who praised Rosenberg's evidence as the more lucid and coherent. [See Jane Jaquette, this volume.] Scott's approach to this distressing episode is first to point out quite rightly the difficulties that feminism has always had in reconciling equality and difference and the impossibility of being presented with such a dichotomous choice. Her solution is to insist that equality inheres in differences, but as Jane Caplan (1989) commented, it is not clear what a politics of differences would look like in practice. How would it differ from pluralism? Denise Riley (1988) reaches a somewhat different conclusion at the end of her recent exploration of the category of "women" in history. She favors a more pragmatic approach whereby feminism calls on a collective identity while being aware of the differences among "women" so that, for example, feminists can deny the neoclassical economists' contention that "women workers" "choose" low-status, low-paid work, thereby denying that the grouping "women workers" has necessary and sufficient validity, but still leaving room for the argument that for some purposes they must be distinguished from all workers. The problem is that this was the very tack that muddied Kessler Harris's argument in the eyes of the judge. It is not yet clear that the new departures in feminist historians' conceptualization of their work will make it any easier than before for feminist activists to find an effective voice.

HOW FAR, HOW FAST?

It seems from the outside that other disciplines, notably sociology, anthropology, and literary criticism, have made greater strides than history in accepting gender as crucial concept for analysis. Women's history has sold a lot of books but it remains on the periphery of the male historical establishment's vision. It is sometimes tempting not to worry about this—feminist historians have produced extremely interesting work, drawing on the theoretical insights of feminist theory and of feminist work in other disciplines—and maybe this is the way forward. Separatism can be attractive, but it will not achieve a fundamental shift in the way history is written, nor will it necessarily secure a place for younger women in the academic world, although there is much more to be said professionally for women's caucuses and committees. In Britain, women members of the Economic History Society have just set up such a group, almost 20 years after the Berkshire Conference on the History of Women was reconstituted in the United States. The integration of women within history and the historical profession is, I think, crucial, but "professionalization" does raise issues about the relationship between women's history and the women's movement. When I returned to the Berkshire Conference in the mid-1980s, I was saddened by some of the ways in which women's history signalled that it had "arrived" in American academic life—it had become as important to find a female patron as it had used to be to find a male one. Historical work was largely devoured by the women's movement of the 1970s. The new departures signalled by the use of gender and deconstruction have reinvigorated debate among feminist historians, but in insisting on the study of epistemological categories and in moving away from the preoccupations with consciousness and collective identity that feminism shared with the Left, ways of inserting the results of such work firmly back into feminist politics are not so clear.

BIBLIOGRAPHY

Caplan, Jane. (1989, January 9/16). Gender is everywhere. *Nation*, pp. 62–65.

Davies, Natalie Zemon. (1975–1976, Winter). Women's history in transition: The European case. *Feminist Studies. 3*, 88–103.

Davidoff, Leonore & Hall, Catherine. (1986). *Family fortunes.* London: Hutchinson.

Gordon, Linda. (1977). *Woman's body, woman's right.* New York: Viking Penguin.

Hinton, James. (1973). *The first shop stewards movement.* London: Allen and Unwin.

Hollis, Pat. (1987). *Ladies elect.* Oxford: Oxford University Press.

Hufton, Olwen. (1971). Women in revolution, 1789–1796. *Past and Present, 53*, 90–108.

Kaluzynska, Eva. (1980). Wiping the floor with theory—A survey of writings on housework. *Feminist Studies,* 6.

Kelly, Joan. (1984). *Women, history and theory.* Chicago: University of Chicago Press.

Leavitt, Judith Walzer. (1980, Autumn). Birth and anaesthesia: The debate over twilight sleep. *Signs, 6,* 147–164.

Lewis, Jane. (1980). *The politics of motherhood: Child and maternal welfare in England 1900–1989.* London: Croom Helm.

Lewis, Jane. (1991). *Women and social action in late Victorian and Edwardian England.* Cheltenham: Edward Elgar.

Lown, Judy. (1989). *With free and graceful step.* Oxford: Polity Press.

MacLaren, Angus. (1978). *Birth control in nineteenth century England.* London: Croom Helm.

Macmillan, James. (1988, September). European women and women's history. *Historical Journal, 31,* 745–751.

Milkman, Ruth. (1987). *Gender at work.* Chicago: University of Illinois Press.

More, Charles. (1980). *Skill and the English working class 1870–1914.* London: Croom Helm.

Osterud, Nancy Grey. (1986). Gender dividions and the organisation of work in the Leicestershire hosiery industry. In Angela V. John (Ed.), *Women's employment in England 1800–1918* (pp. 65–70). Oxford: Blackwells.

Pugh, Martin. (1989). Self-defeating efforts. *Times Literary Supplement,* 27/1–2/2, 83.

Riley, Denise. (1988). *"Am I that name?" Feminism and the category of "women" in history.* Minneapolis: University of Minnesota.

Rowbotham, Sheila. (1973). *Hidden from history.* London: Pluto Press.

Scott, Joan. (1986). Gender: A useful category for historical analysis. *American Historical Review, 91,* 1053–1075.

Scott, Joan. (1988). *Gender and the politics of history.* New York: Columbia University Press.

Taylor, Barbara and Phillips, Ann. (1980). Sex and skill. *Feminist Studies, 6,* 79–88.

Chapter 14

The Impact of Feminism on the Natural Sciences

Marian Lowe

Women working in various scientific disciplines in the late 1960s began developing feminist ideas, just as women in other fields did. However, the role of feminism in the natural sciences has evolved raher differently from its role in the social sciences and the humanities. While feminism has probably not changed the dominant perspective of any of the disciplines, at least in a number of the humanities and social sciences feminists have created niches in which to reexamine and begin to recreate assumptions and methodologies. Alternative ways to practice sociology, anthropology, or literary criticism, for example, based on feminist scholarship are available within the boundaries of the professions. With two notable exceptions, the same thing has not happened in the natural sciences. A number of people, primarily women scientists, have had some success in understanding why women do not enter science and engineering and helping to change this circumstance. However, the disciplines themselves are largely untouched.

The difficulty in affecting the natural sciences arises from their special position. Since the seventeenth century, scientific rationalism has defined what we accept as reality. It organizes our way of viewing the universe, our place in it and even our images of gender. The largely unconscious world view that science provides is so pervasive that most of us, if we consider the matter at all, assume it is not only a correct one but also the only possible one. It is held to be independent of society and history, unaffected by the characteristics of individual scientists. For those who hold these beliefs, and this includes most scientists, feminism can clearly have nothing to say about science. Thus, no niches have been carved out for alternative feminist scholarship in fields such as chemistry, physics, or most of biology and at this point it is far from clear even what the basis of such scholarship might be.

This is not to say that feminists have had nothing to say about the natural sciences. Feminists, both scientists and nonscientists, have created two areas of feminist scholarship and practice: in women's reproductive biology within medical science [see Renate Klein, this volume] and in behavioral studies in biology. More recently, critical examinations of the social origins of scientific knowledge and the interactions of gender with the foundations of contemporary science have appeared. However, this work has come largely from the outside, from historians, philosophers and sociologists of science. In some cases, the critics have had training in one of the scientific disciplines and have even been practicing scientists, but their critique of science has come when they have put themselves in the position of outside observer. This is quite different from the way feminist scholarship has developed in the social sciences and humanities and reflects both the strength of scientific orthodoxy and the small number of women, let alone feminists, within the natural sciences.

It is noteworthy that the two main areas of feminist research that have developed within the natural sciences have both been in the life sciences, where gender is an important attribute. These feminist research areas are also ones that have direct effects on women's lives. Furthermore, the greater number of women scientists working in the life sciences has made a stronger feminist voice possible there. In spite of this, however, basic research priorities even in biology have not been affected by feminism.

Below, I will give a summary of the evolution of feminist projects in and about the sciences and then suggest directions for future work. While assessing this description of the role of feminism in the sciences, keep in mind both the rigidity of conventional scientific thinking and the lack of numbers to provide support for alternatives.

WOMEN'S PARTICIPATION IN SCIENCE

In the late 1960s, as the feminist movement began to develop, women scientists, particularly in the United States, began to be concerned about the fact that they were usually few and far between. It is not that women had not noticed this before, but the observation took on new significance with the appearance of the women's movement. At the beginning of the 1970s in the United States, women made up about 9% of all scientists and engineers, ranging from less than 1% of engineers and about 4% of physicists to about 15% of biologists (National Science Foundation, 1986). The situation in other countries with substantial scientific work-forces varied in detail, but overall was similar. Furthermore, women's position was considerably worse than these figures indicate, because most women were concentrated in the lower ranks of each field. In the highly visible and prestigious research positions, women constituted a tiny handful (J. R. Cole, 1981; Linda Dix, 1987; Lilli Hornig, 1984).

The situation in chemistry, the largest of the physical sciences, is instructive. The schools in the United States that offered a doctorate in chemistry in 1972 had a total faculty of about 4,000. Of these, an estimated 50 women, just over 1%, had the rank of assistant professor or above. The top five departments in chemistry, which granted about 7% of their Ph.D.s to women, had no women faculty. The numbers were somewhat better in the biological sciences, but women were still a distinct minority. In all scientific fields women were largely outside the informal structures and networks that integrate people into a discipline and allow them to prosper.

Widespread recognition developed among women scientists that a problem existed, while a token response came from male colleagues. Most of them, both women and men, however, saw no real inconsistency between the overwhelming predominance of men in science and the claim that scientific fact should be independent of the observer. Many men made the assumption that women simply were not capable of doing science. Masculine characteristics defined the norm and women were seen as defective. Feminists countered with the assumption that women had the same potential for success in scientific careers as men, but sexism and faulty socialization were barriers (Ana Berta Chepelinski, Marian Lowe, Nancy Tooney, & Martha Verbrugge, 1972; Violet Haas & Carolyn Perucci, 1984; Sue Rosser, 1988; Alice Rossi, 1965; Naomi Weisstein, 1970). The problem was not just outright discrimination (although that existed), but also that girls were socialized so that they turned away from science and, according to some, did not develop the proper personality for it. The male definition of the norm for doing successful science was implicitly accepted. Hence, most of the strategies to increase women's participation in science have amounted to trying to make women act and appear more like men.

Feminist scientists have used a number of different tactics to make scientific careers accessible to women and at the same time to educate male colleagues: publication of statistics; studies of attitudes of girls and boys toward science; studies of teachers' behavior in science classrooms; support for enforcement of affirmative action; formation of women's groups in professional organizations as well as formation of separate professional organizations; fellowships to make women scientists more visible; various pilot projects for increasing girls' interest in science and for changing mathematics and science education for them (L. H. Fox, L. Brody, & E. Tobin 1980; Janet Buter Kahle, 1985; Shirley Malcolm, 1983). We should note that these projects were taking place at a time when women's participation in public life and particularly in wage labor was changing dramatically. However, science has appeared to be particularly resistant to women entering.

By the end of the 1980s, in the United States the overall participation of women had risen to 13% of the total in science and engineering and the percentage of women among those just entering the fields was considerably higher. However, it is important to note that the proportion of women as a group who got degrees of all kinds in this period went up even more rapidly, so that the proportion of women who entered the natural sciences rather than the humanities or the social sciences actually went down for a time in 1970s.

By many criteria, women are currently somewhat better integrated into the scientific community than they were in the early 1970s. However, this integration is tenuous, at best. In the United States, for example, women do not receive tenure at the same rate as their male colleagues, so that the wave of women who entered research positions in the late 1970s and 1980s may be receding (Harriet Zuckerman, 1987). Furthermore, the percentage of females going into science appears to have peaked in the last few years and may be going down (B. Vetter & E. Babco, 1986; William LeBold, 1987). A continuing problem is that scientific careers are still widely seen as appropriately male professions, requiring stereotypically masculine intellectual and personality traits. Thus, women scientists to some extent still must have two different identities—as female and as scientist. The psychic cost of a career in science can be high for women, because being both a women and a scientist involves a conflict between two sets of characteristics seen as mutually exclusive.

THE HISTORY OF WOMEN IN SCIENCE

A companion project to the attempts to lower barriers for women in science has been historical and biographical studies of women scientists (Louis Bucciarelli & Nancy Dworsky, 1980; Vivian Gornick, 1983; Evelyn Fox Keller, 1983; Ann Hibner Koblitz, 1983; Olga Opfell, 1978; Elizabeth Patterson, 1983; Ann Sayre, 1975). Biographies of prominent women scientists provide evidence that at least some women have made major contributions to science, although the numbers are few.

A number of feminists have faulted this approach for obscuring problems due to gender by reinforcing the idea that the history of science is the history of exceptional individuals, now including some women. However, it seems to be inevitable that even when authors do not focus on gender issues, these appear when the subject is women in science. Indirectly, these studies have served to illuminate the position of science as a social institution and particularly its interrelationship with gender.

Several studies have aimed at trying to understand the context in which women scientists developed and worked in earlier periods (Pnina Abir-am & Dorinda Outram, 1987; Margaret Rossiter, 1982). Rossiter's work has provided important information on the interactions of science and gender in nineteenth century America by studying the ways in which women practiced science and the mechanisms that either limited them or exlcuded them from scientific professions. It is instructive—and rather chastening—to find from her work that many of the twentieth century projects designed to increase the number of women in science are much the same as those used by women during the nineteenth century for the same purposes.

The collection by Abir-am and Outram looks at a wide range of women scientists and particularly asks how the distinction between the public and private realms, which developed at the same time as our scientific institutions, has affected the participation of women in science. The kind of work displayed in this volume uses the insights of other feminist historical work to illuminate studies of women scientists.

CRITIQUES OF BIOLOGICAL DETERMINISM

In the late 1960s, behavioral scientists propounded a number of theories trying to show how sex differences had evolved in humans. At the same time, others claimed that the observed difference in the average IQ between blacks and whites was due to genetic differences. By the early 1970s biologists had joined in, with theories that attempted to demonstrate that differences in behavior in women and men, black and whites or the rich and the poor had a biological basis. The list of biological candidates produced by various studies is long and has included most possible differences in brain structure and functioning and a wide array of hormonal differences. The most influential of these theories has proven to be a theory, sociobiology, that takes most of its material from evolutionary biology (E. O. Wilson, 1975). The theories have not remained academic curiosities, because the media has shown a tremendous appetite for stories about such claims of biological determinism. Both feminism and changes in women's roles had made work on sex differences interesting again after 50 years of disregard.

When theories about biological determinism began to reappear, women in biology and a number of other disciplines in both the natural and social sciences immediately became concerned about what the creators of these theories were saying about the origins of sex differences in behavior. A large critical body of work now exists examining the methodology of a number of the theories (Lynda Birke, 1986; Ruth Bleier, 1983; Anne Fausto-Sterling, 1985; Elizabeth Fee, 1986; Ruth Hubbard & Marian Lowe, 1979; Marian Lowe & Ruth Hubbard, 1983; Janet Sayers, 1982; Stephanie Schields, 1975). Different writers have pointed to the way that scientists' beliefs, particularly gender bias, have influenced the conclusions that they draw, because those theories that justify social inequities such as sexism and racism are more likely to be accepted than other theories derived from the same observations. Other researchers have examined the history of such theories and their work has given additional support to the idea that a political component exists to this supposedly objective scientific work. In fact, analyses of the development and dissemination of biological determinist theories make good case studies for demonstrating the role of science in the creation of ideology about women's nature.

A disturbing trend has been the appearance of a number of feminist versions of bio-deterministic theories in response to sociobiology and other works. Alternative evolutionary and hormonal theories have appeared. In addition, results from works on brain lateralization have been widely adopted, with a left brain versus right brain dichotomy identified with male versus female thinking. These ideas attempt to counter the stories of mainstream biological determinists which accept the male stereotype as the norm and devalue women. They attempt instead to assert the legitimacy of the cultures and values that are typical of women's worlds. These theories, however, have no better basis than any of the others.

As the critiques of biological determinist theories developed, feminists began questioning whether any work on gender could be objective. The further suspicion began to appear that perhaps all of biology was affected by ideas about gender and therefore by extension, was not objective. These were the same kinds of concerns that were then being raised by feminists in the social sciences. Thus, the studies of biological determinism have been important in leading feminists to think about the social nature of scientific inquiry. However, it is not clear what effect, if any, feminist critics have had on mainstream work on sex differences.

REPRODUCTION AND THE WOMEN'S HEALTH MOVEMENT

At the same time that women scientists were calling attention to the lack of women in the natural sciences and critics of the emerging biological determinist theories were pointing out the effects of gender bias, women began to take up questions concerning reproduction and women's health. Abortion rights was one of the first major causes of the women's movement and quickly led to questioning of the medical profession, mostly by women who were neither scientists nor doctors. Women felt that medical knowledge was incomplete and biased where reproduction and women's health were concerned and set about filling the gaps. In doing so, they developed a different kind of knowledge about medical phenomena from that supplied by medical science. This challenge to medical expertise is exemplified by the collectively created handbook, *Our Bodies Ourselves* (Boston Women's Health Collective, 1984). [See Joan Mulligan; and Carole Ogelsby and Christine Shelton, this volume.]

By the mid-1970s feminists had constructed critiques of this particular form of supposedly rational knowledge—scientific medicine. Not only was current knowledge in medicine seen as gender-laden, but feminists began tracing the historical roots as well (Barbara Ehrenreich & Deidre English, 1979; Carroll Smith-Rosenberg & Charles Rosenberg, 1973). This work challenged the objectivity of the medical knowledge produced by male experts. Feminists suggested that it was distorted by male prejudice and, further, that feminism offered a better, more rational scientific thought.

The contribution of the work on reproduction and women's health to the feminist analysis of science has been immense. It has offered alternative visions of how science might be practiced and has illuminated many aspects of the politics of science. However, its role as exemplar of an alternative feminist science (Rita Arditti, Renate Duelli Klein, & Shelly Minden, 1984; Anne Fausto-Sterling, 1985; Karen Messing, 1983) is necessarily limited. The scientific research is focussed directly on humans and gender is explicit in the subject matter. Both of these factors have particular effects on the design of research procedures and the role played by the experimenter. Thus, the outlines of a feminist research program in reproduction and women's health cannot be generalized even to the rest of biology, much less to the physical sciences.

GENDER AND SCIENCE: FEMINIST
SCIENCE AND EPISTEMOLOGIES

All of the threads of feminist work in the sciences have led to a recognition that science is a social product and to a questioning of the foundations of science. Given the role of science in defining our reality these are profound questions. If scientific fact is a product of a particular society and affected by the social framework of the scientists producing the knowledge, then how do we know what we know? What is reality? What is objective knowledge? These are the kinds of questions that were part of the development of contemporary science and they have now reappeared.

Feminists have not been alone in questioning the idea of science as independent of the society and of those who generate scientific knowledge. Others, also rejecting the value neutrality of science, have looked at the degree to which science is permeated by ideas of domination and have questioned the idea of one true reality (Paul Feyerabend, 1975; Boris Hessen, 1971; Thomas Kuhn, 1970; William Leiss, 1972; Edgar Zilsel, 1942). Feminists have added the recognition that gender is one of the basic components of our mental framework and as such must affect the production of all scientific knowledge. Feminist work on specific questions has eventually led to the idea that masculinity and science are in some way strongly connected.

The first full-blown examination of the way gender might be embedded in science came in studies of the scientific revolution (Brian Easlea, 1981; Carolyn Merchant, 1980). Merchant's work identified the distinguishing characteristic of science as domination, originating in male traits. She looked both at the way men treated women and the way they treated nature and concluded that the scientific revolution of the sixteenth and seventeenth centuries was part of a triumph of masculinity over both women and nature. As a result, the characteristics of men and of science are now the same.

Others have suggested that the historical interrelationship between science and gender was somewhat more complicated than the work by Merchant and others indicates (Marian Lowe, 1990; Maureen McNeil, 1987). Our contemporary ideas of masculinity were themselves shaped in part by characteristics needed for the science that appeared with the scientific revolution. Furthermore, science emerged from a complex of material conditions, of which gender relations are just one part. The relations of a capitalist economy need to be considered, as well.

Object relations theorists also have identified the origins of the domination that marks scientific practice in masculine behavior (Nancy Chodorow, 1978; Evelyn Fox Keller, 1984). They see the development of an urge to dominate as characteristic of males but not females, because of differences on boys' and girls' relationships to their mothers.

The work based on object relations is presented as a universalizing theory, but has been criticized as culture laden. Several authors have observed that the characteristics attributed to gender differences in our culture change both historically and cross culturally. [See Mary Roth Walsh, this volume.] Even within our culture social identities are much more complex than is suggested simply by gender and the interrelationship between creating knowledge and social identity is similarly complex. Thus, the causal links suggested by object relations theorists simply do not hold.

A number of writers have suggested that a science developed by females would be very different. A distinctive feminist science would arise from distinctive female experiences (Rita Arditti, 1980; Ruth Bleier, 1983; Anne Fausto-Sterling, 1985; Elizabeth Fee, 1981; Evelyn Fox Keller, 1984). This "standpoint" position says that women (or feminists) will have a different, and according to most, a truer view of nature and of our relationship to it, because of women's identity as a group. This alternative science is possible, but has not been developed by men because of the dualities and limitations imposed by the dominant, rigid masculine gender role, which is tied to male domination and privilege. Several writers using a Marxist framework have come to similar conclusions about the possibility of a more valid science arising from women's experiences, but ground it in the material conditions of women's lives (Nancy Harstock, 1983; Hilary Rose, 1986).

The point is made by several feminists (Elizabeth Fee, 1986; Sandra Harding, 1986; Marian Lowe, 1990) that in order to understand science we must understand its relationship to power. The social institutions of gender and science interact through their relationship to power, as does science with other social institutions, such as race. Scientific knowledge is a result of, and a reflection of, the power relations in the culture within which it developed. Science looks masculine because males have power and because science is a tool of power, but for the same reasons science also looks white, European, and bourgeois. Thus, for example, attempts to try to understand why there are few women scientists can be only partially successful if the focus remains purely on women and not on power relations in all of their manifestations.

WHERE DO WE GO FROM HERE?

Attempts to formulate a new, feminist epistemology based on analyses of how gender affects knowledge often result in theories that paint a large picture, but are difficult to pin down in details. We clearly need to develop our epistemological notions further. At the same time we need to begin to connect our rather abstract theorizing with the real world and real problems. To begin with, we need to understand better just how science is affected by social factors, not only in areas that are directly connected with gender but in those which are not. I suggest that we begin to analyze the way both power and ideas about gender help to construct our current body of knowledge and the way it is used. As a part of this program, we need to examine specific cases that demonstrate the cultural and political nature of objective knowledge.

Objectivity is a slippery concept. It usually is used to refer to the ability to acquire value-free knowledge or some kind of absolute truth. In reality, objectivity is a cultural creation of those with power within a given field. Questions about the world are clearly determined by social values, within, of course, the framework of the current development of theory and the available data base. Answers to these questions can be better or worse (more on this a little later) and to that extent one can speak of objectivity. However, abstract objectivity does not exist. When we try to compare the validity of knowledge created by two different groups, we find that we are not really comparing the same thing. Groups with different points of view will have different aims in seeking knowledge and different criteria for what constitutes a "better" or successful answer to a question. Inevitably they will need to know different things in order to meet these criteria. Thus, scientific knowledge is shaped by the reason one has for acquiring it. It is particular.

Only when one group is dominant, as is now the case, can we have the illusion of one true picture of reality. This group defines the questions and the criteria used to judge answers to those questions. By their criteria, any other point of view is not objective. When no dominant group exists, different views of world may exist simultaneously, each providing objective information.

This is not relativism, but a matter of politics. The questions that a scientist asks and the constraints on what kinds of answers will be accepted as valid are determined by a particular social point of view. However, within those constraints, "better" and "worse" do exist. The actual answers to questions do depend on the world out there and should correspond to it. Depending on the degree of correspondence, then, what a given scientist finds may be more or less objective.

In assessing this objectivity we need to recognize that a strict dichotomy between socially determined questions and scientifically objective answers does not exist. Besides the constraints on what is acceptable as evidence, further limitations arise from prevailing social beliefs. Real scientists inform their work with the same assumptions, values, and attitudes that underlie the rest of their lives. The idea of an impartial observer is nonsense. Standards of objectivity that prevail in any branch of science at any given time are not absolute, but are determined by the internal and external politics of the scientific community.

One of the most unsettling implications of this view of objectivity is that we must give up certainty. Since Descartes, science has been seen as the source of certain knowledge about the natural world, untainted by human culture. However, we now encounter indications that no such thing is possible. This is not to say that we must accept the validity of all points of view. Instead we must develop ways of assessing the limitations on our understanding.

Our intuitive feeling is that a real world exists out there and that some answers to a given question are better than others. We have reason to believe this. Because of knowledge acquired over the last three or four centuries, the reality is that we can make new organisms and new chemicals. Birth control pills do keep women from getting pregnant. We can find out, in the face of doctor's claims to the contrary, that fetal monitors do not cut the rate of infant mortality. Genetic engineering does allow the expression of genes to be modified and $E = mc^2$ is close enough to reality that it leads to nuclear weapons. But this reality now exists because someone asked particular questions for particular reasons.

In order to evaluate data or a theory, we need to be absolutely clear what question is being asked and why it is being asked. We need to know who did the work and for whom. With this knowledge, we will have some idea of the ways the observer will affect the observation, recognizing that one can try to minimize the observer effect, but can not eliminate it. The most important factor, perhaps, is who stands to gain by particular findings.

In our present society the results of almost all modern scientific research are selectively far more useful to large, wealthy organizations than they are to ordinary people (Brian Martin, 1979). Science is concerned with providing profit for these organizations, solving military problems or providing social stability, so that there is no threat to the established social order. The process of defining scientific research and setting standards of objectivity results in standards that systematically favor these results.

Biochemists, for example, are unlikely to have considered the environmental consequences of molecules created for the drug industry, would not feel responsible for environmental problems they caused even if they knew about them, and would refuse to consider the morality of making a particular molecule, regardless of its intended use. They are working within a framework of domination of nature and they have successfully solved a problem even when they develop molecules that often directly or indirectly disrupt the environment. Interaction with the environment is just not defined to be part of the problem and by the standards of their field they are doing objective science. In fact, if they were to decide on moral grounds that a particularly offensive product should not be made, they would be acting in a nonobjective way. These standards allow scientists to develop new profitable products or techniques without any social responsibility and allow external control of the directions of scientific research.

We can expect sciences developed by feminists to be different from present-day science, just as a science developed by a group of working class men would be or a science developed by a group of American Indians. Just how different depends on the political programs of the groups. Feminists and other progressive movements have a number of different aims: a commitment to social change rather than social stability, redistribution of wealth, egalitarian social relations, integrating public and private life, doing away with expertise as it currently exists, and protecting the environment [See Irene Diamond, this volume.] Different kinds of questions clearly flow out of these concerns, but all of them have to do with changing power relationships. We can begin to see different kinds of research priorities emerging, which will likely bring with them new methods and organizations of work. Thus, even though they must necessarily be tentative, discussions of new, alternative science need to be grounded firmly in a political program.

Much of the feminist political program already implies that science should be transformed into an enquiry compatible with environmental integrity and egalitarian human relations. Various programs to develop alternatives based on these principles exist around the world. One approach to a feminist alternative in an applied area is a Canadian project to involve users in the design and development of a computer network. If this project, which is in its beginning stages, is to be successful, it needs not only the development of nonhierarchical relationships, but also the design and development of distinct technologies (Margaret Lowe Benston, 1988).

Developing a new scientific base is a formidable intellectual and political challenge. Our current scientific perspective is so embedded in our ways of knowing that it is difficult even to conceive of an alternative. Feminist perspectives exploring the roles of power and gender in shaping science offer the best starting point, at present, for developing an understanding of science that will help us transform it into a less destructive, less limited model of the world, but they are only a beginning. We need both scientists and nonscientists committed to understanding science as a social creation and to reshaping it. However, it is proving to be extremely difficult for feminists to manage a conventional career in science while carrying out feminist analyses of it. In the social sciences and humanities, feminist analyses have come primarily from feminists within the disciplines. In the physical sciences, the incompatibility of scientific and social analyses shifts feminist critiques outside these disciplines, so that women in the physical sciences cannot integrate the practice of science and the practice of feminism. Even trying to function separately is very difficult, because the perspectives of science and feminism clash. This difficulty is a measure of the magnitude of the problem facing us.

BIBLIOGRAPHY

Abir-am, Pnina & Outram, Dorinda. (Eds.). (1987). *Uneasy careers and intimate lives.* New Brunswick: Rutgers University Press.

Arditti, Rita. (1980). Feminism and science. In R. Arditti, P. Brennan & S. Cavrak (Eds.) *Science and liberation.* Boston: South End Press.

Arditti, Rita, Klein, Renate Duelli & Minden, Shelly. (Eds.). (1984). *Test-tube women,* London: Pandora Press.

Benston, Margaret Lowe. (1988a). Feminism and system design: Questions of control. In W. Tomm (Ed.), *The effects of feminist approaches on research methodologies.* Toronto: Wilfred Laurier Press.

Benston, Margaret Lowe. (1988b). Women's voices/Men's voices: Technology as language. In Cheris Kramarae (Ed.), *Technology and women's voices.* New York: Routledge & Kegan Paul.

Birke, Lynda. (1986). *Women, feminism and biology.* New York: Methuen.

Bleier, Ruth. (1983). *Science and gender.* Elmsford, NY: Pergamon Press.

Boston Women's Health Collective. (1984). *The new our bodies ourselves: A health book by and for women.* New York: Simon & Schuster.

Bucciarelli, Louis & Dworsky, Nancy. (1980). *Sophie Germaine: An essay in the history of the theory of elasticity.* Dordrecht: Reidel.

Chepelinski, Ana Berta, Lowe, Marian, Tooney, Nancy, & Verbrugge, Martha. (1972, July). Women in chemistry: Part of the 51% minority. *Science for the People,* 10–17.

Chodorow, Nancy. (1978). *The reproduction of mothering.* Berkeley: University of California Press.

Cole, J. R. (1981). Women in science. *American Scientist, 69,* 385–391.

Dix, Linda. (Ed.). (1987). *Women: Their underrepresentation and career differentials in science and engineering.* Washington, DC: National Academy Press.

Easlea, Brian. (1981). *Science and sexual oppression: Patriarchy's confrontation with women and nature.* London: Widenfeld & Nicolson.

Ehrenreich, Barbara & English, Deirdre. (1979). *For her own good: 150 years of the experts advice to women.* New York: Doubleday.

Fausto-Sterling, Anne. (1985). *Myths of gender.* New York: Basic Books.

Fee, Elizabeth. (1979). Nineteenth century craniology: The study of the female skull. *Bulletin of the History of Medicine, 53,* 415–433.

Fee, Elizabeth. (1981). Is feminism a threat to scientific objectivity? *International Journal of Women's Studies 4,* 213–233.

Fee, Elizabeth. (1986). Critiques of modern science: The relationship of feminism to other radical epistemologies. In Ruth Bleier (Ed.), *Feminist approaches to science.* Elmsford, NY: Pergamon Press.

Feyerabend, Paul. (1975). *Against method.* London: NLB.

Fox, L. H., Brody, L., Tobin, D. (Eds.). (1980). *Women and the mathematical mystique.* Baltimore: Johns Hopkins University Press.

Gornick, Vivian. (1983). *Women in science: Portraits from a world in transition.* New York: Simon & Schuster.

Harding, Sandra. (1986). *The science question in feminism.* Ithaca: Cornell University Press.

Hartsock, Nancy. (1983). The feminist standpoint: Developing the ground for a specifically feminist historical materialism. In S. Harding & M. Hintikka (Eds.), *Discovering reality: Feminist perspectives on epistemology, metaphysics, methodology and philosophy of science.* Dordrecht: Reidel.

Haas, Violet & Perucci, Carolyn. (Eds.). (1984). *Women in scientific and engineering professions.* Ann Arbor: University of Michigan Press.

Hessen, Boris. (1971). *The economic roots of Newton's principia.* New York: Howard Fertig.

Hornig, Lilli. (1984). Women in science and engineering: Who so few? *Technology Review, 87,* 29–41.

Hubbard, Ruth & Lowe, Marian. (Eds.). (1979). *Genes and gender II: Pitfalls in research on sex and gender.* New York: Gordian Press.

Kahle, Janet Butler. (Ed.). (1985). *Women in science.* Philadelphia: Falmer Press.

Keller, Evelyn Fox. (1983). *A feeling for the organism.* San Francisco: Freeman.

Keller, Evelyn Fox. (1984). *Reflections on gender and science.* New Haven, CT: Yale University Press.

Koblitz, Ann Hibner. (1983). *A convergence of lives, Sofia Kovalevskia: Scientist, writer, revolutionary.* Boston: Birkhauser.

Kuhn, Thomas. (1970). *The structure of scientific revolutions* (2nd ed.). Chicago: University of Chicago Press.

LeBold, William. (1987). Women in engineering and science: An undergraduate research perspective. In L. Dix (Ed)., *Women: Their underrepresentation and career differentials in science and engineering.* Washington, DC: National Academy Press.

Leiss, William. (1972). *The domination of nature.* Boston: Beacon Press.

Lowe, Marian & Hubbard, Ruth. (Eds.). (1983). *Woman's nature: Rationalizations of inequality.* Elmsford, NY: Pergamon Press.

Lowe, Marian. (1990). *The foundations of science and gender in contemporary culture.* In preparation.

Malcolm, Shirley. (1983). *An assessment of programs that facilitate increased access and achievement of female and minorities in K-12 mathematics and science education.* Washington, DC: AAAS.

Martin, Brian. (1979). *The bias of science.* Marrickville, Australia: Southwood Press.

McNeil, Maureen. (1987). Being reasonable feminists. In M. McNeil (Ed.), *Gender and expertise.* London: Free Association Books.

Messing, Karen. (1983). The scientific mystique: Can a white lab coat guarantee purity in the search for knowledge about the nature of women? In M. Lowe and R. Hubbard (Eds.), *Woman's nature: Rationalizations of inequality.* Elmsford, NY: Pergamon Press.

Merchant, Carolyn. (1980). *The death of nature.* San Francisco: Harper & Row.

Mosedale, S. S. (1978). Science corrupted: Victorian biologists consider "The Woman Question." *Journal of the History of Biology, 11,* 1–56.

National Science Foundation. (1986). *Women and minorities in science and engineering.* Washington, DC: U.S. Government Printing Office.

Opfell, Olga. (1978). *The lady laureates: Women who have won the Nobel Prize.* Metuchen, NJ: Scarecrow Press.

Patterson, Elizabeth. (1983). *Mary Somerville and the cultivation of science, 1815–1840.* The Hague: Nijhoff.

Rose, Hilary. (1983). Hand, brain and heart: A feminist epistemology for the natural sciences. *Signs: Journal of Women in Culture and Society, 9,* 73–90.

Rose, Hilary. (1986). Beyond masculinist realities: A feminist epistemology for the sciences. In R. Bleier, (Ed.), *Feminist approaches to science.* Elmsford, NY: Pergamon Press.

Rosser, Sue. (Ed.). (1988). *Feminism within the science and health care professions.* Elmsford, NY: Pergamon Press.

Rossi, Alice. (1965). Women in science—Why so few? *Science, 148,* 1196–1201.

Rossiter, Margaret. (1982). *Women scientists in America.* Baltimore: The Johns Hopkins University Press.

Sayers, Janet. (1982). *Biological politics: Feminist and anti-feminist perspectives.* London: Tavistock.

Sayre, Ann. (1975). *Rosalind Franklin and DNA.* New York: WW Norton.

Schields, Stephanie. (1975). Functionalism, Darwinism and the psychology of women. *American Psychologist, 30,* 739–754.

Smith-Rosenberg, Carroll & Rosenberg, Charles. (1973). The female animal: Medical and biologic views of woman and her role in nineteenth-century America. *Journal of American History, 60,* 332–356.

Vetter, B. & Babco, E. (1986). *Professional women and minorities: A manpower data resource service* (6th ed.). Washington, DC: Commission on Professionals in Science and Technology.

Weisstein, Naomi. (1970). Kinder, kuche and kirche. In R. Morgan (Ed.), *Sisterhood is powerful.* New York: Vintage Books.

Wilson, E. O. (1975). *Sociobiology: The new synthesis.* Cambridge: Harvard University Press.

Zilsel, Edgar. (1942). The sociological roots of science. *American Journal of Sociology, 47,* 312–325.

Zuckerman, Harriet. (1987). Persistence and change in the careers of men and women scientists and engineers. In L. Dix (Ed), *Women: Their underrepresentation and career differentials in science and engineering.* Washington, DC: National Academy Press.

Chapter 15

Nursing and Feminism[1]
Caring and Curing

Joan E. Mulligan

THE MORE THINGS CHANGE, THE MORE THEY REMAIN THE SAME

Nursing has been and is a little valued, underpaid, overworked health-threatening woman's occupation in which few women occupy top management positions. In the United States, changes have been taking place in the extended and expanded responsibilities carried by nurses in adult health, public health, maternal–child health and intensive care services delivered through community group medical practices (GMP) and health maintenance organizations (HMOs). These practitioners carry responsibility for management of minor acute and chronic medical problems, freeing physicians for the complex problems. In general, American nurses have a smaller domain of practice than do nurses in Great Britain and elsewhere. In the 1980s, as in the 1960s, nurses continue to air publicly their many disagreements with each other and to form specialty groups. Such activities diminish their power to influence power holders in the resolution of practice problems such as staffing and reimbursement.

Little change seems to have occurred in the past 20 years. Yet, publishing history suggests otherwise if what publishers accept reflects the market value of a discipline. Beginning in 1900 with the *American Journal of Nursing,* there are now at least 520 English language nursing journals currently published. Four American journals focus on research: *Nursing Research* (NR); *Advances in Nursing Science* (AINS); *Research in Nursing and Health* (RINH) and the *Western Journal of Nursing Research* (WINR). These four journals reflect the confidence nurses have in their ability to study their knowledge and their confidence that this knowledge defines the differences between nursing and medicine; caring and curing.

WHO PROTESTED? WHO LISTENED?

The earliest record of protest by a nurse against women's powerlessness is found in Florence Nightingale's *Cassandra* (1852). Nightingale, sanitary engineer and biostatistician but known primarily for her association with nursing (F. B. Smith, 1982), protested the waste of "women's passion, intellect, activity . . . " (p. 25) and proclaimed, "the time has come when women must do more than the 'domestic hearth' " (p. 52). The social morés of Victorian society stifled any opportunity for women's growth, except in the roles of hostess, wife, and mother. It took Nightingale 9 years of family conflict before she left home in that world to enter nurse training (Florence Nightingale, 1979, p. 11). More recently, Virginia Cleland's (1971) article drew attention to the existing sexism in nursing at a time when it was believed that attracting men to the profession would enhance the status of and increase monetary rewards for nurses. (This idea was not considered sexist.) In the same city and month that the Equal Rights Amendment (ERA) failed (Washington, DC, 1982), the *Radical Feminist Nurses Network* was born (Peggy Chinn, 1982); called *Cassandra* to acknowledge Nightingale's essay, the network was intended as a means for feminist nurses to share knowledge, initiate research and to preserve the story of nursing (Gretchen La Godna, 1982).

At best, most nurses are liberal feminists. They want equal access to the power of decision making and the reward system in their corporate world. They want recognition for caring and nurturing equal to that given for curing and repairing. Criticism in the discipline relates more to nurses' lack of power to gain power than to power distribution itself.

The publicity given to feminists who wanted to increase women's admission to medical schools served to demean the few gains enjoyed by nurses (Margaret Sandelowski, 1981, p. 159). But at the same time, nurse-authored publications drew attention to the plight of nurses. For example, Marlene Grissum and Carol Spengler (1976) examined the socialization of women to be mothers and housewives. They explored the assertion by psychologists and psychiatrists that woman's "primary motivation in life, based on her true nature, is to become a companion to a man and to become a mother" (p. 3). They examined the stereotypic roles for women and how these roles and the consequent socialization of women to be mothers and housewives impact on the socialization of female nurses in the male-dominated health care world. They used this analogy to describe a world in which the nurse is "symbolic mother" and the physician is "symbolic father" paired in nonsymbolic power imbalance. These authors challenged nurses to understand the structure of power and the use of power to gain creditability for nursing to develop a "significant social movement that could lead to important reforms and improvements within the health care system" (p. 301). The authors' plea for nurses to create a unified movement in the health care system, similar to that in the larger women's movement, remains unanswered. Denise Benton (1977), Phyllis Kritek and Laurie Glass (1978), Margaret Sandelowski (1981), Janet Muff (1982), Peggy Chinn and Charlene Wheeler (1985), and Claire Fagin and Pamela Maraldo (1988) are nurse academics who see feminist analyses as an important contribution to professional survival. Yet with the exception of the Radical Feminist Nurses' Network, no nursing organization has articulated a feminist analysis of male-dominated medical care and its consequences for nursing.

HISTORIOGRAPHY: NURSING'S PAST AND PRESENT

While the histories of women's work, and the documentation of medical abuse of women's minds and bodies burgeoned between 1960 and the mid-1980s, little attention was given nurses or their contributions to women's health. In Women's Studies programs, feminists often discriminated against this group of women while supporting the struggle of other working women. In fact, the struggle of nurses to control their practice is generally portrayed unsympathetically by feminist writers (Barbara Melosh, 1982; Susan Reverby, 1987). Jo Ann Ashley brought to her writing the perspective of an historian who was also a nurse; thus her 1976 analysis of the enduring power imbalance between nurses and physicians differs from that of others.

Although the feminist movement led to increased enrollment of women in the "male professions" and opened apprenticeships to women, the movement served the "female professions" poorly. The omission of references in feminist writings to support nursing as a valued occupation suggests feminist scholars ignored its existence. In the absence of feminist recognition, nurses' contributions to women's health are virtually invisible and the achievement of equitable economic returns made more difficult. Although helpful to individuals and small groups of nurses, the feminist movement has been harmful to the public image of nursing.

A few nurses have received public recognition. There are 27 nurses listed in *Notable American Women* (Edward T. James, Janet W. James, & Paul S. Boyer, 1971; Barbara Sicherman, Carol Green, Irene Kantrow, & Harriette Walker, 1980). Seven of these (Dix, Mahoney, Wald, Sanger, Dock, Breckenridge, & Goodrich) championed women's right to vote and to control their fertility; opposed war; worked to relieve the suffering of the poor and to educate immigrant women. They strove to improve the condition of women, children, and nurses but left traditional women's roles unchallenged. With the exception of Wilma Scott Heide, nurse and early president of the National Organization for Women (NOW) (Eleanor Haney, 1985), there is no visible passion for social justice in nursing's present leaders. That passion has been replaced by a passion for the generation of knowledge and the ongoing struggle to separate nursing practice and knowledge from medical practice and knowledge. Leaders in the 1980s are in the world of bureaucratic academia and medical care. They direct their energies to scholarship and management. It can be said that feminism enabled some nurses to pursue power in their bureaucracies.

It is at the international level that nurses appear to be in a position to demonstrate leadership. Although nurses are being called upon to provide the leadership needed to reach the World Health Organization (WHO) goal of Health for All (HFA) by the year 2000 (Halfdan Mahlar, 1986, Dame Nita Barrow, 1986), they must contend with the decisions made by the male physician dominated, Geneva based organization (Martha Quivey, 1989). Nurses, most of whom are women, are expected to be the leaders in this male defined and male directed health care movement.

CHANGE IN PRACTICE
AND ITS ANTECEDENTS

The women's health movement has dismantled many of the underpinnings supporting sexist medical treatment of women. The feminist analyses of physicians' portrayal of women in textbooks (Diane Scully & Pauline Bart, 1973) and Naomi Weisstein's (1971) critique of psychologists depiction of women's true nature and the audacity of the Boston Women's Health Book Collective members to claim their bodies as their own, have affected every aspect of reproductive and emotional health services, and thus nurses and nursing, because changes in nursing practice accompany changes in medical practice.

For example, the re-emergence of midwives and nurse-midwives in America is attributable to the women's health movement. From the lay midwives in California and Tennessee (May Ina, 1975) to the establishment of free standing birth centers (Ruth Lubic, 1981), liberal and radical women's health activists unnerved insurers, attorneys, nurses, and physicians caring for childbearing women. Feminist demands for the right to one's body (Boston Women's Health Book Collective, 1971), including fertility control, have made prominent the adversarial relationship between women and their physicians.

A strong academic response to the women's health movement occurred at the College of Nursing, University of Illinois–Chicago. Here the academic legitimacy of women's health as a focus for education, research, and practice was established when nurse faculty members sought and received in October, 1984, a United States Public Health Service grant to support masters and doctoral education of nurses for practice and research in women's health. Whereas early women's health activists concentrated on informing other women about the risks to their reproductive health from American medical care, these women's health nurse academics went beyond the reproductive system to examine and find ways to reduce risks to other body systems. The relationship between work related stress and cardiovascular disease in men is well established. When data on women were analyzed a similar relationship was found (Suzanne Haynes & Manning Feinleib, 1980). Faculty members initiated teaching programs about risk reduction for inner-city women. They have led the way to a different understanding of, for example, the menstrual cycle (Alice Dan, Effie Graham, & Carol Beecher, 1980) and substance abuse (Tonda L. Hughes, 1987). The bimonthly publication of *Nursing Scan in Women's Health* (Beverly McElmurray & T. L. Hughes, 1987, 1988, 1989), begun in 1985, is an outgrowth of this scholarship. Subscribing to the belief that women's lived experience (Angela B. McBride & William L. McBride, 1981) is a legitimate base for research, University of Illinois–Chicago nurse faculty members have exchanged knowledge with inner-city women to improve their health and to widen the base of nurse faculty research. Unlike other disciplines, where the scholarship stimulated by feminist analyses is easily located and identified, feminist analyses of nursing is difficult to identify and, thus to describe. New priorities and directions derived from the women's health movement are clearer in the area of research.

STATISTICAL CERTAINTY

As the examples above indicate, a few nurse academics have begun to recognize that controlled experimental design is not the only route to new knowledge or the re-examination of old knowledge, yet the lived experience as the origin of research questions has had limited acceptance among nurse academics. Many reject the subjective experiences of women as real data. The focus on controlled design is driven by two forces: federal funding which reflects male selected priorities (U.S. Department of Health and Human Services [USDHHS], 1988) and the tenure review process. There is an uneasiness with experiential data, a rejection of alternative descriptions of reality and a reliance on the male definition of true science. The methodological issues emerge from the tension between those academics who claim equality for experiential, descriptive research in an environment that awards status to prescriptive research. Because its origins derive from the life experiences of the subjects, the knowledge generated by experiential researchers may be more trustworthy and enduring than is the knowledge generated by controlled experimentation.

What is important to everyone is the light shed on women's experience and interpretation of these experiences generated by the experiential approach to research. One tenet held by feminist nurse academics establishes the subjects as participants in the design, the conduct, and the interpretation of the research. However, few nurse academics can risk subscribing to that tenet. Obstacles to implementing new research approaches include the previously mentioned funding sources, the tenure process, human subjects review committees and the editors of professional journals.

IGNORANCE IS BLISS

The mainstream nursing response to feminist scholarship is to ignore it. Textbooks, for example, continue to contain sexist descriptions of women (Ruth Elder, Winnifred Humphrey & Cheryl Laskowski, 1988). Using textbooks as an indicator, it can be seen that curriculum content remains essentially unchanged by feminist scholarship. Feminist scholarship has had little impact on academic nursing or on nursing practice. Academic nursing has paid little attention to this scholarship although recent publications (Claire M. Fagin & Pamela J. Maraldo, 1988, Joan E. Lynaugh & Claire M. Fagin, 1988) suggest more nurse academics are recognizing the importance of feminist scholarship to nursing.

PATRIARCHAL EDICTS PREVAIL

The advancement to tenure for nurse academics is governed by standards set by mostly male faculties. The research, publication, service and teaching records of nurse academics are expected to be the equivalent of academics in disciplines long at home in academia. Because nursing's home in academia is of short duration, the opportunities to establish research programs, obtain research funds, recruit graduate and postgraduate students are fewer than for other academics. Little academic support exists for the argument that male-defined tenure requirements discriminate against nurse academics and that nurses should have a longer time period to establish their tenure credentials. The tenure process protects the power base of male faculty; it subverts nurse knowledge development. Despite the fact that most nurse academics must demonstrate knowledge in two fields (nursing and the discipline of their doctoral study), they have had limited success in dealing with mostly male opposition to their scholarship. Whether this dual preparation serves to disadvantage nurse academics is an open question. Although there are doctoral programs in nursing, currently the majority of doctorally prepared nurses have earned their doctorates in disciplines such as sociology, anthropology, physiology.

SCIENCE TO THE RESCUE

Many of the technological and social–political changes which have occurred over the past 20 years are attributable to biomedical research and its applications. The application of this research to the female reproductive system has reaped benefits for the researchers, their institutions and many women. However, the National Women's Health Network (a Washington, DC-based public interest, nonprofit, membership, organization attending exclusively to women's health issues), journalists (e.g., Gena Corea, 1977), reproductive health activists (e.g., Barbara Seaman & Gideon Seaman, 1977) and others claim the wholesale application of this knowledge was, is or may be harmful to women (Cynthia L. Orenberg, 1981). [See Renate Klein, this volume.]

The consequences for women of this technology applied to the management of reproduction has been the creation of "mother machines" (Gena Corea, 1985). The consequences for some nurse academics has been research directed away from personal responses to the events of reproduction and toward finding ways to study women's responses to the technological management of pregnancy and to assist women to adjust to this management. Many birthing women do not recognize the nurse as important to their reproductive outcome or the nurse's head, heart, and hands as their protectors. The tensions in the nurse–physician–pregnant women triad continue. The extent to which biomedical technology and information has been applied to other aspects of women's health is less well documented than is the application to reproductive health. New technologies used on women's cardiovascular, endocrine, respiratory, and renal systems also need scrutiny. [See Carole Ogelsby & Christine Shelton, this volume.]

It is in the social–political arena that the discipline has benefited most from feminist analyses of inequalities in the competition for federal research funding and employment opportunities. When the National Center for Nursing Research was established in 1986 and housed in the physician-dominated National Institutes of Health, it represented a political unity new to the discipline. The Center places nurses in vigorous, equal competition with others for scarce federal research funds. Although public health nurses filing pay discrimination suits against their employing agencies have yet to win (see Dody Cotter, 1985), these nurses led the way for others to initiate claims under the 1963 Federal Equal Pay Act which prohibits pay differentials where men and women do equal work requiring equal skill in similar conditions. Nurses have benefited from employment changes resulting from actions of the larger women's movement (Dody Cotter, 1985, p. 221–222; Connie Vance, Susan Talbot, A. B. McBride, & D. J. Mason, 1985, pp. 27–28). For example, attention to women's safety in the work place drew attention to employee safety hazards in hospitals thus leading to procedures for the reduction of injury and illness risks in the very hazardous work environment of hospitals.

Students in the discipline have access to biomedical and social–political knowledge generated by nurse and other academics. For the most part, they continue to value more the biomedical knowledge and its application to hospitalized persons over the equally important but less visible sociopolitical aspects of their discipline.

NURSE–PHYSICIAN TENSIONS CONTINUE

The slowly emerging respectability of subjective phenomenon and the declining credibility of the objective as a basis for research questions may be the major contribution of feminist knowledge to the discipline in academia. The inclusion of social–political course work (Yale Nurse, 1987, p. 5), the increasing numbers of nurses elected to state office or serving as legislative aides to state and federal legislators are attributable to the larger women's movement.

As was noted previously, it is hard to document the direct application of feminist knowledge to the discipline, although strong inferences may be drawn to support the conclusion that the women's movement has had an impact on the discipline at the national level. At the local and state level, nurses continue to practice in male-dominated institutions where, as other employees receive increased benefits, so do nurses. Nurse academics benefit from improved opportunities as opportunities for other academics increase. What will endure in the work place is the tension between nurses and male decision makers. Risks to the financial and other benefits of academia rest in the actions of state and federal governments and their committees which allocate funds for research and salaries. The decisions underlying appropriations reflect the current values of elected officials. For example, federal funding for nursing education during the Truman Administration (1945–1953) reflected the value placed on nursing services.

My analyses of current and past histories of the discipline suggest it is more resistant to change because of the past and because of the bureaucratic structures in which it is housed and practiced.

EMERGING SOCIAL HISTORY
OF NURSING

In sum, feminist knowledge has had an influence on some nurse academics and some nurses in practice. It is perhaps more accurate to say that the larger women's movement rather than feminist nursing knowledge has most influenced the discipline and some nurses. Nurses, like others, lack information about their immediate and distant past. Feminist scholars have made abundantly clear that the lack of an historical foundation must be corrected if women are to regain, retain and obtain further gains. The recent histories of nursing indicate an emerging feminist scholarship (Celia Davies, 1980; Robert Dingwall, Anne Marie Rafferty & Charles Webster, 1988; Ellen C. Lagemann, 1983).

Unlike nurses in other countries, many American nurses lack employment benefits such as maternity leave, job protection, and assured payment for their own medical care. Gains made are fragile and may be damaged in an economic downturn. As the demographics of America change and as women realize that they will be in the work force for most of their lives, the discipline may expect to attract fewer young adult but more mid-adult Euro-Americans and young adult Hispanic, Native, and African Americans. Nursing has been a means of exit from one social class to another. It is reasonable to expect that it will continue to be a route to new opportunities for older Euro-Americans and younger Hispanic, Native, and African Americans. Additionally, the academic community and professional organizations presently are vigorously recruiting and financially supporting ethnic applicants to nursing. These students can be expected to bring cultural heritages and career expectations which may conflict with those held by Euro-American nurse academics.

Important questions center around communication and image. How will feminist knowledge be transmitted to the young? How will it be interpreted by the media, especially television? How can nurse academics and practicing nurses persuade the media of the equality of their scholarship and caring skills with those of other academics and those who practice cure? What arguments need to be made to redistribute the medical care dollar to give comparable rewards to nurses? (P. Maraldo, 1989). Will feminist scholarship and analyses of political events continue to stimulate constructive response from the larger community? Both must continue if women, and especially nurses, are to experience their true potential and the discipline of nursing made welcome in the feminist world.

NOTE

1.   International readers are reminded that in the United States, most nurses are educated in colleges and universities, and that, unlike other countries, access to payment for care depends on employment or economic status.

BIBLIOGRAPHY

Ashley, Jo Ann. (1976). *Hospitals, paternalism and the role of the nurse.* New York: Teacher's College, Columbia University.

Barrow, Dame Nita. (1986, April). Leadership for health for all—Actual and potential global perspective. Paper presented at the International Encounter on Leadership in Nursing For Health for All, Tokyo, Japan. Geneva, Switzerland: World Health Organization, Division of Health Manpower Development.

Benton, Denise. (1977). A study of how women are reflected in nursing textbooks used to teach obstetrics and gynecology. *Nursing Forum, 26*(3/4), 269–297.

Boston Women's Health Book Collective. (1971). *Our bodies, ourselves.* New York: Simon & Schuster.

Boston Women's Health Book Collective. (1984). *The new our bodies, ourselves.* New York: Simon & Schuster.

Chinn, Peggy. (1982, October). *Cassandra: Radical Feminist News Journal, 1*(1), 2.

Chinn, Peggy, & Wheeler, Charlene. (1985). Feminism and nursing. *Nursing Outlook, 33*(2), 74–77.

Cleland, Virginia. (1971, August). Sex discrimination: Nursing's most pressing problem. *American Journal of Nursing, 71,* 1542–1547.

Corea, Gena. (1977). *The hidden malpractice: How American medicine treats women as patients and professionals.* New York: William Morrow.

Corea, Gena. (1985). *The mother machine.* New York: Harper & Row.

Cotter, Dody. (1985). Fantasy, fact and finding. A case study of Nurse, Inc. suit against the city and county of Denver. In Diana J. Mason and Susan J. Talbott. (Eds.), *Political action handbook for nurses* (pp. 216–222). Menlo Park, CA: Addison-Wesley.

Dan, Alice, Graham, Effie, & Beecher, Carol. (Eds.). (1980). *The menstrual cycle: A synthesis of interdisciplinary research.* New York: Springer.

Davies, Celia. (Ed.). (1980). *Rewriting nursing history.* London: Croom Helm.

Dingwall, Robert, Rafferty, Anne Marie, & Webster, Charles. (1988). *An introduction to the social history of nursing.* London: Routledge & Kegan Paul.

Elder, Ruth, Humphrey, Winnifred, & Laskowski, Cheryl. (1988). Sexism in gynecology textbooks: Gender stereotypes and paternalism, 1978 through 1985. *Health Care of Women International, 9,* 1–17.

Fagin, Claire M., & Maraldo, Pamela J. (1988). Feminism and nursing: Do women have a choice. *Nursing Outlook, 9*(7), 364–367.

Grissum, Marlene, & Spengler, Carol. (1976). *Women, power and health care.* (1st ed, p. 1–15, 24). Boston: Little Brown.

Haney, Eleanor. (1985). *Feminist legacy: The ethics of Wilma Scott Heide and company.* Buffalo, NY: Margaret Daughters.

Haynes, Suzanne, & Feinleib, Manning. (1980). Women, work, and coronary heart disease: Results from the Framingham 10-year follow-up study. In Phyllis W. Berman and Estelle R. Ramey (Eds.). (April, 1982). *Women: A developmental perspective* (proceedings of a research conference). (November 1980). Bethesda, MD: DHSS, PHS, NIH, (NIH Publication No. 82–2298). (See also Lois M. Verbrugge)

Hughes, Tonda L. (1987, April). Chemical impairment in nursing. In A. Dan and D. Nissen (Eds.), *New directions in women's health* (proceedings of a workshop, pp. 15–16). Chicago, IL: University of Illinois, College of Nursing.

Hines, Darlene Clark. (1989). *Black women in white: Racial conflict and cooperation in the nursing profession, 1890–1950.* Bloomington, Indiana: Indiana University Press.

Ina, May and the farm midwives. (1975). *Spiritual midwifery.* Summerstown, TN: The Book Publishing Company.

James, Edward T., James, Janet W., & Boyer, Paul S. (Eds.). (1971). *Notable American women 1607–1950.* Cambridge, MA: The Belknap Press of Harvard University.

Keddy, Barbara, Acker, Kelly, Hemeon, Dianne, MacDonald, Donna, MacIntyre, Anne, Smith, Thayne, & Vokey, Brenda. (1987). Nurses' work world: Scientific or 'womanly ministering'? *RFR/DFR (Resources for Feminist Research), 16*(4), 37–39.

Kritek, Phyllis, & Glass, Laurie. (1978). Nursing: A feminist perspective. *Nursing Outlook, 26*(3), 182–186.

Lagemann, Ellen C. (Ed.). (1983). *Nursing history: New perspectives, new possibilities.* New York: Teachers College, Columbia University.

La Godna, Gretchen. (1982, October). Cassandra: A report of the beginning. *Cassandra: Radical Feminist News Journal, 1*(1), 1.

Lubic, Ruth. (1981). Evaluation of an out-of-hospital maternity center for low risk patients. In Linda Aiken (Ed.), *Health policy and nursing practice,* (pp. 90–116). New York: McGraw/Hill.

Lynaugh, Joan E., & Fagin, C. M. (1988). Nursing comes of age. *Image: The Journal of Nursing Scholarship, 20*(4), 184–190.

Mahlar, Halfdan. (1986). Why leadership for health for all. Keynote address International Encounter on Leadership in Nursing For Health For All. Tokyo, Japan. Geneva, Switzerland: World Health Organization, Division of Health Manpower Development.

Mahler, Halfdan. (1981). Health 2000: The meaning of "health for all by the year 2000." *World Health Forum,* 2(1), 5–22.

Maraldo, P. (1989, June). Home health care should be the heart of a nursing sponsored national health plan. *Nursing and Health Care,* 10(6), 300–306.

McBride, Angela B., & McBride, William L. (1981). Theoretical underpinning in women's health. *Women and Health,* 6(1/2), 37–55.

McElmurray, Beverly, & Hughes, T. L. (Eds.). (1987, 1988, 1989). *Nursing scan in women's health.* J. B. Lippincott, Bimonthly publication. Previously published (1985–1986) by Women's Health Exchange, College of Nursing, University of Illinois-Chicago.

Melosh, Barbara. (1982). *The physicians hand: Work culture and conflict in American nursing.* Philadelphia: Temple University Press.

Muff, Janet. (Ed.). (1982). *Socialization, sexism, stereotyping: Women's issues in nursing.* St. Louis: CV Mosby.

Nightingale, Florence. (1979). *Cassandra.* (With introduction by Myra Stark). Old Westbury, NY: The Feminist Press. (Original work published 1852.)

Orenberg, Cynthia L. (1981). *DES: The complete story.* New York: St. Martens Press.

Quivey, Martha. (1989, July). Lecture delivered at the University of Wisconsin–Madison. School of Nursing, Community Health Nursing Practicum Students. (M. Quivey is the Associate Director for Research and Development, City of Oslo, Norway and Vice President of International Council of Nurses, Geneva, Switzerland.)

Reverby, Susan. (1987). *Ordered to care: The dilemma of American nursing 1850–1945.* New York: Cambridge University Press.

Sandelowski, Margaret. (1981). *Women, health and choice.* Engelwood Cliffs, NJ: Prentice Hall.

Sicherman, Barbara, Green, Carol, Kantrow, Irene, & Walker, Harriette. (Eds.). (1980). *Notable American women: The modern period.* Cambridge, MA: The Belknap Press of Harvard University Press.

Scully, Diane, & Bart, Pauline. (1973). A funny thing happened on the way to the orifice. *American Journal Sociology,* 78, 1045–1050.

Seaman, Barbara, & Seaman, Gideon. (1977). *Women and the crises in sex hormones.* New York: Rawson Associates Publisher.

Smith, F. B. (1982). *Florence Nightingale: Reputation and power.* London: Croom Helm.

U.S. Department of Health and Human Services. (Weekly publication), National Institute of Health. *NIH guide for grants and contracts.* Baltimore, MD: Room BHB No. 8, Building 31.

Vance, Connie, Talbott, Susan, McBride, A. B., & Mason, D. J. (1985). Coming of age: The women's movement and nursing. In D. J. Mason and Susan W. Talbott (Eds.) *Political action handbook for nurses* (pp. 23–37). Menlo Park, CA: Addison-Wesley.

Verbrugge, Lois M. (1976a, Winter). Sex differences in morbidity and mortality in the United States. *Social Biology,* 23, 275–296.

Verbrugge, Lois M. (1976b, December). Females and illness: Recent trends in sex differences in the United States. *Journal of Health and Social Behavior,* 17, 387–403.

Verbrugge, Lois M. (1983, March). Multiple roles and physical health of women and men. *Journal of Health and Social Behavior,* 24, 16–30.

Verbrugge, Lois M. (1989, September). The twain meet. Empirical explanations of sex differences in health and mortality. *Journal of Health and Social Behavior,* 30, 282–304.

Weisstein, Naomi. (1971). *Psychology constructs the female.* Sommerville, MA: New England Free Press. Also in Robin Morgan (Ed.). (1970). *Sisterhood is powerful.* New York: Random House.

World Health Organization. (1987). *Report leadership for health for all; The challenge to nursing, A strategy for action.* Geneva: Division of Health Manpower Development, World Health Organization (WHO/HMD/NUR/86.1). (Contact Regional WHO offices for information on Regional Health For All (HFA) activities.)

Yale Nurse. (1987, April). Health policy and nursing practice. New Haven, CT: Yale School of Nursing.

Chapter 16

Exercise and Sport Studies
Toward a Fit, Informed, and Joyful Embodiment of Feminism

Carole A. Oglesby
Christine M. Shelton

It is impossible to document the impact of feminism on the human movement disciplines without setting forth the context of this discipline within the dualistic structure of the academy. The mind–body dichotomy of Cartesian philosophy has dominated the Western academy for decades (at least). Academe is only now admitting the possibility of a sport and/or exercise discipline viewed as integral to the study of science and culture. In the United States, from the period of the dawning of the mandates for public education extended to boys and girls (including the eventual creation of the colleges for women) to the early 1960s, three lines of thought are discernible with regard to this dicipline: (a) school-based physical exercises and other activity forms were tolerated by academicians at the behest of some medical experts and humanistic educators, as an antidote to the long, inactive hours of schooling which were corollary to the pursuit of a formal education; (b) competitive athletics evolved for males designed along a military model and ostensibly controlled by college presidents through the National Collegiate Athletic Association (NCAA); (c) the training of teachers and administrators of physical education and athletic programs was believed to be adequately accomplished through normal schools and in-formal mentor experiences offered by the organizations that controlled collegiate and other forms of educational sport.

A complete understanding of the history, sociology, and politics of exercise and sport studies is, of course, impossible here. (Our bibliography provides some beginnings for interested readers.) Suffice it to say that the past 30 years has been marked by the emergence of a new "interdisciplinary discipline" utilizing a large portion of the traditional liberal arts to examine the movement behavior of men and women. Partly because the physical education of the past was sex separate, the influence of women on physical education and sport has been pronounced and thus it should be no surprise that the developments in our field of the past 30 years have been deeply influenced by feminism. The influence has been neither predictable nor coherent and seldom explicitly welcomed, but deep nonetheless. We will attempt, in the material that follows, to catalogue the influence through our answers to the questions posed by the editors of this text. We add, with regret, that we are not able in this chapter to chronicle the story of women's sport around the world. Our personal experiences with contacts in other English speaking countries (Great Britain, Canada,

Australia) and in Latin America and the Caribbean convince us: (a) that we would not be able to find a place where the road was easier than ours and (b) each country's story is unique, exciting, and filled with its own heroines. These are histories and dramas which beg to be written, though we have not been able to attempt that here.

WOMEN IN THE DISCIPLINE
20 YEARS AGO

To grasp the impact of feminism on exercise and sport studies, two caveats must be remembered. The first is that exercise and sport studies was, until approximately the past 15 years, almost totally sex-segregated. On the one hand were beliefs, policies, programs for girls and women and on the other, those for boys and men. Very little was identical. Integration might have proceeded someday by evolutionary drift but it was catapulted by Title IX of the 1972 Education Amendments. This integration is, of itself alone, one of the most profound effects of feminism on this area. Title IX states:

> No person in the United States shall, on the basis of sex be excluded from participation in, be denied the benefits of, or be subjected to discrimination under any education program or activity receiving Federal financial assistance.

A second note to be made is that there are differential considerations of feminist thought on the "sporting life of participants/athletes" as compared to effects on the leader and scholar.

The status of women in exercise and sport science was one of virtual total separation from men in the field and autonomy in the rationalization and conduct of programs. In certain respects this may have seemed a status to be treasured, but there were at least two significant "down sides" to the situation. First the sphere of autonomy was very limited. The "mainstream" (collegiate sport, national amateur sport, networks from high school sport to college sport to business–community leadership) basically ignored, and was ignorant of, the woman's system. The second problematic aspect was the self-perception of women in this area as potential "outcasts," both to traditional academic scholarship and to the "normal" pursuits of women. A climate of near phobic insistence on the image of acceptability was stifling (J. Felshin, 1974).

Women's sport programs were built upon a distinctly different philosophy from that of men and the approach that women scholars took in defining "women's physical education" was conceptually distinct as well. As expected, the "women's discipline" was more holistic, integrated, social–science and natural science balanced, and theoretical more than empirical, as compared to the men's approach.

In the period from the early 1960s to mid-1970s, the near simultaneous pressure to create a coherent discipline of exercise and sport science (as different from earlier views of physical education as solely a special form of teacher training) and to sex-integrate departments, organizations, and programs, resulted in a short term dominance of the "men's approach" to leadership, to programs and to disciplinary structuring. For example, in the latter case, a host of "subdisciplinary organizations" have sprung up (sport sociology, sport psychology, sport history, sport philosophy, sport management) in what seems to us, a hyperspecialization orientation. Today, the so-called "splintering" of the discipline has been identified as a very troubling trend by the physical education higher education association. The leadership of the field within the changeover period has not been equally shared by men and women. One of the hopes of the future is that the traditional "women's way" will be reasserted by an aware, new, sex-integrated leadership group.

One last consideration in regard to this topic is the problem of locating the research and theory work of women scholars in this field prior to 1970. The extensive work of women scholars and leaders was primarily distributed within the community of women physical educators and markedly in speeches, workshops, and other forms of oral transmission. Thus, literature searches by electronic means of today turn up little. This is not a simple problem for our field (of course we are not alone with it) but, for the moment, we recommend that interested persons look to the unpublished graduate theses of the colleges and universities with notable women's physical education programs and/or contact the offices of the National Association for Girls and Women in Sport (NAGWS), American Alliance of Health, Physical Education, Recreation, and Dance (AAHPERD), 1900 Association Drive, Reston, VA 22091, for archival material. It is woefully apparent that considerable bibliographic work is needed in this discipline, work which would be international in scope.

FIRST SIGNS OF FEMINIST INFLUENCE

In the early 1960s, protests began to surface which dealt primarily with the status of sport programs and secondarily to the limiting effects of cognitive-based stereotypes concerning what was and was not "appropriate" sports activity for women. The "establishment" national professional association for women sport leaders is the National Section (NS), Division (D), or National Association (NA) for Girls and Women's Sports. It has existed in one form or another since 1899. From the early 1930s to early 1960s, this organization had strictly enforced "appropriate" sports formats for females and (informally of course) exerted strict control over training and policy formulation in physical education and sport. Sport sociologists (M. A. Boutilier & L. San Giovanni, 1983) have lambasted this organization as retrogressive. By today's standards it surely was. Our thought is that the women leaders of this organization placed the highest priority on women's exercise for health and sought to create a preserve where women would be "safe" and encouraged to engage in an active lifestyle by all. By the early 1960s, many women leaders believed that girls and women's sport were going to be taken over by the NCAA if the women's organization did not open more competitive, high level sports for females. The Division of Girls and Women's Sport (DGWS) accomplished this by creating another organization, the Association for Intercollegiate Athletics of Women (AIAW) to sponsor and promote collegiate championships for women. This organization was very successful from 1971 to 1981, but was, at that time, literally put out of business by NCAA.

The support of the AIAW, to counteract effects of the NCAA, was about all the professional women of the period could manage and they were not able to mount the 50 separate campaigns which would have been necessary to maintain their control at the state high school level. The effect of Title IX-based changes, to open sports opportunities for females, was to increase participation rates and financial support greatly and to begin a marked decline in the proportion of women sport leaders at all levels. In our opinion it is one of the "unsung heroine" facts that, in spite of never ending turmoil and erosion of power, the women's sport organizations and their leaders have unselfishly never paused for a moment in their fight to support and enlarge the Title IX and Civil Rights Restoration Act effects.

The scholarly efforts of women physical educators have dealt largely with the production of empirical data and theory which debunked stereotypes concerning the limitation of females for sport and other nontraditional areas. Three classic pieces of work in this vein are Dorothy Harris' (1972) *Proceedings of the Penn State Conference in Sport,* Gerber, Felshin, Berlin, & Wyrick (1974) *The American Woman in Sport,* and Oglesby's (1978) *Women and Sport: From Myth to Reality.*

The DGWS/NAGWS, and later the Women's Sports Foundation, has had loose ties with the "Women's Movement" of the 1960s, 1970s, and 1980s. Feminists who created Title IX were a little surprised, and perhaps dismayed we believe, by the dominance of the sports issue with regard to Title IX acceptance, but they never wavered in their firmness on the issues. The NAGWS gave the Movement one of its finest symbols in creating and implementing the Torch Run (Seneca Falls to Houston) to lead into the National Women's Conference. This cooperation was begun with contacts between NAGWS and the International Women's Year Commission. Through the 1970 and 1980 period, AIAW and NAGWS were active with the Washington based National Coalition of Girls and Women in Education. An example of this cooperation's present extension is the involvement of NAGWS academic women in a think tank concerning the legal/theoretical basis for maintenance of women's colleges. A common thread was perceived between arguments for sex-segregated sports for women, in addition to, and liberating, organizations like Little League, and those concerning maintenance of the Smiths and Mt. Holyokes in addition to opening previously male institutions to women.

"TRADITIONAL SPORT" AND "SPORT-FOR-WOMEN"

Physical education began in schools as medical gymnastics. It consisted of exercise systems which were thought to counteract the effects of schools' enforced inactivity of children. The role of these medically based exercises was particularly debated, and ultimately supported, for girls and women, albeit that the debate focused heavily on the deficits of females for sport and activity. This topical area is perhaps best catalogued in the histories of the founding of the American women's colleges. From invisibility, women's place in sport evolved to a sex segregated and trivialized position and in academe into a sex segregated and diametrically different shape in the field of exercise and sport science. It is our contention that, since the 1930s to the contemporary period, at least two differing sport and sport science constructs have been created: that of "traditional sport" and "sport-for-women." A sample of the characteristics of these two cultural forms are as follows:

Traditional (Men's) Sport	*Sport for Women*
Business-oriented	Educational oriented
Star/spectator focus	Participant/mass focus
Specialized/particularistic	In balance with other life interests
Institutional support	Limited to self-support
Risky	Safe
Active	Passive
Dominant	Subordinate
Aggressive	Cooperative

The effect of feminism has opened the possibility of a transformed sport which integrates the best of both previous forms. At the present, the traditional sport form appears dominant for males and females, although the hope of transformation is certainly not gone (M. Duquin, 1978).

Because of the existence of the mirror "women's physical education" discipline, from the formation of the American Physical Education Association (1885) to the period of Title IX-based integration movements, there have been innumerable foremothers in our field. Like nursing positions, and the dean of women's positions, being a physical educator was one of the few relatively sure places for women to survive in American higher education. The lives of some of these important pioneer scholars are catalogued in many works of the bibliography. One of the problems we see at present is adequate recognition of these women in that Exercise and Sport Science has, increasingly, moved towards a collection of fairly autonomous subspecializations which almost mirror a miniature College of Arts and Science and which have "fathers" but no "mothers." Because the women in our field tended towards a perspective which was holistic more than narrowly specialized; theoretical and ethical more than empirical; service-focused more than self or field aggrandizing, they are virtually forgotten or unknown entities to the fields' new professionals. The "correcting" and amplification of our history, as a discipline, is an unfinished task.

NEW RESEARCH PRIORITIES AND DIRECTIONS

There are several research and theory areas which a feminist stance has elicited in our field. One area deals with the outer limits of women's physical–psychological potential. *Challenging the Men* (K. Dyer, 1982) is a book about women's chances of defeating men in head-to-head competition. In a broader light, many researchers are studying the strengths and weaknesses of the male and female bodily systems, at varying points along the life span, without some of the previous stifling stereotypic assumptions. The 1983 "New Agenda for Women and Sport," an activist, theorist, visioning conference, identified six of these pervasive myths to be dispelled:

1. Sport masculinizes women.
2. Sports are medically risky for women.
3. The female body is inadequate for sports performance.
4. Women are not interested in sports.
5. Women are not psychologically tough enough for sports.
6. Present financial resources are adequate for women's sports.

We know, for example, that women from Japan, Canada, and England attended the New Agenda Conference and returned to their countries to form "Women's Sport Foundations." Canada has been particularly successful in attracting the attention of government to the solutions of some of these problems.

NEW METHODOLOGIES

In the physiological–biomechanical area women were almost never subjects until the 1980s. For ease of filming anatomical landmarks in motion, and for collecting blood and gas samples, rectal temperatures, and the like, it had always seemed "simpler" for male researchers to work on male subjects. We think it also likely that there was great hesitation in taking female subjects close to maximal energy expenditure. Thus, virtually all of what was "known" about "athletes" was known about males. It is exciting today to see male and female researchers utilizing similar techniques to answer the fundamental psycho–physical questions which remain unanswered about human performance. [See Joan Mulligan, this volume.]

In addition to the lack of data on female subjects up until the 1980s, there is a second methodological issue that must be noted with historical biophysiological data. This is the truism that "normal" population females, even in high school and college samples, were basically sedentary whereas their male counterparts were much less so. Thus, seemingly innocuous studies of reaction times and the like, of male/female college freshmen, were not accurately designed to test similarly "untrained" subjects. Well-designed studies today, focusing on gender differences, will pretest and group male/female samples which are functioning at equivalent levels on the variables under study.

In the psycho–social realm, one of the major methodological flaws in research in this discipline was to ignore the distinction between sex (biogenetic assignment) and gender identity. The psychological studies of athletes of the period before 1980, utilized bipolar masculine/feminine scales of the standard trait inventories and often revealed at least one or two high-masculine or low-feminine variables. It remained for the Bem-like inventories, which gave female athletic performers the opportunity to reveal their high-expressive *and* high instrumental orientations, to present a more complete picture of the gender orientation of the female athlete.

One last contribution of the feminist perspective to research methodology is the not-so-subtle pressure to expand the research focus *beyond* the bounds of the elite-only level to examine the biopsycho–social orientation of all movement performers across age range, racial group, and able/disabled status.

RESPONSES OF THE ATHLETIC "ESTABLISHMENT"

Watzlawick (1978), a family systems psychologist, has suggested that people often declare that new thinkers (like feminists for example who see problems with old ways of being) are either "mad" or "bad" and oppose changes in thinking with all the energy they can muster. This kind of dynamic has been played out ferociously in physical education and athletic associations. The facts that spilled out during the Title IX debate period, concerning lack of funding for girls and women's sport, lack of pay for coaches and officials, anachronist rules and policies, and the like, were denied and/or "explained" by the most bizarre and contradictory rhetoric. When further denial was finally patently impossible, the athletic establishment claimed that the reality existed because that was the way females desired it or maintained that equity changes would "be the death" of males' athletics.

The passing of time has seen many desirable changes occur but two backlash ramifications have been painful to witness. One is that the increase in desirable conditions for leadership of girls and women's sport, paired with the perception that the sport experience is fundamentally the same for boys and girls, has created a situation where coaching, officiating, and administering women's sport is a "good job" for a man. Because men are perceived to be "better qualified" for many sport leadership posts, the percentage of female sport leaders has dropped precipitously. A second backlash element has been the destruction of many "women's" organizations. The affirmative concept of requiring a place in the mainstream organization *and* "a place" (organization) of one's own has been difficult to maintain. The list of "fallen" women's sport and physical education organizations is lengthy. Women are moving into leadership of previously "men only" organizations, and this is to be lauded, but the pace is agonizing.

The specter of homophobia is used by men to win many of these political battles with the women's sport and physical education organizations. The scenario goes like this: (a) women (feminists) begin a very successful campaign to build a women's sport organization; (b) the mainstream sport establishment opposes the *costly* idea of equity for females; (c) the establishment, clearly losing the battle to "keep women's sport from growing," proclaims that now they really want to help so they will just "take over" the women's organizational program (e.g., NCAA destroys AIAW, 1983); and (d) the women's group opposes the take over at which point the rhetoric begins on a not-so-subtle basis . . . "why don't you want to join us; why do you want to be all by yourselves in this; is something wrong with you?" This dynamic is prevalent to the degree that collegiate women coaches include, in recruitment brochures, pictures of themselves with husband and children if possible, and *at least* all dressed up in fashion attire if single, in order to blunt the implications of lesbianism which come from other male and female coaches. The concept of dealing with this problem by system-wide homophobia awareness projects is just beginning to surface. Women in sports have a history of denial and, what Felshin has called "apologetics" to cope with the fears they held about the appropriateness of their place in sport. Thus, an overt, explicit feminist consciousness has been particularly wrenching in this regard, though to be sought.

SUMMARY AND CONCLUSION

The potential contribution of sport feminist knowledge to women's lives is something we believe in deeply. We see that the "academic feminist" may have some biases that work against her knowledge development in this area. She may, for example, reject competition, equating it with dominance and the patriarchy. We, sport feminists, define sport competition as a mutual quest for excellence wherein the quality of the challenge is precisely what facilitates personal growth. Thus, such a quest may be defined as an ultimate expression of care for self and other.

The "academic feminist" may have, without full consciousness, rejected her body because "it" has been made alien and "it" has been defined as her inferior realm. The consciousness of the sport feminist, including knowledges and techniques about the *enabling* of the body and the *joyful integration* of self embodied, is the treasure we bring forward, not always to a warm welcome. The dialogue needed between "academic feminists" and "sport feminists" should be seen, we believe, as a dialogue between people speaking different languages. We believe bilingual "translators," are needed to create a new integration.

The biggest challenge, we believe, for sport feminism today is to describe and promulgate a transformed sport. "Old" sport, "traditional" sport is that cultural product which honors and creates the traditional unrelieved masculine. The fact is, however, that sport, created as it is by men and women who possess and reflect both the "masculine and feminine" qualities, has integral to it a "feminine" aspect. Sport is perfected as a human experience when its animus and anima are recognized and celebrated. Women who pursue sport experience so they can win in the "cut throat" world of business, are as lost in the traditional concept of sport as are men. The great sociologist Jessie Bernard pointed out that the next century will require the community building qualities of human culture as never before; thus, she said, this is not the time to devalue the traditional feminine. If we all can enable the "feminine" in sport to be seen and honored, surely we can find it anywhere.

POSTSCRIPT

The editors wanted each chapter to bring in international considerations. We really have been unable to do this. We each have international experience: Chris was a Peace Corps volunteer in Venezuela for 2 years and 1 year in Puerto Rico. She has served as director of the NAGWS Latin American Project featuring biannual professional conferences on women's sport in the hemisphere. Carole has traveled as a speaker and sport administrator with the World University Games since 1971, visiting the socialist countries of Eastern Europe, England, Italy, Scandinavia, as well as being involved with the Latin American Project. We know just enough to know we know little. Nowhere we have been has been "better or healthier" for women's sport than in the United States. The problems we have seen are remarkably similar, although at times in different external guises. As much progress as there has been, we are only at the beginning. Sport is a cultural form which seems to supply many provocative metaphors. We see the most appropriate one to end this section as that of the relay team in track. There have been many "laps" run by sport feminists but the race is only begun. Each of us must simply run her best course and look for, indeed train, those in the next generation to whom the baton of effort can be passed. Thus it is, "till our race be won."

BIBLIOGRAPHY

Arnold, E. H. (1924, October). Athletics for women. *American Physical Education Review, 24*(8), 452–457.

Bell, M. (1926). Why girls should play girls' basketball rules. In *Spalding athletic library basketball for women* (pp. 70–71). New York: American Sports Publishing Company.

Bell, M. (1938). The doctor advises. In *Official basketball guide 1938–1939*. New York: National Section on Women's Athletics, A.S. Barnes.

Birrell, S. (1984). Studying gender in sport: A feminist perspective. In N. Therberge & P. Donnelly (Eds.), *Sport and the sociological imagination*. Fort Worth: Texas Christian University Press.

Birrell, S. & Richter, D. (1987). Is a diamond forever? Feminist transformations of sport. *Women Studies International Forum, 10*(4), 395–409.

Boutilier, M. A. & San Giovanni, L. (1983). *The sporting woman*. Champaign, IL: Human Kinetics.

Bouve, M. (1931, March). Ethel Perrin—Humanist. *The Sportswomen, 7*, 7–8.

Brooks, G. A. (1981). *Perspectives on the academic discipline of physical education*. Champaign, IL: Human Kinetics.

Coakley, J. J. (1986). *Sport in society* (3rd ed.). St Louis: Time Mirror/Mosby.

Corbett, D. (1981). *Learned social identity of the Black female athlete/nonathlete*. Presentation at North American Society for the Sociology of Sport, Fort Worth, TX.

Duquin, M. (1978). The androgynous advantage. In C. Oglesby (Ed.), *Women and sport: Myth to reality*. Philadelphia: Lee & Lebiger.

Dyer, K. (1982). *Challenging the men: The social biology of female sporting achievement*. New York: University of Queensland Press.

Felshin, J. (1974, January). Triple option for women in sport. *Quest, XXI*, NAPECW and NCPEAM.

Garrison, F. (1929, February). Amy Morris Homan—An appreciation. *The Sportswomen, 5*(6), 7–8.

Gerber, E. (1971). *Innovators and institutions in physical education*. Philadelphia: Lea & Febiger.

Gerber, E. (1975). The controlled development of collegiate sport for women, 1923–1936. *Journal of Sport History, 2*(1), 1–28.

Gerber, E., Felshin, J., Berlin, P., & Wyrick, W. (1974). *The American women in sport.* Reading, MA: Addison-Wesley.

Hall, M. A. (1985). How should we theorize sport in a capitalist patriarchy? *International Review for Sociology of Sport, 20*(1–2), 109–116.

Harris, D. (1972). *Women and sport: A national research conference.* Penn State HPER Series No. 2, University Park, Penn State Press.

Hart, B., Hasbrook, C., & Mathes, S. (1986). An examination of the reduction in the number of female interscholastic coaches. *Research Quarterly for Exercise and Sport, 57*(1), 68–77.

Hough, T. (1901). The physiological effects of basketball. In *Spalding athletic basketball for women* (pp. 15–19). New York: American Sports.

Hult, J. S. (1985). The governance of athletics for girls and women: Leadership by women physical educators, 1899–1949. *Research Quarterly for Exercise and Sport, Centennial Issue,* 64–77.

Howell, R. (1982). *Her story in sport: A historical anthology of women in sports.* West Point, NY: Leisure Press.

Lee, M. (1924, January). The case for and against intercollegiate athletics for women and the situation as it stands today. *American Physical Education Review, 26*(11), 13–19.

Lee, M. (1929, July). Sports and games—an educational dynamic force. *Playground and Recreation,* 223–225.

Lee, M. (1931, May). The case for and against intercollegiate athletics for women and the situation since 1923. *Research Quarterly, 2*(2), 93–127.

Lee, M. (1932a). A survey of athletic and gymnastic costumes used by American girls and women. *Research Quarterly, 3*(1), 5–47.

Lee, M. (1932b). *The underlying principles in athletics for girls and women.* Paper presented at the Women's Division of National Amateur Athletics Federation, Reston, VA: (WNDAAF Collection) AAHPERD Archives.

Lee, M. (1937). *The conduct of physical education.* New York: A. S. Barnes.

Lee, M. (1977). *Memories of a bloomer girl.* Washington, DC: American Association of Health, Physical Education, and Recreation.

Lee, M. (1978). *Memories beyond bloomers.* Washington, DC: American Association of Health, Physical Education, and Recreation.

Lee, M. (1983). *A history of physical education and sports in the USA.* New York: John Wiley & Sons.

Locke, M. C. (1959). *A biographical study of Agnes Rebecca Wayman.* Unpublished doctoral dissertation, Springfield College, Springfield, MA.

Lucas, J. A. & Smith, R. A. (1982). Women's sport: A trail of equality. In R. Howell (Ed.), *Her story in sport: A historical anthology of women in sport* (pp. 239–256). West Point, NY: Leisure Press.

Lumpkin, A. (1986). *Physical education: A contemporary introduction.* St. Louis: Times Mirror/Mosby.

Massengale, J. D. (1987). *Trends toward the future in physical education.* Champaign, IL: Human Kinetics.

McGinnis, J. M. (1984, November/December). The national children and youth fitness study. *Journal of Physical Education, Recreation, and Dance, 55,* 19–23.

Nixon, J. A. (1918). The beneficial results and dangers of basketball. In *Spalding athletic library basketball for women* (pp. 70–71). New York: American Sports.

Nixon, J. E. & Jewett, A. E. (1980). *An introduction to physical education.* Philadelphia: Saunders College/Holt, Rinehart, and Winston.

Oglesby, C. (Ed.). (1978). *Women and sport: From myth to reality.* Philadelphia: Lea and Febiger.

Oglesby, C. (1981). *The paradox of racial stereotyping in physical education and sport: Black is inferior or Black is best?* Amherst: University of Massachusetts, Project TEAM, Women's Educational Equity Act Program.

Oglesby, C. (1984). Interaction between gender identity and sport. In J. M. Silva and R. S. Weinberg (Eds.), *Psychological foundations of sport* (pp. 387–399). Champaign, IL: Human Kinetics.

Perrin, E. (1928). Introduction. In S.W. Frymir *Basketball for women.* New York: A.S. Barnes.

Perrin, E. (1941, October). Ethel Perrin—An autobiography. *Research Quarterly, 12*(3), 682–685.

Ponthieux, N. & Barker, D. (1967). Relationships between race and physical fitness. *Research Quarterly, 36*(3).

Puhl, J., Brown, C. H., & Voy, R. O. (1988). *Sport science perspectives for women,* Champaign, IL: Human Kinetics.

Rintala, J. & Birrell, S. (1984). Fair treatment for the active female: A content analysis of the *Young Athlete* magazine. *Sociology of Sport Journal, 1*(3), 231–250.

Rosenberg, R. (1982). *Beyond separate spheres.* New Haven: Yale University Press.

Sloan-Green, T., Oglesby, C., Alexander, A., & Franke, N. (1981). *Black women in sport.* Reston, VA: American Alliance of Health, Physical Education, Recreation, and Dance.

Spears, B. & Swanson, R. A. (1983). *History of sport and physical activity in the United States.* Dubuque, IA: William C Brown.

Spears, B. (1979). Success, women, and physical education. In M.G. Scott and J.J. Hoferek (Eds.), *Women as leaders in physical education and sports.* Iowa City: University of Iowa Press.

Teriot, N. (1986). Towards a new sporting ideal: The women's division of the national amateur athletic federation. *Frontiers, 3*(1), 1–6.

Theberge, N. (1987). Sport and women's empowerment. *Women's Studies International Forum, 10*(4), 387–393.

Trilling, B. M. (1929, August). The playtime of a million girls or an Olympic victory—Which? *The Nations Schools, 4*(2).

Twin, S. L. (1979). *Out of the bleachers: Writings on women and sport.* Old Westbury, NY: The Feminist Press, McGraw-Hill.

von Borries, E. (1951). *The history and functions of the national section of women's athletics.* Washington, DC: National Section of Women's Athletics.

Watzlawick, P. (1978). *The language of change: Elements of therapeutic communication.* New York: Norton.

Wayman, A. R. (1938). *A modern philosophy of physical education.* Philadelphia: W.B. Saunders.

Wayman, A. R. (1925). *Education through physical education.* Philadelphia: Lea & Febiger.

Wayman, A. R. (1924, November). Women's athletics—All uses—No abuses. *American Physical Education Review, 24*(9), 517–519.

WDNAAF. (1936). *Report of medical advisory committee.* Reston, VA: (WDNAAF Collection) AAHPERD Archives.

Wells, C. L. (1985). *Women, sport, and performance: A physiological perspective.* Champaign, IL: Human Kinetics.

Weston, A. (1962). *A making of American physical education.* New York: Appleton-Century-Crofts.

Williams, J. F. & Hughes, W. L. (1930). *Athletics in education.* Philadelphia, W.B. Saunders.

Women's Sport Foundation. (1983). *New agenda for women and sport.* New York: Author.

Wood, T. D. (1883). Some unsolved problems in physical education. *Proceedings of the Eighth Annual Meeting of the American Association for the Advancement of Physical Education,* 9–11.

Chapter 17

What's a Nice Feminist Like You Doing in Journalism and Mass Communication?

Lana F. Rakow

WHERE WE STARTED

Women in journalism and in mass communication education and research were all but invisible as students and faculty members 20 years ago. To give an example of how invisible they were, one of the organizations in the discipline in the United States, the Association for Education in Journalism (AEJ) (it later added Mass Communication to its name) had only nine women at its annual convention in 1965 (Maurine Beasley & Kathryn T. Theus, 1988). Founding mothers of the organization's Committee on the Status of Women, which was started only a few years later, have told us that women faculty members were so isolated at those earlier conventions that they were not able to even identify each other—any woman at the convention was assumed to be a male faculty member's wife. By 1970 to 1971, only 11% of the organization's 1,200 members were women, no women appeared on the convention program that year, no women were officials or sat on any of the organization's committees and only 7% of the contributors of major articles in the main professional journal, *Journalism Quarterly,* were women (Maurine Beasley & Kathryn T. Theus, 1988, p. 39).

Women's position in media industries and as students was little better. For example, because large newspapers hired very few women, the Columbia University of Graduate School of Journalism maintained a 10% quota on women students, a system discontinued only in 1968 (Maurine Beasley & Kathryn T. Theus, 1988, p. 39). The feminist movement, which began picking up momentum in the late 1960s and early 1970s, both critiqued the role of the media in portraying women as happy domestic servants and consumers and bore the brunt of media ridicule as the news media sought to contain and disparage the movement and its critique.

Given the few women and their precarious position in journalism and mass communication education and research programs such a short time ago and given the centrality of the media in knowledge and myth production recognized early on by feminists, we have had our work cut out for us.

HOW WOMEN RESISTED

In the middle of this dismal picture of the discrimination faced by women inside, outside, and around the media in this time period, a group of courageous women demanded that attention be directed at the situation. A paper by Ramona Rush, Carol Oukrop, and Sandra Ernst, reporting on their research findings on the status of women in journalism education, was presented at AEJ's 1972 convention. Among their recommendations was that a Committee on the Status of Women be appointed (Nancy Sharp, Judy Van Slyke Turk, Edna F. Einsiedel, Linda Schamber, & Sharon Hollenbeck, 1985, p. 1). That committee continues to be an active agitator for women. Also in 1972, Donna Allen founded the Women's Institute for Freedom of the Press in Washington, DC, a non-profit organization that is a network for women working to change the structure of media sysems into one that enables all people to speak for themselves and be heard. The Institute's periodical, *Media Report to Women,* now published by Communication Research Associates in Silver Spring, Maryland, has, since 1975, provided an avenue for academic and activist women, inside and outside of the media, to be in touch with each other and share information and research. The tenets of the organization still hold as much radical potential for changing the means of knowledge production and distibution as they did in 1972. (See the *Directory of Women's Media* published by the Institute [Martha Leslie Allen, 1989] for more information about the Institute and its principles.)

Women inside media industries, many sympathetic to the feminist movement if not an active part of it, also challenged their employers' hiring and assignment practices and their coverage of women's issues and the feminist movement. Feminist activists outside the media demanded changes in women's magazines (remember the occupation of the editorial offices of *The Ladies' Home Journal?*) and challenged the licenses of some broadcast stations. (The history of this activism in England and the United States can be found in Maurine Beasley & Sheila Gibbons, 1977; Josephine King & Mary Scott, 1977; and Ethel Strainchamps, 1974).

Academic research on media content seemed to pick up momentum through the 1970s. Content analyses of the representation of women in media content and documentation of women's employment status appeared regularly in journalism and mass communication journals, culminating in several major works: Gaye Tuchman, Arlene Kaplan Daniels, and James Benet's *Hearth and Home: Images of Women in the Mass Media* (1978), Matilda Butler and William Paisley's *Women and the Mass Media* (1980), Helen Baehr's *Women and Media* (1980), and Margaret Gallagher's global summary, *Unequal Opportunities: The Case of Women and the Media* (1981). In the 1980s a change occurred in academic research. Rather than traditional kinds of research documenting women's statistical place, feminists began to create an identity and an approach they dared to call feminist scholarship. It distinguished itself from previous gender research because of its self-avowed political nature (calling attention to the fact that all research and theory is political) and its interest in doing research *for* women, starting from the perspective of women. This research has connected feminists in communication with feminist scholarship in other disciplines— sociology, history, and literary criticism, in particular—making the study of mass communication far richer and more complex.

Feminist groups within several academic communication organizations have become important places for feminists to challenge the politics of the field. The Committee on the Status of Women of AEJMC (Association for Education in Journalism and Mass Communication), the Feminist Scholarship Interest Group (founded in 1985 with programming begun in 1986) of the International Communication Association, and the Women's Caucus of the Speech Communication Association are such groups. Women from the International Association for Mass Communication Research began *Sex-Roles Within Mass Media* in 1981 and sponsor feminist programming in that organization.

CHALLENGING ASSUMPTIONS

Most of the starting assumptions of journalism and mass communication research actively sustain a system of communication that is detrimental to women. These assumptions include:

- A definition of news that ensures that men and their activities will be made known and defined as normal and that women and their activities and concerns will be invisible or denigrated if outside the boundaries of acceptability for women.
- An unquestioned United States belief in the rightness of using the First Amendment to preserve the speaking rights of those who already have them, without being the least troubled by the legal and social sanctions against women speaking or having access to the means to reproduce speech.
- A Western faith in the "free market" of technology and information that leads to media imperialism in much of the rest of the world and threatens the economic and social standing of women in many cultures.
- An acceptance of the media's construction of "woman" as a happy domestic consumer or a heterosexual sex object, white, and middle class. Marketing research, long a mainstay of mass communication research, has been most interested in finding out how to best construct an image of women that will fit their own profit interests while maintaining male dominance.
- A major blindspot about who owns and controls the media, ignoring the fact that our media structure permits a few large corporations to make enormous profits telling the major stories in the culture while denying that opportunity to most people, in particular white women and people of color.
- A concern about media "effects" based on a concern about the moral behavior of the "masses" (that is, does the media make "them" violent, lazy and politically apathetic, over-stimulated, lowbrow?). It is interesting that despite several decades worth of research concerned about the media's effect on making "people" violent, researchers did not concern themselves with how and why men become violent toward women. [See also Susanne Kappeler, this volume.]

These basic tenets are being challenged with great difficulty. Despite feminist research that has demonstrated the arbitrariness and injustice of these assumptions, the media remains essentially unchanged and academic educators and researchers have changed little about what they do and believe. For example, Catherine East and Dorothy Jurney's study *New Directions for News* (1983) demonstrated that even according to the news media's own definitions of news, women are badly treated and receive little coverage. Coverage by the news media of the feminist movement and of women's issues remains invisible, shallow, or disparaging. Attempts by feminists to pass city ordinances protecting women from pornography have been met with horror, outrage, and ridicule from both the liberal and the radical elements of the discipline. Catharine MacKinnon's book *Feminism Unmodified: Discourses on Life and Law* (1987) is nearly undiscussable at AEJMC, while Andrea Dworkin's book *Intercourse* (1988) has been self-confidently ridiculed by men in programs of the International Communication Association as if no one could possibly disagree with them. Market researchers continue to present papers at conferences, and publish them in journals, that discuss such matters as whether or not "female nudity" makes an advertisement more effective.

Despite such strong evidence that the discipline is essentially unchanged, we have to remind ourselves that feminist scholarship within it is only a few years old and that we have made remarkable progress in our ability to organize, program, and do our work. A sign of that progress is evident in the fact that at the 1989 annual convention of AEJMC, the plenary session was devoted to the topic of feminist scholarship. We are at least making ourselves heard.

Elsewhere in the world, women are developing better means of communicating with each other and raising issues of concern to them, as evidenced by the work of *Win News,* a quarterly publication with information about women's activities world-wide; the publication of the International Women's Tribune Centre's *Women Using Media for Social Change* (1984); the formation of the Council of Communication Organizations: A Women's Network, which is planning a global gathering of representatives; and the publication of periodicals by women in various countries, such as the magazine published by the *Manushi* collective in New Delhi, India (see Leslie Steeves' [1989] synthesis of global communication trends concerning or affecting women).

ASKING NEW QUESTIONS

Given the pervasiveness of these assumptions which are detrimental to women, feminist scholars have had to rethink almost completely what the study of mass communication ought to be and do. Whereas women in AEJMC have until only recently been most concerned about the status of women as educators, researchers, and media professionals, feminist scholars who have gathered together through the Feminist Scholarship Interest Group of the Internaitonal Communication Association and those affiliated with the Women's Caucus of the Speech Communication Association (which sponsored its first session on feminist work in 1986), have been more likely to make deep challenges to the discipline by asking new research questions and setting new priorities. We have looked at the world of communication from the point of view of women. We ask questions which men never thought to ask: What is going on—what is gender, anyway?—when the media show us women and men? How does the media keep women in our places? What do women think about what we encounter in the media, and do we make sense of it and with it (e.g., romance novels and soap operas)? How is male dominance justified and made natural through the media? How are women silenced? What are the interconnections between all aspects of communication, language, speech, organizing, publicly communicating, which were previously assumed to be discrete areas of study? What impact does technology have on women? How have women managed to be active communicators, writing, publishing, producing, telling their own stories and experiences? How have women changed the media? What would they *like* to change? (For a small sampling of feminist work that asks new and interesting questions, see the articles in the special feminist issues of *Communication,* [Ellen Wartella & Paula A. Treichler, 1986] and *Journal of Communication Inquiry* [Haeryon Kim & David Tetzlaff, 1987]; as well as Rosemary Betterton, 1987; Sharon Bramlett-Solomon, 1989; Jackie Byars, 1987; Rosalind Coward, 1985; Jane Gaines, 1986; Cheris Kramarae, 1988; Ann Moyal, 1989; Janice A. Radway, 1984; Ann Russo & Cheris Kramarae, 1990; and Liesbet Van Zoonen, 1988. [Also see Lourdes Torres, this volume.]

DISCOVERING WOMEN-CENTERED METHODOLOGIES

Traditional research methods of mass communication could not get at these kinds of questions. The acceptable research methodologies were quantitative content analyses, quantitative surveys, and laboratory experiments. To put research at the service of women rather than at the service of media industries, marketers, or the government, feminist scholars in communication (along with feminist scholars in other disciplines), have had to try new methodologies, such as other ways to interpret texts and images than quantitative content analysis, other forms of interviewing than the predetermined survey, other ways of understanding women's experiences than the laboratory experiment. We have been interested in breaking down the subject–object dichotomy between researchers and the researched. Participant observation and ethnography are currently two methods attracting interest, and these methods are yielding much richer accounts of what women experience and think. [See Shulamit Reinharz, and Liz Stanley, this volume.] We have needed to look in different places for what we study; for example, researchers didn't think to find soap operas and romance novels of interest until feminist scholars came along, and media historians paid little attention to the history of women's media. (For discussions about methodology in communication, see Nina Gregg, 1987; Angela McRobbie, 1982; Janice A. Radway, 1986; and Lana F. Rakow, 1987.)

HOW MEN HAVE RESPONDED

Mainstream researchers (conservative, liberal, and "critical") have responded in several ways to feminists and feminist scholarship. On one hand, there has been an attempt to make feminist scholarship part of a pluralistic approach to communication, that is, proclaiming feminist scholarship as one of a number of acceptable ways that scholars can study communication. On the face of it, this response seems to signal a welcome to feminist scholars. It permits some feminist programming at conferences here, a feminist article in a journal there, a feminist put on an editorial board over there. Just like those who wish to study news, or magazines, or new technologies, feminist scholars can have their "equal opportunity" to be one of the many. This is, of course, nothing less than cooptation, because feminist scholarship is about the *transformation* of the discipline, not about its accommodation (see Lana F. Rakow, 1989). All areas of communication practice and study need to be changed; our goal is not "permission" to do our own work as long as we do not bother anyone else.

Another form of cooptation has come from those who claim themselves to be our friends and supporters. There are men who have found it useful to jump on a feminist bandwagon in an attempt to control and contain it while deriving professional recognition. They edit books and journals which include feminist work, they choose feminist scholars to be on programs and serve on committees, and they may even attempt to "do" feminist work themselves. Not coincidentally, the feminists whose work they valorize tend to be critical of other feminists or are "safe" in their unwillingness to challenge the deep-seated sexism of the men around them. Needless to say, radical feminism is seldom represented because it does not meet these two tests, or, in their words, is "untheoretical." Consequently the direction and critique of feminism is shifted and blunted and its development reshaped into an acceptable and unpolitical offshoot of some "more encompassing" theoretical enterprise, such as postmodernism. An example of how some men have responded to feminist scholar-

ship—by becoming intellectually interested without changing their own oppressive behaviors—occurred at a recent communication conference panel on the subject of men and
feminism. The panel—all men—took up every minute of the program for their own talk
about feminist scholarship leaving no time for audience discussion, but they were outraged
and insulted when feminists in the audience pointed out the irony in what they had done.
This incident is not the only example of men's rudeness toward women or toward feminist
work in the field of communication (see Dale Spender, forthcoming).

Another response to feminist scholarship may be building momentum. Feminist scholars
in communication—many of whom are graduate students and assistant professors—are
reporting experiences of not getting job offers because they are feminist scholars and of not
being renewed in their positions. It may now be somewhat easier for a woman to be hired
and promoted than it was 20 years ago. In fact, in some areas of study, women are the
majority of students and the majority of employees in the industries (this is true for
journalism and public relations). They can be elected to the office of president of AEJMC,
ICA, and SCA. They have more representation in journals and on panels. Feminist women,
however, are not as popular. For example, a woman on the communication faculty of a large
U.S. research institution told this story. She heard the men of her department discussing an
open faculty position. "Well, I suppose we could hire a woman," one of them said, "as long
as she's like the two we've already got." (Nonthreatening? Won't rock the boat?) Indeed,
a woman who is not a feminist scholar was offered the position over the feminist scholar
the department had also interviewed. In another case, a man on the faculty of a communication department was explaining to a woman that his department had recently hired a
feminist scholar. "But she's not like any feminist scholar you've ever met," he said, visibly
showing his relief. "She's nice, she's not pushy like all the rest."

Despite men's preference for "nice" women, however, feminist scholars in communication are finding jobs and they are finding support from each other to give them the strength
to continue their work in sometimes cold and alien environments. The support can be found
in the various feminist groups and caucuses of the professional associations, where deep
freindships have developed among women who never see each other except at yearly
conferences. Long-distance telephone and letter relationships develop between women—
often from different countries—who have never met but who share a common research
interest or career situation. A wonderful network of feminists in communication is developing that will increase our ability to survive and make a difference in our institutions and our
field.

But we must also be alert to men's efforts to keep feminists out of their departments.
Feminist scholars must not get lost in the content of our studies and ignore our professional
status. Two indicators should serve as a warning that efforts may be made to contain
feminists. In ICA, the Feminist Scholarship Interest Group (FSIG) grew out of and became
distinct from what is now called the Task Force on Professional Development—Women.
As feminists directed their energy toward the development of FSIG and toward feminist
scholarship, we neglected the Task Force. We have suddenly been confronted with the
knowledge that two men have been appointed to the Task Force, and the group has decided
to focus its attention on the professional development of "people in general" (according to
the 1989 conference program book). In AEJMC, the Committee on the Status of Women
has faced strong pressure that challenged the right of the group to sponsor programming.
Could it be an accident that the challenge came just at the time that a feminist scholar
became chair of the committee and feminist scholarship was programmed for the first time?

HAVE WE MADE CHANGES?

Though it has been difficult to make inroads into the core of the discipline and outside our pockets of self-claimed space, it is now increasingly difficult for male scholars to ignore feminist work. They seem aware that new and exciting things are going on, yet few trouble themselves to read it and come to understand it, let alone to be changed by it. Graduate students, and many undergraduates, too, however, seem more likely than ever before to seek out feminist scholarship, despite the difficulty of doing so. Feminist scholars are few and far between on faculties; some students face outright hostility in their attempts to do feminist reading and research in regular courses. Feminist scholarship in communication is being published here and there in journals—not always communication journals—and books cover only particular issues or areas of the discipline, so that figuring out what feminist scholarship is all about can be a daunting task. Fortunately, undergraduate courses on women and the media are taught all across the country (Marion Marzolf is reported to have taught the first such course in 1971 at the University of Michigan [Maurine Beasley & Kathryn T. Theus, 1988, p. 42]) and graduate courses in feminist theory and related topics are being developed (despite the fact that department heads, deans, and other faculty have been known to resist them on the grounds that such courses are "too specialized"). The graduate students interested in feminist scholarship who are now fighting their own battles for survival promise to be the next generation of women who will be able to make a real difference.

OTHER RESISTANCE

Despite all the insights feminist scholars have brought to the complexity of understanding representations of gender, to our appreciation of women as active meaning makers and communicators, to our awareness of the role of the media in producing knowledge at the expense of women, journalism and mass communication education and research seems particularly resistant to doing anything about it. This would seem to be so not only because the men in the discipline have status and power to lose if feminist scholarship and its point of view of the world become prevalent, but also because the discipline has been so beholden to media industries for so long. AEJMC, for example, receives considerable amounts of money from the Gannett Foundation, the benevolent arm of this media conglomerate. To question the structure of our media system and the rights of media industries to own and control them is, shall we say, not well supported.

THE DIRECTION WE NEED TO TAKE

The current situation for women and for feminist scholarship in journalism and media studies is an ambiguous one for the moment, but we should soon see signs of important change. Women worldwide are participating in important efforts to change or subvert the media or use it for our own purposes. And despite efforts to resist us, there are now too many more feminist scholars coming out of the starting gate to keep us back. When feminist scholars begin to get tenure, serve in large numbers on editorial boards, edit the journals, and hold the organizations' elected positions, then will we be able to do something about what we have learned, and the connections between feminist activism inside and outside the academy will become more apparent. Soon the days of thinking that a nice feminist won't dare rock the boat will be over.

BIBLIOGRAPHY

Allen, Martha Leslie (Ed.). (1989). *Directory of women's media*. Washington, DC: Women's Institute for Freedom of the Press.

Baehr, Helen (Ed.). (1980). *Women and media*. Oxford: Pergamon Press.

Beasley, Maurine & Gibbons, Sheila. (1977). *Women in media: A documentary source book*. Washington, DC: Women's Institute for Freedom of the Press.

Beasley, Maurine H. & Theus, Kathryn T. (1988). *The new majority: A look at what the preponderance of women in journalism education means to the schools and to the professions*. Lanham, MD: University Press of America.

Betterton, Rosemary (Ed.). (1987). *Looking on: Images of femininity in the visual arts and media*. London: Pandora.

Bramlett-Solomon, Sharon. (1989, May). *Press portrayal of black women in the Civil Rights Movement: The invisible freedom vanguards*. Paper given at the International Communication Association Conference, San Francisco, California.

Butler, Matila & Paisley, William. (1980). *Women and the mass media, Sourcebook for research and action*. New York: Human Sciences Press.

Byars, Jackie. (1987). Reading feminine discourse: Prime–time television in the U.S. *Communication, 9*, 298–303.

Coward, Rosalind. (1985). *Female desires: How they are sought, bought and packaged*. New York: Grove Press.

Dworkin, Andrea. (1988). *Intercourse*. New York: Free Press.

East, Catherine & Jurney, Dorothy. (1983). *New directions for news*. Washington, DC: Women Studies Program and Policy Center of The George Washington University.

Gallagher, Margaret. (1981). *Unequal opportunities: The case of women and the media*. Paris: UNESCO.

Gaines, Jane. (1986, Fall). White privilege and looking relations: Race and gender in feminist film theory. *Cultural Critique*, 59–69.

Gregg, Nina. (1987). Reflections on the feminist critique of objectivity. *Journal of Communication Inquiry, 11*(1), 8–18.

International Women's Tribune Centre. (1984). *Women using media for social change*. New York: Author.

Kim, Haeryon & Tetzlaff, David (Eds.). (1987, Winter). The feminist issue. *Journal of Communication Inquiry, 11*(1).

King, Josephine & Scott, Mary (Eds.). (1977). *Is this your life? Images of women in the media*. London: Virago.

Kramarae, Cheris (Ed.). (1988). *Technology and women's voices: Keeping in touch*. New York: Routledge & Kegan Paul.

MacKinnon, Catharine A. (1987). *Feminism unmodified: Discourses on life and law*. Cambridge, MA: Harvard University Press.

McRobbie, Angela. (1982). The politics of feminist research: Between talk, text, and action. *Feminist Review, 12*, 46–57.

Moyal, Ann. (1989). The feminist culture of the telephone. People, patterns and policy. *Prometheus, 7*(1), 5–31.

Radway, Janice A. (1984). *Reading the romance: Women, patriarchy, and popular literature*. Chapel Hill: University of North Carolina Press.

Radway, Janice A. (1986). Identifying ideological seams: Mass culture, analytical method, and political practice. *Communication, 9*, 93–123.

Rakow, Lana F. (1987). Looking to the future: Five questions for gender research. *Women's Studies in Communication, 10*, 79–86.

Rakow, Lana F. (1989). Feminist studies: The next stage. *Critical Studies in Mass Communication, 6*(2), 209–214.

Russo, Ann & Kramarae, Cheris (Eds.). (1990). *The radical women's press of the 1850s*. London: Routledge & Kegan Paul.

Sharp, Nancy W., Turk, Judy VanSlyke, Einsiedel, Edna F., Schamber, Linda, & Hollenback, Sharon, (1985). *Faculty women in journalism and mass communications: Problems and progress*. Syracuse, NY: Gannett Foundation.

Spender, Dale. (in press). Unprofessional conduct in language research: Why don't men listen? *Discourse and Society*.

Steeves, H. Leslie. (1989). Gender and mass communication in a global context. In Pamela J. Creedon. (Ed.), *Women in mass communication: Challenging gender values*. Beverly Hills: Sage Publications.

Strainchamps, Ethel (Ed.). (1974). *Rooms with no view: A woman's guide to the man's world of the media*. Compiled by Media Women's Association. New York: Harper & Row.

Tuchman, Gaye, Daniels, Arlene Kaplan, & Benet, James (Eds.). (1978). *Hearth and home: Images of women in the mass media*. New York: Oxford University Press.

Van Zoonen, Liesbet. (1988). Rethinking women and the news. *European Journal of Communication, 3*(1), 35–53.

Wartella, Ellen & Treichler, Paula A. (Eds.). (1986). Feminist critiques of popular culture. *Communication, 9*(1).

Chapter 18

Women and the Law

Jocelynne A. Scutt

In the late 1960s, few law students, legal practitioners, members of the magistracy and judiciary, or professors and lecturers in law were women. This was so in the common-law countries of New Zealand, Australia, the United States of America, Canada, and other countries colonized by Great Britain, including the Pacific island states and countries on the African and Indian continents. In the nineteenth and early-twentieth centuries, women demanded entry into universities and into the legal profession. This struggle occurred throughout the common-law world.

That the struggle was necessary reflects the position of women generally as subjects in law. In the nineteenth century, a married woman (a "feme covert" or "covered woman") had no personhood; her personhood was subsumed in that of her husband upon marriage. Even before marriage, a woman lost her right to control any property she might have, in that upon betrothal, if she gave away such property, her husband had a right to renounce the gift and recover the property once they were legally wed. It was considered that a woman had no right to attend university on two counts: first, because universities were established for the training and teaching of men and were not places for women; and secondly, because women were not "persons," so that if regulations referred to "persons" as being entitled to enter university and study there, courts said they did not refer to women. The same arguments were made against women's entry to the legal profession.

The first woman to graduate in law in Australia (when women were finally permitted university entrance) was Ada E. Evans, from the University of Sydney, in 1903. It was not until 1921 that she was admitted to the practice of law, because the *Legal Practitioners Act* of New South Wales, referring as it did to "persons" with qualifications being entitled to practice law, was interpreted not to include women. Ada Evans lobbied, together with supporters, for the passage of the *Women Legal Practitioners Act* granting women with the requisite qualifications (e.g., a Bachelor of Laws degree) to practice law. This problem was confronted earlier in the United States. Karen Berger Morello reports in *The Invisible Bar* (1986) that the first woman lawyer in America was Margaret Brent, who arrived in the colonies in 1638. No other practicing women lawyers have yet been discovered before 1869 when Mary E. Magoon practiced in Iowa County. Belle Babb Mansfield passed the Iowa state bar examination in June 1869. In the year she was admitted to practice, Myra Colby Bradwell was refused the right by the Illinois Supreme Court, despite her passing the bar exam. In Britain, women were refused the right to practice law on the grounds of being "nonpersons" if married, and potential nonpersons if unmarried—because at any time (ran the argument) they could marry, thus demoting themselves from personhood. In 1914, the House of Lords held Miss Bebb, a graduate of Oxford University, was not entitled to practice law because she was a woman, not a person.

Just as in Australia women won the right to practice law by lobbying for laws to be changed, women in the United States and Britain also won that right. In Canada, a Privy Council decision in 1930 held women in that country were persons, on the grounds that the *British North America Act* had intended laws to be applied with greater liberality than laws subsisting in England in 1867, when the Act was passed. (The Canadian court had held that women were not "persons," and that decision was appealed to the Privy Council, a division of the English House of Lords set up to deal with appeals from the colonies.)

In the early 1970s, although there were no formal impediments in common-law countries to women attending universities, studying law and applying successfully to be admitted to the practice of law, informal barriers existed. Karen Berger Morello writes of her own experience in 1971 when she decided to pursue a legal career:

> . . .The resistance to women lawyers was still substantial. In college my prelaw adviser suggested that as a woman, I was better suited for marriage than for law school. A law professor I once greatly admired boasted that he placed all the women students in one of two classes so he could enjoy teaching the other one. A county prosecutor's office in New York City hired male students for criminal law internships but offered me, then a third-year law student, a typing job. After I passed my bar examination a prominent New York attorney suggested hiring me at a salary considerably lower than what the men were earning. When I refused, pointing up to the difference in pay, he asked, "Are you married?" I said I wasn't. "Well, then, what's a single girl need with all that money—let the guys buy you dinner." (Karen Berger Morello, 1986, p. xi)

The number of women law students began to equal the number of men law students, or at some universities to outstrip them, by the mid 1970s. I attended law school at the University of Western Australia from 1965 to 1968, graduating in 1969. In my first year, there were 4 women to about every 100 men. Cynthia Fuchs Epstein (1983), Karen Berger Morello (1986) and Jane H. Mathews (1982) point out that for the United States and Australia, although women are now attending and graduating from law school in high numbers compared with twenty years ago, substantial differences exist in legal careers for women and men. The experience of other common-law countries is similar. Cynthia Fuchs Epstein found a significant increase in women partners in Wall Street law firms:

> Nowhere is the "old boy" network so characteristic of the formal and informal structure of an occupation as in the "establishment bar"; nowhere is tradition more important and the impact of background status so pertinent both to recruitment and to the style of doing work. These firms have constituted the quintessential upper-class male culture. . . .

> Of the 1,520 partners distributed among the large New York firms in 1977, 29 were women. This represented almost a tenfold increase since 1971. In 1956, Erwin Smigel found only one woman partner, and when I surveyed those same firms in 1968, that number had only increased to three. A survey made of women partners in Wall Street firms in 1979 showed an increase to 34. By summer 1980 there were 41; at that time, of 3,987 partners in the top fifty law firms in the country, 85 were women. . . . Today about 3.5% of all partners are women. A survey in 1982 shows that slightly less than 10% of the large firms (including some of the giants, such as Sullivan and Cromwell with 219 lawyers) have *no* women partners. (Cynthia Fuchs Epstein, 1983, pp. 178–179)

For Britain and Australia, the figures are less positive: women entering partnerships frequently do so on less advantageous terms. Sometimes they are unaware of the differentials.

With appointments to the magistracy (the lowest level of courts) and judiciary, men far outstrip women. For the highest courts, in the 1970s the first woman (Bertha Wilson) was appointed to the Supreme Court of Canada; there are now three women serving on that court. Sandra Day O'Connor was appointed to the Supreme Court of the United States in 1981; Mary Gaudron was appointed to the High Court of Australia in 1986. In Britain, when the first woman was appointed to the judiciary, the major issue appeared to be whether she should be titled "Mrs. Justice." She was! Nonethless, women are slowly making their way onto all levels of courts in the United States and other countries. In Australia, the greatest representation of women is on the Family Court (5 women, and approximately 50 men). In civil-law countries (Europe and countries previously colonized by Continental states), judges are members of the public service, so women have greater representation than in common-law countries. But men continue to hold the positions on the higher courts (e.g., the Constitutional Court in Germany).

From the nineteenth century (and before), women have protested their position in law. Agitation resulted in changes to women's property rights in marriage, custodial and guardianship rights of children of a marriage, access to public office and various professions, women's position as victims of violent and sexual crimes and women's position as criminals, particularly in relation to prostitution and imprisonment. Agitation continued in the 1960s and 1970s. The most significant overall critique was published by Karen DeCrow in 1974—*Sexist Justice: How Legal Sexism Affects You* (1974)—commencing with a general discourse on the misogyny of the law, a critique of "equal protection" under the United States Constitution, and coverage of discrimination in money and employment, estate law, family law, abortion, women and husbands' and fathers' family names, access to education, criminal law and criminology and the Equal Rights Amendment. Apart from this encompassing work, criminology (crime, offenders and punishment) was a major subject of feminist critique. In the United States, the writings of Meda Chesney-Lind, Laura Crites, Rita Simon and Dorie Klein were significant. (Freda Adler's 1975 *Sisters in Crime* was a regressive step, asserting "women's liberation" was "turning women to crime.") In 1979, Kathleen Barry's *Female Sexual Slavery* covered worldwide kidnapping, prostitution, and exploitation of women and girls (see Jane Caputi, this volume). In 1982, D. Kelly Weisberg edited *Women and the Law,* an historical and contemporary perspective in two volumes of women as offenders in the United States. In the United Kingdom, Carole Smart published *Women, Crime and Criminology* in 1976. Jocelynne Scutt's articles on women and crime appeared from the early 1970s in legal and criminological journals in Britain, Australia, Europe and Africa.

Discussions in legal and criminological journals on rape—particularly evidence laws— also injected feminist analysis into the law. Articles and books appeared in the 1970s: Susan Brownmiller's *Against Our Will: Men, Women and Rape;* writings by Diana E.H. Russell, Julia R. Schwendinger, Noreen Connell and Cassandra Wilson (1974); Lorenne Clark and Debra Lewis (1977); Barbara Toner's *The Facts of Rape* (1982) in Britain; and Jocelynne Scutt in Australia, New Zealand, Britain and Africa. Contemporary work was published on criminal assault in the home (following a tradition established in the mid 1800s by Frances Power Cobbe in her article on "wife torture"), with Erin Pizzey's *Scream Quietly or the Neighbours Will Hear* in the United Kingdom and Sue E. Eisenberg and Patricia L. Micklow in the United States (see *Women's Rights Law Reporter,* 1977). Rape in marriage became a focus with articles published from the mid 1970s in law journals in the United States, Britain, Europe, Africa and Australia, and with Diana Russell's book, *Rape in Marriage*, published in 1982.

Much of the writing that was critical of the law in this period was published in sociological or criminological journals, as well as some in historical journals. However, there were breaks-through into "straight" legal journals such as the *Harvard Law Review* and the *Australian Law Journal.*

Agitation about the framework and application of law to women came from grassroots and from individuals working within the academy and profession. The grassroots action centered around rape and criminal assault at home, expanding in the 1980s into child sexual abuse and father-daughter rape, wife killing and women prosecuted for marital murder. Leading texts were the United States' work of Ann Jones in *Women Who Kill* and Florence Rush in *The Best-Kept Secret: Sexual Abuse of Children* in 1980, followed by Judith Herman in *Father-Daughter Incest* in 1981; in the United Kingdom, work by Susan S.M. Edwards in *Women on Trial* in 1984, Jane Caputi in *The Age of Sex Crime* in 1988, Jalna Hanmer and Shiela Saunders in *A Well Founded Fear* in 1984, Elizabeth Wilson in *What is to be Done About Violence Against Women* in 1983; and in Australia, Elizabeth Ward in *Father-Daughter Rape* in 1984 and Jocelynne Scutt in *Even in the Best of Homes: Violence in the Family* in 1983, covering bashing, rape and sexual abuse of children at home, rape in marriage, woman bashing and marital murder (see Jane Caputi, this volume).

Feminist agitation has reframed rape laws in the United States, Canada, Australia and New Zealand, although feminists remain dissatisfied with the formulation and application of the laws. Changes in Michigan where new laws were crafted by women, including law professor Virginia Blomer Nordby, provided a base for rape law reform in the United States and Australia while also affecting the Canadian and New Zealand efforts. In the United Kingdom, feminist lobbying has impinged less. Rape laws remain out of step: for example, rape in marriage remains "no crime" in Britain. In Australia, all states make rape in marriage criminal.

Feminists have ensured that violence in the family is on governmental agendas and have helped to bring changes to enforcement of laws against these crimes. But feminists remain dissatisfied with the police, courts and governments.

Pornography as violence against women has raised feminist grassroots agitation. In the legal arena, in the 1980s Andrea Dworkin and Catharine A. MacKinnon first took up the challenge in the United States. Articles have been published in Australia and evidence given to a Joint Parliamentary Committee of the federal parliament proposing similar reforms. In New Zealand, a Ministerial Committee of Inquiry raised some feminist perspectives on pornography. Although incitement to racial hatred has been incorporated into antidiscrimination laws in one Australian state (New South Wales), no laws have been passed making pronography unlawful as discrimination against women. In Britain, some parts of the feminist movement appear to be bogged down in promale civil libertarianism, although the feminist perspective on pronography as violence against women has gained some attention. (See Susanne Kappeler, this volume.)

There is little doubt that the law has distorted women's experience and many laws have been designed with men, not women, in mind. The common law built up over centuries, under the direction of judges who determined what the law would be. Judges did this through case law: each case heard by a judge could provide a new facet of law or a new legal rule. Judges were obliged to operate by precedent and continue to be required to do so. This means they apply rules from earlier cases. But if a judge does not like the earlier rule, he can "distinguish" it from the case he (or more rarely, she) is deciding. He then devises a rule to cover the case to his liking. Predominantly male views thus color the law.

Case law clearly discriminates against women. The cases holding women were not "persons" and therefore not entitled to enter universities, hold public office, be elected to parliaments and local councils, enter various professions such as medicine and law, and enter various trades, show a clear bias. Only a man (or a colonized woman) could hold that a woman is not a person. Albie Sachs and Joan Hoff Wilson, in their book *Sexism and the Law* (1978), provide a comprehensive account of the relevant cases and judicial bias. Yet some judges—like the judge who determined upon Belle Mansfield's right to practice law in Iowa—specifically held out against biased interpretation of the law designed to keep women out.

Rape laws provide a clear illustration of the law's (and judges') refusal to accept women's reality and a wholesale trend toward accepting a false picture as "truth." Chief Justice Hale in seventeenth century Britain considered women were not to be trusted when they reported rape, and this has formed the basis of rape law in the United States, Canada, New Zealand, Britain, Australia and other common-law countries ever since. He manufactured a rule that juries should be warned that the charge of rape is a charge "easily made" and hard to be defended against, "tho the accused be ever so innocent." Hale also said that no married woman could be raped by her husband, because upon consent to marriage, she gave up any right to withhold consent to sexual intercourse. (Ironically, this "rule" meant that a man could rape his wife with impunity, so long as it was rape in the missionary position. If the parties agreed to an act of sexual intercourse involving penile-anal penetration, that would be criminal despite consent and despite a marriage contract. "Buggery" was a crime, whatever the circumstances, under common law.) Evidence laws surrounding rape were constituted differently from evidence laws in other crimes, in that the woman could be questioned about her sexual history and general conduct, even years before the event occurred, without the accused's history or credibility being questioned. There was a general assumption that deceit is a sex-linked characteristic: a characteristic possessed by women (and small children), and from which men remain immune.

In marital murder and crimes of assault against women married to their assailants, the law similarly shows bias. It was not recognized by judges until toward the end of the nineteenth century that it was criminal for a man to beat his wife. In a case decided in 1861, (*R. v. Jackson*) the majority held that a man did not have the right to kidnap his wife when she had left him and did not want to return. But some of the judges contemplated circumstances where a husband might rightly keep his wife imprisoned if she had not already left him—but was intending to go on a shopping spree, and he feared that she might spend all "his" money.

Rules of provocation and self-defense have been clearly developed with men in mind, not women. If a person is charged with murder, a plea of provocation can be put forward, which (if accepted) results in a conviction for manslaughter instead of murder. The classic example of provocation given is that of a husband coming home to find his wife engaged in the act of adultery with another man. Losing control, and in the midst of passion, the husband grabs a gun, or knife, or uses his hands to kill the man, the woman, or both. He can plead provocation and be acquitted of murder. Is it likely that this scenario would fit any woman? What woman has a gun or knife conveniently at hand for an occasion such as this? What woman is strong enough to strangle her husband or her husband's lover? What woman would do it if she could, anyway? And what man commits acts of adultery in his own home? Most go elsewhere—because they have the money for the hotel room or can go to the woman's home. If the woman does find her husband in the act of adultery, it is more likely that she will be devastated by the event, convinced that she has brought it on herself. If she goes away to think about it, then returns to kill, she has placed herself outside the rules relating to provocation and will be guilty of premeditated murder, not being consumed by passion, and therefore a murderess.

With self-defense, in common law it is necessary to show that the person doing the killing was in direct and real fear of being murderously attacked, and that the force used to fend off this attack was reasonable. This is generally expressed as the person who is prosecuted for murder having to show that attacking fists were met with fists. Obviously, if a man is attacked with fists, it makes sense to say he should retaliate with fists, rather than a knife. If attacked by a knife, it is reasonable to expect him to retaliate with a knife, rather than a gun or an axe. But for a woman, it makes little sense to expect her to retaliate against the fists of a man with her own fists, unless she has undergone specific training in fighting or self-defense. For the woman attacked by a man wielding fists, it is reasonable to retaliate with a knife. But the common law has not interpreted reasonableness in this way. The classic test of reasonableness is "what does the reasonable *man* do?," what would "the man in the street" do? The law has generally distinguished the reasonable man as male. A woman is not a "reasonable man."

In family law, women's work (paid and unpaid) is given no common-law recognition in assessing women's right to a proportion of the amount of property accumulated during marriage. Australia, through the 1975 *Family Law Act,* gave the first recognition in a common-law jurisdiction to the unpaid contribution made by women in the home, to the accumulation, maintenance and conversation of property in marriage. California, in the United States, followed, as did New Zealand. Canada gives this work some recognition. But there is no acknowledgment in family law that women's work is equal to men's work, just as there is no acknowledgment in industrial law that women's work in the paid workforce is equal to the work of men. Equal pay acts were fought for and gained by women in Britain and the United States, and in Australia women fought for recognition of equal pay, and equal pay for work of equal value, through Industrial Commissions. Although laws and decisions formally recognize women's right to equal pay, equal pay remains elusive. In the United States, women earn approximately 71 cents for every (full-time) male dollar; in Australia, the ratio is approximately 69 cents, when full-time and part-time paid work are taken into account, and 81 cents full-time work. The ratios are no better in Canada or in Britain, as pointed out by Jennifer Corcoran in her 1986 article in *Women's Studies International Forum.*

Women's work in the field of law has resulted in challenges to everything that the law stands for: the supposed neutrality of the law; the supposed "favor" with which the law looks upon women in criminal law and family law in particular, but in other fields of law as well; the biases harbored by those putting the law into effect, including judges, magistrates and police. Problems are created in the legal system by the sexist teaching of lawyers and by defective teaching in other disciplines; for example, sexist approaches being taught in social work, psychology, psychiatry, and medicine. Questions of new reproductive technologies and genetic engineering have also taken a different complexion because feminists have played a prominent role in highlighting the antiwoman nature of these procedures and the laws which have been developed to deal with them. Prominent in this debate are Gena Corea and Janice Raymond in the United States, Jalna Hanmer in the United Kingdom, Robyn Rowland in Australia and Renate Klein in Europe and Australia. (See Renate Klein, this volume.)

One of the problems with the law, and with new ways of looking at legal issues, is that sexism is built into the system itself, so that feminist impacts sometimes appear to be merely tinkering or embroidery at the edges. However, many of the campaigns have sought to challenge the very structure and authority of the law—with varying degrees of success. But it is instructive that major law journals have published contributions to the debate, thus giving them a legitimacy in areas which previously would not have given any ground to feminist ideas. Women have also played a prominent role in formal law reform efforts—for example, in various Law Reform Commissions in Australia, some in Canada, and less so in the United Kingdom. Women's Commissions, or Advisory Councils, or Consultative Councils, in Australia, Canada, New Zealand and the United States have made some contributions to legal debate and law reform, despite having to work within governmental structures and the strictures that follow from that.

In terms of significant methodological issues, the major development was to actually talk to, and listen to, women. This was an important advance in the legal system and in research relating to the legal system. Previously, men's experiences were at the root of the system and permeated the system, without women's experience, knowledge, voices, and reality having any relation to the way laws were focused, drafted and applied.

The legal mainstream has responded in a variety of ways to feminist pressures. Some reactions have been ungracious and defensive; some reactions have been welcoming. In the field of rape law reform, for example, it was clear that the law was not working satisfactorily. Proposed changes to rape laws prompted some reaction in the mainstream, but generally there has been acceptance—at least to some degree—of feminist proposals in Canada, the United States, New Zealand and Australia. Again, the United Kingdom has provided greater difficulties. For example, when asked in the mid 1980s to look again at the question of rape in marriage, the Law Commission continued to refuse to acknowledge a need to amend the law by making rape in marriage a crime, just as rape of a stranger is a crime, despite this change having been adopted by most common-law jurisdictions around the world. The Commission continues to be obsessed with the idea that women (particularly wives) tell lies, that the false complaints will be the order of the day. In Sweden, where the law was changed in 1965 to make rape in marriage a crime, there has been no rash of rape in marriage charges.

In the area of child sexual abuse, there has been a significant backlash, even before there was a significant move forward in the law and legal system. This is being experienced most clearly in the United States, in the United Kingdom (since the misreporting and misrepresentation of the so-called "Cleveland Affair"—as reported by Beatrix Campbell) and in South Australia. A backlash against feminist efforts in the area of rape law reform is also arising in Australia, centered upon South Australia, where a criminal law organization was set up in the mid 1980s specifically as a response to "feminist fiddling" with the laws relating to rape: this was explicitly stated in the material sent to lawyers who were seen as prospects for joining the organization.

There have also been considerable efforts by men's groups to agitate against feminist advances in family law, particularly with regard to custody and access as visitation, and to the acknowledgment of women's entitlement to some property, as a consequence of unpaid work in the home. The law does not give adequate recognition: it does not recognize women's *property rights* as a consequence of unpaid work; it does, however, give an *equitable right* to women in property accumulated by the paid efforts of the husband and the unpaid efforts of the wife. That is, any entitlement of the wife rests upon the discretion of the judge making the determination or, where the parties settle the matter without going to court, upon what the lawyers think is the appropriate value to place on the contribution of the woman to the property.

There has also been considerable backlash against women's work in the field of child sexual abuse, as it applies to fathers seeking access to children of the marriage or to custody of those children. Men's groups have been established around this issue to fight back against what are said to be methods used by women to "get back" at their husbands.

In some respects, men's resistance has not had to operate within the legal system. Because some of the changes brought about have been made parallel to the legal system, mainstream lawyers, judges and others have not had to directly confront the changes. For example, in the field of equal opportunity laws in Australia, the approach has been not to require the mainstream courts to administer these laws, but to have them administered by tribunals or boards which are not a part of the "real" legal system. This has allowed the courts to continue operating without any acknowledgment of the principles of equal opportunity. Appeals go from the boards or tribunals to the regular courts. This has meant that the courts do not have to deal, on a daily basis, with human rights and women's rights. It would be preferable to have the laws administered by the courts, which would not then be able to maintain a distinction between property rights and human and/or women's rights, dealing with the former as matters of the moment, the latter as irrelevant to the legal process.

Within the legal system, where courts in contemporary times have had to deal with matters related to women, sometimes feminist perspectives have been incorporated into decisions; sometimes they have not. One American feminist analyzed the United States Supreme Court's decisons on the 14th Amendment requirement that there be equal treatment of citizens and the failure of the Court to find "sex" as a suspect category, whereas "race" had been held clearly to be a suspect category. She succinctly expressed the view that this was because the judges of the Supreme Court did not go home to live with Black American citizens, but they did go home to live with women who were their wives. (With race a suspect category, any law which is founded in a racial distinction has to be proven by the body making the law to be nonracist. If it were not a suspect category, the onus of proving it racist would lie on the party protesting about the discriminatory effects of the law. Where sex is not a suspect category, women protesting discrimination on grounds of sex bear the onus proving the relevant law is sex discriminatory.)

The law is relatively easy to subvert when it comes to those areas which were drafted with feminist principles in mind. Just as some judges in the past were able to find women not "persons" to keep them out of universities and some professions, whilst other judges operating under similar laws found women were entitled to those privileges, today it is possible for judges to take divergent views on what laws mean and what the spirit of the law is. In the United States, some courts have found sexual harassment to be unlawful on grounds of sex, where the acts done could apply equally to a man or a woman, or where the sexual harasser harassed men as well as women. Other decisions have held that acts can be discrimination on grounds of sex if they are directed at women alone; if the man harasses both sexes, it cannot be sexual harassment. Some courts have held that discrimination on grounds of pregnancy is sex discrimination, because only women can suffer it. Others have held it is not discrimination for the same reason. This divergence is possible under laws which are framed in identical terms. The difference lies in the attitudes of the judge determining what the laws mean and in other factors relating to culture, socialization, and social mores.

Men have protected their power base in the law in a number of ways. Police have done so by convincing too many Women's Movement women that police need more powers, so harnessing women to a campaign by police to increase their power base. Lawyers in private practice and in the academic world have protected their power base by working to ensure that men continue to be appointed as professors and lecturers in law schools, where law can continue to be taught from a sexist perspective. Women have broken through, and in some cases men have worked to ensure that women have access; however, law schools remain dominated by men. It is more difficult for women to break into areas of corporate law and tax and relatively simple to work in family law and (in Australia at least) criminal law, where much of the work is done on legal aid, and is therefore not lucrative. Women do work in the corporate and tax areas, and women are appointed as in-house counsel to large corporate entities. But is remains true that women tend to be concentrated in areas of law seen as "women's fields" or "suitable for a woman." This also means that particular areas of law are themselves downgraded: family law should be an important legal field, dealing as it does with issues of real moment, affecting people's lives, yet it is seen as "easy" and "not important," or less important than corporate issues which involve large sums of money, or tax avoidance and evasion which again involve large sums.

Numerous male authorities have been challenged in law and the legal system. Women have demonstrated against judges' rulings in Canada, the United States, Australia, Britain and New Zealand, particularly in regard to rape cases. When the English House of Lords brought down the 1976 decision in *Morgan's case* that if a man honestly believes the woman is consenting to sexual intercourse, his act will not be rape, even if she was not consenting and it is unreasonable of him to think that she was (that is, objectively no one would have thought her to be consenting), women demonstrated in the streets of London, Sydney, and other Australian capital cities. In the United States, instances have occurred where judges have said women "were provocative" or "led the man on" in rape cases, and women have lobbied successfully to have the judge replaced at the next election. In 1985 in Melbourne, Australia, a judge held that a man could not be prosecuted or convicted for raping his wife, because the rape took place in the (former) matrimonial home when, after leaving her husband, the wife returned to collect some clothing. Demonstrations and agitation from women led to the almost instantaneous passage of an Act amending the *Crimes Act,* so that rape in those circumstances was classified as a crime.

Challenges have been made through writing in legal journals and journals in associated disciplines, such as sociology and criminology or penology. They have also been made in the courtroom, by feminist legal practitioners, and in the offices of solicitors and attorneys. They have been made in law schools as well. Numerous universities and other institutions of higher education include feminist perspectives in the law school curriculum. In the 1970s, such courses were established in law schools in the United States, as "Women and the Law" courses. Such courses were also established later in universities and other institutions in Canada, Britain, the United States and New Zealand. In the 1980s there has been a tendency for these courses to be watered down into "Gender and the Law" in some institutions. A problem with these courses is, however, that they are optional rather than part of the mandatory curriculum. And the students who attend already have some modicum of consciousness about the issues. The students (and professors) who should be involved, and who have the greatest necessity for being exposed to the issues, do not enroll or attend. They see these courses (if they see them at all) as "mickey mouse" or irrelevant to the real task of becoming a lawyer.

Feminist contributions in the legal field have a considerable potential for enriching understandings. It is, however, vital to recognize the fundamental role played by the law in women's oppression, and equally to recognize that the law can be used to benefit women and (at minimum) to illuminate ways in which patriarchy has operated, and continues to operate, to exploit and oppress women. The law is supremely resistant to feminist ideas and ideals because it is based in patriarchal beliefs. The law was originally designed to assist the powerful in retaining their power. It has played its part well. However, the structure of the law is not monolithic. There are male judges and male lawyers who have been prepared to stand out against the prevailing orthodoxy and to support arguments based in the rights of women and the injustice of denying women rights and privileges. The law has had to accommodate some women as lawyers and even as judges. It can also work to co-opt those women. But feminist lawyers continue to resist co-optation and to an extent succeed, which means that they are able to bring issues relevant to women and the liberation of women into the legal arena, where they get a public airing—and, sometimes, decisions in favor of women and feminist perspectives.

There can be little doubt that feminist knowledge has made an impact, at least among women and among (some) women law students and (some) women engaged in the teaching of law and the practice of law. It also cannot be doubted that it has had an impact on courts and the judiciary and on legislatures. Just as in early times feminist knowledge and agitation had an impact on the legal system, with the passage of legislation giving women rights to practice law and medicine, enter universities, run for public office, own property though married, and the like, this knowledge and agitation has had an impact on the legal system of today with equal opportunity and antidiscrimination or sex discrimination laws, laws relating to abortion, laws relating to equal pay and a recognition of women's unpaid work contribution to property accumulation in marriage, and laws relating to violence against women, particularly rape in marriage and changes to substantive rape laws.

However, just as feminist knowledge and feminist gains in other disciplines and spheres might be said to have a tenuous hold, it must be acknowledged that in the law it is always possible for backward steps to be taken—even backward leaps. But that there are equal numbers of women now going to law school in numerous countries, and that women are making in-roads into all areas of law, even corporate and tax laws in industrialized societies, means that it will be difficult to "turn back the tide." The law is in a totally different position today from the nineteenth century.

Currently, although the numbers of women in the various legislatures are not impressive (they in no way equate with the numbers of men), women are playing a significant role in some legislatures. For example in Australia, at the state level, two (Western Australia and Victoria) have women premiers and there are three additional women ministers of the crown; at the national level, two women hold ministerial positions. Virtually all these women would accept the appellation "feminist" and would endeavor to operate in accordance with feminist principles. Women are members of Congress and state legislatures in the United States, and of provincial legislatures and the federal legislature in Canada, and of parliaments in New Zealand and the United Kingdom, who also adhere to feminist beliefs and endeavor to act in accordance with feminist principles.

Organizations such as the National Organization for Women (NOW) in the United States and the Women's Electoral Lobby in Australia and New Zealand have played a significant role in lobbying for legislative changes. NOW is currently involved in a campaign to ensure that the gains won in relation to women's right to an abortion (via the 1973 Supreme Court case *Roe* v. *Wade*) are not lost, despite the current composition of the Supreme Court and their 1989 decision in the case *Webster* v. *Reproductive Health Services*. The 1973 decision would not have been possible without feminist agitation about women's autonomy and right to control our own bodies and lives. A campaign such as that currently underway by NOW would not have been possible 30 years ago. Similarly in Australia, women in Western Australia and in New South Wales are gearing up for a campaign to eliminate abortion from the *Crimes Act* and *Criminal Code,* so that no woman or her medical practitioner could be prosecuted for terminating a pregnancy at the woman's request. Abortion laws in Australia are framed in terms of what judges have ruled will not be an unlawful pregnancy-termination operation. Rather than a positive right to abortion, the law holds that in certain defined circumstances (for the life and health of the mother, psychological and phsyical), abortion is not unlawful and therefore not subject ot criminal prosecution.

Changes continue to be required in the area of marriage and property rights for women: the law must be changed to recognize that women's contributions to property are equal to those of men, whether by direct financial contribution or unpaid work in the home. Rape laws require further modification, so that it is clear beyond doubt that consent is irrelevant in cases of rape involving grievous bodily and/or mental harm (just as consent is irrelevant in other assaults or attacks involving grievous bodily harm); and in other cases of sexual assault, consent should be defined so that what is *not* consent—in women's terms—is set down without any doubt being able to be engendered about whether a woman has consented to sexual intercourse or not. Those jurisdictions which do not recognize rape in marriage as a crime must acknowledge this offense.

Laws relating to the sexual assault of children, particularly sexual molestation and rape of children by their fathers, must be enforced so that children are not placed in the invidious position of having to continue on access or child visitation to abusive fathers. Women should not be obliged to endure months of imprisonment, as has been so in the United States (Dr. Elizabeth Morgan is a prime example), where they have conerns about the sexual integrity of their children yet are required to stand by silently, sending them on access or visitation despite that concern. Phyllis Chesler's (1986, 1987) work (published in *Mothers on Trial: The Battle for Children and Custody)* has brought this problem starkly to attention—but more attention must be paid by those in authority and positions of power, particularly judges in family and divorce law.

Experimentation on women's bodies in the field of health—through new reproductive-technology programs and techniques, genetic engineering and the introduction of various devices and drugs (such as the so-called boon drug—another one—RU486)—must be outlawed. Changes are also required in relation to consent to medical treatment and the need for medical practitioners to explain, in easily understood language, the content and implications of various forms of treatment. (See Joan Altekruse and Sue Rosser, this volume.)

The potential for positive changes in the law, in the ways the law treats women, as well as in access to the law and positive ways for women to use it, is considerable. The way the law operates is fundamental to all women's lives. Whether women wish to be covered by various laws or not, the fact is that the law intrudes into every aspect of women's lives. It is therefore imperative that women who have legal training maintain direct connections with the broader Women's Movement. A tendency arises amongst women who have professional training, and particularly training which takes them into male-dominated fields, to forget our origins in the Women's Movement and to forget our real reason for existence—namely, to make this world a better world for women. To fight against this, women in professions such as the law have to take positive steps into the outside world. Women who are outside the formal legal system also do the women within it a favor by intruding into their domain and "keeping them true" to feminist ideals. The biggest issue for women in the law, and for the law and women, is for women who have gained some foothold in the system not to isolate themselves from the real world of women and from the issues confronting women in that world.

BIBLIOGRAPHY

Adler, Freda. (1975). *Sisters in crime: The rise of the new female criminal.* New York: McGraw-Hill.

Barry, Kathleen. (1979). *Female sexual slavery.* New York: Prentice-Hall. (1981, New York: Avon).

Brownmiller, Susan. (1975). *Against our will: Men, women and rape.* London: Secker and Warburg.

Campbell, Beatrix. (1988). *Unofficial secrets—child sexual abuse: The Cleveland case.* London: Virago Press.

Caputi, Jane. (1988). *The age of sex crime.* London: The Women's Press.

Chesler, Phyllis. (1986, 1987). *Mothers on trial: The battle for children and custody.* Seattle, WA: Seal Press.

Chesney-Lind, Meda. (1974, July). Juvenile delinquency: The sexualisation of female crime. *Psychology Today,* p. 44.

Chesney-Lind, Meda. (1979). Chivalry re-examined: Women and the criminal justice system. In Lee H. Bowker (Ed.), *Women, crime and the criminal justice system* (p. 197), Lexington, MA: Lexington Books.

Chesney-Lind, Meda. (1988). Girls and status offences: Is juvenile justice still sexist? *Criminal Justice Abstracts, 20*(1), 144.

Clark, Lorenne N.G. & Lewis, Debra. (1977). *Rape: The price of coercive sexuality.* Toronto: Women's Press.

Cobbe, Frances Power. (1869). *Criminals, idiots, women and minors: Is the classification sound?* 9 Ireland, Manchester, UK.

Cobbe, Frances Power. (1878). Wife torture in England. *Contemporary Review, 55.*

Connell, Noreen & Wilson, Cassandra (Eds.). (1974). *Rape: The first source book for women.* New York: New American Library, Plenum Publishing.

Corcoran, Jennifer. (1986). Law and the promotion of women. *Women's Studies International Forum, 9*(1), 19.

Crites, Laura. (1976a). Women offenders: Myth vs reality. In Laura Crites (Ed.), *The female offender.* Lexington, MA: D.C. Heath.

Crites, Laura. (1976b). *The female offender.* Lexington, MA: D.C. Heath.

DeCrow, Karen. (1974). *Sexist justice: How legal sexism affects you.* New York: Random House.

Director of Public Prosecutions v Morgan, 61 Criminal Appeal Reports 136 (1975)

Edwards, Susan S.M. (1984). *Women on trial: A study of the female suspect, defendant and offender in criminal law and criminal justice system.* Manchester, UK: Manchester University Press.

Eisenberg, Sue E. & Micklow, Patricia L. (1977). The assaulted wife: "Catch 22" revisited. *Women's Rights Law Reporter, 3* (Spring, Summer), 151.

Epstein, Cynthia Fuchs. (1983). *Women in law.* New York: Anchor Books/Doubleday.

Griffin, Susan. (1979). *Rape: The power of consciousness.* San Francisco: Harper & Row.

Hanmer, Jalna & Saunders, Shiela. (1984). *Well founded fear.* London: Hutchinson.

Hanmer, Jalna & Saunders, Shiela (Eds.). (1984). *Women, violence and crime prevention.* Yorkshire, UK: West Yorkshire County Council.

Hanmer, Jalna & Stanko, Elizabeth. (1985). Stripping away the rhetoric of protection: Violence to women, law and the state in Britain and the U.S.A. *International Journal of the Sociology of Law, 13,* 357.

Herman, Judith Lewis, with Hirschman, Lisa. (1981). *Father-daughter incest.* Cambridge, MA: Harvard University Press.

Jones, Ann. (1980). *Women who kill.* New York: Holt, Rinehart and Winston. (Published with new material 1981, New York: Fawcett Columbine.)

Klein, Dori. (1973). The etiology of female crime: A review of the literature. *Issues in Criminology, 8*(2), 3.

Klein, Dori & Kress, June. (1976). Any woman blues: A critical overview of women, crime and the criminal justice system. *Crime and Social Justice, 5,* 34.

Mathews, Jane. (1982). The changing profile of women in law. *Australian Law Journal, 56,* 634.

Morello, Karen Berger. (1986). *The invisible bar—The woman lawyer in America: 1638 to the present.* Boston: Beacon Press.

People v Rincon Pineda, 538 P. 2d 247, 14 Cal. 3d 864, 123 Cal. Rptr 119 (1975).

Pizzey, Erin. (1974). *Scream quietly or the neighbors will hear.* Harmondsworth, UK: Penguin Books.

Rush, Florence. (1980). *The best-kept secret: Sexual abuse of children.* Englewood Cliffs, NJ: Prentice-Hall.

Russell, Diana E.H. (1982). *Rape in marriage.* New York: Macmillan.

Sachs, Albie & Wilson, Joan Hoff. (1978). *Sexism and the law: A study of male beliefs and judicial bias.* Oxford: Martin Robertson.

Schwendinger, Julia R. & Schwendinger, Herman. (1983). *Rape and inequality.* Beverly Hills, CA: Sage Publications.

Scutt, Jocelynne A. (1983). *Even in the best of homes: Violence in the family.* Carlton, Australia: McCulloch Publishing. (Published with updated chapter 1990, Ringwood, Australia: Penguin.)

Segal, Lynne. (1983). *What is to be done about the family?* Harmondsworth, UK: Penguin.

Simon, Rita J. (1976). *Women and crime.* Lexington, MA: D.C. Heath & Co.

Smart, Carol. (1976). *Women, crime and criminology.* London: Routledge & Kegan Paul.

Toner, Barbara. (1982). *The facts of rape.* London: Arrow Books.

Ward, Elizabeth. (1984). *Father-daughter rape.* London: The Women's Press.

Weisberg, D. Kelly (Ed.). (1982). *Women and the law: The social historical perspective.* Cambridge, MA: Schenkman Publishing Company, Inc. In two volumes.

Wilson, Elizabeth. (1983). *What is to be done about violence against women?* Harmondsworth, UK: Penguin.

Chapter 19

Women Deserve Spatial Consideration

(or, Geography Like No One Ever Learned in School)

Joni Seager

This is not a global survey. Although the intellectual course of the discipline is surprisingly similar around the world, specific references, dates, and examples used in this article are particular to the American situation, unless otherwise noted. Separate histories of women and geography in most other countries are yet to be written.

A TWENTY-YEAR RETROSPECTIVE

Geography is a hybrid discipline, an awkward coalition of physical earth study, social science spatial analysis, and humanistic place study. Thus, while some geographers measure soil movement in river systems, others examine the structure and design of urban space, and still others ponder the meaning and evolution of "sense of place." It is this abundance that makes the discipline exciting and vibrant. Although all the subfields of geography are linked by a central concern for "the why of where," this diversity in research and theoretical approach has provoked an interminable disciplinary identity crisis—geographers constantly argue among themselves about what Geography is. One side effect of this professional insecurity is the prevailing ethos that geographers should strive to locate and legitimate their work by measuring it against what is held to be "good" and "rigorous" science (as measured by the most conventional icons). Even humanistic geographers find it hard to escape the allure of scientific legitimacy. In consequence, the representation of women within Geography, and the treatment of women as subjects of study, is more comparable to the situation in the physical sciences than to it is to other social sciences or humanities.

All of which is to say that 20 years ago, women were not in the university classrooms, nor in the textbooks, nor in the minds of most geographers. A 1973 survey of the geographical literature (Wilbur Zelinsky, 1973a) produced absolutely no citations on the subject of women. As an undergraduate Geography major at the University of Toronto in the early 1970s, I never once heard a classroom discussion of the role of women in the world, not even in the two-year-long Population Geography courses that I took—which, in

With thanks to Eve Gruntfest, Susan Hanson, Bonnie Loyd, Tamar Mayer, Janice Monk and Linda Peake for information and guidance.

retrospect, is an amazing feat, given that these courses focused primarily on how and why human populations expand and decline. As a Geography student at Toronto, the only professional woman I encountered was the department secretary.

This is not surprising. In the academic year 1971–1972, there were only 54 women teaching in graduate Geography schools in all of North America[1], more than half of whom held an academic rank of assistant professor or lecturer (Wilbur Zelinsky, 1937b). By 1979–1980, the ranks had swelled to a total of 80 women geographers teaching in the Canadian and American network of 146 graduate schools (Wilbur Zelinsky, Janice Monk, & Susan Hanson, 1982); in Britain in the 1970s, women represented an average of 7% of university geography lecturers (Women & Geography Study Group, 1984). Nor were women visible as researchers. In the decade of 1961–1971, women authored fewer than 5% (on average) of the articles published in the five major American professional journals of Geography (Wilbur Zelinsky, Janice Monk, & Susan Hanson, 1982); in Spain in the similar period, about 6% of geography journal authors were women (M. Dolores Garcia-Ramon, Margarida Castaner, & Nuria Centelles, 1988).

Women had slightly more presence in the Association of American Geographers (AAG), the largest professional geographers' association in the world. In 1967, there were 529 women members—or about 13% of total AAG membership[2]. But even here, women represented the anomalous "other": special excursions and activities "for the ladies" (i.e., wives of geographers) were still being scheduled for the annual AAG meetings as late as 1973.

The overview of women in the discipline provided by academic or academic-related measures is somewhat misleading. Women have always been numerically more important in the fields of *applied* geography than in academia: women are well represented in jobs and as cartographers, population assessors for census bureaus, and geographic education institutes. But these women tend not to participate in academic forums, nor do they publish in the disciplinary journals. For a realistic view of the state and status of women in Geography, it is important to remember that because of the applied versus academic split, there is a strata of women's participation in Geography that has always been relatively invisible, and remains so today.

EMERGING FEMINIST CRITIQUES

The year 1973 was a threshold for the emergence of feminist geography in North America and Great Britain[3]: the first articles about women and geography were published in Geography journals. Three survey articles appeared assessing the dismal state of women in the discipline (Peggy Lentz, 1973; Wilbur Zelinsky, 1973a; Wilbur Zelinsky 1973b), and, perhaps more importantly, the first substantive articles on the geography of women appeared (Pat Burnett, 1973; Bonnie Loyd, 1973). From 1973 on, there was an exponential growth in the geographical literature on women, and in 1976 the first bibliography of American materials on geography and women was compiled, containing more than 60 references (Bonnie Loyd, 1976).

The first substantive feminist critiques of the field, although clearly catalyzed by popular feminist organizing, did not draw on the theory and praxis of the larger women's movement, but rather grew out of radical movements already present within the discipline. The first feminist wave drew on the philosophical strengths of Marxist critiques of mainstream "scientific" Geography, and several of the early articles on women and geography were published in the radical geographical journal, *Antipode*. The work of Marxist geographers pointed the way in particular for feminist questioning of the assumptions of geographical models of urban development—and reconstructing urban geography is now a central strand in the feminist geography repertoire. The extent of the link between Marxist frameworks and feminist critiques varied considerably across the discipline, and from country to country. In Great Britain, for example, the Marxist and feminist, and especially the socialist and feminist, link was stronger from the start than in the United States and remains so today.

Radical and feminist geographers still share critiques of the field, and some prominent feminist geographers pursue historical materialist research, but the bloom is largely off the rose: the theoretical and methodological discordance resulting from the attempt to combine Marxist and feminist critiques (that "unhappy marriage", as it is often called) became apparent early on. Further, by the late 1970s, women in geography (as in the women's movement at large) were largely disenchanted with the very male and often misogynist left wing. The phase of cooperation between Marxism and feminism in American Geography was ephemeral: the Marxist did not pursue feminist analysis, nor did American feminists, in general, persist in Marxist research. (In Great Britain and Australia, the feminist and Marxist link, and more so the feminist and socialist link, is proving to be more durable.) Nonetheless, the presence of a radical caucus in Geography, which was relatively well established by the early 1970s, was crucial to early feminist efforts.

Because the boundaries of geographical study overlap a number of other disciplines, influences from other disciplines were particularly important in the early development of feminist geographical critiques. For example, Esther Boserup, an economist, was among the first to suggest that women are victimized by conventional international development policies (Esther Boserup, 1970), and her work broke ground for what is now a major subfield in Geography—the study of women and international development. [See Claudia Salazar, this volume.] Early feminist analysis of women's perceptions of and relationships to both natural and "man-made" landscapes (Bonnie Loyd, 1975a, 1975b; Nancy Wilkinson, 1979) drew heavily on feminist research in history and architecture. Feminist geography continues to draw strength from multidisciplinary contributions.

The 1973 surge in feminist publishing followed women's organizing that had been underway in the profession for at least two years prior. The first visible agitation in the field focused on issues of women's equity and representation within the profession—as in many disciplines, these were the issues that brought women's organizing out of the closet. The Committee on the Status of Women in Geography (CSWG), a permanent subcommittee of the AAG, was formed in 1971 to assess and monitor the status of women geographers; a special discussion panel on women in geography was convened for the first time at the AAG conference in 1972, followed by similar panels in 1973 and 1974. Feminist research organizing took a few more years to emerge: in 1975 the first issue of *Women and Environments* was published, a journal that continues to be on the cutting edge of feminist research in geography: in the United States, the "Geographic Perspectives on Women" research group within the AAG was formed in 1979, the first year that the "specialty group" structure was in place and that such a group could be formed; equivalent groups in Canada and Great Britain coalesced in the late 1970s.

MAKING WOMEN INVISIBLE

Geography in the 1960s and 1970s was burdened by a language that pointedly excluded women, analytical tools that left the female half of the world in the dark, and an all male ethos that smothered women in classrooms and conference meeting halls.

The language of Geography was an early warning of the extent to which the existence of women on earth was denied: geographers' libraries are lined with books from the 1960s and 1970s with titles such as *Plants, Man and Life, The Man-Made Environment,* and *Man's Role in Changing the Face of the Earth.* For decades, "human geographers"—that is those geographers who study human relationships to space and place, as opposed to the physical earth–science side of the discipline—used a single phrase to summarize the focus of their field: the "man–land tradition." This phrase represented the central organizing principle of a whole branch of the discipline; it also unintentionally described the literal focus of geographers' interests: the *man*–land relationship.

Susan Hanson and Janice Monk, two feminist geographers, have categorized some of the ways in which women were made invisible by conventional geographical research (Janice Monk & Susan Hanson, 1982; Janice Monk, 1988):

1. Many geographical research questions are incompletely framed; scholars may write about areas of life in which women and men both participate, but men's experiences are presumed to represent both. Standard urban geography texts describe suburbia, for example, solely through the eyes of male residents, ignoring the fact that women's lives and men's lives in suburban environments are completely different. "Head of household" (always presumed to be male) sampling was standard fare in geographical surveys. Men were portrayed in geography textbooks as the sole agents of geographical change—it was men who built and lived in cities, men who farmed, and men who made resources policy.
2. If women are discussed, authors often assume stereotypical and fixed gender roles, and additionally may bring a Western bias to discussion of women's lives in other cultures.
3. Research themes that directly address women's lives, such as child care, women's legal rights, or unpaid work, are neglected.
4. Brief recognition may be given to gender differences, but their significance is dismissed in making generalizations.

The exclusion of women from the geographical field of vision is not a problem of superficial or transient gender blindness. Many of the problems, above, suggest deeply embedded, structural flaws in geographical analysis and theory. The "scientific" and positivist approach to gathering knowledge, which has been so enticing to geographers, incorporates a stance of anonymity, neutrality, objectivity, and universality. By shaping geographical research in a mod of scientific neutrality, the assumption of collectivity takes precedence over the possibility of difference in geographers' research (Tamar Mayer, 1989). Feminist theory makes clear the ways in which an illusion of universality serves as a source of women's oppression and undergirds sexist ideology—by attempting to present the "neutral" in describing human relationships to space and place, geographers mask the potential conflicts between the interests of men and women, and between particular groups of both men and women.

The humanist tradition within Geography, which has always stood as an alternative to positivist hegemony, has not welcomed feminist geography either. Humanist geography, with its concern with agency (i.e., individuals), as opposed to structuralist geography, which emphasizes structures such as class, might have been expected to differentiate between individuals in terms of their gender—but it never did Marxist geography, humanist geography, phemonenological geography (which had its heyday in the late 1970s), cultural geography, historical geography: researchers in these fields have not taken up feminist critiques or analysis, nor have they particularly encouraged feminist participation in their caucuses and meetings.

NEW DIRECTIONS FOR GEOGRAPHY

Feminist geographers, working from within a heavily male and science-aspirant discipline, faced an uphill battle to legitimate feminist geography—especially when it began to dawn on other geographers that the feminists were calling for a reassessment of most of the basic principles of the discipline. Within human geography, the first step meant a reassessment of the relationships between people and space, place, environment, landscape—the lived spatial contexts within which we all conduct our daily affairs. Geographers had long accepted that the relationship of groups or individuals to environment is an interactive process influenced by class, political power, and race, the inclusion of gender in this analytical assemblage was (and is) considerably more controversial.

Three interlocked observations served as the departure point for feminist geography (Joni Seager, 1985):

1. that space is gendered; that is, the design and use of space—like all other cultural constructs—is determined in part by ideological assumptions about gender roles and relations (for example, the related spatial dichotomies of public and private, work and home, city and suburb)
2   that, in turn, spatial relations help to maintain and shape culturally specific notions of gender behavior (for example, when suburbia becomes a geographic "trap" for women, isolating them from public services and work opportunities)
3. that gender is one of the interpretive lenses influencing our relationship to environment (women's perception of "safe" and "unsafe" environments, for example, is markedly different from men's).

From these fundamental principles, three distinct but interrelated research tracks have emerged: some feminist research has focused on identifying the distinctive "geography of women," the world of women that is different from the world of men; some research examines the consequences for women of living in a world designed by patriarchy and dominated by patriarchal spatial arrangements; and, some research has extended the analytical borders of the discipline by introducing gender as a category of explanation and theory.

Feminist geography is now on the leading edge of the discipline. Feminist geographers are recasting old geographical problems and rewriting theory, and are forging completely new areas of research and new methodologies. A quick survey of the feminist geographical literature suggests its broad sweep.[4]

Spatial Patterns of Diversity

Feminist geographers have clearly undercut the assumption that descriptions of men's lives and men's worlds represent a universal norm. By specifically asking geographical questions about women's daily lives—about women's access to resources, about the spatial structures that are the context for women's work and home lives, about women's access to waged work, about women's status globally—feminists have exposed the very clear differences between men and women, and among women (Mary Ellen Mazey & David Lee, 1983; Joni Seager & Ann Alson, 1986; Janet H. Momsen & Janet Townsend, 1987). With this new understanding of the distinctiveness of women's lives, and of the differences in women's lives around the world, geographers have been participants in the creation of a new research and policy field—women and international development.

Women and Environmental Response

Geographers have joined with researchers from a number of other disciplines in introducing gender into the study of environmental perception. In so doing, they are rewriting conventional geographical and historical wisdoms: we find that European women had a very different view than men of European encounters with the American west (Annette Kolodny, 1984; Nancy Wilkinson, 1979); women and men do not share a common perception of the American Southwest (Vera Norwood & Janice Monk, 1987); and worldwide, women assess urban environments differently than men, in terms of perceived opportunity, safety, and access (Shirley Ardener, 1981; Briavel Holcomb, 1984; Gerda Wekerle, Rebecca Peterson, & David Morley, 1980). Further, environmental perception studies have made visible the differences among women (in terms of ethnicity, class, and race), and changes over time in women's relationships to landscape.

Environments of Women

Following from the understanding that women and men operate differently in common environments, some feminist geographers have turned to study women's environments—domestic space (Bonnie Loyd, 1975a, 1975b; Roger Miller, 1983; Joni Seager, 1988), lesbian communities and specifically designed women's spaces (Polly Wynn Allen, 1988; Alison Hayden, 1984; Heresies, 1981). [See also Leslie Weisman, this volume.] These are all environments previously overlooked by geographers, and still overlooked by most male geographers.

Gender & Urban Theory

Recent feminist geographical research establishes that women and men are not equal or equivalent urban users and actors. Women's urban experience is inadequately represented by conventional urban theories and models that describe the development and consequences of different urban forms. As feminist scrutiny turns to our cities, it becomes apparent that the differences between men and women run through all aspects of urban life: in commuting patterns and transportation use, in patterns of housing and homelessness, in labor force participation and work opportunities, and in the use of urban social space (Ruth Fincher, 1987; Susan Hanson & Ibipo Johnson, 1987; Briavel Holcomb, 1984; Jo Little, Linda Peake, & Pat Richardson, 1988; Geraldine Pratt & Susan Hanson, 1988; Joni Seager, 1986; Catherine Stimpson, 1980; Sophie Watson & Helen Austerberry, 1986; Gerda Wekerle, Rebecca Peterson, & David Morley, 1980).

MAINSTREAM RESPONSES

The fact that Geography is a divided field diminishes the influence of feminist critiques across the discipline. Physical geographers can claim (with some justification) that feminists have not demonstrated the significance of gender to their objects of study; indeed, there does not seem to be an applicable feminist critique of soil movement, river flow, or rock formation. Feminist critiques of the *practice* of science and of the ways that scientific knowledge is structured, introduced in other disciplines by scholars such as Evelyn Fox Keller and Sandra Harding, may well be generally applicable to Geography-as-science, but they have not been broached by feminists in the field. There has been some recent interest in identifying the gender divisions of labor in geographical field work; when a team of geographers prepares to camp out for a summer to measure some physical phenomenon, the role of women and of men in the daily life and hierarchy of the field camp seems significantly different. The practice of physical geography, and particularly the field camp tradition, thus seems to be coming under some feminist scrutiny. But by and large, as it now stands, half the discipline can claim that feminist theory has little to do with them, and they have no reason to hide their indifference.

Among the human geographers, the primary reaction to feminist critiques appears to be a mild and benign curiosity. There is very little obvious acrimony. Most geographers have learned not to openly scoff when feminist topics are raised, and in some quarters there is genuine interest and respect—feminist geography is seen by some to be a leading edge of the field. But on the other hand, this may be the tolerance of the mighty. There are, after all, only a handful of active feminist geographers relative to the "malestream," and although we appear to have an influence greater than our numbers, there is no real threat at this time to the male hegemony in Geography.

Because it continues to be the case that the overwhelming share of the literature on the geography of women is generated by women, the spread of feminist geography is limited by the extent to which women themselves are present and prominent in the profession. Current data on the memberships of various specialty groups in the AAG shows a strong association between gender and specialty. The specialty groups with the highest proportions of women are those associated with "social concerns," such as Medical Geography, Aging, Population, and Environment. The most male-dominated groups include Transportation Geography, Soviet Studies, and Climatology (Michael Goodchild & Donald Janelle, 1988). The spread of feminist geography is further limited by the fact that the women geographers who are specialists in fields such as cartography and physical geography are not likely to generate or deal with research issues on women.

The prospects for feminist geography are thus almost totally dependent on the persistence and strength of a minority culture (women) in the discipline. So, to fully assess the response to feminist geography, one has to further inquire about the treatment of women within the field. The "men's club" atmosphere of the discipline, which is palpable at every national or international geographers' gathering, perpetuates a cycle that keeps women's presence low. And we find that although feminist geography, per se, may not be the object of disdain, women often are—either by omission or commission. Women in geography must fight for every gain, and the battles often rage around the most mundane and humble symbols. Some recent examples:

- As in most professions, members can identify their specialized interests by topical category; thus, on the annual AAG membership forms, geographers can identify their work by selecting from 50 categories such as "climatology" or "population geography" or "land use." After a decade of lobbying, it was only in 1987 that the AAG allowed "gender" to be included on the list of topical specialties.
- Few of the major American or Canadian professional geography journals have a non-sexist language editorial policy, although some individual editors do impose nonsexist standards at their own discretion. The Council of the Association of American Geographers recently passed a nonsexist language policy, but the presence of this policy remains to be publicized, and enforcement is weak.
- A much feted textbook published in 1985 reprinted a series of cartoons (originally circulated in the 1960s) to illustrate the struggle in the field between qualitative and

quantitative interests (see cartoon, page 221): The male author, when challenged, did not concede that these cartoons depicted scenes of violence against women, denied that they were offensive to women, and did not understand complaints that they categorized women (and particularly women geographers) as "the other."

• In the late 1970s, there was a national women's campaign in the United States to ask professional and trade organizations not to hold conferences in states that had not ratified the ERA. Over 250 scholarly and professional organizations, including all of the major social science associations, supported this boycott. In 1978, the AAG membership voted against the boycott, and proceeded with plans to hold its conference in a nonratified state. (The Association is not consistently conservative—10 years earlier, by contrast, the AAG Executive Committee decided to move the annual meeting out of Chicago in response to the political boycott called in the aftermath of the 1968 riots).

Many disciplines have "biology-is-destiny" arguments hidden in their intellectual recesses that are paraded out to dismiss women. Geographers have their own particular proprietary strategy to silence feminist critics: the debate about male and female differences in spatial skills (the assumption being that men have superior spatial skills). The spatial skills debate periodically rears its head in the geographical literature, usually introduced by a disgruntled male author in a flourish to establish definitively and "scientifically" that women are deservedly lesser peers in the discipline (see, for example, Wolf Roder, 1977). Whereas most geographers dismiss this debate out of hand, it's a constant thorn and its use as a diversionary tactic is skillful.

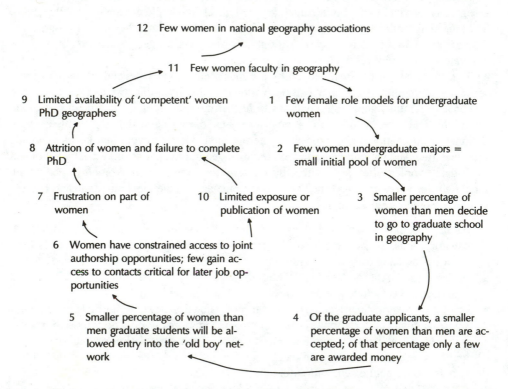

Chain of events in the structural discrimination hypothesis for explaining the limited number of women in geography. *Source:* Zelinsky, 1982; reprinted with permission.

The abduction of
Geographia by
Quantifactus.
Source: Gould,
1985; reprinted with
permission.

A CHANGING DISCIPLINE?

There is no question that the face of Geography as a discipline now bears the imprint of feminism. Feminist panels at national conferences are among the most popular and are widely acknowledged to be the most exciting; student interest in feminist geography is high, and growing; the blatant use of sexist language in textbooks and course materials has been greatly diminished (Tamar Mayer, 1989); articles on feminist geography (and on feminism within geography) are accepted for publication in most of the mainstream geographical journals; geographers' associations in the United States, Canada, Britain, and Australia now have active feminist caucuses; strong feminist networks have been forged in The Netherlands, West Germany, and Spain. In 1988, the International Geographic Union, a prestigious association, ratified the formation of a Gender and Geography Study Group within the IGU. In many ways, feminist geography is now "hot."

But it is hard to estimate the extent to which this wave of interest and acceptance represents a fad. By and large, our successes have not yet translated into structural change within the discipline. A few statistics illustrate the recalcitrance of the discipline: women are still far outnumbered by men at all levels of professional activity, and the disproportion is greatest toward the upper end of the scale. In Canada, Spain, and Great Britain, women currently represent only up to 9% of all fulltime geography faculty in colleges and universities; in the United States, 12% to 13%. In 1987, 27% of the female members of the AAG were employed in colleges or universities, compared to 50% of the men who were so employed. The Geographic Perspectives on Women group of the AAG, the largest feminist geographers' study group in the world, has at best 150 members; the British equivalent, the IBG Study Group, counts nearly 100 members (Jo Little, Linda Peake, & Pat Richardson, 1988).

The late 1980s trend within Geography in the United States, Canada, and Great Britain (and probably elsewhere) is toward a specialty known as "Geographic Information Systems" (GIS), which is basically an advanced form of remote sensing. By far, the most research applications and the most new jobs are in GIS, a subfield that is having an inordinate influence on geography because of available funding from government and scientific research establishments. Geography's embrace of GIS is escalating the militarization of the field (most GIS money comes from the military, even if funneled through other government agencies), and is reinforcing dependence on scientific and positivist paradigms—a trend that, for reasons noted elsewhere, is bound to undercut feminist influences in the discipline.

Other indicators reflect different aspects of the problem. For example, it is now possible to find an occasional listing for a geography teaching position seeking applicants to teach a cross-listed course with women's studies; but there has yet to be a job advertised in the United States for someone to primarily teach feminist geography. Feminist geography is still treated very much as a sideline, not as a legitimate and full specialization in itself. The overwhelming majority of geography departments in the United States and Canada have no course offerings in feminist geography; where such courses are offered, they are typically taught by marginalized parttimers, and often are a once-only offering. There is no "center" for feminist geography—no place a student can go to find a cluster of feminist geographers; many departments have never had a woman on staff, and still don't. Several of the feminist geographers who are most active within the American and Canadian feminist network do not hold teaching positions.

The channels of communication within feminist geography thus still operate largely outside the main structures of the discipline. Although there is a journal (*Women and Environments*) and most national feminist caucuses have a newsletter, communication and exchange of ideas among feminist geographers still depends very much upon personal contact. While this fosters an important "old girl" network, it does not necessarily foster permanence or structural support.

CONCLUSION

Geographers study place, space, landscape—the lived contexts of everyday life. Around the world, geographers are involved in developing policy for a wide range of public and social planning undertakings—in urban planning, transportation system planning, housing policies, hazards protection, international development policies, water supply, resources allocation, among others. A feminist interpretation of the socio-spatial structure and conditions of society, and a feminist restructuring of the discipline of Geography, can have wide-ranging consequences. But (to use a geographical metaphor), although we have established a permanent camp in the foothills, the central *massif* remains to be scaled.

NOTES

1. For comparison, there were 1,675 men teaching in graduate Geography schools in the same year.
2. This figure was tabulated by Frederick Rechlin, and passed on to the author by Janice Monk.

3. Feminist critiques in other countries appeared much later—for example, not until the early 1980s in Spain [Garcia-Ramon, Castaner, & Centelles, 1988].

4. The categories used in this survey were suggested by Janice Monk's 1988 work.

BIBLIOGRAPHY

Allen, Polly Wynn. (1988). *Building domestic liberty: Charlotte Perkins Gilman's architectural feminism.* Amherst, MA: University of Massachusetts Press.

Ardener, Shirley. (1981). *Women and space.* London: Croom Helm.

Berman, Mildred. (1977). Facts and attitudes on discrimination as perceived by AAG members: Survey results. *The Professional Geographer, 29*(1), 70–76.

Boserup, Esther. (1970). *Women's role in economic development.* London: Allen & Unwin.

Bowlby, Sophie, Foord, Jo, & McDowell, L. (1986). The place of gender in locality studies. *Area, 18*(4), 327–331.

Burnett, Pat. (1973). Social change, the status of women, and models of city form and development. *Antipode, 5*(1), 57–62.

Fincher, Ruth. (1987). Social theory and the future of urban geography. *The Professional Geographer, 39,* 9–12.

Garcia-Ramon, M. Dolores, Castaner, Margarida, & Centelles, Nuria. (1988). Women and geography in Spanish universities. *The Professional Geographer, 40*(3), 307–315.

Goodchild, Michael & Janelle, Donald. (1988). Specialization in the structure and organization of geography. *Annals of the Association of American Geographers, 78*(1), 1–28.

Gruntfest, Eve. (In press). Geographic perspectives on women: A status report. In Gary Gaile & C. Wilmott (Eds.), *Geography in America.* Boston: John Wiley & Sons.

Hanson, Susan & Johnson, Ibipo. (1985). Gender differences in work-trip lengths. *Urban Geography, 21,* 139–148.

Hanson, Susan & Pratt, Geraldine. (1988). Spatial dimensions of the gender division of labor in a local labor market. *Urban Geography, 9,* 180–202.

Hayden, Dolores. (1984). *Redesigning the American dream.* New York: W. W. Norton.

Hayford, Alison. (1974). The geography of women: An historical introduction. *Antipode, 6*(2), 1–19.

Holcomb, Briavel. (1984). Women in the city. *Urban Geography, 5,* 247–254.

Kolodny, Annette. (1984). *The Land Before Her.* Chapel Hill, NC: University of North Carolina Press.

Lentz, Peggy. (1973, June). A too silent majority. *The Monadnock, 47,* 59–60.

Libbee, Michael. (1980). Geographic research and women. *Transition, 9*(4), 2–5.

Little, Jo. (1987). Women and geography study group: A report. *Area, 19,* 368.

Little, Jo, Peake, Linda, & Richardson, Pat. (Eds.). (1988). *Women in cities: Gender and the urban environment.* London: Macmillan.

Loyd, Bonnie. (1973, October). Male and female differences in spatial mobility. *Proceedings of the AAG, Middle States Division, 7,* 23–25.

Loyd, Bonnie. (1975a). *The home as a social environment and women's landscape.* Paper presented at Annual Meeting of AAG, Milwaukee, WI.

Loyd, Bonnie. (1975b). Woman's place, man's place. *Landscape, 20*(1), 10–13.

Loyd, Bonnie. (1976). Women and geography: A resource list. *Exchange Bibliography #1159.* Berkeley, CA: Council of Planning Librarians.

Loyd, Bonnie. (1981). Women, home, and status. In James Duncan (Ed.), *Housing and identity.* London: Croom Helm.

Mackenzie, Suzanne, Foord, Jo, & Breitbart, Myrna. (Eds.). (1984). Women and the environment [Special Issue]. *Antipode, 16*(3).

Mackenzie, Suzanne. (1980). Women's place—Women's space: A geographical study of women. *Area, 12,* 947–949.

Making room: Women and architecture [special issue]. (1981, March 11). *Heresies, 3.*

Mayer, Tamar. (In press). Consensus and invisibility: The representation of women in human geography textbooks. *The Professional Geographer.*

Mazey, Mary Ellen & Lee, David. (1983). *Her space, her place: A geography of women.* Washington, DC: AAG.

McDowell, Linda & Peake, Linda. (1989). Women in British geography revisited: The same old story. *Journal of Geography in Higher Education, 13,* 2.

Miller, Roger. (1983). The Hoover in the garden: Middle class women and suburbanization, 1850–1920. *Environment and planning D: Society and Space, 1,* 73–87.

Momsen, Janet H. (1980). Women in Canadian geography. *Canadian Geographer, 24*(2), 177–183.

Momsen, Janet H. & Townsend, Janet. (1987). *Geography of gender in the third world.* Albany, NY: State University of New York Press.

Monk, Janice. (1984). Approaches to the study of women and landscape. *Environmental Review, 8*(1), 23–33.

Monk, Janice. (1988). *On not excluding half of the human world.* Presentations from the Conference on Feminist Geography, Instituut voor Sociale Geografie, Amsterdam.

Monk, Janice & Hanson, Susan. (1982). On not exluding half of the human in human geography. *The Professional Geographer, 34*(1), 11–23.

Norwood, Vera & Monk, Janice. (1987). *The desert is no lady: Southwestern landscapes in women's writing and art.* New Haven, CT: Yale University Press.

Pratt, Geraldine & Hanson, Susan. (1988). Gender, class, and space. *Environment and Planning D: Society and Space, 6,* 15–35.

Roder, Wolf. (1977). An alternative interpretation of men and women in geography. *The Professional Geographer, 29*(4), 397–399.

Seager, Joni. (1985). How to put women on the map. *Women's Review of Books, 2*(5), 9–10.

Seager, Joni. (1986, October). Women are the housing wars' wounded. *Sojourner: The women's forum,* 17–18.

Seager, Joni & Olson, Ann. (1986). *Women in the world: An international atlas.* New York: Simon & Schuster.

Seager, Joni. (1988). *"Father's chair": Domestic reform and housing change in the progressive era.* Unpublished doctoral dissertation, Clark University, Worcester, MA.

Stimpson, Catharine, Dixler, Elsa, Nelson, Martha J., & Yatrakis, Kathryn B. (Eds.). (1980). Women and the American city [Special Issue]. *Signs 5,*(3).

Watson, Sophie & Austerberry, Helen. (1986). *Housing & homelessness: A feminist perspective.* London: Routledge & Kegan Paul.

Wekerle, Gerda, Peterson, Rebecca, & Morley, David. (1980). *New space for women.* Boulder, CO: Westview Press.

Wilkinson, Nancy. (1979). Women on the Oregon trail. *Landscape, 23,* 42–47.

Women and Geography Study Group of the IBG. (1984). *Geography and gender: An introduction to feminist geography.* London: Hutchinson.

Zelinsky, Wilbur. (1973a). The strange case of the missing female geographer. *The Professional Geographer, 25*(1), 101–106.

Zelinsky, Wilbur. (1973b). Women in geography: A brief factual account. *The Professional Geographer, 25*(2) 151–165.

Zelinsky, Wilbur, Monk, Janice, & Hanson, Susan. (1982). Women and geography: Review and prospectus. *Progress in Human Geography, 6*(3), 317–366.

Chapter 20

Women's Studies for a "Women's" Profession
Theory and Practice in Library Science

Susan E. Searing

The discipline of Library Science, now typically dubbed "Library and Information Science," is an applied field with a duel identity. As a subject for scholarly inquiry, it is usually pursued at the graduate level. A masters degree is the credential that separates true "librarians" from everyone else who works in libraries. Persons aspiring to careers teaching Library Science or directing university libraries earn doctorates. Feminist perspectives on teaching and research inevitably influence and challenge the progress of scholarship within schools of Library Science.

As an applied field, Library Science is practiced on every college and university campus. As members of the academic community, librarians contribute in concrete ways to the educational process. The application of the principles of Library Science to daily library operations results, ideally, in carefully selected acquisitions, usefully cataloged collections, and efficient reference services. On this everyday level, librarianship is affected by feminist politics and changing gender relations in the workplace. By the same token, the activities of librarians, both as individuals and as a professional bloc, have an impact on the shape of Women's Studies scholarship.

This essay will discuss Library Science in the United States as it is studied and taught *and* as it is practiced. I will review, quite selectively, historical writings on librarianship, studies of the status of women librarians, and applied research on the practice of librarianship, and will suggest topics overdue for feminist analysis and action.

The disciplinary boundaries of Library Science, like those of Women's Studies, are fuzzy. The field shares interests with social history, literature, sociology, psychology, education, communications, and computer science, as well as management and public policy studies. Some Library Science faculty consider themselves social scientists and believe that rigorous quantitative research will yield solutions to problems in library service and management. Others argue that librarianship is essentially a humanistic art, unquantifiable yet teachable.

Whether Library Science possesses its own unique theories or methods is debatable, but the field does lay claim to a distinct body of principles and a code of professional ethics, which are inculcated during the education and training of professional librarians. It is there, within the realm of values, that librarianship's intersection with feminism becomes most productive and, paradoxically, most problematic.

"Information equals power" is the basic credo of Library Science. The profession believes that individuals possess a basic human right to information (the full range of print, audiovisual, and electronic media), and that "a person's right to use a library should not be denied or abridged because of origin, age, background, or views" ("Library Bill of Rights," Article 6). It is hardly surprising, given this democratic outlook, that Library Science concerns itself with the unserved and the underserved. Urban public libraries in the nineteenth century positioned themselves as informal schools to help "Americanize" new immigrants. In the early twentieth century, book mobiles began bringing culture and good reading to isolated rural families. In the 1970s, librarians established intensive "reference and referral" services, presenting themselves as *the* source for information on community services and organizations. In the 1980s, libraries in many communities launched adult literacy classes and after-school programs for latch-key children. Many librarians reacted to the women's liberation movement by acquiring print and audiovisual materials on a range of women's issues, dismantling barriers to the use of such resources (e.g., sexist catalog headings), and mounting informational public programs for female audiences (Kay Ann Cassell & Kathleen Weibel, 1980). As Women's Studies gained visibility, academic librarians argued passionately for separate book budgets, new journal subscriptions, and the appointment of Women's Studies subject experts to library staffs. They designed library modules tailored to Women's Studies classes, prepared special reading lists and research guides, and participated actively in faculty development seminars. At the national level, the American Library Association (ALA) has advanced a liberal agenda for social change through its support of issues ranging from antiapartheid to the Equal Rights Amendment. The service ethic and sense of mission that pervade so many female-intensive occupations lie at the core of Library Science's self-image.

According to the 1980 U.S. census, women constitute 82.6% of librarians, a percentage that has changed little over the course of the twentieth century. As a "women's profession," librarianship shares many values and strategies with feminism. Just as early scholars of Women's Studies concentrated on recovering women's "lost" history and culture, so librarians have enlarged their understanding of their profession by examining the contributions of women.

LIBRARY HISTORY AS WOMEN'S HISTORY

Kathleen Weibel and Kathleen M. Heim assembled a groundbreaking anthology of primary and secondary sources that celebrated women's work in librarianship while revealing a legacy of sex discrimination. Their collection opens with Melvil Dewey's resurrected essay, "Women in Libraries: How They Are Handicapped" (Kathleen Weibel & Kathleen M. Heim, 1979). Biographers chronicled the lives of exemplary female librarians (Laurel A. Grotzinger, 1975, 1978, 1983; Sharon McCaslin, 1990; Leila Gaston Rhodes, 1983; Margo Sasse, 1973), as other historians sought to uproot the stereotype of the prim, authoritarian spinster (Rosalee McReynolds, 1985; Judy Newmyer, 1976). Barbara Brand delved for the causes of librarianship' perpetuation as a women's calling (Barbara E. Brand, 1983a; 1983b), and Nancy O'Brien related how concerted efforts to recruit more men failed raise the profession's overall status (Nancy Patricia O'Brien, 1983).

A particularly lively debate swirls around the question of women's roles in the development of free public libraries. Revisionist scholars point to a gap between the democratic ideology of the public library and its actual impact, arguing that, in reality, American libraries have promoted the conservative goal of reinforcing mainstream culture and middle-class values. Dee Garrison, for example, takes late-nineteenth-century librarians to task for inhibiting professionalization and valorizing "feminine" attributes, including noble self-sacrifice, gentle domesticity, and attention to detail, and thus stunting the development of libraries as important public institutions (Dee Garrison, 1973). Mary Biggs (1982) claims that librarians strayed down the path of conservatism when they drew an analogy between their social mission and that of the public schools. Suzanne Hildenbrand (1983) provides a counterpoint, systematically challenging Garrison's assumptions and methods and offering an alternative feminist model for interpreting women's roles in American library history.

The project of rewriting library history as women's history continues. The ALA's Committee on the Status of Women in Librarianship (COSWL) has completed a minority women librarians oral history project. These historical studies not only "right the record" but also offer role models and traditions to younger women embarking on library careers.

FILTERING OUT WOMEN

"When I look into the future," Melvil Dewey proclaimed at the turn of the century, "I am inclined to think that most of the men who will achieve this greatness [as librarians] will be women" (Melvil Dewey, 1899). For nearly a century, Library Science has looked inward at its own sex ratios, yet the advent of the women's movement raised new, pressing questions about male dominance within a female-intensive field. A sizeable body of research explores the status of women in the library workforce. Recent writings on this topic are thoroughly documented in a two-volume bibliography sponsored by COSWL (Kathleen Heim & Katharine Phenix, 1984; Katharine Phenix, Lori Goetsch, Sarah Watstein, & Mary Ellen H. Landry, 1989). In addition, excellent review essays in *Signs* (Anne E. Brugh & Benjamin R. Beede, 1976) and *Frontiers* (Katharine Phenix, 1987) summarize the key issues and statistical findings. Consequently, I will highlight only a few representative studies here.

Anita Schiller set the stage for subsequent research by gathering baseline data, identifying problems, and suggesting an analytical framework for proposing solutions (Schiller, 1970; 1974). She zeroed in on gender differences in salaries, position levels, and participation in ALA but also pointed to other troublesome inequities. Heim, providing a more detailed overview of statistical evidence, concluded that "a decade of activism [the 1970s] on the part of women librarians has resulted in no clear improvement in status" (Kathleen Heim, 1982, p. 42). The percentage spread varies depending on the source of the data, yet all salary studies document a male advantage that is only slowly diminishing. (See, for example, David R. Dowell, 1988; Jacqueline Goggin, 1984; Kathleen Heim & Leigh S. Estabrook, 1983; and Jean Meyer Ray, 1987.)

In a field where women already predominate numerically, affirmative action focuses on moving more women into management positions. Numerous researchers have looked at women library directors and middle-level administrators, hoping to discern patterns in such things as academic preparation, marital status, geographic mobility, and personality that correlate with successful careers. Study after study disproves the notion that women are themselves to blame for their underrepresentation in library administration. Robert Swisher and Rosemary Ruhig DuMont (1984) propose an analytical framework for understanding the "filtering" process that produces the inequitable gender distribution in academic libraries. Most other researchers are content to document discrimination without advancing explanatory theories.

A few researchers have incorporated feminist concepts and methods into studies of psychological sex differences among librarians. Robert L. Turner (1980) used the Bem

Sex-Role Inventory to refute earlier findings that Library Science students (both male and female) were abnormally "feminine." Rosann Webb Collins and Richard Eggleton (1980) measured "fear of success" among future librarians. Jill Moriearty and Jane Robbins-Carter (1985) examined the importance of faculty role models to women Library Science students. Paul F. DuMont and Rosemary Ruhig DuMont (1989) looked for a correlation between managerial aspiration and positive attitudes toward technology, hypothesizing (incorrectly, as it turned out) that the paucity of women in library administration reflected their allegedly negative attitudes toward computers. These investigations exemplify how feminist scholarship in other areas has been brought to bear on the issue of gender imbalances within librarianship.

Not all the research, nor all the proposed solutions, focus on individual actions. In the 1980s, librarians launched campaigns for job analyses and salary adjustments, based on the feminist concept of comparable worth. A decade earlier, working through the ALA, they established formal collegial networks and committees to enhance both the status of women in the profession *and* the service provided to library users. A succinct history of feminist organizing from 1977 to 1981 appears in the introduction to the first volume of *On Account of Sex* (Kathleen Heim & Katharine Phenix, 1984). Sarah M. Pritchard also touches on this history in her inspiring essay, "The Impact of Feminism on Women in the Profession" (1989).

HOW TO FIND IT

Feminism has not only made a difference in the lives of librarians, but also in the experiences of those who use libraries. To assess the impact of feminism on the applied side of Library Science, we must turn to descriptive case studies and calls to action, in addition to scholarly writings.

Library Science arguably achieves its purest theoretical expression in the processes of classification and cataloging. Feminists have pointedly questioned the value systems that underlie the standard American classification schemes—the Dewey Decimal and Library of Congress (LC) systems—but a sustained analysis is still lacking (Nancy Humphreys, 1987). The creation of any subject-based call number sequence reflects a positivist belief that all knowledge can be divided neatly into use categories. Surrounded by new interractive information technologies in an intellectual climate of postmodernism, this assumption can only strike us as naively old fashioned.

Call numbers group works on similar topics together physically to facilitate browsing, but browsing is seldom effective in an interdisciplinary field like Women's Studies. Robert L. Mowery (1989) has shown that, even within the limited subfield of women's literature, books are scattered throughout the stacks. Small resource centers devoted solely to women's materials have sometimes modified the LC or Dewey classifications or created alternative systems, but college and university libraries cannot realistically make such sweeping changes.

When browsing doesn't suffice, one must rely on library catalogs. Computerized catalog systems promise to revolutionize the ways we organize and access information, yet there has been scant feminist commentary on their potential, even by those who prize the nonlinear, contextual (female?) thought processes that hypertext and other software breakthroughs promise. Admittedly, the radical potential often seems remote. Electronic library catalogs today are essentially mechanized card catalogs; they still require a linear mode of searching and prior knowledge of library indexing rules. Therefore, feminist librarians have concentrated on reforming existing cataloging practices to better meet researchers' current needs.

Feminist-inspired reforms have included common-sense policy reversals, such as identifying a woman author by the name under which she published rather than her legal married name (thus replacing "Margaret Ossoli" with "Margaret Fuller," for example). Building on the work of feminist linguists, librarians denounced the misrepresentation inherent in subject headings like "Founding fathers" and the absurdity of Victorian constructions like "Women—Social and moral questions." They waged a loud campaign against the "as" headings—"Women as doctors," "Women as teachers"—because they implied the peculiarity and inappropriateness of women in professional roles. Many of the proposed alternatives, such as the simpler forms "Women doctors" and "Women teachers," were eventually adopted (Sanford Berman, 1971; Joan K. Marshall, 1977). But language and social conditions are constantly in flux, so catalogers continue to press for updated, socially responsible terminology (Sanford Berman, 1989; Edith Maureen Fisher, 1986). The *Women's Thesaurus* (Mary Ellen S. Capek, 1987), a collaborative creation of feminist scholars, indexers, and librarians, offers a visionary prescription for women-centered cataloging and indexing. Meanwhile, three librarians have compiled the ultimate guide to existing Library of Congress subject headings, *Women in LC's Terms* (Ruth Dickstein, Victoria A. Mills, & Ellen J. Waite, 1988).

The conceptual problems of library catalogs are mirrored and multiplied in the diverse indexing systems encountered in discipline-based reference tools. As more and more journal indexes become available via computer, librarians are reevaluating their coverage of women's issues (Suzanne Hildenbrand, 1986a; Sarah M. Pritchard, 1984) and voicing the needs, as yet unmet, for an electronic bibliographic database devoted to Women's Studies.

As academic libraries grow increasingly complex, offering a wider range of media and sophisticated access systems, librarians are promoting formal classroom instruction in library research methods. When done skillfully, such instruction moves well beyond the old-fashioned library tour to a critical discussion of how libraries organize information. Ellen Broidy (1987) argues that library instruction is crucial in Women's Studies because of the field's nontraditional, interdisciplinary, and politicized content. By positing a feminist rationale for librarians' presence in the classroom, she challenges and reshapes the prevailing theories of library pedagogy. Susan G. Williamson, Nicole Hahn Rafter, and Amy Cohen-Rose (1989) describe a model program for involving students in hands-on bibliographic research.

Librarians are also concerned with the library users who pose questions at the reference desk. In an unusual experiment, Roma M. Harris and Gillian Michell (1988) observed that judgments about the adequacy of reference service varied depending on the sex-appropriateness of the question. When a man asked for information on repairing a washing machine, for example, observers deemed a simple factual answer sufficient. But when a woman made the same inquiry, the observers faulted librarians for not providing additional instruction in information-seeking strategies that would "include" the library user in the process of finding the answer. Although further research is warranted, this study suggests that, at least in certain circumstances, gender stereotypes may influence the content and/or the style of information exchanges between librarians and library users.

Several writers have addressed the needs of specific types of users. Harris (1988) interviewed battered women and drafted a typology of their information needs, based not on the perceptions of librarians or social workers but on the women's own responses. Peggy G. Glover (1985) outlined strategies for serving mid-life women. Using her own experiences at the Library of Congress as a model, Sarah Pritchard (1987) demonstrated how a librarian specializing in women's issues can tailor services for scholars and policymakers. Even general feminist overviews admonish librarians "to shed stereotypes about the average user and to acknowledge and learn about the complex world in which women live" (Neel Parikh & Ellen Broidy, 1982, pp. 295-6). Working directly with the public, librarians are often the first to feel the need for new specialized bibliographies, directories, and other tools, and many have compiled and published such sources.

The development, evaluation, and preservation of library collections are always central concerns. Beth Stafford's directory (1990) supplies basic comparative data on the size, budgets, and subject strengths of Women's Studies holdings in academic libraries. Joan Ariel (1987) assembles a wealth of information in her pragmatic guide to selection and acquisition, while Sherre H. Dryden (1988) dispenses advice to enthusiastic but underfunded collection builders. Betty Glass (1990) highlights the importance of collecting materials on women of color.

Because no library is comprehensive, directing advanced researchers to specialized collections remains an important component of good library service. Hildenbrand (1986a) gathered in-depth profiles of major women's libraries and archives in North America. Researchers in the New York City area are blessed with a unique guide prepared by a committee of feminist librarians (Women's Resources Group 1988).

RESEARCH DIRECTIONS

As we have seen, Library Science incorporates feminist theories, methods, and politics into examinations of the field's own history, studies of the status of librarians, and applied research on library collections and services. I will conclude this essay by listing a few additional topics that are ripe for feminist analysis and action.

1. In the subfield of library history, researchers have begun to look beyond the "exceptional" women pioneers and leaders. Further research on "ordinary" women who founded, worked in, and used libraries could yield new insights into women's roles in the public sphere at the local level.

2. Historical research on women of color as librarians and consumers of library services is sorely underdeveloped. And there exist no scholarly studies of lesbian librarians, although the ALA was the first professional association in the United States to sanction a Gay and Lesbian Task Force, more then two decades ago.

3. How future librarians are socialized into the profession is another question worth raising. How are students' perceptions of specializations (e.g., public vs. behind-the-scenes work, service to children vs. service to adults, academic libraries vs. public libraries) shaped by the Library Science curriculum and classroom climate? Tales have emerged of African American students being pushed toward public library work so they can serve "their" communities, of Asian Americans being encouraged to choose careers in cataloging because they allegedly excell at detailed work but are too shy and retiring to staff a public desk, and so on. Anecdotal evidence, shored up by statistics, likewise suggests a subtle but persistent tracing of women into work with children and men into work with computers. [See Susanne Damarin, this volume.] As Suzanne Hildenbrand has pointed out (1989), the low salaries and status accorded those who specialize in children's services and cataloging, the *most* female-intensive career choices in librarianship, make sex-segregation within the field a serious problem.

4. A number of scholars have looked at how women break into library management; fewer have asked what they do once they're there. Do female library directors act differently than their male peers? Do they practice a conscious style of "feminist management?" At the peak of their careers, do they still rely on mentors, networks, or other female support systems?

5.   The entrance of more women into management compels a fresh look at libraries as organizations. Most libraries function as hierarchical bureaucracies within larger bureaucratic structures, such as city governments, universities, public schools, and corporations. Is this the healthiest or most efficient system for a predominantly female enterprise? Are the class divisions between credentialled librarians and skilled para-professionals a barrier to effective library service? Is automation a leveling force? Lori A. Goetsch (1986) has asked some penetrating questions in this regard.

6.   A class-based analysis of the profession might answer several questions. For example, does the insistence on a masters degree perpetuate a homogenous, middle-class, mostly white labor pool? Or does librarianship, no longer prized as a genteel career for educated daughters of the upper class, offer upward socio-economic mobility to lower-middle-class women and men?

7.   Even if we focus narrowly on academic libraries, the area of library practice suggests almost limitless opportunities for research. For example, librarians should be asking how interdisciplinay scholars negotiate information systems that are grounded in a disciplinary view of the world. A survey of Women's Studies scholars by Margo Anderson and Susan Searing (1989) offers a bare beginning to this rich and complex area of study.

8.   The provision of library collections and services to Women's Studies programs deserves better documentation and analysis. Grace Jackson-Brown's survey of women's research centers (1988) serves as a model. Beth Stafford's data on college and university collections (1990) must be updated regularly to chart national trends. We also need a clearer understanding of how library budgets for Women's Studies are allocated and defended, and how librarians with widely varying academic backgrounds acquire and maintain current subject expertise in Women's Studies.

9.   As the explosion in publishing forces librarians to measure the quality as well as quantity of their holdings, we must devise more sensitive tools for evaluating Women's Studies collections. A just-created "conspectus"—a detailed conceptual map based on Library of Congress call numbers—will permit many libraries to treat Women's Studies as a distinct field when they undertake self-assessments. How the findings will be used, however, is as yet unknown. Hopefully, libraries will cooperate to acquire a broader range of women's publications, especially from abroad, and will share responsibility for preserving fragile materials, including women's liberation pamphlets and newspapers printed on cheap paper a mere generation ago.

CHANGES MAKING CHANGES

Generally speaking, Library Science has borrowed feminist theory and method from other disciplines rather than developing its own. However, I believe that librarians' singular vision and real-world expertise can contribute to the shaping of interdisciplinary feminist theory in at least two vital areas.

The first is the vexing debate over pornography and censorship. The feminist community at large is deeply divided on the issue. [See Susan Kappeler, this volume.] As a group, librarians staunchly defend the freedom to read as a natural extension of the freedom of expression and oppose any laws or rulings intended to limit access to sexually explicit materials. Their stance is not based on abstract principle alone but on experience. Librarians have risked loss of job and reputation to keep *Ms.* and *Our Bodies, Ourselves* on the shelves, to preserve children's access to books depicting nontraditional gender roles, and to build diverse collections for *all* members of the reading community, including racial, ethnic, and sexual minorities. In striving to reconcile their received professional ethics with the conflicting feminist viewpoints on pornography, librarians may achieve unique insights worth sharing with the wider women's movement.

Librarians could also contribute new perspectives to discussions of the literary–cultural canon and the sociology of knowledge. Dale Spender, Joanna Russ, Lynn Spender and others have shown how the female half of human knowledge and creativity is obscured and displaced by the patriarchy [see Berenice Carroll, this volume], especially the closed systems of publishing, reviewing, and literary criticism. The library is missing from these critiques of "gatekeeping" institutions, yet librarians hold the keys to vast storehouses of knowledge. Thanks to the prescient librarians of the past, the works of many "lost" women authors remain stored in dusty corners of libraries, awaiting rediscovery. Today's information explosion forces librarians to make value judgments and hard choices every day that will affect future scholarship. Grappling concretely with decisions about ordering, cataloging, microfilming, and the like, present-day librarians may reach new understandings of how knowledge structures are constructed, how meanings are encoded in such mundane items as call numbers and index entries, and how, in turn, the information structures themselves shape what questions are asked and what answers are found.

BIBLIOGRAPHY

Anderson, Margo, & Searing, Susan. (1989). *Surveying Women's Studies research needs.* Unpublished manuscript.

Ariel, Joan (Ed.). (1987). *Building women's studies collections: A resource guide.* Middletown, CT: Choice.

Berman, Sanford. (1971). *Prejudices and antipathies: A tract on the LC subject heads concerning people.* Metuchen, NJ: Scarecrow Press.

Berman, Sanford. (1989). Compare and contrast, or, the unexamined cataloging record isn't worth inputting. *Collection Building, 9,* 36–42.

Biggs, Mary. (1982, Fall). Librarians and the "Woman Question": An inquiry into conservatism. *Journal of Library History, 17,* 409–428.

Brand, Barbara E. (1983a, Fall). Librarianship and other female-intensive professions. *Journal of Library History, 18,* 391–406.

Brand, Barbara E. (1983b). Sex typing in education for librarianship, 1870–1920. In Kathleen M. Heim (Ed.), *The Status of Women in Librarianship* (pp. 29–49). New York: Neal-Schuman.

Broidy, Ellen. (1987). Bibliographic instruction in women's studies: From the grassroots to the ivory tower. In Mary Reichel & Mary Ann Ramey (Eds.), *Conceptual frameworks for bibliographic education: Theory into practice* (pp. 86–96). Littleton, CO: Libraries Unlimited.

Brugh, Anne E., & Beede, Benjamin R. (1976, Summer). Review essay: American librarianship. *Signs, 1,* 943–955.

Capek, Mary Ellen S. (Ed.). (1987). *A women's thesaurus.* New York: Harper & Row.

Cassell, Kay Ann, & Weibel, Kathleen. (1980, Fall). Public library response to women and their changing roles. *RQ, 20,* 72–75.

Collins, Rosann Webb, & Eggleton, Richard. (1980, January). Fear of success theory and librarians. *International Library Review, 12,* 49–63.

Dewey, Melvil. (1899, January). The ideal librarian. *Library Journal, 24,* 14.

Dickstein, Ruth, Mills, Victoria A., & Waite, Ellen J. (1988). *Women in LC's terms: A thesaurus of library of congress subject headings relating to women.* Phoenix: Oryx Press.

Dowell, David R. (1988, May). Sex and salary in a female dominated profession. *Journal of Academic Librarianship, 14,* 92–98.

Dryden, Sherre H. (1988, Spring). Building a women's studies library with no curriculum, budget or administrative support. *Feminist Teacher, 3,* 10–13.

DuMont, Paul F., & DuMont, Rosemary Ruhig. (1989, Spring). The information professional and the new technology: An investigation of possible differential responses by gender. *Library Trends, 37,* 510–520.

Fisher, Edith Maureen. (1986). Women of color: Observations about library access. *Ethnic Forum, 6,* 117–127.

Garrison, Dee. (1973, Winter). The tender technicians: The feminization of public librarianship, 1876–1905. *Journal of Social History, 6,* 131–159.

Glass, Betty J. (1990). Information needs of minority women and serial resources. *Reference Librarian* no. 27/28: 289–303.

Glover, Peggy G. (1985). *Library services for the woman in the middle.* Hamden, CT: Library Professional Publications.

Goetsch, Lori A. (1986, Summer). Librarianship, professionalization, and its impact on work environment. *NWSA Perspectives, 4,* 7–8.

Goggin, Jacqueline (1984, Summer). The feminization of the archival profession: An analysis of the 1982 salary survey as it pertains to women. *American Archivist, 47,* 327–330.

Grotzinger, Laurel A. (1975, July). The proto-feminist librarian at the turn of the century: Two studies. *Journal of Library History, 10,* 195–213.

Grotzinger, Laurel A. (1978, May). Women who spoke for themselves. *College and Research Libraries, 39,* 175–190.

Grotzinger, Laurel A. (1983). Biographical research of women librarians: Its paucity, perils, and pleasures. In Kathleen M. Heim, (Ed.) *The status of women in librarianship* (pp. 139–190). New York: Neal-Schuman.

Harris, Roma M. (1988, Fall). The informations needs of battered women. *RQ, 28,* 62–70.

Harris, Roma M., & Michell, Gillian. (1988, Winter). Home insulating and home births: Do patrons' sex-typed questions influence judgements about the competence of reference librarians? *RQ, 28,* 179–184.

Heim, Kathleen. (1982). The demographic and economic status of librarians in the 1970s, with special reference to women. In Wesley Simonton (Ed.), *Advances in librarianship* (Vol. 12, pp. 1–45). New York: Academic Press.

Heim, Kathleen, & Estabrook, Leigh S. (1983). *Career profiles and sex discrimination in the library profession.* Chicago: American Library Association.

Heim, Kathleen, & Phenix, Katharine. (1984). *On account of sex: An annotated bibliography on the status of women in librarianship, 1977–1981.* Chicago: American Library Association.

Hildenbrand, Suzanne. (1983). Revision versus reality: Women in the history of the public library movement, 1876–1920. In Kathleen M. Heim (Ed.), *The status of women in librarianship* (pp. 7–28). New York: Neal-Schuman.

Hildenbrand, Suzanne (Ed.). (1986a). *Women's collections: Libraries, archives, and consciousness.* New York: Haworth Press.

Hildenbrand, Suzanne. (1986b, Fall). Women's studies online: Promoting visibility. *RQ, 26,* 63–74.

Hildenbrand, Suzanne. (1989, September 1). "Women's work" within librarianship: Time to expand the feminist agenda. *Library Journal, 114,* 153–155.

Humphreys, Nancy. (1987, Fall). Beyond standard forms of information organization: A woman's classification system for libraries. *Feminist Collections, 9,* 9–14.

Jackson-Brown, Grace. (1988). *Libraries and information centers within women's studies research centers.* (SLA Research Series, no. 3). Washington: Special Libraries Association.

Library Bill of Rights. (1939). Chicago: American Library Association. (Rewritten in 1948; amended in 1961, 1967, 1980.)

Marshall, Joan K. (1977). *On equal terms: A thesaurus for nonsexist indexing and cataloging.* New York: Neal-Schuman.

McCaslin, Sharon. (1990, March). The displacement of Mary Jones. *American Libraries, 21,* 186–191.

McReynolds, Rosalee. (1985, November 1). A heritage dismissed. *Library Journal, 110,* 25–31.

Moriearty, Jill, & Robbins-Carter, Jane. (1985, Fall). Role models in library education: Effects on women's careers. *Library Trends, 34,* 323–341.

Mowery, Robert L. (1989). Women in literature: A study of library of congress subject cataloging. *Cataloging and Classification Quarterly, 9,* 89–99.

Newmyer, Judy. (1976, January). The image problem of the librarian: Femininity and social control. *Journal of Library History, 11,* 44–67.

O'Brien, Nancy Patricia. (1983). The recruitment of men into librarianship, following World War II. In Kathleen M. Heim (Ed.), *The Status of Women in Librarianship* (pp. 51–66). New York: Neal-Schuman.

Parikh, Neel, & Broidy, Ellen. (1982, December). Women's issues: The library response. *Wilson Library Bulletin, 57,* 2295–2299.

Phenix, Katharine. (1987). The status of women librarians. *Frontiers, 9,* 36–40.

Phenix, Katharine, Goetsch, Lori, Watstein, Sarah, & Landry, Mary Ellen H. (1989). *On account of sex: An annotated bibliography on the status of women in librarianship, 1982–1986.* Chicago: American Library Association.

Pritchard, Sarah M. (1984, Fall/Winter). Developing criteria for database evaluation: The example of women's studies. *Reference Librarian, 11,* 247–261.

Pritchard, Sarah M. (1987). Linking research, policy, and activism: Library services in women's studies. *Reference Librarian, 20,* 89–103.

Pritchard, Sarah M. (1989, August). The impact of feminism on women in the profession. *Library Journal, 114,* 76–77.

Ray, Jean Meyer, & Rubin, Angela Battaglia. (1987, January). Pay equity for women in academic libraries: An analysis of ARL salary surveys, 1976/77–1983/84. *College and Research Libraries, 48,* 36–49.

Rhodes, Lelia Gaston. (1983). Profiles of the careers of selected Black female librarians. In Kathleen M. Heim (Ed.), *The Status of Women in Librarianship* (pp. 191–205). New York: Neal-Schuman.

Sasse, Margo. (1973, January 15). Invisible women: The children's librarian in America. *Library Journal, 98,* 213–217.

Schiller, Anita R. (1970, April). The disadvantaged majority: Women employed in libraries. *American Libraries, 1,* 345–349.

Schiller, Anita R. (1974). Women in librarianship. In Melvin J. Voight (Ed.), *Advances in Librarianship* (Vol. 4, pp. 103–147). New York: Academic Press.

Stafford, Beth. (1990). *Directory of women's studies programs and library resources.* Phoenix: Oryx Press.

Swisher, Robert, & DuMont, Rosemary Ruhig. (1984, April). Sex structuring in academic libraries: Searching for explanations. *Library Quarterly, 54,* 137–156.

Turner, Robert L. (1980, May). Femininity and the librarian—Another test. *College and Research Libraries, 41,* 235–241.

Weibel, Kathleen, & Heim, Kathleen M. (Eds.). (1979). *The role of women in librarianship, 1876–1976.* Phoenix: Oryx Press.

Williamson, Susan G., Rafter, Nicole Hahn, & Cohen-Rose, Amy. (1989, March). Everyone wins: A collaborative model for mainstreaming women's studies. *Journal of Academic Librarianship, 15,* 20–23.

Women's Resources Group of the Greater New York Metropolitan Area Chapter of the Association of College and Research Libraries, and the Center for the Study of Women and Society of the Graduate School and University Center of the City University of New York. (1988). *Library and information sources on women: A guide to collections in the greater New York area.* New York: Feminist Press.

Chapter 21

The Entry of Women to the Education of Men

Dale Spender

THE POSITION OF WOMEN
20 YEARS AGO

Because of its many facets it is difficult to conceptualize education as a cohesive discipline; like the disciplines of sociology or history, education does have a body of knowledge which can be critiqued but unlike many other disciplines the term "education" also refers to institutions. Encompassed in the ambit of education are governmental departments, schools, colleges and universities, along with policies and practices associated with everything from teacher training to the development of a technically competent work force.

There is nonetheless an educational enterprise which to some extent can be identified and analyzed; cross-culturally an effort is being made to systematically transmit the valued information of the society, particularly to the younger generation. The rationale for this provision is that the individual and the community are better served by the encouragement of intellectual and personal development and that the economy is better served when the workforce is skilled or "professional."

And this educational enterprise in all its complexity has been—and still is—primarily in the hands of men.

From the sixteenth century and until relatively recently in the western world, education was confined almost exclusively to males. In Britain, during the Reformation Henry VIII abolished the religious teaching orders and the process effectively wiped out educational opportunity for girls. Completely excluded formally from education (and professional occupations) women in nineteenth century Britain worked untiringly for educational opportunity for their own sex (there were comparable campaigns in other countries as well). Entrenched male resistance was encountered with each new demand and basically took two forms. The first was to demonstrate that women would not benefit from education and to this end there was a "great brain debate" (where the data were continually changed but the interpretation that male brains were superior remained constant) and with this went evidence provided by a reputable medical profession that women's uteruses would atrophy and their brains would burst if they were subjected to the rigors of education (see Carol Dyhouse, 1978). The second preventive measure was simply to refuse to give women entry; for example, the obstacles that men erected to prevent women from participating in medical education, in both Britain and the United States, and the violent male response to the admission of women to Cambridge (see Rita McWilliams-Tullberg, 1975, for further discussion).

But by the 1960s it was stated that women "have largely won the battle for equal educational opportunity with men" (Kathleen Ollerenshaw, 1961, p. 14). That women had not taken advantage of the technically equal educational availability was quite another matter and the failure was frequently attributed to the women themselves.

What was not routinely recognized at the time was the extent to which the culture of education had remained a masculist preserve. Few, if any, voices in the 1960s asserted that all that women had won was the right to sit in on the education that men had designed for themselves—one which did not even include reference to women's struggle for educational rights!

Although women were included in the system it was at the lowest levels; they could well comprise the majority of school teachers (though not of colleges or universities) and the majority of students (until the legal leaving age) but the higher the status in the educational hierarchy, the fewer women were to be found.

Writing her ground-breaking survey of the patriarchal scene in 1978, Dorothy Smith was concerned to show how women had been excluded from the production of theory in general and from the formulation of educational theory in particular. Documenting the way that theory has materialized in western culture, she argues that for centuries men have checked only with men in constructing their explanations of the world; with the result that "women have been largely excluded from the work of producing the forms of thought and the images and symbols in which thought is expressed and ordered. There is a circle effect," argues Dorothy Smith and, "The circle of men whose writing and talk was significant to each other extends backwards in time as far as our records reach. What men were doing was relevant to men, was written by men, about men, for men." (p. 281).

To be without representations of one's experience, to be deprived of an encoded heritage or valued culture is to be oppressed; it is to be existentially denied, to be outsider, invisible, the other.

What women needed in this context argued Adrienne Rich (1979–1980) and Jessie Bernard (1989) was to name themselves and produce their own knowledge. Women had to be convinced "that their own experiences were as valid as those of men," and "that they had as much right to define the human situation as men did . . . they were deserving in their own right, that they did not have to be like men to be worthy" (p. 414).

To Eileen Byrne (1987, who declared that 97% of the government of education was male) it was demonstrable that women were receiving an inferior education as a result of this sex bias. It was inferior in men's terms in that girls did not enjoy the same resources nor gain the same qualifications as boys, particularly in mathematics or science. And it was inferior in women's terms in that it did not spring from women's experience of the world, resonate women's values, or consolidate or clarify the goals and aspirations of women's lives.

So through no ill will men could conceive of the best education and the most successful outcome as one which suited their purposes and reflected their sense of world order, including the positioning of themselves as the central, and superior gender.

These values—which construct a double standard—were at the center of educational policy and provision more than two decades ago and helped to establish a climate in which it was *normal* for boys to be successful, and *normal* for girls to perform at a reduced level. Any departure from these *norms* could be problematic; so when boys did not do well at reading, for example, it was clear that remedial reading teaching was called for. But when girls did not do well at maths and science this did not challenge expectations, get represented as a problem, or lead to the immediate introduction of remedial science education for the female sex.

As Katherine Clarricoates (1987) demonstrated, this double standard at the core of educational theory and practice was responsible for the theft of the intellectual and creative capacity of girls. For when boys did not do well a range of rationalizations was available to maintain the belief that they were bright but that some external factor was interfering with the result (for further discussion and the manifestation of this process in teacher training see Dale Spender, 1984): conversely when girls did do well their success did not always count—it could be discredited on the grounds of luck, or conformity.

In the 1960s there were few women theorists or policy makers to critique or challenge these discriminatory practices. Most of the researchers were male, most of the problems they perceived were the product of their own experience, and most of the research they conducted was on their own sex. When not invisible, females could still be inexplicable— *non-data*—as Sandra Acker (1980) stated when she analyzed the findings of educational research. It was the females who did not fit the theory derived from male behavior who were seen as the problem rather than the inherent limitations and bias of the theories themselves.

> Witkin is puzzled as 'the findings for girls in secondary modern school were not anticipated.' For Synge, the high educational aspirations of rural girls were 'contrary to expectations.' Robinson and Rackstraw admit 'at present we have no supportable explanation to offer for these occasional sex differences in performance.' Liversidge is surprised that working class girls' occupational aspirations don't differ much between those in grammar schools and in modern schools, unlike those of boys. And Robertson and Kapur go so far as to say that results for women students are bizarre. (Sandra Acker, 1980, p. 9)

And this was the position of women in the discipline of education two decades ago; where even the competitive method of teaching and learning was geared to male experience (see Virginia Woolf, 1938). Paradoxically, whereas the majority of those delivering education in many countries were women, most, if not all of the package they were presenting, was meant for males.

FIRST FEMINIST PROTESTS

The first feminist protests against men's education came from outside the discipline and to some extent are inseparable from the women's movement itself. For it was the recognition that women's reality was not reflected in valued or validated knowledge and that women's experience was not taken into account in the education system which provided part of the impetus for "the revolution." From the outset the demand for knowledge by and about women—and in a form which was consistent with women's view of the world—was central to the analysis of women's oppression, and liberation.

In the 1960s women started to suspect that all was not as it should be—or might be—and they went in search of information on women's lives. (Betty Friedan, 1963, played a prominent part in planting the doubts in the United States and Juliet Mitchell, 1971, was a pioneer in questioning the "natural" relationship between the sexes and the arrangements of society.) And when their search proved frustrating and fruitless, when women could find little or nothing in established knowledge which answered their questions or suited their purposes, there was really no alternative but to invent or construct their own knowledge for themselves. And this is where consciousness-raising sessions materialized and played such a crucial role in producing women's meanings and in representing women's view of the world.

The very existence of consciousness-raising groups was an indictment of traditional educational theory and practice. To some extent women began to do informally what men had done formally (and with funding) for hundreds of years; to sit around, to encode understandings which came from their own experience, and to check with one another and reach a consensus as to the accuracy and adequacy of the explanations. And to write up these findings—in newsletters, magazines, books, and journals—and transmit the information to other women who were asking similar questions and confronting similar "absences" in the conventional wisdom.

So a tradition was formed. And as women began to protest about their absence from encoded knowledge and the curriculum, and from educational theory and practice, and as they began, cross culturally, to generate information and understandings about women they not only provided a critique and challenge to education, they also established a demand for a new discipline.

DENIAL OF WOMEN'S EXPERIENCE

Within the history, philosophy, and practice of education, the contribution of women has been systematically obscured and eclipsed. This has been the case with individual women and with earlier women's movements, and there is no better example of the wholesale denial and exclusion of an extensive area of information than that of women's campaigns for education itself.

It cannot be because it lacks excitement or interest, nor that it involved but a few women, endured for but a short period, or was an abysmal failure, that women's struggle for education (on most continents) has not featured in mainstream educational records. So frequent were the battles, so many the victories, that it is surprising that so much recent and remarkable evidence could have been so effectively removed. (Many of the women who were part of the early 1960s protest must have had living grandmothers who fought for educational and occupational rights earlier this century and it is a mark of the power and pervasiveness of patriarchal authority that their version of reality could be so readily repressed or disbelieved [for further discussion of this process, see Dale Spender, 1990].)

From Mary Astell (1668–1731) who in 1696 called for the creation of a women's college in Britain, to the Bluestockings, and the scientific writings of Mary Somerville (1780–1872); from Harriet Martineau (1802–1876) who wrote 1,400 editorials on the education of girls (not to mention the first social science textbook and the first popular series on economics) to the dedicated efforts of Barbara Bodichon (1827–1891) and Emily Davies (1830–1921) who established Girton College, Cambridge, along with many, many more women who, despite the fact that few women today may ever have heard of them or know the extent of their indebtedness, conducted educational campaigns that were spectacularly successful (for further discussion, see Dale Spender, 1990).

In the United States, Margaret Fuller (1810–1850) introduced her "conversations" for women (and created women's studies courses in the process) and Mary Jane Paterson defied the odds to become the first Black female college graduate in 1862. Antoinette Brown Blackwell crossed the barriers to become the first ordained woman minister and Sophia B. Packard and Harriet E. Giles founded Spelman College for Black women in 1881.

And these are just the bare bones of this fascinating and illuminating history (see Beverly Guy-Sheftall & Patricia Bell Scott, 1989a, for further discussion about the "gaps"). And the same problem of nonexistence in the mainstream educational knowledge base arises in relation to women theorists. Mary Wollstonecraft, for example, in 1792, wrote one of the most impressive and incisive analyses of equal educational opportunity and she began her treatise with a scathing critique of Jean Jacques Rousseau. She exposed the absurdity and injustice of his double standard which would have men educated for the world, and women for men; yet to this day it is Rousseau who is still quoted as the brilliant educational theorist (with his concept of liberty requiring the enslavement of half the population causing no conceptual difficulty in a masculist educational environment). Yet, to my knowledge there is no mainstream course in educational philosophy which gives credit to the theories of Mary Wollstonecraft.

So, too, do Piaget and Lawrence Kohlberg—whose work was undertaken entirely on boys—dominate the child development arena, whereas the outstanding contribution made by Maria Montessori is devalued or denied.

As recently as 1938 Virginia Woolf wrote a convincing condemnation of the competitive practices of the education system. She made a causal connection between men's education and war and violence, and argued that women would be better served by remaining "outsiders." But her brilliant critique, and Adrienne Rich's alternative vision of a woman-centered university, have not found a praised or permanent place in educational theory or practice.

It was Mary Wollstonecraft who argued that the two sexes would not be seen to be equal until they were both equally resourced; it was her contention that the last male bastion to fall would be that of intellectual competence. With its refusal to acknowledge the intellectual contribution of women, past or present, and with its capacity to deny women's intellectual and creative ability in the classroom, education continues to construct the intellectual inequality of the sexes.

NEW RESEARCH PRIORITIES AND DIRECTIONS

Consciousness-raising sessions produced new questions and new knowledge which were soon labeled as *Women's Studies* and referred to in the 1970s as "the academic arm of the women's movement." To claim that this new area of intellectual endeavor simply set new research priorities and pointed women scholars in a new direction is to do a great disservice (and to drastically underestimate) the radical nature of this new discipline [for further discussion see Pat Cramer and Ann Russo, this volume]. It was both a challenge to existing educational conventions and a resource for "revolution."

As Marilyn Boxer (1989) has stated: "During the decade of the 1970s, with a momentum and magnitude which defied an overall retrenchment of higher education (in the United States), women's studies grew to include thousands of courses on hundreds of campuses across the nation, more than three hundred of which established integrated women's studies programs (including a few departments). "Innovative in structure as well as content", their continued expansion offers a challenge to patriarchy and precepts of postfeminism—and "reflects an extraordinary expansion in scholarship about women" (p. 185). While the United States may have led the way, the model of Women's Studies programs have been adopted cross-culturally with courses firmly established in places as different and distant from each other as Scandinavia, South America, Japan and Australia.

The emergence of Women's Studies outside the discipline served as a base for critiquing education and creating new directions within the discipline. The issue of women's education was of such fundamental interest in both Women's Studies and to women in departments of education that there was not, and often still is not, an obvious dividing line between these two scholarly areas. Both began to question educational theory and practice and its significance for women.

It was not just in terms of content that educational provision was challenged; it was also in terms of philosophy and process. Feminist educational theorists asked why education was competitive, why it was arranged hierarchically, why those who pursued knowledge were divided into knowers and nonknowers. The very concept of authority was scrutinized and frequently found wanting by feminist educationalists.

Everything was open to reconceptualization from the arrangement of classroom furniture to the images in textbooks. (What are the assumptions that underlie the arrangement of separated desks, asks Elizabeth Dodson Gray (1989)? "Clearly it is because we conceptualize an education as a solitary and autonomous experience" (p. 336)—a context in which cooperation can be called cheating. Which is why it is neither a feminist joke nor a frivolous suggestion that before learning can take place, the furniture must be rearranged, preferably in a circle.)

There was widespread criticism of the way in which girls were required to defer to boys with some of the initial explanations bordering on "blaming the victim": that it doesn't pay for a girl to be too bright could be seen as fear of success rather than as another part of the pattern of the denial and repression of female intellectuality.

Feminists produced an astonishing range of critical and substantive materials which were fed back into the curriculum (though often only in sexism and education courses). The result of this energetic effort has been that there are now women's alternatives to male literature and history programs, and there are experiments, studies, pilot schemes on single-sex teaching along with new curriculum materials in science and mathematics. (Jayne Johnston, Curtin University, Western Australia, has participated in the development of a calculus text which is a narrative and which has been taken up enthusiastically by girls, while boys are having some difficulty with this unfamiliar format.)

There are professional publications, (e.g., *Gender and Education,* and *Feminist Teacher*) and a plethora of books, curriculum documents and course outlines which testify to the enormous success of the enterprise. Summarizing the extent to which feminist educational theory and practice have changed educational institutions and society, Marilyn Boxer (1989) has said that "the process began as a politics" and "became a passion." Its transformation of the curriculum is "more than a question of women's rights. It is essential to the fulfillment of the university's commitment to the search for truth" (p. 199). With its "criticism of the fragmentation of knowledge into discrete disciplines," its critique "of the separation of modes of learning into affective and cognitive, and of the compartmentalization of individual lives into professional and personal pursuits," feminist educational philosophy not only reflects a "wholeness" but emphasizes the necessity "of resolving the conflict between scholarship and politics" (p. 193).

CHALLENGE TO METHODOLOGY

That women had been omitted from encoded knowledge—or else conceptualized as deviant—was one issue, but that the academic community did not find this bias scandalous, and move as quickly as possible to remedy the situation when alerted to the error of their ways, was another matter entirely. And the discipline which was considered most culpable was education. It had been in the ideal position to take as its brief the investigation of knowledge production. Instead of the "poor cousin" syndrome (often the status of education) it could have been one of the most influential disciplines had it taken as its range of reference the examination of the origins of knowledge, the nature of proof, the relationship between knowledge and politics. No educational institution should conduct its business without reference to its own processes, and education as a discipline was well situated to have monitored—what was being researched and taught; by whom; for what purposes (and indeed, who was providing the funding). Gatekeeping, how it worked, who and what was let in and kept out, could have been (and some would say should have been) at the core of educational research and scholarship.

But so total has been the (white, heterosexual, and ablebodied) male control of the production and legitimation of knowledge that for years virtually no analysis or criticism of the process was encouraged."Internal" debates about the efficacy of one methodology in contrast to another persisted, but all took place within the largely unquestioned framework of "scientific dogma" which assumed the impartiality of the schemata and the objective nature of its proof.

It's very different now. There's no longer a notion of a monodimensional reality, an ordered world, in which there is one set truth awaiting discovery. And it is no coincidence that the move from one truth to multiple truths, from a single prescribed reality to the fragmentation of postmodernism, has taken place at the same time that feminist educationalists have challenged the male monopoly on definitions of truth, proof, and order. (Even scientific dogma has not been immune; with theories of chaos and processes of imaginative speculation launching physics into the realm of postmodernism.)

Women were looking for an inclusive rather than an exclusive way of knowing, which led them to place a positive value on diversity. Instead of replicating the mind-set of the male model—declaring that what one knows is all that there is to know—feminist educational method was formulated with the aim of taking limitations into account, and with attempting to go beyond them.

For example, it is not sufficient to add white women to white men's history for apart from the fact that adding women in itself can change the representation of men, there are other categories which have to be introduced and analyzed. For the history of white men is primarily the history of the publicly famous—a category which is not particularly applicable to women who historically have been confined to the private sphere (or the invisible work force). And even in terms of women's educational history, it cannot be assumed that in simply recovering the records of white women who got to college that they would begin to tell the full story. As Beverly Guy-Sheftall and Patricia Bell Scott (1989b) make clear, there are numerous questions which need to be answered about Black women who went into higher education in the United States, the pressures they faced from family, institutions, society and how they are different from those faced by white women if we are to have an adequate understanding about women's educational history (and its relationship to men). And this is only a beginning.

Working class women, migrant women, returning women, (mature age women) Australian Aboriginal women, and American Indian women (in themselves very diverse groups, see Robbi Ferron, 1989), women with disabilities, and lesbians, all have different educational histories and experiences which must be taken into account if there is to be an accurate and authentic coverage of women's educational history.

It is this inclusiveness and interconnectedness (as distinct from the old linear cause and effect model), this disposition for soft data, for narrative and ethnological studies, for participant-observation—for an *ecological world view*—which is often characteristic of the feminist challenge to traditional educational measurements. It is the new research directions in curriculum content and construction, in classroom processes and teaching practices, that have become the hallmark of feminist educational theory. But above all it is the inclusion of an examination of the nature of knowledge production and the part it plays in perpetuating power that distinguishes feminist educational knowledge from the traditional premises and practices of the discipline.

MAINSTREAM RESPONSE

Men occupied the powerful positions in education—and constituted the mainstream—and this enabled them to ignore some of the protests and challenges which came from feminists. Initially numerous strategies were available to them to discredit feminist efforts; from pronouncements that women's research topics did not fall within the discipline parameters, to assertions that the research methods were unreliable, political, subjective, and the prevailing atmosphere was one in which feminist scholarship was treated as suspect.

Not surprisingly, women "defied the evidence" (see Elaine Reuben, 1978) and started to produce knowledge about women for inclusion in the curriculum (sexist ideology, cooperative teaching practices, assessment of single sex education, work loads of women teachers, women teachers and promotion and ambition, sexual harassment, sexism and reading, sexism and sex education, boy talk in the classroom, racism and homophobia, etc.). But when these proposals were put forward for new courses the following objections were likely to be encounteed as Elizabeth Minnich (1989) has made clear:

> Should you teach a course that is only about women? Isn't it peculiar to talk about the (history, literature, psychology . . .) of women without mentioning men (the assumption being that to talk about women is to exclude men, an assumption that reverses the usual, that to talk about men is to include women). Did you choose the works (authorities, research reports, etc.) because they are good or because they are by women? If another faculty member brings in a syllabus in which not a single woman author is represented and not a single book that deals with women is included, no such questions are asked. (p. 277)

To this she adds, "a list of white authors writing about themselves is still not seen as exclusive." And in the context of the intellectual double standard and the way in which the male mainstream can discredit the scholarship of women, it is in order to include the assertion that males who do research on males are considered to be scholars, whereas females who do research on females are perceived as trouble-makers and political agitators. By such means is knowledge gendered and graded.

Another mainstream response which can effectively accommodate feminist critiques and "threatening" innovations, is to provide a small space, a metaphorical footnote, so that it simply cannot be stated that feminist knowledge has not been taken into account. One lecture on sexism, one guest speaker to cover sexist practices in the classroom, one teaching video on boys classroom behavior and then the old theory and practice can proceed without being fundamentally modified.

It is partly because the discipline has proved so resistant to change that more feminist scholarship (and activity) takes place outside the discipline rather than inside. Women have developed an alternative educational practice—though it is one which at this stage has not been systematically identified and studied and suggests itself as a major topic for analysis in the future.

To some extent educated women's culture *is* a literary culture, (witness the explosion of women's publications in the last two decades) with women looking to books for information, guidance, *education*. More women buy books and this enables them to share a common information culture and engage in (informal) seminars, lectures, discussions on a topic which generally falls outside conventional educational and curriculum parameters. And nowhere is this division between the formal patriarchal education and the informal education of women more apparent than in the bookshops on university campuses. When on average less than 7% of the writers taught within the university are women, campus bookshops can be crammed with books by, about, and for women, few of which are prescribed texts for any courses; but all of which are purchased and read by women.

MEN'S OPPOSITION

"Though women's participation in the educational process at all levels has increased in this century," states Dorothy Smith (1978), it "remains within marked boundaries" and among the most important is that "which reserves to men control of the policy-making and decision-making apparatus in the educational system" (p. 287). By blocking the appointment of women to positions of influence—where they would be able to introduce women's knowledge into the discipline and the academy—male opposition has erected an effective barrier to feminist theory and practice. For while women have increased their participation at the student level (and now comprise 52% of all enrollments in the United States and gain 50% of the undergraduate and masters' degrees, Carol Pearson, Donna Shavlik, & Judith Touchton, 1989, p. 27), there is considerable evidence that their presence in the upper echelons has declined. Certainly there are fewer women's colleges (so fewer opportunities for women principals, M. Elizabeth Tidball, 1989) and sex discrimination laws in some countries have been used to open up headships of female establishments to men, without male establishments being opened to women.

It is still in order for women's education to be controlled by men even though it is demonstrable that the education provided is designed to produce "the best men;" but the idea that men's education should be controlled by women—and worse, that it should *reflect* women's priorities—is still anathema in education, and society. It is also further evidence of the intellectual double standard which decrees the positive nature of male intellect and the suspect and deviant nature of women's intellectual ability. In Britain and Australia, where single sex schools (and colleges) have become co-educational institutions there has been an increase in the number of male principals and a corresponding decrease in the number of women in charge (see M. Elizabeth Tidball, 1989, for further discussion of the disadvantages experienced by women in the United States, particularly page 168). As Carol Pearson, Donna Shavlik, and Judith Touchton (1989) state "Women hold only 10% of all college and university presidencies and only a handful of those in research institutions. If all women administrators at the dean's level and above were equally distributed among all the institutions, there would be only 1.1 per institution" (p. 5).

The absence of women "at the top" has further implications according to M. Elizabeth Tidball (1989); "the development of young women of talent into achieving adults is directly proportional to the number of same-sex role models to which they have access" (p. 164). If it is the case that young women do need the example and support of more experienced and successful women to see themselves attaining comparable achievements, then it could be quite an efficaceous form of male resistance to obstruct women's entry to positions of role model and mentor for the next generation.

But as many feminist researchers have found, having the numbers for women is no guarantee of influence either; (after all, women are more than 50% of the population). In New Zealand, only 1 in every 37 elementary teachers is male but so strategically has women's path to promotion been blocked (and so easy has it been made for men) that of these very few men, one in three becomes a principal. And this astonishing ratio (I am assured by many authorities) has nothing to do with sex discrimination; it is that men display more suitable leadership qualities.

This points to another form which male opposition can take; it is that of identifying and valuing the activities customarily undertaken by men and of then declaring them the desirable and necessary attributes for promotion. So for example, in the New Zealand context, the fact that men ordinarily take up more space (verbal and physical), that they conduct school assemblies, train football teams, and are seen to administer public chastisement and praise, is taken to be more in keeping with responsibility than the invisibles performed by women (counseling, conducting the clinic, managing relationships and interactions so as to avoid public confrontations). Describing the characteristics that men display as those required for leadership and promotion and then deciding that these characteristics are more prevalent and better developed in men, has to afford one of the best examples of circular reasoning available; but by the same token it is still a useful tactic for it can help to keep women out of influential positions.

But there's another factor which must also be taken into account; there are women classroom teachers who enjoy their work, who see it as a valid end in itself and who do not seek promotion. As the expansionary/progress model of industrialization which assumes the desirability of bigger and better is increasingly being challenged, perhaps it is not so problematic to be satisfied with what one has and even to insist that teaching, rather than policy making, can serve society better. In this context, is the classroom teacher who refuses promotion a wise woman, or does she lack ambition? Of course this scenario begs the question of whether women could become administrators and reorganize teaching so that it was perceived as an end in itself and accorded more value.

Men do not have to be the majority to exert influence as Margaret Wilkerson (1989) makes clear, "Women students are a numerical majority in higher education, yet their needs and interests are often a low priority. At the same time white males may be in a minority in the college or university but in fact have more power to define the college's goals and values." So money goes to football fields on campuses and not to child care facilities; so even the leisure needs of men can be held to be more important than the livelihood needs of women. This is part of the evidence that men count more than women; it is a manifestation of the principle that the experience, feelings, egos of men are more important than those of women.

So it is permissable, even preferable, to provide girls with boys' toys for play; and teaching about male experience, presenting male models, and fostering the development of male values can be seen as improving and extending the education of girls. But give boys the toys initially associated with girls, dress them in skirts or teach them "sissy" girls' subjects or female values, and long and loud will be the objections to the lowering of models, and standards. This is one of the most powerful and pervasive forms of male opposition to the inclusion of women in education; it is a primary means of keeping women *invisible*.

Feminist educators have recently drawn attention to the extent to which girls are verbally abused within the mixed sex classroom (see Sue Lees, 1987, for further discussion and documentation of the use of *slut* and *slag* and for general discussion of the American classroom). But perhaps even worse than the abuse itself is the failure of many teachers to take this form of harassment seriously with the result that girls learn they are not entitled to a safe place, not even in the protected environment of the classroom (see Roberta M. Hall & Bernice R. Sadler, 1982).

Sexual harassment is another form of male opposition which is used extensively to keep women in their place in the education system, and it is practiced from a very early age as Valerie Walkerdine (1987) has made chillingly clear. She quotes an interchange between a teacher, Miss Baxter, about 30 years old, and Annie (age 3) and two boys, Sean and Terry, (age 4) in a nursery school:

> The sequence begins when Annie takes a piece of Lego to add on to a construction that she is building. Terry tries to take it away from her to use himself and she resists. He says:
>
> *Terry:*   You're a stupid cunt, Annie.
>
> The teacher tells him to stop and Sean tries to mess up another child's construction. The teacher tells him to stop. Then Sean says;
>
> *Sean:*   Get out of it Miss Baxter paxter.
> *Terry:*   Get out of it Miss Baxter the knickers paxter knickers, bum.
> *Sean:*   Knickers, shit, bum.
> *Miss B:*   Sean, that's enough, you're being silly.
> *Sean:*   Miss Baxter, knickers, show your knickers
> *Terry:*   Miss Baxter, show your bum off.
> (they giggle)
> *Miss B:*   I think you're being very silly.
> *Terry:*   Shit Miss Baxter, shit Miss Baxter.
> *Sean:*   Miss Baxter, show your knickers your bum off.
> *Sean:*   Take all your clothes off, your bra off.
> *Terry:*   Yeah, and take your bum off, take your wee-wee off, take your clothes off, your mouth off.
> *Sean:*   Take your teeth out, take your head off, take your hair off, take your bum off, Miss Baxter the paxter knickers taxter.
> *Miss B:*   Sean, go and find something else to do please (p. 167).

With this sort of harassment beginning at such an early age and directed towards a female adult authority figure it is no wonder that it is a form of behavior which permeates the ethos of educational institutions. Mary M. Leonard and Brenda Alpert Sigall (1989) state that "40% of undergraduate women all over the country report experiencing sexual harassment from male students, faculty and staff. Graduate and undergraduate women alike are affected and few know what steps to take to protect themselves." And, they add, "women continue to report sexist jokes, less eye contact, fewer follow up questions, and other covert dismissal behavior by professors plus critical omission of materials on and by women in the classroom" (p. 231).

Not only are all these oppositional strategies intimidatory, there is ample evidence which suggests that they work. Women can be intimidated and their confidence and judgement undermined. Reared with the intellectual double standard which attributes "brightness" to males, which socializes females to be modest and even to camouflage their own intellectual ability, it is no wonder that women (who can meet harassment from preschool boys) can discount or distrust their own competence even when they do obtain better grades than men. ("Research in general shows that women get higher grades than men in both high school and college," but "Even though women enter college with better records of high school performance, they do not have as high expectations of performing well in college," Anne L. Hafner, 1989, p. 37).

The same mark can mean something different to teachers depending on the students' sex.

(See Dale Spender, 1984 and 1989, for the way "poor" results in maths and science were perceived as "something being wrong with the system" for boys, but the same marks were taken by trainee teachers as an accurate indication of the poor ability of girls.) And the same mark can mean something different to students; girls can think they are lucky to get good grades while boys can believe they deserve them. Much depends on the starting level of confidence and self-esteem; and an educational system which daily conveys the message that males and male experience are valued and that females have done little of note or praise which is worthy of inclusion in the curriculum, routinely replenishes the confidence of one sex and reduces that of *the other*.

And of course, if all subtle measures fail, there is always "might is right" to fall back on. One of the most widespread and workable oppositional strategies used by boys today in school to prevent women from entering their territory is that of physically forcing them out of the system. In schools in Australia and Britain the only way that girls can be guaranteed time at the computer in some classes is by banning the boys' entry to computer rooms on specific days. But in some (male controlled) educational circles and some areas of (male controlled) society, there is a feeling that this arrangement is not fair; another indication of the priority of male needs and of the pressure placed on education to accommodate them.

EXTENT OF CHANGES IN THE DISCIPLINE

Feminist scholarship has probably had the greatest impact on curriculum, partly because almost every feminist publication can be claimed as making some contribution to the general curriculum. (In my own case, in the late 1970s, when asked what I would like to teach in women-centered courses, I came to the grim realization that there were virtually no readily available texts I would choose to use [apart from some blatantly sexist materials which provided excellent examples of injustice, inhumanity and irrationality] because the books I wanted did not exist, I began to research and write the ones I needed for my own teaching purposes. I also became involved in reclaiming relevant women writers from the past and in persuading publishers to reprint them.)

The entire explosion of feminist knowledge—indeed the very contents of this volume—can be seen as part of the educational change if the discipline itself takes on the production, legitimation, and distribution of knowledge as its proper and primary concern. Which of course is what feminist educationalists have done, and in the process they have drastically changed the parameters and the premises. Whereas 20 years ago it would have been possible to assert (without threat of much contrary evidence) that women had not done anything worthy of inclusion in the cultural traditions—and hence their absence from the curriculum—such a position would be difficult to maintain in the contemporary context. With all the reclaiming work that has been done on every aspect of human endeavor, from women writers, inventors, and conservationists, from women scientists, artists, educators, and pacifists, to women spirtualists, adventurers, philsophers, and politicians, the question of whether women have made any contribution to the community should have been laid to rest; what still persists is the matter of whether this contribution ranks with that of men. But arguments about whether women measure up to men's standards are qualitatively different from those about women's invisibility.

Publications have also made their presence felt in relation to the curriculum, and educational explanations. Academic monographs, popular texts, reprints, past and present fiction, professional literature through to magazines, and their availability and accessibility have all worked to change what is known and how it is known; and to establish the reality of women's experience and achievements. So widespread and pervasive has this distribution of knowledge been that it is understandably tempting to assert that it has been women who have generated an information revolution and that it is one of feminism's greatest and most enduring successes. And although it would be foolish to discount or devalue this remarkable output, it is realistic to include a caveat.

For it is possible that one of the reasons that women's presses and women's publications have enjoyed such unparallelled success, is that print is no longer the primary information medium; because the area of print is no longer contested by the powerful and privileged in the way it used to be.

The association with print, with a literary culture, is well within the traditional confines of women's subjects. Talking, reading, writing—the arts and humanities—(as distinct from maths and science) have been the areas where women have enjoyed their greatest success. And it is interesting to note that another form of resistance to their achievement is in the making. Currently there is a tendency to favor the sciences at the expense of humanities, and on the spuriously sexist grounds that science and technology justify expenditure as they generate wealth (and are the breadwinners) while social sciences and humanities are a *cost* to the community (i.e., the consumers of wealth). It should not prove to be too difficult to bring such a schemata into disrepute; to argue that guns, weapons, bombs, fighter planes, submarines and the like, generate wealth, while drama, opera, art, music, libraries, philosophy, ideas, explanations, and forms of community support and development are a *cost* which society cannot afford, is hardly tenable.

Apart from the establishment of women's studies, one of the greatest gains of the last two decades has been the opening up of college and university education to mature women in the western world.

"Who are returning women? While no technical definition is widely used returning women are generally thought of as over twenty five years of age and with a history of delay or interruptions in their education. They are drawn from every racial, ethnic and regional group" (Jean F. O'Barr, 1989, p. 91). So many of them have there been that in the United States, "By 1986 women over twenty five constituted 24% of all post-secondary students" (p. 93). The reasons for the return of these women are numerous. They range from divorce, and the need to earn a living to the desire for an education in its own right. And the implications of this female presence in the halls of learning have also been interesting and far-reaching. First of all there is no equivalent group of "returning men" so a distinct literature has been generated on the problem of returning women (particularly in relation to angry/threatened male partners). There is also an expanding literature on the satisfaction this form of education affords (see for example Irene Thompson and Audrey Roberts, 1985—which is representative of this genre and which appears to have no parallel in men's educational experience). And then there is the manner in which the success of these women makes a mockery of traditional grading and entry requirements; for it appears that these women—many of whom were *failures* at school leaving age— attain disproportionately so many academic honors that being either a high achiever in school finals *or* a mature woman, is the recipe for reaping scholarly awards.

As Anne L. Hafner (1989) has stated one of the changes which is occurring among college women is that they report a greater interest in business and status than earlier generations, and a corresponding loss in altrusim and social concern. Which may or may not be a bad thing

Women show a 35% increase in being better off financially . . . (and) . . . Although the percentage of women who wanted to be in business on their own declined from 1966 to 1976, it has increased by 12% since 1976. The number of women who want to be experts in finance has also increased from 6% to 22% since 1966. In addition, the percentage of women who think it important to have administrative responsibility for others has doubled (21% to 41%) and large increases are also seen in obtaining recognition (from 36% to 59%) and being an authority in one's field (from 61% to 69%). From 1966 to 1985, women declined in their belief that it was important to develop a meaningful philosophy of life (down 21% from 1976). Declines are also observed in women's belief that it is important to help others in difficulty (down 10%) and in participation in community action programs (down 8% from 1976). (p. 39).

There could be some substance to the assertion that if you give females an education based on male values it should not come as a surprise if male values are adopted by female students; but perhaps this is one of the tasks for feminist educational research in the future.

And while as yet it may be too early to assess all the changes that feminism has made, it's not too early to identify the areas that show little sign of modification

Since the early 70s women have begun to be taken more seriously by higher education and many changes have occurred, still institutions remain fundamentally at the core, unchanged, and the values governing the establishment of priorities and the making of difficult decisions often do not include women or the issues that they deem critical (Carol Pearson, Donna Shavlik, & Judith G. Touchton, 1989, p. 7)

Virginia Woolf would not have been at all surprised.

SPECIFIC CONTRIBUTIONS

One of the most notable contributions that feminist education theory and practice has made has been that of extending the "one world" curriculum of white males to encompass the multiworld view. While in practice the goal may not have been achieved, (and to represent the unique realities off all groupings within society may not even be achievable) the fact it is considered good practice ideologically, to *aim* for an inclusive knowledge base is in itself an immeasurable advance on the old stated aims of equating excellence, norms, and universality with the particularities of the white, heterosexist male view.

An extension of this principle has been the analysis that feminist educational research has provided in relation to the concepts of *equal* education versus the *same* education. In British educational circles this debate has a distinctive history; when the first two women's colleges were established at Cambridge University in the nineteenth century, one of the critical issues was whether women should set up for themselves the *same* education as men, or whether they should develop an education system which was consistent with their interests as women.

Girton College went for the *same* education; the rationale behind this approach was that women's education would not count unless it was exactly the same as that undertaken by men. But at Newnham the philosophy was somewhat different; there was so much that was wrong with men's education, the reasoning went, why would women want to emulate it if they were in a position to devise their own? The counter argument to the Newnham stand was that if women did anything different it would assuredly be viewed as deficient—as an inferior form of education, and to some extent this allegation cannot be refuted. But by the same token it would be difficult to maintain the assertion that Girton (now coed) was seen to provide the *same* education as that offered by men, or even that in following the male line it was anything other than "an imitation."

In 1961 the United Nations passed the resolution that females should have:

The same choice of curricula, the same examinations, teaching staff with the same qualifications of the same standard, and school premises and equipment of the same quality, whether the institutions are coeducational or not (quoted in Eileen Byrne, 1987, p. 25).

To Eileen Byrne the stipulation of *the same* constituted a safeguard and it is the principle she wishes to see preserved in the interest of equal educational opportunity for girls; for when British educationalists introduced the specious concept of *equivalent* (or equal) instead of the *same,* it was used to justify the separation of subjects on the basis of sex. It was a means of educating the boys for work and the girls for domestic life—another version of Rousseau's arrangement but this time in a context of providing an *equally* relevant and equivalent education for the sexes.

But there are still huge problems with accepting the principle of *sameness* as many feminists have pointed out, particularly when girls are being provided with the *same* education that was designed to produce the best men! For the *same education* does not result in the *same learning experience* as Elizabeth Minnich (1989) makes clear:

... We have seen Black people admitted to institutions that continue to offer the same curriculum they offered when Black people were excluded ... an overwhelmingly if not exclusively all-white curriculum. . . . (But) . . . The full absurdity of assuming that a Black woman, studying a curriculum that is by and about white men is having the same experience, is learning the same things as a white man studying alongside of her is still not fully evident to some educators. (p. 286)

CURRENT ASSESSMENT AND FUTURE OUTLOOK

There can be no doubt about the changes that feminist educational theory and practice have made to the curriculum, to the awareness of classroom dynamics and the role of teachers'—and society's—expectations in the construction of gender and social inequality. The amount of information which ranges from sexism in children's books to epistemological analysis and which has been produced over the last 25 years is extraordinary. But the extent to which this information has infiltrated the mainstream and the extent to which it will endure is another matter.

Male opposition is not the only obstacle to the inclusion of the new and challenging knowledge of women as an integral part of the curriculum. Although there are individual men and interest groups of men who act as "gatekeepers" determining what is of the subject and what is not, what is the nature and quality of the work which is acceptable and what kind of people are to be admitted to their ranks, there are also females who have been initiated into the discipline, who sometimes because they are "suspect" can see their role as upholding the standards they were taught in an even more committed and rigid manner than some of their male peers. This form of female behavior can be used in a variety of ways against the inclusion of women's issues and the research, policy, and curriculum agenda as Dorothy Smith (1978) pointed out.

At the other end of the scale, are the young women students who stand in a different relationship to the feminist knowledge base from those who have constructed it. So much feminist theory and practice has been forged by women (now in midlife) who realized 20 years ago that if they wanted knowledge about women and their own lives they had to construct it themselves. This was an exciting and involved process. Of course it encompassed issues about the role of the knowledge-maker in the knowledge making and the relationship between knowledge and politics. But for the new generations of students who are the inheritors—rather than the bequeathers of a body of knowledge, and who cannot be held accountable for their "failure" to participate in the initial construction—the relationship to theory and practice is very different.

But more fundamental than the generation gap is the change in the information medium; it has been asserted that every 50 years women's knowledge is eclipsed or suppressed; it disappears so that women must start from scratch, and reinvent the wheel again:

> The entire history of women's struggle for self-determination has been muffled in silence over and over. One serious cultural obstacle encountered by any feminist writer is that each feminist work has tended to be received as if it emerged from nowhere; as if each of us had lived, thought and worked without any historical past or contextual present. This is one of the ways in which women's work and thinking has been made to seem sporadic, errant, orphaned of any tradition of its own. (Adrienne Rich, 1979–1980, p. 11)

As we move into the era of electronic transmission of information it seems clear that unless women's knowledge is included in the database to be transmitted, it could disappear from our "screens" entirely. While the advent and achievements of the women's presses have played an admirable role in educating women, in providing the basis for a common culture, a reservoir of authoritative authors, experiences and realities, perhaps we should look on books and the outsider literary culture which women have forged as only *one* educational medium. Perhaps the best hope for endurance is when women's knowledge is encoded in multimedia (e.g., Cheris Kramarae & Dale Spender, forthcoming).

And, of course, there are other knowledge based issues to be explored; how far should women take on the existing educational framework, and how far should they develop something entirely different which envisages a very different society? Is the woman who wants to do her Ph.D. on the meaning of life, or who writes a reference for another woman valuing her humanity over her hierarchy, her own worst enemy, or is she a font of wisdom?

The knowledge making possibilities for feminist educationalists are infinite, and exciting.

BIBLIOGRAPHY

Acker, Sandra. (1980, April 8). *Feminist perspectives and the British sociology of education.* Paper presented at the annual conference of the British Sociological Association, Lancaster, UK.

Astin, A. W. (1978). The undergraduate woman. In Helen S. Astin & W. Hinsford (Eds.), *The higher education of women.* New York: Praeger.

Arnot, Madeleine & Weiner, Gaby. (Eds.). (1987). *Gender and the politics of schooling.* London: Hutchinson/The Open University.

Bernard, Jessie. (1973). My four revolutions: An autobiographical history of the ASA. In Joan Huber (Ed.), *Changing women in a changing society* (pp. 11–29). Chicago: University of Chicago Press.

Bernard, Jessie. (1989). Educating the majority. The feminist enlightenment. In Carol S. Pearson, Donna L. Shavlik, & Judith G. Touchton (Eds.), *Educating the majority: Women challenge tradition in higher education.* New York: Macmillan.

Bogart, Karen & Traux, A. (1983, June). *Sexual harassment in academe: A new assessment.* Symposium presented at the annual conference of the National Women's Studies Association, Columbus, OH.

Boxer, Marilyn J. (1989). Women's studies, feminist goals, and the science of women. In Carol S. Pearson, Donna L. Shavlik, & Judith G. Touchton (Eds.), *Educating the majority. Women challenge tradition in higher education* (pp. 184–204). New York: Macmillan.

Bunch, Charlotte & Pollack, Sandra. (1983). *Learning our ways: Essays in feminist education.* Trumansburg, NY: The Crossing Press.

Byrne, Eileen. (1987). Education for equality. In Madeleine Arnot & Gaby Weiner (Eds.), *Gender and the politics of schooling* (pp. 23–34). London: Hutchinson/The Open University.

Clarricoates, Katherine. (1987). Dinosaurs in the classroom–The "hidden" curriculum in primary schools. In Madeleine Arnot & Gaby Weiner (Eds.), *Gender and the politics of schooling* (pp. 155–165). London: Hutchinson/The Open University.

Desjardins, Carolyn. (1989). The meaning of Gilligan's "Different Voice" for the learning environment. In Carol S. Pearson, Donna L. Shavlik & Judith G. Touchton (Eds.), *Educating the majority: Women challenge tradition in higher education* (pp. 134–146). New York: Macmillan.

Digest of Educational Statistics. (1987). Table 157, First Professional Degrees Conferred by Higher Institutions of Education by Sex of Student, Control of Institution and Field of Study, 1981–82 to 1984–85, Washington DC: Center for Education Statistics, Office of Educational Research and Improvement, U.S. Department of Education.

Duffy, Yvonne. (1989). Enhancing the effectiveness of postsecondary education for women with disabilities. In Carol S. Pearson, Donna L. Shavlik & Judith G. Touchton (Eds.), *Educating the majority: Women challenge tradition in higher education* (pp. 114–120). New York: Macmillan.

Dyhouse, Carol. (1978). Towards a "feminine" curriculum for English schoolgirls. The demands of ideology 1870–1963. *Women's Studies International Quarterly, 1*(4), 297–312.

Ferron, Robbi. (1989). American Indian women in higher education. In Carol S. Pearson, Donna L. Shavlik, & Judith G. Touchton (Eds.), *Educating the majority: Women challenge tradition in higher education* (pp. 80–89). New York: Macmillan.

Fraser, Antonia. (1984). *The weaker vessel: Women's lot in seventeenth century England.* London: Weidenfeld & Nicolson.

Friedan, Betty. (1963). *The feminine mystique.* Middlesex: Penguin.

Gabelnick, Faith & Pearson, Carol S. (1989). Recognizing the diversity of women's voices by psychological type. In Carol S. Pearson, Donna L. Shavlik, & Judith G. Touchton (Eds.), *Educating the majority: Women challenge tradition in higher education* (pp. 121–133). New York: Macmillan.

Gould, Jane S. (1989). Women's centers as agents of change. In Carol S. Pearson, Donna L. Shavlik, & Judith G. Touchton (Eds.), *Educating the majority: Women challenge tradition in higher education* (pp. 219–229). New York: Macmillan.

Gray, Elizabeth Dodson. (1989). The culture of separate desks. In Carol S. Pearson, Donna L. Shavlik, & Judith G. Touchton (Eds.), *Educating the majority: Women challenge tradition in higher education* (pp. 333–345). New York: Macmillan.

Guy-Sheftall, Beverly & Bell Scott, Patricia. (1989a). Finding a way. Black women students in the academy. In Carol S. Pearson, Donna L. Shavlik, & Judith G. Touchton (Eds.), *Educating the majority: Women challenge tradition in higher education* (pp. 47–56). New York: Macmillan.

Guy-Sheftall, Beverly & Bell Scott, Patricia. (1989b). Black Women's Studies: A view from the margin. In Carol S. Pearson, Donna L. Shavlik, & Judith G. Touchton (Eds.), *Educating the majority: Women challenge tradition in higher education* (pp. 205–218). New York: Macmillan.

Hafner, Anne L. (1989). The "traditional" undergraduate woman in the mid-1980s: A changing profile. In Carol S. Pearson, Donna L. Shavlik, & Judith G. Touchton (Eds.), *Educating the majority: Woman challenge tradition in higher education* (pp. 32–46). New York: Macmillan.

Hall Roberta M. & Sandler, Bernice R. (1982). *The classroom climate: A chilly one for women.* Project on the Education and Status of Women, Washington, DC. Association of American Colleges.

Kramarae, Cheris & Spender, Dale. (Eds.). (forthcoming) *International Encyclopedia of Women's Studies,* Elmsford, NY: Pergamon Press.

Lees, Sue. (1987). The structure of sexual relations in school. In Madeleine Arnot & Gaby Weiner (Eds.), *Gender and the politics of schooling* (pp. 175–187). London: Hutchinson/The Open University.

Leonard, Mary M. & Sigall, Brenda Alpert. (1989). Empowering women student leaders. A leadership development model. In Carol S. Pearson, Donna L. Shavlik, & Judith G. Touchton (Eds.), *Educating the majority: Women challenge tradition in higher education* (pp. 230–249). New York: Macmillan.

Macaulay, Catherine. (1790). *Letters on education.* Reprinted 1974, Gina Luria (Ed.), New York: Garland Publishing.

Martineau, Harriet. (1838). *How to observe: Morals and manners.* London: Charles Knight.

McNaron, Toni A. H. (1989). Mapping a country: What Lesbian students want. In Carol S. Pearson, Donna L. Shavlik & Judith G. Touchton (Eds.), *Educating the majority: Women challenge tradition in higher education* (pp. 102–113). New York: Macmillan.

McWilliams-Tullberg, Rita. (1975). *Women at Cambridge: A men's university—though of a mixed type.* London: Victor Gollancz.

Melendez, Sara E. & Petrovich, Janice. (1989). Hispanic women students in higher education. In Carol S. Pearson, Donna L. Shavlik & Judith G. Touchton (Eds.), *Educating the majority: Women challenge tradition in higher education* (pp. 57–68). New York: Macmillan.

Minnich, Elizabeth Kamarck. (1989). From the circle of the elite to the world of the whole: Education, equality and excellence. In Carol S. Pearson, Donna L. Shavlik, & Judith G. Touchton (Eds.), *Educating the majority: Women challenge tradition in higher education* (pp. 277–293). New York: Macmillan.

Mitchell, Juliet. (1971). *Women's estate.* Middlesex: Penguin.

O'Barr, Jean F. (1989). Reentry women in the academy: The contributions of a feminist perspective. In Carol S. Pearson, Donna L. Shavlik, & Judith G. Touchton (Eds.), *Educating the majority: Women challenge tradition in higher education* (pp. 90–101). New York: Macmillan.

Ollerenshaw, Kathleen. (1961). *Education for girls.* London: Faber & Faber.

Pearson, Carol S., Shavlik, Donna L., & Touchton, Judith G. (Eds.). (1989). *Educating the majority: Women challenge tradition in higher education.* New York: Macmillan.

Rich, Adrienne. (1979–1980). *On lies, secrets and silence: Selected prose 1966–1978.* New York: W W Norton.

Reuben, Elaine. (1978). In defiance of the evidence. *Women's Studies International Quarterly, 1*(3), 215–218.

Rogers, Barbara. (1988). Men only: *An investigation into men's organizations.* London: Pandora.

Shakeshaft, Carol. (1986, March). A gender at risk. *Phi Delta Kappa,* pp. 499–503.

Smith, Dorothy. (1978). A peculiar eclipsing: Women's exclusion from man's culture. *Women's Studies International Quarterly, 4,* 281–296.

Solomon, Barbara Miller. (1985). *In the company of educated women: A history of women in higher education.* New Haven, CT: Yale University Press.

Spender, Dale & Sarah, Elizabeth. (Eds.). (1980/88). *Learning to lose.* London: The Women's Press.

Spender, Dale. (1990). *Women of ideas—and what men have done to them.* London: Pandora.

Spender, Dale. (1984). Sexism in teacher education. In Sandra Acker & David Warren Piper (Eds.), *Is higher education fair to women?.* Society for Research in Higher Education, and National Foundation for Educational Research, Slough.

Spender, Dale. (1989). *Invisible women: The schooling scandal.* London: The Women's Press.

Spender, Dale. (Ed.). (1981b). *Men's studies modified: The impact of feminism on the academic disciplines.* Elmsford, NY: Pergamon Press.

Spender, Dale. (1981a). Education: The patriarchal paradigm and the response to feminism. In Dale Spender (Ed.), *Men's studies modified: The impact of feminism on the academic disciplines.* Elmsford, NY: Pergamon Press.

Stimpson, Catherine & Cobb, Nina Kressner. (1987). *Women's Studies in the United States.* (Available from The Ford Foundation, P.O. Box 559, Naugatuck, CT.)

Thompson, Irene & Roberts, Audrey. (Eds.). (1985). *The road retaken—Women reenter the academy.* New York: Modern Language Association.

Thorne, Barrie. (1989). Rethinking the ways we teach. In Carol S. Pearson, Donna L. Shavlik &

Judith G. Touchton (Eds.), *Educating the majority: Women challenge tradition in higher education* (pp. 311–325). New York: Macmillan.

Tidball, Elizabeth M. (1989). Women's colleges: Exceptional conditions, not exceptional talent, produce high achievers. In Carol S. Pearson, Donna L. Shavlik, & Judith G. Touchton (Eds.), *Educating the majority: Women challenge tradition in higher education* (pp. 157–172). New York: Macmillan.

Walkerdine, Valerie. (1987). Sex, power and pedagogy. In Madeleine Arnot & Gaby Weiner (Eds.), *Gender and the politics of schooling* (pp. 166–174). London: Hutchinson.

Wilkerson, Margaret B. (1989). Majority, minority, and the numbers game. In Carol S. Pearson, Donna L. Shavlik, & Judith G. Touchton (Eds.), *Educating the majority: Women challenge tradition in higher education* (pp. 25–31). New York: Macmillan.

Wollstonecraft, Mary. (1792). *Vindication of the rights of woman.* Joseph Johnson, London: Penguin.

Woolf, Virginia. (1938). *Three guineas.* London: The Hogarth Press.

Yamauchi, Joanne Sanae & Tin-Mala. (1989). Undercurrents, maelstroms, or the mainstream? A profile of Asian Pacific American female students in higher education. In Carol S. Pearson, Donna L. Shavlik & Judith G. Touchton (Eds.), *Educating the majority: Women challenge tradition in higher education* (pp. 69–79). New York: Macmillan.

Chapter 22

The Impact of Feminism on Sociology in the Last 20 Years

Liz Stanley

Summarizing the impact of feminism in sociology is no easy matter, for 'a discipline' is a complex entity. Moreover, sociology takes radically different forms in different countries; my review is written from the viewpoint of a British feminist sociologist and where possible I make brief comments about such differences. The Reference List provides further reading on the topics discussed.

THE POSITION OF WOMEN IN SOCIOLOGY 20 YEARS AGO

In *Men's Studies Modified* (Dale Spender, 1981), Helen Roberts (1981a) reviewed the impact of feminism on sociology to date and provided useful information about an earlier generation of proto-feminist work, specifically that of Marjorie Spring Rice (1939), Pearl Jephcott (1949), and Alma Myrdal and Viola Klein (1956). With benefit of hindsight and the "recovery" work of post–1981 feminist sociology, much more feminist and proto-feminist work from that period and earlier could now be added. Thus it is important to keep in mind that at least two previous generations of feminists have left their mark on the discipline, and that feminist sociology goes back to the work of Harriet Martineau and Flora Tristan.

It is useful to distinguish between the position of women in the discipline (a) organizationally, as students, researchers and teachers; (b) as the objects of research, "research subjects"; and (c) as the subjects of sociological theory, along with men.

In Great Britain, currently the majority of undergraduate sociology students are women; probably the majority of graduate students are male, although this is difficult to gauge given the paucity of evidence for higher education as a whole. Certainly increasing numbers of graduate sociologists are women, particularly those registered parttime. Most short-term contract research workers are women who are overqualified for the insecure and badly paid

Rosemary Deem, Janet Finch, David Morgan, Dale Spender, and Sue Wise provided me with detailed comments on draft versions of this paper for which I am very grateful. A spoken version of this paper was delivered at the Soviet Summer School, held at the University of Manchester in the summer of 1989, an experience which has confirmed for me just how far western sociology has traveled in a feminist direction during the last 20 years.

work they do. One result of the reduced funding of higher education in Britain is that a research *career* in sociology is now almost impossible, and the few teaching appointments that are made go disproportionately to men. Most teachers of sociology work in a variety of further education colleges rather than higher education (polytechnics and universities) or in schools (although some sociology is taught in school settings); by and large this majority neither do research nor publish. Women are concentrated in the least secure, worst paid jobs in each of these institutional settings; if they are women of color, this tends to be even more pronounced. The further up the organizational hierarchy, the fewer women. Twenty years ago the "shape" of women studying or employed in the discipline in Britain was very similar to this except there was a smaller proportion of women to men at all levels and particularly in further education; also the discipline as a whole was much smaller.

As research subjects, 20 years ago women's lives were studied only in specific subject areas. Ann Oakley (1974), for example, argued that it was only in relation to "the family" that women's presence had truly registered with male sociologists and even here only in particular ways (e.g., not seeing that housework and childcare constitute work).

Sociology produces different varieties of theory. The most prestigious—"social theory"—was then and still is written at such a level of abstraction that it is difficult to tell whether the writer intended that women should be included or excluded. Indeed, it is difficult to tell whether *men* are included or excluded except as "theoretical puppets." Gender seems to be conceived as existing at some lower level of generalization than that conventionally ascribed to "theory."

In British sociology 20 years ago, most theoretical work was of the kind Robert Merton termed "middle range": underpinning empirical research (as conducted via a number of different methods or techniques), and/or being derived from such research. Often very explicitly indeed, both the research and the theory was concerned with men only. One example was noted by Joan Acker (1973) regarding "class"; and there were a myriad of others, many of which were the concern of my own doctoral research (outlined later).

Succinctly, the position of women in sociology 20 years ago can be summarized as invisible, marginal, misrepresented, or entirely absent. However, even in advance of an organized feminist critique there were rumblings of discontent, even downright disbelief (see Meg Stacey [1981] for a powerful feminist critique of "structural" features of the role of theory and ideas in the discipline). It was women students and teachers of the sociological generation of approximately 1968 to 1974 that began to ask awkward questions and so initiated the now honored feminist sociological tradition of "being difficult."

THE FIRST FEMINIST CRITIQUES

The first four pieces of feminist sociological work that made an impact in Britain were: (a) Betty Friedan's (1963) critique of functionalism, the work of Talcott Parsons in particular (which for me joined C. Wright Mills's equally singeing remarks on Parson's work); (b) Jessie Bernard's (1973) powerful autobiographically located criticisms of sexisms in sociological theory and method; (c) Joan Acker's (1973) analysis of sexism in stratification theories, class theory, and its research in particular; and (d) Ann Oakley's (1974) overview of sexism in sociology in general, in work on deviance, stratification, power, the family, industry, and work, in particular.

Interestingly, apart from Oakley's this work was American in origin, although Hannah Gavron's research (1966), discussed later, provided a basis for comprehending and assimilating it in Britain.

In 1973 I had just started Ph.D. research, become totally disenchanted with the so-called

"Left," had been involved in gay movement national organization and a local lesbian group for the previous 2 years, and was familiar with more general feminist literature. Initially there seemed no point of contact between my political commitment to feminism and my great interest in sociology. So I fell upon the emerging feminist sociological literature as manna in a wilderness, along with a host of material from also emergent radical and reflexive sociology. My doctoral research started as an investigation of women's work and leisure, but then became a 1976-completed investigation of "the sociology of gender" (its title), dealing with sociology's misrepresentation of sexual divisions in the family, work, and class; and the epistemology of how such subject areas could be feministically conceptualized and investigated.

Kathryn Ward and Linda Grant (1985) identify the four major themes within the feminist critique as: (a) the omission and underrepresentation of women as subjects; (b) the focus on "male" topics and relevancies; (c) the recognition that sociology's paradigms, models, and methods distort women's experiences; and (d) the necessity to move away from treating male experience as the norm. They identify the fourth as the most radical, seeing it as "recasting" the discipline. They identify the first theme as producing "addition" only, and suggest that the second and third themes constitute "modifications" only and are thus merely revisionist. There are problems with this evaluation.

First, it denies the potentially revolutionary impact of criticisms of bias and "maleness." Second, it fails to take account of the prime position of "social theory" and epistemology within sociology: any feminist recasting of the discipline necessarily centers a critique of precisely "paradigms, models, and methods" (or what I would prefer to term epistemology); and certainly my own work with Sue Wise has largely focused on emphasizing precisely this point (e.g., Liz Stanley & Sue Wise, 1983a, 1990).

The "baseline" feminist critique, in pinpointing omissions, misrepresentations, and the existence of "male topics," added up to something very powerful, that "scientific" sociology was actually highly partial, largely if not exclusively reflecting the assumptions and experiences of men (as sociologists and as "subjects"), and was therefore open to incontrovertible criticism *on its own terms*. Relatedly, this critique pointed the way to two later developments. One was the feminist focus on "method," specifically identifying methods as "male" or "female" according to whether they were quantitative or qualitative. The other (and with hindsight actually in conflict with the first) was the then largely implicit feminist critique of "knowledge," particularly the awareness that there were knowledge*s*, each valid in their own terms but in practice in conflict.

Feminism does not live by critique alone: it constitutes a positive and constructive impulse within sociology as in other disciplines. The many contributions to the feminist critique were joined by a swiftly increasing body of feminist sociology that started to reconstruct sociological subject areas. Ann Oakley (1974), for instance, provided one of the first detailed studies of housework as work. Her research was greatly influenced by the earlier research of Hannah Gavron (1966); and both formed an early contribution to a feminist reworking that has completely reconceptualized understandings of "work" in mainstream British sociology (for example Duncan Gallie, 1988; Ray Pahl, 1988). Similar early feminist reworkings can be found in the various contributions to *Another Voice* (Marcia Millman & Rosabeth Kanter, 1975); and in Great Britain in particular the two collections edited by Diana Leonard Barker & Sheila Allen (1976 a&b) that derived from the 1974 British Sociological Association Annual Conference, which was organized around the theme of sexual divisions. A number of comments on these reworkings are worth making, given future developments.

The first concerns Arlene Kaplan Daniels's (1975) prescient remarks concerning the implications of feminist ideas for the "sociology of knowledge," for what we now call "epistemology" or theories of knowledge. Her work points to recent feminist interest in the implications of epistemology for "methodology" or perspective as well as for "methods" in the sense of specific research techniques (see Shulamit Reinharz 1979 and this volume; Helen Roberts 1981b; Liz Stanley & Sue Wise 1983a, 1983b; Gloria Bowles & Renate Duelli-Klein 1983; Dorothy Smith 1987; Shulamit Reinharz and Lynn Davidman 1989; Liz Stanley 1990; and the introduction to Sandra Harding [1987] for a feminist philosopher's use of these terms).

The second concerns the significant number of contributions by men to both of the Diana Leonard Barker and Shiela Allen collections. These point to the later development of "men's studies" and its more acceptable face, in the form of sociological men seriously and in good faith questioning their own past and present working practices in the light of feminist ideas (for example, Ronnie Frankenberg [1975] still seems a useful rethinking of community studies research). [See also Lillian Robinson, this volume.]

The third, which leaps at contemporary readers, is that few of these unanswerable criticisms and accompanying positive suggestions for better sociological work have had impact on the subject areas discussed. For instance, Lyn Lofland's (1975) analysis of the "thereness" of women in urban sociology can still act as a blueprint for change in urban sociology, a still exciting and largely unfulfilled program of ideas.

Margrit Eichler (1985) has identified four successive phases in the development of feminism within sociology, recognizing that each now coexists and the development continues. In British feminist sociology a slightly different route developed: (a) "Sex roles" was associated with the kind of work carried out by and about women before the advent of the feminism in the late 1960s—one example is Alva Myrdal and Viola Klein's work (1956), referred to earlier. (b) The "feminist critique" followed. (c) There then developed a "sociology of women" (e.g., Sarah Delamont, 1980), which conceptualized women's lives in relation to ideas about socialization and the life-cycle; this was in important ways dependent upon the "sex role theory" underpinning the dominant model of "socialization." (d) This was followed by a growing interest in a "feminist sociology," seeking to recast the discipline by working from "women's perspective as a radical critique of sociology" (with key work here being done by Canadian Dorothy Smith [1974, 1978, 1979, 1987]); and out of which has developed ideas concerning a *"women's* standpoint" research position (Sandra Harding, 1987). (e) Alongside this has been the development of a distinct feminist epistemology derived from a specifically *"feminist* standpoint" (e.g., Liz Stanley & Sue Wise, 1983a, 1990). (f) Relatedly, recognizing "difference" as well as "sameness" among women (Michele Barrett & Mary McIntosh, 1985) but also between feminists, and the existence of "feminist postmodernism" (as Sandra Harding, 1987, and Denise Riley, 1987 refer to it), has increasingly made it apparent that there are standpoints, no one of which can claim a priori grounds for greater validity, whatever one might want to claim about what is politically and ethically preferable. I refer to these developments in later sections.

BASIC TENETS DEVALUING WOMEN

Feminist sociology, then, has provided powerful criticisms and exciting suggestions concerning the subject areas of the discipline, but relatively few of these have resulted in radical change (those that have, will be outlined later). Kathryn Ward and Linda Grant (1985) suggest that among the reasons for the limited impact of feminist critiques are (a) the relatively few women involved at editorial level in professional journal publication; (b) the focus by women authors on areas of social life which concern women. Also from the United States comes the explanation of Judith Stacey and Barrie Thorne (1986). They attribute the absence of a basic transformation of sociology—unlike what they contend has happened (I would disagree) in anthropology, history and literature—to (a) the functionalist containment of feminism as gender roles or sex roles; (b) the limiting of gender to the status of a "variable" only; and (c) the ghettoization of feminism within marxist sociology.

Judith Stacey and Barrie Thorne's first two reasons are characteristics of "mainstream sociological feminism" in America. However, their relevance to an explanation of the impact of feminism in British sociology is doubtful, for the influence of functionalist and social psychological ideas about "gender roles" has been minimal here. Their third reason similarly speaks to the American experience and a parochial evaluation of marxist sociology, for in Britain the impact of marxist analytic ideas on the sociological mainstream is powerful to the extent that it must be counted as part of that mainstream. Certainly the influence of feminist ideas on British marxism cannot be doubted, but this does not have any "ghettoization" connotations. In addition, the presence of a powerful marxism feminism has also ensured that feminist sociologists in general have been concerned with the production of theory and research concerned with employment and with "work" conceived more widely. It is no coincidence that conceptualizations of and substantive research on work have formed British feminist sociology's major impact on the mainstream (I discuss other important feminist impacts later in the chapter).

In spite of reservations concerning its dimensions, I agree with Judith Stacey and Barrie Thorne that there *has* been a containment of feminism within sociology in Great Britain as in America and would account for its British containment in the following closely interlinked ways (for different views, see Mary Maynard, 1990; Ann Oakley, 1989).

The Containment of Feminism

Ann Oakley's (1974) discussion of sexism in sociology identified the sources of its perpetuation as: (a) the origins of sociology in the concerns identified by Marx, Weber and Durkheim; (b) the organizational maleness of the profession; and (c) the ideology of gender, which justified supposedly differential characters, behaviors, roles, and lives of women and men and assigned "importance" to the latter only. Fifteen years later, these three factors remain the most crucial means of containing not only feminist ideas but also feminist sociologists. To them I would add the following.

First: The work of Marx, Weber, and Durkheim is each more complex on the "question of women" and indeed the question of men than Oakley allows (and see here R. A. Sydie's [1987] reexamination of them from a feminist perspective). What *is* important is an almost fetishistic attitude toward "MarxWeberDurkheim" as a totemic structure within the discipline, to which has been added small accretions of other male social theorists—"andSchutzParsonsHabermasGarfinkelFoucault" (or variations thereon). In other words, there is still a privileging of particular styles of theorizing over "merely" empirical work but also over other kinds of theorizing and theorists. Neither feminist theory in general nor the work of women sociologists "count," have this kind of "weight" or credibility: there are no "Founding Mothers" (although I can see no good feminist reason for fetishism about the work of women any more than about men).

Second, Oakley does not discuss what has become increasingly a topic of feminist attention to the entire apparatus of Scientism (Habermas's phrase), in which there is a privileging of what "scientists" do, in both the natural and the social sciences, in sociology in particular. What has caught our collective attention is that such critiques must not exclude academic feminism itself (see Margrit Eichler [1980] for an excellent example of how constructive this can be). We too are part of this institutional apparatus, and we need to be aware of the implications regarding our positions as "social scientists," as researchers and theoreticians, vis-à-vis "women." Also for women, for feminists in particular, membership of the category "social scientist" is double-edged, for the assumptions and values of Scientism ("knowledge" is single and unseamed; objectivity is essential; value-commitment is taboo) can be and often are used to devalue, dismiss or deny the work of feminist sociologists. [See also Shulamit Reinharz, this volume.]

NEW PRIORITIES AND DIRECTIONS FROM FEMINISM

The existence of a strong feminist presence within British sociology has led to various new directions in theory and research. Perhaps the most important are: (a) an emphasis on "sexual divisions" (Diana Leonard Barker & Sheila Allen, 1976 a&b); (b) an attention to "public–private" definitions and separations (Eva Gamarnikow, June Parvis, Daphne Taylorson, & David Morgan, 1983); (c) a focus on questions of method; (d) a concern with crime and criminality and the treatment of women within the criminal justice system (Carol Smart & Barry Smart, 1978; Susan Edwards, 1984, 1989; Frances Heidensohn, 1985), but also in particular the degrees and kinds of male violence (Ruth Hall, 1985; Jalna Hanmer & Sheila Saunders, 1984; Jalna Hanmer & Mary Maynard, 1987; Liz Kelly, 1988; Jan Pahl, 1985; Sue Wise & Liz Stanley, 1987 [see also Jane Caputi, this volume]); (e) the analysis of "work" and its relationship not only to employment but also "family life" and the operations of the informal economy (Rosemary Deem, 1986, 1988; Janet Finch, 1989; Janet Finch & Dulcie Groves, 1983; Sylvia Walby, 1988); (f) attention to the gendered nature of the hidden and formal educational curricula and also to the dynamics of girls' lives in and out of school (Rosemary Deem, 1978; Christine Griffin, 1985; Vivienne Griffiths, 1988; Gaby Weiner, 1985 [see also Dale Spender, this volume]); and (g) concern with both "difference" and similarity in women's lives, principally but not exclusively in relation to the stringent criticisms of black feminists (as responded to by white feminists, see Michelle Barrett & Mary McIntosh, 1985; Caroline Ramazanoglu, 1986; Denise Riley, 1987) regarding the hegemonic role of white feminists and their ideas in the construction of what 'feminism' is.

Some of these areas of development are shared with feminist sociology in other Western countries. However, the form they have taken differs, as does the impact made on mainstream sociology. The areas of development which have had the greatest mainstream impact in Great Britain are, first, "sexual divisions," which has resulted in a generally much higher level awareness of the existence of power as a condition of social life and so of relationships between men and women; and second, the gendered nature of all forms of work and leisure. These are followed in approximate order of impact by the recognition of power within the family and of the existence and prevalence of male violence.

Although as yet not of such great significance, it is nonetheless clear there is a growing feminist concern with "practical ethics," with a principled *feminist* approach to the conduct of empirical research. Thus it is no coincidence that much of the discussion of ethics has been conducted as a part of the feminist discussions of methods (Lorraine Code, Sheila

Mullet, & Christine Overall, 1987; Susan Sherin, 1987; and in Great Britain, Janet Finch, 1984; Ann Oakley, 1981; Liz Stanley & Sue Wise, 1983a; Sue Wise, 1987).

NEW FEMINIST METHODS

In much the same way that the feminist presence in sociology has been characterized by successive and overlapping phases of development, so the interest in questions of "method" has also been characterized by successive developments. Jessie Bernard's (1973) now classic contribution to the feminist critique was, among other things, concerned with identifying and criticizing "male methods." Similar arguments were made by many other feminists (including Helen Roberts 1981a, although a more complex note, ironically, was sounded in this collection by David Morgan, 1981), the logic of which was to confirm reservations concerning the nature and use of survey research; these were shared with what has become known as the "critique of positivism" within sociology.

Helen Roberts (1981b, p. 25) succinctly summarizes the problem identified by feminists as "some methodologies and research situations may systematically prevent the elicitation of various kinds of information and . . . certain methodological assumptions and techniques may limit the researcher's vision and produce questionable findings." Her answer was to utilize interviewing approaches. A number of other contributions to *Doing Feminist Research* (Helen Roberts, 1981a) similarly see interviewing as *the* feminist answer to the problem, perhaps the best known of which is Ann Oakley's (1981) account of "interviewing women." Subsequently Janet Finch's (1984) discussion of the feminist dynamics of interviewing identified not only its strengths and possibilities, but also some of its more worrying aspects. However, it is only recently (e.g., Jane Ribbens, 1989) that interviewing has been placed in perspective as not the easy answer to all feminist research ills as some have treated it.

In spite of feminist criticisms of "male methods," many feminist sociologists have utilized quantitative approaches, including the use of survey method to serve feminist aims and answer feminist questions (see chronologically, Alison Kelly, 1978; Toby Epstein Jayaratne, 1983; Hilary Graham, 1983, 1984; Jalna Hanmer & Sheila Saunders, 1984; Ruth Hall, 1985). This constitutes a rejection of the identification of "hard" and "male" with quantification, recognizing that how research is set up and conducted, the questions it seeks to explore, and the uses its results are put to, can all provide good feminist reasons for quantification. In addition, it is often supposed (I argue erroneously, see Liz Stanley, 1990) that large-scale research allows generalizations about whole populations to be made and that nonquantified research does not.

Alongside run two more dubious arguments, one is that feminists must use "numbers" because this is what the mainstream will take notice of; the other is that the critique of method is "really" about some women's inability to do quantitative work. I reject the first argument including for its assumptions that "the mainstream" is worth joining in an unreconstructed form, and that the intellectual problematics with quantification can be ignored. The second argument is a patronizing dismissal of other feminists' deeply felt intellectual and political convictions and is completely uncceptable.

Although having its origins in the first stages of the feminist critique, discussions of a distinctly feminist approach to constructions of knowledge, of epistemology, in sociology have been greatly developed in recent years (Gloria Bowles & Renate Duelli Klein, 1983; Shulamit Reinharz, 1979; Shulamit Reinharz & Lynn Davidman, 1989; Dorothy Smith, 1974, 1978, 1979, 1987; Liz Stanley, 1990; Liz Stanley & Sue Wise, 1983a, 1983b). Critics of such developments (e.g., Michele Barrett, 1987; Sue Clegg, 1985; Dawn Currie, 1988;

Dawn Currie & Hamida Kazi, 1987) have rejected what they have dubbed "feminist methodology" on the grounds of its purported "essentialism," biologically-based ideas about women's innate difference from men. Additionally, such critics also reject the idea that (true) knowledge can ever be plural: fundamentally theirs is an adherence to the assumptions and standards of foundationalist science.

Whether termed "women's standpoint" or "feminist postmodernism" (as in Sandra Harding, 1987), discussions of feminist epistemology are concerned not with method but rather with fundamentally recasting the way we understand the nature and product of "knowledge"—not only feminist knowledge but *all* knowledge (and these are the grounds on which I dispute Kathryn Ward and Linda Grant's [1985] evaluation of the feminist critique of paradigms, models, and methods). It is here, in relation to the sociology of knowledge, that feminism's greatest promise for a truly radical transformation of the discipline lies.

RESPONSE TO FEMINISM
FROM THE MAINSTREAM

In spite of earlier statements about the "mainstream," it is actually difficult to pinpoint exactly what this is and so what its response has been. Is the mainstream determined by the British Sociological Association (BSA)? If so, then its central organization and elected members' committees are thoroughly feminized, as are its national annual conferences; its many study groups, however, are sometimes much less positively responsive to feminism (although this changes over time depending on who is involved in them). But by no means all sociologists are members of the BSA—indeed, the majority are not. The mainstream, then, might be seen as mainstream journals; in which case in Great Britain a significant number of these are positively responsive to feminist work and/or have feminist representation at editorial level. So is it constituted by other forms of publishing? Again, the situation is complex. Certainly there are few academic publishers that do not have extensive feminist lists and there is still a lively demand for more. The teaching of gender issues, and the production of theory and research, shows similar complexities.

Pinpointing the "mainstream" in a different way directs attention to the organizational apparatus of professional sociology in higher education. In sociology there is a clear "hierarchy of credibility" (Howard Becker, 1971); some ideas, writings, and persons "count" more than others, and are accorded greater intellectual "weight." One good indication of this hierarchy in Great Britain concerns appointment to professorial chairs, for this is not only the concern of the particular university but also of those outside professional advisors it draws into the appointments procedure; and an even smaller proportion of women hold chairs than are senior lecturers in British sociology. Another concerns lecturing appointments in general: the BSA Equality of the Sexes Sub-Committee has found that of the 19 latest (to July, 1990) appointments to sociology lectureships in British universities, only seven were of women, and this in spite of funding council level recognition that the gender imbalance in the discipline is a severe problem.

This position could be taken as the product of active discrimination, a conspiracy albeit one carried out covertly. However, a more plausible explanation focuses on the "hierarchy of credibility," which collects into it evaluations of presentational styles, of types of publications, of areas of research and so forth which evaluate what male sociologists do as having greater professional credibility. The mainspring of this process depends upon the shared beliefs and values of a hegemonic ascendency in the discipline, in which those appointed and published are themselves like, and produce work which is similar to, those who people the gatekeeping levels of the discipline. A simple example of this hierarchy of credibility can be seen in a recent statement made to me: an interest in the work of philosopher Ludwig Wittgenstein is general sociology, while one in the work of philosopher Sandra Harding is feminism only.

Howsoever the sociological "mainstream" is defined, its responses are both difficult to pin down and complex in their operation. In some areas of sociological work there has been a positive response to feminism and in others not. Identifying with any precision where exactly the sources of resistance are is difficult, given that there are also sources which accept and even welcome feminist ideas. However, it is clear, given the heavily gendered nature of the organizational structure of sociology in higher education, that there are indeed resistances, refusals, and rejections.

DEFENSIVE AND OFFENSIVE STRATEGIES OF MEN IN SOCIOLOGY

The responses to feminism of men in sociology include "jobs for the boys" and a hierarchy of credibility which largely fails to accord feminism and feminists their due; but these are mixed with acceptance and a positive response beyond what anyone 20 years ago would have thought possible. A further response, which similarly demonstrates the complexity of the position, is the responsive or offensive strategy of "men's studies" (Harry Brod, 1987; Robert Connell, 1983, 1987; Jeff Hearn, 1987; David Morgan, 1975, 1981, 1985, 1987a, 1987b).

Many feminists dismiss men's studies as yet one more male hegemonic form, this time presented as politically "right-on." Others welcome its development, for if the discipline is ever to radically change then its male practitioners have to change to the same degree. These arguments are discussed at length elsewhere in this book. [See Lillian Robinson, this volume.] My own position encompasses both reactions, for I perceive two major stands within men's studies and find the first objectionable and welcome the second.

The first strand colonizes feminist ideas, seeing its practitioners as the true guardians of sexual political theorizing. Here the emphasis is on taking over and reworking feminist ideas and seeing no problems in doing so. In the second strand masculinities and their production in all spheres of social life, including within sociology, are the topic of investigation and analysis; and by doing so a powerful critique of the "malestream" sociological mode of production is produced.

It is important that feminism develops a response to both strands. One way forward is for men's studies to become a focus of feminist analysis (e.g., Marianne Hester, 1984; Liz Stanley, 1984b), in precisely the way other areas of male activities (as assailants, as trade unionists defending male privilege . . .) have become topics of feminist analysis.

HOW EXTENSIVE IS THE CHALLENGE OF FEMINISM IN SOCIOLOGY?

It is extraordinarily difficult to say how extensive the feminist challenge in sociology is. In terms of *possibilities,* its challenge is almost unlimited; *in practice* the area of its greatest possible impact is one shied away from by many feminist sociologists. This concerns the sociology of knowledge, the definition and construction of knowledge and the specification of who are and who are not 'knowers.' It is shied away from for two main reasons, by two probably different groups of feminist sociologists.

First, there is a nervousness about entering into this particularly prestigious area of sociology of "high theory" engaged in not only by "MarxWeberDurkheim" but also by all those later social theorists who constitute the "names" of the discipline (and precisely none of whom "happen" to be female). One of the prime pieces of ideological rhetoric that serves to keep women in (what many men see as) our place within sociology is the mystique that attaches to "theory" as completely different from reading, thinking, researching, and writing. One way of subverting this self-perpetuating cycle of exclusion and removal is for feminist sociologists to insist that all sociological products are written in such a way that the product is grounded in a detailed account of its own labor process (and see here Liz Stanley, 1984a, 1990). This would demonstrate very clearly indeed that theory and research are by no means as distinct as this rhetoric would have us believe.

Second, although through the years, there has been general acceptance by feminists that there are knowledge*S* (Judith Cook, 1983; Margrit Eichler, 1985; Judith Cook & Mary Fonow, 1986), there are some who dissent. Margrit Eichler (1985) proposes that one of the four fundamental feminist epistemological propositions is that male and female viewpoints differ systematically and women's is arguably better because it incorporates both a knowledge of "overdogs" and also that of "underdogs." This proposition is unacceptable for some feminist sociologists for reasons derived from the foundationalist Scientistic conviction that there is one single unseamed reality "out there" composed of facts which adequate researchers can establish as the "truth" about social life. Succinctly, theirs is the conventional academic view that knowledge, true knowledge, is one and indivisible—and that it is feminist "experts" who establish what this is.

THE SPECIFIC CONTRIBUTIONS OF FEMINISM

Beyond any doubt the most important contribution feminism has made to sociology is through the feminist critique. Its basic message—that by using its own standards of science sociology could be easily and incontrovertibly shown to be riddled with the values and assumptions of sexism which led it either to misrepresent or render invisible the lives and experiences of women and girls—still resounds in the discipline. Like Adam after the expulsion from Eden, the sociological male has forever lost his innocence; and while open sexist attitudes as well as research and writing continues, there is a wide recognition that this is indeed sexism.

One of the reasons the feminist critique has been so effective is because of the prior existence of a well-argued critique of positivism in sociology. Many feminist newcomers to sociology tend to think that feminism invented the critical sociological wheel, whereas without this other critique feminist ideas would have made little impact, certainly not of the degree and long-lastingness they have had.

Additionally, feminist work has fundamentally changed three substantive subject areas, including the most basic assumptions brought to these fields of study. These are the sociology of the family (David Morgan, 1975, 1985; Chris Harris, 1983; Paul Close & Rosemary Collins, 1986; Julia Brannen & Gail Wilson, 1987; Janet Finch, 1989); the sociology of work; and the study of male violence (see earlier references for these two latter areas). Family sociology now is predicated upon treating power as a dimension of family life and recognizing that both gender and age are crucially important to any understanding of family life. The sociology of work now turns upon the recognition of the close interdependence of work—committed and obligated activities and time—in each of the "three economies" (the formal economy, the informal economy, the domestic economy) and the gender as well as race and class nature of its distribution. The sociology of crime and deviance now accepts not only the high prevalence of domestic and public violence towards women and children, but also the crucial gender, age and race aspects of how crimes, innocence, blame, and guilt, and other related concepts are produced and used.

OVERALL ASSESSMENT

Feminist sociology, like Thursday's child, has far to go. There is still much to be gloomy and angry about. However, there are significant areas of change and important gains have been made, and these must not be forgotten. I would like briefly to raise some issues not dealt with in the previous sections, but which seem important to the future of feminist sociology.

1. For many feminist sociologists there is a still unresolved tension between wanting feminist change and a gut-level belief in the privileged role of scientists, and including feminist experts on other women's lives. Ten years ago a friend said she couldn't understand why so many academic feminists complained about their promotion and that they didn't get the same grants and 'honors' as male colleagues, for all to proclaim oneself a revolutionary *and* expect preferential treatment was surely to have missed the point of revolution! What strikes me in 1990 is how depressingly respectable many feminist academics are. During the next 10 years I hope that more of us will cultivate taking intellectual and political risks and thumbing our noses to orthodoxy. We may not end up as supposedly key members of the discipline, but surely we'll have a better time than now.

2. The discovery of difference by some feminist sociologists strikes a very wry note for those of us who, by virtue of being lesbians, black, working class, disabled, have *lived* difference for a good deal of our lives. It is only because black feminism has effectively forced white to recognize its existence, take it seriously, that *any* kind difference is on the academic feminist agenda. And race and racism is still only minimally on the agenda in feminist sociology as anything other than a variable (and for a discussion of the kind of rethinking that needs to be done at an epistemological level, see Patricia Hill Collins, 1986a, 1986b, 1991). I sincerely hope that other kinds of difference will be taken as seriously, and no more, than race and racism should be at all levels of feminist sociological practice. I hope that on this score we will do a good deal better during the next 20 years than we have in the last.

3. Some readers may be surprised at the minimal appearance of women's studies in this essay. Certainly the vast majority of British academic feminists are convinced of the value of more interdisciplinary ways of working together. However, for many there are reservations concerning claims that women's studies is a discipline in its own right, even more concerning the elitism of its British focus on higher degrees. Of course there are passionate proponents of a women's studies approach as the way forward for academic feminism (see Roisin Battel, Renate Duelli Klein, Catherine Moorhouse & Christine Zmroczek, 1983) and graduate courses in women's studies are proliferating. The issues on either side are complex; but as yet there has been little published writing that takes seriously the reservations sketched out above (for one exception, see Liz Kelly & Ruth Pearson, 1983).

4. The relationship between feminism and sociology is a complex one, and in Great Britain parallels the relationship between marxism and sociology. Feminism has its own separate existence, as an immensely important program of personal and political change, one which has had far greater impact in some nonwestern countries than the so-called "first world." Feminism has its own now worldwide stage; however, it is also a presence on a sociological stage. Originally a bit part, it has moved through minor roles and must now

be counted one of the protagonists, albeit one whose importance may be disputed by some of the other actors. The sources of its importance and the disputes are complexly intertwined and center upon those features of the discipline so clearly identified by the feminist critique. In particular, feminism presents an unanswerable case for the existence of sexism, bias, subjectivity, as the hallmark of mainstream sociology as indeed "malestream" sociology. Feminism, then, is a very threatening presence within a discipline which has almost unthinkingly adopted Scientistic ideologies and practices. It is because of this that I have argued feminism can make its greatest contribution to the discipline at the level of epistemology, although this is not to deny the continuing importance of other feminist contributions, in particular to theory and research within various traditional subject areas of sociology, such that at least some have undergone fundamental transformations.

Overall, sociology has been unusually positively responsive to feminist ideas, in spite of the resistances, and there *is* the possibility for a radical transformation of the discipline. One sign of this is the way that the discipline has in the recent past provided a base for feminists who have felt unwelcome in or driven out of other disciplines. And another is the surely quite remarkable impact of antipositivist ideas on sociological theory and practice over the last 25 years or so.

Finally, I am uncomfortably aware that I have said little about the funding of higher education in Great Britain, as the backcloth against which the drama of feminism in sociology is being played out. There are now relatively few appointments, postgraduate awards, or research grants because of budget cut-backs. People are much more cautious, the general academic mood is less buoyant. Thus funding issues affect the position of both women and feminism in the discipline in complex ways which I am unable to outline in this chapter.

BIBLIOGRAPHY

Insofar as possible I have provided British feminist references in this chapter, and similarly with the bibliographic material referenced below. Most of what appears here has been described in the text, so only the most important/useful of the non-referenced material is annotated below.

Acker, Joan. (1973). Women and social stratification: A case of intellectual sexism. In Joan Huber, (Ed.), *Changing women in a changing society* (pp. 174–183). Chicago: University of Chicago Press.

Barker, Diana Leonard & Allen, Sheila. (Eds.). (1976a). *Sexual divisions and society*. London: Tavistock.

Barker, Diana Leonard & Allen, Sheila. (1976b). *Dependence and exploitation in work and marriage*. London: Longman.

Barrett, Michele. (1987). The concept of "difference." *Feminist Review, 26,* 29–41.

Barrett, Michele & McIntosh, Mary. (1985). Ethnocentrism and socialist-feminist theory. *Feminist Review, 20,* 23–47.

Battel, Roisin, Duelli Klein, Renate, Moorhouse, Catherine, & Zmroczek, Christine. (Eds.). (1983). So far, so good—so what? Women's studies in the UK. *Women's Studies International Forum, 6,* 3.

Becker, Howard. (1971). *Sociological Work.* London: Allen Lane.

Bernard, Jessie. (1973). My four revolutions: An autobiographical history of the ASA. *American Journal of Sociology, 78,* 773–801.

Bowles, Gloria & Klein, Renate. (Eds.). (1983). *Theories of women's studies*. London: Routledge & Kegan Paul.

Brannen, Julia & Wilson, Gail. (Eds.). (1987). *Give and take in families* London: Allen & Unwin.

Brod, Harry. (Ed.). (1987). *The making of masculinities: The new men's studies.* London: Allen & Unwin.

BSA Standing Committee on the Equality of the Sexes. (1986). Teaching gender—struggle and change in Sociology. *Sociology, 20,* 347–361.

Clegg, Sue. (1985). Feminist methodology—fact or fiction? *Quality and Quantity, 19,* 83–97.

Close, Paul & Collins, Rosemary. (Eds.). (1986). *Family & economy in modern society.* London: Macmillan.

Code, Lorraine, Mullett, Sheila, & Overall, Christine. (Eds.). (1987). *Feminist perspectives: Philosophical essays on methods and morals.* Toronto: University of Toronto Press.

Collins, Patricia Hill. (1986a). Learning from the outsider within: The sociological significance of black feminist thought. *Social Problems, 33,* 14–332. (emphasizes how black women are multiply 'outsider', and that this provides a distinct epistemological position, which should be seen as a sociological strength)

Collins, Patricia Hill. (1986b). The emerging theory and pedagogy of black women's studies. *Feminist Issues, 6,* 3–17. (a continuation of Collins 1986a but focusing on pedagogical issues; both highly recommended reading)

Collins, Patricia Hill. (1990). *Black feminist thought.* London: Allen & Unwin.

Connell, Robert. (1983). *Which way is up?* Sydney: Allen & Unwin.

Connell, Robert. (1987). *Gender and power.* Oxford: Polity Press.

Cook, Judith. (1983). An interdisciplinary look at feminist methodology: Ideas and practice in sociology, history and anthropology. *Humboldt Journal of Social Relations, 10,* 127–152.

Cook, Judith & Fonow, Mary. (1984). Am I my sister's gatekeeper? Cautionary tales from the academic hierarchy. *Humanity and Society, 8,* 442–452.

Cook, Judith & Fonow, Mary. (1986). Knowledge and women's interests: Issues of epistemology and methodology in feminist sociological research. *Sociological Inquiry, 56,* 2–29.

Currie, Dawn. (1988). Re-thinking what we do and how we do it: A study of reproductive decisions. *Canadian Review of Sociology & Anthropology, 25,* 231–53.

Currie, Dawn & Kazi, Hamida. (1987). Academic feminism and the process of de-radicalisation: Re-examining the issues. *Feminist Review, 25,* 77–98.

Daniels, Arlene. (1975). Feminist perspectives on sociological research. In Rosabeth Kanter & Marcia Millman (Eds.), *Another voice* (pp. 340–380). New York: Anchor.

Deem, Rosemary. (Ed.). (1978). *Women and schooling.* London: Routledge & Kegan Paul.

Deem, Rosemary. (1986). *All work and no play: The sociology of women and leisure.* Milton Keynes: Open University Press.

Deem, Rosemary. (1988). *Work, unemployment and leisure.* London: Routledge & Kegan Paul.

Delamont, Sara. (1980). *The sociology of women.* London: Allen & Unwin.

Edwards, Susan. (1984). *Women on trial.* Manchester: Manchester University Press.

Edwards, Susan. (1989). *Policing 'domestic violence'.* London: Sage.

Eichler, Margrit. (1980). *The double standard: A feminist critique of feminist social science.* London: Croom Helm.

Eichler, Margrit. (1985). And the work never ends: Feminist contributions. *Canadian Review of Sociology & Anthropology, 22,* 619–44.

Fee, Elizabeth. (1986). Critiques of modern science: The relationship of feminism to other radical epistemologies In Ruth Bleier (Ed.), *Approaches to science* (pp. 42–56). New York: Pergamon Press. (self-explanatory title; very useful paper in an excellent collection)

Finch, Janet. (1984). It's great to have someone to talk to: The ethics and politics of interviewing women. In Colin Bell & Helen Roberts (Eds.), *Social researching: Politics, problems, practice* (pp. 70–87). London: Routledge & Kegan Paul.

Finch, Janet. (1989). *Family obligations and social change.* Oxford: Polity Press.

Finch, Janet & Groves, Dulcie. (Eds.). (1983). *A labour of love: Women, work and caring.* London: Routledge & Kegan Paul.

Frankenberg, Ronnie. (1976). In the production of their lives men (?). . . . In Diana Leonard Barker & Sheila Allen (Eds.), *Dependence and exploitation in work and marriage* (pp. 25–51) London: Longman.

Friedan, Betty. (1963). *The feminine mystique.* Harmondsworth: Penguin.

Gallie, Duncan. (Ed.). (1988). *Employment in Britain.* Oxford: Blackwell.

Gamarnikov, Eva, Purvis, June, Taylorson, Daphne, & Morgan, David. (Eds.). (1983). *The public and the private.* London: Heinemann.

Gavron, Hannah. (1966). *The captive wife.* Harmondsworth: Penguin.

Gould, Meredith. (1980). The new sociology. *Signs 5,* 459–468.

Graham, Hilary. (1983). Do her answers fit his questions: Women and the survey method. In Eva Gamarnikov, June Purvis, Daphne Taylorson, & David Morgan (Eds.), *The public and the private* (pp. 132–146). London: Heinemann.

Graham, Hilary. (1984). Surveying through stories. In Colin Bell & Helen Roberts (Eds.), *Social researching: Politics, problems, practices* (pp. 104–124). London: Routledge & Kegan Paul.

Griffin, Christine. (1985). *Typical girls.* London: Routledge.

Griffiths, Vivienne. (1988). From playing out to dossing out: Young women and leisure. In Erica Wimbush & Margaret Talbot, (Eds.). *Relative freedoms: Women and leisure.* Milton Keynes: Open University Press.

Hacker, Helen Mayer. (1951). Women as a minority group. *Social Forces, 30,* 60–69.

Hall, Ruth. (1985). *Ask any woman.* Bristol: Falling Wall Press.

Hanmer, Jalna & Maynard, Mary. (1987). *Women, violence and social control.* London: Macmillan.

Hanmer, Jalna & Saunders, Sheila. (1984). *Well-founded fear.* London: Hutchinson.

Harding, Sandra. (1986). *The science question in feminism.* Milton Keynes: Open University Press.

Harding, Sandra. (Ed.). (1987). *Feminism and methodology.* Milton Keynes: Open University Press.

Harris, Chris. (1983). *The family and industrial society.* London: Allen & Unwin.

Hearn, Jeff. (1987). *The gender of oppression.* Brighton: Wheatsheaf.

Heidensohn, Frances. (1985). *Women and crime.* London: Macmillan.

Hester, Marianne. (1984). Anti-sexist men: A case of cloak and dagger chauvinism. [Special Issue] *Women's Studies International Forum, 7,* 33–38.

Huber, Joan. (Ed.). (1973). *Changing women in a changing society* Chicago: University of Chicago Press.

Jayaratne, Toby Epstein. (1983). The value of quantitative methodology for feminist research. In Gloria Bowles & Renate D. Klein (Eds.), *Theories of women's studies* (pp. 140–161). London: Routledge & Kegan Paul.

Jephcott, Pearl. (1949). *Girls growing up.* London: Faber.

Kanter, Rosabeth & Millman, Marcia (Eds.). (1975). *Another voice.* New York: Anchor.

Kelly, Alison. (1978). Feminism and research. *Women's Studies International Quarterly, 1,* 225–232.

Kelly, Liz. (1988). *Surviving sexual violence.* Oxford: Polity Press.

Kelly, Liz & Pearson, Ruth. (1983). Women's studies: Women studying or studying women? *Feminist Review,* 15, 76–80. (raises some of the often ignored feminist problematics of Women's Studies as a source of 'expertise' on women's lives)

Lofland, Lyn. (1975). The 'thereness' of women: A selective review of urban sociology. In Rosabeth Kanter & Marcia Millman (Eds.). *Another voice* (pp. 144–170). New York: Anchor.

Maynard, Mary. (1990). The reshaping of sociology? Trends in the study of gender. *Sociology, 24,* 269–290.

Millman, Marcia & Kanter, Rosabeth Moss. (1975). *Another voice: Feminist perspectives on social life and social science.* New York: Anchor Books.

Morgan, David. (1975). *Social theory and the family.* London: Routledge.

Morgan, David. (1981). Men, masculinity and the process of sociological enquiry. In Helen Roberts (Ed.), *Doing feminist research* (pp. 83–113). London: Routledge & Kegan Paul.

Morgan, David. (1985). *The family, politics and social theory.* London: Routledge & Kegan Paul.

Morgan, David. (1987a). Masculinity and violence. In Jalna Hanmer & Mary Maynard (Eds.), *Women, violence and social control.* London: Macmillan.

Morgan, David. (1987b). *It will make a man of you.* Studies in Sexual Politics no. 17, Sociology Department, University of Manchester, England.

Myrdal, Alva & Klein, Viola. (1956). *Women's two roles.* London: Routledge & Kegan Paul.

Oakley, Ann. (1974). *The sociology of housework.* London: Martin Robertson.

Oakley, Ann. (1981). Interviewing women: A contradiction in terms. In Helen Roberts (Ed.), *Doing feminist research* (pp. 30–61). London: Routledge & Kegan Paul.

Oakley, Ann. (1989). Women's studies in British sociology. *British Journal of Sociology, 40,* 544–564.

Pahl, Jan. (Ed.). (1985). *Private violence and public policy.* London: Routledge & Kegan Paul.

Pahl, Ray. (1984). *Divisions of labour.* Oxford: Blackwell.

Pahl, Ray. (Ed.). (1988). *On work.* Oxford: Blackwell.

Ramazanoglu, Caroline. (1986). Ethnocentrism and socialist-feminist theory: A response to Barrett and McIntosh. *Feminist Review, 22,* 83–86.

Reinharz, Shulamit. (1979). *On becoming a social scientist.* San Francisco: Jossey-Bass.

Reinharz, Shulamit, Bombyk, Marti, & Wright, Janet. (1983). Methodological issues in feminist research: A bibliography of literature in women's studies, sociology and psychology. *Women's Studies International Forum, 6,* 437–454. (essential source material for an exploration of epistemological as well as methodological issues; to be supplemented by the bibliography in Stanley & Wise 1990)

Reinharz, Shulamit & Davidman, Lynn. (Eds.). (1989). *Social science methods: Feminist voices.* Elmsford, NY: Pergamon Press.

Ribbens, Jane. (1989). Interviewing: An "unnatural situation?" *Women's Studies International Forum, 12,* 579–592.

Riley, Denise. (1987). *Am I that name? Feminism and the category of 'women' in history.* London: Macmillan.

Roberts, Helen. (1981a). Some of the boys won't play anymore: The impact of feminism on Sociology. In Dale Spender (Ed.), *Men's studies modified* (pp. 73–81). Oxford: Pergamon Press.

Roberts Helen. (Ed.). (1981b). *Doing feminist research.* London: Routledge & Kegan Paul.

Roberts, Helen. (1981c). Women and their doctors. In Helen Roberts (Ed.) *Doing feminist research* (pp.7–29). London: Routledge & Kegan Paul.

Sherin, Susan. (1987). A feminist approach to ethics. *Resources for Feminist Research, 16*(3), 25–28.

Smart, Carol. (1977). *Women, crime and criminology.* London: Routledge.

Smart, Carol & Smart, Barry. (1978). *Women, sexuality and social control.* London: Routledge & Kegan Paul.

Smith, Dorothy. (1974). Women's perspective as a radical critique of sociology. *Sociological Quarterly, 44,* 7–13.

Smith, Dorothy. (1978). A peculiar eclipsing: Women's exclusion from men's culture. *Women's Studies International Quarterly, 1,* 281–296.

Smith, Dorothy. (1979). A sociology for women. In Julia Sherman & Evelyn Beck (Eds.), *The prism of sex: Essays in the sociology of knowledge* (pp. 135–187). Madison, WI: University of Wisconsin Press.

Smith, Dorothy. (1987). *The everyday world as problematic: A feminist sociology.* Canada: Northeastern University Press. Milton Keynes: Open University Press.

Spender, Dale. (Ed.). (1981). *Men's studies modified.* Oxford: Pergamon Press.

Spring Rice, Margery. (1939). *Working class wives.* London: Penguin.

Stacey, Judith & Thorne, Barrie. (1985). The missing revolution in sociology. *Social Problems, 32,* 301–316.

Stacey, Meg. (1981). The division of labour revisited or overcoming the two Adams. In Philip Abrams, Rosemary Deem, Janet Finch, & Paul Rock (Eds.), *Practice & progress: British sociology 1950–1980* (pp. 172–190). London: Allen & Unwin.

Stanko, Elizabeth. (1985). *Intimate intrusions: Women's experience of male violence.* London: Routledge & Kegan Paul.

Stanley, Liz. (1984a). How the social science research process discriminates against women. In Sandra Acker & David Warren Piper (Eds.), *Is higher education fair to women?* (pp. 189–209). London: Nelson.

Stanley, Liz. (1984b). Whales and minnows: Some sexual theorists and their followers. In Sue Wise

& Liz Stanley (Eds.), *Men and sex: A case study in sexual politics* [Special Issue]. *Women's Studies International Forum, 7,* 53–62. (shows the means by which feminism is made to vanish by supposedly "radical" men, here in relation to sexual theory)

Stanley, Liz. (Ed.). (1990). *Feminist praxis: Method, theory and epistemology in feminist sociology.* London: Routledge & Kegan Paul.

Stanley, Liz & Wise, Sue. (1979). Feminist research, feminist consciousness and experiences of sexism. *Women's Studies International Quarterly, 2,* 359–374.

Stanley, Liz & Wise, Sue. (1983a). *Breaking out: Feminist consciousness and feminist research.* London: Routledge & Kegan Paul.

Stanley, Liz & Wise, Sue. (1983b). "Back into the personal" or: Our attempt to construct "feminist research." In Gloria Bowles & Renate D. Klein (Eds.), *Theories of women's studies* (pp. 192–209). London: Routledge & Kegan Paul.

Stanley, Liz & Wise, Sue. (1990). Method, methodology and epistemology in feminist research processes. In Liz Stanley (Ed.), *Feminist praxis: Method, theory and epistemology in feminist sociology.* London: Routledge & Kegan Paul.

Sydie, R. A. (1987). *Natural women cultured men: A feminist perspective on sociological theory.* Milton Keynes: Open University Press.

Walby, Sylvia. (Ed.). (1988). *Gender segregation at work.* Milton Keynes: Open University Press.

Ward, Kathryn & Grant, Linda. (1985). The feminist critique and a decade of published research in sociology journals. *Sociological Quarterly, 26,* 139–157.

Weiner, Gaby. (Ed.). (1985). *Just a bunch of girls.* Milton Keynes: Open University Press.

Westkott, Marcia. (1979). Feminist criticism of the social sciences. *Harvard Educational Review, 49,* 422–430.

Wise, Sue. (1987). A framework for discussing ethical issues in feminist research: A review of the literature. In Vivienne Griffiths, Maggie Humm, Rebecca O'Rourke, Janet Batsleer, Fiona Poland, & Sue Wise (Eds.), *Writing feminist biography 2: Using life histories* (pp. 47–88). Studies in Sexual Politics no. 19, Sociology Department, University of Manchester, England. (comprehensive review of the feminist and sociological literature on ethics in research to that date)

Wise, Sue & Stanley, Liz. (1987). *Georgie porgie: Sexual harassment in everyday life.* London: Pandora Press.

Chapter 23

Home Economics
Feminism in a Hestian Voice

Patricia J. Thompson

Home economics represents a paradox in relation to contemporary feminism and the new scholarship on women. Some feminists of the "second wave" expected the family, not the state, to "fade away." Home economics seemed an embarrassing anachronism that would fade away, too. That has not been the case. My choice to enter home economics more than 20 years ago expressed my wish to identify with a woman's field where (I hoped) my intellectual life would be free of male domination. I believed then (and I still believe) that academic and intellectual freedom for women and men includes the choice of discipline— even one Marjorie East calls "a female field" (1980, p. 134). My choice predated the founding of most Women's Studies programs, but L. B. Cebik (1975) argues convincingly for the commonalities between home economics and Women's Studies. Canadian home economist Patricia Saidak (1986) call home economics the first Women's Studies. My entry into home economics (after studies in international law and social studies education) predated publication in March 1971 of a special issue of *What's New in Home Economics* (a magazine for home economics teachers) devoted to "Home Economics and Women's Liberation." The anonymous author of the article "Anatomy is Destiny: (Or is it?)" provided a brief history of the women's movements of the nineteenth and twentieth centuries and maintained that:

> Home Economics . . . must offer a girl studies that can help her find her identity as a woman and determine how she fits into our fast-changing society. [To do this] girls need a good understanding of the feminist movement. . . . (1971, p. 14).

The author advised that boys be involved in such study because their lives would be affected by any change in the roles of women requiring changed responsibility for child care and household management.

This essay seeks to make a case for reconciliation between feminists who share concern for women and their families and home economists (both feminist and nonfeminist) who see their field as serving women by treating the private or domestic domain as being as worthy of serious study as the public or civic domain.

270

WHEN RIVALRY CHALLENGES
SISTERHOOD

The first confrontation between home economics and modern feminism occurred when Robin Morgan keynoted the annual meeting of the American Home Economics Association (AHEA) held in Denver, Colorado, 1972. She addressed her audience as "the enemy" and characterized the field as "conservative and hypocritical." She urged the "younger sisters" (ageism was not then a feminist buzzword) to get out of the field, warning them

> you run the risk of becoming obsolete. Those institutions that home economics has been hooked into are dying, and they are dying even without the feminist revolution. One out of three marriages ends in divorce, the nuclear family is breaking down, the system is crumbling. It's your choice whether you're going to crumble with that system and stand in the way while history rolls over you or whether you're going to move with it. I hope you will join us—but we're going to win in any event. ("What Robin Morgan said," 1973, p. 13)

Not surprisingly, many home economists (who perceive themselves as prowoman and as advocates for the family) became defensive and resisted feminist influence. Jean Cooper (1972) expressed surprise that the leadership of the Women's Liberation movement (as it was then called) did not perceive home economics as "a major and natural ally" (1972, p. F-21). A senior home economics student at Eastern Mennonite College (which one might expect to be ultraconservative) expressed her gratitude that the *Journal of Home Economics* "is finally speaking to the Women's Liberation issue" and said "I'd like to see more about the relationship of home economics to the Women's Movement . . . " (Erma Weaver, 1972, pp. 2, 64). As an organizational initiative, AHEA formed the Women's Role Committee chaired by Virginia Y. Trotter (later Secretary of Education). Committee member Susan F. Weis observed that "the home economics profession has suffered because it was representing women's interests and needs. . . . " (*Journal of Home Economics,* 1973, p. 12). The solution, she believed, was to include men and boys in its mission. Concerned with women's changing experiences and their impact on family life, home economists remained responsive to the same issues that concerned feminists while serving as advocates for women, children, and families. Why, then, is home economics so often scapegoated by feminists as part of the problem rather than part of the solution? Perhaps home economics had grown complacent in the 1940s, but it had also recognized the strains and challenges of women's changing roles in and after two world wars. It needed to get "shook up" in the 1960s and 1970s! One consequence of this was a long period of soul-searching and self-examination among members of the profession that culminated in a theoretical–philosophical position paper which proposed a new mission statement:

> The mission of Home Economics is to enable families to build and maintain systems of action that lead to (1) maturing in individual self-formation, and (2) to enlightened, cooperative participation in the critique and formulation of social goals and the means for accomplishing them. (Marjorie Brown & Beatrice Paolucci, 1978, p. 23)

This statement answers a basic feminist criticism, namely the dubious value of a single model of "family." It might surprise those who think home economics advocates "compulsory heterosexuality" to learn that there are gay Home Economists (women and men) and that there are gay couples in home economics who find its mission acceptable. The attraction of Home Economics (as a knowledge system, not a system for the perpetuation of conventional gender roles) is thus not boundaried by gender orientation. (Patricia J. Thompson, 1984b).

272 Patricia J. Thompson

Home economics maintains its critique of society from the standpoint of the domestic discourse territory. I call this distinctive standpoint, mode, and voice Hestian, after the goddess Hestia, archetypal protector of "hearth and home" (Patricia J. Thompson, 1986a). Hestia's domain contrasts with the patriarchal public sphere under the protection of Hermes, the trickster god of communication. Judith Albert (1989) has noted the persistence of "Hestian" imagery in the views of the nineteenth century educator Elizabeth Peabody, whose position contrasted with the "Minervan" view of Margaret Fuller. It is hard, as Carol Gilligan, Jean Victoria Ward, and Jill McLean Taylor (1988) report, for a "different voice" to be heard in patriarchal society. Perhaps the early critique of home economics by feminists was partly due to having a "deaf ear" for the Hestian voice. We must ask about the effects of applying Hermean categories, language, logic, and ethics to a voice coming from the Hestian standpoint *before* we understand fully what an extrapatriarchal standpoint looks and sounds like.

HOME ECONOMICS: THE ECOLOGY OF EVERYDAY LIFE

Helen LeBaron Hilton, then dean of Home Economics at Iowa State University (1972), observed that a full history of the nineteenth century women's movement in the United States must account for two social reform movements: suffrage and domestic science– home economics. From its beginnings as "domestic science" in the mid-nineteenth century Land Grant Colleges to its formal founding in 1908, home economics recognized that women (both rural and urban) were educationally deprived. Its aim was to integrate essential knowledge from the sciences, social sciences, and humanities and communicate it to women in nonspecialist (vernacular) language. The knowledge needed to address the timeless certainties and perennial problems of everyday life became available to women.

Home economics units and departments were sometimes the only ones to welcome and support women scholars. Women's "need to know" generated research and curricula in such extrapatriarchal subjects as family relationships and child development, food and nutrition, textiles and clothing, housing, furnishings, and design, and the management of such household resources as time, energy, and finances. It also raised questions of ethics and esthetics from a woman-centered, Hestian perspective. When feminist scholars began to recover the forgotten history of "women worthies," they praised such early domestic science–Home Economics leaders as Catherine Beecher, Ellen Swallow Richards, and Marion Talbot. But when these women (and others) are mentioned, it is often as "firsts" in educational, social, and scientific endeavors controlled by patriarchy rather than as women contributors to a "modern" Hestian tradition that is now over a century-and-a-half old.

Women who in the past plied their scholarly trades in departments of home economics are often pitied because they were not admitted to male-dominant departments or disciplines. Maresi Nerad (1987a, p. 159; 1987b, p. 78) characterizes working in a home economics department as a "female ghetto." Would she make the same claim for women historians, political scientists, sociologists, biologists, or chemists who today pursue feminist interests in Women's Studies? Some women are fourth-generation home economists. Barrie Thorne and Glenna Spitze are women sociologists whose mothers, Alison Thorne and Hazel Taylor Spitze, had distinguished careers in home economics. The educational philosopher Jane Roland Martin's mother was a home economics teacher. We need to ask what kind of intellectual orientation these mothers were able to bequeath their daughters. Did their daughters not enter home economics because of its devaluation by patriarchal standards? Do women cluster in departments of low prestige and status (Maresi Nerad,

1987a, p. 157), or do *all* the places where women predominate experience low or negative status? Whose standpoint do we adopt in interpreting data? That of male reality-definers in the power structure or that of the women who are oppressed by them?

The Family as an Ecosystem

As early as 1833, Lydia Maria Child advocated a conserving approach toward family resource management, stating that "The true economy of housekeeping is simply the art of gathering up all the fragments so that nothing be lost. I mean fragments of *time* as well as *materials"* (1833, p. 1). In the same spirit of "Yankee frugality," Vassar-educated, Massachusetts Institute of Technology (MIT)-trained Ellen Swallow Richards (together with like-minded colleagues—female and male) founded the new discipline of Home Economics in 1908. [See also H. Patricia Hynes, this volume.] One goal was to gather up the neglected scraps of knowledge everyday women need to improve and enrich their own and their families' everyday lives. Richards believed that if people work with the "environmental principle" superimposed on their everyday lives they grow more conscious of what to do and what not to do with it (Robert Clarke, 1973, p. 114). This idea has been elaborated on by Nancy C. Hook and Beatrice Paolucci (1970); Margaret Bubolz, Joanne Eicher, and Susan Sontag (1988); and Margaret Bubolz and Susan Sontag (1988). By virtue of its ecosystem paradigm of the household or family unit, home economics is sometimes called "Human Ecology." The view of some feminists (Judith Stacey, 1983) that the family is the source of women's oppression proves problematic for home economics. Only in traditional patriarchy is the family defined, misleadingly, solely as an affectionally bonded unit. Recognizing the family as an ecosystem, that is, a "life support system" for its members, makes it possible to empower the family in relation to other systems and for home economists to make global ecological connections. [See also Maxine Baca Zinn, this volume.]

Ecosystems Thinking

Systems theory postulates that a change in one part of a system affects other parts of the system to a lesser or greater degree. Systems thinking liberates home economics (perhaps more than traditional, male-defined disciplines) from the linear, binary polarities of patriarchal categories. Home economics studies the demands (inputs) made on the family– planetary ecosystem to provide food, shelter, clothing, and child and elder care as problems in the ecology of everyday life. To do this, it integrates knowledge from its own research and from other disciplines. A holistic, systems perspective enables home economists to identify the interrelationships, interdependencies, and interconnections between the family and other systems by using such value-neutral terms as input, throughput, output, and feedback (Ann A. Hertzler & Carol Owen, 1984; Diane Kieren, Eleanore Vaines & Doris Badir, 1982; Eleanore Vaines, 1989). As a metadiscipline that focuses on the household and family as an ecological unit, home economics is uniquely positioned to incorporate feminist reconceptualizations of the disciplines of knowledge (Linda Peterat, 1989; 1990).

NEEDED: EPISTEMOLOGICAL EQUITY FOR HOME ECONOMICS

Home economics is vulnerable to misunderstanding and misrepresentation by both male and female scholars. For example, the first volume of the *History of Women Philosophers*

(Mary Ellen Waithe, 1987) reinforces rather than challenges the destructive stereotyping by males of home economics. Waithe reports:

> I mentioned to a male colleague that I had located some writings by Pythagorean women philosophers. He replied. . . . "but weren't they just writing about—heh, heh— [sic] home economics? . . . I could see how a superficial glance at the . . . works . . . could leave an impression that the Pythagoreans did write about home economics [sic]. Their topics included child rearing and the role of women in ancient society. But a closer, complete reading of the materials . . . belied such a conclusion. These philosophers were analyzing how the Pythagorean concept *harmonia* applied to the structure and running of the state, and to the structure and running of the family, viewed as a microcosm of the state. They discussed how a woman might apply that principle in raising children to become just, harmonious individuals, and how a woman might apply that principle to other areas of her daily life. This wasn't home economics, this was applied ethical theory, complete with a psychology of moral development, a theory of familial obligation, and much, much more. (Mary Ellen Waithe, 1987, p. xi)

Such dismissive references to home economics deny home economists the right to speak in their own voice and to argue on historical, philosophical, and theoretical grounds that what Waithe claims (purely as a matter of unsupported opinion) is *not* "home economics" is indeed "home economics!" Comparison of Pythagorean *harmonia* with the family ecosystem perspective evokes the Hestian mode and voice alluded to earlier. There have always been some men who share the Hestian perspective of home economics. What happens when males are welcomed to a traditionally "female" field? The male presence, presumed at first to lend legitimacy to a women's department, can prove subversive. The number of males from patriarchal (Hermean) disciplines who join home economics units and rise to become department chairs and deans is disproportionate to their numbers in the field. Women accept male norms as the price of membership in male-dominant enterprises. Males resist being resocialized into "female" norms of scholarship and collegiality. Do they fear becoming "feminized?" Once in the field, some males have been critical, assuming a "blame the victim" posture. They want the field to conform to standards prevailing in patriarchal disciplines. Males—and females who accept patriarchal (Hermean) norms—actively campaign to eliminate home economics and claim its disappearance a "victory" for women (Patricia J. Thompson, 1989b).

THE NAME OF THE GAME

Feminists note that the "power to name," to devise language that reflects women's authentic experience from their own standpoint, is denied them. (See Lourdes Torres, this volume.) Name change contributes to the invisibility of home economics. Is name change supported by those who are embarrassed to be associated with a field dominated by women and therefore low in status and prestige? Perhaps. In some universities home economics has been renamed "Human Ecology," "Family and Consumer Studies," or "Applied Human Development." Name change often presages the elimination of the department or unit. Patriarchal denial of the right of home economics faculties to "keep" their disciplinary name and to direct their own destinies has not been challenged by feminists or by Women's Studies faculty. At the University of Maryland, I am told, the Women's Studies faculty voted *against* including home economists.

HOME ECONOMICS, FEMINISM,
AND THE NEW SCHOLARSHIP

Marjorie M. Brown, professor emerita at the University of Minnesota and a respected philosopher of home economics, suggests three categories that can help to address feminist issues in home economics: (a) feminism as abstract individualism and public self-interests; (b) feminism that is publicly and politically passive while intensely private, and in which power inheres in the feminine qualities of the delicate lady or the coquettish sex kitten; and (c) feminism in which woman identifies herself both with the family as a private social group and politically with or against the public realities of her epoch in history (Marjorie M. Brown, 1985, Vol. I, p. 358).

Feminist home economists in the Feminism and Family Studies section of the National Council on Family Relations (NCFR) have assumed leadership in the re-vision of the Family Relationships and Child Development subject matter area of home economics. They look at what it means to be a feminist practitioner in family studies, the difficulty of translating feminist vision into practice, and the need for a practical literature on feminist family programming (Alexis J. Walker, Sally S. Martin, & Linda Thompson, 1987). Katherine Allen (1988; 1989) offers a framework for integrating feminist perspectives into home economics research and family studies courses. One way to think about this problem, she advises, is illustrated by Anne Cameron's novel *Daughters of Copper Woman*. Allen points out that from the male perspective an Indian man has multiple wives. The woman's view is that several women share one husband!

Women's interest in the family crosses age, race, educational level, class, nationality, culture, and ethnicity. Home economists seek to empower all women to work with men to create families that are more appropriate human environments (Jane Kwawu, 1989). Home economics has long had international networks. The International Federation of Home Economics (IFHE) was founded in Fribourg, Switzerland, in 1908 and later moved to Paris (Linda Nelson, 1984, p. 150). The American Home Economics Association has been affiliated with IFHE since 1915. IFHE meets quadrennially and has met twice in the United States—in 1958 in College Park, Maryland, and in 1988 in Minneapolis, Minnesota. The latter meeting was held about one month after the National Women's Studies Association met in the same place. Home economists from some 60 nations attended the Minneapolis Congress which addressed such internatinal concerns as world hunger, homelessness, the exploitation of women workers, AIDS education, child welfare, infant and maternal nutrition, aging in cross-cultural perspective, and the changing status of women and the shifts of family life worldwide. Although some home economists attended NWSA, no members of local Women's Studies faculties attended the Congress. Osuala (1987) emphasizes the potential role of home economics departments in African universities (in collaboration with international agencies) to carry on research to meet the needs of both rural and urban women. Home economists have been active worldwide in improving the conditions of rural women in developing countries. An overview of the challenges being met by home economists working in developing countries is provided in *Looking Toward the 21st Century: Home Economics and the Global Community* (Sally K. Williams, Dorothy L. West, & Eloise C. Murray, 1990).

From 1908 on, the AHEA went through decades of holding racially segregated meetings. This was in part due to the existence of segregated home economics units in the historically Black institutions of the South. During the era of intense "civil rights" movements, AHEA voted to remove "all barriers against the cooperation of all fully qualified members in the work of the Association at local, state, and national levels" (Helen Pundt, 1980, p. 320). Three African-American university professors, Gwendolyn Newkirk, Mildred Barnes Griggs, and Virginia Caples have served as president of the predominantly white AHEA. Most scholarly work by African-American home economists (as evidenced by the writing of Jean Cooper, Mildred Barnes Griggs, Flossie Byrd, and theorist Gloria M. Williams) is more notable for its academic vision grounded in home economics than a personal vision grounded in racial identity. Early in 1980, the biracial Coalition for Black Development in Home Economics was founded to provide networking and mentoring opportunities for minority members of the profession with both African-American and white professionals. These efforts resulted in publication of the ground-breaking book *Empowerment Through Difference: Multicultural Awareness in Education* (1988) edited by Herma Barclay Williams.

A conjoint masters thesis, *Home Economics and the Challenge of Feminism* (Susan A. Hoye & Rose H. Merrell, 1983), cites work by Nancy Chodorow, Jean Baker Miller, Jean Bethke Elshtain, and Carol Gilligan. The conjoint team was composed of one African-American and one white graduate student. In teaching home economics and Women's Studies courses (cross-listed at Lehman), I have assigned (in addition to Robert Hill's *Strengths of Black Families*), Adrienne Rich's *Of Woman Born,* Dale Spender's *Men's Studies Modified,* Jean Baker Miller's *Toward a New Psychology of Woman,* and Mary Field Belenky, Blythe McVicker Clinchy, Nancy Goldberger, and Jill Mattuck Tarule's *Women's Ways of Knowing.*

TEXTUAL POLITICS AND HOME ECONOMICS

A major difference between home economics and Women's Studies is the existence in middle, junior, and senior high school of state-mandated home economics curricula. However, presenting feminist research and the new scholarship on women in school textbooks is not without peril. As this essay was being written, three of my own texts were submitted for adoption in Texas. One called *Lifeplans* (Thompson & Faiola-Priest, 1990a) (for senior high school students of both sexes) was criticized in public hearings for its "feminist bias." The text refers to Carol Gilligan's and Nancy Chodorow's work, as well as to other women scholars. Kay Sparkman stated that her objections to listing the text in Texas were the author's preoccupation with sexism, gender differences, and "sexual stereotypes" (Kay Sparkman, 1989, p. 135–136). What's a home economist to do when the field is castigated by the Left as "too conservative" and the New Right as "too feminist?" Feminists have been properly critical of the content of school texts, but nowhere was there one to raise her voice to rebut Mrs. Sparkman's antifeminist critique of a home economics textbook.

Doris Badir, current president of the IFHE and a special adviser on gender equity to the president of the Unviersity of Alberta, Canada, addressed the Minneapolis IFHE Congress on the importance of feminism in the research, theory, and practice of home economics. In *Home Economics and Feminism* (1988) she called home economics a profession of women working for women, a profession which has as its focus the dailiness of women's lives. It sees the dailiness of life as always with us but not necessarily the prerogative or responsibility of women. It is ready to bring together the knowledge and understanding of the lives of women have led and are leading in the private world of the home with the insights and understandings of feminist scholars (Doris Badir, 1988, pp. 16–17).

Is It Time for Home Economics to Come Out of the Feminist Closet?

Annie Dillard advised writers of the urgency to "give voice" to their own astonishment (1989, p. 1). This essay was written both with a sense of urgency and a sense of astonishment. Some questions raised by the editors of this volume don't apply to home economics in the same way they do for women working within established masculinist disciplines. There are differences among home economists as there are among feminists. By and large, feminists have distanced themselves from home economists. It is rare for home economists to be invited to particiate in "interdisciplinary" conferences, and their names are not found among the consulting editors on feminist journals, even when articles in them refer to home economics.

Over the past two decades, the "marriage failure" rate has risen from one in three to one in two. Have women's lives improved? We must redirect our thinking about what is central and ultimately the most significant location for a meaningful human existence. Home economics does not rest on an essentialist argument about "women's nature" but on an essentialist argument about *human* nature, namely, that to remain human there are needs to be met and tasks to be done, and they must be done consciously and creatively through the emancipatory exercise of choice. The time is fast approaching when feminists will need to take into account the role of the family (variously defined) in human life. To do so, will mainstream feminists heed the Hestian voice of home economics?

BIBLIOGRAPHY

Albert, Judith Strong. (1989). The debate in women's studies: Contradictory role models in the nineteenth century—Margaret Fuller and Elizabeth Peabody. *Women's Studies International Forum, 12*(4), pp. 463–473.

Allen, Katherine R. (1988, January). Integrating a feminist perspective into family studies courses. *Family Relations, 37*(1), 29–41.

Allen, Katherine R. (1989). Integrating research with a feminist perspective. Home Economics Division research presession. American Vocational Association Annual Meeting. Orlando, FL. November 30, 1989.

"Anatomy is destiny . . . " [Or is it?]: A look at the women's liberation movement. (1971, March). *What's New in Home Economics,* 10–14.

Badir, Doris. (1988). Home economics and feminism. In Eleanore Vaines, Doris Badir, & Dianne Kieren (Eds.), *People and Practice. International Issues for Home Economists, 1*(3).

Belenky, Mary Field, Clinchy, Blythe McVicker, Goldberger, Nancy, & Tarule, Jill Mattuck. (1986). *Women's ways of knowing.* New York: Basic Books.

Bovy, Barbara. (1984). Feminist research: Implications for home economics education. In Patricia J. Thompson (Ed.), *Knowledge, Technology and Family Change.* (pp. 293–316). 4th Yearbook of the Teacher Education Section of the American Home Economics Association, Bloomington, IL: McKnight Publishing Co.

Brown, Marjorie M. (1985). *Philosophical studies of home economics in the United States: Our practical-intellectual heritage; Vols. I, II.* East Lansing, MI: College of Human Ecology, Michigan State University.

Brown, Marjorie, & Paolucci, Beatrice. (1979). *Home economics: A definition.* Washington, DC: American Home Economics Association.

Bubolz, Margaret. (1988, April). *Use of an ecological perspective in home economics.* Paper presented at the National Conference for Integration in Home Economics, Chicago, IL.

Bubolz, Margaret M., & Sontag, M. Suzanne. (1988). Integration in home economics and human ecology. *Journal of Home Economics, 71,* 28–31.

Byrd, Flossie. (1970, June). A definition of home economics. *Journal of Home Economics, 62*(6), 414–416.

Cameron, Anne. (1988). *Daughters of Copper Woman:* San Francisco: Spinster Books.

Cebik, L. B. (1975, January). Women's studies and home economics. *Journal of Home Economics, 67,* 27–30.

Child, Lydia Maria. (1833). *The American frugal housewife* (12th ed.). Office of Educational Services, The Ohio State University Libraries.

Clarke, Robert. (1973). *Ellen Swallow: The woman who founded ecology.* Chicago, IL: Follett.

Cooper, Jean. (1972, April). Home economics and the women's movement. *Forecast for Home Economics, F,* 11–13.

Definitive Themes in Home Economics and Their Impact on Families: 1909-1984. (1984). Washington, DC: American Home Economics Association.

Dillard, Annie. (1989, May 28). Write till you drop. *The New York Times Book Review, 1,* 23.

East, Marjorie. (1980). *Home economics: Past, present, and future.* Boston, MA: Allyn & Bacon.

Ehrenreich, Barbara & English, Deirdre. (1979). *For her own good: 150 years of expert's advice to women.* Garden City, NY: Anchor-Doubleday.

Elshtain, Jean Bethke. (1981). *Public man, private woman. Women in social and political thought.* Princeton, NJ: Princeton University Press.

Elshtain, Jean Bethke (Ed.). (1982). *The family in political thought.* Amherst, MA: University of Massachusetts Press.

Gilligan, Carol. (1982). *In a different voice: Psychological theories and women's development.* Cambridge, MA: Harvard University Press.

Gilligan, Carol, Ward, Jean Victoria, & Taylor, Jill McLean. (With Betty Bardige). (1988). *Mapping the moral domain.* Cambridge, MA: Harvard University Press.

Hertzler, Ann A., & Owen, Carol. (1984, May). Culture, families, and the change process. *Journal of the American Dietetic Association., 84*(5), 535–540.

Hill, Robert. (1971). *The strengths of black families.* New York: Emerson Hall.

Hilton, Helen LeBaron. (1972, April). Now that women are liberated. *Journal of Home Economics, 64,* 3–5.

Hook, Nancy C., & Paolucci, Beatrice. (1970, May). The family as an ecosystem. *Journal of Home Economics, 62,* 315–317.

Hoye, Susan A. & Merrell, Rose H. (1983). *Home economics and the challenge of feminism.* Unpublished master's thesis, Herbert H. Lehman College, CUNY, Bronx, NY.

Hultgren, Francine Holm & Coomer, Donna Leonhard (Eds.). (1989). *Alternative modes of inquiry in home economics research.* 9th Yearbook. Teacher Education Section of the American Home Economics Association. Peoria, IL: Glencoe.

Hunt, Caroline L. (1942, 1958, 1980). *The life of Ellen H. R. Richards.* Washington, DC: The American Home Economics Association.

Kwawu, Jane. (1989, April). *Family planning as a contribution to economic security and family survival.* Paper presented at the First All-Africa Home Economics Conference. Accra, Ghana. In Eleanore Vaines, Doris Badir & Diane Kieren (Eds.), *People and practice: International issues for home economists, 1*(4).

Kieren, Dianne, Vaines, Eleanore, & Badir, Doris. (1984). *The home economist as a helping professional.* Winnipeg, Canada: Frye.

The Lake Placid Conferences on Home Economics. (1899-1908). Washington, DC. The American Home Economics Association.

Merrell, Rose H., Hoye, Susan A., & Thompson, Patricia J. (1984). Home economics, feminism, and the family. In Patricia J. Thompson (Ed.), *Knowledge, technology, and family change* (pp. 265–292). 4th Yearbook of the Teacher Education Section of the American Home Economics Association. Peoria, IL: Bennett & McKnight.

Miller, Jean Baker. (1976). *Toward a new psychology of woman.* Boston: Beacon Press.

Nelson, Linda. (1984). International ventures. In *Definitive themes in home economics and their impact on families: 1909-1984* (pp. 149–162). Washington, DC: American Home Economics Association.

Nerad, Maresi. (1987a). Gender stratification in higher education: The Department of Home Economics at the University of California, Berkeley, 1916-1962. *Women's Studies International Forum, 10*(2), 157–164.

Nerad, Maresi. (1987b). The situation of women at Berkeley between 1870 and 1915. *Feminist Issues, 7*(1), 67–80.

Osuala, Judith D. C. (1987). Extending appropriate technology to rural African women. *Women's Studies International Forum, 10*(5), 481–487.

Paolucci, Beatrice, Hall, Olive, & Axinn, Nancy. (1977). *Family decision-making: An ecosystem approach.* New York: John Wiley & Sons.

Peterat, Linda. (1989). Re-search and re-form: A feminist perspective in Home Economics research. In Francine Holm Hultgren & Donna Leonhard Coomer (Eds.), *Alternative modes of inquiry in home economics research* (pp. 211–219). 9th Yearbook. Teacher Education Section of the American Home Economics Association. Peoria, IL:Glencoe.

Peterat, Linda. (1990, Winter). The promise of feminist research for home economics. *Canadian Home Economics Journal, 40*(1), 33–36.

Pundt, Helen. (1980). *AHEA: A history of excellence.* Washington, DC: American Home Economics Association.

Ralston, Penny. (1978). Black participation in home economics: A partial account. *Journal of Home Economics, 70*(4), 34–37.

Reddin, Nancy E. (with J. Estelle Reddin). (1987). A new view of home economics. *Common Ground, 5*(5), 5–6.

Rich, Adrienne. (1986). *Of woman born: Motherhood as experience and institution.* New York: W W Norton.

Saidak, Patricia. (1986, November 7–9). *Home economics: The first women's studies.* Paper presented at the CRIAW Conference, Moncton, NB, Canada.

Sparkman, Kay. (1989, July 10–11). Testimony from the public hearings on Home Economics textbook submittals, Austin, TX.

Spender, Dale. (1981). *Men's studies modified.* Elmsford, NY: Pergamon Press.

Stacey, Judith. (1983, Fall). The new conservative feminism. *Feminist Studies, 9*(3), 559–583.

Thompson, Patricia J. (1984a). *Knowledge, technology, and family change.* 4th Yearbook of the Teacher Education Section of the American Home Economics Association. Peoria, IL: Bennett & McKnight.

Thompson, Patricia J. (1984b). Home economics: A knowledge system not a gender system. In Patricia J. Thompson (Ed.), *Knowledge, technology, and family change* (pp. 317–341). 4th Yearbook of the Teacher Education Section of the American Home Economics Association. Peoria, IL: Bennett & McKnight.

Thompson, Patricia J. (1986a, January/February). Home economics and the Hestian mode. *Illinois Teacher of Home Economics*, 87–91.

Thompson, Patricia J. (1986b, Autumn). Beyond gender: Equity issues in home economics education. *Theory Into Practice*, 276–283.

Thompson, Patricia J. (1987). Emancipatory education: Is home economics the missing link? *Journal of Home Economics Education, 36*(3), 5–18.

Thompson, Patricia J. (1988a). Hestian feminism. Paper presented at the Sixth Annual Women's Scholarship Conference, *Women and the environment: Old problems, new solutions.* Lehman College, CUNY, Bronx, NY, 10468.

Thompson, Patricia J. (1988b, June). *A Hestian framework for science and technology.* Paper presented at the National Women's Studies Association, Minneapolis, MN.

Thompson, Patricia J. (1988c). Hestian education: The minority view of praxis. In Herma Barclay Williams (Ed.), *Empowerment through difference. Multicultural awareness in education* (pp.

329–349). 8th Yearbook of the Teacher Education Section of the American Home Economics Association. Peoria, IL: Glencoe.

Thompson, Patricia J. (1988d). *Home economics and feminism: The Hestian synthesis.* Charlotte-town, PEI, Canada: Home Economics Publishing Collective.

Thompson, Patricia J. (1988e, November). *The Hestian paradigm: Reconciling feminist and family theory.* Paper presented at the National Council on Family Relations, Philadelphia, PA.

Thompson, Patricia J. (1989a, April). *Beyond the gender wars: Is Hestian feminism the answer?* Paper presented at the South Central Women's Studies Association Meeting, Houston, TX.

Thompson, Patricia J. (1989b). The rape of a discipline: Home economics under attack. ERIC ED 301 123.

Thompson, Patricia J. (1989c). Theory-building in home economics. In Francine Holm Hultgren and Donna Leonhard Coomer (Eds.), *Alternative modes of Inquiry* (pp. 95–116). 9th Yearbook. Teacher Education Section of the American Home Economics Association. Peoria, IL: Glencoe.

Thompson, Patricia J., & Faiola-Priest, Theodora. (1990a). *Lifeplans* (2nd ed.). Cincinnati, OH: South-Western Publishing.

Thorne, Barrie & Yalom, Marilyn. (1982). *Rethinking the family.* New York: Longman.

Vaines, Eleanore. (1989, April). *Systems theory, systems thinking, and ecological systems approach related to home economics.* Paper presented to the National Meeting on Integration in Home Economics, Chicago, IL.

Vaines, Eleanore. (1990, Winter). Philosophical orientation and home economics: An introduction. *Canadian Home Economics Journal, 40*(1), 6–11.

Waithe, Mary Ellen (Ed.). (1987). *A history of women philosophers: Vol. I. Ancient women philosophers 600 B.C.–500 A.D.* Boston: Martinus Nijhoff.

Walker, Alexis J., & Thompson, Linda. (1984). Feminism and family studies. *Journal of Family Issues, 5,* 545–570.

Walker, Alexis J., Martin, Sally S. Kees, & Thompson, Linda. (1988, January). Feminist programs for families. *Family Relations 37*(1), 17–22.

Weaver, Erma. (1972, October). Women's lib advocate. Letters to the editor, *Journal of Home Economics, 64*(7), 2, 64.

What Robin Morgan said. (1973, January). *Journal of Home Economics, 65*(1), 13.

Williams, Gloria M. (1984). The esthetics of everyday life. In Patricia J. Thompson (Ed.), *Knowledge, technology, and family change* (pp. 215–236). 4th Yearbook of the Teacher Education Section of the American Home Economics Association. Peoria, IL: Bennet & McKnight.

Williams, Gloria M. (1988). Race and ethnicity in home economics: theoretical and methodological issues. In Herma Barclay Williams (Ed.), *Empowerment through difference. Multicultural awareness in education* (pp. 46–86). 8th Yearbook of the Teacher Education Section of the American Home Economics Association. Peoria, IL: Glencoe.

Williams, Herma Barclay (Ed.). (1988). *Empowerment through difference. Multicultural awareness in education.* 8th Yearbook of the Teacher Education Section of the American Home Economics Association. Peoria, IL: Glencoe.

Williams, Sally K., West, Dorothy L., & Murray, Eloise C. (Eds.). (1990). *Looking toward the 21st century: Home economics and the global community.* 10th Yearbook. Teacher Education Section of the American Home Economics Association. Peoria, IL: Glencoe.

Chapter 24

Women and Language
From Sex Differences to Power Dynamics

Lourdes Torres

In the 1970s, as the feminist movement grew, feminists turned their attention to the virtual invisibility of women in all fields of study. Language was identified as an important area of study given its centrality and interrelation with almost all other crucial issues. This is not to suggest, however, that the subject of women and language had not been addressed much earlier. In the 1860s and 1870s, feminists were writing and talking about the impact on their lives of naming practices in law, organized religions, and marriage customs that represented women as dependent or trivial (Lana Rakow & Cheris Kramarae, 1990). Barrie Thorne, Cheris Kramarae, and Nancy Henley (1983) trace the origin of interest in language and the sexes to early twentieth century anthropology. These studies generally considered language in nonwestern cultures. One of the first linguists to discuss "women's" language was Otto Jesperson (1922) in the text, *Language: It's Nature, Development, and Origin*, which dedicated one chapter to reviewing studies that discussed women's language. Jesperson provides a variety of unsubstantiated stereotypes of women's speech which are still part of "folklinguistics" today. Aside from the occasional consideration of their "aberrant" speech behavior, studies in mainstream linguistics with women as their focal point are rare.

The publication of Robin Lakoff's *Language and Women's Place* in 1975 is often taken as the point when research in women and language really took off. Lakoff was one of the first to make a connection between women's subordinate position and their speech; she provides a theory that seeks to explain women's "lady-like," speech in terms of women's uncertainty and politeness. Lakoff's claims that women's language is characterized by tag questions, passives, and intensifiers were drawn from her casual observations rather than from empirical research. Subsequent studies on the issues raised by Lakoff have challenged many of her observations (Barrie Thorne et al., 1983). The questions asked have become increasingly more complex as researchers have realized that the question of sex or gender differences in language is intimately related to other issues such as race, social class, and social roles. It is now clear that one cannot speak of universal sex differences in language.

The same year, 1975, saw the publication of two other books on the subject, Mary Ritchie Key's *Male/Female Language* and *Language and Sex: Difference and Dominance*, edited by Barrie Thorne and Nancy Henley. Although both texts also deal with language and sex issues they did not generate the reaction and response accorded to Lakoff's text. Alette Olin Hill (1986) speculates that *Language and Women's Place* was more influential because the book "goaded others into irritation" and also, perhaps, because it presented a deficiency model of women's language which the mainstream, of course, found attractive. Lakoff's (1975) book, which in some ways supported Jesperson's stereotyped assertions, was followed by a series of publications which attempted to empirically respond to her assertions.

PROBLEMS IN AND WITH SOCIOLINGUISTICS

In the area of theoretical linguistics, where a distinction is made between what we know about language (competence) and how we use language (performance), issues of women's language have not been dealt with because they are considered performance issues and therefore irrelevant to the study of formal grammar. Mainstream sociolinguists, specifically those who work within a correlational, variationalist framework tend to treat sex as one more variable among the list of variables usually studied. If differential frequency of use of a variable is found (and this is not always the case) these are often merely described rather than explained. When explanations are offered they are usually inadequate.

Deborah Cameron and Jennifer Coates (1985) critique the three common explanations for the sex differential in language usually offered in sociolinguistic studies. These are: (1) women's conservatism accounts for their use of more formal variants, (2) women's status accounts for their sensitivity to prestige form and therefore their higher frequency of use of these forms (3) women do not have the strong ties to vernacular culture and therefore do not feel pressure to adhere to vernacular norms. All three "explanations" are inadequate in that they are sexist, characterizing all women as a class with stereotyped attributes.

Of these three approaches, the third which comes out of network analyses (Jenny Cheshire, 1982; Susan Gal, 1979; Leslie Milroy, 1980) seems to hold the most promise. Network analyses, most of which deal with working class communities, seek to study variation at the level of the subculture of speakers; this approach avoids relying solely on abstract categories such as class, age and sex, and seeks rather to understand how the social networks that people maintain interact with these variables and effect speech patterns. Unfortunately, so far most network studies have either focused solely on male networks (William Labov, 1973) or like other sociolinguistic studies have defined male linguistic behavior as the norm from which to analyze women's linguistic production. Cheshire (1982), for example, constructs a vernacular culture index for boys on the basis of their attitudes toward activities such as fighting, carrying weapons, and participating in criminal activities. The vernacular index for girls focuses on swearing, playing hooky, and stealing. This index of vernacular loyalty is obviously a derivative of the boys' index which emphasizes delinquent behavior. It seems unsatisfactory to conclude as Cheshire does that girls don't participate to the same degree that boys do in vernacular culture; rather we must investigate what girls networks look like and then construct an index based on the values that predominate in that group. The challenge is to avoid defining vernacular culture exclusively according to masculine criteria.

Cheshire (1982) does demonstrate however, that in networks of boys and girls she studied different variants functioned differently in relation to the vernacular norms. For some variants girls scores were more "nonstandard" than the scores of the boys and vice versa. This finding challenges the assumption that women will always produce the more conservative forms.

Cameron and Coates (1985) conclude their review by calling for more empirical research, but they caution that " . . . it must not be done within a framework which assumes male behavior and male norms are prototypical. Explaining sex difference does not mean explaining the usage of women after all. It means devising methods equally applicable to all informants, so that we can gauge the importance of sex in the complex system of intersecting social relations that supports linguistic variation" (p. 149).

NEW RESEARCH PRIORITIES AND DIRECTIONS

Feminist research has sought to produce analyses which do not assume that all things are equal and removed from a political arena. Dale Spender, in *Man Made Language* (1980), for example, presents an analysis premised on the idea that differences or perceived differences in language are produced in a context where women are a subordinate group and men are in a position of power. The insistence on linking language and power issues is an important development in research on women and one that opens it up to the usual critiques that such analysis is not objective, or scholarly. Feminists have argued that the issue is not really what the differences between male and female language are, but rather how gender differences are constructed and perpetuated in order to maintain the status quo. Spender's (1980) project is to undermine the status quo, to show how language is used to rationalize male supremacy and male power. She argues that males have appropriated the means for advancing their world view and that they control the mechanisms for legitimizing their perspective (p. 230). This argument has been criticized by some feminists (for instance Deborah Cameron, 1985) as being deterministic and therefore pessimistic about the possibility of enacting change. Cameron (1985) argues rather that language is indeterminate and that speakers are free to create meanings, further that meaning is plural, flexible and must always be negotiated, therefore it is impossible to speak of male control of the language (p. 141).

However, as both Cameron and Spender acknowledge, men do seem to control the means by which their particular perspectives are privileged, through their control of political, religious, and literary discourses. Whereas theoretically we are all free to engage in creating meaning, Spender demonstrates that it is men's meanings that are sanctioned and propagated. Cameron points out that feminists must analyze the origins and mechanism of this control in different social and historical moments. [See Cheris Kramarae, this volume.] It seems to me that this is exactly the project that Spender (1980, 1984) and many other feminists are engaged in.

As Thorne, Kramarae, and Henley (1983) point out, the literature on women and language increasingly is looking at language use within the social context where it occurs and analyzing the various factors which influence women and men's linguistic options. Analyses such as those offered by Patricia Nichols (1983), Pamela Fishman (1983), and Victoria De Francisco (1989) demonstrate how differences in language use are determined by the position of the speakers in a specific social context. A context sensitive analysis will consider, as Nichols states, that, "the linguistic choices made by both men and women are always constrained by the options available to them, and these options are available always and only within the context of a group which shares rules for the use and interpretation of language" (Patricia A. Nichols, 1983, p. 66).

Work that is contextualized according to the specifics as a particular community demonstrate that it is naive to expect women (or men) to always behave in a particular way in terms of the production of, for example, certain linquistic variables. This is especially true given that most English language studies produced in the field of women and language continue to be based on Western, white middle-class models. Recent work on language and people of color in the United States (Bea Medicine, 1987; Patricia C. Nichols, 1983; Marsha Houston Stanback, 1985; Ana Celia Zentella, 1987; Lourdes Torres, 1990) and language use in non-western cultures (the collection of articles in Susan Philips, Susan Steele, & Christine Tanz, 1987) questions the most basic generalizations made in the field. For example a generalization perpetuated from Labovian type studies is that women's language tends to be more conservative or standard, as revealed from their use of more complete surface form realizations. Women are said to refrain from the process of deletion and the use of substandard forms to a greater extent than men. Studies by Janet Shibamoto (1987) of a Japanese community and of Elinor Ochs (1987) of a Samoan community contradict this tendency. Women are not always the ones to more frequently produce the more standard variant, and the use of variants is not always interpreted the same way as they are in the Western context. These studies also point out the importance of looking at gender as it interacts with other variables such as age, status, and speech event.

MAINSTREAM RESPONSE TO RESEARCH ON WOMEN AND LANGUAGE

The mainstream has responded to the research on women and language by using several strategies. One has been to dismiss the work as being irrelevant to specific research agendas. A related strategy is to simply ignore the existence of the many analyses of women's language and power produced during the last 20 years. This is the strategy found in recent books intended for general audiences by two well-known linguists, *You Just Don't Understand* (1990) by Deborah Tannen and *Talking Power* (1990) by Robin Tolmach Lakoff. Both authors attempt to deal with women's language and miscommunication issues outside of a context of power relations. Tannen's book, which deals with miscommunication between the sexes, treats difference as if it were a neutral concept. Departing from a two cultures framework, Tannen argues that misunderstandings occur because men and women have different styles of talk which they have acquired through their sex specific socialization experiences. Henley and Kramarae (1990) critique the two cultures theory for among other limitations failing to consider what these differences come to mean in a hierarchical society, and also for failing to make the necessary links between differences and power relations.

Lakoff, in *Talking Power,* also ignores much of the recent research on language, gender, and power when she reasserts many of her original (Robin Lakoff, 1975) stereotypes of women's language. She continues to speak of universal characteristics of women's language without considering how race, class, or context might interact with gender. While Lakoff does consider power issues in various institutions, her analysis is inadequate because as Sally McConnell-Ginet (1991) in a review of *Talking Power* points out, Lakoff fails "to question the basic assumptions and institutions underlying existing patterns of exercising and distributing power." Both texts attempt to analyze aspects of women's language without confronting issues of social power and male dominance; while this means that they offer little explanatory power it also might explain why the texts have such a popular appeal.

Another mainstream response to the research on women and language has been to trivialize the work. In the area of generic pronouns, for example, Wendy Martyna (1983) demonstrates how the media and the academy have sought to undermine the significance of research findings which suggest that "generics" are not neutral, and to trivialize the attempts made to create and promote nonsexist alternatives to the current situation. Feminists have not been dissuaded by such strategies and continue to challenge attempts to dismiss the issues. Maija S. Blaubergs (1980) deconstructs the classic arguments men use to argue against changing sexist language. Women persist in the production and promotion of guidelines for nonsexist usage (Francine Wattman Frank & Paula Treichler, 1989; Casey Miller & Kate Swift, 1980; Aileen Pace Nilsen, 1987; and many more). At least in some areas of society these issues have been taken up and there has been progress. Some newspapers, journals, publishing houses, and government agencies now endorse nonsexist guidelines (Marlis Hellinger, 1984; Wendy Martyna, 1983). The constant pressure by women is beginning to have an effect, despite Lakoff's (1975) claim that language change would have to be preceded by societal change.

Although academics continue to dismiss feminist claims about male control of the language, maintaining that language is neutral and arbitrary, feminists continue to produce analyses that demonstrate how language, gender, and power issues are intimately connected (Catharine MacKinnon, 1987; Cherríe Moraga & Gloria Anzaldúa, 1981; Adrienne Rich, 1980; Dale Spender, 1980, 1984). Women are exploding the myth of the neutrality of language (Cheris Kramarae, 1981; Sally McConnell-Ginet, 1989; Casey Miller & Kate Swift, 1976; Dale Spender, 1980; Susan J. Wolfe, 1989). Feminist analyses have offered women an understanding of why they often feel that the language is inadequate to express their perspectives; the analyses also demonstrate how women are socialized to be silent. Kramarae and Jenkins (1987) review strategies women are using in order to "take back the power of language and talk." Women are creating new terms and expressions to articulate their experience from their perspective (Cheris Kramarae, Paula Treichler, & Ann Russo, 1985). They are recovering words that have been used against them (Mary Daly, 1978), and reclaiming "nonstandard" varieties that are generally condemned, such as codeswitching (Cherrie Moraga, 1983; Gloria Anzaldúa, 1987), and working class dialects (Judy Grahn, 1978). Nan Van Den Bergh (1987) argues that renaming is an important part of feminist ideology tied to issues of power, "Changing language raises consciousness. It brings to public attention the deceptions inherent within words in order to disspell them. Through such an exorcism, renaming makes public a political statement, and it empowers the group by giving it a sense of control over life. Renaming is the politics of personal experience. Therefore, the way in which one names one's experience has profound implications extending beyond the individual" (p. 134).

CHANGES IN THE DISCIPLINE

Over the last 20 years the discipline of women and language has grown extensively and the range of topics being addressed has widened tremendously as can be seen in the bibliography complied by Cheris Kramarae, Barrie Thorne, and Nancy Henley (in Barrie Thorne, Cheris Kramarae & Nancy Henley, 1983). Major topics included in their bibliography are: gender marking and sex bias in language structure and content, stereotypes and perceptions of language use, sex differences and similarities in language use—linguistic components, conversational interaction, genre and style, children and language, language varieties in American English, and nonverbal aspects of communication. Rather than focusing on language in cross-sex situations there is a proliferation of studies on the use of language by women in same-sex contexts. The 1983 bibliography is six times larger than the similar bibliography put together by Barrie Thorne and Nancy Henley in 1975. Unfortunately the studies continue to be based primarily on the white, middle-class, heterosexual experience. Works which deal with research on the language of people of color and gay people are rare.

Some studies that do deal with women of color in the United States, provide critiques of the ethnocentric analysis that characterizes much of the literature on women and language, and suggests different frameworks that can be used to study the situation of people of color. Stanback (1985) argues that Black women's experience has always been understood to be the same as the Black experience (read Black male) or women's experience (read white women). She documents how two factors, (a) Black women's experience in the work force, and (b) their ambivalent relationship with both white and Black cultural forms (Marsha Houston Stanback, 1985, p. 179) shape their communicative patterns and create a "double-consciousness." Black women share a tradition with Black men of having to work in the public domain, whereas white women's work has traditionally been restricted to the home domain. This participation in both public and private domains influences their linguistic options. When studied at all, Black women are found to be as fluent as men in manipulating Black vernacular English and in participating in speech events such as signifying and sounding. However, given that Black women also participate in white culture they are also affected by white middle-class norms which dictate that they assume a more subordinate role in cross-gender conversations. The idea of "double consciousness" appears to be a concept that may be relevant for other people of color who must engage in constant code-switching between the cultures they participate in.

Bea Medicine (1987), in an analysis of the communication patterns of American Indian women, points out the multiple functions of women fulfilled through their language. They serve as the keepers of the traditions; it is women who pass on the legends, proverbs, and other cultural information inherent in linguistic patterns which tend to be lost in translation to English. At the same time women often have a better grasp of English, compared to men, and therefore they serve as mediators between Indian and white societies. Finally women, as primary socializing agents, are the ones who decide the code or codes to be taught to the children. Medicine (1987) points out that this choice is contingent on a number of factors and varies among tribal groups and individual ideologies.

Ana Zentella (1987) in an analysis of the role of women in linguistic change in a New York, Puerto Rican situation, critiques Robin Lakoff's (1975) claim that the fact that women "code-switch" (i.e., alternate between an assertive variety and a more "lady-like variety") renders them indecisive and deficient in both codes. In the Spanish–English bilingual context, code-switching has been found to convey a profound knowledge of the language structures involved (Shana Poplack, 1979). Zentella points out that women have been found to engage more frequently than men in intrasentenial code-switching (the switching to a second language within the same sentence), which demands the most proficiency in both codes. As in the American Indian and Black communities the various roles women fulfill demand that they control various codes and that they are able to switch codes according to the context. The linguistic reality of women of color appears to entail a constant switching of codes; while white women, as a subordinate group must also engage in frequent code-sitching, the situation is obviously more complex in the case of women of color when the variables of race and ethnicity are considered.

DIRECTIONS FOR THE FUTURE

Cheris Kramarae (1986) critiques sociolinguistics and in a challenging proposal suggests that the field focus the research of the next decade on gender as the organizing principal of language studies. Because gender is a category which interacts with all other categories such as age, ethnicity, race, occupation, and class, it would be useful as a point of departure from which to analyze the variation and diversity inherent in human language. Not surprisingly, the sociolinguistic community has not raced to embrace this challenge.

Such a focus would be illuminating especially given a critical reading of the crucial category "gender." Catharine MacKinnon (1987) provides some suggestive directions in this regard. For MacKinnon gender is first an inequality of power, and only as a result is it a question of difference. Usually the meaning of gender is construed in terms of sameness or difference, but there is no neutral sameness, rather man becomes the standard from which sameness or difference is measured. MacKinnon argues that we must therefore get away from the idea of gender as difference to the idea of gender as dominance. [See Jacqueline Zita, this volume.] This approach does not assume that sex differences are naturally coded as difference, rather that this coding is the result of the prior differential which is power. The difference defined as sex difference only becomes important as a consequence of power. MacKinnon (1987) states, "One of the most deceptive antifeminisms in society, scholarship, politics, and the law is the persistent treatment of gender as if it is truly a question of difference, rather than treating the gender difference as a construct of the difference gender makes" (pp. 8–9).

When studies are contextualized in a particular social and economic context the element of power can not be divorced from the analysis (Nancy Henley & Cheris Kramarae, 1990). The concept of power must also be understood as more complex than, for example, merely the control one group exerts over another. Rather power needs to be analyzed as a more dynamic, flexible, and relational concept than it has in the past, as suggested by Cheris Kramarae, Muriel Shultz, and William O'Barr (1984). Susan Philips, Susan Steele, and Christine Tanz, (1987) in their book on cross-cultural language and gender differences, caution against an analysis which sees women as always associated with spheres which have little legitimate power because in different societies power is identified in different ways. For example Joel Sherzer (1987) argues that for Kuna Indians of Panama men and women achieve authority through different speech events—the men through religious and political forums and the women through cultural and economic spheres. Therefore it would be misguided to assume that women lack some means of authority in this culture. Although this is true, Philips argues,

> . . . Such arguments should not obscure distinctions among what is overwhelmingly dominant, what is more common than not, what is rare, and what is nonexistent. In this book all societies documented have major political public-speaking roles and speech genres in which women's significant verbal involvement is rare. And there are no examples of public activities in which men rarely participate in major speaking roles and speech genres. To the extent that such roles and forms of speech exert control and influence over men's and women's lives, the men have more power and control than the women. (Susan Philips 1987, p. 9).

The challenge then is to produce theoretical frameworks that explain the interaction of language, gender, and power based on insight from historically specific studies of Western and non-Western cultures, which connect language use to gender, where gender is not treated as just a difference or an individual characteristic, but as a matter of social relations and power. From a feminist perspective, research on language and gender is undertaken to empower women by exposing the lie of the neutrality of language, and exposing the mechanisms which legitimize the meanings of the powerful over the meanings of the powerless. The ultimate goal is to transform the "muted" position of women across cultures and continents.

BIBLIOGRAPHY

Anzaldúa, Gloria. (1987). *Borderlands/La frontera.* San Francisco: Spinsters/Aunt Lute Book Company.

Blaubergs, Maija S. (1980). An analysis of classic arguments against changing sexist language. In Cheris Kramarae (Ed.), *The voices and words of women and men.* Oxford: Pergamon Press.

Cameron, Deborah. (1985). *Feminism & linguistic theory.* London: Macmillan Press.

Cameron, Deborah & Coates, Jennifer. (1985). Some problems in sociolinguistic explanation of sex differences. *Language & Communication, 5*(3).

Cheshire, Jenny. (1982). *Variation in an English dialect: A sociolinguistic study.* Cambridge: Cambridge University Press.

Daly, Mary. (1978). *Gyn/Ecology: The metaethics of radical feminism.* Boston: Beacon Press.

DeFrancisco, Victoria. (1989). Marital communication: A feminist qualitative analysis. Unpublished doctoral dissertation, University of Illinois.

Fishman, Pamela M. (1983). Interaction: The work women do. In Barrie Thorne, Cheris Kramarae, & Nancy Henley (Eds.), *Language, gender, and society.* Rowley: Newbury House.

Frank, Francine Wattman & Treichler, Paula. (1989). *Language, gender and professional writing.* New York: Modern Language Association.

Gal, Susan. (1979). *Language shift.* New York: Academic Press.

Goodwin, Marjorie Harness & Goodwin, Charles. (1987). Children's arguing. In Susan Philips, Susan Steele, & Christine Tanz (Eds.), *Language, gender, & sex in comparative perspective.* Cambridge: Cambridge University Press.

Grahn, Judy. (Ed.). (1978). *True to life adventure stories: Vol. I* New York: Crossing Press.

Hellinger, Marlis. (1984). Effecting social change through group action. In Cheris Kramarae, Muriel Shultz and William O'Barr (Eds.), *Language and power.* Beverly Hills: Sage.

Henley, Nancy & Kramarae, Cheris. (1990). Gender, power and miscommunication. In Nikoks Coupland, Howard Giles, & John Wiemann (Eds.), *Problem talk and problem contexts.* Newbury Park, CA: Sage.

Hill, Alette Olin. (1986). *Mother tongue, father time.* Bloomington: Indiana University Press.

Jespersen, Otto. (1922). *Language: Its nature, development and origin.* Hemel Hemstead: Allen & Unwin.

Key, Mary Ritchie. (1975). *Male/female language.* Metuchen, NJ:Scarecrow Press.

Kramarae, Cheris. (1981). *Women and men speaking.* Rowley, MA: Newbury House.

Kramarae, Cheris. (1986, May). A feminist critique of sociolinguistics. *Journal of the Atlantic Provinces Linguistic Association, 8,* 1–22.

Kramarae, Cheris & Jenkins, Mercilee M. (1987). Women take back the talk. In Joyce Penfield (Ed.), *Women and language in transition.* Albany, NY: State University of New York Press.

Kramarae, Cheris, Treichler, Paula, & Russo, Ann (1985). *A feminist dictionary.* New York: Pandora Press.

Kramarae, Cheris, Shultz, Muriel, & O'Barr, William (Eds.). (1984). *Language and power.* Beverly Hills: Sage.

Labov, William. (1972). *Sociolinguistic patterns.* Philadelphia: University of Pennsylvania Press.

Labov, William. (1973). The linguistic consequences of being a lame. *Language and Society, 2,* 1.

Lakoff, Robin. (1975). *Language and women's place.* New York: Harper & Row.

Lakoff, Robin Tolmach. (1990). *Talking power: The politics of language in our lives.* New York: Basic Books.

MacKinnon, Catharine. (1987). *Feminism Unmodified.* Cambridge: Harvard University Press.

Martyna, Wendy. (1983). Beyond the he/man approach: The case for nonsexist language. In Barrie Thorne, Cheris Kramarae, and Nancy Henley (Eds.), *Language, gender, and society.* Rowley: Newbury House.

McConnell-Ginet, Sally. (1988). Language and gender. In Frederick J. Newmeyer (Ed.), *Linguistics: The cambridge survey, Vol. IV. Language: The socio-cultural context.* Cambridge: Cambridge University Press.

McConnell-Ginet, Sally. (1989). The sexual (re)production of meaning: A discourse-based theory. In Francine Wattman Frank and Paula Treichler (Eds.), *Language, gender and professional writing.* New York: Modern Language Association.

McConnell-Ginet, Sally. (1991, March). "Talking politics" a review of *Talking power. Women's review of books, 8*(16), 13–14.

Medicine, Bea. (1987). The role of American Indian women in cultural continuity and transition. In Joyce Penfield (Ed.), *Women and language in transition.* Albany, NY: State University of New York Press.

Miller, Casey & Swift, Kate. (1976). *Words and women: New language in new times.* New York: Anchor Press.

Miller, Casey & Swift, Kate. (1980). *The handbook of nonsexist writing: For writers, editors and speakers.* New York: J. B. Lippincott.

Milroy, Leslie. (1980). *Language and social networks.* Oxford: Basil Blackwell.

Moraga, Cherríe. (1983). *Loving in the war years.* Boston: South End Press.

Moraga, Cherrie & Anzaldúa, Gloria (Eds.). (1981). *This bridge called my back.* Watertown, MA: Persephone Press.

Nichols, Patricia C. (1983). Linguistic options and choices for Black women in the rural south. In Barrie Thorne, Cheris Kramarae, & Nancy Henley (Eds.), *Language, gender and society.* Rowley: Newbury House.

Nilsen, Alleen Pace. (1987). Guidelines against sexist language: A case history. In Joyce Penfield (Ed.), *Women and language in transition.* Albany, NY: State University of New York Press.

Ochs, Elinor. (1987). The impact of stratification and socialization on men's and women's speech in Western Samoa. In Susan Philips, Susan Steele, & Christine Tanz (Eds.), *Language, gender and sex in comparative perspective.* Cambridge: Cambridge University Press.

Penfield, Joyce. (Ed.).(1987). *Women and language in transition.* Albany, NY: State University of New York Press.

Philips, Susan, Steele, Susan, & Tanz, Christine (Eds.). (1987). *Language, gender & sex in comparative perspective.* Cambridge: Cambridge University Press.

Poplack, Shana. (1979). Sometimes I'll start a sentence in Spanish y termino en español: Towards a typology of code-switching. *Working Papers #4.* New York: Centro de Estudios Puertorriqueños.

Rakow, Lana & Kramarae, Cheris. (Eds.). (1990). *The revolution in words.* New York: Routledge & Kegan Paul.

Rich, Adrienne. (1980). *On Lies, Secrets and Silence: Selected Prose 1966-1978.* New York: WW Norton.

Sherzer, Joel. (1987). A diversity of voices: men's and women's speech in ethonographic perspective. In Susan Philips, Susan Steele & Christine Tanz (Eds.), *Language, gender, and sex in comparative perspective.* Cambridge: Cambridge University Press.

Shibamoto, Janet S. (1987). The womanly women: Manipulation of stereotypical and nonstereotypical features of Japanese female speech. In Susan Philips, Susan Steele, & Christine Tanz (Eds.), *Language, gender, and sex in comparative perspective.* Cambridge: Cambridge University Press.

Spender, Dale. (1980). *Man made language.* London: Routledge & Kegan Paul.

Spender, Dale. (1984). Defining reality: A powerful tool. In Cheris Kramarae, Murial Shultz, & William O'Barr (Eds.), *Language and power.* Beverly Hills: Sage.

Stanback, Marsha Houston. (1985). Language and Black women's place: Evidence from the Black middle class. In Paula Treichler, Cheris Kramarae, & Beth Stafford (Eds.), *For alma mater: Theory and practice in feminist scholarship.* Urbana: University of Illinois Press.

Tannen, Deborah. (1990). *You just don't understand: Women and men in conversation.* New York: William Morrow.

Thorne Barrie, & Henley, Nancy. (Eds.). (1975). *Language and sex: Difference and dominance.* Rowley: Newbury House.

Thorne, Barrie, Kramarae, Cheris, & Henley, Nancy. (Eds.). (1983). *Language, gender and society.* Rowley: Newbury House.

Torres, Lourdes. (1990). Spanish in the United States: The struggle for legitimacy. In John Bergen (Ed.), *Spanish in the United States: Socialinguistics Issues.* Washington, DC: Georgetown University Press.

Treichler, Paula, Kramarae, Cheris, & Stafford, Beth. (Eds.). (1985). *For alma mater: Theory and practice in feminist scholarship.* Urbana: University of Illinois Press.

Trudgill, Peter. (1972). Sex, prestige and linguistic change in urban British English of Norwich. *Language & Society, 1,* pp. 179–95.

Van Den Bergh, Nan. (1987). Renaming: Vehicle for empowerment. In Joyce Penfield (Ed.), *Women and language in transition.* Albany, NY: State University of New York Press.

Wolfe, Susan J. (1989). The reconstruction of word meanings: A review of the scholarship. In Francine Wattman Frank & Paula Treichler (Eds.), *Language, gender and professional writing.* New York: Modern Language Association.

Women speaking from silence [Special issue]. (1991, October). *Discourse & Society, 2*(4).

Zentella, Ana Celia. (1987). Language and female identity in the Puerto Rican community. In Joyce Penfield (Ed.), *Women and language in transition.* Albany, NY: State University of New York Press.

Chapter 25

Psychology and Feminism

Mary Roth Walsh

BEFORE THE KNOWLEDGE EXPLOSION

Psychology has nothing to say about what women are really like, what they need and what they want, essentially, because psychology does not know. (Naomi Weisstein, 1968, p. 268)

Naomi Weisstein's famous words summed up the state of knowledge in psychology in the late 1960s but, unfortunately, this lack of knowledge did not translate into more careful treatment of women patients. Phyllis Chesler's ground breaking book, *Women and Madness* (1972, reissued 1989), went on to document how health professionals abused their women patients with tranquilizers, sexual seduction, hospitalization against their will, shock therapy, and lobotomies and then insulted them with labels such as "too aggressive," "promiscuous," "ugly," "old," "disgusting," or "incurable."

Psychological science had so little to offer women patients because the profession had shut out women researchers who tried to develop the field. In the 1890s, for example, a small number of women social scientists had launched an attack on the Victorian notion that sex differences were proof of female inferiority. One of the leaders in this struggle was Helen Thompson [Woolley], who did a brilliant doctoral dissertation in 1903 at the University of Chicago on the psychology of women. She demonstrated that the intellectual similarities between the two sexes far outweighed any differences (Helen Thompson, 1903). The noted sociologist, William Isaac Thomas, who had earlier defended the notion that there were significant differences between men and women, hailed her research findings as "probably the most important contribution to this field" (Rosalind Rosenberg, 1982, p. 81).

Leta Stetter Hollingworth, another brilliant pioneer, coauthored several articles with Thompson and established a remarkable record for herself. Before she received her Ph.D. from Columbia University in 1916, Hollingworth had already published a book and nine scientific papers on the psychology of women. Her research and writing has a strikingly modern flavor: she criticized the social forces that pressured women into becoming mothers, a situation that later feminists would label "the motherhood mandate" (Leta Stetter Hollingworth, 1916; Nancy Felipe Russo, 1979, p. 7). Hollingworth also rejected the notion, widely accepted by leading psychologists at the time, that men tended to have a wider range of intellectual abilities than women, an idea known as "the variability thesis."

In her research, she also attacked the popular view that women's cognitive abilities declined during menstruation (Leta Stetter Hollingworth, 1914a, 1914b).

Pioneers like Helen Thompson Woolley and Leta Stetter Hollingworth made important early twentieth century contributions to feminist scholarship and then, suddenly, their work in this area stopped. Helen Thompson Woolley had a good reason, she was never able to obtain an academic position that enabled her to continue her research (Elizabeth Scarborough & Laurel Furumoto, 1987). Leta Stetter Hollingworth, on the other hand, joined the faculty at Columbia University; yet she, too, stopped doing research and writing on the psychology of women. When she died in 1939, scholars like Laurel Furumoto, (1987, 1988) who have carefully searched for historical traces of the lives of women psychologists, claim women were "on the margins" of the profession while men dominated the high status research and theory building areas. Women physicians confronted sex discrimination in 1915 by founding the American Medical Women's Association but women psychologists remained isolated and tended to avoid organizations. After a brief skirmish of organizing during World War II and the formation of the National Council of Women Psychologists, members quickly voted to change their organization's title to the more gender neutral, International Council of Psychologists. Soon afterward, the group elected a man as president and men became the majority on the board of directors. In 1959, when Cynthia Deutsch, a beginning psychotherapist, asked the group to sponsor a study of discrimination against women psychologists, she was told that the organization no longer was interested in this topic and it had shifted its focus to international issues (Mary Roth Walsh, 1985c)

THE BEGINNINGS OF A
FEMINIST PSYCHOLOGY

Female psychologists, spurred on by the women's movement, demonstrated against employment discrimination at the 1969 and 1970 American Psychological Association (APA) conventions and in the process organized the Association for Women in Psychology (AWP). In addition to expanding women's role in the profession, the AWP also sought to encourage feminist psychological research on women and women's issues. Following four years of protest and pressure, the APA accepted a petition to form a division on the psychology of women (Division 35) in 1973. Some 800 members responded to the first call for applications for the new division, an important step forward for the field of the psychology of women because it insured an institutional base for legitimizing and formalizing research devoted to women. At the same time the APA also established an office for women's programs and a committee on women is psychology, both of which are still in existence. Most important, special task forces issued reports on a number of topics ranging from guides for nonsexist language, reports on sex bias and sex role stereotyping in psychotherapeutic practice to the development of guidelines for nonsexist research (APA, 1977, 1988; Annette M. Brodsky & Rachel T. Hare-Mustin, 1980; Florence L. Denmark, 1977; Maureen McHugh, Randi Koeskie & Irene Hanson Frieze, 1986).

The law became a major ally in women's struggle for advancement in the professions (George LaNoue & Barbara A. Lee, 1987) in 1972 when Congress amended the Civil Rights Act of 1964 to apply to institutions of higher education and American women could sue colleges and universities for discriminating against them. These lawsuits, or the threat they posed, opened opportunities for women to gain faculty positions, do research, teach, and establish women's research centers. These institutional structures have enabled feminist scholarship to sustain itself.

Sue Wilkinson (1990) has recently described the very different experiences of women psychologists in Great Britain, Israel, Argentina, and Italy. The one thing we can conclude for sure about women's organizing efforts is that such activities stimulated the growth and development of feminist scholarship. Because of space limitations, my account here will concentrate on the knowledge contributions of American psychologists but the transformation in American psychology has clearly been fueled, in part, by the brilliant writing of feminists from other countries as Dale Spender documents in *For the Record: The Making and Meaning of Feminist Knowledge* (1985). For example, Germaine Greer, one of these early feminist writers, was born in Australia and educated at Cambridge University in England and her book, *The Female Eunuch* (1971) was originally published in London, but when it was reprinted in the United States it very quickly became a best seller. Greer singled out psychology for special attack, charging that psychotherapy played "an extraordinary confidence trick"on women. She argued: "Psychologists cannot fix the world so they fix women" (p. 83); though, as she pointed out, they did not even manage that very well.

THE FEMINIST CHALLENGE
TO PSYCHOLOGY

The feminist challenge encompassed almost every aspect of psychology from grand theoretical issues to specific research methodologies and therapeutic practices. No single individual came under greater attack than Sigmund Freud. As Josephine Donovan (1985) has commented, what Betty Friedan called the "feminine mystique" could just as easily be called the "Freudian mystique" (p. 105). Feminist critics also focused on the research practices of psychologists who relegated female subjects to the periphery of their research interests. As Virginia O'Leary (1977) pointed out, sex was generally considered a "nuisance variable to be controlled, not investigated" (p. 3). John Atkinson's (1958) study of achievement motivation is a case in point. Although Atkinson devoted more than 800 pages to this topic, all of the research on sex differences can be found in one footnote (Matina S. Horner, 1972). According to Mary Brown Parlee, researchers' habits of ignoring women and viewing male behavior as the prototype of human behavior resulted in "distored facts and omitted problems" which, in turn "perpetuated pseudo-scientific data relevant to women." (1975, p. 124). To make matters worse, women with real problems were encouraged to seek the cause in themselves. To cite just a few examples: violence against women was explained, in part, by female masochism [see Susan Kappeler, and Jane Caputi, this volume]; women's anger by "raging hormones;"and female underachievement in mathematics by genetic deficiencies (Mary Roth Walsh, 1987).

NEW RESEARCH PRIORITIES
AND DIRECTIONS RESULTING
FROM FEMINIST ACTIVITY

The introduction of feminism into psychology led to the jettisoning of some theories, the revision of others, and the charting of new directions for the field (Rachel T. Hare-Mustin & Jeanne Marecek, 1990; Jeanne Marecek, 1989). In some cases, old theories have been transformed through a feminist dialectic. A case in point is the attempt to reinterpret and reapply Freudian theory. At first, the rebirth of feminism seemed to create a consensus among feminist psychologists that psychoanalysis was a means of social control and dangerous to women's mental health. In the mid-1970s some feminists such as Juliet Mitchell (1974) attempted to build a bridge between psychoanalysis and feminism, arguing that Freud's theories had an important descriptive power, explaining male and female development within a patriarchal society. Others like Helen Block Lewis (1986) have argued that "feminist themes have always been intrinsic in Freud's work" (p. 3). The British writer Janet Sayers (1986) has taken Lewis' observations one step further; she contends that psychoanalysis is a necessary building block for feminism's focus on social change. Nancy Chodorow (1978, 1989), on the other hand, has viewed psychoanalytic theory as a jumping off point in developing her view of the essential female phenomenon of mothering which divides society into public (masculine) and private (feminine) spheres. Nevertheless, feminist criticism of Freudian theory remains strong. Hannah Lerman (1986a), for example, argues that women cannot benefit from any attempt to revive psychoanalysis because it is "fundamentally flawed" (1986b, p. 6). In her view, the theory not only neglects and denigrates women, but it also ignores the uniqueness of women's life experience.

Other theories that once constituted a psychology of women, or more appropriately, in Nancy Henley's words, "a psychology against women" (1974, p. 20), have been either discarded or reexamined from new perspectives. Prior to the rebirth of feminism in the 1960s, there was a consensus that the role strain attached to work outside the home posed serious physical and mental health threats for women. Like much of psychology's misunderstanding of women, this concept was based on unproven assumptions rather than real research. An impressive number of empirical studies beginning in the 1970s has demonstrated that the benefits of multiple roles far outweigh the strains and these additional roles increase a women's chances for well-being (Debra Froberg, Dwenda Gjerdingen, & Marilyn Preston, 1986, p. 81).

Finally, some feminist psychologists, such as Sandra Lipsitz Bem, have taken the psychology of women in new directions. Bem came to prominence as the result of her work on androgyny, a term referring to people who are high on both feminine and masculine traits. She then equated androgyny with mental health and created the Bem Sex Role Inventory (1981a,b), an instrument to measure androgynous traits. Psychologists immediately climbed on the bandwagon and some clinicians even began to discuss how to "androgynize" exclusively masculine or feminine clients (Peter B. Zeldow, 1982, p. 401). Like any major theorist, Bem's work also stimulated a considerable amount of controversy. Bernice Lott, for example, rejected the notion that there are separate feminine and masculine ways of behaving. "To label some behaviors as feminine and some as masculine," she charged, "is to reinforce verbal habits which undermine the possibility of degenderizing behavior" (1981, p. 178). Interestingly, Bem has also had second thoughts about her earlier research. In her new work on gender schema theory, Bem now argues that masculinity and femininity are the products of a belief system that organizes our world into masculine and feminine components (Sandra Lipsitz Bem, 1987).

The one study that has attracted both popular and academic attention is Carol Gilligan's book, *In a Different Voice,* (1982). Two writers even go so far to say that Gilligan has "inalterably changed our understanding of human psychology" (Karen Johnson & Tom Ferguson, 1990, p. 38). Carol Gilligan focuses criticism on Kohlberg's stage theory of moral development that locates women at level 3, characterized by a regard for "what pleases or helps others," while it places men at the more mature level 4, which focuses on a concern with law and justice. Gilligan charges that Kohlberg and most other psychologists have erred in adopting male behavior as the norm. She notes the paradox that the traits traditionally associated with the "goodness" of women—caring and sensitivity to others— are the very same characteristics that render them relatively inferior on moral–judgment scales.

Gilligan has been praised for challenging the male bias in previous theories on moral development, but her work has also stimulated considerable controversy. For example, Catherine G. Greeno and Eleanor Maccoby (1986) argue that because Gilligan ignores more recent work which does not show men scoring at higher levels, she is attacking a straw man. There is also the question of whether Gilligan, by basing a theory of moral development in part on the responses of women to abortion, has built sex bias into her work. Others have criticized her abortion research from a different perspective, noting that in failing to consider the race, religion, class, or ethnicity of her subjects, Gilligan ignores variables that may be more influential than gender in determining moral decision making (Judy Auerback, Linda Blum, Vicki Smith, & Christine Williams, 1985).

Feminists have also voiced concern over the effect that Gilligan's work will have on the political advancement of women. Recently, Mary Brabeck (1989) edited a major collection of essays representing some of the diverse responses to the "ethic of care" hypothesis and in the process she has opened up new possibilities for dialogue among scholars and empirical investigators in the field. Whether or not Gilligan's earlier conclusions will be used to support traditional sex-role stereotypes, it is clear that her research findings contrast sharply with those of earlier feminist psychologists in the 1970s who developed concepts such as androgyny to minimize the significance of sex differences. Now, in the 1990s, Gilligan and her colleagues are focusing their attention on young girls and attempting to avoid "the muddle of gender comparisons" altogether (Francine Prose, 1990, pp. 23,25).

MAJOR METHODOLOGICAL ISSUES AND CRITIQUES OF THE NEW APPROACHES TO KNOWLEDGE

In another chapter in this volume, Shulamit Reinharz (1991) analyzes the feminist research methodology debate which is extremely complex and which encompasses all of the academic disciplines. In each field of knowledge there are idiosyncratic concerns. For example, Anne Peplau and Eva Conrad (1989) have recently completed a very systematic study of feminist research methodology in psychology and they conclude that any research method can be sexist and that "no method comes with a feminist guarantee" (p. 379). They recommend that feminist researchers become skeptical of the limitations of all research methods. Because many psychologists consider the experimental method to be essential to the study of psychology, they cite the work of Rhoda Unger (1981) who has pointed out that certain sex differences are more likely to be documented in naturalistic settings such as homes and offices. In the experimental conditions of a laboratory setting, people may self-consciously monitor their behavior and distort the data collection process. Peplau and Conrad also point to the fact that many prominent studies in the psychology of women such as Matina Horner's (1972) work on the fear of success, Sandra Bem's (1981a,b) work on androgyny and Carol Gilligan's (1982) work on moral development have broken new ground but still have used traditional research methodology.

THE ACCESSIBILITY OF THIS NEW KNOWLEDGE TO STUDENTS: THE ROLE OF TEXTBOOKS

Although there have been few published studies documenting the extent to which new research on women has been mainstreamed into textbooks for students, a very ambitious project is now underway. Sharyl Bender Peterson (1989) is in the process of doing content

analyses of the 46 top-selling introductory psychology and 15 top-selling lifespan development textbooks published in the United States. In a preliminary report, she concludes that
women are still "grossly under represented" in the textbooks she has reviewed: historical
coverage of women's contributions to the field of psychology is ignored and research on
women is presented in stereotyped and negative contexts. On the other hand, there are also
some small but hopeful signs of change. For example, Sandra Brehm and Saul Kassin,
authors of a 1990 textbook in social psychology, begin their chapter on the social perception
of groups (which includes such topics as stereotyping, sexism, prejudice, and racism) with
a case study and photograph of Ann Hopkins, who recently won a 1989 United States
Supreme Court Decision protesting sex discrimination which denied her a partnership in her
accounting firm. Susan Fiske, a social psychologist, helped win the case when she testified
how gender stereotypes distort the perceptions of competent women.

Other authors are also beginning to include the new research on women in their
introductory psychology textbooks as well. David Myers (1986, 1989) has a separate
chapter on gender in both editions of his introductory psychology textbook. Carol Tavris
and Carole Wade [Offir] authors of the feminist book, *The Longest War: Sex Differences
in Perspective* (1977, 1984, new edition forthcoming) have just issued the second edition
of their introductory psychology textbook which they claim integrates gender and culture
into mainstream psychology discussions throughout their book (1990, p. xix). Similarly,
Margaret Matlin, author of the feminist text, *The Psychology of Women* (1987), is in the
process of writing an introductory psychology textbook which she claims will also explicitly mainstream the new research on women and gender (in press).

Although mainstreaming efforts are important, separate psychology of women courses
are still desperately needed to serve as a catalyst for change (Mary Roth Walsh, 1985a,b).
When a 1972 APA task force was called to evaluate the status of women in the profession,
it could only locate 32 psychology departments in the entire United States that offered a
course on the female life experience (APA, 1972). When I tried to document efforts to
mainstream the new research on women in the undergraduate curriculum, I discovered that
only 209 schools (23%) in the Microfiche College Catalogue Collection listed at least one
undergraduate course focusing on the female life experience (Mary Roth Walsh, 1985a).
Other surveys report similar findings: APA's Educational Affairs office surveyed 1,210
psychology department heads in 4-year colleges and found only 24% had courses on
women or gender issues (C. James Scheirer & Anne M. Rogers, 1985). Margaret Matlin
(1989) has conducted a survey of 440 full-time faculty, identified by a national marketing
firm as the total number of United States faculty who teach gender related courses. Matlin's
survey confirms the fact that the most popular title for gender courses is still the "Psychology of Women." Other titles such as the "Psychology of Gender" are much less common
and the majority of colleges and universities still do not offer a single psychology course
focused on women or gender issues despite the fact that women are 60% to 90% of the
undergraduate psychology majors on many campuses.

CONTRIBUTIONS OF PSYCHOLOGY
TO FEMINIST KNOWLEDGE

Hester Eisenstein (1983) views psychology as one of the most basic of all the academic
disciplines in terms of its potential to affect women's lives. Jean Baker Miller (1976/1986)
goes even further in *Toward a New Psychology of Women* when she argues that women play
a human role that no other suppressed group plays: women are entwined with men in
intimate and intense relationships in the family where the human mind is formed. When

women leave the family, they move into a gendered educational system and a world which clearly disadvantages women in their quest for knowledge. Mary Field Belenky, Blythe McVicker Clinchy, Nancy Rule Goldberger and Jill Mattuck Tarule (1986) have issued an invitation for others to join them in their effort to construct a theory that explains how women learn about the world. As Mary Brabeck (in press, citing Mary Field Belenky et al., p. 59), notes, perhaps it is no coincidence that so many of women's characteristic "ways of knowing" are also sex stereotypes such as women's intuitive rather than rational way of perceiving the world. She also calls attention to the devastating statistics on sexual abuse reported by the 75 women cited in their study: 38% of those in schools and 65% of those in social agencies had been subjected to incest, rape or sexual seduction by males in authority over them. Incest was reported by one of every five college women and one of every two women from social agencies.

ASSESSMENT OF THE CURRENT SITUATION IN PSYCHOLOGY

Clearly, psychology has been transformed from a profession that, in Naomi Weisstein's words, had "nothing to say about women" to one that now has a great deal to say about them. For example, in 1975 the journal *Sex Roles: A Journal of Research,* began publication, followed a year later by the *Psychology of Women Quarterly* and now a new journal, *Feminism and Psychology: An International Journal* will begin publication in 1991. In addition, there are dozens of more specialized journals that publish research on the psychology of women such as the *Journal of Women and Aging, Journal of Gay and Lesbian Psychotherapy,* and *Women and Therapy.* Practically every mainstream psychology journal has increased the number of articles it publishes on psychology of women issues (Kay Deaux, 1984, 1985; Bernice Lott, 1985; Brinton Lykes & Abigail Stewart, 1986). The five most recent textbooks designed for college courses on the psychology of women represent still another dimension of this knowledge explosion (Janet Shibley Hyde, 1991; Bernice Lott, 1987; Margaret Matlin, 1987; Mary Roth Walsh, 1987; and Juanita H. Williams, 1987). The size of the fourth edition of Janet Hyde's 1991 textbook, *Half the Human Experience: The Psychology of Women,* stands in sharp contrast to the relatively brief version she published 15 years ago. Workshops on teaching the psychology of women have paralleled the growth in knowledge about women. During the past seven years I have organized 10 different programs on teaching the psychology of women. Though these sessions began as short "conversation hours" at conferences, they have now expanded into all-day workshops at the American Psychological Association's annual meetings (Mary Roth Walsh, 1988a, 1988b, 1988c, 1990).

In an earlier period, faculty teaching courses on women may have found it difficult or impossible to locate published research on women's issues; now faculty find it difficult to read and assimilate all that is available. Our teaching workshops are designed to help faculty keep up with the rich array of resources now available and to demonstrate how teaching can be enriched by projects and interesting exercises that involve students in their learning. All of the following authors have edited resource guides for teaching: Alice G. Sargent (1985); Sharon Golub and Rita Jackaway Freedman (1987); Phyllis Bronstein and Kathryn Quina (1988); and Michele Paludi (1990). The Bronstein and Quina volume has separate chapters on women from a number of different cultural perspectives: Asian-Americans, African-Americans, Chicanos, lesbians, handicapped women, and the psychology of poverty. In addition, Christine C. Iijima Hall (1989) has published a bibliography on Black females in the United States from 1967 to 1987. An even more specialized source is Laurie Williams'

(1990) bibliography which focuses on Black feminist theory and experience. In fact, the field has become so large that libraries now have separate reference books with extensive bibliographies on dozens of psychology of women topics such as gender and nonverbal communication, assertiveness training for women, and feminist psychoanalytic psychology.

Another measure of the increased maturity of the field of the psychology of women is the fact that debates within the field are no longer just between feminists and nonfeminists. In my recent book on debates in the psychology of women, I view the growing diversity of views within the field as a very positive development and I see the continued flow of new ideas and rival claims as essential to growth in the field. Debates can stimulate the development of the field of the psychology of women by encouraging open discussions that challenge the biases of researchers (Mary Roth Walsh, 1987).

Finally, it is important to point out that the changes that have taken place in psychology over the past 20 years do not constitute a panacea. Critics have pointed out that we still have a long way to go if our goal is to conduct truly nonsexist research (Brinton Lykes & Abigail Stewart, 1986; Maureen McHugh, Randi Koeske & Irene Hanson Frieze, 1986). Another area of concern is the continuing resistance to affirmative action legislation. Phyllis Bronstein and her colleagues (1986, 1988, 1989) and Suzanna Rose (1986) have called attention to the difficulties that women psychologists experience in getting and keeping academic jobs. Statistics show, for example, that in graduate departments offering a doctoral degree, women comprise only 13% of the tenured faculty. Letters from Rogers Elliott (1987, 1989), published in the American Psychological Association's *American Psychologist*, indicate the deep seated resistance toward women that still exists. Elliott argues that women are equally successful in getting jobs even though they are not equally qualified, that women are being hired in proportion to their percentages in the applicant pool, and that affirmative action programs are not needed. After 4 years of letters back and forth between the disputing parties, Phyllis Bronstein and Joyce Pfenning (1989) recently began their final rebuttal letter by informing Professor Elliott that if he *acts* on his beliefs, he will violate the law because institutions receiving federal funds are required to make special efforts to recruit, employ, and promote qualified members of under represented groups. As long as affirmative action policies are implemented and sex discrimination laws are enforced, feminist psychology has a major ally in advancing its research and publishing agenda in the 1990s—at least in the United States.

BIBLIOGRAPHY

American Psychological Association. (1972). Report on the task force on the status of women in psychology. (Available from the Women's Program Office of the American Psychological Association).

American Psychological Association. (1977). Guidelines for nonsexist language change sheet for the APA Publication Manual. Washington, D.C.: Author.

American Psychological Association. (1988). Women in the American Psychological Association, 1988. (Available from the Women's Program Office of the American Psychological Association).

Atkinson, John. W. (Ed.). (1958). *Motives in fantasy, action and society: A method of assessment and study.* New York: Van Nostrand.

Auerback, Judy, Blum, Linda, Smith, Vicki, & Williams, Christine. (1985). Commentary: On Gilligan's *In a different voice. Feminist Studies, 11*(1), 149–161.

Belenky, Mary Field, Clinchy, Blythe McVicker, Goldberger, Nancy Rule, & Tarule, Jill Mattuck. (1986). *Women's ways of knowing: The development of self, voice, and mind.* New York: Basic Books.

Bem, Sandra Lipsitz. (1981a). *Bem Sex Role Inventory Professional Manual.* Palo Alto, CA: Consulting Psychologists Press.

Bem, Sandra Lipsitz. (1981b). Gender schema theory: A cognitive account of sex typing. *Psychological Review, 88,* 354–364.

Bem, Sandra Lipsitz. (1987). Reprint of two articles in response to the question: "Is Androgyny a Solution?" In Mary Roth Walsh (Ed.), *Psychology of women: Ongoing debates.* New Haven, CT: Yale University Press.

Brabeck, Mary M. (Ed.). (1989). *Who cares? Theory, research, and educational implications of the ethic of care.* New York: Praeger.

Brabeck, Mary M. (in press). Recommendations for reexamining women's ways of knowing, *New Ideas in Psychology.*

Brehm, Sharon S. & Kassin, Saul. (1990). *Social psychology.* Boston: Houghton Mifflin.

Brodsky, Annette M. & Hare-Mustin, Rachel Hare. (1980). *Women and psychotherapy: An assessment of research and practice.* New York: Guilford Press.

Bronstein, Phyllis & Pfenning, Joyce. (1988). Misperceptions of women and affirmative action principles in faculty hiring: Response to Elliott's comment on Bronstein et al. *American Psychologist, 43*(8), 668–669.

Bronstein, Phyllis & Pfenning, Joyce. (1989). Beliefs versus realities: Response to Elliott. *American Psychologist, 44*(12), 1550.

Bronstein, Phyllis & Quina, Kathryn. (Eds.). (1988). *Teaching a psychology of people: Resources for gender and sociocultural awareness.* Washington, DC: American Psychological Association.

Bronstein, Phyllis, Black, Leora, Pfenning, Joyce, & White, Adele. (1986). Getting academic jobs: Are women equally qualified–and equally successful? *American Psychologist, 41*(3), 318–321.

Chesler, Phyllis. (1989). *Women and madness.* Garden City, NY: Doubleday. (Reprint of 1972 book with new introduction.)

Chodorow, Nancy. (1978). *The reproduction of mothering.* Berkeley: University of California Press.

Chodorow, Nancy. (1989). *Feminism and psychoanalytic theory.* New Haven, CT: Yale University Press.

Deaux, Kay. (1984). From individual differences to social categories: Analysis of a decade's research on gender, *American Psychologist, 39*(2), 105–16.

Deaux, Kay. (1985). Sex and gender. *Annual Review of Psychology, 36,* 49–81.

Denmark, Florence L. (1977). The psychology of women: An overview of an emerging field. *Personality and Social Psychology Bulletin, 3,* 356–367.

Deutsch, Cynthia. (1959). National-International Women in Psychology Archives, n.p. Akron, Ohio.

Donovan, J. (1985). *Feminist theory.* New York: Frederick Ungar.

Eisenstein, Hester. (1983). *Contemporary feminist thought.* Boston: G. K. Hall.

Elliott, Rogers. (1987). Getting academic jobs: Women appear to be equally successful without being equally qualified. *American Psychologist, 42(2),* 188.

Elliott, Rogers. (1989). Preferential hiring of women in psychology is unwarranted and unwise: Reply to Bronstein and Pfenning. *American Psychologist, 44*(12), 1549–1550.

Froberg, Debra, Gjerdingen, Dwenda, & Preston, Marilyn. (1986). Multiple roles and women's mental and physical health: What have we learned? *Women and Health, 11*(2), 79–96.

Furumoto, Laurel. (1987). On the margins: Women and professionalization of psychology in the United States, 1890–1940. In Mitchell G. Ash & William R. Woodward (Eds.), *Psychology in twentieth-century thought and society.* Cambridge: Cambridge University Press.

Furumoto, Laurel. (1988). Shared knowledge: The experimentalist, 1904–1929. In Jill G. Morawski (Ed.), *The rise of experimentation in American Psychology.* New Haven, CT: Yale University Press.

Gilligan, C. (1982). *In a different voice: Psychological theory and women's development.* Cambridge, MA: Harvard University Press.

Golub, Sharon & Freedman, Rita Jackaway. (1987). *Psychology of women: Resources for a core curriculum.* New York: Garland.

Greeno, Catherine C. & Maccoby, Eleanor. (1986). How different is the "different voice?" *Signs: Journal of Women in Culture and Society, 11*(2), 310–16.

Greer, Germaine. (1971). *The female eunuch.* New York: McGraw-Hill.

Hall, Christine C. Iijuima. (Ed.). (1989). *Black females in the United States: A bibliography from 1967 to 1987.* Washington DC: American Psychological Association.

Hare-Mustin, Rachel T. & Marececk, Jeanne. (Eds.). (1990), *Making a difference: Psychology and the construction of gender.* New Haven, CT: Yale University Press.

Henley, Nancy. (1974). Resources for the study of psychology and women. *R.T.: Journal of Radical Therapy, 4,* 20–21.

Hollingworth, Leta Stetter. (1914a). Variability related to sex differences in achievement. *American Journal of Sociology, 19,* 510–30.

Hollingworth, Leta Stetter. (1914b). Functional periodicity: An experimental study of the mental and motor abilities of women during menstruation. *College Contributions to Education, 69.* New York: Teacher's College, Columbia University.

Hollingworth, Leta Stetter. (1916). Social devices for impelling women to bear and rear children. *American Journal of Sociology, 22,* 19–29.

Horner, Matina S. (1972). Toward an understanding of achievement-related conflicts in women. *Journal of Social Issues, 28*(2), 157–176.

Hyde, Janet Shibley. (1991). *Half the human experience: The psychology of women* (4th ed.). Lexington, MA: DC Health.

Johnson, Karen & Ferguson, Tom. (1990). *Trusting ourselves: The Sourcebook on psychology for women.* New York: Atlantic Monthly Press.

LaNoue, George R. & Lee, Barbara A. (1987). *Academics in court: The consequences of faculty discrimination litigation.* Ann Arbor, MI: University of Michigan.

Lerman, Hannah. (1986a). *A mote in Freud's Eye: From psychoanalysis to the psychology of women.* New York: Springer.

Lerman, Hannah. (1986b). From Freud to feminist personality theory: Getting here from there. *Psychology of Women Quarterly, 10*(1), 1–18.

Lewis, Helen Block. (1986). Is Freud an enemy of women's liberation? In T. Bernay & D.W. Cantor (Eds.), *The psychology of today's women: New psychoanalytic visions.* New York: Lawrence Erlbaum.

Lott, Bernice. (1981). A feminist critique of androgyny: Towards an elimination of gender attributions for learned behavior. In Clare Mayo & Nancy M. Henley (Eds.), *Gender and nonverbal behavior* (pp. 171–80). New York: Springer-Verlag.

Lott, Bernice. (1985). The potential enrichment of social/personality psychology through feminist research and vice versa. *American Psychologist, 40*(2), 155–64.

Lott, Bernice. (1987). *The psychology of women.* Monterey, CA: Brooks/Cole.

Lykes, Brinton & Stewart, Abigail (1986). Evaluating the feminist challenge to research in personality and social psychology: 1963–1983. *Psychology of Women Quarterly, 10,* 393–412.

Marecek, Jeanne. (Ed.). (1989). Theory and method in feminist psychology. Special Issue of *Psychology of Women Quarterly, 13*(4).

Matlin, Margaret. (1987). *The psychology of women.* New York: Holt Rinehart & Winston.

Matlin, Margaret. (1989). Teaching psychology of women. *Psychology of Women Quarterly, 13*(3), 245–261.

Matlin, Margaret. (in press) *Psychology.* Fort Worth, TX: Holt Rinehart & Winston.

McHugh, Maureen, Koeske, Randi & Frieze, Irene Hansen. (1986). Issues to consider in conducting nonsexist psychological research: A guide for researchers, *American Psychologist, 41*(8), 879–890.

Miller, Jean Baker. (1976/1986). *Toward a new psychology of women.* Boston: Beacon Press.

Millet, Kate. (1969). *Sexual politics.* Garden City, NY: Doubleday.

Mitchell, Juliet. (1974). *Psychoanalysis and feminism.* New York: Random House.

Myers, David. (1986, 1989) *Psychology* (1st ed., 2nd ed.). New York: Worth.

O'Leary, Virginia. (1977). *Toward understanding women.* Monterey, CA: Brooks Cole.

Paludi, Michele A. (1990). *Exploring/teaching the psychology of women: A manual of resources.* Albany, NY: State University of New York Press.

Parlee, Mary Brown. (1975). Review essay: Psychology. *Signs: Journal of women in culture and society, 1*(1), 119–58.

Peplau, Letitia Anne & Conrad, Eva. (1989). Beyond nonsexist research: The perils of feminist methods in psychology. *Psychology of Women Quarterly, 13*(4), 379–400.

Peterson, Sharyl Bender. (1989, November). *The nature and effects of gender-biased psychology curriculum: And some suggestions for implementing change.* Paper presented at the conference, Gender in Academe: The Future of our past. University of South Florida.

Prose, Francine. (1990, January 7). Confident at 11, confused at 16. *New York Times Magazine.* pp. 22–25; 37–40, 46.

Reinharz, Shulamit. (1991). The principles of feminist research: A matter of debate. In Cheris Kramarae & Dale Spender (Eds.), *The knowledge explosion: Generations of feminist scholarship.* Elmsford, NY: Pergamon Press.

Rose, Suzanna. (Ed.). (1986). *Career guide for women scholars.* New York: Springer.

Rosenberg, Rosalind. (1982). *Beyond separate spheres: Intellectual roots of modern feminism.* New Haven, CT: Yale University Press.

Russo, Nancy Felipe. (Ed.). (1979). The motherhood mandate [Special issue]. *Psychology of Women Quarterly, 4*(1).

Sargent, Alice G. (1985). *Beyond sex roles* (2nd ed.). St. Paul: West Publishing Co.

Sayers, Janet. (1986). *Sexual contradictions: Psychology, psychoanalysis, and feminism.* London: Tavistock.

Scarborough, Elizabeth & Furumoto, Laurel. (1987). *Untold lives: The first generation of American women psychologists.* New York: Columbia University Press.

Scheirer, James & Rogers, Anne M. (1985). *The undergraduate psychology curriculum: 1984.* Washington DC: American Psychological Association.

Spender, Dale. (1985). *For the record: The making and meaning of feminist knowledge.* London: The Women's Press Limited.

Tavris, Carol & Offir, Carole. (1984). *The longest war: Sex differences in perspective.* San Diego: Harcourt Brace Jovanovich. (Original edition published 1977).

Thompson, Helen (1903). *See* [Woolley], H.T.

Unger, Rhoda K. (1981). Sex as a social reality: Field and laboratory research. *Psychology of Women Quarterly, 5,* 646–653.

Wade, Carole & Tavris, Carol. (1990, 1987). *Psychology* (2nd ed.). New York: Harper & Row.

Walsh, Mary Roth. (1985a). The psychology of women course: A continuing catalyst for change. *Teaching of Psychology, 12*(4), 198–203.

Walsh, Mary Roth. (1985b). The psychology of women course and clinical psychology. *The clinical psychology of women, 1*(2), 4–7.

Walsh, Mary Roth. (1985c). Academic professional women organizing for change: The struggle in psychology. *Journal of Social Issues, 41*(4), 17–28.

Walsh, Mary Roth. (1987). *Psychology of women: Ongoing debates.* New Haven, CT: Yale University Press.

Walsh, Mary Roth & Van Ormer, Alice. (1988a). *Study guide for psychology of women: Ongoing debates.* New Haven, CT: Yale University Press.

Walsh, Mary Roth. (1988b). Conference Report: Teaching and learning about the psychology of women: A workshop for undergraduate and graduate faculty (report on American Psychological Association preconvention workshop, New York City, August, 1987). *Signs: A Journal of Women and Culture,* 886–891.

Walsh, Mary Roth. (1988c). Undergraduate update: Courses on women's issues flourishing. *APA Monitor: American Psychological Association Monthly Newspaper, 19*(5), 38.

Walsh, Mary Roth. (Ed.). (1990). Resources for 1990 workshop on teaching and learning about women. Sponsored by the Division of the American Psychology of Women (Division 35) of the American Psychological Association.

Weisstein, Naomi. (1968, October). "Kinder, Kuche, Kirche" as scientific law: Psychology constructs the female. Paper presented at the American Studies Association Meeting, University of California, Davis. Reprinted in R. Morgan, (Ed.) (1970). *Sisterhood is powerful: An anthology of writings from the women's liberation movement* (pp. 205–220). New York: Vintage Books.

Williams, Juanita H. (1987). *Psychology of women: Behavior in a biosocial context.* New York: WW Norton.

Williams, Laurie. (Ed.). (1990). *Psychology of Black Women: A feminist bibliography.* Available from Loraine Obler, Program in Speech and Hearing Sciences, CUNY Graduate School, 33 West 42 St., New York, N.Y. 10036

Wilkinson, Sue. (1990). Women organizing within psychology. In Eric Burman (Ed.), *Feminists and psychological practice.* London: Sage.

[Woolley], Helen Thompson. (1903). *The mental traits of sex: An experimental investigation of the normal mind in men and women.* Chicago: University of Chicago Press.

Zeldow, Peter. (1982). The androgynous vision: A critical examination. *Bulletin of the Menninger Clinic, 46*(5), 401–13.

Chapter 26

Economics

Marilyn J. Waring

I'm responding to your request as a political economist. It's an odd title—I think most women I know are political economists. The "discipline disciples" would undoubtedly disagree, but in this context I use the words to make it clear that I'm not about to talk about U-shaped curves, stocks or shares, banking or the specifics of what is called "microeconomic."

According to Baron Lionel Robbins (1969) the authoritative definition of economics is "the study of human behavior in disposing of scarce means which have alternative uses to satisfy ends of varying importance." The major twentieth century British economist, John Maynard Keynes (1936), called economics "a method rather than a doctrine, an apparatus of the mind, a technique of thinking which helps its possessor to draw correct conclusions."

Theory is used, first of all, to decide what facts are relevant to an analysis. Only some everyday experiences are stated, recognized, and recorded by economic theory. Overwhelmingly, those experiences that are economically visible can be summarized as *what men do*.

Most propositions in economics are explained and illustrated by using words and mathematics. These are seen to be alternative languages that are translatable into each other. Mathematical formulas assist the illusion that economics is a value-free science: propaganda is less easily discerned from figures than it is from words. The process of theorizing takes place when economists reason about simplified models of an actual economy or some part of an economy. From this model, "factual predictions" are made. Clearly, if you do not perceive parts of the community as economically active, they will not be in your model, and your "correct conclusions" based on the model will not include them.

The belief that value results only when (predominantly) men interact with the marketplace, means that few attempts are made to disguise this myopic approach.

For example, Baron Lionel Robbins (1957), an economist who was a member of the British House of Lords, wrote:

> The propositions of economic theory . . . are all *assumptions* involving in some ways *simple* and *indisputable* facts of *experience*. . . . We do not need controlled experiments to establish their *validity*: they are so much *"the stuff of our everyday experience* that they have only to be stated to be recognized as *obvious*." [Emphasis added.] (pp. 140–142)

Whatever else Baron Robbin's "everyday experience" may have included, it would not account for the everyday experience of almost all the women on the planet.

Feminist theorist Sheila Rowbotham (1973) reminds us:

> Language conveys a certain power. It is one of the instruments of domination. . . . The language of theory—censored language—only expresses a reality experienced by the oppressors. It speaks only for their world, for their point of view. (pp 32–34)

And something else happens to language in its colonizing by male theorists.

Xenophon coined the word "oikonomikos" to describe the management or rule of a house or household. In general usage, the word "economy" still retains some links with its Greek origins. *Roget's Thesaurus* (Norman Lewis, 1964) lists as synonyms management, order, careful administration, frugality, austerity, prudence, thrift, providence, care, and retrenchment (p. 165). These synonyms are unlikely candidates for what is called the "science" of economics. The meaning of words, our words, change inside a "discipline."

When I look at the index of any major journal of economics it is difficult to think of subjects that have remained unscathed in terms of invasion by this discipline. Nobel prizewinner Paul Samuelson, professor of economics at Massachusetts Institute of Technology, writes:

> In recent years, economists have begun to infiltrate the field of demography. This is part of the imperialist movement in which we economists try to apply our methodologies to everything—to the law, to the sociology of the family, courtship, marriage, divorce, and cohabitation. (1985, p. 167)

But women are generally presumed to know little about economics, or the world's or a nation's economy. Yet a "simple and indisputable fact of everyday experience" is that most women know how to be economical, to use things sparingly, to cut down on expenses. For some this knowledge and skill sustains the lives of themselves and their children from one hour or one day to the next.

The "imperialist movement of economists" has an awesome power. They say, for example, that many of the things I value about life in New Zealand—its pollution-free environment; its mountain streams with safe drinking water; the accessibility of national parks, walkways, beaches, lakes, kauri and beech forests; the absence of nuclear power and nuclear energy—all count for nothing. They are not accounted for in private consumption expenditure, general government expenditure, or gross domestic capital formation (see Marilyn Waring, 1989).

It is not surprising then that their empire "values" the manufacture, storage, transportation, and use of weapons; the causes of pollution and the costs of cleaning it up; the maintenance of defense forces; and the purchase of, for example (legally or illegally), drugs, including narcotics, alcohol, pharmaceuticals and tobacco, and pornography.

This "science" which in its empire building attempts to have forces of occupation in all "important" disciplines, is afflicted with a problem common in many of these essays. Women are present when they are in "male" territory, or as dependents, liabilities, or welfare. Otherwise they are invisible. Economics achieves this by categorizing the way the majority of women on the planet live their lives as "unoccupied," "nonproductive" and "economically inactive." They do not *work*. Their *labor* (both productive and reproductive), has no "value."

Since the debate between Thomas More and Thomas Hobbes on the "political" and "moral" distinctions in "value," this word (derived from the Latin *valere*, meaning "to be strong or worthy") has been colonized by "economics" to carry the narrow connotation of the "market." This abuse of language is a further common finding of feminist scholars when examining patriarchy's "disciplines."

For centuries many feminist women have been critical of the outrageous abuses of women, in both theory and practice, made in the name of economics. They have included novelists and poets, philosophers, and activists for peace, the environment, the suffrage. They have been grassroots activists, writers, or held political office. They are found in all countries, races, religions, cultures. But they are seldom called "economists."

Some women have written classics that will be found under "economics" in a library catalog. Charlotte Perkins Gilman, Olive Schreiner, Joan Robinson and Esther Boserup are examples, in the last century, of Western women in this category. But it would be unusual to find all four on reading lists for undergraduates in economics in western universities.

Harvard economist and liberal U.S. writer John Kenneth Galbraith writes:

> That many women are coming to sense that they are instruments of the economic system is not in doubt. But their feeling finds no support in economic writing and teaching. On the contrary, it is concealed, and on the whole with great success, by modern neoclassical economics—the everyday economics of the textbook and classroom. This concealment is neither conspiratory nor deliberate. It reflects the natural and very strong instincts of economics for what is convenient to influence economic interest—for what I have called the conventional social virtue. It is sufficiently successful that it allows many hundreds of thousands of women to study economics each year without their developing any serious suspicion as to how they will be used. (1980, p. 41)

Robin Morgan (1989) has written that one of the ingenuous tools of the patriarchy is its capacity for demarcation. [See also Cheris Kramarae, this volume.] This tool assists the assertion that Rachel Carson's *Silent Spring* (1979), Mary O'Brien's *The Politics of Reproduction* (1983), or Jessie Bernard's *The Female World* (1981) are not about economics. It also assists the political ghettoization of the planetary concerns of the majority of the human species as "women's issues."

In the past 20 years, many of those thought of as "feminist economists" by their economic colleagues probably prepared papers on subjects such as equal pay, women and their invisibility in development projects, the effects of the more-market mentality on public policy and women and children, pay equity, capitalism and patriarchy, and sex-role stereotyping. But there are changes, as multidisciplinary approaches to feminist research leave the patriarchal demarcative defenses in ruins. The more recent work of feminist women writers, academicians, policy makers, and activists challenges all the basic roles, principles, conceptual frameworks, descriptive functions, and perceived outcomes of the theory, science, profession, practice, and institutionalization, of economics. In this they challenge one of patriarchy's fundamentals: the myth of an objective and value-free science, the myth of this discipline being devoid of self-interest.

Take my own work in the field of the United Nations System of Nation Accounts (UNSNA), an international system of economic measurement. Any annual report of the World Bank, the International Monetary Fund (IMF), United Nations (UN) agencies, or national governments, is based on national account statistics. The UN uses national accounts to assess annual contributions, and to appraise the success of regional development programs. Aid donors use the UNSNA to identify deserving cases, "need" being determined by "per capita gross domestic product." The World Bank uses these figures to identify nations that most urgently need economic assistance. Multinational corporations use the same figures to locate new areas for overseas investments. Companies project the markets for their goods on the basis of the national accounts projections and plan their investment, personnel, and other internal policies.

And that's only part of the story. For individual countries the uses made of national accounts and their supporting statistics are manifold and have far-reaching effects. They are used for creating frameworks or models for the integration of economic statistics generally, they are used to analyze past and current developments in the national economy, and are the basis of projections of the possible effects of changes in policy or other economic changes. They are used to quantify all areas of what is considered the national economy so that resource allocation decisions can be made accordingly. Governments project public service investment and revenue requirements for the nation—and plan new construction, training, and other programs necessary to meet those needs—all by using their national accounts. They are used to forecast short and medium term future trends. They are also used internationally to compare one nation's economic performance with another's.

The national accounts by themselves do not indicate what economic policies a government should implement. They are simply a mechanism—but one which operates for specific ends. The appropriate size of the budget deficit or correct amount of any taxation cuts, for example, cannot be inferred directly by the national accounts. Policy measures are based on a *selective* understanding of economic statistics. The national accounts just record a pattern of economic activity. But from the outset, the figures are rigged.

Early national income accounts were evolved to justify paying for wars (Marilyn Waring, 1989). Since the institutionalization of national income accounting by the United Nations, however, the motive has expanded. A major reason that only cash generating activities are taken into account is to ensure that countries can determine balance of payments and loan requirements—not as a comparative exercise, but as a controlling exercise. Those to whom money is owed (First World governments, multinational banks, and multilateral agencies) now impose this system on those who owe them money. They are only interested in seeing the *cash generating* capacity of the debtor countries, not their *productive* capacity. But whatever the change of motive, two things are constant. Those who are making the decisions are men, and those values which are excluded from this determination are those of our environment, and of women and children.

The question of what entails "economic activity" revolves around the question of value. It is said that obvious exclusions from such activity are goods and services on which no one could put a market price because their values are spiritual, psychological, social, or political. It is then argued that women's role as socializers, as articulators of class and gender ideology, and as (too often the easy) collaborators in reproducing the conditions of their own subordination, has no value. Yet nonprofit organizations such as churches and clubs are included as productive services in the national accounts; so are therapists and voluntary agencies where the cost of production is met by members and benefactors. Agents of social reproduction in education, law enforcement, and policing are included, as are political campaigners, and government administrative services on the grounds that the services have an economic price in terms of the cost of labor, capital, and materials to produce them. An infant born through the new "test-tube" technology or womb implant, or a child raised in an institution, are considered "products." Those who bring the fetus to term in the laboratory, or who care for the child in the orphanage or juvenile facility are seen as workers. They are economically active. But a mother, daily engaged unpaid in these activities, is "just a housewife."

The current state of the world is the result of a system that attributes little or no "value" to peace. It pays no heed to the preservation of natural resources or to the labor of the majority of its inhabitants or to the unpaid work of the reproduction of human life itself—as well as its maintenance and care. *The system cannot respond to values it refuses to recognize.*

Typical of the emphasis such an analysis provides are the Elements for an Alternative Economic Analysis proposed by a meeting of women economists in Athens in 1989 prior to the World Congress of the International Economists Association. The Workshop, involving women from 14 countries, was sponsored by the Mediterranean Women's Studies Institute and the International Research and Training Institute for the Advancement of Women (INSTRAW). The conceptual framework "to assess the impact of theories and policies on women and development" were:

1. The examination of all theories and policies to determine the structural forms of discrimination, invisibility and oppression.
2. The inclusion of gender divisions in all micro– and macroeconomic analyses.
3. The expansion of the parameters of mainstream economic and policy analysis to include those dimensions traditionally described as "social cultural and political" (the "soft" approach) from a gender perspective.

A listing of the "main elements" determined "acceptable to all participants involved" demonstrates the range of fundamental questions which feminist knowledge has brought to economics.

1. A strictly economic approach does not capture the complexities of development, a process determined by the interdependence of social, cultural, environmental, and political dimensions. Therefore, economic theory and empirical analysis should incorporate these dimensions, on a gender basis.
2. Economic science should extent its scope beyond the market to cover production of "human welfare" and incorporate that part of the nonmonetized economy which includes production within the household, housework, childcare, and emotional labor, (nurturing children, spouses, personal relations).
3. Economic short term policy, programs, and projects often have negative social, environmental, and political consequences, particularly for women and children. Therefore, economic research, analysis, and planning should have a long-term framework, with long-term and medium-term policy implications and objectives.
4. *The Household* as unit of economic analysis does not fully represent nor measure the rights, needs and priorities of women. The unit of analysis for economic research and policy should be *individual* members of the household. This would facilitate assessment of intrahousehold relations and the distribution of resources, income and labor and bring about changes in favor of women.
5. Economists and others need to pay closer attention to the adverse effects of the debt crisis and structural adjustment policies on women in general and women in low income countries in particular.
6. The current revision of national accounts (SNA) should include the economic activity of women in the informal sector and housework.
7. The political use (and abuse) of crude indicators such as GNP and aggregate rates of employment leads to policy decisions which have negative impact on women's lives (e.g., employment, fiscal policies, and social security schemes).
8. It is necessary to have a better understanding of quantitative and qualitative data about women in employment, their working conditions, and their pay, and in the widest sense their contribution to the economic life of all the countries.

9. Existing data and indicators do not fully take into account important aspects of women's employment, unemployment, and underemployment.
10. Existing techniques of data collection and analysis should be improved and internationally standardized to fully capture the conditions of work and life of women (such as unpaid family work, employment contracts, temporary and seasonal work, part-time and self-employment).
11. Macroeconometric model builders usually neglect and ignore data and information on gender differences even when available (such as in the employment sector). This leads to inaccurate estimates of the employment impact of public policies.
12. Social, political, and cultural dimensions based on gender analysis should be better integrated in economic analysis, research, and policy recommendations.
13. It should be recognized that fiscal systems discriminate against women's work and therefore social security rights. They should not reinforce the dependent status of women. The tax system should be reformed (so as not to penalize women's work) by implementing separate assessment of women's earnings.
14. Like women, nature is frequently taken for granted. It is undervalued, exploited, and being depleted for future generations. Planning for future development should include a set of indicators emphasizing the preservation of natural resources and encourage policies leading to sustainable development.
15. To create conditions of equity for women and sustainable development, it is urgent that the following research and policy steps be taken:

- Identification of distinct characteristics and conditions of three areas: The unpaid work in the household for production of human welfare in the households; the cultivation of renewable natural resources; and the extraction and processing of nonrenewable resources.
- An analysis of the interplay and dynamics between these three areas in the totality of the human economy.
- The development of new methods and measures for taking these distinct components of human economy into consideration in economic policies and decisions for future development.

Such are the issues that arise when women from different cultures and nation-states meet together to discuss "economics." But as with all spheres of feminist scholarship, the fundamental principles of (male) economics clash with the informed multi- and cross-disciplinary debate in which other feminist scholars engage. Historian Gerda Lerner's (1986) work, for example, arguing that women's reproductive power was the first private property amassed by men, and that domination over women provided the model for men's enslavement of other men, is a basic challenge to what have been seen as classical and neoclassical fundamentals of "economics."

If the definition of "slavery" is still "a person who does not possess their own labor for sale," then all the work done by feminists on marriage and housework, as well as on dowry, and in particular on the extent and range of women's unpaid work, is of particular significance for "economics."

The writing and research of women such as Gena Corea, Maria Mies, Robyn Rowland, and Renate Klein on the new medical technologies (see *Issues in Reproductive and Genetic Engineering: Journal of International Feminist Analysis*) the work of sociologists such as Mary O'Brien in her book *The Politics of Reproduction* has had particular significance for me in my work on the basic absence of any feminist concept of reproduction from "economics." [See also Renate Klein, this volume.]

I believe that one of the key challenges feminism will offer "economics" in the 1990s concerns "reproduction" for it seems perfectly obvious to me, at both a theoretical and practical level, that reproduction is the primary exchange, and thus the primary principle, of economics.

There's a considerable distance yet to travel. Much of our work in male economics is still that of exposure: for example, the United Nations rules consider that most of the work done by most women is "of little or no importance" (Marilyn Waring, 1989, p. 63). This work involves unraveling the jargon, demystifying and exposing the propaganda.

The tools that other feminist scholars adapt, use and share in their work are creating a tremendous impetus to expose what the grass roots women's movement has always known about patriarchal economics. Their lives, as evidence, are the food for the growing feminist scholarship which will overwhelm patriarchal demarcations into so-called disciplines, and restore a comprehensive all-encompassing general science, which more truly reflects women's lives on this planet, and the good-humored chaos of the universe.

BIBLIOGRAPHY

Bernard, Jessie. (1981). *The female world*. New York: Free Press.

Boserup, Ester. (1970). *Women's role in economic development*. New York: St. Martin's Press.

Carson, Rachael. (1979). *Silent spring*. Hammondsworth, Middlesex: Penguin.

Delphy, Christine. (1984). *Close to home: A materialist analysis of women's oppression*. (Diana Leonard, Ed. & Trans.). Amherst: University of Massachusetts Press.

Galbraith, John Kenneth. (1980). In Andrea D. Williams. (Ed.), *Annals of an abiding liberal*. New York: New American Library.

Gilman, Charlotte Perkins. (1966). *Women and economics*. New York: Harper & Row.

Keynes, J. M. (1936). *The general theory of employment, interest and money*. London: Macmillan. (Second edition published 1965).

Kulm, Annette & Wolpe, Anne Marie. (Eds.). (1978). *Feminism and materialism: Women and modes of production*. London: Routledge & Kegan Paul.

Lerner, Gerda. (1986). *The creation of patriarchy*. New York: Oxford University Press.

Lewis, Norman. (Ed.). (1964). *The new Roget's thesaurus of the English language in dictionary form*. New York: C.P. Putnam's Sons.

Mies, Maria. (1986). *Patriarchy and accumulation on a world scale*. London: Zed Books.

Morgan, Robin. (1989). *The demon lover*. New York: W.W. Norton.

O'Brien, Mary. (1983). *The politics of reproduction*. London: Routledge & Kegan Paul.

Robbins, Lionel. (1957). In Tjalling C. Koopmans (Ed.), *Three essays on the state of economic science*. New York: McGraw-Hill.

Robbins, L.C.R. (1969). *An essay on the nature and significance of economic science*. London: Macmillan.

Robinson, Joan. (1962). *Economic philosophy*. London: Watts.

Rowbotham, Sheila. (1973). *Woman's consciousness, men's world*. Baltimore: Penquin.

Samuelson, Paul A. (1985, May). Modes of thought in economics and biology. *American Economic Review*, 75, 167.

Schreiner, Olive. (1978). *Women and labour*. London: Virago.

Waring, Marilyn. (1989). *If women counted*. San Francisco: Harper & Row.

Chapter 27

Designing Differences
Women and Architecture

Leslie Kanes Weisman

Until the end of the nineteenth century any man or woman engaged in building could call himself or herself an architect. Architecture did not establish itself in the United States as a formal profession until the founding of the first academic programs at the Massachusetts Institute of Technology (1868), Cornell University (1871) and the University of Illinois (1897) and the enactment of the first licensing law in Illinois in 1897. The establishment of architecture as a profession, like law and medicine, depended upon excluding women and the rank and file from its membership. In the latter case, the self-proclaimed builder's appropriation of the name architect infuriated professionals, who believed themselves to be engaged in a higher form of art, removed from the practicalities of mere construction and the vulgarities of popular taste. In turn, builders, journalists, and citizens accused architects of extravagance, arrogance, an obsessive concern with "ideal beauty" and a neglectful disinterest in the economic and functional issues of daily life.

To protect themselves from populist attacks, in 1857 architects established their own professional organization, The American Institute of Architects (AIA). By the end of the century the lines were clearly drawn. Architects would design unique public and ecclesiastical buildings and elegant mansions for those who could afford to pay for them; the provision of moderate-cost dwellings for countless anonymous families across the country would be left to builders and not surprisingly, to women.

Although specialization in domestic architecture and interior design afforded women some status, men ensured that it would be low by proclaiming these specialties as unworthy of their own professional abilities and considerations. "The planning of houses . . . is not architecture at all" (*The American Architect and Building News,* September 30, 1876).

PROFESSIONAL TRAINING

Entry into the profession was historically accomplished either by gaining practical experience as an apprentice in the atelier of a master architect, or by obtaining a formal architectural education. Both routes presented formidable obstacles for women. Professional journals alleged that office work and field supervision were unhealthy, unsuitable, and at best awkward for a lady clothed in female "raimant." Editorials warned architects not to hire women: "contractors do not like to build from their plans; people with money to spend do not like to entrust its expenditure to a woman [and] the office manager is certain to fall in love with her" (*The Journal of the American Institute of Architects*, 1951).

Whereas the personal prejudice of individual males made it difficult for women to obtain professional training through apprenticeship, discriminatory policies in the academy made its equally difficult for women to obtain architectural degrees. Although by law the land-grant colleges were coeducational, they openly discouraged women from applying and completing the required course of study. The private schools, under no obligation to equality, simply refused women admittance.

THE CAMBRIDGE SCHOOL FOR WOMEN

These egregious policies indirectly led to the establishment of a unique architectural school open only to women. In 1915, Henry Atherton Frost, then a young instructor at the Harvard School of Architecture, was asked to tutor a woman in architectural design; (Harvard refused to instruct women directly). He agreed to do so in his own office. Soon five other women joined and the program quickly expanded to a three-and-a-half year curriculum staffed by Harvard's best faculty. During its 27 year history the school enrolled nearly 500 women, the majority graduating to become able and active practitioners either with a certificate issued in the early days, or with a degree made possible by the school's affiliation with a degree-granting institution, Smith College). In 1941, when Smith refused to continue supporting the enterprise, largely for financial reasons, Frost and others waged a huge battle to get the currently enrolled students into Harvard to finish their study. Finally Harvard agreed to let women in on a temporary basis until the end of the war, very probably to counter their own low wartime enrollment. After the war, the Cambridge School never reopened and Harvard's "commitment" to women waned considerably.

The percentage of women in architecture in the United States has gone up and down, but has remained consistently small. Between 1950 and 1970 the proportion of women architects declined from 3.8% to 3.6%. In 1975 about 4.3% of all architectural personnel were women; by 1985 it had risen to 11.3%.

The enrollment of women students in collegiate schools of architecture is generally increasing, making up 30% of the bachelor's programs and 40% of the master's programs in 1985–1986. However, enrollment patterns are very uneven among schools; in some women may number as high as 50%; in others there are too few to count. The same is true for women faculty.

PROFILES OF DISCRIMINATION

Throughout the 1950s, 1960s and early 1970s, the education and employment experiences of women in architecture paralleled those of other professional women in male-dominated fields. In the schools students were not taken seriously; there was a paucity of women professors and among them, the design studio "master" was a rarity. In architectural practice women made less money than men and in the large firms were clustered in lower status ancillary specialties and were promoted less. Few had achieved associate or partner status; fewer still had their own practices.

THE NEW FEMINISM VERSUS
THE OLD PROFESSIONALISM

Beginning in the late 1960s, the "new" lessons of feminism were causing many women architects and architectural educators to shift their energies from proving they could work in a man's field to challenging architectural praxis itself. Advocates of change within the established profession sought to identify and eliminate various forms of discrimination and to develop an affirmative action plan; to promote careers for women in architecture and to help prepare them for the professional licensing exams; and to revise the traditional office work structure to incorporate flexible and part-time schedules helpful to women with families.

Advocates of change outside the established profession began to form women's design collectives in which all members participated equally in decision making; the inherent conflict between the profit motive and the social responsibility of the architect was resolved by paying members only for work done and using the profits to subsidize projects beneficial to women; and in which the professional practitioner identified with nonprofessionals as clients and collaborators by accepting and respecting their values, life experiences and aesthetic preferences, even when they violated the canon of the "architect's architecture."

Beginning in 1974, major conferences were organized in established architecture schools by women students and faculty. While we argued about whether we should be "women first" or "architects first" and how or if we could be both, in the short span of one year we developed a very supportive network the educational benefits of which were quickly apparent. For example, five of us, each teaching in a different part of the United States, informally organized a design studio consortium to collaborate on developing prototypes for midwife-run birth centers.

THE WOMEN'S SCHOOL
OF PLANNING
AND ARCHITECTURE

But the most imaginative feminist innovation in architectural education of the time, logically, had nothing to do with the conventional university setting. In 1974, I was one of seven women who started the Women's School of Planning and Architecture (WSPA)—the only school of its kind to be completely conceived of, founded, financed, and run by women for women. During its years of operation, 1975–1981, it was known and highly regarded internationally both by feminists and establishment schools of architecture and planning. Each of our two-week summer residence programs, held on different college campuses, brought together about 60 diverse women.

Our courses and learning methods were not available in traditional schools. We discussed new ways to practice architecture, which clients to serve, how energy conscious design could assist the economic development of low income groups, learned carpentry, evaluated how environments support and hamper women's daily activities by comparing our personal experiences, and learned about the politics and ideology of urban planning by interviewing women (mostly nonprofessionals) active in their own neighborhoods. WSPA was an innovative model of education, community and professional responsibility where we pursued important goals in ways we believed were honorable.

THE EXCEPTIONAL ONE AND
THE HANDMAIDEN

Historically, high-spirited women who dared trespass upon the inviolable male domain of architecture, followed one of two career paths; they stayed single and developed independent practices of extraordinarily high professional standards or they married architects and formed professional partnerships in which their work was largely attributed to their husbands. Julia Morgan (1872–1957) is a classic example of the former. Morgan designed an estimated 800 buildings during some 50 years of private practice in the San Francisco Bay Area. She graduated from the University of California at Berkely in engineering in 1894 and the Ecole des Beaux Arts in Paris in architecture in 1901 (and was the first woman to receive degrees in these subjects from either school). Yet despite her remarkable career as America's most prolific woman architect, the scope and merit of her architectural achievements remain largely unrecognized. The reasons? Her responsiveness to her clients' diverse architectural tastes coupled with her tendency to eschew all publicity suggests why less than half of her buildings have been identified. Further, over half of the buildings Morgan designed were for women, commissioned by women clients, including clubs and sorority houses, retirement houses, dormitories and schools, a gymnasium, and a number of YWCA's (Sara Holmes Boutelle, 1988).

In contrast to Julia Morgan's independent office practice, Marion Mahony Griffin (1871–1961) was dependently hidden in the architectural shadows cast by two male giants—the pre-eminent American architect, Frank Lloyd Wright—in whose Chicago office she worked for some 14 years as the gifted delineator of some of "Wright's" most acclaimed work, and Walter Burley Griffin, a colleague in Wright's office whom she married in 1911. When the two won the competition for the Australian capital of Canberra in 1912, Mahony wrote: "I was proud . . . for my husband's sake. I can never aspire to be as great an architect as he but I can best understand and help him and to a wife there is no greater recompense" (Anne Griswold Tyng, 1989, p. 78). Small wonder that today she is best remembered in Australia, where she lived and worked for almost a quarter of a century, as Walter Burley Griffin's wife-helper.

ARCHITECTURE: NO PLACE FOR WOMEN

In architectural practice, the mechanisms that marginalize women are the same as in other professions: an emphasis on a full-time professional life at the expense of personal and family life; the reliance on an exclusive "old-boy's network" as a means of achieving status and advancement and a professional mystique in which male competence and "character" are the "norm." In architectural education, the design studio format disadvantages women faculty and the jury review process, women students. Within the prestigious studio, the teacher (mentor) privately tutors the student (protege). The studio "master" is a supremely male figure, either a captain-at-the-helm (star designer) who commands respect through sheer presence, or an architectural coach (avuncular buddy). For students, competing for individual recognition among peers is fundamental in the studio and the review process of their completed work by a jury of expert critics. Both situations create an inherent conflict for women who are socialized to place cooperation and sharing ahead of their own individual achievements. In architecture, accommodation, a "female trait," is negatively interpreted as a lack of aesthetic conviction.

OLD PROBLEMS, NEW INSIGHTS

In the last decade, feminist architects, sociologists, historians, planners, geographers, and environmental psychologists have created a new field of research known as women and environments. Five dominant directions emerged to guide our work.

Spatial Dichotomies

The first emphasized the gender-based spatial dichotomies produced by industrial capitalism: the segregation of workplace and dwelling, cities and suburbs, and private life from public existence. Academicians analyzed how proscriptive residential zoning prevents the establishment of neighborhood-based commercial services essential to women and prohibits home occupations which would make the combination of work and family roles easier. Architects and planners proposed designing new forms of congregate and cohousing in neighborhoods that would encourage personal support, companionship, and the sharing of domestic tasks.

Environmental Fit

The second paradigm provides empirical research on the "fit" between the activities that characterize women's daily lives and the design of dwellings, neighborhoods, and cities. For example, inner-city neighborhoods that are often labeled as deteriorating and disorganized by planners, frequently provide precisely the kinds of services that divorced mothers need: child care, schools, public transportation, shopping, apartment houses, welfare, and social services.

Environmental Equity

The third direction analyzes how women are unfairly disadvantaged and rendered invisible by public policies and practices relating to housing, transportation, and social services. For example, public housing policy is evaluated relative to its impact on the poor, not women. Yet the vast majority of the poor in the United States are women and children. As a result, public housing is virtually a female ghetto; women head over 90% of households. In addition, public transportation designed to accommodate commuters during peak rush hours, does not adequately address the needs of the countless employed mothers who take their children to day care centers en route to their jobs and pick them up along with the groceries on their way home at night. The fare structure and the scheduling and routing of busses and trains does not support this travel pattern.

Female Principles in Architecture

The fourth theme articulates the special sensibilities, attributes, and priorities women bring to architecture. For some that has meant searching for a woman's cultural heritage and archetypal female imagery in architecture derived from sources in the matrifocal Paleolithic and Neolithic cultures. Others have developed hypotheses on "female" and "male" principles in architecture based on gender socialization; still others have tried to define women's environmental values and perceptions by looking outside the profession. For example, between 1974 and 1975, Noel Phyllis Birkby and I asked women of all kinds to draw their environmental fantasies (Noel Phyllis Birkby & Leslie Kanes Weisman, 1975, 1977).

Eventually patterns emerged: the need to control privacy and access to others, the inclusion of multiple use spaces that accommodate changes in activities and relationships, and a preference for natural, sensuous materials. More recent feminist research on women's moral and psychological development helped "place" these design proclivities within the framework of women's socialization toward an ethic of care and the need to sustain relationships.

Woman Made Space

The fifth area of research is focused on the ways women have historically shaped the built landscape. An excellent and inspiring collection of articles, books, and public exhibitions have been produced documenting the past and present work of women architects, landscape architects, planners, and designers. The contributions made by women peripheral to professional practice are of equal importance. Since the early 1900s women have authored books of domestic advice that have shaped our national values and our homes; developed models of cooperative housekeeping in which kitchenless houses and apartment hotels with communal dining, laundry, and day care would free women to work outside the home by paying other women to provide domestic services; and, at the turn of the century, women established over 100 settlement houses in the immigrant ghettos and slums of America's cities to reform inadequate housing, neighborhood blight, and inhumane institutions. Women have also played a leading role in neighborhood beautification programs, urban sanitation and public health, historic preservation, and the parks and recreation movement.

NEW PROBLEMS, NEW METHODS, PARTICIPATORY RESEARCH AND DESIGN

Unconventional methods have been devised to produce this extensive body of knowledge. Participatory research joins professionals and women's groups in a consultative process in which the former encourages the latter to examine critical issues in urban planning and building design in light of their own experiences and aspirations. The purpose is to develop planning and design guidelines that reflect women's needs and a plan of action to put these into practice. A similar method employed by feminist architects—participatory design—involves women directly in designing the buildings they will use through input obtained in interviews and guided design exercised. User participation involves a considerable amount of consumer education and often raises the client's expectations, standards, and self-esteem. When women define their own problems and objectives, professionals gather more trustworthy data, develop better categories and more accurately articulate the needs of clients "without voices." In turn, women, who are the primary users of shelters and service technologies, develop the capacity to understand, analyze, and change their situation, and to better speak for themselves.

THE POLITICS OF SELF-HELP

At the community level, women organize to solve the problems that directly affect them. In the United States, women have formed self-management tenant organizations in some of the country's most shameful public housing developments, transforming these "projects" from places of neglect to homes that are safe and clean. Women worldwide have led rent strikes, formed housing committees, and sheltered themselves and each other. They have created centers for day care, health care, battered and homeless women and children, marched together to "Take Back The Night", reclaiming the public streets from pornographers, led sit-ins to protest segregation, occupied vacant houses as urban squatters because "their" governments will not provide for them, and established peace camps at the sites of nuclear missile depots in defiance of the male war machine. The politics of self-help is at the epicenter of the production of feminist environmental knowledge.

ACADEMIC ALLIANCES

Academic alliances is a fourth method. Opportunities to teach and conduct research on women and environments have been created in large measure by unorthodox relationships among women faculty and students who understand, that as women and feminists, they have more in common with each other than with their respective "peer" groups. Although the formal invitation I received to teach a graduate course on feminism in architecture and planning was from the male department head at Massachusetts Institute of Technology, it came because the women students in architecture, planning, and women's studies collectively demanded the course and put forth my name. They needed the feminist input; likewise, the ability of graduate students to undertake feminist theses depends upon the presence of an established, influential professor. Logically, those most qualified are women faculty who are feminists, whose disproportionately small numbers, low status, and uneven distribution throughout U.S. architecture schools makes the provision of such expertise difficult if not impossible. Much of the best work has been produced by women in different environmental disciplines collaborating on research grants, team teaching, consulting to community and government groups, and editing and writing books and articles.

THE IMPACT OF WOMEN AND ENVIRONMENTS KNOWLEDGE ON CURRENT ARCHITECTURAL EDUCATION AND PRACTICE

Convincing evidence now exists that women, to the extent that their roles differ from men's, use, perceive, and design environments differently and have different environmental needs. Yet there is little evidence that the fundamental challenge posed by feminist values and environmental design research has had any effect on the dominant mode of architectural thought. For the most part, architecture is still taught by, practiced by, the content determined by, and controlled by men. The integration of feminist theory, content, and pedagogy within the standard curriculum is entirely dependent upon the feminist consciousness of those teaching; and most architects still practice in traditional ways, serving clients who commission projects that have little to do with social justice and nothing to do with benefiting women.

Feminism requires an architectural practice characterized by cooperation over competition, holistic design over design specialization, and a concern for the development of people over technology. But competition among architects for jobs is increasing not decreasing (as exemplified in the expanded emphasis the average office must now place on marketing and public relations). And with the recent growth in the complexity of modern buildings, the profession has been transformed from a collection of self-employed general practitioners into a community of huge firms staffed by specialists, often concentrating on specialized building types.

HOUSING AND SOCIAL JUSTICE

However, whereas most architects believe that inexorable technological forces will seriously influence the future of architectural practice, they are increasingly participating, at the same time, in designing socially responsible housing. Today almost all architecture curricula include studio problems on affordable housing, shelters for the homeless and underprivileged, and innovative housing designs for nonnuclear family households. Architectural journals have recently published a spate of excellent, newly built housing projects designed by North American architects for nonprofit community and philanthropic organizations responding to the burgeoning need for diverse shelter care provision. Unquestionably, the literature on women and environments has informed and influenced these designs. As more for-profit developers discover the large and varied clientele awaiting such housing alternatives, we will see more of them; and women—of all ages and incomes—will benefit most from these solutions.

THE SPATIAL DIMENSIONS OF WOMEN'S LIVES

In asking how the social construction of gender shapes environmental form, meaning, use and relations among people, women in the environmental fields are helping women (and men) better to comprehend the experiences of our daily lives and the cultural assumptions in which they are immersed. [See also Joni Seager, this volume.] Environmental design research and practice is providing new blueprints for redesigning the built landscape in ways that support women and foster relationships of equality and environmental wholeness. Perhaps more than any "women's issue" the need for shelter has begun to unite women globally in a sisterhood of purpose that crosses the destructive boundaries of race, class, and nationalism. Through international networking among women at United Nations sponsored events, and conferences organized by the International Interdisciplinary Congress on Women during the past decade, there is an increasing realization that the shelter needs of women in developing countries parallels those of low income women in North America. From First World slums and public housing projects to Third World squatter settlements, women live in appallingly overcrowded, hazardous, unsanitary dwellings. Worldwide poverty among women means that many can only afford limited infrastructural services such as pit latrines, public water hydrants, open drains and unpaved roads. Lack of adequate sanitation increases health risks. In Bangladesh and Middle Eastern countries where the purdah system segregates the sexes, women who do not have private toilets are forced to defecate on rooftops and relieve themselves only before sunrise or after sunset which causes severe medical problems.

Women's universally low wages means that fewer housing units are affordable and that household income is frequently insufficient to meet the eligibility criteria for subsidized housing. The high illiteracy rate among women limits their access to information on the availability of subsidized housing schemes which is typically published in newspapers and public notices by housing authorities; and the complexity of the application forms and required documentation further prevents women from being successful applicants. In many countries women's legal standing denies them the right to own land, which means they cannot protect themselves and their children from domestic instability and violence, or provide collateral to gain access to credit or capital.

An estimated one-third of the world's households are now headed by women. In parts of Africa and many urban areas, especially in Latin America, the figure is greater than 50%; in the refugee camps in Central America and the public housing projects of North America the figure exceeds 90%. Yet the universal favoritism bestowed upon the male-headed family guarantees that the selection process for recipients of affordable rental and subsidized housing will screen out female-headed households. Further, households headed by women are more likely to be involuntarily displaced from their housing than any other households.

Homelessness among women, a common and widespread occurrence in many Third World cities, is burgeoning across the United States as increasing displacement and domestic violence force women on to the streets and into the welfare hotels and shelters where they are once again frequently the victims of male sexual assault and abuse. Women refugees, made homeless and widowed by political upheaval and war, are systematically subjected to rape in the camps while they await resettlement.

As women from the First World and Third World countries share their varied housing experiences and strategies, they increase their ability to control their housing and communities, thereby claiming greater control over their own lives, futures, and the welfare of their children. The increasing realization among diverse women of their mutually urgent need for safe shelter is contributing to a growing solidarity among white women and women of color, migrant, native, rural, peasant, displaced, and refugee women and with those whose shelter situation is affected by the apartheid regime in South Africa.

WHAT MORE IS NEEDED?

But much more research is needed comparing the environmental needs of women in developing and more developed countries. We know little about the differences among ethnic women in urban neighborhoods; disabled and lesbian women and their isolated worlds; or how the divorced mother copes with a suburban environment organized for two-parent nuclear families. Women need to be made aware of their shelter rights and their potential to influence government policy. They need self-sufficiency training in home maintenance, repair, weatherization, and finance in accessible forms and languages. Women's use of the workplace and other public environments like shopping malls, airports and civic buildings, have received little attention. We need to know why and when women feel safe or threatened in cities and suburbs. To honor and make visible women's contributions to society, we must locate and preserve sites of historic importance to women.

Architecture exists fundamentally as the expression of an established social order. It is not easily changed until the society that produced it is changed. The scale, complexity and cost of buildings and human settlements, and the myriad layers of decision making by regulatory authorities, public participation, government, and financial institutions, create an overburdened and painfully slow process. Built space is socially constructed; and like the syntax of language, the spatial arrangements of buildings and communities reflect and reinforce the nature of gender, race, and class relations in society.

The nature of the built environment is such that it can suggest the world transformed as well as the means for its transformation. If we are to design a society in which all people matter, more architects and planners need to become feminists and more feminists need to concern themselves with the design of our physical surroundings.

BIBLIOGRAPHY

The History of Architectural Education and Practice and Women's Current Place Within It

Anderson, Dorothy May. (1989). The Cambridge school, an extraordinary professional education. In Ellen Perry Berkeley with Matilda McQuaid (Eds.), *Architecture: A place for women* (pp. 87–98). Washington, DC: Smithsonian Institution Press.

Berkeley, Ellen Perry. (1980). Architecture: Toward a feminist critique. In Gerda R. Wekerle, Rebecca Peterson, and David Morley (Eds.), *New space for women* (pp. 205–218). Boulder: Westview Press.

Berkeley, Ellen Perry, with Matilda McQuaid. (Eds.). (1989). *Architecture: A place for women*. Washington, DC: Smithsonian Institution Press.

Boutelle, Sara Holmes. (1988). *Julia Morgan, architect*. New York: Abbeville Press.

Cole, Doris. (1973). *From Tipi to skyscraper*. Boston: I Press.

Making Room: Women and architecture. (1981). *Heresies: A Feminist Publication on Art and Politics, 3*(3).

Martin, Rochelle. (1986). The difficult path: Women in the architectural profession. Unpublished doctoral dissertation. School of Architecture, University of Michigan.

Martin, Rochelle. (1989). Out of marginality, toward a new kind of professional. In Ellen Perry Berkeley with Matilda McQuaid (Eds.), *Architecture: A place for women* (pp. 229–235). Washington, DC: Smithsonian Institution Press.

Rubbo, Anne. (1988). Marion Mahony Griffin: A portrait. In the exhibition catalog, *Walter Burley Griffin: A review*. Sydney: Monarch University Gallery.

Torre, Susana (Ed.). (1977). *Women in American architecture: A historic and contemporary perspective*. New York: Whitney Library of Design.

Tyng, Anne Griswold. (1989). From muse to heroine, toward a visible creative identity. In Ellen Perry Berkeley with Matilda McQuaid (Eds.), *Architecture: A place for women* (pp. 171–185). Washington, DC: Smithsonian Institution Press.

Weisman, Leslie Kanes with Noel Phyllis Birkby. (1983). The women's school of planning and architecture. In Charlotte Bunch & Sandra Pollack (Eds.), *Learning our way: Essays in feminist education* (pp. 224–245). Trumansburg, NY: Crossing Press.

Weisman, Leslie Kanes. (1989). A feminist experiment: Learning from WSPA then and now. In Ellen Perry Berkeley with Matilda McQuaid (Eds.), *Architecture: A place for women* (pp. 125–133). Washington, DC: Smithsonian Institution Press.

Wright, Gwendolyn. (1977). On the fringe of the profession: Women in American architecture. In Spiro Kostoff (Ed.), *The architect* (pp. 280–308). New York: Oxford University Press.

Wright, Gwendolyn. (1980). *Moralism and the model home: Domestic architecture and cultural conflict in Chicago, 1873–1913*. Chicago: University of Chicago Press.

Important Writings on Cross-Disciplinary Feminist Research on Women and Environments

Ardner, Shirley (Ed.). (1981). *Women and space: Ground rules and social maps*. New York: St. Martin's Press.

Keller, Suzanne (Ed.). (1981). *Building for Women*. Lexington, MA: Lexington Books and DC Heath.

Matrix Collective. (1984). *Making space: Women and the man-made environment*. London: Pluto Press.

Mazey, Mary Ellen & Lee, David K. (1983). *Her space, her place: A geography of women*. Washington, DC: Association of American Geographers.

Weisman, Leslie Kanes. (1992). *Discrimination by design: A feminist critique of the man-made environment.* Urbana-Champaign: University of Illinois Press.

Wekerle, Gerda R. (1980, Spring). Women in the urban environment. *Signs, 5,* 188–214.

Wekerle, Gerda R., Peterson, Rebecca, & Morley, Robert. (Eds.). (1980). *New space for women.* Boulder, CO: Westview Press.

Women and Environments. Published quarterly by the Centre for Urban and Community Studies, 455 Spadina Avenue, Toronto, Ontario, Canada, M5S2G8.

Women and Geography Study Group of the TBG. (1984). *Geography and gender: An introduction to feminist geography.* London: Hutchinson.

Women's Aesthetic Values and Environmental Priorities in Architecture

Birkby, Noel Phyllis & Weisman, Leslie Kanes. (1975, Summer). A woman-built environment: Constructive fantasies. *Quest, Future Visions, 2*(1).

Birkby, Noel Phyllis & Weisman, Leslie Kanes. (1977, May). Women's fantasy environments: Notes on a project in process. *Heresies, 1*(2), 116–117.

Franck, Karen A. (1989). Toward a feminist approach to architecture, a framework based on women's ways of knowing and analyzing. In Ellen Perry Berkeley with Matilda McQuaid (Eds.), *Architecture: A place for women* (pp. 201–216). Washington, DC: Smithsonian Institution Press.

Kennedy, Margrit. (1981). Toward a rediscovery of feminine principles in architecture and planning. *Women's Studies International Quarterly, 4*(1), 75–81.

Kennedy, Margrit. (1981). Seven hypotheses on male and female principles in architecture. *Making Room: Women and Architecture. Heresies: A Feminist Publication On Art and Politics, 3*(3), 12–13.

Lobell, Mimi. (1989). The buried treasure: Women's ancient architectural heritage. In Ellen Perry Berkeley and Matilda McQuaid (Eds.). *Architecture: A place for women* (pp. 139–157). Washington, DC: Smithsonian Institution Press.

Weisman, Leslie Kanes. (1981). Women's environmental rights: A manifesto. In *Making Room: Women and Architecture. Heresies: A Feminist Publication On Art and Politics, 3*(3), 6–8.

Weisman, Leslie Kanes. (1992). *Discrimination by design: A feminist critique of the man-made environment.* Urbana-Champaign: University of Illinois Press.

Women and Housing

Birch, Eugenie Ladner. (1985). *The unsheltered women: Women and housing in the 80's.* New Brunswick: Rutger's Center for Urban Policy Research.

Cooper, Clare. (1975). *Easter Hill Village: Some social implications of design.* New York: Free Press.

Franck, Karen A. & Ahrentzen, Sherry. (Eds.). (1989). *New households, new housing.* New York: Van Nostrand Reinhold.

Hayden, Dolores. (1981). *A grand domestic revolution: A history of feminist designs for American homes, neighborhoods and cities.* Cambridge: MIT Press.

Hayden, Dolores. (1984). *Redesigning the American dream: The future of housing, work, and family life.* New York: W W Norton.

Moser, Caroline O. N. & Peake, Linda. (Eds.). (1987). *Women, human settlements and housing.* New York: Tavistock.

McClain, Janet & Doyle, Cassie. (1984). *Women and housing: Changing needs and the failure of policy.* Toronto: James Lorimer.

Watson, Sophie & Austerberry, Helen. (1986). *Housing and homelessness, A feminist perspective.* London: Routledge & Kegan Paul.

Citations Previously Listed of Interest to a General Feminist Readership

Berkeley, Ellen Perry, with Matilda McQuaid. (Eds.). (1989). *Architecture: A place for women.* Washington, DC: Smithsonian Institution Press.

Hayden, Dolores. (1984). *Redesigning the American dream: The future of housing, work, and family life.* New York: W W Norton.

Making room: Women and architecture. (1981). *Heresies: A Feminist Publication on Art and Politics, 3*(3).

Torre, Susana (Ed.). (1977). *Women in American architecture: A historic and contemporary perspective.* New York: Whitney Library of Design.

Weisman, Leslie Kanes. (1992). *Discrimination by design: A feminist critique of the man-made environment.* Urbana–Champaign: University of Illinois Press.

Chapter 28

Noise Makers, Sound Breakers
Music and Musicology in the United States

Elizabeth Wood

Across all women's activities in American music in the past 20 years there has been a contradictory pattern of simultaneous losses and gains. In 1900, music was one of five leading female professions. By 1960, comparable with turn-of-the-century census reports, women comprised 57.1% of musicians and music teachers but in the period 1970 to 1980, although the labor force increased by 41%, the proportion of women employed in music declined. Adrienne Fried Block's (1988) statistical analysis suggests two reasons for this change: First, an overall shrinkage in available positions throughout the profession has had serious effects upon women and especially women of color; second, inequities have persisted in hiring patterns and policies.

Block reveals that in the academy, although the number of qualified women in music has dramatically increased in greater proportion than the national average for all fields, fewer trained women are hired in music than in the national average for *all* academic jobs; predictably our gains, though still slight, have arisen in smaller colleges in part-time, lowest level, untenured positions both in teaching and administration. Twice as many women teach part-time as do those in tenured positions; Block also reports a disturbing drop in women music education faculty who prepare future school music teachers. In 1950, women gained 12.5% of all doctorates in music which increased tenfold in 1985 to 35.9%, in addition to 52.8% of bachelor's and 50% of master's degrees. However, in specialist music schools and major universities, the more prestigious, secure and better-paid positions continue to be held by men who also compete more profitably for jobs in performance, criticism, publishing, recording, arts funding, and the business side of music (Adrienne Fried Block, 1988, p. 81–82, 84, 88; cf. Carol Neuls-Bates, 1976; & Barbara Hampton Renton, 1980).

However, Judith Tick's (1986) essay documenting this period demonstrates that outside the academy in the areas of orchestral employment, popular music, and conducting, women have made small but striking gains. In 1942, only 31 women were employed in all American orchestras but, after the major symphonies integrated women in 1945 and instituted screened auditions, the numbers of women orchestral players increased from a mere 8% in 1947 to 26.3% in 1982, although the greater proportion of these (40%) worked in smaller low-budget community orchestras. In popular music, including rhythm and blues and country music, the numbers and status of women fell between 1950 and 1970 from the 1940s figures until opportunities especially for black women's groups rose during the 1980s when women comprised some 40% of pop chart singers (Judith Tick, 1986, pp. 550–557; Sue Steward & Sheryl Garratt, 1984, pp. 41, 50, 99). A prestigious, authoritative position in music is conducting: in the 1930s, a handful of women conductors mostly worked, when they worked, with all-women symphonies but by 1985, 61 women held professional appointments in both mixed and women's choral, operatic, and orchestral groups (Judith Lang Zaimont, Catherine Overhauser, & Jane Gottlieb, 1987, pp. 52–54).

Women singers continue to reap their greatest successes in opera, notably many outstanding black artists since Marian Anderson's pathbreaking debut in 1955 with the Metropolitan Opera, but few women composers of opera meet with similar rewards. Across all genres, creative women fare less well in a field still dominated by men. Although some 40 women composers taught in university-based electronic music studios in the early 1980s, overall numbers of tenured academic women composers have fallen, a situation that affects access to grants, commissions, and recordings. In 1970, the Schwann catalog listed among hundreds of recordings only 26 women composers; between 1954 and 1982 women's compositions comprised only 5% of the total recordings issued by CRI, a leading contemporary music label. Public and corporate funding for women's music has long been parsimonious. Although the Guggenheim Foundation in 1970 alone more than doubled its awards given women in the preceding 40 years, of grants by the National Endowment for the Arts 9% went to women composers in 1973–1980 but only 3.3% in 1987 (Judith Tick, 1986, p. 555; Adrienne Fried Block, 1988; cf. Carol Neuls-Bates, 1976).

In the early 1970s, women's status both as historical subjects and active agents came into focus as the impact of the women's movement, similar to feminist waves in the 1890s and 1930s, brought a renewal of composer organizations and women's music groups and festivals. Increasing numbers of scholars and students produced scholarly monographs, editions, essays, bibliographies, and dissertations that sought to retrieve lost traditions (Elizabeth Wood, 1980). Beyond academic boundaries, a significant market was developing for and by women in a popular music often with a radical lesbian message "springing from feminist consciousness, utilizing women's talent" (Judith Tick, 1986, p. 555) and performed by women's bands and soloists, in which the political economy of the genre, its production, presentation, distribution, promotion and finances, was controlled by feminist collectives (Heresies, 1980, pp. 88–90; Karen Petersen, 1987, pp. 203–212; Sue Stewart & Sheryl Garratt, 1984, pp. 129–137).

The "Firsts" in a string of "firsts" in the 1970s, the sounds of protest against discrimination in all aspects of music, and the stirrings of political activism to take control of women's musical profile and production, began outside the academy among individual composers and performing artists in every field. Not all called themselves feminist but those who transformed personal outrage into activism were closely identified with the women's movement. Several were highly regarded with established careers; many worked independently and often in radically innovative ways outside mainstream music. In common, all had encountered and some had conquered persistent sexist barriers and bias against women's creativity and the economic exploitation and aesthetic trivialization of women's talent.

In 1970, the avant-garde composer Pauline Oliveros (1984) fired the first Press salvo berating a critical and historical bias against "Lady Composers;" composer Julia Smith (1970) published the first directory of American women composers; and in New York Mimi Stern-Wolfe formed a consciousness-raising Women Musicians' Collective (Heresies, 1980, pp. 91–92). Ten years after conductor Sarah Caldwell founded the Opera Company of Boston (1958), the Opera Orchestra of New York began its annual opera recordings and revivals under founder-conductor Eve Queler. In 1973, a feminist collective who had worked on *The Furies*, a radical paper, started the first of several women-owned companies with Olivia Records; other collectives organized the first annual National Women's Music Festival and Michigan Women's Music Festival in 1974. In that year, singer Judy Collins codirected the first feminist documentary film on the conductor Antonia Brico, and in 1975 composer Nancy Van de Vate founded the first international activist organization, The International League of Women Composers. In 1976, a collective produced the first annual *Ladyslipper Resource Guide and Catalog of Records and Tapes by Women*. In 1978, jazzwomen organized the first Women's Jazz Festival in Kansas and the Universal Jazz Coalition in New York, and published their first annual directory of jazz performers (Linda Dahl, 1984, pp. 187–192). Independent recording labels were formed for jazz by Rosetta Reitz (Rosetta Records) and for art music by Marnie Hall (Leonarda Productions), followed in 1979 by the creation of the Women's Independent Label Distribution Network.

In the areas of musicology and music education and in response to the development of both Women's Studies and American Music studies, African-American women formed a Society of Black Composers and researched Black musical foremothers. In 1972, Adrienne Fried Block led a group of teachers and scholars to establish a Committee on the Status of Women within the College Music Society who published in 1976 the first report on women in the profession; sponsored open meetings, panels and lecture-recitals; and nominated women for national office. In New York City in 1976, four composers, Annea Lockwood and Ruth Anderson at Hunter College, Doris Hays and Beth Anderson at the New School, created the first college courses on women's music (Jane Bowers, 1977, pp. 11–15). A student at Hunter, Jeannie Pool, privately printed a research and resource guide to women's musical history (Jeannie G. Pool, 1977) and in 1980 initiated the formation of a National Congress on Women in Music. This has since grown into a broad-based international network of activists, scholars, and representatives from the music business who have met in New York; Los Angeles; Mexico City; Paris; Atlanta, Georgia; and Heidelberg "to promote an international exchange of information, to form an organizational basis for conferences and meetings, to promote creative work, networking, and advocacy of women in music, and to recognize outstanding women" (ICWM, 1988; see Edith Borroff, 1987, pp. 335–346).

This essay concentrates upon the United States, but the women's music revolution of the 1970s resonated across the world as feminist groups such as Berlin's "Musikfrauen," Cologne's "Frau und Musik," London's "Feminist Improvisation Group," Chicago's "Women's Liberation Rock Band," Amsterdam's "Vrouw & Muziek," and Rome's "Il Canzoniere Femminista," to name only a few, were formed to celebrate and promote women's musicmaking.

WHO WAS LISTENING

None of these outrageous developments were honored or even heard in a conservative discipline whose authorities, like Ulysses's sailors, sternly plugged their ears so as not to be rendered dumb or transformed into wild beasts by the dangerous siren-songs of feminist sound, thought, theory, and critique.

Because the study of music "travels behind the latest chariots . . . of intellectual life in general" (Joseph Kerman, 1985, p. 17), its negligence toward women and the late-coming of feminism and postmodernism into its arena is hardly surprising. In common with visual and performance arts (including fine art, film, theater, and dance), the music discipline comprises both practical and scholarly pedagogical traditions, usually integrated in the same institution but sometimes autonomous, derived from the performance-oriented technical skills-training conservatory and the humanistic, liberal arts academy. Whether in theory, history, performance, or composition, their curricula and methodology are almost exclusively based on the quaint artifacts of Western art music 1750–1850, "a musical culture of which only remnants still exist, and (which) has little relevance to music in the last half of the twentieth century" (Jon Appleton, 1989, p. B2).

Academic musicological positivism, transported to America by immigrant Europeans in the 1930s, has concentrated on accumulating data (on "great" men, "great" works) with scant regard for interpreting that data. Musicology's Eurocentric, elitist perspectives that have devalued criticism and cultural diversity view with defensive suspicion the activities of its younger sibling, ethnomusicology (founded as a professional society in 1954), whose relatively more innovative cross-cultural critique, drawing upon anthropology and the social sciences, has been more welcoming to feminist ideas and approaches. Until quite recently, many musicologists viewed jazz, honored as a national treasure by the U.S. Congress in Resolution 57 of December 1987, as a kind of bastard relation.

The two-faced misogynist heritage of Western music history, epitomized in bourgeois nineteenth-century gender ideology and morality, glamorized, eroticized, and exploited exceptional singers and virtuoso performers as it sanctified maternal muses who sacrificed their talents to nurture famous husbands and brothers. Parallel to a gendered constructor tonality whose climaxes and closures enact patterns of power, violence, and oppression, Western music-masters constructed a gendered hierarchical scale of valued genres, styles, instruments, and institutions that restricted and devalued women's permissible talents and assigned tasks. For instance, keepers of the musical canon have consistently denied, while burying evidence to the contrary, that if and when they choose to do so, women are intellectually and artistically capable of creating large-scale, professional, public, heroic and so-called "masculine" genres such as operas, symphonies, Masses, and concertos, and have consigned and trivialized women's work to intimate, amateur, domestic, decorative, and so-called "feminine" genres such as parlor songs, hymns, and piano morsels.

As material reality outran ideology, in the 1940s a psychologist, Carl Seashore, insisted that "great" women composers were still conspicuously absent from the canon *not* for want of emancipation, endurance, native talent, education, intelligence, musical temperament, nor "in any form of limitation by heredity . . . nor in present limitations of opportunity, environment, or women's peculiar obligations" to marriage and maternity. His explanation lay in distinctive biologically determined male and female urges: "Woman's fundamental urge is to be beautiful, loved, and adored as a person; man's urge is to provide and achieve in a career. It is the goal that accounts for the difference" (Carl E. Seashore, 1940, pp. 42, 44, 72).

DEALING WITH MEN'S RESISTANCE

As in every field of artistic and creative expression, some women internalized or succumbed to oppression, whereas others refused to be silenced, valorized their status as outsiders, and celebrated difference. Two late nineteenth-century pioneers represent polar positions on the continuum of feminist protest in music. The militant British suffragette, lesbian, professional composer, conductor, and writer, Ethel Smyth (1934), derived from her own exceptional experience an analysis of the "sex antagonism" that fuels the "Male Machine" that contrives to drive women out, and urged women to unite to fight as she had done for equal rights to confront and compete with men on male turf (Ethel M. Smyth, 1934, pp. 1–57; Elizabeth Wood, 1983, pp. 132–136). Sophie Drinker (1948), a married, middle-class amateur singer in Philadelphia, inspired by the women's chorus who met in her home for 15 years to search for a repertory composed by women, wrote the first ethnographic and historical survey of women's music-making that celebrated music's links with women's spirituality and the universal power of female song in ancient myth, ritual, iconography, community, and everyday life. Drawing on the work of then-contemporary European musicologists Yvonne Rokseth, Kathi Meyer, Marie Bobillier, the historian Mary Beard, classicist Jane Harrison, and anthropologist Ruth Benedict, Drinker invented an essentialist, feminist music historiography that discarded notions of the canon, ignored individual genius, and thereby "rendered her book invisible to the professional musicological community" (Sophie Drinker, 1948, pp. xi–xv; Ruth A. Solie, 1989).

Feminist research priorities in the 1970s understandably replicated traditional musicological concerns: essential data gathering in biography, bibliography, discography, and music editions provided evidence and tools to restore lost women to the historical record. The nature and scope of the research was new and often raised issues of class, race, and gender, but initial findings were atheoretical, intended to compensate for flawed or distorted texts and to contribute to existing historical and conceptual frameworks (Marcia T. Citron, 1990).

RECENT WORK

During the 1980s, more sophisticated feminist work on the female subject has begun to attract attention from critics of and within musicology. Nancy Reich's (1985) biography of Clara Schumann, one of few women to be recognized in music history but always as interpreter and muse, draws upon previously unexamined sources and psychoanalytic theory to examine such themes as Schumann's childhood, marriage, motherhood, female friendships, compositions, and daily life. Daphne Duval Harrison's (1988) study of Black blues singers raises questions about women's power and sexuality and an emerging feminist style in lyrics and performance during the 1920s. In two recent collections, feminist ethnomusicologists discuss the ways musical behavior transculturally "is not only enmeshed in social concepts of sexuality but can also serve to reinforce and define gender identity" (Ellen Koskoff, 1987, pp. 1–23), while a survey of 800 years of Western art music uncovers new knowledge and perspectives that illuminate women's musical work and the socio-cultural forces that have shaped it (Jane Bowers & Judith Tick, 1986).

Until the appearance of textbooks by Carol Neuls-Bates, James Briscoe, and Diane Jezic, the study of women in music was largely unintegrated with, and inaccessible to, both interdisciplinary Women's Studies and introductory music courses, in part due to the specialized knowledge, time, and money required to locate and obtain primary sources, scores, and audio-visual materials (James Briscoe, 1987; Diane Jezic, 1988; Carol Neuls-Bates, 1982; see Barbara English Maris, 1988). While music dissertations on women's topics have doubled in the past decade, at all levels of music education the mainstream textbooks remain insensitive toward women and minorities (T. J. Anderson, 1982; Diane Jezic & Daniel Binder, 1987, pp. 445–469). Roberta Lamb (1987) reports that "it is possible for a student to pursue studies in music from elementary school through university and never encounter music composed by women" (Roberta Kay Lamb, 1987, pp. 8, 11, 23).

Although musicology continues to resist diversity, an interdisciplinary approach, new technologies, and contemporary music to protect and privilege its elite Eurocentric boundaries, the more marginal interdisciplinary specialties of American music and ethnomusicology are more encouraging of feminist insights and more likely to feature feminist work in their conferences, journals, and newsletters.

However, in 1988 the national American Musicological Society for the first time solicited feminist papers and panels for its annual meeting. This welcome change, urged within the profession by feminist scholars, coincided with the discovery and appropriation to music study by some leading male and female musicologists of advanced literary and film theory, semiotics, deconstruction, and the New Historicism (e.g., Richard Leppert, 1989; Arthur Groos & Roger Parker, 1989, Richard Leppert & Susan McClary, 1987). It appears from their work that fruitful areas at present for feminist music critique are sociocultural studies of musical production, and deconstruction of music's gendered meanings relative to and represented in musical iconography, opera librettos, and song texts (see e.g., Jacques Attali, 1985; Linda Phyllis Austern, 1989; Austin B. Caswell, 1988; Catharine Clément, 1988; Susan G. Cusick, 1988; Jenny Kallick, 1988; Susan McClary, 1991; Ruth A. Solie, 1988).

How far or securely such very recent scholarly advances can make a difference to the status of women in music as subjects and agents, or to women's lives, remains to be seen. Scholars and teachers need to confront the political agendas in music, our weakening links with feminist activism, and our perceived irrelevancies among young and especially minority women students.

If feminist work on music is to become relevant to Women's Studies, we must adopt feminist theoretical frameworks advanced by the other disciplines and design radical courses and resources for the teaching of history, theory, composition, performance, and music education that acknowledge music's diversity and contemporaneity and the centrality of women's experiences, including those of our students.

Similarly, directors and designers of courses and programs in Women's Studies need to take into account that the majority of our students belong to an international techno-electro generation that is literate, passionate, and informed about today's music—about rock, jazz, Gospel, rhythm and blues, folk, rap, mixed-media, and performance art idioms, to name a few—and that needs opportunities to study the multicultural heritage of living women and their living music across the former boundaries of time, place, gender, and genre.

BIBLIOGRAPHY

Anderson, T. J. (Ed.). (1982). *Racial and ethnic directions in American music*. College Music Society Report Number 3.

Appleton, Jon. (1989, April 19). The college music curriculum is in pressing need of reform. *The Chronicle of Higher Education*. B2.

Attali, Jacques. (1985). *Noise: The political economy of music* (1977). (Brian Massumi, Trans.). Minneapolis: University of Minnesota Press.

Austern, Linda Phyllis. (1989, Autumn). *Sing againe syren*: The female musician and sexual enchantment in Elizabethan life and literature. *Renaissance Quarterly 42*(3), 420–48.

Block, Adrienne Fried. (1988). The status of women in college music, 1986–87. *Women's studies/women's status: CMS report No. 5*, 79–158. Boulder, CO: The College Music Society.

Borroff, Edith. (1987). Spreading the good news: Conferences on women in music. In Judith Lang Zaimont, Catherine Overhauser & Jane Gottlieb (Eds.), *The musical woman: An international perspective, Vol. II 1984–1985*. (pp. 335–346). Westport, CT: Greenwood Press.

Bowers, Jane. (1977). Teaching about the history of women in western music. *Women's Studies Newsletter, 5*(3), 11–15.

Bowers, Jane & Tick, Judith. (Eds.). (1986). *Women making music: The Western art tradition, 1150–1950*. Urbana: University of Illinois Press.

Bowers, Jane. (1988, November). *Feminist scholarship and the field of musicology*. Paper presented at the American Musicological Society Annual Meeting, Baltimore, MD.

Briscoe, James (Ed.). (1987). *Historical anthology of music by women*. Bloomington, IN: Indiana University Press.

Caswell, Austin B. (1988, November). Ariane et Barbe Bleue: A feminist opera? Paper presented at the American Musicological Society Annual Meeting, Baltimore, MD.

Citron, Marcia J. (1990, Winter). Gender, professionalism, and the musical canon. *The Journal of Musicology*, 102–117.

Clément, Catherine. (1988). *Opera, or the undoing of women* (1979). Forword by Susan McClary (Betsy Wing, Trans.). Minneapolis: University of Minnesota Press.

Cusick, Susan G. (1988, November). Francesca Caccini's *La Liberazione di Ruggiero dall'isola d'Alcina (1865): A feminist misreading of Orlando Furioso*? Paper presented at the American Musicological Society Annual Meeting, Baltimore, MD.

Dahl, Linda. (1984). *Stormy weather: The music and lives of a century of jazzwomen*. New York: Pantheon.

Drinker, Sophie. (1948). *Music and women. The story of women in their relation to music*. New York: Coward-McCann. (Reprinted 1975, Washington, DC: Zenger Publishing.)

Groos, Arthur & Parker, Roger. (Eds.). (1989). *Reading opera*. Princeton: Princeton University Press.

Harrison, Daphne Duval. (1988). *Black pearls: Blues queens of the 1920s*. New Brunswick: Rutgers University Press.

Heresies: A Feminist Publication on Art & Politics (1980). *Women and music*. Number 10. New York: Heresies Collective.

International Congress on Women in Music. (1988). Membership Directory. Lomita, CA: Cambria Records & Publishing.

Jezic, Diane. (1988). *Women composers: The lost tradition found*. New York: Feminist Press.

Jezic, Diane & Binder, Daniel. (1987). A survey of college music textbooks: Benign neglect of women composers. In Judith Zaimont, Catherine Overhauser, & Jane Gottlieb (Eds.), *The musical woman: An international perspective, Vol. II, 1984–1985* (pp. 445–469). Westport, CT: Greenwood Press.

Kallick, Jenny. (1988, November). *Representing Lulu: Félicien Champsaur, Frank Wedekind, and Alban Berg*. Paper presented at the American Musicological Society Annual Meeting, Baltimore, MD.

Kerman, Joseph. (1985). *Contemplating music: Challenges to musicology*. Cambridge: Harvard University Press.

Koskoff, Ellen (Ed.). (1987). *Women and music in cross-cultural perspective*. Westport, CT: Greenwood Press.

Lamb, Roberta Kay. (1987). Including Women Composers in Music Curricula: Development of Creative Strategies for the General Music Class, Grades 5-8. Ed.D. diss. Teachers College, Columbia University.

Leppert, Richard. (1989). *Music and image: Domesticity, ideology, and socio-cultural formation in eighteenth-century England*. Cambridge, MA: Cambridge University Press.

Leppert, Richard & McClary, Susan. (Eds.). (1987). *Music and society: The politics of composition, performance, and reception*. Cambridge: Cambridge University Press.

Maris, Barbara English. (1988). A preliminary check-list of selected films and videos featuring women in music. In *Women's Studies/Women's Status*. College Music Society Report No. 5, 159–204. Iowa City: University of Iowa Press.

McClary, Susan. (1991). *Feminine endings: Music, gender, and sexuality*. Minnesota: University of Minnesota Press.

Neuls-Bates, Carol (Ed.). (1976). *The status of women in college music: Preliminary studies*. College Music Society Report No. 1. Iowa City: University of Iowa Press.

Neuls-Bates, Carol (Ed.). (1982). *Women in music: An anthology of source readings from the Middle Ages to the present*. New York: Harper & Row.

Neuls-Bates, Carol. (1984). Creating a college curriculum for the study of women in music. In Judith Lang Zaimont, Catherine Overhauser & Jane Gottlieb (Eds.), *The Musical Woman: An International Perspective Vol. I, 1983*. Westport, CT: Greenwood Press.

Oliveros, Pauline. (1984). And don't call them lady composers. In *Software for people: Collected writings 1963–1980* (pp. 47–51). Baltimore: Smith Publications. (Originally printed in *The New York Times*, 1970, September 13, 2, 23, 30).

Petersen, Karen. (1987). Women-identified music in the United States. In Ellen Koskoff (Ed.), *Women and music in cross-cultural perspective* (pp. 203–212). Westport, CT: Greenwood Press.

Pool, Jeannie G. (1977, October). *Women in music history: A research guide*. New York: Privately printed.

Reich, Nancy B. (1985). *Clara Schumann: The artist and the woman*. Ithaca, NY: Cornell University Press.

Reich, Nancy B. (Ed.). (1988). An annotated bibliography of recent writings on women in music. In *Women's Studies/Women's Status*. College Music Society Report No. 5, 3–77. Iowa City: University of Iowa Press.

Renton, Barbara Hampton. (1980). *The status of women in college music, 1976–1977: A statistical study*. College Music Society Report No. 2. Iowa City: University of Iowa Press.

Robertson, Carol E. (1987). Power and gender in the musical experiences of women. In Ellen Koskoff (Ed.), *Women and music in cross-cultural perspective* (pp. 225–244). Westport, CT: Greenwood Press.

Seashore, Carl E. (1940, March). Why no great women composers? *Music Educators Journal*. (Reprinted in *Music Educators Journal*, January, 1979, 42, 44, 72).

Smith, Julia (Ed.). (1970). *A directory of American women composers*. Chicago: National Federation of Women's Clubs.

Smyth, Ethel M. (1934). *Female pipings in Eden* (pp. 1–57). London: Peter Davies.

Steward, Sue & Garratt, Sheryl. (1984). *Signed, sealed and delivered: True life stories of women in pop*. Boston: South End Press.

Solie, Ruth A. (1988, Spring). *Whose life?: The gendered self in Schumann's* Frauenliebe *songs*. Paper presented at the Music and Literature Conference, Dartmouth College, NH.

Solie, Ruth A. (1990, June). *Women's history and music history*. Paper presented at the Eighth Berkshire Conference on the History of Women, Rutgers University.

Tick, Judith. (1986). Women in music. In H. Wiley Hitchcock & Stanley Sadie (Eds.), *The new Grove dictionary of American music* (pp. 550–557). London: Macmillan.

Wood, Elizabeth. (1980, Winter). Women in music: A review essay. *Signs: Journal of Women in Culture and Society, 6*(2), 283–297.

Wood, Elizabeth. (1983, Spring). Women, music, and Ethyl Smyth: A Pathway in the politics of music. *The Massachusetts Review, 24*(1), 125–139.

Zaimont, Judith Long, Overhauser, Catherine, & Gottlieb, Jane. (Eds.). (1984). *The musical woman: An international perspective, Vol. I, 1983*. Westport, CT: Greenwood Press.

Zaimont, Judith Long, Overhauser, Catherine, & Gottlieb, Jane. (Eds.). (1987). *The musical woman: An international perspective, Vol. II, 1984–85*. Westport, CT: Greenwood Press.

PART II

DEBATES

Chapter 29

The Personal Cost of the Feminist Knowledge Explosion

Susan S. Arpad

After two decades of feminist struggle, women's studies has been institutionalized at my university, which mandates women's studies classes as part of the general education curriculum. Consequently, most of my teaching assignment these days consists of classes of Introduction to Women's Studies. Some of my students come into the classes with curiosity, even enthusiasm, but most come with a great deal of resistance, based in apathy, self-satisfaction, or even outright hostility. Therefore, I choose many of their early reading assignments to give them evidence of the misogyny of the great western thinkers. Last week some of my women students rebelled. One said:

> I read Thomas Aquinas. And I read Rousseau. But I was so angry by the time I finished Rousseau that I couldn't bear to read Freud. If I get any angrier, no one will talk to me. My boyfriend groans everytime I mention my women's studies class and even my mother tells me to lighten up.

I've been teaching women's studies classes for 13 years and I recognize these conversations as a sign that the student's consciousness is beginning to change. It's a sign of success, but, as we've written elsewhere (Susan S. Arpad & Joseph J. Arpad, 1980), consciousness-changing also is disruptive, even painful. The students who undergo this change of consciousness often experience it as a change from order to chaos. It is a radical change, questioning the fundamental nature of everything they know. Although they experience the world differently, they still retain old habits, customs, and behavior patterns. Life still revolves around old social and cultural relationships. Consequently, students feel almost schizophrenic—split between the old self and the new, between the old familiar

Some of the examples and ideas presented here have been printed before in Susan Arpad, "Burnout," *Women's Studies International Forum*, *9*(2), (1986), pp. 207–213. In delving further into the subject, with Joseph Arpad, I entered into areas in which we are doing other collaborative scholarship about the formation, maintenance, and changing of personal and cultural consciousness. This article was co-authored with Joseph Arpad. We chose to use my voice because most of the experiences mentioned here were mine. Currently, we are both teaching women's studies courses at California State University, Fresno. In addition to the people who contributed to the earlier article, we would like to thank the following for helping to develop these ideas further: Kathryn Adamsky, Marcia Bedard, Jane Caputi, Sandy Coyner, Zelda Detroit, Meridith Flynn, Marilyn Hoder-Salmon, Renate Klein, Sharon Showman, Ellen Silber, Judith Stitzel, Rochella Thorpe, and Judith Treesburg.

world and the world as they now see it. Consciousness-changing leads, at least temporarily therefore, to instability. At its worst, it can lead to a kind of psychological breakdown. At its best, it necessitates a period of adjustment, in which the individual experiences an unaccustomed self-consciousness while strained social and cultural relationships are re-negotiated. In either case, the feelings of estrangement can be acute.

In the same week as the conversation about Rousseau and Freud, I received a letter from a former student who has recently enrolled in a doctoral program in women's history. She wrote in part: "This is a thank-you-and-an-assertion-of-happiness letter. It sounds corny, but I wake up excited every morning because I love my work." I recognize that working in women's studies can evoke both emotional states—positive and negative. On a daily basis, I talk to students and colleagues who are euphoric as a result of their change of consciousness; they see the world with unaccustomed clarity and they feel expansive because of the budding of their self-esteem. I also talk to other students and colleagues who are stuck in a stage of anger or despair. We prefer to see only the positive, but, as feminists, we have to accept the negative personal consequences of feminism as well.

In 1938 Virginia Woolf wrote in *Three Guineas* about the alienation women would experience if they attempted to live in the patriarchal world of the professions and at the same time, pursued "the rights of all—all men and women—to the respect in their persons of the great principles of Justice and Equality and Liberty." Such women would have to join the "Society of Outsiders"—enduring alienation, with little more than a "private psycho-meter" to guide their attempts to create moral actions in an immoral world. Woolf's essays have become classics in the feminist canon; we recognize her wisdom, but, for the most part, we have tried to ignore the loneliness and despair that feminists all have experienced as members of the Society of Outsiders. In an introduction to Emma Goldman's autobiography, we find that Goldman deliberately did not mention the monumental depressions she suffered from time to time because she was afraid it would discourage others from joining the struggle (Emma Goldman, 1982).

Five years ago, I resigned from a position as director of a Women's Studies program. At the time, I attributed my discouragement to "burnout": the result of a "craziness" caused by too much work and too little time to do it, multiple and conflicting roles, lack of institutional support, caring too much, failing to achieve an ideal society, and realizing how effectively external institutions could thwart my efforts. I went back to my department, where I was a tenured full professor and where my colleagues supported my disciplinary and interdisciplinary scholarship and teaching. I gradually recovered my energy, but my feelings of dis-ease remained. In the years since that experience, I have returned to Women's Studies and I have come to the conclusion that, while burnout is endemic among feminists, "burnout" alone is not an adequate concept to explain what happened to me and what I see happening to others involved in Women's Studies. The responses to my article on "Burnout" (Susan S. Arpad, 1986) also convinced me that there is something else gnawing away at our innards.

Although the concept of "alienation" has been explored by psychologists, sociologists, and social theorists in many different contexts, I am not aware of anyone who has used the concept to look at what happens to individual feminist scholars. Without a language and a forum to discuss our experiences of alienation, each of us thinks that it is our personal inadequacy that makes us feel despair. Our avoidance of the topic leads us to dismiss the older folk of academic feminism who have dropped by the wayside as "cynical" or "just burned out." [See also Robyn Arianrhod, this volume.] We experience anger and alienation at what feels like "betrayal" on the part of sisters, but are constrained by ideals of sisterhood from acting on those feelings. We need to recognize in a public forum that, while the constant tensions of living with ambivalence and contradiction can be fruitful, they are not always positive; for many of us, the personal cost of doing feminism in the academy has been the ongoing painful experience of alienation. Let me give some examples.

ALIENATION AS MARGINALITY

I recognize that, as a woman, I am a marginal human being; I live in a society where at any time I can be dismissed, trivialized, ignored, or brutalized. I recognize this intellectually, but as my self-esteem as an academic increases, as my feelings of integrity and authenticity as a feminist become more and more a part of my everyday consciousness, I tend to forget my marginality. I work very hard to be liked, to fit in. As a director of a Women's Studies program, much of my work day is spent fostering a feminist perspective in the academy—in its administration, in its curriculum, in its faculty, and in its general environment. As I have some successes, I again forget about my marginality. Consequently, each time I encounter an event that reminds me of my marginality, I am shocked, I feel betrayed. I am never quite prepared because each time it happens, it is slightly different.

For example, there is all the gratuitous violence toward women. A colleague was walking down a sidewalk, feeling good because the class she had just finished went well. A car, with two young men in the front seat and loud music blasting from the open windows, annoyed her as an invasion of her peaceful state of mind. As the car pulled away, she read the bumper sticker: IT'S MISTER TO YOU, BITCH. Momentarily, she was filled with rage.

Weekly, even daily, I hear ugly, bizarre, painful stories of incest, rape, physical and psychological battering, sexual harassment, economic and social injustice told by women. [See Jane Caputi, this volume.] Although most Women's Studies faculty I know, including myself, will not formally counsel students, we accept a responsibility for helping them to find ways for working through problems. We recognize that as students become more aware of the world around them and as they begin to break the silences, they will need to speak about the specific realities of women's oppression. For many of the students, these stories are personal; for me, they are political. I want to act, but there's nothing I can do to alleviate my anger and fear. My academic colleagues sense my anger and fear and avoid me. As people avoid me, I experience my marginality again.

In one of my recent classes, two student couples who were opposed to feminist ideas because of their religious and political beliefs, repeatedly used body language to show the other students their disrespect for me and their disregard for the course material. They regularly challenged factual information, keeping me on the defensive. They argued with all theories; they explained why each example isn't a problem. Under the guise of intellectual freedom and maintaining an intellectual dialogue of dissent, they were able to keep me from doing my best. I was always fearful that I would say something wrong, always second-guessing the examples I used, limiting my repertoire in response to their challenge. I felt paranoid, until I remembered Long Beach State University and the University of Washington, whose women's studies programs have been in the courts over just such challenges. [See Pat Cramer & Ann Russo, this volume.] I dreaded entering that classroom because of the atmosphere of antagonism; other students in the class would become silent. When I attempted to talk to colleagues in Ethnic Studies and in Chicano-Latino Studies about this classroom harassment, I was given suggestions for improving my teaching. The reality I experienced, even among those I considered my closest allies, had been dismissed. Again, I recognized my marginality, my vulnerability.

On my campus, the women's studies program has become institutionalized, with large student enrollments, faculty contracts, and strong administrative support; in my day-to-day worklife, I sometimes think of myself as just another worker in the institution. Last year, when the Women's Studies program proposed a "Critical Thinking About Sex and Gender" course to our general education committee, a committee member responded that it was good to have feminists teaching required general education courses like Introduction to Women's Studies, which were opposed to things like rape and violence to women. But, he continued, that same feminist bias that enabled them to teach the general education course, meant that Women's Studies faculty could not teach a critical thinking course. A year later, we continue to fight for the course; each time a demand for proof of our "impartiality" is met, another is made. In many ways, I am reminded of my marginality.

ALIENATION AS BEING THE OUTSIDER

Perhaps the most disturbing situations are those in which my understanding of what is happening in a situation is so different from the understanding of others around me that I question my sanity. I feel like the woman in the horror movie (e.g., *The Stepford Wives*) whose experience is repeatedly denied by the outside world; I wonder who is crazy. One of the sources of this crazy-making is the experience of always being the outsider. Because I perceive events differently from most other people, I feel always alienated from the community. When I try to describe the experience of pain of alienation, my experience is frequently trivialized or denied. Dr. Mary Rowe's (1977) description of these ordinary alienating events as "micro-inequities" is one of the most useful conceptualizations of crazy-making that I have read:

> These minutiae [of sexism] are usually not (practically speaking) actionable; most are such petty incidents that they may not even be identified, much less protested. They are however important, like the dust and ice in Saturn's rings, because, taken together, they constitute formidable barriers. . . . Micro-inequities are of a fiendish efficiency in maintaining unequal opportunity, because we cannot change the personal characteristic which leads to the inequity. Micro-inequities are woven into all the threads of our work life and of American education. They are "micro," not at all in the sense of trivial, but in the sense of micro-economics (which looks at the process and effect of decision-making at the level of individuals and firms). . . . It is hard to deal with micro-inequities because each one by itself, appears trivial. Because the victim finds it hard to be sure what happened. Because we are all so used to it, we don't notice. Because victims who are female and/or black are also socialized not to make a fuss, lest they get sacked or isolated or put down or called sick.

ALIENATION AS DENIAL OF ONE'S EXPERIENCE

I remember, in an earlier women's studies job, being a member of an ad hoc committee appointed to investigate the status of women and minorities on our campus. The committee had decided that previous studies provided ample quantitative evidence of sexism and racism; we would, instead, gather stories, hoping that by retelling these stories and, thus, exposing the pain caused by sexism and racism, our report would persuade our readers to act. We were interviewing two middle-aged, white, male administrators in the student affairs area and we had been discussing rape and other forms of violence that women experience. When the tape recorder was turned off, one man commented that "women were their own worst enemies." When asked what he meant, he told a story about a woman student who had been drinking with her female roommate; when she became very in-toxicated, the roommate took her to a fraternity house where "a train was pulled on her" (gang rape). The second man joined in, telling in detail a similar story. For twenty minutes the story telling session continued, the details becoming ever more graphic and porno-graphic. Everyone in the room found the stories appalling; no one, except for myself, found the *telling* of the stories appalling. Later, when I explained to a friend that I thought the two administrators were "getting off" on the stories, he laughed and said that I was imagining things. Susan Griffin (1971) wrote persuasively about how men sometimes receive a vicarious titillation from retelling stories about violence done to women, but when I suggest it to my colleagues, the response is denial.

At moments like this, my estrangement becomes immediate. His experience and con-sciousness are so different from mine that there is no shared wisdom on which we can base our communication. To communicate my awareness of the world, I must create a rhetorical argument that will allow him to share my consciousness. If I choose to argue, I use my energy to help one more person comprehend one idea or experience. If I choose not to argue, I am condemned to live in a community which excludes my experience and my consciousness. Almost everything, it seems, must be argued.

ALIENATION AS BETRAYAL

The difference of consciousness also happens within the feminist community and then I experience the difference as "betrayal." As I think back on my years of experience as a director of an academic women's studies program, I remember with pain and deep regret scenes of dichotomizing, denial, and scapegoating: a group of lesbian students angrily confronting a bisexual professor about her overtly heterosexual lifestyle; a women's studies professor living a "private" life as a battered wife; a women's studies faculty committee scornfully demanding that a student feminist organization "get their act together," stop discussing, and start making decisions; a women's studies administrator withdrawing a proposal to create a women's center at the university because the school's feminist factions could not agree about the governance of the center; radical feminists arguing about which actions were "politically correct"—sometimes done with humor but othertimes done with barely disguised venom. Some of the recurring dichotomies that divide the feminist com-munity are arguments about process versus product, academic excellence versus self-discovery, separatism versus working within patriarchal institutions, elitism versus egal-itarianism, revolution versus reform, individual versus cooperative decision making, and more versus less political action. Most divisive, perhaps, have been the charges and countercharges around issues of racism and ethnocentrism. [See Rose Brewer, this volume.] When these divisions occur, those on one side of the issue or the other must feel alienated from the group. When both sides feel alienated, the community usually dissipates, leaving festering feelings of betrayal.

ALIENATION AS ESTRANGEMENT

In any or all of these situations, my feelings of alienation can become so acute that my reaction is "outlandish" and I experience further feelings of estrangement and even shame. A colleague told me that last year, in a large public meeting of regional and state dignitaries, when she was asked at the last minute to shorten her remarks to a couple of minutes because the program was too long, she publicly refused and explained to the audience with much vehemence that women were always being shunted aside and that she would be heard! She went home worrying about how the audience had received her rebellion. Another colleague, after bursting into tears in a women's studies advisory committee meeting, regretted that she had to get to a situation of desperate emotional need before others would believe that something needed to be changed. She worried that her colleagues "thought I was having a breakdown." In public meetings, I am sometimes shocked by sexist remarks and, without thinking, boo or hiss loudly and then am startled by the stares of the others in the room.

CONCLUSION

I suspect that many of my readers will recognize themselves in many of these situations. Although we share similar experiences, most of us experience them in isolation, amplifying our feelings of inadequacy by our silence. To enable us to deal with alienation individually and institutionally, we need to examine the concept of alienation caused by our feminist worldview.

We have long recognized that knowledge—particularly knowledge gained by taking a critical perspective of social reality—creates alienation. We associate this kind of alienation with artists, philosophers, and great thinkers, who step outside the world to gain perspective on it, to gain a new vision of it. In the last 20 years, many such "great thinkers" in women's studies have stepped outside our social construction of reality to give us a new perspective, a new vision. These thinkers undoubtedly experienced the pain of their alienation, but they also experienced the joy of their creativity, the satisfaction of communicating their insights, and the expansiveness of sharing their feminist consciousness with the rest of us.

Whenever a person has her or his consciousness raised by the "great thinkers and doers" in women's studies, there is an accompanying feeling of estrangement from the dominant patriarchal consciousness. In existential terms, this development of a feminist consciousness means that the person becomes a subject, not an object, an authentic self rather than "the other." These feelings of integrity, of authenticity, are the base from which creative work can be done. It is probably necessary, therefore, to accept the inevitability of some kind of pain in return for the creative potential we derive from our intellectual alienation. The question becomes how to cope with the pain.

We frequently use *alienation* to describe any process that is intrinsically dehumanizing, but, as Walter Kaufmann points out (Richard Schacht, 1970), we would do better to limit our use of it to describing *estrangement from something*. When I think about the situations described above and ask what it is that I feel estranged from, I am surprised to find, in most cases, it is from misogynist males and patriarchal social conventions—things that I do not care to be associated with in the first place. It is a false consciousness (perhaps, my feminine socialization to want everyone to love me, to want to affiliate with everyone) which leads me to experience this alienation negatively; I would be wiser to be apprehensive for my physical well-being and to be prepared to defend myself vigorously. When I experience the pain of estrangement, I should ask myself, "Is this a social group I want to identify with?" Often, as with the students who want to teach rather than learn, or the macho colleagues who "get off" on telling rape stories, the answer is an obvious NO. Just recognizing this helps me to cope with the pain.

More problematic are the situations where I do want to affiliate with the group but not on the terms that are being dictated to me, as in the case of being restricted from teaching critical thinking courses because "feminists can't be critical thinkers." As Judith Stitzel points out very persuasively (1986), although I don't share a common consciousness of reality with all or even most of my colleagues, we work together, we share some common goals, and periodically, we fight common enemies. There are some honorable things we do together. This *is* my community. I want my voice heard, too. To remain within the academy and to continue to struggle against a patriarchal consciousness and the patriarchal institution means that I will have to learn ways of coping with the inevitable alienation.

Even more problematic is the occasional, but painful, estrangement from other feminists. As I indicated above, I have become a pragmatist; as an academic, I have chosen to remain within the institution and work for change. The tensions and conflicts with which I live may be balanced by the institutional support I receive. This is a compromise position and I understand that there is a constant potential of being coopted. I understand that others have chosen other political and institutional positions; I recognize that many women have been "deflected" from an academic position (see Robyn Arianrhod, this volume). Feminists live different lives and have differing points of view. For many reasons—whether philosophical differences about ideals, political differences about strategies, or momentary lapses of generosity and forbearance—as feminists, we have fought among themselves. Living constantly with the tensions of alienation and feeling always that there is not enough time to do all we need to do, unfortunately, sometimes I tend to forget the importance of community celebration. I need to remind myself regularly to make time and space for communion with feminist men and women who are living different lives: whether in a playful game of bocce on the lawn, in ritual theater such as "At the Foot of the Mountain" presents, in the many community celebrations of the annual National Women's Studies Association meetings, or in a consciousness-raising group. Healing and affirmation of common goals is essential when living with alienation.

These thoughts are meant as suggestions for further discussion. If we are to continue to pursue a knowledge explosion and a transformation of consciousness within the academy, we are going to continue, as individuals, to live with alienation. We need to address the problem of alienation directly.

BIBLIOGRAPHY

Arpad, Susan S. (1986). Burnout. *Women's Studies International Forum, 9*(2), 207–213.

Arpad, Susan S. & Arpad, Joseph J. (1980). Consciousness changing in the women's studies classroom. In Cynthia L. Berryman & Virginia A. Eman (Eds.), *Proceedings of the Conference on Communication, Language, and Sex.* Newbury House, Rowley, Massachusetts.

Fisher, Berenice. (1986). Over the long haul: Burnout and hope in a conservative era. *Frontiers, 8*(3), 1–7.

Goldman, Emma. (1982). *Living my life: An autobiography of Emma Goldman.* Introductions by Meridel Le Sueur and Candace Falk. Salt Lake City, UT: Peregrine Smith Book. (Original work published 1931.)

Griffin, Susan. (1971, September). Rape: The all-American crime. *Ramparts.* Quoted by Sheila Ruth. (1980). *Issues in Feminism* (pp. 300–313). Boston: Houghton Mifflin Company.

Rowe, Mary. (1977). The saturn's rings phenomenon: Microinequities and unequal opportunity in the American economy. In Patricia Bourne & Velma Parness (Eds.), *Proceedings of the NSF Conference on Women's Leadership and Authority,* University of California, Santa Cruz, California.

Schacht, Richard. (1970). *Alienation.* New York: Doubleday.

Stitzel, Judith. (1986). Meditations of a middle-aged administrator. *Women's Studies International Forum, 9*(2), 203–205.

Woolf, Virginia. (1938). *Three guineas.* New York: Harcourt Brace & World.

Chapter 30

To Acknowledge and to Heal
20 Years of Feminist Thought and Activism on Sexual Violence

Jane Caputi

One of the most significant achievements of the Women's Liberation Movement has been the naming of *sexual violence* as a systematic form of patriarchal oppression. The term itself, however, is somewhat obscure. Many feminists prefer to make explicit who is responsible for sexual violence, and who is victimized by it, by using "male violence," "violence against women," or *gynocide*, defined by Andrea Dworkin (1976, pp. 16, 19) as: "the systematic crippling, raping, and/or killing of women by men. . . . The relentless violence perpetrated by the gender class men against the gender class women."

Two decades of feminist activism and research have revealed an immense scope and complexity of phallic violence as a diverse set of practices both individual and institutional. Current debate on this issue includes: sexual harassment (Catharine A. MacKinnon, 1979); battery (R. Emerson Dobash & Russell P. Dobash, 1979; Del Martin, 1976); rape—stranger, marital, and acquaintance (Pauline Bart & Patricia O'Brien, 1985; Susan Brownmiller, 1975; Angela Y. Davis, 1981; Susan Griffin, 1971; Diana E. H. Russell, 1974, 1989, 1990; Peggy Reeves Sanday, 1990; Robin Warshaw, 1988); incest (Florence Rush, 1980; Diana E. H. Russell, 1986); molestation; sexual slavery (Kathleen Barry, 1979; Kathleen Barry, Charlotte Bunch & Shirley Castley, 1984); medical violence (Gena Corea, 1985a), forced sterilization, particularly of women of color in the United States (Angela Y. Davis, 1989), denial of contraception or abortion, unnecessary gynecological operations (Gena Corea, 1985a; Mary Daly, 1978; Miranda Davis, 1989 [see Renate Klein, this volume]), medical experimentation (Gena Corea, 1985); purdah; genital mutilation (Mary Daly, 1978; Angela Y. Davis, 1989; Asma El Dareer, 1982; Nawal El Saadawi, 1980; Adi Gevins, 1987; Olayinka Koso-Thomas, 1987), women-burning, dowry murders, and socially compelled suicide (Miranda Davies, 1983; S. Islam & J. Begum, 1985); female infanticide; violent, objectifying and degrading images of women in all forms of mass and elite culture, paradigmatically pornography (Jane Caputi, 1987; Laura Lederer, 1980); pornography itself as both a depiction and practice of sexual violence (Kathleen Barry, 1979; Andrea Dworkin, 1981; Susan Griffin, 1981; Catherine A. MacKinnon, 1987; Diana E. H. Russell, 1988 [see also the debate in Susanne Kappeler, this volume]); compulsory heterosexuality

I would like to thank Deborah Cameron for reading and commenting on a first draft of this manuscript.

(Adrienne Rich, 1980); and sexual torture and murder (Deborah Cameron & Elizabeth Frazer, 1987; Jane Caputi, 1987; Barbara Smith, 1981). For an excellent survey of the various forms of violence against women in Africa, Asia, and Latin America, as well as a discussion of feminist organizing against violence on both the international and grassroots levels, see Lori Heise (1989) and the publications of the Center for Global Issues and Women's Leadership, directed by Charlotte Bunch. See also Diana E. H. Russell and Nicole Van de Ven (1976), Mary Daly (1978), Diana E. H. Russell (1984), Elizabeth Stanko (1985), Jalna Hanmer and Mary Maynard (1987), and Miranda Davies (1983, 1987).

In a 1978 essay, June Jordan (1981) linked the rape of an individual woman to the "multitudes now suffering rape" in South Africa; she is one of many African-American feminists who have pinpointed the connections between forms of violence against individual women and neo-colonial violence against peoples and nations (Angela Y. Davis, 1985, 1989). Angela Davis (1989, p. 50) called upon feminists to recognize that "the systematic oppression of women in our society cannot be accurately evaluated except as it is connected to racism and class exploitation at home and imperialist aggression and the potential nuclear holocaust that menace the entire globe." Angela Davis (1981), bell hooks (1981), and Barbara Smith (1981) among others have explored the ways that battery, torture, rape were quintessential elements of Black women's enslavement in North America as well as the ways that these patterns of devaluation and abuse continue into present day attitudes toward and violences against Black women, e.g., the racist stereotype of the Black woman as "whore." Native American Women's advocacy groups, e.g., the Sacred Shawl (Tasina Wakan), a battered women's resource shelter on the Lakota Sioux Reservation, trace many patterns of violence against Native women to the destruction of traditional Native society accomplished by European-Anglo colonialism and genocide (Marla N. Powers, 1986, pp. 173–178). Paula Gunn Allen (1990, p. 4) directly attributes violence against women in Native American communities to the "devaluation of women that has accompanied christianization and Americanization." Moreover, since the mid 1970s many feminists have drawn connections between violence against women and phallotechnic violence against the Earth and other beings (Jane Caputi, 1987; Andrée Collard with Joyce Contrucci, 1988; Mary Daly, 1978; Mary Daly, 1984; Angela Y. Davis, 1989; Francoise d'Eaubonne, 1974; Susan Griffin, 1978; Carolyn Merchant, 1980; Diana E. H. Russell, 1989; Vandana Shiva, 1988; Alice Walker, 1988). [See also Joni Seager, and Irene Diamond, this volume.]

In the past two decades feminists have named, documented and analyzed an immensity of sexual violence. In the beginnings of the movement, this meant overcoming a deeply entrenched cultural resistance; as two women regretfully noted in 1971: "When an individual woman manages to see that rape is an act which oppresses and degrades her and limits her freedom, when she sees it as political and useful to all males, she cannot count upon support from other women. Many women believe that rape is an act of sick men or is provoked by the female" (Barbara Mehrhof & Pamela Kearon, 1973, p. 233). This situation was soon to change as organizing against sexual violence became a major focus among activists, particularly in the United States, where in the early 1970s rape became "the feminist issue" (Anne Edwards, 1987). Anne Edwards (1987) writes that a single issue approach first characterized feminist theory and activism, but that this later expanded into an awareness of such violence as a "unitary phenomenon" which works to reproduce and maintain male dominance. For early response of feminists to a wide range of sexual violence issues see Frédérique Delacoste and Felice Newman (1981), Wini Breines and Linda Gordon (1983), Irene Diamond (1980), and Ann Russo (1987).

BACKGROUND

Although it is easier to document individual, published theoretical works on sexual violence, credit for introducing and expanding awareness of this issue belongs to both activists and theorists. Kate Millett in *Sexual Politics* (1970) was one of the first to argue that patriarchy depended upon the use of force to maintain itself "both in emergencies and as an ever-present instrument of intimidation" (p. 60) and to proffer a political analysis of sexual violence. [See also Elise Boulding, this volume.]

In 1971 Susan Griffin published her classic article "Rape—the All-American Crime," raising key issues including:

> The close interconnection between sexuality, aggression and violence as the primary component of masculinity in many societies; a difference in degree only, not quality, between rape and "normal" heterosexual intercourse; the contradiction between men as predators on and guardians or protectors of women; the paradox that femininity, socially constructed as the complement of masculinity, not only undermines women's capacity for sexual (and social) self-determination but actually increases their physical and psychological vulnerability to male attack; the perception of rape as more a political than a sexual act, one which represents the collective domination of men over women and thus is an act akin to terrorism; and the failure of the legal and judicial systems to extend to women the support, protection and redress their injuries deserve. (Anne Edwards, 1987, pp. 18–19)

Beginning in 1972 feminist activists were founding rape crisis centers throughout the United States, Canada, and England, organizing self defense classes, and lobbying legislatures to change sexist rape laws (Jennifer Temkin, 1986). In India, anti-rape activism (and anti-battery and dowry-murder) became a major focus of a primarily middle-class movement (Miranda Davies, 1983, pp. 179–185) and women in other non-Western countries such as Peru, Jamaica, Brazil, South Africa, Pakistan, and Nicaragua continue to organize against rape and battery (Lori Heise, 1989). Battered Women's Shelters have opened in Thailand (Miranda Davies, 1987, pp. 205–207) and other Third World countries including Brazil, India, and Mexico. Feminist-based movements opposed to trafficking in women and sexist exploitation by First World men continue to organize (Miranda Davies, 1987).

This interchange between theorists and activists marked other issues including wife beating (Kersti Yllö & Michele Bograd, 1988) and pornography (Laura Lederer, 1980). In exploring incest, survivor's first person accounts began to appear in the United States in the late 1970s (Louise Armstrong, 1978; Kathleen Brady, 1979) coincident with the first theoretical and feminist analyses (Judith Herman, 1981; Florence Rush, 1980). An important narrative by a survivor of the pornographic film industry, Linda Lovelace's *Ordeal* (Linda Lovelace & Mike McGrady, 1980) also came out at this time. Crucial also to academic awareness and understanding of sexual violences where the battered women's shelter and rape crisis center movements; the formation of support groups for survivors of such things as rape, incest, battery, prostitution; the calling of special issue conferences; and the work of activist groups such as Women Against Pornography, 358 W. 47th St., New York, NY 10036.

CONFRONTING CULTURAL MYTHS

In the efforts to name and resist the various forms of sexual violence, feminists simultaneously have had to confront deeply ingrained social beliefs. Catharine MacKinnon (1982, p. 529) summarizes some of these social beliefs that deny women's experiences of sexual violence: "notions that women desire and provoke rape, that girls' experiences of incest are fantasies, that career women plot and advance by sexual parlays, that prostitutes are lustful, that wife beating expresses the intensity of love."

Blaming women for male violence, particularly *victim-blaming*, is perhaps the most prevalent social myth denying women's experience of sexual violence. From incest (Judith Herman, 1981, pp. 36–49) through rape (Rochelle Albin, 1977, pp. 427–429) and sexual murder (Jane Caputi, 1987, pp. 65–83), agents of malestream thought and institutions frequently blame the victim—as well as the perpetrator's wife, mother, sister, and women in general—rather than the perpetrator himself.

Rochelle Albin (1977) notes, "Freud bequeathed to us the notion of rape as a victim-precipitated phenomenon." In 1971 Menachem Amir explicitly applied this idea to rape, finding that the victim is sometimes a "complementary partner" in her own rape (Menachem Amir, 1971, p. 266). Pauline Bart (1979) lists additional social myths which deny women's experience of rape and subvert justice in rape cases: the double standard (that women who have been sexually active are "bad" and that such "bad" women can't really be raped); the idea that women lie about rape and that corroboration is required to prove that rape happened; the "ideology of the rapist as mentally ill"; "the ideology of the imperative nature of male sexuality." For a summary and analysis of these and other rape myths see Martha Burt (1980).

Belief in victim precipitation has similarly influenced social attitudes toward wife abuse (Wini Breines & Linda Gordon, 1983, p. 518). Other social myths are the idea of the home as "haven" or "safe" place (Elizabeth A. Stanko, 1988), the doctrine of "privacy" in family relationships (Elizabeth Pleck, 1987), and the notion that violence is mutual between spouses and that there is actually a "battered husband syndrome." Moreover, sexist ideology in more subtle forms frequently pervades even those theories which seem to take sexism into account. Wardell, Gillespie and Leffler (1983) conclude social scientific depiction of battered wives is still rooted in patriarchal biases: "She is considered to differ from officially unbattered women, and her purported differences are assumed to play some role in her own victimization."

In cases of incest two predominant stereotypes, the "seductive daughter" and "collusive mother," work to shift the blame from the father to the female members of the family (Wini Breines and Linda Gordon, 1983; Judith Herman, 1981; Florence Rush, 1980). See also Florence Rush (1980) and Judith Herman (1981) for their criticism of Freud's categorization of his patients' descriptions of incest as "fantasy."

FEMINIST METHOD

Catharine MacKinnon writes (1987, p. 5): "Since 1970 feminists have uncovered a vast amount of sexual abuse of women by men . . . The reason . . . [for this] is that feminism is built on believing women's accounts of sexual use and abuse by men." Believing women's accounts has led to redefinitions of violence itself, based upon women's experiences and responses, to include incidents that do not necessarily involve physical attack. It has also led to methods of research which involve extensive interviewing, particularly in the case of rape, by interviewers sensitized to issues of rape and the myths which surround it (Diana E. H. Russell, 1990, pp. 227–241; 1984, p. 48).

In the early 1970s, feminist theorists at first tended to focus upon one issue. However, by the end of the decade feminists were starting to approach sexual violence as a more unified phenomenon, naming connections among various types of sexual abuse. Anne Edwards (1987) identifies Mary Daly's *Gyn/Ecology* (1978) as a particularly significant work in the development of feminist method and theory. Daly finds the legitimating roots of gynocide in patriarchal myth, underscores her earlier claim that rapism is the fundamental model of oppression, identifies a "sado-ritual syndrome" that underlies patriarchal atrocities across cultures and time periods. [See Cheris Kramarae, this volume, for further discussion of patriarchy.]

Feminist research consistently challenges the standard dictum of objectivity; it is not just "about women" but is "dedicated to advocacy *for* women" (Michele Bograd, 1988, p. 15) and must develop theories and models that accurately reflect women's experience. Studying wife abuse, Lee Ann Hoff (1988) calls for "collaborative feminist research" between researcher and subject and insists upon the importance of making values explicit when embarking upon a sensitive research topic.

One of the most important general theoretical statements on feminist method in relation to sexual violence is contained in two rich and complex articles by Catharine MacKinnon (1982; 1983). In these she locates "sexuality as the primary social sphere of male power" (1982, p. 529) a realization which grows out of feminist practice in confronting sexual violence. Also crucial is the feminist method of consciousness raising; knowledge gained in this way accurately reflects the previously erased women's perspective and thus definitively counters "objectivity" which MacKinnon perceives as a guise for the male point of view (1983). She further critiques the prior feminist notion of rape (Susan Brownmiller, 1975) as a violent, but not a sexual act (1983, p. 646). Earlier, and without reliance upon male authorities, Andrea Dworkin (1981, 1985) had argued that sex, like everything else in a male supremacist culture, is constructed and defined in male supremacist terms. Thus, modes of oppression and enactments of domination and power including incest, rape, battery, torture, and murder, are themselves defined and understood as "sex" and used as a primary means of oppression.

Several theoreticians including Carole Vance and Ann Snitow (1984) reject the notion that sex is the "cornerstone of women's oppression." Irene Diamond and Lee Quinby (1984, 1988) express a wariness with MacKinnon's attempt "to unify feminism via sexuality and its control." They reject the notion that sex is "the measure of identity and the instrument of truth" and find specifically that MacKinnon's view of sexuality leads her into a "language of control" which they see as participating in, not challenging, patriarchal scientized culture.

THE MALE RESPONSE

Particularly on individual issues, various male academics have entered into the debate on violence against women. Much of the social scientific literature on wife-beating and the relation of pornography to violence is generated by men, material used by feminist academics, though frequently criticized for its sexist biases (Laurie Wardell, Dair L. Gillespie, & Ann Leffler, 1983).

Particularly antagonistic to feminist analysis on the issue of rape are some sociobiologists who have attempted to undercut feminist analysis of rape as a form of patriarchal terror by proffering a genetic determinist view of rape as an "evolutionary strategy" (Randy Thornhill, Nancy Thornhill, & Gerard Dizinno, 1986). For a critique of this see Suzanne Sunday and Ethel Tobach (1985).

In a well-received book on child sexual abuse, John Crewdson (1988) argues that pornography is quite unrelated to such abuse and that women probably abuse children as much as men do. Both contentions are highly suspect; in regard to the latter, David

Finkelhor and Diana Russell (1984) posit that a female perpetrator figures in probably 5% of abuse of girls and 20% in the abuse of boys.

Social scientists Neil Malamuth and Edward Donnerstein (together and separately) have conducted research on such topics as male proclivity to rape, male sexual arousal in response to both sexual and nonsexual depictions of violence, and depictions of violence against women in mainstream media. They conclude (1984) that depictions of sexualized violence can desensitize men to violence against women, but hesitate to draw causal links between actual violence and depictions of such acts.

Recently, the *Attorney General's Commission on Pornography Final Report* (1986) found that a causal relationship did exist between exposure to sexually violent materials and aggression toward women. This has been widely disputed by the malestream, vehemently by such humanities scholars as Walter Kendrick (1987), who, cloaking himself in a defense of free speech, opposes censorship of any kind. In an overview of social scientific research, Edward Donnerstein, Daniel Linz, and Steven Penrod (1987) point out that only when it is combined with violent imagery does sexually explicit material cause dangerous reactions. They reject the Attorney General's commission's claim that sexually violent materials constitute the majority of present pornographic materials. Moreover, they believe that mainstream representations are the most common and perhaps the most important and dangerous source of depictions of sexual violence.

DEBATES WITHIN FEMINISM

As already noted, issues of sexual violence have served to unify feminists of differing tendencies over a long period; activists and theorists, radicals and socialists remain in broad agreement that such violence is a serious political problem and that support services for women experiencing violence should be a priority. However certain divisions among feminists have emerged. African-American feminists (bell hooks, 1981; Angela Y. Davis, 1981) have criticized racist assumptions in Susan Brownmiller (1975) and Diana E. H. Russell (1974). bell hooks (1981), Barbara Omolade (1985), and Angela Davis (1981, 1989) further criticize the insensitivity of the white-led antirape movement to the concerns of women of color: that is, by neglecting the vulnerability of Black domestic workers to white male employers; by focusing on legal redress, when that would ensure that Black men would be unfairly labeled and prosecuted as rapists due to the racist myth of the Black rapist. Angela Davis, while excoriating the practice as undeniably misogynistic, examines the racism in much of the Western feminist critique of clitoridectomy (Angela Y. Davis, 1989). Similarly, AAWORD (African Women for Research and Development) issued a statement criticizing some Western agitation against genital mutilation as paternalistic. At the same time, they unequivocally condemned the practice, called for its total eradication, and exhorted African women to take leadership in that campaign (AAWORD, 1983).

One of the greatest feminist divisions in the United States and England has centered on the issue of *pornography*. Many antipornography feminists distinguish between pornography, that is, sexually explicit material "that represents or describes degrading or abusive sexual behavior so as to endorse and/or recommend the behavior as described" (Helen Longino, 1980, p. 44) and *erotica* "sexual representations that are premised on equality" (Diana E. H. Russell, 1988). Antipornography feminists generally have found pornography to be a key institution in the promotion of an ideology of male supremacy (Irene Diamond, 1980, p. 192; Susanne Kappeler, 1986). Moreover, some feminists maintain that pornography itself is a form of forced sex (Kathleen Barry, 1979; Andrea Dworkin, 1981; Catharine A. MacKinnon, 1987). Andrea Dworkin (1985) stresses that pornography is not "only" pictures, but that in many instances women are violated in the *making* of pornography. As testimony to the Attorney General's Commission on Pornography (1986) reveals, male abusers regularly use pornography in sexual abuse by making women act out scenarios depicted in pornography. Diana Russell (1988) also offers an original argument that pornography is causally related to rape in that it predisposes (or intensifies a predisposition in) some men for rape, and that it also undermines some men's internal and social inhibitions. Andrea Dworkin and Catharine MacKinnon (1988) have drafted a civil rights antipornography ordinance as a legal alternative to censorship that defines pornography as the "graphic sexually explicit subordination of women through pictures and/or words" that includes one or more of a set of eight qualifiers such as "women are presented as sexual objects who experience sexual pleasure in being raped." The ordinance has been passed into law in several United States cities, but has been overturned in the courts as a violation of the first amendment. It also has aroused a significant opposition among some feminists.

Such feminists argue that pornography, by which they mean sexually explicit representations in general, including those of behaviors often seen as deviant (e.g., sadomasochism), has a useful role in enhancing the sexual freedom and pleasure of women whose sexuality has too often been suppressed or molded into acceptable and oppressive forms by patriarchy (Carole Vance, 1984; Ann Snitow, Christine Stansell, & Sharon Thompson, 1983). Many "pro-sex" feminists say that antipornography feminists speak of sex only in terms of victimization and thereby deny women's pleasure in sex and sexual depictions. They argue that antipornography theory is grounded in the patriarchal construct of good girl–bad girl, which denied "good" women access to sexual pleasure (Ellen Willis, 1983). In *Women Against Censorship* (Varda Burstyn, 1985), nine North American feminists argue against the basic feminist antipornography position. For example, Lisa Duggan, Nan Hunter, and Carole Vance (1985) gather specific arguments against the Dworkin/MacKinnon bill: it would trust the patriarchal state to enforce feminist objectives; its criteria are too vague; it assumes that sexuality is only a realm of victimization for women. R. Amy Ellman (1989) disagrees; drawing on the lesson of the Holocaust, she shows how the Nazis systematically withdrew civil rights from Jews and argues that women must demand redress from the state or become ever more vulnerable.

A number of discussions of "the feminist sexuality debates" appeared in a forum in the U.S. journal, *Signs*. Ann Ferguson (1984) calls for the adoption of a transitional feminist sexual morality, while urging feminists to continue to explore the dimensions of a feminist erotica as well as all the various dimensions of sexual equalization: race, class, parent–child, and kinship–friendship networks. Carole Vance and Ann Snitow (1984) argue that antipornography feminists conflate pornography with violent pornography, privilege explicit sexual representations as the most effective conveyors of misogyny, inaccurately see sex as the "root cause of gender oppression," and neglect an exploration of female sexuality in its diversity.

A related debate also arose among feminists in the 1980s over the practice of sadomasochism. Groups such as Samois and spokeswomen such as Pat Califia argued in favor of lesbian sadomasochism as a valid and liberating form of sexuality (Samois, 1981). Others argued that sadomasochistic sex ineluctably stemmed from patriarchy's eroticization of dominance and submission as well as its construction of male subjecthood and female objectification, and was utterly opposed to feminist values (Deborah Cameron & Elizabeth Fraser, 1987; R. R. Linden, D. R. Pagano, & Diana E. H. Russell, 1990).

Another related debate concerns the role of sex trade workers. Several recent works reject some feminist definitions that see sex trade workers only as "victims," and not as women who sometimes choose this work. There are many different positions among sex

trade workers as represented by the various organizations such as COYOTE, US PROS-
titutes, and WHISPER (Frédérique Delacoste & Priscilla Alexander, 1987). Some of these
include a criticism of dominant feminist attitudes toward prostitution as reflecting variously: middle-class morality, reflecting again a division between "good girls" and "bad
girls"; racism, because although the majority of sex trade workers are white, those most
vulnerable to police harassment and crimes against them are women of color; and a lack
of class consciousness in understanding the economic reasons for prostitution (Laurie Bell,
1987; Frédérique Delacoste & Priscilla Alexander, 1987). Toby Summer (1987) is a former
prostitute who argues that prostitution is a form of female slavery and the "ultimate
systematic expression of male supremacy" (p. 42). Internationally, feminist movements in
Japan, Thailand, and the Philippines among other nations have organized against racist and
sexist exploitation of women as prostitutes (Kathleen Barry, Charlotte Bunch, & Shirley
Castley, 1984; Miranda Davies, 1987).

CONCLUSION

There can be little doubt that consciousness raising around issues of sexual violence has
made a significant difference in academic pursuits. Such investigations are necessarily
multidisciplinary, encompassing the social sciences, jurisprudence, the humanities and
sciences. Particularly in the social sciences a radical reorganization of research interests and
goals has occurred; major scholars, both female and male, now define their expertise in
some area related to sexual violence.

Feminist theory and activism around issues of sexual violence have enabled women to
break the silence surrounding subjects like rape and incest, has lessened our shame and guilt
about being abused, has provided networks of mutual support and resources (shelters, crisis
centers), and achieved law reform in various areas (Jennifer Temkin, 1986). Laws concerning domestic abuse in some U.S. states have been rewritten and now are much more
effective in protecting abused women (M'liss Switzer and Katharine Hale, 1987); only six
U.S. states remain in which marital rape is not a crime. Twenty years of feminist activism
has resulted in the creation of many organizations designed to help individual women,
lobby for legal reform, raise consciousness, and further feminist research, including: WHIS-
PER (Women Hurt in Systems of Prostitution Engaged in Revolt); US PROS (United States
Prostitutes Collective); VOICES (Victims of Incest Can Emerge Survivors); the National
Coalition Against Domestic Violence; the National Clearinghouse on Marital Rape; the
Gabriela Network; Sisters in Support Across the Pacific, and, in Los Angeles, the Black
Coalition Fighting Back Serial Murder. Rape crisis centers and battered women shelters
now frequently are found in major cities. Laws concerning domestic abuse in some U.S.
states have been rewritten and now are much more effective in protecting abused women
(Switzer & Hale, 1987). [See Jocelyn Scutt, this volume, for further discussion on violence
and law.] Feminist consciousness informs popular U.S. media productions, to name only
two: *The Burning Bed* (a 1984 made-for-TV movie about an abused wife who kills her
batterer) and the 1988 Hollywood film *The Accused* (about gang rape). Feminist novels with
themes of outrage against violence against women, such as Alice Walker's award-winning
The Color Purple (1982), have reached immense audiences.

Feminist researchers and writers continue to delve more deeply into the histories of
various forms of sexual abuse (Elizabeth Pleck, 1987) and to direct attention to derivative
forms such as lesbian battering (Kerry Lobel, 1986). Recent research confirms the incidence
of date and/or acquaintance rape as the most frequently committed form of rape in the
United States (Robin Warshaw, 1988). Other feminist writers investigate survival strategies

(Pauline Bart & Patrician O'Brien, 1985) or tell inspirational and educational narratives of successful resistance (Emily Culpepper, 1985; Ginny NiCarthy, 1987). Another recent development is the production of guidebooks to assist women in the process of healing from various forms of sexual abuse (Ellen Bass & Laura Davis, 1988).

We must continue to network and to forge international ties, with Western women continuing to acknowledge indigenous women's leadership and to analyze how racist and imperialistic domination furthers sexual exploitation. Violence against women in non-Western countries is a focus for increasing activism. *Sisterhood is Global* (Robin Morgan, 1984) covers 70 countries and offers statistics on and discussion of rape, incest, sexual harassment, battery, prostitution, and "those practices specifically aimed at and injurious to women" (p. xxi). Morgan notes that frequently no data could be found, for "these are still the 'unspeakable issues' in most parts of the globe. As long as they remain unspoken and unresearched an enormous amount of human suffering will continue to go unacknowledged and unhealed" (p. xxiii). This, precisely, is the continuing task of the international feminist movement against violence against women: to acknowledge and to heal.

BIBLIOGRAPHY

African Women for Research and Development. (1983). A statement on genital mutilation. In Miranda Davies (Ed.), *Third world/second sex*: Vol. 1 (pp. 217–220), London: Zed Books.

Albin, Rochelle. (1977). Psychological studies of rape. *Signs: Journal of Women in Culture and Society, 3*, 423–435.

Allen, Paula Gunn. (1990, July). Violence and the American Indian woman. *Common ground— different planes: The Women of Color Partnership Program Newsletter*, pp. 4, 7, 14–15.

Amir, Menachem. (1971). *Patterns in forcible rape*. Chicago: University of Chicago Press.

Armstrong, Louise. (1978). *Kiss daddy goodnight*. New York: Pocket Books.

Attorney General's Commission on Pornography, Final Report. (1986, July). Washington, DC: U.S. Department of Justice.

Barry, Kathleen. (1979). *Female sexual slavery*. Englewood Cliffs, NJ: Prentice-Hall.

Barry, Kathleen, Bunch, Charlotte, & Castley, Shirley. (1984). *International feminism: Networking against female sexual slavery/report of the global feminist workshop to organize against traffic in women, Rotterdam, the Netherlands, April 6–15, 1983*. New York: International Women's Tribune Center.

Bart, Pauline. (1979). Rape as a paradigm of sexism in society—Victimization and its discontents. *Women's Studies International Quarterly, 2*, 347–357.

Bart, Pauline, & O'Brien, Patricia. (1985). *Stopping rape: Successful survival strategies*. Elmsford, NY: Pergamon Press.

Bass, Ellen, & Davis, Laura. (1988). *The courage to heal: A guide for women survivors of sexual abuse*. New York: Harper & Row.

Bell, Laurie. (1987). *Good girls/bad girls: Feminists and sex trade workers face to face*. Seattle, WA: Seal Press.

Bograd, Michele. (1988). Feminist perspectives on wife abuse: An introduction. In Kersti Yllö & Michele Bograd (Eds.), *Feminist Perspectives on Wife Abuse* (pp. 11–27) Beverly Hills, CA: Sage.

Brady, Kathleen. (1979). *Father's days: A true story of incest*. New York: Dell.

Breines, Wini, & Gordon, Linda. (1983). The new scholarship on family violence. *Signs: Journal of Women in Culture and Society, 8*, 490–531.

Brownmiller, Susan. (1975). *Against our will: Men, women and rape*. New York: Simon & Schuster.

Burstyn, Varda. (1985). *Women against censorship*. Vancouver: Douglas & McIntyre.

Burt, Martha. (1980). Cultural myths and supports for rape. *Journal of Personality and Social Psychology, 38*(2), 217–230.

Cameron, Deborah, & Frazer, Elizabeth. (1987). *The lust to kill: A feminist investigation of sexual murder*. New York: New York University Press.

Caputi, Jane. (1987). *The age of sex crime*. Bowling Green, OH: Bowling Green State University Press.

Chapman, Jane Roberts, & Gates, Margaret (Eds.). (1978). *The victimization of women*. Beverly Hills, CA: Sage.

Collard, Andrée with Contrucci, Joyce. (1988). *The rape of the wild: Man's violence against animals and the earth*. London: The Women's Press.

Corea, Gena. (1985a). *The hidden malpractice: How American medicine mistreats women*. New York: Harper & Row. (Original edition published 1977.)

Corea, Gena. (1985b). *The mother machine: Reproductive technologies from artificial insemination to artificial wombs*. New York: Harper & Row.

Crewdson, John. (1988). *By silence betrayed: Sexual abuse of children in America*. Boston: Little Brown.

Culpepper, Emily. (1986). Ancient gorgons: A face for contemporary women's rage. *Women of Power, 3*, 22–24, 40.

Daly, Mary. (1978). *Gyn/Ecology: The metaethics of radical feminism*. Boston: Beacon Press.

Daly, Mary. (1984). *Pure lust: Elemental feminist philosophy*. Boston: Beacon Press.

Davies, Miranda (Ed.). (1983). *Third world/second sex*: Vol. 1. London: Zed Books.

Davies, Miranda (Ed.). (1987). *Third world/second sex*: Vol. 2. London: Zed Books.

Davies, Angela Y. (1981). *Women, race and class*. New York: Random House.

Davis, Angela Y. (1985). *Violence against women and the ongoing challenge to racism*. Latham, NY: Kitchen Table/Women of Color Press.

Davis, Angela Y. (1989). *Women, culture, and politics*. New York: Random House.

d'Eaubonne, Françoise. (1974). *Le feminisme ou la mort* [Feminism or death]. Paris: Pierre Horay.

Delacoste, Frédérique, & Newman, Felice (Eds.). (1981). *Fight back: Feminist resistance to male violence*. Minneapolis, MN: Cleis Press.

Delacoste, Frédérique, & Alexander, Priscilla (Eds.). (1987). *Sex work: Writings by women in the sex industry*. Pittsburgh, PA: Cleis Press.

Diamond, Irene. (1980). Pornography and repression: A reconsideration of "who" and "what." In Laura Lederer (Ed.), *Take back the night: Women on Pornography* (pp. 187–203). New York: William Morrow.

Diamond, Irene, & Quinby, Lee. (1984). American feminism in the age of the body. *Signs: Journal of Women in Culture and Society, 10*, 119–125.

Diamond, Irene, & Quinby, Lee. (1988). American feminism and the language of control. In Irene Diamond & Lee Quinby (Eds.), *Feminism and Foucault: Reflections on resistance* (pp. 193–206). Boston: Northeastern University Press.

Dobash, R. Emerson, & Dobash, Russell P. (1979). *Violence against wives: A case against the patriarchy*. New York: Free Press.

Donnerstein, Edward, Linz, Daniel, & Penrod, Steven (Eds.). (1987). *The question of pornography: Research findings and policy implications*. New York: Free Press.

Duggan, Lisa, Hunter, Nan, & Vance, Carole. (1985). False promises: Feminist antipornography legislation in the U.S. In Varda Burstyn (Ed.), *Women against censorship* (pp. 130–151). Vancouver: Douglas & McIntyre.

Dworkin, Andrea (1976). Remembering the witches. In *Our blood: prophecies and discourses on sexual politics* (pp. 15–21). New York: Harper & Row.

Dworkin, Andrea. (1981). *Pornography: Men possessing women*. New York: Perigee.

Dworkin, Andrea. (1985). Censorship, pornography, and equality. *Trivia: A Journal of Ideas 7*, 11–29. (Originally published in the *Harvard Women's Law Journal, 8*.)

Dworkin, Andrea, & MacKinnon, Catharine A. (1988). *Pornography and civil rights: A new day for women's equality*. Minneapolis, MN: Organizing Against Pornography.

Edwards, Anne. (1987). Male violence in feminist theory: An analysis of the changing conceptions of sex/gender violence and male dominance. In Jalna Hanmer & Mary Maynard (Eds.), *Women, violence and social control* (pp. 13–29). Atlantic Highlands, NJ: Humanities Press International.

El Dareer, Asma. (1982). *Woman, why do you weep? Circumcision and its consequences*. London: Zed Press.

Ellman, R. Amy. (1981). Sexual subordination and state intervention: Lessons for feminists from the Nazi state. *Trivia: A Journal of Ideas, 15*, 50–64.

El Saadawi, Nawal. (1980). *The hidden face of Eve: Women in the Arab world*. London: Zed Press.

Ferguson, Ann. (1984). Sex war: The debate between radical and libertarian feminists. *Signs: Journal of Women in Culture and Society, 10*, 106–112.

Finkelhor, David. (1979). *Sexually victimized children*. New York: Free Press.

Finkelhor, David. (1984). *Child sexual abuse: New theory and research*. New York: Free Press.

Finkelhor, David, & Russell, Diana E. H. (1984). Women as perpetrators. In David Finkelhor, *Child sexual abuse: New theory and research* (pp. 171–185). New York: Free Press.

Gevins, Adi. (1987). Tackling tradition: African women speak out against female circumcision. In Miranda Davies (Ed.), *Third world/second sex* Vol. 2. (pp. 244–249). London: Zed Books.

Griffin, Susan. (1971, September). Rape: The all-American Crime. *Ramparts*, 226–235. Reprinted in Susan Griffin, (1979, 1986). *Rape: The power of consciousness* (pp. 3–24). San Francisco: Harper & Row.

Griffin, Susan. (1978). *Woman and nature: The roaring inside her*. New York: Harper & Row.

Griffin, Susan. (1981). *Pornography and silence: Culture's revenge against nature*. New York: Harper & Row.

Hanmer, Jalna, & Maynard, Mary (Eds.). (1987). *Women, violence and social control*. Atlantic Highlands, NJ: Humanities Press International.

Heise, Lori. (1989, March/April). Crimes of gender. *World-Watch*, 12–21.

Herman, Judith, with Hirschman, Lisa. (1981). *Father-daughter incest*. Cambridge, MA: Harvard University Press.

Hoff, Lee Ann. (1988). Collaborative feminist research and the myth of objectivity. In Kersti Yllö & Michele Bograd (Eds.), *Feminist perspectives on wife abuse* (pp. 269–281). Beverly Hills, CA: Sage.

hooks, bell. (1981). *Ain't I a woman: Black women and feminism*. Boston: South End Press.

Island, S. & Begum, J. (1985). *Women: Victims of violence, 1975–1984*. Dhaka: BRAC Printers.

Jordan, June. (1981). Against the wall. In *Civil wars* (pp. 147–149). Boston: Beacon Press.

Kappeler, Susanne. (1986). *The pornography of representation*. Minneapolis: University of Minnesota Press.

Kendrick, Walter. (1987). *The secret museum: Pornography in modern culture*. New York: Viking.

Koso-Thomas, Olayinka. (1987). *The circumcision of women: A strategy for eradication*. London: Zed Books.

Lederer, Laura (Ed.). (1980). *Take back the night: Women on pornography*. New York: William Morrow.

Linden, R. R., Pagano, D. R., & Russell, Diana E. H. (Eds.). (1982). *Against sadomasochism: A radical feminist analysis*. San Francisco: Frog in the Well.

Lobel, Kerry (Ed.). (1986). *Naming the violence: speaking out about lesbian battering*. Seattle, WA: Seal Press.

Longino, Helen. (1980). Pornography, oppression, and freedom: A closer look. In Laura Lederer (Ed.), *Take back the night: Women on Pornography* (pp. 40–54). New York: William Morrow.

Lovelace, Linda, & McGrady, Mike. (1980). *Ordeal*. Secaucus, NJ: Citadel Press.

MacKinnon, Catharine A. (1979). *Sexual harassment of working women*. New Haven, CT: Yale University Press.

MacKinnon, Catharine, A. (1982). Feminism, Marxism, method and the state: An agenda for theory. *Signs: Journal of Women in Culture and Society, 7*, 515–544.

MacKinnon, Catharine A. (1983). Feminism, Marxism, method and the state: Toward feminist jurisprudence. *Signs: Journal of Women in Culture and Society, 8*, 635–658.

MacKinnon, Catharine A. (1987). *Feminism unmodified: Discourses on life and law*. Cambridge, MA: Harvard University Press.

Malamuth, Neil, & Donnerstein, Edward (Eds.). (1984). *Pornography and sexual aggression*. Orlando, FL: Academic Press.

Martin, Del. (1976). *Battered wives*. San Francisco: Glide.

Mehrhof, Barbara, & Kearon, Pamela. (1973). Rape: An act of terror. In A. Koedt, E. Levine, & A. Rapone, (Eds.), *Radical feminism* (pp. 228–233). New York: Quadrangle/The New York Times Book Co.

Merchant, Carolyn. (1980). *The death of nature: Women, ecology and the scientific revolution*. San Francisco: Harper & Row.

Millett, Kate. (1970). *Sexual politics*. New York: Ballantine Books. (Original edition published 1969.)

Morgan, Robin (Ed.). (1984). *Sisterhood is global: The international women's movement anthology*. New York: Anchor Press, Doubleday.

NiCarthy, Ginny. (1987). *The ones who got away: Women who left abusive partners*. Seattle, WA: Seal Press.

Omolade, Barbara. (1985). Black women and feminism. In Hester Eisenstein and Alice Jardine (Eds.), *The future of difference* (pp. 247–257). New Brunswick, NJ: Rutgers University Press.

Pleck, Elizabeth. (1987). *Domestic tyranny: The making of American social policy against family violence from colonial times to the present*. New York: Oxford University Press.

Powers, Marla N. (1986). *Oglala women: Myth, ritual, and reality*. Chicago: University of Chicago Press.

Rich, Adrienne. (1980). Compulsory heterosexuality and lesbian existence. *Signs: Journal of Women in Culture and Society, 5*, 631–660.

Rush, Florence. (1980). *The best kept secret: Sexual abuse of children*. Englewood Cliffs, NJ: Prentice-Hall.

Russell, Diana E. H. (1974). *The politics of rape: The victim's perspective*. New York: Stein & Day.

Russell, Diana E. H. (1984). *Sexual exploitation: Rape, child sexual abuse, and workplace harassment*. Beverly Hills, CA: Sage.

Russell, Diana E. H. (1986). *The secret trauma: Incest in the lives of girls and women*. New York: Basic Books.

Russell, Diana E. H. (1988). Pornography and rape: A causal model. *Political Psychology, 9*, 41–73.

Russell, Diana E. H. (Ed.). (1989). *Exposing nuclear phallacies*. Elmsford, NY: Pergamon Press.

Russell, Diana E. H. (1990). *Rape in marriage*. Bloomington: Indiana University Press. (Original edition published 1982.)

Russell, Diana E. H., & Van de Ven, Nicole (Eds.). (1976). *Crimes against women: The proceedings of the international tribunal*. Millbrae, CA: Les Femmes.

Russo, Ann. (1987). Conflicts and contradictions among feminists over issues of pornography and sexual freedom. *Women's Studies International Forum, 10*, 103–112.

Samois (Ed.). (1981). *Coming to power: Writings and graphics on lesbian s/m*. Palo Alto, CA: Up Press.

Sanday, Peggy Reeves. (1990). *Fraternity gang rape: Sex, brotherhood, and privilege on campus*. New York: New York University Press.

Shiva, Vandana. (1988). *Staying alive: Women, ecology and survival in India*. London: Zed Books.

Smith, Barbara. (1981). Introduction to "twelve black women: Why did they die?" by the Combahee River Collective. In Frédérique Delacoste & Felice Newman (Eds.), *Fight back: Feminist resistance to male violence* (pp. 67–70). Minneapolis, MN: Cleis Press.

Snitow, Ann, Stansell, Christine, & Thompson, Sharon (Eds.). (1983). *Powers of desire: The politics of sexuality*. New York: Monthly Review Press.

Stanko, Elizabeth A. (1985). *Intimate intrusions: Women's experience of male violence*. London: Routledge & Kegan Paul.

Stanko, Elizabeth A. (1988). Fear of crime and the myth of the safe home: A feminist critique of criminology. In Kersti Yllö and Michele Bograd (Eds.), *Feminist perspectives on wife abuse* (pp. 75–89). Beverly Hills, CA: Sage.

Summer, Toby. (1987, Summer). Women, lesbians and prostitution: A workinglcass dyke speaks out against buying women for sex. *Lesbian Ethics, 2*(3), 33–44.

Sunday, Suzanne R., & Tobach, Ethel. (1985). *Violence against women: A critique of the sociobiology of rape.* New York: Gordian Press.

Switzer, M'liss, & Hale, Katherine. (1987). *Called to account: The story of one family's struggle to say no to abuse.* Seattle, WA: Seal Press.

Temkin, Jennifer. (1986). Women, rape, and law reform. In Sylvana Tomasello & Roy Porter (Eds.), *Rape* (pp. 1–15). Oxford: Basil Blackwell.

Thornhill, Randy, Thornhill, Nancy, & Dizinno, Gerard. (1986). The biology of rape. In Sylvana Tomasello & Roy Porter (Eds.), *Rape* (pp. 102–121). Oxford: Basil Blackwell.

Vance, Carol (Ed.). (1984). *Pleasure and danger: Exploring female sexuality.* Boston: Routledge & Kegan Paul.

Vance, Carole, & Snitow, Ann. (1984). Toward a conversation about sex in feminism: A modest proposal. *Signs: Journal of Women in Culture and Society, 10*, 126–135.

Walker, Alice. (1982). *The color purple.* New York: Harcourt Brace Jovanovich.

Walker, Alice. (1988). *Living by the word: selected writings, 1973–87.* San Diego: Harcourt Brace Jovanovich.

Wardell, Laurie, Gillespie, Dair L., & Leffler, Ann. (1983). Science and violence against wives. In David Finkelhor & Richard Gelles (Eds.), *The dark side of families: Current family violence research* (pp. 69–84). Beverly Hills, CA: Sage.

Warshaw, Robin. (1988). *I never called it rape.* New York: Harper & Row.

Willis, Ellen. (1984). Feminism, moralism, and pornography. In Ann Snitow, Christine Stansell, & Sharon Thompson (Eds.), *Powers of desire: The Politics of Sexuality* (pp. 460–467). New York: Monthly Review Press.

Yllö, Kersti, & Bograd, Michele (Eds.). (1988). *Feminist perspectives on wife abuse.* Beverly Hills, CA: Sage.

Chapter 31

Originality and Creativity
Rituals of Inclusion and Exclusion

Berenice A. Carroll

DEFINING THE ISSUES

"This anthology . . . shows [Jane Addams] as theorist and intellectual—a thinker of originality and daring."

Christoper Lasch, *The Social Thought of Jane Addams* (1965).

"Jane Addams was not an original thinker of major importance. One can find predecessors for almost every one of her ideas. . . . Her importance was not as a manufacturer of ideas, but as their retailer."

Daniel Levine, *Jane Addams and the Liberal Tradition* (1971).

Among the various techniques of depreciation and dismissal of the work of women as intellectuals and scholars, one of the most effective has been denial of its "originality." Affirmations such as the first quotation above about Jane Addams are rare, often ambivalent, and almost always ephemeral, readily dismissed, as in the second quotation, by repressive negations.

Upon close examination, terms such as "original," "innovative," "creative," "unoriginal," "derivative," and so forth are found to be as slippery and insubstantial as are the more generalized stamps of approval such as "excellent," "brilliant," or "first rate." All these terms are essentially barren of substantive meaning and are used with a political rather than an intellectual purpose: to draw invidious distinctions among people and creations, to rationalize and justify a system of rank, privilege, rewards, and control of knowledge. (For further discussion of these points, see Carroll, 1990.)

Twenty years ago women's intellectual works (particularly women's contributions to social and political theory) were so widely dismissed or ignored in the malestream canons as unimportant or nonexistent that the question of their "originality" hardly rose to the surface. Early efforts to recover women's history often accepted uncritically the negative judgments of the malestream elites on women's intellectual work. Thus, for example, the treatment of women intellectuals and scholars in *Notable American Women* (James & James, 1971) was marred by many depreciatory remarks on the "superficial," "constricted," or "derivative" character of their work or on a given writer's generally inferior stature as "not one of the first rank" (see Berenice A. Carroll, 1981, 1990; Dale Spender, 1982, pp. 20–21).

These concepts have been used as weapons of control both in critical scholarship and in academic employment. The intellectual and academic elites have used "originality" to protect their own hegemony and exclude almost all women, as well as most men, from the dominant arenas of discourse, publication, and authority. The same techniques of depreciation used in allegedly scholarly assessments of women's work in literary and historical criticism are used also to exclude women from the ranks of tenured faculty or deny them other rewards and privileges of academic or intellectual professions. [See Mary Ellen Capek, this volume.]

For example, in a recent sex discrimination case (unusual mainly in that it was won by the plaintiff, Kathryn Gutzwiller), documents and testimony at the trial showed that her work had been evaluated as "competent, lucid, in full control of pertinent bibliography, and thorough, but neither creative nor original." The evidence also showed that the author of these judgments had "*not even read* Gutzwiller's manuscript at the time that he informed her" that it "wasn't rich enough or productive enough" to warrant granting her tenure, and that the majority of the professors who voted against her tenure had never read any significant part of her publications (*Gutzwiller v. Fenik*, 1988, pp. 8, 15, 18).

The issues that call for examination here are: First, is there any valid substantive meaning of such terms as "original" or "creative" in this context or are they exclusively empty terms conveying only invidious distinction? Second, to what extent have the repressive uses of these terms obscured the true history and current significance of women's political and social theory? [See Jane Lewis, this volume.] Third, are there alternative conceptions of creativity and value in works of art, science, and intellect that may help to open the way for a serious reconstruction and reassessment of women's theoretical contributions, and for a more democratic concept of "originality" in general? [See Autumn Stanley, this volume.]

TRACINGS

Like all ideas and debates, ideas and debates about "originality" can be traced back for generations and centuries to various forerunners.

The desire to recover and defend the intellectual originality of women dates back at least as far as the elevation in value of "new discoveries" over ancient authority that took place in Renaissance Europe. Christine de Pizan, in *The City of Ladies* (1405), asks Lady Reason to tell of women who "have themselves discovered any new arts and sciences which . . . had hitherto not been discovered or known. For it is not such a great feat of mastery to study and learn some field of knowledge already discovered by someone else as it is to discover by oneself some new and unknown thing" (Christine de Pizan, 1982, pp. 70–71). Similarly, Matilda Joslyn Gage, in the *History of Woman Suffrage*, calls attention to a number of "firsts" among the contributions of women to learning and ideas. For example, of Mercy Otis Warren, Gage wrote: "She was the first one who based the struggle [for independence] upon 'inherent rights,' . . . She was the first person who counseled separation and pressed those views upon John Adams . . . " (Matilda Joslyn Gage, 1978 [1881], p. 57; see also Dale Spender, 1982, pp. 226–252). But here Christine and Matilda Gage accept the notion of "originality" (though they do not use the term), and neither Christine nor her successors in recurrent similar efforts sought to challenge its validity as a criterion of intellectual accomplishment.

At the beginning of the 1970s I became interested in the work of Mary Ritter Beard, in the neglect of her work, and in the evidence in *Woman as Force in History* of a long history of leading women *intellectuals* of whom I had been totally ignorant, despite my doctorate in history (Mary Ritter Beard, 1946; Berenice A. Carroll, 1972).[1] In 1974 I began to teach a course on "Social and Political Thought of Women," and encountered repeatedly, in the limited biographical and critical literature available, the ritual dismissals or depreciatory remarks noted above. In the course of my efforts to explore the problems of recovering and reassessing the contributions of women intellectuals, the need to examine the concept of "originality" itself emerged as increasingly urgent.[2]

Critical analysis of the concept of originality itself dates back at least to the early twentieth century, in the writings of perplexed but fundamentally reverent forefathers, such as William Ogburn, Edwin Boring and Robert Merton (Edwin G. Boring, 1927; Robert K. Merton, 1957, 1965; William Ogburn & Dorothy Thomas, 1922) or of irreverent fore-mothers, such as Mary Parker Follett and Céline Renooz (Mary Parker Follett, 1920; Céline Renooz, 1924; for discussion, see Berenice A. Carroll, 1990). In the past 30 years, the general literature on "originality" or "creativity" has grown substantially. This literature includes some critical examination of the modern preference for "originality" (mainly to be found in literary studies), and of the nature and sources of "creativity" (more to be found in psychology, sociology, education, and fine arts).

But there is hardly any recognition of the functions of these concepts in maintaining a class system of the intellect. There has been little consciousness of the systematic use of such terms to devalue women's work, and little explicit "debate," in the form of sustained discourse over time. The subject is certainly not a regular item on the agenda of any discipline. Questions raised from time to time seem to have fallen back and disappeared in dark seas of nonresponse.

OLD CANARDS AND RESPONSES

In the late 1960s and early 1970s, debate revolved around the old canards: "Where are the female geniuses?" or "Why are there no great women artists?" (Linda Nochlin, 1971). Feminists were conscious of the repressive effects of stereotypes, citing for instance the comment of a University of Chicago professor: "We expect women who come here to be competent, good students but we don't expect them to be brilliant or original" (Robin Morgan, 1970, p. 101), or the widespread notion that "men create culture and women transmit it" (Gaye Tuchman, 1975, p. 171).

Feminists have dealt with these questions and stereotypes in a number of different ways, all implicit in the slogans of the women's liberation activists who proclaimed: "Our history has been stolen from us . . . !" At first they protested that "our geniuses were never taught to read and write," but soon went on to discover that "many of our geniuses were edu-cated—and indeed created much literature and knowledge" (Ann Forfreedom, 1972, p. 205).

One response was implied by the assertion: "Our geniuses were never taught to read and write." This concedes implicitly, as Gaye Tuchman later wrote explicitly, that "women have *not* been frequent creators of culture." Tuchman argued that women "played roles central to the institutional production of culture in specific historical periods," but too readily granted that women had not been "creators" of culture in the conventional sense of authorship or origination (Gaye Tuchman, 1975, p. 191).

A second response, more in the tradition of Christine and Matilda Gage, was to seek out women authors and challenge the male-centered standards for judgment of what was of substantive interest or importance ("technological mode" rather than "aesthetic mode;" "public" rather than "domestic" affairs; "great men" rather than "little women;" "the state" or "class struggle" rather than "personal relations;" etc.). This response led to the great flowering of research into the history of women's literature and art as well as the history of feminism and feminist theory that we have witnessed in women's studies over the past two decades.

A third response was to analyze and confront the techniques used in the suppression or appropriation of women's work, affirming that "our history has been stolen from us" and enumerating the tools of the theft, as in Joanna Russ' *How to Suppress Women's Writing*: "She didn't write it. . . . She wrote it, but look what she wrote about. . . . She wrote it, but she had help . . . " (Joanna Russ, 1983; see Dale Spender, 1982, 1989).

Yet in all these responses, the inherent validity of criteria of judgment such as "originality" and "creativity" was rarely called into question.

In the area of social and political theory, the prevailing belief was that women had made no major "original" contributions such that they would be worthy of inclusion, for example, in texts and anthologies for courses in the history of political philosophy or political theory. This view was (and remains) so widespread that it is hardly possible to single out any particular male authorities as more responsible for it than others. Publishers continue today to send out brochures advertising collections of "masters of political theory" and "texts in the history of political thought" (sometimes authored by women) that feature exclusively male theorists.

The extent of change in the malestream literature has been limited to token representation of women theorists in a number of recent anthologies and texts. These generally offer no more than one selection by a woman theorist, though Volume 9 (Twentieth Century Europe) of the *University of Chicago Readings in Western Civilization* actually includes four women theorists. The token character of these inclusions tends to reinforce the notion that only a handful of women quality as exceptions to the principle that men, not women, are the authors of great and original ideas.

Even many feminist scholars tend to share the same perspective. Thus for example, the recent call for papers for the conference on "Feminism as Catalyst: Bridging the Discourses of the Sciences, Social Sciences, Arts, and Humanities" lists as one of the issues to be addressed: "Why are there so few women theorists and what difference does that make?" (Graduate Women's Studies Conference, 1988). Though the tradition of feminist theory has elicited a growing literature in women's studies, a general interest in women's contributions and originality as theorists has not yet taken hold.

Indeed, even feminist theory is often presented as implicitly or explicitly "derivative," founded in or arising in response to malestream ideas (e.g., liberal individualism or socialist egalitarianism). Malestream philosophy and theory are often seen as defining the frame of reference, both the background and the foreground, in which feminist theory is situated.

PUZZLING QUESTIONS

Have women in writing political theory directed attention to theories or issues "that men would never dream"? This is difficult, almost impossible to say.

It seems evident that men could not—or would not—ever have developed feminist theory in all its diverse manifestations. Yet men were authors of early and influential feminist tracts, such as Poulain de la Barre's *The Woman as Good as the Man; or, The Equality of Both Sexes* (1677; see Hilda Smith, 1982, pp. 116–117) and John Stuart Mill's *Subjection of Women* (1869; see John Stuart Mill, 1970).

In the context of a discussion of "originality," it seems pertinent to ask: Were such writings "original" to these men, or did some women actually originate them?

We do not know whether Poulain wrote under some woman's influence, but we may well ask whether Mill could ever have written *Subjection of Women* without the influence and ideas of Harriet Taylor Mill and her daughter, Mill's stepdaughter, Helen Taylor (see Alice Rossi, 1970). The answer seems to be that he could not have done so, as he himself attributed many of the ideas and much of the motivation for it to them. But Mill also claimed that his ideas on the equality of the sexes were already well formed when he met Harriet, and were indeed a main point of mutual attraction between them when they met, so perhaps he would have gone on to develop these ideas in any case. Or again, one might argue that the circles from which both John Stuart Mill and Harriet Taylor drew their ideas were influenced by earlier feminist women, for example Mary Wollstonecraft and Catharine Macaulay, and this was why Mill was able to dream such ideas, which otherwise would never come to men.

One could argue this around in circles forever. Yet it seems likely that ideas of liberation for any particular oppressed group, which arise spontaneously among members of that group, can never arise spontaneously in the same terms among the oppressors, though the latter may adopt some of them and be in a better position to propagate them. In this sense, women's feminist ideas have surely posed sharper challenges than men would dream. Whether the same can be said for other arenas of theory is more doubtful.

For example, it can be argued that there is in women's theoretical writings a long standing tradition of rejection of male conceptions of dominance, and a recurrent effort to analyze power in populist terms, or in terms of autonomy (Berenice A. Carroll, 1977, 1978b). However, some men have also challenged hierarchy and even male dominance. Did women learn these ideas from them? Moreover, this tradition is by no means uniform among women theorists, nor wholly consistent even within each woman's writings. There have been women theorists who defend or even exalt hierarchical power. Should we maintain that women learn these ideas only from men? Would this not imply that these ideas are indeed "derivative" or "unoriginal," and only certain ideas propounded by women are to be acknowledged as authentically their own? Is it unthinkable that women might have originated ideas of hierarchy? That men may even have learned them from women?

Indeed, the whole question is wrongly posed if we take seriously the challenge to "originality." There can be no private property in ideas and theories. As Mary Parker Follett wrote in 1918, much of her book, *The New State*, had come to her "by wireless": "What we think we possess as individuals is what is stored up from society, is the subsoil of social life" (Mary Parker Follett, 1920, pp. 12–13, 62). Or as Morroe Berger wrote in 1964 in situating the ideas of Madame de Staël: "Ideas may be traced back infinitely because they emerge out of previous ones and out of a social condition that has its origins in previous ones" (Morroe Berger, 1964, p. 37). No idea or theory is created de novo, out of nothing, nor are the ideas of any person identical with those of any other. No human being may dream things totally undreamed by anyone before, yet each may dream things never before exactly dreamed either by men or women.

ARE NEW METHODS NEEDED?

On the surface, no new methods are necessary to generate the knowledge we need in this area—the methods of historical and critical research and analysis should suffice. However, some new approaches are necessary: in particular, broadening of the parameters of search for inclusion of types of texts and subject matter differing from those traditionally accepted as works of "political theory."

Women, excluded for centuries from the academies, the chambers of law, the divinity schools, and similar institutions, have had fewer opportunities or inducements to learn, practice, and publish in the conventional style of the political treatise. To recover their political thought, therefore, it is necessary to turn more often than for men to other forms of expression: fiction and poetry, letters and essays, diaries and autobiographies, periodical articles, speeches and pamphlets, histories, and even textbooks for the school or the home (Berenice A. Carroll, 1978a). The social and political theory of women of color and poor and working class women around the world must particularly be sought through such alternative sources. Poetry and song have often been important vehicles of political expression, particularly under repressive regimes. Admittedly in such works, theory may be implicit rather than explicit, and the problems of interpretation and assessment are multiplied. Yet such forms of expression have been accepted in the traditional canons when written by men, from Plato's dialogues and Dante's poetry to Montesquieu's letters and Sartre's novels and plays. Thus it is not the forms themselves, but the weight of the double standard, that has excluded women's political writings in "nontraditional" forms.

It might also be argued that an approach adopting a conscious bias in favor of women theorists may be not only justified but necessary in order to identify and assess their works in an *un*biased way. We must bear in mind, in dealing with the intellectual history of women, that we are surrounded by profound, centuries-old biases and stereotypes, and that it requires conscious effort to avoid falling prey either to the biases themselves, or to wasteful defensiveness and uncritical apologetics. In this context, we must struggle to free ourselves of the irrational demand that a woman writer be perfect, or near perfect, judged by contemporary values, before her work is worth studying. Indeed, we surely should forgive our foremothers for errors, tedium, contradictions and other flaws at least as readily as we do the prevailing male idols—and we do forgive these idols much. We must favor women with the presumption that we will find much of value in their works if we accord them the same respect, and examine them as carefully, as often, as patiently, and as intently as we have done for the works of men (Berenice A. Carroll, 1978b, pp. 16–17, 1980). And as Dale Spender argued in *Women of Ideas*: "Treating women as positively intellectual and creative . . . in a society which regards them as negatively intellectual and creative, will no doubt be seen as distortion and bias. This gives me little cause for concern: it gives me considerable satisfaction to believe that patriarchy will not know how to use such knowledge biased in favour of women" (Dale Spender, 1982, p. 22).

To some degree, inattention to women's intellectual contributions as such has been perpetuated by class issues in the women's liberation movement. A certain deemphasis of women intellectuals may be seen as responsive to principles of egalitarianism or to criticisms of elitism in the movement. "Women intellectuals" are seen as a small privileged class, largely isolated from and unrepresentative of the masses of women around the world, whose history and experience stand as a higher priority for many feminist scholars. Restoration and evaluation of the work of women intellectuals often has lower priority or may even seem somewhat suspect. On the other hand, stereotypes based on class have led to solipsistic ignorance or dismissal of the theoretical, literary, and artistic contributions of "ordinary" women as not "intellectual."

In rejecting phallocratic dichotomies of mind and body, public and private, with their correlative subordination of the body and the private, feminist scholars have turned their attention primarily to what has been conceived as the everyday life and experience of ordinary women, with emphasis upon sexuality, reproduction, economic roles and status, domestic relations, and political activism. [See Shulamit Reinharz, Jane Jaquette, and Marilyn Waring, all this volume.] Given the suppression and distortion of knowledge about all these in the past, this is a monumental agenda of indisputably essential research. Yet avoidance of the intellectual components of women's lives reproduces the phallocratic dichotomy: though the absolute supremacy of the mind has been challenged, mind and body are still separate, and mind remains implicitly elite and male.

Thus, there is need for both reassessment of the work of women intellectuals, and recovery of the intellectual contributions of women not ordinarily perceived as intellectual.

THE NEED FOR DEBATE

In a very significant sense, there has been no "debate" at all: there has been hardly any response to the contention that a slippery, unsubstantive concept of "originality" has been used to dismiss women's intellectual work; it has been neither challenged nor taken up as a point of departure for further theory or research. Despite *Women of Ideas* and an extensive literature of other works on feminist theory, most malestream scholars are completely unaware of the issues (some seem to remain as oblivious after reading or hearing them presented in a lecture as before). The general pressure of the women's movement to reduce or eliminate sexism in discourse and treat women's contributions with respect has produced some cautious reassessments of the work of a small number of women theorists and their inclusion in courses, texts, and anthologies (Rosa Luxemburg, Hannah Arendt, and a handful of others). But recognition of women's contributions to social and political theory is still very limited, and despite the current emergence of deconstructionism, deconstructing concepts such as "originality" and their role in maintaining a class system of the intellect has not gained a following.

A critique of "originality" and development of alternative concepts of evaluation, however, is essential to the understanding that women (and nonelite men) have had an intellectual life as rich, as "creative," as filled with innovations in theory, literature and art as the male intellectual oligopoly—indeed more truly "original," innovative and creative as those admitted to the ranks of the intellectual ruling classes are recruited and rewarded on condition of conformity to the ideological assumptions, dogmas, strictures, and "standards" of the ruling elites and of respectful adherence to the ideas and methods of the established "authorities."

Yet to the present, there has not been sufficient attention to the critique of concepts such as "originality," "innovation," "creativity," "excellence," and so forth. As a consequence, even feminist studies continue to devalue women's intellectual contributions. This is true not only of earlier assessments by male scholars such as those quoted at the outset concerning Jane Addams, but also within the arena of current feminist scholarship. One example is to be found in a recent review essay in *Signs*. Deirdre David, commenting on Valerie Sanders' *Reason over Passion: Harriet Martineau and the Victorian Novel* (1986), objects to Sanders' "misplaced focus on innovation and influence." David casts doubt on Martineau's *intellectual* innovations and urges instead a focus on the "innovative achievements of Martineau's *career as a professional woman*," in particular her productivity, her feminist "indictments of the exploitation of women," and her "dazzling ability to assimilate and popularize difficult political ideas" (Deirdre David, 1988, pp. 847–848, emphasis added). Despite the approving adjectives, the message here is basically similar to that of the traditional stereotype: Martineau's importance lay in her career, her feminist advocacy, and her role as a popularizer and persuader, not in any innovative contributions or influence in the realm of theory and intellect.

Fortunately, we encounter such remarks less frequently today, and we may hope that our situation is "two steps forward, one step backward" rather than the reverse. My expectations for the future are at least cautiously hopeful.

The important question remains: What more substantive criteria of evaluation of in-

360 Berenice A. Carroll

tellectual and artistic work can be developed to clarify, democratize, or replace "originality" and its entire brotherhood of ritual exclusionary concepts?

NOTES

1. This experience, which Dale Spender calls "Why didn't I know?," seems to be a recurrent one for many women intellectuals, even today, on discovering that their *ideas*, as well as their struggles, have a history in the *writings* of women whose works have been ignored. Spender cites the similar reaction of Mary Daly on reading the work of Matilda Joslyn Gage (Dale Spender, 1982, pp. 3–13, 227).

2. In June 1981, I presented a paper on "The Politics of 'Originality': Women Scholars and Intellectuals" at the Berkshire conference on women's history at Vassar College. Some of the key points of the 1981 paper were noted by Dale Spender in *Women of Ideas: And What Men Have Done to Them* (1982, pp. 20–21, 25). Spender's volume also provides many other examples of the depreciation and dismissal of women's intellectual works. Other versions of my paper were presented in subsequent years, and it was published under the title "The Politics of 'Originality': Women and the Class System of the Intellect" in the *Journal of Women's History* in Fall 1990 (Berenice A. Carroll, 1990).

BIBLIOGRAPHY

Beard, Mary Ritter. (1946). *Woman as force in history*. New York: Macmillan.
Berger, Morroe (Ed.). (1964). *Madame de Staël on literature, politics, and national character*. London: Sidgewick & Jackson.
Boring, Edwin G. (1963). The problem of originality in science. Reprinted in *History, psychology, and science: Selected papers*. New York: John Wiley & Sons. (Original work published 1927.)
Carroll, Berenice A. (1972, Winter/Spring). Mary Beard's *Woman as Force in History*: A critique. *Massachusetts Review, 13*, (1/2), 125–143. Reprinted in Berenice A. Carroll (Ed.), *Liberating women's history: Theoretical and critical issues* (pp. 26–41). Urbana, IL: University of Illinois Press.
Carroll, Berenice A. (1976). *Liberating women's history: Theoretical and critical issues*. Urbana, IL: University of Illinois Press.
Carroll, Berenice A. (1977, November). *Women and power: The mind and the matter*. Lecture presented at the International Conference on Women's History, College Park, MD.
Carroll, Berenice A. (1978a, February). 'To crush him in our own country': The political thought of Virginia Woolf. *Feminist Studies, 4*(1), 99–131. (First presented at the Third Berkshire Conference on Women's History, Bryn Mawr, June 1976).
Carroll, Berenice A. (1978b, March). *Women and the American intellectual tradition*. Paper presented at the American Studies Symposium, Purdue University, West Lafayette, IN.
Carroll, Berenice A. (1980, November). *Minerva in the shadows: Women in intellectual history*. Paper presented at the Nineteenth Century Women Writers Conference, Hofstra University.
Carroll, Berenice A. (1981, June). *The politics of 'originality': Women scholars and intellectuals*. Paper presented at the Berkshire Conference on Women's History, Vassar College, Poughkeepsie, NY.
Carroll, Berenice A. (1990, Fall). The politics of 'originality': Women and the class system of the intellect. *Journal of Women's History, 2*(2), 136–163.
David, Deirdre. (1988, Summer). Review of Valerie Sanders, *Reason over passion*, and other works. *Signs: Journal of Women in Culture and Society, 13*(4), 847–848.
Follett, Mary Parker. (1920). *The new state: Group organization, the solution of popular government*. (First published 1918). New York: Longmans, Green.
Forfreedom, Ann. (1972). *Women out of history: A herstory anthology*. Los Angeles, CA: Ann Forfreedom.
Gage, Matilda Joslyn. (1978). Preceding causes. Reprinted in Mari Jo Burke & Paul Buhle (Eds.),

The concise history of woman suffrage. Urbana, IL: University of Illinois Press. (Original work published in 1881.)

Graduate Women's Studies Conference. (1988). Call for participants, conference on Feminism as Catalyst, March 4, 1989. College Park, MD: University of Maryland.

Gutzwiller v. Fenik. (1988). United States Court of Appeals for the Sixth Circuit, Nos. 86-3852/86-3854/86-3916, decided and filed November 1.

James, Edward, & James, Janet (Eds.). (1971). *Notable American women: Vols. 1–3*. Cambridge, MA: Harvard University Press.

Lasch, Christopher. (1965). *The social thought of Jane Addams*. Indianapolis: Bobbs-Merrill.

Levine, Daniel. (1971). *Jane Addams and the liberal tradition*. Madison: State Historical Society of Wisconsin.

Merton, Robert K. (1957, 1962). Priorities in scientific discovery. Presidential address to the American Sociological Association. *American Sociological Review, 22*, 635–659. Reprinted (1962) Bernard Barber and Walter Hirsch (Eds.), *The Sociology of Science*. New York: Free Press.

Merton, Robert K. (1965). *On the shoulders of giants*. New York: Free Press.

Mill, John Stuart. (1970). The subjection of women. In Alice Rossi (Ed.), *Essays on sex equality: John Stuart Mill and Harriet Taylor Mill*. Chicago: University of Chicago Press. (Original work published 1869.)

Morgan, Robin. (1970). *Sisterhood is powerful*. New York: Random House.

Nochlin, Linda. (1971). Why are there no great women artists? In Vivian Gornick & Barbara Moran (Eds.), *Woman in sexist society* (pp. 480–510). New York: Signet.

Ogburn, William, & Thomas, Dorothy. (1922, March). Are inventions inevitable? A note on social evolution. *Political Science Quarterly, 37*(1), 83–98.

Pizan, Christine de. (1982). *The book of the city of ladies* [1405]. New York: Persea Books.

Poulain de la Barre, François. (1677). *The woman as good as the man: Or, the equality of both sexes*. London: Printed by T.M. for N. Brooks.

Renooz, Céline. (1924). Le monde ancien. *L'Ere de Vérité*. (6 vols., 1921–1928), vol. 2. Paris: Marcel Giard.

Rossi, Alice. (Ed.). (1970). *Essays on sex equality: John Stuart Mill and Harriet Taylor Mill*. Chicago: University of Chicago Press.

Russ, Joanna. (1983). *How to suppress women's writing*. Austin, TX: University of Texas Press.

Sanders, Valerie. (1986). *Reason over passion: Harriet Martineau and the Victorian novel*. New York: St. Martin's Press.

Smith, Hilda. (1982). *Reason's disciples: Seventeenth-century English feminists*. Urbana, IL: University of Illinois Press.

Spender, Dale. (1982). *Women of ideas: And what men have done to them*. London: Routledge & Kegan Paul.

Spender, Dale. (1989). *The writing or the sex ? Or why you don't have to read women's writing to know it's no good*. Elmsford, NY: Pergamon Press.

Tuchman, Gaye. (1975). Women and the creation of culture. In Marcia Millman & Rosabeth Moss Kanter (Eds.), *Another voice: Feminist perspectives on social life and social science*. Garden City, NY: Doubleday.

Twentieth Century Europe. (1987). *University of Chicago Readings in Western Civilization*. Vol. 9, Chicago: University of Chicago Press.

Chapter 32

Where Is Women's Knowledge in the Age of Information?

Suzanne K. Damarin

During the past two decades the theory of information and the computer-based application of this theory to numerous disciplines and practices within society has begun to affect both our day-to-day economic and social transactions and the way we do our work. Computers are changing the relationships between students and teachers and between clients and caregivers; they are changing the nature of work and the relationships among workers and management. Scholars and researchers communicate on electronic networks, do their writing on word processors, gather data via computer interface, structure it using data base software, and analyze it using preprogrammed statistical software packages. There are many other examples.

These effects might be viewed as largely practical matters, issues of concern more to users of technology than to the scholarly disciplines. However, these are not the only effects claimed for information and computer technologies. It has become commonplace to hear or read that we have entered "the computer age" or "the information era," that the computer will have effects unparalleled since the invention of movable type (Evans, 1979), that computers are changing "who can know what" (Seymour Papert, 1980), that computers will surpass humans in at least some aspects of intelligence, that computers are the first exoskeletal stage in the continuing (biological) evolution of humanity (R. Jastrow, 1981; Daiyo Sawada, 1985), and that computers, in the form of robots, will soon be coinhabitants of this planet demanding and deserving the same attention to civil rights and moral obligation as other "minority groups" (Heinz Pagels, 1988).

Before simply dismissing these statements as faddish or fanatical it is important to recognize the amount and quality of attention given to them within the groves of academe. Some philosophers in the analytic and post-analytic traditions devote much time and many pages to arguments that the "intelligence" of computers is generally overrated (Hubert L. Dreyfus, 1972, 1979; Hubert L. Dreyfus & Stuart E. Dreyfus, 1986), that computers cannot think (John Searle, 1984), cannot engage in discourse (Hilary Putnam, 1988), and cannot write poetry (William Barrett, 1986). At the same time philosophers of mathematics (Rudy Rucker, 1987) add "information" to number, space, logic, and infinity as the defining topics of mathematics. From the diverse academic fields of history (Theodore Roszak, 1986), computer science (Joseph Weizenbaum, 1976), political science (Langdon Winner, 1977, 1988) and education (C. A. Bowers, 1988; M. J. Streibel, 1986), among others, come

362

critiques of computer application and culture. Meanwhile, poststructuralists argue that theirs is a philosophy unique to the information era, and Sherry Turkle, one of the rare female voices in all of this discussion, argues that the computer provides us with a "sustaining myth" analogous to Freudian psychology in its power to organize our under-standing of ourselves (1988b). Clearly the computer is a "hot topic" and one must ask "where are the voices of women and of feminism in these debates?"

While feminist scholars work arduously to deconstruct, revision, and recreate the disciplines and institutions created by the patriarchal values of the past (and the present), the new "electronic patriarchy" of computer and information technologies is busy creating a future, not only for themselves, but for all of us. The purpose of this essay is to raise a number of issues surrounding the relationships between and among women, feminism, and the rise of computer technology. The first issues addressed are those of how women and feminism have influenced, and can influence, the nature, development, and application of computer technology. The second set of issues concerns the ways in which computer and information technologies are permeating our work, our discourses, our thinking, and our disciplines, and how they affect the lives and status of women.

WOMEN, FEMINISM, AND THE DEVELOPMENT OF COMPUTERS

The written history of the digital computer often begins with the nineteenth century design and partial construction of the Difference Engine and the Analytical Engine; these machines, though never fully operational, were the invention and the passion of the mathematician Charles Babbage. Working closely with Babbage was Countess Ada Augusta Lovelace (1815–1852) an accomplished female mathematician whose genius allowed her, not only to share in Babbage's vision, but to do what he could not, that is, to describe in writing the theory and operation of the machine and, in the process, to extend his ideas. Thus, it is to Lady Ada Augusta that we owe the knowledge of these "engines," knowledge that was later used, first by George Boole in the development of Boolean Algebra, the algebraic basis of all computer operations, and again in the 1940s by the creators of the first modern computers. The modern computer language ADA, used largely for defense department work, is named in honor of this woman.

Unfortunately, this auspicious beginning of true collaboration between male and female mathematicians in the development of computers has not continued. Among the many "stars" in the brief history of this growing field one finds only a few females: Grace Hopper, the inventor of COBOL, the computer language most popular for business applications; Jean Sammet, who influenced the development of both COBOL and ADA, and was also a prolific writer on the history and characteristics of programming languages; and a handful of other women (Lynn M. Osen, 1974; Teri Perl, 1978). Today the use of initials rather than given names in scientific citations tends to hide any contributions of women but it is probably safe to say that no more than 5–6% of coauthors of scientific papers in computer science are female. In the United States approximately 22% of undergraduate students and 10–12% of doctoral students in computer science are female (William K. LeBold, 1987; Betty M. Vetter, 1988). The situation of women in computer science thus replicates the situation of women throughout the sciences (Sandra Harding, 1986), and there is little hope that it will improve in the near future. [See also H. Patricia Hynes, and Marian Lowe, this volume.] Not only are there predictions that the number of new women being trained in these areas will decline (Betty M. Vetter, 1988), but also, without an increase in the ratio of females to males in the graduate student population the intellectual climate and professionals prospects of women students are unlikely to change (Female Graduate Students . . . , 1983). As will be discussed below a handful of those women who have survived the "rites of passage" into computer science are today seeking feminist solutions to some of the problems of women arising from the application of computers.

Although women seem to be scarce at the core of computer science, there are today many more women who are leaders in areas of study which have grown up at the interfaces of computer science with other disciplines. In fields such as cognitive psychology and educational computing one finds that a number of the leadership voices are those of women. However, it should be noted that as computer science grows within these areas the more "respected" and cited work becomes more technical and the "wisdom" of the root fields becomes less valued. Thus, for example, a "state-of-the-art" text on computer-based instruction (Etienne Wenger, 1987) is based almost entirely upon work in artificial intelligence laboratories and makes hardly a bow in the direction of educational psychology or the psychology of individual differences, both relevant fields to which women have made substantial contributions. This situation portends the replication, within these fields, of the "mathematization of engineering" described by Sally Hacker (1983), and with it a general decline in the influence of women.

Another way in which women might influence computing is as historians, interpreters, and social scientists who are respected within the computer science community (e.g., Margaret Boden, 1977; E. A. Feigenbaum & Pamela McCorduck, 1983; Pamela McCorduck, 1979, 1986; Sherry Turkle, 1980, 1984, 1988a, 1988b). Because the work of these writers is more accessible than technical science to the lay reader, scholars from many fields may find their first introduction to computers in the writings of a woman, even as some earlier scientific readers found their first introduction to computer science in the writings of the "Mother of Invention," Ada Augusta, Countess of Lovelace.

It is through the latter writers that any influence of feminism within the broader community of computer-related sciences can be seen. As Rothschild (1986, 1988) points out, the interaction of the individual person with the computer is depicted much differently by Sherry Turkle (1984) than it is by other (male) writers. Not only is Sherry Turkle's description of the classical Turing test (a means of defining artificial intelligence) more faithful to Turing's original description, but her entire approach places a different value on the human being than is accorded by males writing from a more "scientific" perspective.

Similarly, Pamela McCorduck's (1979) placement of computers in historical perspective is different from the typical male analysis. Rather than viewing computers exclusively in the context of developments in mathematics and engineering, she places them within the context of the desire of humans to "play God" and to create beings of more nearly perfect intelligence. Placing the computer in the lineage of the mechanical "gods" created by the ancients, she contrasts those modern attitudes toward the computer which are derived from classical traditions with those derived Judeo-Christian traditions prohibiting graven images. In the conflict between these two traditions she finds the roots of our ambivalence toward the computer.

WOMEN AND AMBIVALENCE
TOWARD THE COMPUTER

The ambivalence of women toward computers may result from more areas of conflict than those identified by McCorduck. The computer is, after all, *a machine* and thus a part of the male domain often prohibited to women. Among the psychological sequellae of these conflicts are the phenomena of "technostress" (Craig Brod, 1984; Walter M. Mathews,

1980) and "computer anxiety." The latter has been studied extensively, especially in schools and colleges, and gender differences have been found frequently. Although some researchers (Betty Collis, 1987; Jan Hawkins, 1987) find a direct link between females' mathematics anxiety and computer anxiety, others attribute females' anxieties, negative attitudes, or general avoidance to the view that the computer is a masculine instrument. Among the more compelling findings of this body of research is the "we can but I can't" phenomenon; many young women opine that women generally are as capable as males at using computers, but feel that they, personally, are not (B. Collins, 1985). The response of many people to these findings of anxiety, especially of educators concerned with issues of gender equity, is to stress (to female students) that computers are different from mathematics and that it is not necessary to understand mathematics to use computers.

Indeed, this is true at many levels; but there is a danger in this argument as well. At the base of their operations, computers *do* have logical procedures which are represented in logico-arithmetic language and forms. The indoctrination of young women to a point of view which separates computers from mathematics (while young men are studying computer science and programming) seems to ring a familiar refrain: "now, don't you go worrying your pretty little head about that." [See also Robin Arianrhod, this volume.] Surely, as the computer intrudes more deeply into more arenas of scholarly activity and social concern we all need to "worry our heads" about the relationships of computer-based procedural representations of information to the knowledge and wisdom of our fields.

Women as Computer Users

Of course, many women do use computers in nonmathematical ways. The larger portion of women's interactions with computers are not in the roles of scientist or scholar, but rather as users of hardware–software systems (such as word processors and automatic bank tellers), as consumers of computer printouts and computer generated messages, as students in computerized classrooms, as victims of office automation, and as participants in a society in which, increasingly, a computer designed to link people together actually stands between them.

It is probably in connection with office automation that the effects of computers on women's lives have been studied most extensively, not one of the findings of these studies is positive. Women who spend their working lives at video display terminals (VDTs) are subject to serious health problems including chronic back pain, visual deterioration, problem pregnancies, and threats to fertility (Mary Sue Henifin, 1984). Thus the computer poses serious threats to the physical health of women workers; there are also threats to psychological well-being. Word processors and data entry clerks work under continual pressure to produce; each press of the keyboard is monitored by the machine itself and an irrefutable minute by minute record of characters entered is maintained; fluctuations in performance can become occasions for negative evaluations.

Not only does this monitoring produce the stress consequent upon continual surveillance; it also creates secondary stresses in the form of moral dilemmas. Because correcting an obvious error in an existing computer record decreases one's productivity rating, it becomes both tempting to let errors slide and necessary to make judgments as to when the magnitude of the error demands a personal risk. As computers are brought into existing office settings, the old modes of operation in which a clerk or secretary saw projects through from start to finish are displaced by the dissemination of projects across several workers; one obvious effect of this dispersal is the loss of pride in completion, or of a job well done. When work is dispersed hierarchically via a computer network, workers become isolated from each other and exiled from those "higher up" who might add incentives and meaning to the task. The work becomes essentially meaningless and repetitive and lacking in any rewards. Computerization tends to increase any existing isolation of workers and is, therefore, especially pernicious in its effects upon Black women who are twice as likely as white women to be assigned to back room data entry positions (Barbara Garson, 1988; Sally Otos and Ellen Levy, 1983; Judith Gregory, 1983; Heidi I. Hartmann, Robert E. Kraut, & Louise A. Tilly, 1986; Anne Machung, 1988; Shashana Zuboff, 1988).

Arguing that women office workers need to organize Gregory (1983) observes that new office technologies create the potential "to upgrade jobs, skills, and earnings, and to raise the overall standards of living" (p. 260). The writings of other analysts, however, suggest that the overall effect of computer technology in the office is to create a division of the workforce into a technological elite and a group assigned trivialized tasks (Maria Bergom-Larsson, 1982). In this analysis women office workers will not qualify for either group; too highly qualified and paid for the lower class group they will find themselves insufficiently trained in technology for the elite group. As Deborah L. Brecher (1985) observes, one cause of underqualification is the creation by computer developers of separate languages for the same concepts as used in computer science and in wordprocessing; this linguistic separation keeps women from knowing how much they do know, and, thus, "in their place." Critical analyses of the application of computer-based technologies to the workplace indicate that these innovations do not enhance the mobility of women (Cynthia Cockburn, 1988). Generally speaking writers concerned with these issues call for the increased technical training of women and observe that the role of mathematical training is both critical and problematic (Suzanne K. Damarin, 1988a).

Although the business office is currently the locus of the most direct and the deepest intrusion of computers into the lives and work of women, it is not the only area of concern. Computers are increasingly common in the social service areas (Barbara Garson, 1988) where they separate clients from professionals. Educational computing at precollege levels is increasing and with it comes a number of serious problems (C. A. Bowers, 1988; Suzanne K. Damarin, 1988a, 1989b; Jim Ridgeway, 1988; Douglas Sloan, 1984; William D. Taylor & Jane B. Johnsen, 1986). In these and other areas a very real danger is that computer models are being used and studied in place of the "realities" they are intended to reveal. Students (as well as decision makers in high places) using computer simulations can see only those aspects of a situation or process which lend themselves to computer-based procedural representation. Together with knowledge gained and expressed through artistic, aesthetic, metaphoric, and many other ways of knowing, much of the feminist "knowledge explosion" reflected in this volume lies outside the realm of the logic of procedural representation.

THE FEMINIST RESPONSE

In recent years feminists trained in systems analysis and computer science have begun to look at the problem of designing computer applications which are consistent with the needs of the users and which value the knowledge and backgrounds that the users bring to them. Gitte Moldrup Nielsen and Kristine Stougaard Thomsen (1985) have begun to address the design of office automation systems more congenial to the women who use them. Lucy Suchman and Brigitte Jordan (1988) address the issue of the feminist design of computer environments more generally but, consequently, can provide fewer pragmatic solutions for immediate application. The design of such environments is a difficult problem and one deserving far more attention, at both general and specific levels, than it has been given.

The difficulties encountered in this design process are both enormous and deep. The language which comes with the introduction of computers is biased toward the technology and away from humans. The term "wordprocessor," for example, is used first to refer to the hardware–software system and secondarily to the person who operates it; implicit in this usage is the notion that the person becomes a part of the system (and, perhaps, ultimately a dispensable part). The connection of the person to the system is through the "user-inter-face," just as the printer-interface does, the user-interface connects a "peripheral device" (in this case human) to the main computer system. The status of the user in relation to the computer is reflected in the design of the user-interface; this software is specifically designed to allow the computer to send messages (to speak) while creating the illusion that the user is speaking to a computer-listener (Gerhard Fischer & Andreas C. Lemke, 1988). Many other linguistic examples could be cited to illuminate the technological bias implicit in the field; it is important to note that as these terms enter the general discourse of society they bring these biases with them.

The *feminist* designer of computer applications faces the problem of bringing to a situation her knowledge of computer capabilities while leaving behind the biases of the language and structures through which she learned them. She must listen to the potential users, finding and honoring the processes and values which they want to maintain despite computerization. Often this means that she must resist her ability (and inclination) to provide a techno-fix in areas which need no fixing; she must redesign software to avoid unwanted side-effects, and generally deconstruct the myths of computer use. (It is a myth, for example, that computers automatically keep track of key presses by data entry operators; computers have been deliberately programmed to do this!)

To date there have been scant examples of computer applications which incorporate feminist values. Feminist networks (Judy Smith & Ellen Balka, 1988) and the National Women's Mailing List (Jill Lippett, 1988) have been successfully designed by feminists for the feminist community. Attempts to incorporate feminist values into educational software (Suzanne K. Damarin, 1984) have not succeeded as well as hoped, although there are a few nice pieces of "software for girls" on the market (Rhiannon Software, 1985). Continued work in educational computing shows some promise (or at least hope) as new ideas are generated and new approaches tried (Cornelia Brunner, Jan Hawkins, & Margaret Honey, 1988; Nancy Law, 1987; Suzanne K. Damarin, 1989a), but it is a long and difficult process.

There is a very real question as to whether the computer is so heavily valenced against feminist values (Corlann Gee Bush, 1983) that it precludes the development of useful feminist approaches. Whereas some writers might see information and telecommunications technologies as heralds of a new and kinder era, the state of existing applications bespeaks a different reality. In some circles the question is regularly asked: "Are computers ultimately liberating or are they essentially disempowering?" An answer frequently given to this question is that computers will be whatever we make of them. If so, it is time to get busy.

BIBLIOGRAPHY

Barrett, William. (1986). *Death of the soul: From Descartes to the computer*. New York: Doubleday.

Bergom-Larsson, Maria. (1982). Women and technology in the industrialized countries. In P. M. D'Onofrio-Flores & S. M. Pfafflin (Eds.), *Scientific-technological change and the role of women in development*. Boulder, CO: Westview Press.

Boden, Margaret. (1977). *Artificial intelligence and natural man*. Brighton: Harvester.

Bowers, C. A. (1988). *The cultural dimensions of educational computing: Understanding the non-neutrality of technology*. New York: Teachers College Press.

Brecher, Deborah L. (1985). *The women's computer literacy handbook.* New York: New American Library.

Brod, Craig. (1984). *Technostress: The human cost of the computer revolution.* Reading, MA: Addison-Wesley.

Brunner, Cornelia, Hawkins, Jan, & Honey, Margaret. (1988, April). Making meaning: Technological expertise and the use of metaphor. Paper presented to the American Educational Research Association, New Orleans, LA.

Bush, Corlann Gee. (1983). Women and the assessment of technology: To think, to be, to unthink, to free. In J. Rothschild (Ed.), *Machina ex Dea: Feminist perspectives on technology* (pp. 151–170). Elmsford, NY: Pergamon.

Cockburn, Cynthia. (1988). *Machinery of dominance: Women, men, and technical know-how.* Boston: Northeastern University Press.

Collins, B. (1985). Psychological implications of sex in attitudes toward computers: Results of a survey. *International Journal of Women's Studies 8*, 207–213.

Collis, Betty. (1987). Sex differences in the association between secondary school students' attitudes toward mathematics and toward computers. *Journal for Research in Mathematics Education, 18*(5), 394–402.

Damarin, Suzanne K. (1984). Technology and basic skills-mathematics: A courseware development project. In V. P. Hanson & M. Zweng (Eds.), *Computers in mathematics education* (pp. 62–71). Reston, VA: National Council of Teachers of Mathematics.

Damarin, Suzanne K. (1988a, January). *Issues of gender and computer assisted instruction.* Paper presented to the Association for Educational Communication and Technology, New Orleans, LA.

Damarin, Suzanne K. (1988b). *The "women and math problem" in a computer age: Working toward feminist solutions.* Working Paper No. 33, Center for the Study of Women and Society, University of Oregon, Eugene, OR.

Damarin, Suzanne K. (1989a, February). *Toward a feminist meaning for equity: The role of computer technology in science education.* Paper prepared for Association for Educational Communication and Technology, Dallas.

Damarin, Suzanne K. (1989b). Rethinking equity: An imperative for educational computing. *The Computing Teacher, 16*(4).

Dreyfus, Hubert L. (1972; revised 1979). *What computers can't do: A critique of artificial reason.* New York: Harper & Row.

Dreyfus, Hubert L., & Dreyfus, Stuart E. (1986). *Mind over machine.* New York: Free Press.

Evans, Christopher. (1979). *Micromillenium.* New York: Washington Square Press.

Feigenbaum, E. A., & McCorduck, P. (1983). *The fifth generation.* Reading, MA: Addison-Wesley.

Female Graduate Students and Research Staff in the Laboratory for Computer Science and the Artificial Intelligence Laboratory at MIT. (1983). *Barriers to equality in academia: Women in computer science at MIT.* Cambridge, MA: Author.

Fischer, Gerhard, & Lemke, Andreas C. (1988). Construction kits and design environments: Steps toward human problem-domain communication. *Human-Computer Interaction, 3*(3), 179–222.

Garson, Barbara. (1988). *The electronic sweatshop: How computers are transforming the office of the future into the factory of the past.* New York: Simon & Schuster.

Gregory, Judith. (1983). The next move: Organizing women in the office. In Jan Zimmerman (Ed.), *The technological woman: Interfacing with tomorrow* (pp. 260–272). New York: Praeger.

Hacker, Sally L. (1983). Mathematization of engineering: Limits on women and the field. In Joan Rothschild (Ed.), *Machina ex dea: Feminist perspectives on technology* (pp. 38–58). Elmsford, NY: Pergamon Press.

Harding, Sandra. (1986). *The science question in feminism.* Ithaca, NY: Cornell University Press.

Hartmann, Heidi I., Kraut, Robert E., & Tilly, Louise A. (Eds.). (1986). *Computer chips and paper clips.* Washington, DC: National Academy Press.

Hawkins, Jan. (1987). Computers and Girls: Rethinking the issues. In R. D. Pea and K. Sheingold (Eds.), *Mirrors of minds: Patterns of excellence in educational computing.* Norwood, NJ: Ablex.

Henifin, Mary Sue. (1984). The particular problems of video display terminals. In Wendy Chavkin (Ed.), *Double exposure: Women's health hazards on the job and at home* (pp. 69–80). New York: Monthly Review Press.

Jastrow, R. (1981). *The enchanted loom: Mind in the universe*. New York: Simon & Schuster.

Law, Nancy. (1987). Students' creation and interaction with computational representations of their own knowledge structures. In R. Lewis and E. D. Taggs (Eds.), *Trends in computer-assisted education* (pp. 223–228). Oxford: Blackwell Scientific.

LeBold, William K. (1987). Women in engineering and science: An undergraduate research prospective. In L. S. Dix (Ed.), *Women: Their underrepresentation and career differentials in science and engineering* (pp. 49–97). Washington, DC: National Academy Press.

Lippett, Jill. (1988, Autumn). The feminist face of computer technology. *Woman of Power*, 11, 56–57.

Machung, Anne. (1988). Who needs a personality to talk to a machine? In Cheris Kramarae (Ed.), *Technology and women's voices: Keeping in touch* (pp. 62–81). New York: Routledge & Kegan Paul.

Mathews, Walter M. (Ed.). (1980). *Monster or messiah: The computer's impact on society*. Jackson, MS: University of Mississippi Press.

McCorduck, Pamela. (1979). *Machines who think*. San Francisco: Freeman.

McCorduck, Pamela. (1986). *The universal machine: Confessions of a technological optimist*. New York: Harcourt Brace Jovanonich.

Minsky, Marvin. (1986). *The society of mind*. New York: Simon & Schuster.

Nielsen, Gitte Moldrup, & Thomsen, Kristine Stougaard. (1985). In A. Olerup, L. Schneider, & E. Monod (Eds.), Women, work, and computerization: Opportunities and disadvantages. *Proceedings of the first IFIP conference* (pp. 187–194). Amsterdam: North-Holland.

Osen, Lynn M. (1974). *Women in mathematics*. Cambridge, MA: MIT Press.

Otos, Sally, & Levy, Ellen. (1983). Word processing: This is not a final draft. In J. Zimmerman (Ed.), *The technological woman: interfacing with tomorrow* (pp. 149–158). New York: Praeger.

Pagels, Heinz. (1988). *The dreams of reason: The computer and the rise of the sciences of complexity*. New York: Simon & Schuster.

Papert, Seymour. (1980). *Mindstorms: Children, computers, and powerful ideas*. New York: Basic Books.

Perl, Teri. (1978). *Biographies of women mathematicians and related activities*. Menlo Park, CA: Addison-Wesley.

Putnam, Hilary. (1988). Much ado about not very much. In S. Graubard (Ed.). *The artificial intelligence debate: False starts, real foundations*. Cambridge: MIT Press.

Rhiannon Software. (1985). *Jenny of the prairie*. [Computer Software].

Ridgeway, Jim. (1988). Of course ICAI is impossible . . . worse, though it might be seditious. In J. Self (Ed.), *Artificial intelligence and human learning: Intelligent computer-aided instruction*. London: Chapman & Hall.

Roszak, Theodore. (1986). *The cult of information: The folklore of computers and the true art of thinking*. New York: Pantheon Books.

Rothschild, Joan. (1986). *Turing's man, Turing's woman, or Turing's person?: Gender, language, and computers*. Working Paper no. 166, Wellesley College Center for Research on Women, Wellesley, MA.

Rothschild, Joan. (1988). *Teaching technology from a feminist perspective*. Elmsford, NY: Pergamon Press.

Rucker, Rudy. (1987). *Mind tools: The five levels of mathematical reality*. Boston: Houghton Mifflin.

Sawada, Daiyo. (1985). New metaphoric images for computers in education. *Educational Technology* 25(5), 15–20.

Searle, John. (1984). *Minds, brains, and science*. Cambridge, MA: Harvard University Press.

Sloan, Douglas. (1984, Summer). On raising critical questions about the computer in education. *Teachers College Record, 85*(4), 546.

Smith, Judy, & Balka, Ellen. (1988). Chatting on the Feminist Computer Network. In Cheris

Kramarae (Ed.), *Technology and women's voices: Keeping in touch* (pp. 82–97). New York: Routledge & Kegan Paul.

Streibel, M. J. (1986). A critical analysis of the use of computers in education. *Educational Communication and Technology Journal, 34*(3), 137–161.

Suchman, Lucy, & Jordan, Brigette. (1988). Computerization and Women's Knowledge. In *Women, work, and computerization (IFIP Conference Proceedings)*. Amsterdam: North-Holland.

Taylor, William D., & Johnsen, Jane B. (1986). Resisting technological momentum. In J. A. Culbertson and L. L. Cunningham (Eds.), *Microcomputers and education*. Chicago: University of Chicago Press.

Turkle, Sherry. (1980). The computer as Rorshach. *Society, 17*(2), 15–24.

Turkle, Sherry. (1984). *The second self: Computers and the human spirit*. New York: Simon and Schuster.

Turkle, Sherry. (1988a). Computational reticence: Why women fear the intimate machine. In Cheris Kramarae (Ed.), *Technology and women's voices: Keeping in touch* (pp. 41–61). New York: Routledge & Kegan Paul.

Turkle, Sherry. (1988b). Artificial intelligence and psychoanalysis: A new alliance. In S. R. Graubard (Ed.), *The artificial intelligence debate: False starts, real foundations* (pp. 251–268). Cambridge: MIT Press.

Vetter, Betty M. (1988). Where are the women in the physical sciences? In Sue V. Rosser (Ed.), *Feminism within the science and health care professions: Overcoming resistance* (pp. 19–32). Oxford: Pergamon Press.

Weizenbaum, Joseph. (1976). *Computer power and human reason*. San Francisco: W H Freeman.

Wenger, Etienne. (1987). *Artificial intelligence and tutoring systems*. Los Altos, CA: Morgan Kaufmann.

Winner, Langdon. (1977). *Autonomous technology: Technics-out-of-control as a theme in political thought*. Cambridge, MA: The MIT Press.

Winner, Langdon. (1988). Mythinformation. In John Zerzan and Alice Carnes (Eds.), *Questioning Technology* (pp. 163–170). London: Freeman Press.

Zuboff, Shoshana. (1988). *In the age of the smart machine: The future of work and power*. New York: Basic Books.

Chapter 33

Ecofeminist Politics
The Promise of Common Ground

Irene Diamond

I think it is time to put ecology back into feminism, to feel as our own the plight of the earth and shout it. Otherwise feminism and ecology will continue to win only partial gains, buying time. Otherwise the supremacist mentality that rules the affairs of our planet will continue its destructive course and annihilate us all in the name of health, happiness and progress.

Andrée Collard, *Rape of the Wild* (1989).

In a recent issue of *Ms.* magazine Lindsy Van Gelder declared that ecofeminism "was the most exciting new 'ism' in eons" (Lindsy Van Gelder, 1989). Pleased that *Ms.* had finally decided to devote an entire article to a subject dear to my heart, I also found myself feeling somewhat disturbed and slightly uncomfortable by this enthusiastic recognition. Would Vandana Shiva, the Indian ecological activist and theorist who was so central to my own enthusiasm even recognize her concerns and hopes in this catalogue of new items for American feminists? Did it matter that the article gave little or no indication that this new constellation was opening up new ways of seeing the world, new hope across the globe, because of the imaginative local, simultaneously global, actions of a range of activists and artists who rarely saw themselves as forging a new "ism?"

These were some of the questions that this article raised for me. But, because the process of raising questions, rather than enunciating definitive conclusions, is so integral to this new constellation (is this why I'm rebelling at being sandwiched into an "ism?") I have no interest in branding Van Gelder's partial story as false, hopelessly irredeemable, or beyond the fold.[1] Indeed, I appreciated her articulation of ecofeminism's focus on healing rather than conflictual confrontation or what the historian Barbara Epstein has termed its ability "to place conflict between women and men in the context of a holistic social vision" without abandoning "commitment to equality to community, or its critique of male domination" (Barbara Epstein, 1989). Yes there were problems with Van Gelder's account, but the solution was other stories and interpretations, also necessarily partial. The celebration of diversity *and* the interconnectedness of life, the search for common ground is the promise of this new politics.

The discussion of ecofeminism in such arenas as *Ms.*, the *Nation*, and meetings of the National Women's Studies Association is very new, but in fact the strands that led to ecofeminism as an ethic and politics which sees a connection between the domination of women and the domination of nature can be traced to the 1970s.[2] Not surprisingly, as the discussion has become more frequent, debates have arisen as to origins. Precisely because there is no one theorist or leader of this heterogeneous movement and because it has arisen in such diverse locales—there are a range of narratives about ecofeminism's origins.

ORIGINS AND GROUNDING

One of the questions concerning origins is the issue of spirituality. My own view of this debate is that narratives which deny or ignore the spiritual threads of this loose constellation fail to acknowledge some of its most creative features. Why spiritual or mystical views are so often scorned or trivialized in late capitalist societies is a complex issue which cannot be dealt with here. Although I once shared some of the concerns of the skeptics, I have also come to see that the supposed antagonism between active political resistance and spirituality does not hold for the contemporary era. Indeed, individuals who have been inspired and motivated by their beliefs in earth-based spirituality have often been some of the most active and vigilant defenders of the planet. It is they who have been especially innovative in creating prefigurative egalitarian communities which help ground and sustain commitment. As Starhawk, a well-known Witch and political activist in the direct action wing of the peace movement, relates, "Earth-based spirituality provides both an imperative toward action in the world and a source of strength and renewal of the energies that often burn out in political action . . . Instead of replacing political action, earth based spirituality provides a repository of energy that can resurge in new cycles of political momentum. Ecofeminism, arising in the late seventies and eighties, inherits this history" (Starhawk, 1989, p. 176). Not all ecofeminist direct action participants are deeply involved with reemerging Goddess traditions, and not all ecofeminists who identify with Goddess spirituality are involved in the direct action movement; nonetheless the multifaceted efforts of Western feminists to reclaim Goddess imagery and create new stories and narratives of humans and the cosmos in the 1970s form a vital component of what we now label ecofeminism. [See also Carol Christ, this volume.]

This reclamation of Goddess imagery is certainly a significant component of ecofeminism. And it has been especially important in providing alternative images for visions of a more harmonious, ecologically balanced future. But the development of ecofeminism, and the very interest in Goddess imagery, must also be situated within the larger shift within feminism, sometimes referred to as difference feminism, sometimes as cultural feminism, that in the 1970s came to valorize and actively uphold the values and practices associated with women's culture. This shift is not typically associated with ecofeminism, and the positions within this approach to feminism are many and varied; nonetheless, I feel we cannot fully appreciate the roots of ecofeminism if we do not acknowledge this larger context.

RETELLING OF WOMEN'S HISTORY
AND CULTURE

In the United States the work of academic historians such as Joan Kelly-Gadol (1976) and Carol Smith-Rosenberg (1975) on the strength and vitality of women's culture can be viewed as part of this larger context, as can the more specific work revaluing motherhood by such different writers as Adrienne Rich (1976), Nancy Chodorow (1978) and Sara Ruddick (1980). [See also Jane Jaquette, this volume.] In terms of movement politics the focus on women's culture and the development of women's music and cultural institutions were also integral to this shift. The revaluation of the woman–nature connection in the late

1970s and early 1980s by theorists such as Mary Daly (1978), Susan Griffin (1978), Ynestra King (1983) and Carolyn Merchant (1982) who are more specifically identified with ecofeminism needs to be viewed within this larger retelling of women's history and culture.

Retelling, and most especially a retelling which expands our concepts of "progress" and historical time and reclaims what patriarchal accounts have relegated to the dustbins of prehistory or "backwardness," is certainly part of what has enabled ecofeminism to challenge and reframe dominant paradigms. But ecofeminism is considerably more than a new version of history. Indeed, its promise as a planetary vehicle of change stems from its thorough immersion in the post–modern world. Acknowledging—often through the artistic imagination—the opacity of contemporary forms of hegemonic power, ecofeminism as a theory and practice begins by struggling to create new vocabularies to name these forces (see, for example, Paula Gunn Allen, 1986; Mary Daly, 1978; Starhawk, 1987; Ursula LeGuin, 1985). However, unlike many other forms of resistance, it moves beyond the merely discursive and is not mired in the whirlpool of obscurant theory which often goes under the name "deconstructionist." Rather, as the various movements around the world exemplify, ecofeminism at its best is reconstructionist, able to creatively identify ecologically sustainable practices which can heal the wounds of contemporary capital (see for example, the collections *Healing the Wounds: The Promise of Ecofeminism* [Judith Plant, 1989] and *Reweaving the World: The Emergence of Ecofeminism* [Irene Diamond & Gloria Feman Orenstein, 1990]). Movements such as the Indian Chipko struggle which use the act of hugging trees to thwart the deforestation by multinational firms that is despoiling and ravaging the ecosystems upon which the survival of tribal and peasant peoples depends, provide concrete challenges to the logic of development (or what Vandana Shiva [1988] aptly calls "mal-development") as they expose the fragile ties that sustain all life. [See also Claudia Salazar, this volume.] The sabotage acts against nuclear missiles by the women of Greenham Common in Great Britain are an expression of a similar nonviolent resistance. In a somewhat more symbolic vein the use of webs of wool by Western peace activists to encase the pentagon and other bastions of militarism also disrupts as it points to alternative, more connected ways of living. The particular expressions of this mixing of art, ritual, and politics differ in the individual locales where women resist threats to their bodies, homes, and livelihoods, but what unites this loose configuration is a reverence for the Earth and her many creatures and a recognition that the struggle to free women cannot be separated from the struggle to save the Earth. As the 1988 report from the conference "Nari Mukti Sangharsh Sammelan" held in Patna, India, states:

"Women's survival is crucially linked to nature's survival. Women's health, their access to employment, agricultural productivity, crucial daily needs of fuel, fodder, water etc., are all linked to the preservation and regeneration of nature." (Gail Omvedt, Chetna Galu, & Govind Kelkar, 1988, p. 51)

GLOBAL CONCERNS

In my effort to contextualize ecofeminism I have stressed the roots of ecofeminism within feminism. The central role of aesthetics and ritual in ecofeminist political action draws heavily on the strategies for transforming consciousness of radical feminism. Certainly in the absence of a global feminist movement there would be little talk of ecofeminism. At the same time, to more fully appreciate the multifaceted nature of this emergent politics, it also needs to be situated within the global Green or ecological movement. Whereas feminism as a social movement might be viewed as a child of the Enlightenment, paradoxically realizing its fullest potential in the late twentieth century when Enlightenment ideas of human agency, reason, and emancipation have come under intense assault, the contemporary Green movement transcends the political categories of the last two centuries. The particular German Green slogan, "Neither left nor right but in front," may not be endorsed by all Green groups, but I think this expression is a useful indicator of the sensibility that distinguishes "Green" from that of the traditional left. Given women's crucial leadership role in the diverse Green movements across the globe, ecofeminism must also be analyzed, within this post–Enlightenment configuration. Fundamental to Green politics is a challenge to such universalizing truths of European humanism as freedom through so-called "progress" and technological mastery of nature. For the German Green leader Petra Kelly the terms ecofeminism and Green are but different expressions of the new politics. Her book on Green politics is entitled *Fighting for Hope* (1984) and in her foreword to a recent collection on ecofeminism she writes:

> This book is a book of hope, a book about healing wounds. . . . That is what this courageous book is all about. Just repairing the existing system, whether capitalist or state socialist, cannot be an answer for us! Our aim is a nonviolent and ecological–feminist transformation of societal structures. Our aim is radical, nonviolent change *outside*—and *inside* of us! The macrocosm and the microcosm! This has to do with transforming power! Not power over, or power to dominate, or power to terrorize—but shared power; abolishing power as we know it, replacing it with the power of nonviolence or something common to all. (Petra Kelly, 1989)

Kelly's approach to personal and structural change and the importance of self-transformation clearly draws on the feminist notion of the personal as political. Her critique of "power over," like that of Starhawk's in her book *Truth or Dare* (1987), also draws on earlier feminist critiques and the emphasis on power as energy that has been articulated by feminist theorists such as Nancy Hartsock (1983) and others. But in the context of ecofeminism, which calls attention to the value and integrity of not only women, but all the creatures with whom we share the earth, the feminist emphasis on "power as energy" or "power within" becomes transformed. The ecofeminist language of the power of all beings or in Kelly's words, the power "common to all," (1989) empowers at the same time that it acknowledges the limits of human action. Empowerment, in a world where humans are acknowledged to be but a part of the tapestry of life, favors humility and nonviolence. This language is thus particularly appropriate for challenging the Faustian impulses of the contemporary era and bringing to the fore the twin threats of ecocide and nuclear annihilation that this masculine hubris has produced.

TRANSFORMATION OF FEMINISM

The ecofeminist focus on planetary survival has been criticized by some feminists who feel that women's involvement in peace and ecological movements deflects valuable feminist energy from the very immediate struggles against violence against women, a violence which is not merely a theoretical possibility but is part of the grim daily reality of women's lives. (Certainly in the case of rural Third World women the horror of ecological devastation is also already a daily reality.) Others wonder where the feminism is in this involvement. I mention this debate not to refute the charges, as the nature of the charges are not refutable, but to agree that ecofeminism does represent a transformation of feminism. My difference with these critics, however, is that I believe that this transformation not only does not weaken or undermine feminism, but that it enables feminism to more effectively deal with its problematic Enlightenment legacy. [See also Marilyn Frye, this volume.] Moreover, it is even possible that ecofeminism's subtle shift in the language of empowerment may prove more resistant than more traditional strains of feminism have to the manipulations of the language of individual self-actualization endemic to the strivings of late capitalist culture. The political realization of this resistance is by no means given, and I am certainly not claiming that the language of ecofeminism is fully separate from the larger culture's individualistic focus on the self, but I do believe that this language provides a much needed and valuable opening. As Donna Haraway provocatively notes in an essay devoted to devising ways feminists can engage with the world's active agency:

> Ecofeminists have perhaps been most insistent on some version of the world as active subject, not as resource to be mapped and appropriated in bourgeois, Marxist, or masculinist projects. Acknowledging the agency of the world in knowledge makes room for some unsettling possibilities, including a sense of the world's independent sense of humor. Such a sense of humor is not comfortable for humanists and others committed to the world as resource. (Donna Haraway, 1988)

Haraway's discussion of ecofeminists' ability to cope with the limits of human agency and their acknowledgment that the world no longer has a clearer center, points to why ecofeminist politics has some very clear affinities with the cultural constellation known as postmodernism. The more usual characterization—and the primary reason that academic feminist theory has tended to ignore or dismiss it—is the claim that ecofeminism is merely a variant of cultural feminism and hopelessly mired in essentialism and its reunification of *the* female body. The suggestion that ecofeminist politics provide a vehicle for feminist action through its re-evaluation of women and the natural world strike some as naive. These critics fear a reversion to the patriarchal discourse that equates women with passivity. A related concern is the obscuring of differences among women.

Yet as suggested, if we focus on the actual manifestation of the politics, rather than dissecting the texts of a few theorists, we recover what much academic discourse loses. The ecofeminist refashioning of agency, its focus on micropolitics, and its celebration of diversity and place, put it very much in the postmodern orbit. Yet because ecofeminism actively creates, rather than rejects, utopian visions, it is at the same time not fully postmodern. In this sense its critique of universalism is radically different from the nihilism and pessimism of so much male poststructuralist thought.[3] Indeed, ecofeminist practice demonstrates that deconstructive methods can actually clarify the complex (decentered) connections of the self with the world without removing us from participation in the world. It is this political engagement that helps to bring on to the historical stage what the Indian peace activist Corinne Kumar D'Souza terms "the plurality of civilizations" (Corinne Kumar D'Souza, 1989).

ECOFEMINIST ACTIVISM

I am advocating greater attention to the discourse of ecofeminist activism because as Noel Sturgeon, an academic and activist in the U.S. antimilitarist movement, observes "In the present context of the prevalence of antiessentialist feminist theory, "cultural feminist" and "radical feminist" as labels serve to obscure what the direct action movement has to offer feminists: a model of political action which is, in many ways, most suited to a feminist theory which decenters a female subject while constructing a historically contingent, flexible politics of identity from which political demands can be articulated and political struggle carried out" (Noel Sturgeon, 1989, p. 48). Sturgeon is highly critical of the reductive characterizations academic feminist theorists have used in their treatment of the feminist peace movement and feminist activism more generally. Although she does not deny the presence of essentialism within the movement, she argues that the structures and politics of the movement actually destabilize any fixed notions of what women or feminism should be and that a more sympathetic reading would actually discern "positional" constructions of subjectivity. Ironically, it is such relational formulations that are much favored by feminist theorists searching for a way between the twin dangers of extreme essentialism and extreme social constructionism that haunt contemporary feminist thought (Linda Alcoff, 1988; Donna Haraway, 1988).

I have been arguing that the discourse of ecofeminist activism is considerably more complex and diversified than many critics have recognized. Another aspect of this complexity—and one of the more crucial with respect to the movement's promise of common ground—is its explicit and self-conscious antiracism. The notion that white people have a responsibility to analyze the connections between militarism and racism is widely accepted and has been an impetus, for example, in the formation of coalitions working with people of color on the effects of atomic testing in the South Pacific. Wilmette Brown cofounder of the British-based "Black Women for Wages for Housework" explains:

> With the growth of the women's peace movement, symbolized internationally by Greenham, winning is again a living possibility, because white women are taking a lead from Black women in both the metropolis and the Third World, demanding that the military–industrial complex be disarmed and dismantled, and that the military budget be used to meet people's needs, beginning with women and children . . . the women's peace movement is refusing the sexist and racist assumptions and practices of the peace and holistic health movements once and for all. (Wilmette Brown, 1983, p. 85)

LEARNING VERSUS EXPLOITATION

Because of the strong interest in cultures that see the Earth as sacred, support for the preservation of native lands and other struggles and issues of indigenous peoples has also been a focus of activity. Indeed, the imminent sense of spirituality that is said to prevail in Native American cultures has been an important source of inspiration to Western feminists' evolving ecological consciousness. This very interest has itself led to considerable debate about the appropriateness and feasibility of industrialized peoples modeling their behavior on the cultural practices of nonindustrialized peoples. In the contemporary world the lines between genuine learning versus exploitative mimicry or respect and appreciation versus romanticization are not easily discerned. Yet despite these difficulties, the cultural visions offered by indigenous peoples have reinvigorated a much needed discussion regarding the virtues of voluntary simplicity and the possibility of living *with* rather than against the earth.

The theory of ecofeminism is that Western culture has produced a set of hierarchical dualisms—man–woman, mind–body, spirit–matter, human–animal, white–black—which are currently threatening all life. Questioning these dualisms and sustaining cultures that move beyond them, cultures which acknowledge that men and women are both part of a living earth, is what generates ecofeminist politics. This politics does not purport to have the answers, its borders are diffuse and ill-defined, and at its best it avoids apocalyptic visions, grounding itself in its acceptance of the cycles of life and its celebration of pluralism and connectedness. It is this willingness to face the curves along the road that opens the promise of common ground.

NOTES

1. As Susan Griffin so eloquently states in her preface to the British ecofeminist collection, *Reclaim the Earth: Women speak out for life on Earth* (1983), "If there is one idea that can be said to link together all that is said and reported here, this idea is also a feeling. It is a grief over the fate of the earth, that contains within it a joyful hope that we might reclaim this earth. Does this one idea answer all our questions?" It is not meant to. It is meant to make us ask more questions. And it is not necessary that we agree on every point, for what we have in common is not small." The ability to live with the ambiguities and uncertainties of life is central to ecofeminist thought as it is articulated by Griffin. Her work has been central to the development of my own, and I want to acknowledge the inspiration her recent article entitled "The Curves Along the Road" in *Reweaving the World: the Emergence of Ecofeminism* (Irene Diamond and Gloria Feman Orenstein, 1990) for the final sentence of this essay.

2. *The Nation* debate was sparked by Kirkpatrick Sale's article "Ecofeminism—A New Perspective," *The Nation*, September 26, 1987 (pp. 302–305). Letters responding to the article appeared in the December 12, 1987, and January 16, 1988 issues. At the June 1989 annual meeting of the National Women's Studies Association held in Towson, Maryland, there were several very well attended panels on ecofeminism.

3. The terms "postmodernism", "poststructuralist" and "deconstruction" are often used interchangeably in contemporary philosophical and literary theory to refer to methods of analysis which question the foundationalism and unity of the subject in conventional philosophical thought and literary analysis which draw on Enlightenment notions of truth, reason, and agency. These newer methods are associated with such figures as Jacques Derrida, Michel Foucault, and Richard Rorty. Postmodern is more typically used to refer to the contemporary cultural period where these modes of interpretation are reflected in artistic and cultural representations; poststructuralist is more typically used to characterize the mode of thought; and deconstruction to the actual methods used in reading texts.

BIBLIOGRAPHY

Alcoff, Linda. (1988). Cultural feminism versus poststructuralism: The identity crisis in feminist theory. *Signs: Journal of Women in Culture and Society, 13*(3).

Allen, Paula Gunn. (1986). *The sacred hoop: Recovering the feminine in American Indian tradition.* Boston: Beacon Press.

Brown, Wilmette. (1983). In Leonie Caldecott & Stephanie Leland (Eds.), *Reclaim the Earth: Women speak out for life on Earth.* London: The Women's Press.

Chodorow, Nancy. (1978). *The reproduction of mothering: Psychoanalysis and the sociology of gender.* Berkeley, CA: University of California Press.

Christ, Carol P. (1987). *Laughter of Aphrodite: Reflections on a journey to the goddess.* San Francisco: Harper & Row.

Collard, Andrée with Contrucci, Joyce. (1989). *The rape of the wild: Man's violence against animals and the earth.* Bloomington, IN: Indiana University Press.

Daly, Mary. (1978). *Gyn/Ecology: The metaethics of radical feminism.* Boston: Beacon Press.

Diamond, Irene & Orenstein, Gloria (Eds.). (1990). *Reweaving the world: The emergence of ecofeminism.* San Francisco: Sierra Club Press Books.

Epstein, Barbara. (1989). *Radical feminism and the non-violent direct action movement.* Unpublished manuscript.

Gimbutas, Marija. (1989). *The language of the goddess.* San Francisco: Harper & Row.

Gray, Elizabeth Dodson. (1979). *Green paradise lost.* Wellesley, MA: Roundtable Press.

Griffin, Susan. (1978). *Women and nature: The roaring inside her.* New York: Harper & Row.

Griffin, Susan. (1983). Preface. In Leonie Caldecott & Stephanie Leland (Eds.), *Reclaim the Earth: Women speak out for life on Earth.* London: Women's Press.

Haraway, Donna. (1988). Situated knowledges: The science question in feminism and the privilege of partial perspective. *Feminist Studies, 14*(3).

Hartsock, Nancy. (1983). *Money, sex and power.* Boston: Northeastern University Press.

Kelly, Petra. (1989). Foreword. In Judith Plant (Ed.), *Healing our wounds: The promise of ecofeminism.* Philadelphia: New Society Publishers.

Kelly-Gadol, Joan. (1976). The social relations of the sexes: Methodological implications for women's history. *Signs: Journal of Women in Culture and Society, 1*(4).

King, Ynestra. (1983). Toward an ecological feminism and a feminist ecology. In Joan Rothschild (Ed.), *Machina ex dea: Feminist perspectives on technology.* Elmsford, NY: Pergamon Press.

Kumar, Corinne D'Souza. (1989). A new movement, a new hope: East wind, west wind, and the wind from the south. In Judith Plant (Ed.), *Healing the wounds: The promise of ecofeminism.* Philadelphia: New Society Publishers.

LeGuin, Ursula. (1985). *Always coming home.* New York: Harper & Row.

Merchant, Carolyn. (1982). *The death of nature: Women, ecology and the scientific revolution.* New York: Harper & Row.

Omvedt, Gail, Gala, Chetna, & Kelkar, Govind. (1988). *Women and struggle.* A report of the Nari Mukti Sangharsh Sammelan Patna, Kali for Women, New Delhi, India.

Orenstein, Gloria Feman. (1990). *The reflowering of the goddess.* Elmsford, NY: Pergamon Press.

Plant, Judith (Ed.). (1989). *Healing our wounds: The promise of ecofeminism.* Philadelphia: New Society Publishers.

Rich, Andrienne. (1986). *Of woman born: Motherhood as experience and institution.* New York: W W Norton.

Ruddick, Sara. (1980). Maternal thinking. *Feminist Studies, 6*(2), 432–467.

Shiva, Vandana. (1988). *Staying alive: Women, ecology and development.* London: Zed Press.

Smith-Rosenberg, Carol. (1975). The female world of love and ritual. *Signs: Journal of Women in Culture and Society, 1*(1).

Starhawk. (1987). *Truth or dare: Encounters with power, authority, and mystery.* San Francisco: Harper & Row.

Starhawk. (1989). Feminist earth-based spirituality and ecofeminism. In Judith Plant (Ed.), *Healing the wounds: The promise of ecofeminism.* Philadelphia: New Society Publishers.

Sturgeon, Noel. (1989, June). *What does the politics of poststructuralist feminism look like? Ecofeminism, positional feminism and radical feminism revisited.* Paper presented at the annual meeting of the National Women's Studies Association, Towson, MD.

Van Gelder, Lindsy. (1989, January/February). It's not nice to mess with Mother Nature. *Ms.,* 60–63.

Warren, Karen. (1987). Feminism and ecology making connections. *Environmental Ethics, 9*(1).

Chapter 34

Pornography Unmodified

Susanne Kappeler

The transformation of pornography into a feminist issue is perhaps one of the best examples of the revolutionary or explosive potential of feminist knowledge. This transformation is difficult to chart as a linear development, and in the 1990s the issue of pornography certainly shows up the discrepancy between feminist and malestream knowledge in very startling form.

In the 1960s, pornography was generally seen as a "natural" corollary of the "sexual revolution," the "liberalization" of culture as a part of the "sexual liberation." The key issue in pornography was "explicitness": showing, representing, writing about "sex" in an ever more "open" way. Sexual explicitness was one form of rebellion against stuffy old moralists; it therefore becomes almost inextricably linked with progressiveness. Freedom of expression should naturally follow from other freedoms, especially sexual freedom. A number of legal cases against "obscene" books—for example *Lady Chatterly's Lover* in England in 1960, or the translation of *Fanny Hill* in Denmark in 1964—contributed to the growing official consensus that pornography was not "harmful"—where harm was as a matter of course defined in relation to the consumer. Campaigns against legislation—obscenity laws of all kinds—became a priority for liberals and progressives. Denmark and Sweden, which legalized pornography in the late 1960s, became the "meccas" of the sexual liberation for the western world.

The campaign for freedom of expression was increasingly fought by people in the arts as an issue of culture, against the legal framework and against moralists and religious opinion. The relationship between culture and reality was understood as relatively simple: culture was expected to "reflect" the liberalization of life. The key argument was that culture could do no harm; the effect was to separate pornography from its customary sociological and legal context of rape and crime statistics.

Government Commission Reports on Pornography and Censorship, as well as the actual changes in legislation in western countries gives a picture of the malestream attitudes to pornography since the 1960s.

OUTSIDE THE ACADEMY

Feminists began to look at pornography from a feminist perspective in the 1960s: both in consciousness-raising groups and in the context of activist work against male violence against women. [See Jane Caputi, this volume.] However, the prevailing cultural climate made it difficult to know where this issue belonged; its separation from issues of crime and violence and its placing in the context of culture as an issue of freedom of expression put a very effective barrier against feminist critique, especially in western european countries, where it became a widespread feminist issue only in the 1980s.

Kate Millet looked at pornography and literature in *Sexual Politics* (1970), but mainly as a means of reading out male attitudes to women, taking the term "pornography" to refer to a genre of publication not considered "literature." Activist work on sexual violence, however, revealed the close connection between pornography and (other forms of) male violence, and women's actions against billboards, individual films, sex shops, and "Reclaim the Night" marches began to spring up in the mid- to late 1970s. This was very much part of the Women's Liberation Movement, and happening almost exclusively outside of the academy. Laura Lederer's *Take Back the Night: Women on Pornography*, is a crucial publication; it gives a historical perspective on the developing feminist work on and activism against pornography in the United States. Dusty Rhodes and Sandra McNeill (1985) document conferences and activism against sexual violence and pornography in the early 1980s in the United Kingdom. Organizations like Women Against Pornography (founded in the United States, 1979) and Women Against Violence Against Women (founded in United Kingdom, 1981) helped to give a focus to activism against pornography nationwide and to do education and publicity work. Pornography was no longer simply seen as a cultural reflection of male violence in the world (as in the campaign slogan originally coined by Robin Morgan "Pornography the Theory, Rape the Practice"),[1] but as *itself a form of violence against women.*

Andrea Dworkin's book *Pornography: Men Possessing Women* (1981) was the first systematic theoretical study of pornography that pulled together feminist thinking on the issue of pornography from different areas of both activism and theory, making the connections between male power, sexuality, and culture. As a book-length study with some prominence, it also began to have an effect on the academy, "academic feminism," and malestream culture.

Whereas the feminist opposition to pornography had very clearly come from within the Women's Liberation Movement, it by no means had the backing of the whole movement. The fear of association with the Right and with Moralists, as well as doubts as to whether pornography was as important as "actual" violence and discrimination, prevented many women—perhaps those less involved in activist work on violence—from taking up pornography as a feminist issue.

THE ORDINANCE

In 1983, after teaching a joint course on pornography at the University of Minnesota, Andrea Dworkin and Catharine A. MacKinnon were asked by Minneapolis City Council to draw up a feminist law against pornography. This Ordinance is a groundbreaking piece of legislation and a milestone in legislation against pornography in that it is not a censorship law, but a civil law based on the civil rights of women. It defines pornography as sex discrimination, and provides for redress against harm both for women involved in the production of pornography and women harmed in the use of pornography. The effect of this legislative proposal—of a law that enshrines feminist analysis—is far-reaching and has not yet ended. Although the Ordinance was introduced in several states, it was fought against and eventually brought before the Supreme Court in 1986, which reasserted the primacy of the "Freedom of Speech" of the Constitution's Bill of Rights.

However, pornography has as a consequence become very much a topic for the academy, and feminists in the academy—lawyers, sociologists, psychologists, literary critics, art historians, and theorists of the media and culture. Academic cultural theory, strongly influenced by French semiotics and psychoanalysis, has become one of the foremost voices of opposition to feminist analysis of pornography. Whereas the feminist view that culture is structured for a male viewer or reader has been broadly accepted, especially by women in the field, this has recently led to an attempt to formulate a "female cultural gaze," just as the feminist critique of male sexuality has led to a move to turn to "a positive female sexuality." In the United States a broad coalition of lawyers, publishers, and writers or media workers—Feminist Anti Censorship Task Force (FACT)—coordinated a powerful opposition to the Dworkin–MacKinnon Ordinance, and talked of a "split" in the feminist movement. *Caught Looking: Feminism, Pornography and Censorship* (FACT, 1986) was published in direct response to the Ordinance, containing conventional malestream visual pornography and "serious essays by feminists" opposing the Dworkin–MacKinnon position. Feminist activists, however, continue to promote the Ordinance: In the run-up to the presidential elections, Bellingham, Washington, adopted the Ordinance on its voting bill, where it was accepted with a majority of 62%. However, the city failed to defend the Ordinance against opponents who immediately had an injunction put on it (Margaret A. Baldwin, 1989a, 1989b). The Ordinance is also being studied by feminists in other countries as a model for national adaptation. German feminists have drafted legislation based on the Ordinance and proposed it to the Federal government.[2]

CHALLENGING CULTURAL NOTIONS

The chief home truth was that pornography is just "fantasy," unable to do any harm. Harm itself was conceived as a direct effect of reading, hence in the first instance harm to the reader. The connection between a pornographic culture and the behavior of men toward women, where women are the victims of violence, has been the single most contested factor. Women's experience shows that pornography is central to male violence: in direct ways for example in situations of domestic violence; in rapes where pornography is mentioned or copied; in child sexual abuse, where pornography is first shown to children; in prostitution, where pornography serves to "break in" women and serves as a "catalogue;" and in the production of pornography. This experience is consistently denied by malestream argument. On a cultural level, women also argue that the objectification of women in pornography, advertising and high culture is degrading to women and contributes directly to the discrimination against women in society. This again is contested by malestream notions of culture, which take objectification for granted but deem it harmless. The ruling of the U.S. Supreme Court in 1986, although coming out against the Dworkin–MacKinnon Ordinance as being unconstitutional, included in its ruling that pornography contributes to the discrimination against women, and hence to unequal pay at work and to violence against women. [See Jocelynne Scutt, this volume, for further discussion of pornography and legal systems.]

The feminist debate has also challenged the cultural notion of an ungendered, universal cultural subject—reader or spectator—and developed an analysis of the differential relationship of women and men to representation. This is countered by the malestream argument that "women watch and enjoy pornography too." As in so much uninformed opposition to feminism, feminist gender analysis is misinterpreted as being about single biological individuals instead of women and men as social groups. Hence individual males who have not committed violence are held up as apparent counterexamples to the observation that violent crimes against women are committed by men; individual women who enjoy viewing pornography as counterexamples to the fact that the millions of consumers of pornography are male. Rarely is it argued, however, that because some known women have not born children, it isn't women who bear children.

USE OF THE WORD FEMINISM

A feminist critique of pornography opened up a much more comprehensive analysis of culture and society, as pornography became defined as a *system*, not simply as a trashy subgenre of literature and popular culture. It opened up a discussion of pornography as a form of male violence, as a huge business and industry connected to prostitution, and as an ideological tool that pervades malestream culture in all its forms, including the arts. It opened up possibilities for developing feminist legislation in different countries, as well as continued activist work in the women's liberation movement (WLM) and in malestream politics.

The opposition to this critique prefers to debate pornography in the context of sexuality, and questions of "feminist erotica" and "lesbian pornography" from part of the contemporary debate around "positive female sexuality" and lesbian sadomasochism. Academic feminists and women active in cultural and media work are also concerned with a "feminist aesthetic," the visual reappropriation of the female body, and theories of the "female cultural gaze." These different strands of feminist work are not really compatible, and reflect the discrepancies between feminist and malestream thinking. The chief bone of contention, as in the debate about sexuality and lesbian sadomasochism, is the use of the term "feminist": who can legitimately claim it for their position. Hence it is not so much that arguments raised by feminist critique are defeated or proven wrong (or even engaged with), as that other positions dispute the exclusive use of the term "feminist" by claiming it themselves, (e.g., *Caught Looking* [FACT, 1986], with its pro-pornography position, claiming the label "feminist.")

My own position is that "feminist" requires renewed definition and identification as a political perspective which is grounded in (a) the recognition of women's oppression, and (b) a commitment to work towards ending that oppression, with an understanding that no woman is free until all women are free. I therefore sympathize with MacKinnon's use of "feminism unmodified," as meaning the political perspective which identifies, defends and prioritizes the interests of women in every instance, and which therefore brooks no qualification, or subsumption under other political interests such as marxism, liberalism, christianity or libertarianism (see Catharine A. MacKinnon, 1983). "Feminist" pro-pornography positions would then be required to prove the efficacy of pornography in the struggle for all women's liberation from male oppression, rather than relying on individual women's personal pleasure as a criterion. The cooptation of the debate has already been discussed above; but it can be seen in other ways as well, for example, in women's campaigns and organizations which avoid identification as "feminist" (e.g., the emerging Campaign Against Pornography in Great Britain).

The single most useful resource the feminist analysis of pornography has provided is its redefinition of pornography's harm, as harm to women rather than to consumers or cityscapes (zoning concerns in the United States, Indecent Display [Control] Act in Britain).

Other radical shifts in knowledge include the redefinition of pornography as a *system* and an industry, rather than as a cultural subgenre.

METHODS OF ANALYSIS

The new "methods" of analyzing pornography involve a comprehensive feminist theory which refuses to isolate pornography either in a context of crime statistics, or as a product of culture. As an issue it has raised questions about the form and function of culture itself, its involvement in capitalist production, its ideological function in constructing sexuality and the role of women, the prostitution of women, the legal system. Differences in position are due to different starting points, that is different conceptions of what it means to develop a feminist position, and what presuppositions—for example of an academic discipline—are left unquestioned. The most fundamental issue is therefore "what is a feminist methodology?"

As malestream argument locks the issue of pornography into a link with "censorship" rather than gender (viz, the FACT task force taking over those terms defining itself as "against censorship" rather than "for pornography"), freedom of expression and its meaning in a patriarchal society has also become a key issue. A lot, though not all, of the written work on pornography remains therefore political and ideological, rather than a question of "knowledge" and research.

Information in terms of figures about the pornography industry is notoriously difficult to come by, and finance for feminist work on the industry and its effects is mostly lacking.

Accusing feminism of joining forces with the moralist Right, and of being "antisex," are the most frequently used arguments both by malestream and other feminist opposition to the radical feminist critique of pornography which analyses pornography as part of the oppression of women by men.

ALLIANCES AND DEBATES

In practice, there is confusion over whether pornography is a question of "sex" or of "fantasy" or of some fundamental psychoanalytic reality. The opposition to feminist work in this area is phenomenal, and uses the divisions among women as one of its most effective strategies. Thus malestream work on the ideological level has been quick to exploit proponents of lesbian sadomasochism and "feminist erotica" (e.g., Alan Soble, 1986) or to favor "academic feminism" which takes a propornography line, in an attempt to demolish radical feminist analysis. Also, leftists and progressives have consistently combined and (con)fused their opposition to the Right and to legislation against pornography with their opposition to feminist critique, most notably in the opposition to the (U.S. Government) Meese Commission Inquiry into Pornography (named after its chair), and increasingly so in the United Kingdom. Indirectly, then, it is clear that feminist critique has been recognized by the malestream as a considerable political force, even if that recognition often takes the form of attack on, or misrepresentation and suppression of the feminist position. There has been a lot of "debate," yet the most striking feature of it is its lack of engagement with what is actually new in, and central to, the feminist position. Much of the debate is a replay of the arguments evolved in the 1960s as part of the "sexual revolution." Pornographers, the publishing industry, the culture industry, advertising, and the legal profession have joined forces in campaigns against feminist legislative proposals. Tensions have also emerged between women in professional organizations close to such power bases and women of the autonomous Women's Liberation Movement (e.g., between the National Conference on

Women and the Law and feminist lawyer Catharine McKinnon [see Catharine A. MacKinnon, 1987, "On Collaboration," in *Feminism Unmodified*]). In the United Kingdom, a "high" literary publisher, Faber & Faber, has launched its new foray into publishing books on "sex" with a glossy journalistic book on United States and European pornographers (*Porn Gold,* David Hebditch & Nick Anning, 1988). The traditional dividing line between "respectable" culture and "pornography" as a particular market outlet is disappearing.

In the defense against the feminist intervention, the issue of women consumers of pornography has been used most prominently as an attempt to subvert feminist knowledge. This means finding token women who will speak for pornography, either as voluntary and enthusiastic consumers of it, as producers of it (e.g., the daughters of Hugh Heffner of the *Playboy* empire and of Paul Raymond of Raymond's Revue Bar, *Men Only,* who have both become executives and editors of softcore magazines), or as keen models in the production of it. Although prior to the feminist intervention, women's opinion on pornography seemed immaterial, it now seems to be an obligatory gesture to allude to it.

Women's response to this resistance has been very divided, along the lines suggested above. The need for women to be seen to be "pro-sex," and hence, because men have set the terms, also propornography, is still very powerful. The redefinition of the issue of pornography as one of sexuality has been a very effective strategy of male resistance, especially with its concomitant deployment of sexological and psychoanalytical theories. However, within the narrower feminist movement which stands behind the critique of pornography, analysis has developed and progressed, in particular in conjunction with the analysis of sex work, prostitution and trafficking in women.

THE PRESENT AND FUTURE

The most direct contribution of the feminist analysis of pornography to the enhancement of women's lives is its provision of arguments to women who are oppressed by pornography, but have been unable to voice this oppression. The first step towards a resolution of the debate within the WLM would be an engagement with the terms of the new feminist analysis of pornography as sex discrimination, and the recognition of women's oppression through pornography. The denial of other women's oppression in the affirmation of individual women's pleasure seems to me a significant regression from the original aims of feminism.

It is difficult to talk of feminist gains in the public arena, as these are consistently fought and resisted. However, I think that the feminist analysis has made enormous gains within feminism as a theory and as knowledge, and among women. It has helped to bring feminist analysis into many women's lives and to reach constituencies which "theory" alone would not, whereas it is the "feminist opposition" to antipornography feminism which remains firmly grounded in a middle-class and educated elite. I expect that the antipornography campaigns in different countries will continue to gain a mass grassroots base which will enable legal initiatives, even while the malestream seems to be winning the battle on account of its access to the media. The important question to be asking now is how much energy is to be put into the ideological battle with opposition, feminist or malestream, and how much into activism and campaigning for legal measures which will both have effects on the real lives of women, and effects in terms of education and consciousness raising. In other words, the questions which remain are truly political, rather than theoretical.

NOTES

1.   This is an adaptation of the title of a talk Robin Morgan gave many times in the 1960s entitled: "Theory and Practice: Pornography and Rape"; a version of this is published in Laura Lederer [1980; also, Morgan, 1980]. My main focus in this essay is on the United States and the United Kingdom, where information and documentation are more easily available.

2.   See Andrea Dworkin and Catharine A. MacKinnon (1988); this contains a complete documentation of the different versions of the Ordinance as presented in different states, as well as an analysis of the issues. Also Liz Kelly (1985) gives a brief outline of the arguments between Ordinance feminists and FACT; Susanne Kappeler (1988) contains an update and report on the German legislation. *Pornography and Sexual Violence: Evidence of the Links* (1988) is a complete transcript of the Public Hearings on the Ordinance of the Minneapolis City Council in 1983. One West German legislative proposal based on the Ordinance can be found in *Emma Sonderband* 1988; a different adaptation is proposed by Susanne Baer, Vera Slupik, and Hweidemarie Renk, 1988. A short summary of the history of the Bellingham Ordinance can be found in Margaret A. Baldwin (1989).

BIBLIOGRAPHY

Baer, Susanne, Slupik, Vera, & Renk, Hweidemarie (1988). Entwurf eines Gesetzes gegen Pornographie. *Kritische Justiz, 21*(2).

Baldwin, Margaret A. (1989a, Spring). Law and feminism. *Yale Journal of Law, 1*(1). 111–155.

Baldwin, Margaret A. (1989b). Pornography and the traffice in women: Brief on behalf of Trudee Able-Peterson et al., Amici Curiae in Support of Defendant and Intervenor–Defendants, Village Books v. City of Bellingham, 1989.

Dworkin, Andrea (1981). *Pornography: Men possessing women.* London: The Women's Press.

Dworkin, Andrea & MacKinnon, Catharine A. (1988). *Pornography and civil rights: A new day for women's equality.* Minneapolis: Organizing Against Pornography.

Emma (1988, Sonderband [Special Issue]). *Por No*, Alice Schwarzer (Ed.), *Emma Sonderband* 5 (Cologne, February 1988).

FACT (1986). *Caught looking: Feminism, pornography and censorship.* Seattle, WA: The Real Comet Press.

Hebditch, David & Anning, Nick (1988). *Porn gold.* London: Faber & Faber.

Kappeler, Susanne (1988, Spring). International struggles against pornography. *Trouble & Strife, 13.*

Kelly, Liz (1985, Winter). Feminist vs Feminist. *Trouble & Strife, 7.*

Lederer, Laura (Ed.). (1980). *Take back the night: Women on pornography.* New York: William Morrow.

MacKinnon, Catharine A. (1983). Feminism, Marxism, method and the state: Toward feminist jurisprudence. *Signs, 8*(4), 635–658.

MacKinnon, Catharine A. (1987). On Collaboration. *Feminism unmodified: Discourses on life and law.* Cambridge MA: Harvard University Press.

Millett, Kate (1970). *Sexual politics.* New York: Doubleday.

Morgan, Robin (1980). Theory and practice: Pornography and rape. In Laura Lederer (Ed.), *Take back the night: Women on pornography.* New York: William Morrow.

Rhodes, Dusty & McNeill, Sandra (Eds.). (1985). *Women against violence against women.* London: Everywoman Press.

Pornography and sexual violence: Evidence of the links. (1988). London: Everywoman Press.

Russo, Ann (1990). *The Feminist Debates Over Pornography: Civil Rights & Civil Liberties.* Unpublished dissertation, Speech Communication, University of Illinois at Urbana–Champaign.

Soble, Alan (1986). *Pornography: Marxism, feminism and the future of sexuality,* New Haven, CT: Yale University Press.

U.S. Attorney General's Commission on Pornography. (1986). *Final Report.* Washington, DC: Government Printing Office.

Chapter 35

Reproductive Technology, Genetic Engineering, and Woman Hating

Renate Klein

The recognition that reproductive technology is a new form of violence against women, and—in connection with genetic engineering— is fast becoming an instrument of unprecedented control and power over *all* peoples' lives, has been growing slowly since the mid-1970s, especially since the birth of the world's first "test-tube" baby, Louise Brown, in England in 1978. On the one hand it is fair to say that it is a *new* debate. On the other hand, with the exception of the increasingly "high tech" methods used, there is not much "new" in the ideology and practice of "new" reproductive technologies: it is the "old" ideology of power and control over women's (reproductive) lives in the hands of a small group of "experts," usually white, middle-class scientists and doctors in the industrialized West who have sought to control women's bodies at least since the Middle Ages (see Renate Duelli Klein, 1985). Consequently, the analysis of these new technologies by feminists followed in the wake of *prior* feminist criticisms of patriarchal medicine exposing it as "hidden malpractice" (Gena Corea, 1977): dangerous and enforced fertility control such as harmful contraceptives and compulsory sterilization, as well as the growing interest in transsexual surgery (Janice G. Raymond, 1979). Feminist critiques of sciences can be found in the early 1970s (e.g., in the United States by Rita Arditti, 1974; see also Janice G. Raymond, 1979a, 1979b; and Rita Arditti, Pat Brennan, & Steve Cavrak, 1980). In Germany, natural scientists founded an association, Women in Science, in the mid-1970s and at their regular annual meetings consistently exposed Western science as a patriarchal construct and explored concepts for a new feminist science. [See Marian Lowe, this volume.]

Significantly, as in the case of Janice Raymond and Gena Corea, it was often the same individuals who at the end of the 1970s began to incorporate their growing knowledge of the violence and further threat of the new reproductive technologies to women's physical and psychological integrity into their *previous* analyses of patriarchal medicine, surgery, and science. Already, then, their radical analyses indicated how these developments will affect women of different classes and ethnicities, that is increase the exploitation of poor and so-called Third World women. Significantly also (and best analyzed by Gena Corea, 1985), they began to make visible the fact that since the early 1920s men have been experimenting on animals with such technologies as artificial insemination by donor, superovulation, in vitro fertilization, embryo flushing and transfer, embryo experimentation, "surrogacy," and sex determination (see Julie Murphy, 1984). By the mid-1970s, the extension of these technologies to women as human breeders was imminent. Infertile people inevitably became the focus of the expanding patriarchal control of the production of children "made to order" and hence were subjected to commercial exploitation (see Patricia Spallone & Deborah Lynn Steinberg, 1987).

The first conference on the topic of the new reproductive technologies was organized in 1979 in Amherst, Massachusetts and resulted in two publications: *Birth Control and Controlling Birth: Women-Centred Perspectives* and *the Custom-Made Child?: Women-Centred Perspectives* (Helen B. Holmes, Betty Hoskins, & Michael Gross, 1980; 1981). Sociologists Hilary Rose and Jalna Hanmer (in the United Kingdom) published perhaps the earliest article pointing out the "technological fix" of new reproductive technologies (1976; see also Jalna Hanmer & Pat Allen, 1980; Jalna Hammer, 1981; 1983). Canadian theorist Mary O'Brien deserves recognition for her early insights in *The Politics of Reproduction* (1981), in which she introduced the concept of alienation inherent in male reproduction which, as we now know, is chillingly emulated for *women* in the new reproductive technologies: at the moment eggs are "harvested" from a woman's body, after dangerous hormonal bombardment and invasive surgery, parts of her body are being disconnected from her and become available for manipulation (i.e., the manufacturing into embryos by means of adding sperm) and later transfer into the womb of a woman—not necessarily her own[1].

INTERNATIONAL NETWORKS

The awareness that the new reproductive technologies are a *global* feminist issue of concern to *all* women in *all* parts of the world began to be made explicit only in the 1980s. In 1984, an international panel entitled "The Death of the Female?" at the Second International Disciplinary Congress on Women in Groningen, Holland (organized by Becky Holmes, United States and Robyn Rowland, Australia), led to the founding of FINNRET (Feminist International Network on the New Reproductive Technologies). Focusing on sex selection and "choice" (Gena Corea et al., 1985, 1987), the presentations by women from India, the United States, England and Australia, moved the 500 women attending the session to follow Jalna Hanmer's call for an international network which, as its first commitment, undertook the organization of an "Emergency Conference" to take place in 1985 in Sweden.

In 1985, the connection between reproductive technologies and genetic engineering in humans, as well as animals and plants, was spelled out for the first time in the Resolution of the First National Congress Frauen gegen Gen- und Reproduktionstechnologien (Women against Gene and Reproductive Technologies) in Bonn, West Germany, attended by more than 2,000 women. In the same year at the Emergency Conference of FINNRET in Vällinge, Sweden, the 80 delegates from 16 countries changed its name to FINRRAGE (the Feminist International Network of Resistance to Reproductive and Genetic Engineering) to make it clear that FINRRAGE affiliates *resist* these technologies and also, that genetic engineering is an intrinsic component of the threat these technologies present to *all* forms of life. The Conference Resolution supported and expanded the previous German resolution (reprinted in Patricia Spallone & Deborah Lynn Steinberg, 1987, pp. 211–212).

The radical feminist resistance to the new reproductive technologies and genetic engineering—from its beginning to the present—has always been international in its scope, practice, and affiliations: both 1985 congresses were attended by women from the "North" and the "South" and in 1989 FINRRAGE held a conference in Bangladesh attended by 100 women from Asia, Africa, and South America and 30 from Europe, the United States and Australia. FINRRAGE affiliates in 1986 also held conferences in Austria, Australia, Spain, and Hearings at the European Parliament in Brussels. In 1987 the Conseil du Statut de la Femme organized an International Forum "Sortir la Maternite du Laboratoire" in Quebec, Canada, and in the same year, the Austrian Government held Gene Hearings to which the minister for Women's Affairs invited feminist experts, many of them from FINRRAGE. In 1987 Gena Corea, Janice Raymond and Patricia Hynes, together with so-called surrogate mothers such as Elizabeth Kane, were among the founders of the United States coalition against surrogacy. In 1988 the journal, *Reproductive and Genetic Engineering: Journal of International Feminist Analysis* (Pergamon Press) was founded to facilitate and increase the worldwide exchange of feminist theory and praxis with regard to the development of both human and animal and plant biotechnologies and women's resistance to it (see Jocelynne Scutt, 1988; Patricia Spallone, 1989).

THE CLAIMS OF THE GENETIC ENGINEERS AND THEIR PROMOTERS

The promoters and practitioners of reproductive and genetic engineering—mainly male scientists, doctors, and multinational pharmaceutical companies—claim that their tech-nologically "assisted reproduction" will provide thousands of desperate infertile "couples" with the long-desired child—in spite of the evidence that the test-tube baby technology (IVF) is a failed and experimental technology (IVF has a 90-95% *failure rate*). Women are regarded as defect "mother machines" (Gena Corea's term), as "living laboratories" (Robyn Rowland's term) and their well-being and health is threatened with short- and long-term "side" effects from the fertility drugs administered to increase the production of ripe egg cells (e.g., ovarian cysts, hyperstimulated ovaries, blurred vision, the promotion of cancer and premature menopause; see Renate Klein, 1989a and 1989b). At least 20 women have died while on an IVF program, many end up broken in spirit and physically sick after years on the medical treadmill and with their relationships on the rocks. Increasingly, reproduc-tive technology is used for infertile *men* whose *fertile* female partners are subjected to the IVF (or GIFT) procedure and in some cases have been rendered infertile through these "treatments." Increasingly also, they are used for unexplained infertility in a "trial and error" way and for people "at genetic risk."

Genetic counseling and embryo screening is said to prevent the "misery" of a disabled child and provide happy healthy people—whereas, in reality such attempts to decide which life is "worthy" and which "unworthy" amounts to a practice of selection and eradication and is the latest version of eugenicist theory and praxis. The control over what kind of women in which countries will be allowed to have what kind of children (and of what sex?) becomes more and more insidious: from compulsory amnioscenteses (which in India led to the abortion of 78,000 female fetuses between 1978 and 1983; see Forum Against Sex Discrimination and Sex Preselection, 1989) and chorion villus sampling to pre-implantation diagnosis. With this latest "feat" practiced for the first time in England in 1989, "quality control" checks now occur at the level of conception: in a procedure called embryo biopsy a cell from the embryo is examined for chromosomal damage *before* it is implanted in the woman's womb. The reductionist logic is not only deeply discriminatory of disabled people (and what precisely is a disability? who decides?), but also cruel and false as there will always be disabled children and it will be the *mothers* who will be blamed for their existence.

With regard to reproductive technology the feminist analysis is unique because of its *women-centeredness*. It distinguishes itself sharply from the embryo-centered "fetalist" position of the catholic church and the new right (Janice Raymond, 1987). Surrogacy is opposed not because of moralistic reasons ("it goes against the sanctity of the nuclear family") but because it uses women as a commodity: as living incubators to turn a sperm donor's genes into a product—*his* child. Feminists have been the only ones to point out again and again that the availability of living women as producers of "raw materials" (egg cells) necessary for the creation of embryos is the *sine qua non* of embryo research (Robyn Rowland, 1987). Slowly, but encouragingly, this position is now being supported by infertile women who have been themselves through the trauma of IVF and other reproductive technologies (Alison Solomon, 1989). We assert that these technologies do not present "choice" but, on the contrary, close down choices (e.g., the choice to say "no" to infertility treatment).

RESEARCH PRIORITIES

The feminist investigations of the new reproductive technologies and genetic engineering are crucially different from patriarchal research in their conscious rejection of fragmentation and division, thus resulting in the connecting of issues seen as totally different by patriarchal science and medicine. Examples range from infertility/fertility control to genetic engineering/reproductive technology, which from a radical feminist analysis are inextricably linked with one another whereas in the patriarchal logic, they are perceived as totally different topics.

Feminist research on reproductive and genetic engineering can be of "reactionary" or "actionary" orientation. The former builds on previous feminist analyses of patriarchy's efforts to control and dominate women's lives, specifically in the area of reproduction, to suit its need for population control, be it pronatalist or antinatalist. Thus the global interactions of fertility- and infertility-control are examined. Feminists are pointing out how previous "technological fixes" led to the infertility of women and men (e.g., through IUDs, the pill, DES, herbicides, pesticides, and workplace hazards). The feminist analysis also rejects male notions of women's bodies as "diseased," specifically with regard to women's reproductive biology from menstruation to menopause (see Emily Martin, 1987, for an excellent study of this topic). [See also Joan Altekruse and Sue Rosser, this volume.] Technopatriarchal science is further removed from validating the sustaining life energy of the interconnecting forces of complex organisms (e.g., human beings, animals, or plants), by "advances" in gene technology (e.g., recombinant DNA) which speed up the dissection of whole beings to be reassembled according to man's (sic) desire: bits of chromosomes are inserted or removed or even exchanged between species (e.g., from humans into animals or plants or vice versa).

On the "actionary" side of feminist research, many women-centered demands are made and new research questions asked. The desire for children and the urge to mother are re-analyzed in the context of women's continued oppression including emotional violence against women. Importantly, the question of the meaning of "choice" must be explored. We also need to know more about the stigma of infertility and why women undergo procedures that are dangerous and life-threatening to become pregnant and give birth. Specific research projects are being undertaken to understand the life crisis which infertility can create and to devise support systems for women (and men) with a fertility problem or "at risk," so they have a real choice to say "no" to the new reproductive technologies and genetic screening (Renate D. Klein, 1989b, 1989c). And more research needs to be undertaken on the causes of infertility, especially as they relate to the whole person and not just her or his "diseased" parts. Finally, we urgently need further work toward a feminist "ethics of integrity" (Janice Raymond, 1979b; see also Christine Overall, 1987).

NEW METHODS
FOR NEW KNOWLEDGE

A feminist investigation of reproductive and genetic engineering is best characterized by its *organic*[2] and *global* perspective: (a) by reconnecting the compartmentalized bits and pieces the promoters and practitioners of the "Gene Age" produce in their vivisections of women and nature; and (b) by making them visible as part of the global oppression of women by racist (techno)patriarchy.

With regard to reproductive technology we expose the short- and long-term effects of the technologies on the women and the children. The consequences include devastating emotional and economic effects on the majority of its users (90–95%) for whom they fail, and the repercussions of IVF as a source of living women and their bodies as raw material for research and embryo experimentation. This is not confined to those who directly use the technologies but applies to *all* women as a social group, and particularly to poor and Third World women who are more and more likely to be abused as experimental "material" for research that is increasingly becoming regulated in the West. Sex selection, surrogacy, prenatal diagnosis, and the international trafficking in women are all part of the same vicious cycle that keeps women subordinated to men and must be looked at jointly.

We also study the gains that doctors, scientists, businessmen, and governments have made from the technological control over the (in)fertility of women and expose them as the stuff of which the *system of patriarchy is made:* dominating, debilitating, and maiming women's existence and their (our) sense of Self. See Janice Raymond, 1986, for her analysis of patriarchy as heteroreality.

RESPONSE TO FEMINIST WORK

Feminist efforts to expose the new reproductive technologies and genetic engineering have undoubtedly had an impact on society at large, again in some countries (Germany and Australia) more than others (the United Kingdom and the United States). In Australia (and in the state of Victoria in particular), the FINRRAGE perspective is part of the public debate and has had an influence on what IVF doctors call "terribly restrictive legislation" with regard to embryo experimentation and which has indeed led to a slowing down of their research activities (and in the case of two research scientists leaving for the United Kingdom). Specifically, FINRRAGE affiliates have been sought as consultants to law-makers in a number of states. Through the considerable feminist presence in the media, infertile women who consider using the new reproductive technologies are now much better informed about the risks and know which questions to ask of their doctors (who absolutely loathe this feminist input!). Despite these successes, however, the biggest obstacle to put a stop to these dangerous technologies lies in the surviving belief in society at large that the desire for a child justifies any means, even if they have only a remote chance of resulting in a baby. Demands to bring these technologies to a halt because they constitute unethical experimentation on human beings and violate the human rights convention are seen as "going too far."

DEALING WITH THE RESISTANCE

The majority of "technodocs," genetic engineers, and scientists react to our radical analysis with hatred and contempt; sometimes also (to give them the benefit of the doubt) with utter lack of understanding that women with a fertility problem ought not to be looked at as "fertilization failures," "hostile wombs," or "diseased tubes." Another strategy is to try to ignore our work completely—as happened to me in the United Kingdom after the publication of my book *Infertility* (1989b), when with the exception of the *Observer*, no mainstream newspaper would print a review and I was told by a journalist that infertility specialists had dismissed the women's stories in my book as "irrelevant anecdotes."

When ignoring does not work, as in Australia when with the same publication I got primetime television coverage and dozens of radio interviews, two further strategies are employed. The first is to deny the truth of our work as IVF embryologist Alan Trounson did on TV in response to a program in which two women who had been through IVF spoke out against it, and I summarized some of Robyn Rowland's and my findings on the adverse effects of the superovulation drugs (Renate Duelli Klein and Robyn Rowland, 1988). Trounson claimed he had never seen an ovarian cyst due to the drugs. Even his colleagues write about cysts and hyperstimulation as a result of superovulation, the chemical manufacturer mentions it as one of the drugs' "side effects," and in my study of 40 women who had undergone IVF, 9 had developed ovarian cysts.

The other strategy is to recognize that our work cannot be ignored and to integrate part of our analysis into the IVF rhetoric—thereby, however, grossly distorting it. For example, our demand for independent counseling and self-help groups for women (and men) with a fertility problem *before* they have gone near an infertility clinic is approvingly regurgitated by technodocs ("the feminist attitude to counseling is excellent"), and then suggested as counseling *on* the IVF program (which of course helps to keep women on the treadmill and is therefore *not* a feminist strategy). More vicious strategies consist in spreading rumors as in the case of my colleague Robyn Rowland when on one occasion local journalists and overseas visitors were told that she was being sued by a drug company, and therefore was not a reliable source. On another occasion it was said that she was having a nervous breakdown (and again was not worth consulting). Such dirty tricks must mean that we are successful—but they nevertheless indicate that there is an emotional price to pay for the work we do. Perhaps most distressing is a strategy of technodocs in a number of countries (it has happened to me and many of my colleagues in Germany, the United Kingdom, Australia and the United States) to confront us with one of their infertile "patients" who then attacks us as denying her the "choice" to have a child, thus trying to use women's words to discredit us rather than trying to tell the truth about the technologies.

On the positive side, increasingly, our expertise is sought by women's health centers and services who in a number of countries are beginning to offer feminist support, self-help and counseling groups (Ute Winkler and Traute Schönenberg, 1989). Other women's groups such as nurses, feminist sociologists, social workers, anthropologists, women in medicine, law societies, and women's studies ask FINRRAGE affiliates to speak at seminars and courses at universities and explore the topic. Maria Mies and other FINRRAGE affiliates report from Germany that they are in high demand as speakers by union women, consumer groups, housewives associations, and protestant women's groups who agree with their radical position. In Australia the magazine of the Australian consumer organization, Choice, published a damning report on IVF clinics (October, 1989), much of it derived from (unacknowledged) FINRRAGE material.

DISAGREEMENTS
AMONG FEMINISTS

There is predictable opposition to the radical feminist position within the patriarchal framework but there is also disagreement from other feminists. Some liberal feminists in Great Britain (see Michelle Stanworth, 1987), some members of the "Global Network on Reproductive Rights," and, best organized, a group of academic women in the United States with a core working group at Rutgers University disagree with the FINRRAGE position as taking away "choices" from individual women, and reproach FINRRAGE for being "into censorship," "luddites," "over-the-top," and "simplistic." Sometimes FINRRAGE is accused of being against motherhood—but then at other times the network is accused of being "essentialist" and *into* motherhood (preferring the "natural way" of having children to the one of "technologically assisted reproduction"). In the view of Lori Andrews, a research attorney with the American Bar Association, the new reproductive technologies constitute "reproductive alternatives," and, when regulated carefully, can benefit individual women by providing them with a healthy child (Cohen & Taub, 1988; 1989). German sociologist Maria Mies has criticized this view as "legitimation for the new reproduction industry" by encouraging "the full-fledged commercialization of reproduction" in which the integrity of the human person is lost in favor of "the dividual" who sees her (or his) body as property and is hence free to sell or swap parts of it (e.g., wombs, egg cells, embryos, etc.) The liberalism underlying the ideology of the "supermarket of reproductive alternatives," Mies posits, "is a perversion of everything that ideology of feminism stands for" (Maria Mies, 1988, p. 225). Australian lawyer, Jocelynne Scutt, discussing Andrews' advocacy of surrogate motherhood comments that "Andrews' failure to acknowledge the political nature of the world in which we live . . . is a monumental leap back into 'world-before political consciousness' " (Jocelynne Scutt, 1990, p. 76).

Reproductive liberals sometimes accuse the FINRRAGE position as "absolutist." As Janice Raymond writes:

> Increasingly, opposition is translated as absolutism. "Absolutism" is becoming one of those abused words that is used frequently to discredit the position of those who take a strong and often passionate stand against something . . . "*A single oppositional stance" is out of fashion in feminism, as is outrage, passion, and explicit political activism.* (Emphasis added, 1989, p. 140)

The insistence on a "detached" view (unpleasantly reminiscent of the claims about "objectivity") fits into the current "Zeitgeist" of postmodernist, deconstructionist theory enthusiastically adapted by feminists from French philosophers (men) which, by using exactly the same tools on texts as reproductive and genetic engineering on women and nature—cutting, dividing, dissecting—posit that there is no such thing as "reality"—and in fact "woman." They thereby feed the liberal ideology of "everything goes" and lead to political apathy. Theory devoid from praxis is in—passionate action grounded in *experience* is out! The multitudes of subjectivities are all equal. It remains to be seen if the virus of such thinking currently reproducing itself virulently among academic feminists in western countries will continue to survive. This division amongst women plays into the hands of the technologists who pit "good" (sensible) reproductive liberals against "bad" (crazy, over the top) radicals. [See Barbara Pope, this volume, for discussion of disagreements among feminists.]

GROWING INTEREST

The most important contribution of the radical feminist resistance to reproductive and genetic engineering is undoubtedly its organic and international discussion of the threat these technologies pose for women and all life. Specifically, our work enables those who might consider becoming consumers of the technologies, for example infertile women, to put a framework to their already existing uneasiness about the technologies and makes it possible for them to say "no" to the use of the technologies. Through the existence of our international network the *multidimensional* nature of the problem of technological "progress" is highlighted: the complex links are made obvious, the need to work together and to respect our diversity is made explicit. The many topics raised, for example the meaning of motherhood, the role of heterosexuality, the internalization of the "technological fix" in our own minds, the pro- and antinatalist forces in population control movements and above all (techno)patriarchy's recurring disrespect for life in all its forms—including women's—to name just a few, revitalize feminism because these are topics going to the *roots* of women's oppression. With the exception of the previously mentioned reproductive liberals, interest in the FINRRAGE position by the Women's Liberation Movement in general is growing. In order to reduce differences between the reproductive liberals and the radical feminists, the former would need to change their compartmentalized view of these technologies to a holistic one which includes a historical analysis, the impact on Third World women and the connections between biotechnologies on humans, plants, and animals. Above all, I believe the reproductive liberals need to acknowledge reproductive and genetic engineering as a fundamental *threat* to the lives of present, and, even more so, future generations of women and all life on earth by a ruthless, profit-oriented, life- and women-hating technopatriarchy. (See Irene Diamond, this volume, for a discussion of ecofeminism.)

EXPECTATIONS OF FUTURE

Despite opposition from radical feminists and other concerned members of the community it remains to be seen if the rat-race in human and nonhuman biotechnology can be stopped: after all, it is, after the computer industry, the new "hope" for financial gains in the future. The question is, will those of us who genuinely disagree with the death-dance of split cells and split women be strong enough to counter the enormous financial powers behind the empire of reproductive and genetic engineering? Will we find enough allies to join us in the resistance: women (and a few men) whose "thinking heart and feeling mind" (Janice Raymond's expression, 1986) offer the passion and intelligence of a life-loving philosophy that makes the consumers reject these "miracle" technologies?

Indian physicist Vandana Shiva believes that it is possible. She trusts women's well-known capacity for survival and quotes women's resistance against logging—the Chipko movement—in India (Vandana Shiva, 1989). Maria Mies and other German women are hopeful too; they believe that "ordinary" people have had enough of technological fixes that produce disasters such as Chernobyl and Bhopal. (Indeed Europeans' trust in "experts" in white labcoats suffered a big blow when their incompetence became obvious after the events in Chernobyl.) On the other hand, feminists in the United Kingdom may be less optimistic because the tight-knit media cum science alliance is so difficult to infiltrate. And radical feminists in the United States are angry about the prevalence of liberation thought and the general cowardice—including some feminists'—to take a stand and speak their minds. On the pessimistic side too, it needs to be pointed out that violence against women in all forms continues to be a most distressing issue globally (consider the December 1989 murder in Canada of 14 female engineering students by an "ordinary" man "simply" because he hated feminists.)

My hope is, however, that multidimensional and international radical resistance will be continuing to alert people to what is going on. FINRRAGE affiliates will continue to publish books (e.g., the Bangladesh Proceedings and Robyn Rowland's *Living Laboratories*, both 1991). Hopefully, also, in the area of reproductive technologies the critical voices of women who have undergone IVF, testing and/or genetic screening of their embryos and other prenatal invasions will increase public consciousness in the same way they have done in the area of surrogacy in the United States. Maybe then, by the time the next technical "advance" is announced, for example that, as in cows, it is possible to mature immature eggs outside women's bodies (so that a slice of any woman's ovary will do for the production of embryos which can then be transferred into any "surrogate" woman), or the further development of the artifical womb, grassroot resistance will be strong enough to demand a stop before more women are hurt. FINRRAGE plans a further international conference in Brazil in 1991 and an International Tribunal on Medical and Scientific Crimes against Women; both events will further increase public knowledge about the danger and damage of biotechnologies.

One of the most important areas of radical feminist theory and action to pursue in the future is to continue to expose (techno)patriarchy's iron grip on women as the material and emotional producers and reproducers of its dominant culture. A lot of input into counter-active feminist education (such as women's studies on all educational levels) is needed to emphasize the embodied rights of women to decent healthcare, water, food, and shelter as well as physical and psychological dignity and integrity, and to teach respect for the wholeness and interdependencies between all peoples and all life forms on earth. Above all, however, globally women must continue to resist in order to survive: (techno)patriarchy needs to end—or we will all end with it.

NOTES

1. Frequently, when reviewing the history of feminist discussions on reproductive technology, Shulamith Firestone, the author of *Dialectic of Sex* (1970) is mentioned as an advocate because, as she proposed, it would free women "from the tyranny of reproduction" (p. 193). Without wanting to discount the importance of Firestone's groundbreaking book, her ideas on test-tube babies were not grounded in practice. Put differently, it would take eight more years before the first test-tube child was actually born. Furthermore, Firestone, in 1970 an ardent supporter of the contraceptive pill, which she saw as a technological miracle enhancing women's liberation, 20 years later confronted with all the evidence—social and medical—against the pill might well have changed her mind after feminist analyses had began to pinpoint the dangers of the new reproductive technologies for women (unfortunately, she did not respond to our invitation to write a comment on *Test-Tube Women* in 1983).

2. This expression came up for the first time in an interview with Angela Miles at the National Women's Studies Association Conference in Baltimore, Maryland, June 1989, and I want to thank Angie for her stimulating discussion which led us to the introduction of this term which I think excellently characterizes resistance to gene and reproductive technologies.

BIBLIOGRAPHY

Arditti, Rita. (1974). Women as objects: Science and sexual politics. *Science for the People, 6*(5), 8–32.

Arditti, Rita, Brennan, Pat, & Cavrak, Steve. (1980). *Science and liberation.* Boston: South End Press.

Arditti, Rita, Klein, Renate Duelli, & Minden, Shelley. (Eds.). (1984–1989.) *Test-tube women: What future for motherhood?* London: Pandora Press.

Choice. (1989, October). IVF: A plea for honesty. *Journal of the Australian Consumer Association,* 17–25.

Cohen, Sherrill, & Taub, Nadine. (Eds.). (1988). *Briefing handbook: Reproductive laws for the 1990s.* Newark, NJ: Women's Rights Litigation Clinic, and Institute for Research on Women, Rutgers Law School.

Cohen, Sherrill, & Taub, Nadine. (Eds.). (1989). *Reproductive laws for the 1990s.* Clifton, NJ: Humana Press.

Conseil du statut de la femme. (1988). *Sortir la maternité du laboratoire.* [Motherhood from the laboratory]. Quebec: Gouvernement du Quebec.

Corea, Gena. (1977/1985). *The hidden malpractice: How (American) medicine mistreats women.* New York: Harper Colophon.

Corea, Gena. (1985). *The mother machine: Reproductive technologies from artificial insemination to artificial wombs.* New York: Harper & Row.

Corea, Gena, Klein, Renate Duelli, Hanmer, Jalna, Holmes, Helen B., Hoskins, Betty, Kishwar, Madhu, Raymond, Janice, Rowland, Robyn, & Syeinbacher, Roberta. (1985/1987). *Man-made women: How new reproductive technologies affect women.* London: Hutchinson; Bloomington: Indiana University Press.

FINRRAGE-UBINIG. (1991). Proceedings from 1989 Bangladesh Conference, Dhaka.

Firestone, Shulamith. (1970). *The dialectic of sex.* London: Paladin.

Forum Against Sex Determination and Sex Pre-Selection. (1989). *Campaign against sex discrimination and sex pre-selection in India: Our experience.* Bombay: Author.

Frauen gegen Gentechnik und Reproduktionstechnik [Women against gene- and reproductive technology]. (1986). Dokumentation zum Kongress von 19.-21.4. 1985 in Bonn. Köln: Verlag Kölner Volksblatt.

Hanmer, Jalna. (1981). Sex-predetermination, artificial insemination and the maintenance of male-dominated culture. In Helen Roberts (Ed.), *Women, health and reproduction.* London: Routledge & Kegan Paul.

Hanmer, Jalna. (1983). Reproductive technology: The future for women? In Joan Rothschild (Ed.), *Machina ex dea.* Elmsford, NY: Pergamon Press.

Hanmer, Jalna, & Allen, Pat. (1980). Reproductive engineering—The final solution? In Brighton Women and Science Collective (Ed.), *Alice through the microscope: The power of science over women's lives.* London: Virago.

Holmes, Helen B., Hoskins, Betty, & Gross, Michael. (Eds.). (1980). *Birth control and controlling birth. Women-centered perspectives.* New Jersey: Humana Press.

Holmes, Helen B., Hoskins, Betty, & Gross, Michael. (Eds.). (1981). *The Custom-made child? Women-centered Perspectives.* New Jersey: Humana Press.

Klein, Renate Duelli. (1985/1987). What's 'new' about the 'new' reproduction technologies? In Gena Corea et al. (Eds.), *Man-made women.* London: Hutchinson Press, Bloomington: Indiana University Press.

Klein, Renate. (1989a). *The exploitation of a desire: Women's experiences with in vitro fertilisation.* Geelong, Australia: Deakin University Press.

Klein, Renate D., (Ed.). (1989b). *Infertility: Women speak out about their experiences of reproductive medicine.* London: Pandora Press.

Klein, Renate. (1989c). Women with a fertility problem: An increasing group of clients for feminist therapists. *Feminist Therapy Newsletter, 5*(2), 11–17.

Klein, Renate/Rowland, Robyn. (1988). Women as test sites for fertility drugs: Clomiphene citrate and hormonal cocktails. *Reproductive and Genetic Engineering: Journal of International Feminist Analysis, 1*(3), 251–274.

Klein, Renate, Raymond, Janice G., & Dumble, Lynette T. (1991). *RU486: Misconceptions, myths, and morals.* Spinfex Press: Melbourne/Institute on Women and Technology. Cambridge, MA: MIT.

Martin, Emily. (1987). *The woman in the body: A cultural analysis of reproduction.* Boston: Beacon Press.

Mies, Maria. (1988). From the individual to the dividual: In the supermarket of 'reproductive alternatives.' *Reproductive and Genetic Engineering: Journal of International Feminist Analysis, 1*(3), 225–238.

Murphy, Julie. (1984). Egg farming and women's future. In Rita Arditti, Renate Duelli Klein, & Shelley Minden (Eds.), *Test-tube women: What future for motherhood?* London: Pandora Press.

O'Brien, Mary. (1981). *The politics of reproduction.* London: Routledge & Kegan Paul.

Overall, Christine. (1987). *Ethics and human reproduction: A feminist analysis.* Winchester, MA: Unwin Hyman.

Raymond, Janice G. (1979a). *Fetishism, feminism and genetic technology.* Paper presented at the American Association for the Advancement of Science meeting in Houston, Texas.

Raymond, Janice G. (1979b). *The Transsexual Empire.* London: The Women's Press.

Raymond, Janice G. (1986). *A passion for friends. Toward a philosophy of female affection.* Boston: Beacon Press.

Raymond, Janice G. (1987). Fetalists and feminists: They are not the same. In Patricia Spallone & Deborah Lynn Steinberg (Eds.), *Made to order. The myth of reproductive and genetic progress.* Elmsford, NY: Pergamon Press.

Raymond, Janice G. (1989). At issue: Reproductive technologies, radical feminism and socialist liberalism. *Reproductive and Genetic Engineering: Journal of International Feminist Analysis, 2*(2), 133–142.

Rose, Hilary, & Hanmer, Jalna. (1976). Women's liberation: Reproduction and the technological fix. In Steven Rose & Hilary Rose (Eds.), *The political economy of science.* London: Macmillan.

Rothschild, Joan. (Ed.). (1983). *Machina ex dea: Feminist perspectives on technologies.* Elmsford, NY: Pergamon Press.

Rowland, Robyn. (1987). Making women visible in the embryo experimentation debate. *Bioethics, 1*(2), 179–188.

Rowland, Robyn. (1991). *Living laboratories: Women and reproductive technologies.* Melbourne: Macmillan, Bloomington: Indiana University Press.

Scutt, Jocelynne. (Ed.). (1988). *The baby machine. Commercialisation of motherhood.* Melbourne: McCulloch Publishing.

Scutt, Jocelynne. (1990). [Review of *Between strangers: Surrogate mothers, expectant fathers, and brave new babies* by Lori Andrews]. *Reproductive and Genetic Engineering: Journal of International Feminist Analysis, 3*(1), 73–76.

Shiva, Vandana. (1989). *Staying alive. Women, ecology and survival in India.* New Delhi: Kali for Women.

Solomon, Alison. (1989). Infertility as crisis: Coping, surviving—and thriving. In Renate D. Klein (Ed.) *Infertility: Women speak out about their experiences of reproductive medicine.* London: Pandora.

Spallone, Patricia. (1989). *Beyond conception: The new politics of reproduction.* London: Macmillan.

Spallone, Patricia, & Steinberg, Deborah Lynn. (Eds.). (1987). *Made to order. The myth of reproduction and genetic progress.* Elmsford, NY: Pergamon Press.

Stanworth, Michelle. (Ed.). (1987). *Reproductive technologies: Gender motherhood and medicine.* Cambridge England: Polity Press.

Winkler, Ute, & Schönenberg, Traute. (1989). Options for involuntarily childless women. In Renate D. Klein (Ed.), *Infertility: Women speak out about their experiences of reproductive medicine.* London: Pandora.

Chapter 36

The Condition of Patriarchy

Cheris Kramarae

Many feminists use the word frequently, suggesting it represents the most important concept of the feminist movement. Many feminists never use the word, arguing that it explains nothing and promotes confusion and racism. While the word patriarchy was around before the current resurgence of the women's movement and Women's Studies courses (Veronica Beechey, 1979), the concept of patriarchy has been recreated in the past two decades to analyze the origins and conditions of men's oppression of women. This re-wording has come from feminists with a variety of political perspectives. This essay reviews feminists' discussions on whether the concept of patriarchy provides promise or pitfall for our understanding of a long and wide history of men's nastiness to women.

One of the reasons I am interested in the ways researchers have used the concept is that in my work on women and communication and technology in the nineteenth and twentieth centuries, I have always *deliberately* avoided mentioning patriarchy, even when giving documentation of enduring restrictions, inequalities, and oppressions. Because patriarchy has not been a classic theoretical concept in traditional academic work, I, and many others I have talked with, have worried about whether it is too simplistic a catch-all concept, which, in saying so much, says too little. For many of us, the *thought* of using the term occurs much more frequently than the actual use of the word. In much academic feminist analysis, patriarchy has been a hidden concept, even when central.

In a wide-ranging search, I have gathered hundreds of articles and books, dealing with forms of inequality and inequity in a number of countries, which do make use of the word. There are not as many definition statements; even authors of books and articles which include the word in the title do not always include a definition, evidently assuming that patriarchy has a common-sense meaning, at least within feminist writing and talking.

The definitions which *are* given variously stress the origins, structure, and effects of a social system considered anathema to feminism and feminists. The definitions of patriarchy given below (sometimes in truncated form) summarize many of the concerns.

As Gerda Lerner (1986) points out in *The Creation of Patriarchy*, in recent years most feminists writing in English have used the term to mean the institutionalization of male dominance of women, rather than the system in which the father holds legal and economic

I thank Lana Rakow for her comments on an early draft of this essay.

power over the other members of his household, which is the older more narrow meaning of the term (p. 239). (However, see Joanna Liddle and Rama Joshi for their use of the more traditional meaning in their analysis of the authority of the father over the females and younger males in a household [1986, p. 52].)

Many of the definitions call attention to the pervasive and systemic organization of patriarchy. Kate Millett (1971) describes patriarchy as consisting of every system of power in society, including the military, industry, technology, universities, science, political offices, finances, and religion. She does not rank these institutions in terms of their overreaching control. More recently Sally Hacker (1989) does, in her critique of the military. She writes that the practices and ideology of patriarchy are embedded in military institutions, which, in large part, define masculinity (pp. 27, 56–57). [See also Elise Boulding, this volume.] Patriarchy is, in her analysis, a general form of male domination which includes control of sensuality, emotions, and passion. (See also Christine Ball, 1986.) Mervat Hatem (1986), in her study of patriarchy in eighteenth century Egypt, adds that primary and contradictory concerns of patriarchy are (1) the ideal of heterosexual intimacy and (2) the domination of women by men. She argues that discussions of patriarchy need to include study of homophobia and of sexual and class rivalry among men, general conditions which need to be studied in particular periods and locations.

Sylvia Walby (1990) writes of six structures, relatively autonomous, used by men to dominate, oppress and exploit women: the patriarchal mode of production (women's household labor expropriated by husband or cohabitees); patriarchal relations in paid work with women poorly paid and excluded from good jobs; the bias toward patriarchal interests in policies and actions of state; male violence (e.g., rape, wife beating, sexual harassment); patriarchal relations in sexuality (e.g., compulsory heterosexuality and sexual double standard); and patriarchal cultural institutions (e.g., religions, education, media) (pp. 20–21). In this analysis, patriarchy is a system of social structures and practices in which men oppress and exploit women; the dominant forms of patriarchy vary over time and between different social groups.

The definitions often mention *change* within an enduring general oppression. Zilah Eisenstein (1981) writes of patriarchy as a durable sexual hierarchy which changes form through different economic systems. She is critical of those theorists, such as Mary Daly (1978), who use the term to refer to control that covers all recorded history, collapsing rather than sorting out the particular economic and political forms (Zillah R. Eisenstein, 1981, p. 18).

What Mary Daly, more than most, does include is discussion of *pain*:

Patriarchy is "1: society manufactured and controlled by males: FATHERLAND; a society in which every legitimate institution is entirely in the hands of males and a few selected henchwomen; society characterized by oppression, repression, depression, narcissism, cruelty, racism, classism, ageism, objectification, sadomasochism, necrophilia. . . . 2: the prevailing religion of the entire planet . . . " (Mary Daly, 1987, pp. 87–88)

Many of the definitions discuss patriarchy in relation to *capitalism*, some highlighting the need to consider material conditions. One of the best known is Heidi Hartmann's (1976, 1983) definition of patriarchy as " . . . a set of social relations which has a material base and in which there are hierarchical relations between men, and solidarity among them, which enable them to control women." Patriarchy and capitalism are, she writes, interlocking systems (pp. 194–195). Jane Flax (1979) writes that patriarchy is an " . . . historical force with a material and psychological base" in which gender determines whether a person is excluded or included in whatever is esteemed by society" (pp. 22–23). According to Sally

Alexander and Barbara Taylor (1980), patriarchy is an unequal social structure that is a product of capitalism and of a system of sexual division. This concept, they write, allows women to see through experiences to the processes underlying the experiences. During the past decade there appears to be somewhat less interest in trying to determine the origins of men's domination of women and more interest in understanding the current processes. (Christine Delphy, 1984, p. 17, points out that finding the birth of patriarchy would not explain its present existence.) Yet most of the discussions about patriarchy mention the women's *continued* subordination to men. Barbara Ehrenreich (1991) cautions that folding the patriarchy into capitalism ignores pre-capitalism patriarchy, and lets the human agents of patriarchy off the hook.

Some of the definitions of patriarchy stress the importance of seeing the connections among the official and unofficial, and the macro and micro techniques used to oppress women. Robin Morgan (1989) argues that *separation* is a fundamental technique of patriarchy, enforced by every institution, every day: "If I had to name one quality as the genius of patriarchy, it would be compartmentalization, the capacity for institutionalizing disconnection." The feminist inspection of patriarchy requires *noticing* the connections among all the events, structures, and atrocities of our lives, including the divisions of national borders, the splits of science from art, intellect from emotion, the personal from political, sex from love, material from spiritual, law from justice, and the categories and divisions of sex, age, race, ethnicity, sexual preference, height, weight, class, religion, physical ability, *ad nauseam* (pp. 51–52). Charlotte Bunch (1990) points out that "patriarchy has systematically utilized diversity as a tool of domination in which groups are taught that certain powers and privileges are the natural prerogatives of some people" (p. 50). In white-dominated countries we are taught, early in life, that white males "naturally" have more power. Bunch points out that although many feminists have challenged the "naturalness" of male supremacy, feminists must also challenge the domination in other areas.

Some writers point out that white women are likely to have more trouble than women of color at seeing (or wanting to see) the interlocking systems of what are presented to us as dispersed events. Cherríe Moraga (1983) writes, "What women of color suffer in our families and relationships is, in some way, inherently connected to the rape of women in our neighborhoods, the high suicide rate of American Indians on reservations, attacks on Black gays and disabled people in New York City bars, and the war in El Salvador" (p. 134).

These can be seen as *global* connections, as an interlocking system of racial, sexual, political, and economic oppressions intended to control the earth, white women, people of color, and feelings, and to war against connectedness with one another (Susan Cady, Marian Ronan & Hal Taussig, 1986, p. 8).

QUALIFYING, DEFINING TERMS

Because the word has often been used, seemingly carelessly, to refer to a universal, transhistorical system of male domination without specific reference to the changing nature of male domination, some theorists have looked elsewhere for terminology or have altered the "patriarchy" terminology and definitions to try to capture the diversity, specification, and longevity of men's oppression. for example, the system of male domination has been defined as:

• A stratified *sex-gender system*, a system of arrangements which transforms biological sexuality into products of human activity. Gender relationships, which are not the same as relationships of production (Gayle Rubin, 1975, p. 159).

- *White male system*, the dominant system of beliefs, actions and institutions. The resulting oppression takes many forms, including the oppression of some white males, particularly those who are not middle or upper class, and heterosexual (Anne Wilson Schaef, 1981).

- *Racist patriarchy*, a power system "where whiteskin privilege is a major prop" which has different entrapments for Black women and white women, and which has a wider range of pretend choices and rewards for white women who identify with patriarchal power (Audre Lourde, 1984, pp. 118–119).

- *Capitalist patriarchy*, the underground of the capitalist system. They are global systems which are intertwined. The most powerful guardians of capitalist patriarchy are: the state, the law, the church, and gynecologists (Maria Mies, 1986, pp. 37–38).

REACTIONS TO THE USE OF "PATRIARCHY" IN ACADEME

Initially one might think that patriarchy should work well as a concept for use in academe, because it is an abstract (if keenly felt) concept which speaks not so much of individual experiences as enduring, interlocking systems of oppression. Male academics who have established the rules of acceptable academic theorizing are rather fond of positing universal statements about the relationships of women and men. They have, for example, used the categories *women* and *men* for centuries. They do not argue that the basic relationships between men and women change a lot over time and geographical location, or that the terms *women* and *men* need to be constantly redefined. So we might, for a moment, think that a word for the long term relationship between women and men would be a standard term widely accepted in scholarly literature. But of course patriarchy, as used recently by feminists, contains not only discussion of the widely spread, and enduring hierarchical relationship between women and men, but also a *critical* analysis of the ideas, practices and institutions of men, yesterday and today, including their educational ideas, practices, and institutions. (We have even been known to point out that *men* as super-special humans couldn't exist, without men's construction of *women*, as inferior humans.) Most men academics, the gatekeepers for most scholarly journals, are not going to welcome the use of patriarchy [See Lillian Robinson, this volume.] They might be willing enough to accept the use of it in the older, narrower sense of the fathers holding power over the other members of their households. "Hey, that's serious stuff but that's not me," could be the response. However, as used by most western feminists today as an historical process of sex-segregated jobs, and global exploitation of women, the definition does not exonerate the individual man.[1]

UNRESOLVED PROBLEMS

The problems with the concepts of patriarchy are recognized by many others. For example, some men and women doing postmodern criticism in various social studies and humanities disciplines point out the dangers and inaccuracies which come from using a model of patriarchy which does not explicitly recognize the specificity of each woman's situation. In postmodern theorizing there are no grand theories, no universals. Certainly most concepts of patriarchy do stress commonalities across people, times, places, situations, rather than individual differences, and thus are out of synch with the new theorizing. But postmodern theories themselves are not noted for close attention to the lives of specific women in different times, places, situations. (Lots of talk about readers and responders, but where *are* the workers?) In her critique of contemporary literary criticism and its focus on primarily western male texts, Barbara Christian (1988) writes about the prevailing theoretical language which mystifies rather than clarifies the literature and lives of people of color. She writes that the white scholars expressing new dissatisfaction with their own literary orientation continue to ignore the dissatisfaction and critiques present for ages in the literature of people of color, focusing rather on "deconstructing" the traditional prevailing works, using "the same forms, style, and language of that tradition, forms that necessarily embody its values" (p. 73). Does some of the current white folks' academic interest in postmodern criticism come precisely from the way it diverts attention from the words of people of color and from the depth, ubiquitousness, and intractability of white men's domination of women and people of color?

Barbara Christian also includes a critique of "French feminist theorists," and their too uniform, simplistic ideas about a biological "female language," a concept which ignores the facts that gender is a *social* construct, and that people's relationships to their languages differ (pp. 75–76). She is critical of "the tendency toward monolithism" in theorizing, so we can assume that she would also be very wary of casual uses of the term patriarchy which ignored the differing races and ethnic and class backgrounds of women and men. Her work does, however, caution us to closely examine the motives of those who foster theories which tell women who are struggling against rulers that once again they have it wrong.[2]

There are other reasons for theorists to avoid using the word. As a number of women of color point out, the patriarchy model seems to give primacy to sexual politics. For example, Evelyn Nakano Glenn (1988) gives a detailed critique of the patriarchy analysis model as it is used to encompass the experiences of all women. The problems with the use of what she calls the Marxist-feminist model of patriarchy are implied in her questions:

To what extent [does the patriarchy model] apply to the experiences of racial ethnic women? To what extent does the private-public split and women's association with the domestic sphere exist for racial ethnic women? To what extent has economic dependence on men been an important basis for racial ethnic women's subordination? To what extent do struggles over allocation of house-hold labor create gender conflict in racial ethnic households? (p. 89)

Some of this critique is perhaps more accurately directed to the use of the patriarchy term as it was used in the 1970s. Her comments suggest that many women of color have potentially two simultaneously existing systems of patriarchy to contend with. For example, the patriarchy of Asian-American culture existing within dominant white patriarchy.

Although most noncolored feminists are still very slow in listening to the particulars of the lives of women of color, there *is* now much more discussion about the misleading masculinist public–private division. For example, Mary O'Brien and Sheila McIntyre (1986) give us a description of law as the social institution which is in charge of the ideological and cultural reproduction of the separation of the public (what men do) and the private (what women do). Both are controlled, of course, by the legal system which decrees that we divide activities up into the two realms but then exerts male control over both realms. For example, birthing is a private realm event, but the certificate naming the father or recording the absence of a father's name is a public legal document.

Another reason some theorists give for avoiding the use of the term patriarchy is that there are many conflicting definitions. (That is true, of course, of many other terms that are widely used in feminist literature. See, for example, the many definitions of feminism in *A Feminist Dictionary* [Cheris Kramarae & Paula Treichler, with Ann Russo, 1985].)

BETTER TERMINOLOGY?

As Vicky Randall (1987) argues, the lack of agreement about the definition of "patriarchy" is not grounds to abandon discussion about it. She suggests, however, that there is little necessity for using the term to refer to far-reaching subordination of women when the terms male dominance or male supremacy would do instead (p. 20). A problem with this latter terminology is that it does not remind us of the durability of the oppression of women. Women with whom I've discussed these issues indicate that they think these terms would be no more acceptable to the gatekeepers of academic journals than the word patriarchy. Feminists discuss these issues frequently, usually paying a lot more attention to their language than most antifeminists in academe, as evidenced in part by these concerns about the value and limitation of the term patriarchy.

Maledom was a term used by some nineteenth century "strong-minded women" and their supporters to describe the interlocking system of oppression of women (Lana Rakow & Cheris Kramarae, 1990). Today, some women suggest the word sexism. (e.g., Catherine Itzin, 1985, regards patriarchy and sexism as synonymous systems of male power.) Perhaps because more men are now (jokingly) using the words "sexist" and "sexism," even for defining themselves and their behavior, these words have now become more acceptable even in academic writing. We could ask whether sexism could do as well as patriarchy does to refer to a general system of male domination? Many feminists have used it in this way. Marie Shear defines sexism as a virulent social disease (personal communication). Betsy Warrior calls it the oldest form of institutionalized oppression (1971, p. 1). Dale Spender calls sexism the foundation stone of learning and education in a male-controlled society (1982, p. 37). All refer to a generalized organization of the oppression of women. However, the words sexist and sexism are perhaps most frequently used to refer to *specific* individuals and practices which manifest male domination.[3]

Men often make joking apologies for their own sexist behavior ("I guess I'm just a sexist pig, huh?"), ignoring or trivializing their part in the networks of personal exchanges, and formal policies which support men's domination. Our use of the term patriarchy can be mimicked ("If you think the patriarchy is getting *you* down, just listen to what the matriarchy did to me today"), but it refers clearly to men's domination. We haven't heard men talk yet about "reverse patriarchy." So it would seem useful in some of our analyses of men's domination including the power relationships (many and varied) underlying women's oppression. Not as an all-purpose term, but as one term which can, if used with care, caution, and inclusion, help challenge men's aggressive oppression of women which exists and has, in many forms, for many years. The care, caution, and inclusion would recognize that women of color and men of color share racist oppression, although in different ways (see Audre Lorde, 1984). Just as there is no pradigmatic "woman," there is no paradigmatic "man."

THE RACISM OF PATRIARCHY

As Elizabeth Spelman (1988) suggests, white, middle-class women's talk about "woman" or "women" has the effect of making certain women—white, middle-class women—the paradigmatic examples of "woman." When white women talk about others they use the qualifiers "Black" or "Hispanic" or "Asian-American" or "poor" (p. 186). White women's attempts to talk about "woman" or "women" will, she argues, undermine attempts to talk about differences among us (p. 3). This is a critical caution, a caution which *could* be used to carry us into discussion of the relationship of the problems of terms and concepts such as sisterhood (see Maria Lugone, and Rose Brewer, this volume; also Bonnie Thornton Dill, 1983), essentialism, postmodernism, grand theorizing, plurality, and patriarchy. And a caution which could encourage us to ask if there are times that discussions of commonalities among women can be used without ignoring the differences? For example, might the use of the concept patriarchy make it easier to us to see international terrorism? To see the ecological impact of men's continual work to control women?

Everything *can* be related and commonalities can be found most everywhere. What *is* connected in the ideological convictions which govern academic, disciplines and debates is determined by practical, political, economic priorities. These are not benign, nor intended to be. Certainly many men for many years have tried to control women in a variety of ways, and it is to our benefit to see the connections among the men and the ways. The danger is that attention to these connections effaces other oppressions.

Discussions of patriarchy can lead to talking about women as an undifferentiated mass. As stated in the January 1979 editorial in *Manushi*, a journal published by women in India:

> Isn't life very different for a tribal woman, a Dalit woman in rural India, a factory worker, a clerk, a doctor, a university student, a middle-class or working-class housewife, an air hostess, a woman in purdah, or a common prostitute? (Mandhu Kishwar & Ruth Vanita, 1984, p. 242)

Their essay continues, however, to present common predicaments and to stress the wisdom of helping each other to see connections in these women's lives to put an end to all forms of exploitation based on sex, class, caste, religion, and race. Liz Stanley notes that people invoking the category *working class* are not accused (by deconstructionists or others) of essentialism. We recognize that the term stands for a social construction of a group of people with large internal differences yet facing a common material reality and a common exploitation by other groups who are responsible in varying ways and degrees for the exploitation (Liz Stanley, 1990, p. 152). So, too, for *women*.

In sum, patriarchy is a social theory—a way to describe the world we live in—just as capitalism, democracy, imperialism, and monarchy are social, political, and economic theories. (Note how monolithically those other terms are used, without objections.) Giving our description a name is a way to call attention to our understanding, and to work for change. There is no reason that we can't incorporate aspects of other social theories and descriptions *into* patriarchy, to discuss capitalistic, racist patriarchy.

We need to listen well to women who talk about multiple identities and oppressions. We need to exercise caution that we don't make quick invocations of *women* as a category. We also need to continue our *overview* of the depth and interconnectedness of women's oppression by men. These are related, not conflicting, activities.

NOTES

1. Other fabricated concepts such as "class" and "race" have been extensively used by social scientists. These are also very problematic concepts. Yet they are customarily used by social scientists as if they are categories that exist apart from the classist, racist people who have developed them.

2. The discussion of what is and is not happening in literary criticism is particularly important given that in North American and the United Kingdom literary criticism (rather than, for example, economics, political science, or sociology) has, at present, a primacy in feminist theorizing, for reasons that need more exploring.

3. In addition, "sexist" and "sexism" seem to be used increasingly by men to describe women and their actions as unfair to men. Similarly, whites often use the words "racist" and "racism" to

criticize people of color when they take action to alter the relationships between people of color and people of noncolor.

BIBLIOGRAPHY

Alexander, Sally & Taylor, Barbara. (1980, February). In defence of 'patriarchy.' *New Statesmen, 1,* 161.

Ball, Christine. (1986, Fall). Women, rape and war: Patriarchal functions and ideologies. *Atlantis 12*(1), 83–91.

Barrett, Michele. (1980). *Women's oppression today: Problems in marxist feminist analysis.* London: Verso.

Beechey, Veronica. (1979). On patriarchy. *Feminist Review, 3,* 66–82.

Bunch, Charlotte. (1990). Making common cause: Diversity and coalitions. In Lisa Albrecht & Rose M. Brewer (Eds.), *Bridges of Power* (pp. 49–60). Philadelphia: New Society Publishers.

Cady, Susan, Ronan, Marian, & Taussig, Hal. (1986). *Wisdom's feast: Sophia in study and celebration.* San Francisco: Harper & Row.

Christian, Barbara. (1988, Spring). The race for theory. *Feminist Studies, 14*(1), 67–80.

Coward, Rosalind. (1983). *Patriarchal precedents: Sexuality and social relations.* London: Routledge & Kegan Paul. (Especially pp. 270–273)

Curthoys, Ann. (1988). *For and against feminism: A personal journal into feminist theory and history.* Sydney: Allen & Unwin.

Daly, Mary. (1978). *Gyn/Ecology: The metaethics of radical feminism.* Boston: Beacon Press.

Daly, Mary, in cahoots with Jane Caputi. (1987). *Webster's first new intergalactic wickedary of the English language.* Boston: Beacon Press.

Delphy, Christine. (1984). *Close to home: A materialist analysis of women's oppression.* London: Hutchinson.

Dill, Bonnie Thornton. (1983, Spring). Race, class, and gender: Prospects for an all-inclusive sisterhood. *Feminist Studies, 9*(1), 131–150.

Ehrenreich, Barbara. (1991). War for war's sake. *Z Magazine, 4*(3), 23–25.

Eisenstein, Zillah R. (1979). Developing a theory of capitalist patriarchy and socialist feminism. In Zillah R. Eisenstein (Ed.), *Capitalist patriarchy and the case for socialist feminism.* New York: Monthly Review Press.

Eisenstein, Zillah R. (1981). *The radical future of liberal feminism.* New York: Longman.

Flax, Jane. (1979, Summer). Women do theory. *Quest, 5,* 20–26.

Glenn, Evelyn Nakano. (1988). Racial ethnic women's labor: The intersection of race, gender and class oppression. *Review of Radical Political Economics, 17*(3), 86–108.

Hacker, Sally. (1989). *Pleasure, power, and technology: Some tales of gender, engineering, and the cooperative workplace.* Boston: Unwin Hyman.

Hartmann, Heidi. (1976, 1983). Capitalism, patriarchy, and job segregation by sex. In Elizabeth Abel & Emily K. Abel (Eds.), *Women, gender and scholarship.* Chicago: University of Chicago Press.

Hatem, Mervat. (1986, Summer). The politics of sexuality and gender in segregated patriarchal systems: The case of eighteenth- and nineteenth-century Egypt. *Feminist Studies, 12*(2), 250–274.

Itzin, Catherine. (1985). Margaret Thatcher is my sister: Counselling on divisions between women. *Women's Studies International Forum 8*(1), 73–83.

Kaufman, Michael. (Ed.). (1987). *Beyond patriarchy: Essays by men on pleasure, power, and change.* Toronto: Oxford University Press.

King, Ynestra. (1986). Healing the wounds. In Alison M. Jaggar & Susan R. Bordo (Eds.), *Gender/body/knowledge: Feminist reconstructions of being and knowing.* New Brunswick: Rutgers University Press.

Kishwar, Madhu & Vanita, Ruth. (1984). We shall re-examine everything. *In search of answers: Indian women's voices from Manushi* (pp. 242–245). Londo: Zed Books Ltd.

Kramarae, Cheris & Treichler, Paula, with the assistance of Ann Russo. (1985). *A feminist dictionary.* London: Routledge/Unwin Hyman.

Lerner, Gerda. (1986). *The creation of patriarchy.* New York: Oxford University Press.

Liddle, Joanna & Joshi, Rama. (1986). *Daughters of independence: Gender, caste and class in India.* London: Zed Books (Kali for Women).

Lourde, Audre. (1984). *Sister outsider: Essays and speeches.* Trumansburg, NY: The Crossing Press.

Mies, Maria. (1986). *Patriarchy and accumulation on a world scale: Women in the international division of labour.* London: Zed.

Millett, Kate. (1971). *Sexual politics.* New York: Avon Books.

Moraga, Cherríe. (1983). *Loving in the war years.* Boston: South End Press.

Morgan, Robin. (1989). *The demon lover: On the sexuality of terrorism.* New York: W W Norton.

O'Brien, Mary & McIntyre, Sheila. (1986). Patriarchal hegamony and legal education. *Canadian Journal of Women and the Law, 2*(1), 69–95.

Rakow, Lana & Kramarae, Cheris. (1990). *The revolution in words: Righting women 1868–71.* London: Routledge & Kegan Paul.

Randall, Vicky. (1987). *Women and politics: An international perspective.* Chicago: University of Chicago Press.

Rowbotham, Sheila. (1979, December 21/28). The trouble with 'patriarchy.' *New Statesman,* 970–971.

Rubin, Gayle. (1975). The traffic in women. In Rayna Reiter (Ed.), *Toward an anthropology of women.* New York: Monthly Review Press.

Schaef, Anne Wilson. (1981). *Women's reality: An emerging female system in the white male society.* Minneapolis: Winston Press.

Spelman, Elizabeth V. (1988). *Inessential woman: Problems of exclusion in feminist thought.* Boston: Beacon Press.

Spender, Dale. (1982). *Invisible women: The schooling scandal.* London: Writers & Readers Publishing.

Stanley, Liz. (1990). Recovering *women* in history from feminist deconstructionism. *Women's Studies International Forum, 13*(1/2), 151–157.

Walby, Sylvia. (1990). *Theorizing patriarchy.* Oxford: Basil Blackwell.

Warrior, Betsy. (1971, July). Slavery or a labor of love? *No more fun and games: A journal of female liberation, 5,* 29–41.

Chapter 37

Sisterhood and Friendship as Feminist Models

María C. Lugones
(in collaboration with Pat Alake Rosezelle)

"SISTER" WITHIN A WHITE FEMINIST
CONTEXT, "HERMANA", "COMPAÑERA"
(MARÍA LUGONES)

Sisterhood and friendship have been proposed by feminists as *the* relationships that women need to foster or recognize among ourselves if our liberation from sexist oppression is to end. Sisterhood is thought of sometimes in feminist discourse as a metaphorical ideal and sometimes as a metaphor for the reality of relationships among women. In thinking of sisterhood as a metaphorical model, white feminists have not rethought or reconstructed the concept of sisterhood. They adopted it "as is" and extended it metaphorically to the relations among all women, not just to biological sisters. In contrast, friendship has only been thought of as a feminist ideal, not as a concept that captures actual relations among women. But when friendship, both as a concept and a relationship among women, is presented in feminist discourse it is not friendship "as is" that is being considered. Rather friendship is presented as the *product* of feminist theory and practice, both by white feminists and feminists of color.[1]

I begin this essay by explaining why sisterhood is neither an appropriate metaphor for the existing relations among women nor an appropriate ideal for those relations when put forth by white feminists. But we cannot narrow the investigation just to a white feminist context. The possibility of cross-cultural and cross-racial bonding depends on cross-cultural and cross-racial investigation. Thus I will also explain the meaning of "hermana" among Latinos and Latinas and contrast "hermana" and "compañera." In the next section, Pat Rosezelle will comment on the use of "sister" in the Black community. In the last section I will examine the concept of friendship and recommend a particular understanding of friendship, pluralist friendship, as a very demanding feminist ideal. Alongside this demanding ideal, I will recommend compañerismo as providing the conceptual model that will carry us through the reconstruction of ourselves towards pluralist friendship.

Sister

Sisterhood, the metaphor of kin, is about egalitarian kinship bonding. Kinship bonding itself is a kind of resilient and "unconditional"[2] bond that may, but need not, be accompanied by deep appreciation and respect. Unlike some other kinship relations, sisterhood distinguishes itself by being an egalitarian relation between women.

So understood, sisterhood is an odd model for white/Anglo-american women to adopt as the relationship to recognize or create among white/Anglo women. An odd model for several reasons. First, the white/Anglo-american family has not been known to contemporary white/Anglo feminists as an extended kinship network of support, but as a troubled and unstable relation among a few individuals. Second, the Anglo-american family has been severely scrutinized and criticized by white/Anglo feminists as an oppressive institution. Whether there are any salvageable aspects of the institution is also a matter of feminist concern. But I have not seen any analysis or defense of sisterhood in this light. That is, I have not seen any analysis or defense that places sisterhood as a relationship which is very much a part of the white/Anglo family and thus includes in the analysis the critique of the contemporary white nuclear family in the United States. Or is it that white feminists are not thinking of the white/Anglo family when proposing sisterhood as a metaphor for either the existing or ideal relationship among women?

As we will see in the next section, Pat Rosezelle understands the use of "sister" by white women as unrelated to the American white nuclear family. She sees this use as related to The Black use of "sister" which white women learned about during the Civil Rights movement. Pat's text makes even clearer the need for an analysis and defense of the use of the term "sister" by white women.

Sisterhood is not a good model to describe the *reality* of the relationship between white women and women of color in the United States given that sisterhood is an egalitarian relationship and the relationship between white/Anglo women and women of color is far from being an egalitarian one.

Sisterhood is also not a good model for white feminists to propose in describing the *ideal* relation between white women and women of color given the theory and practice of white feminism. The theory and practice of white/Anglo feminism have not succeeded in including egalitarianism across differences. Rather, they have tended to ignore differences. Sameness, not equality, has been stressed, through the exercise of what Elizabeth Spelman (1988) calls "boomerang perception": "I look at you and come right back to myself. In the United States white children like me got early training in boomerang perception when we were told by well-meaning white adults that Black people were just like us—never, however, that we were just like Blacks." Thus, white feminists are not theoretically or practically in a good position vis a vis women of color to propose sisterhood as a model for our relationships.

If we are to take the model seriously, then the "unconditionality" of sisterhood begins to be problematic because it is potentially burdensome to women of color. We are to stand by as sisters, no matter what, when a bond is being pressed that is conceptually but not practically inconsistent with our erasure. If the bond is unconditional, it is to be upheld even when the relationship is not egalitarian, caring, affirming. It is to be upheld even when the relationship is destructive, denying. So, though sisterhood is supposed to be egalitarian and thus conceptually inconsistent with the erasure of some of the parties to the relation, nonegalitarian practice presses the unconditional clause into service. And our erasure is precisely what we witness in most white feminist theory and practice. So, there is a significant tension between the egalitarian and the unconditional sides of sisterhood. A bond that is unconditional is not broken because the relation has ceased to be or has not yet become egalitarian. This tension creates an ambiguity when the relationship is posed as an ideal by white women without a clear inclusion of difference in their theorizing. Given the theory and practice of white feminism, women of color have every reason to believe that we are both being presented with a true egalitarian ideal and being put in a position to honor this unconditional bond while white women are "messing up" with racism.

Hermana, Compañera

The term "hermana" (sister) is not used politically among Latinas. The term "hermana" like the term "hermano" bear the mark of the commitment to aid one's siblings through life in Latino extended families. It is used metaphorically in times of crisis when one wants to offer a deep sort of empathy, sympathy and practical support. At such times one embraces a woman and says, meaningfully, "hermana." This can be done *only* by siblings and by solid, responsible, close friends. It is a litmus test of the trueness of a close relation. It feels fake otherwise. And, of course, there is a breach in the lack of authenticity.

The term that is used among Latinos for the sort of relation that consists of joining forces and efforts and imagination in common political struggles is "compañera." "Compañera" does not require the depth of emotional attachment, empathetic and sympathetic communication that "hermana" and "amiga" (friend) require.

"Compañera" connotes egalitarianism, but the egalitarianism is one of companionship and participation in common political struggle. The personal is very political in this concept. The term is also used for companionship through life, but the political tone is always there. This extension of the term "compañera" or "compañero" to personal intimate relationships is derivative from the political use and is itself political. The relation for which it is used must be experimental and must, if the term is to be used appropriately, stand *in contrast to* the traditional burgeois husband–wife relation and in contrast with the traditional man–mistress relation.

"Compañera" can be and is used within hierarchies. You can call someone higher up in a political organization "compañera," although there is some tension there. The term is most at home in an egalitarian political companionship where everyone shares the rights and burdens of political struggle. So, I am counting egalitarianism as parts of its meaning.

It is very important that the term does not connote unconditional bonding. The struggle is that about which the parties to the relationship are companions. So, if someone ceases to be involved or interested in, or betrays the struggle, the relationship is at an end with respect to that person.

I have argued so far that sisterhood is not a good model for the actual or ideal relationship among white/Anglo women or among white/Anglo women and women of color. Pat Rosezelle adds further reasons for this claim.

As Pat Roszelle indicates below, the term "sister" has a very different and well anchored history among Black Americans. When Black feminists use the term in the expression "Third World sisters" they are extending to all women of color a different metaphor than the one used by white feminists, a metaphor that is charged with the history of political use of the terms "brother" and "sister" in the Black community.

"SISTER"
(PAT ALAKE ROSEZELLE)

"Sister," "my Sister," "Sister-love," "the sister," "Sister-friend," "a Sister," "Sister outsider." Terms of endearment, a name as title/authority, a greeting as acknowledgment of being and respect. "Sister," the word as conveyer. "Sister." Two syllabes that have the ability to instantly establish a sense of community, status, and affection. "Sister," a people's history, struggles, victories and power. "Sister," a sense of familial tie where there is no blood, women trusting, celebrating, loving and being bound to other women. All this and more is the legacy of "Sister" in the African-American community.

The slave experience is the beginning of "sister" and "brother." When a people are bastardized, raped, and fragmented from their families, they have to create family. Then it is a political act to call those who are not your blood, but who are your people "brother" and "sister." It is a political act to call "brother" and "sister" the very people who are given no respect out of racism and out of racism are called by names you would call children or by service names. In a society where whites call Black men and women "uncle" or "aunt" instead of "Mr." or "Mrs.", it is a political act for Blacks to call each other "brother" or "sister." It is a political act of saying "I am connected to you." When I think of Black women who gave birth at the same time that a white mistress was giving birth and they had to nurse a white child and sometimes watch their own children die of starvation and I think that they then would be called "auntie," I see that name as the epitome of a vile insult. In this context, "brother" and "sister" become a way of redeeming, of respect, of resistance.

The church is the other way that "brother" and "sister" get used. I think there is a connection. There is a cross fertilization between the resistant slave and how "sister" and "brother" are used in the church, in the conscious church as opposed to the colluding church. "Brother" and "sister" become respect as someone of authority, someone who is an elder, someone who has something to give. In a lot of ways, "brother" and "sister" are code for what "Mr." and "Mrs." are in the larger society.

And then "sister" takes on another meaning, that separates it from "brother." "Sister" as saying respect for this female, not buying into the racism that says that she is loose, lewd or promiscuous because she has been raped in a rape that as a slave she had no control over. And so, "sister" is maintained in a way that even when Black men are not called "brothers," a Black man will show his respect by saying to this strange female that he is just meeting, "sister." This is all part of Black community.

In *Personal Politics*, Sarah Evans made a wonderful political decision as a feminist. She decided that she couldn't talk about white feminism in this country without talking about white women in the Civil Rights movement and the problems: women with white skin privilege reclaiming themselves as females and at the same time being in the contradiction of being abusive of their racist privilege. Where else can a white woman go in the late 1960s and receive the kind of respect and support that white women got in the Civil Rights movement because she was an ally in a brutally dangerous situation? But at the same time all the issues around Black men and sexism were there.

White women shared this experience with the Black community, an experience that was very freeing spiritually as well as politically for them. They began to try and use the language of this experience. But when they would call "sister" to Black women, Black women were angry because there was also the issue of these white women with Black men. The issue was whether when you reach out to me and call me "sister," you are reaching to me or reaching past me to my Black man.

When white women left the movement or were expelled—because both things happened—they felt politically and spiritually encompassed in this community of resistance. That meant that when they moved on to begin to organize other white women around issues of sexism, sisterhood was the only experience they had, not alien, away from the white male. It was the only model they had of what the community looked like, people resisting and fighting. And so they took it. I don't believe that they took it as thieves. I believe they took it to try and connect. But at the same time there was something oppressive. In fighting sexism white women only dealt with what was like them[3].

When Sarah Evans writes, it is clear that the connection she took from the Civil Rights movement is sisterhood. But that connection becomes lost in the history of the women's movement. The movement develops a racism all its own and white women don't even know that the root of their white feminism comes out of the Civil Rights movement. And so "sisterhood" has no meaning into the second generation of white women who were not part of the Civil Rights movement. Those women who were involved were taking with them the one thing that made sense as resistance against the white male structure.

So, "sisterhood," a term that arose out of resistance to enslavement and racism, comes to be used by white women as a way of resisting the white male domination. While women learned from the Black community to use the term in resistance of white male domination, but they did not unlearn their racism and so they came to misuse the term. White women forgot what they learned and began using the term "sister" as if all women were alike; they began to erase Black women. White women came to embrace the racism that they were fighting when they learned to call each other "sister."

PLURALIST FRIENDSHIP
(MARÍA LUGONES)

There has been little political use of the term "friend" and not much theoretical examination of the concept in the history of thought, feminist or otherwise. I find friendship interesting in the building of a feminist ethos because I am interested in bonding among women across differences. Friendship is a kind of practical love that commits one to perceptual changes in the knowledge of other persons. The commitment is there because understanding the other is central to the possibility of loving the other person practically. Practical love is an emotion that involves a commitment to make decisions or act in ways that take the well-being of the other person into account. Because I think a commitment to perceptual changes is central to the possibility of bonding across differences and the commitment is part of friendship, I think that friendship is a good concept to start the radical theoretical and practical reconstruction of the relations among women.

Unlike "sister" which presupposes the institution of the family and takes as a model a particular relation within the institution of the family, friendship is not an institutional relationship. It does not have any legal or other institutional components. Friendship is not a normal relation. There are no rules specifying the duties and rights of friends. Rather, in friendship, one is guided by a concern for the friend in her particularity. This is an aspect of friendship that cannot be up for reconstruction without losing the concept, as one would lose the concept of sisterhood if one were to think it *apart* from family. But there is a lot of room for making feminist sense of the meaning of the well-being of the friend in all her particularity.

We cannot propose unconditional love among women as a model at a time when there is so much abuse among women across class and racial lines. Unconditionality is not necessarily a good thing. This is another reason for the adoption of friendship as a feminist ideal: the bond of friendship is not unconditional. In friendship there are failures of friendship that would terminate the relation. Friendship is practical and wholly individuated love that is not unconditional. Friendship as a political vision points to a very different understanding of human organization *because* the particularities of each person are so important, the love is wholly individuated. That is why it is an anarchist ideal.

In the remaining paragraphs, I will add to the concept of friendship an element that is the result of my understanding of the varied realities, worlds, of women. The element is plurality. Not all of the worlds we inhabit construct us as oppressed and one does not find white/Anglo values, norms, and institutions as dominant in all of them. If reality is complex, plural, then our bonding must honor this plurality. If our bonding misses the complexity of reality, then it will necessarily erase some of us. It will only be the illusion of bonding as it will be among women given some construction of them that falsifies them. To put it another way: if you remake me in your image, then the bonding between us is not really between us but between you and your double. You confuse me with your double and that confusion erases and harms me. White women have tended to engage in this falsification and denial *because* racism demands a simplification of reality. White women have tended to remake women of color in their own image. Racism demands that the world as told by whites be all there is to the world. (Think of Adrienne Rich's 1979 account of white solipsism.)

So, if there is more than one way of understanding reality or more than one reality,[4] and friendship is significantly constituted by understanding of the other—friendship, that is, is not love that misses the point—then friendship must embrace this plurality. Pluralist friendship must carry with it a commitment to an understanding of the realities of the friend. One needs to understand the logic of these different realities. In becoming conversant with these realities one comes to see oneself as constructed in that reality in ways different from the ways one is constructed in the reality one started from (see María Lugones, in press a). Thus pluralist friendship enhances self-knowledge.

Because I do think that reality and our selves in it are plural (María Lugones, in press b), I describe a friendship that takes plurality into account. I think that different positions in the racist, ethnocentric state define different realities with their own logic and their own semantics. We also exist in the worlds of those who are differently positioned than ourselves in the racist, ethnocentric state. Thus, each one of us is many selves. Pluralist friendship is a kind of practical love that includes a multivocal communication, a dialogue among multiple selves. A dialogue among people who are fluent in the ways of their own position in the racist and ethnocentric state and in the ways of people who are differently positioned than themselves.

Friendship across positions of inequality has to be worked for rather than discovered or found. One needs to shift the focus of one's attention in ways that are epistemically very demanding. The shift in focus requires a dislodging of the centrality of one's position in the racist, ethnocentric, capitalist, patriarchal state in one's own self-concept. This entails a profound transformation of one's self.

As we have seen this is a very ambitious ideal, a political relation. One of its difficulties lies in its depending on understanding the subtleties of racism in ways that many white/Anglo women may not. In this regard, women of color have an epistemic advantage, they have access to knowledge that white/Anglo women lack.[5] From this epistemic advantage, we can posit feminist pluralism. White women can justify their adoption of this ideal through their acceptance of our epistemic privilege. But such acceptance cannot be very helpful as a guide in their relations to women of color. Rather white/Anglo women need to come to understand our varied realities.

Though pluralist friendship is part of my vision of feminist community, I think we are very far from this ideal. We are very far apart *epistemically*, in a way that makes the ideal hard to grasp for white/Anglo women. I don't think this ideal can carry us through the destruction of the capitalist, patriarchal, racist, ethnocentric state. Therefore, I suggest the term "compañera" for the political relation that can carry women through the destruction of racism and racist ethnocentrism.

NOTES

1.   Sisterhood is a frequent metaphor in feminist discourse. So, here I am not just referring to the use of "sisterhood" in the literature of the movement. Even though Robin Morgan's *Sisterhood is powerful* (1970) was an early work, the use of sisterhood is still common in feminist discussions. "Friendship" is less used. It is used most often in lesbian and/or anarchist feminism. See, for example, Janice Raymond's *A Passion for Friends* (1986) and María Lugones and Elizabeth Spelman's "Have we got a theory for you!" (1983)

2.   The "unconditionality" of the bond has very unclear limits. Gays and lesbians are a common and interesting example of the limits of kinship as people who often find themselves without kin, disowned.

3.   This again reminds us of "boomerang perception" and its power. As Bernice Johnson Reagon (1983) says, "You don't really want Black folks, you are just looking for yourself with a little color to it."

4.   Think here of bell hooks' *Feminist Theory: From Margin to Center* (1984), where margin and center are either two realities or two aspects of one reality known only to people of color and proletarians. The white bourgoisie only knows the center. Think also of Nancy Hartsock's (1983) two levels or reality, both of which are real: the reality of the managers, capitalists, patriarchs and the reality of women–proletarians. Think also of my own "worlds" in "Playfulness, 'world'-travelling and Loving Perception" (1987).

5.   There is quite a bit of work that attributes epistemic privilege to women of color. Uma Narayan's "Working Together Across Difference" (1988), bell hooks' *Feminist Theory: From Margin to Center* (1984), and Alison Jaggar's *Feminist Politics and Human Nature* (1983) are examples.

BIBLIOGRAPHY

Evans, Sara. (1979). *Personal politics: the roots of women's liberation in the civil rights movement and the new left.* New York: Knopf.

hooks, bell. (1984). *Feminist theory: From margin to center.* Boston: South End Press.

Hartsock, Nancy. (1983). The feminist standpoint: Developing the ground for a specifically feminist historical materialism. In Sandra Harding & Merrill Hintikka (Eds.), *Discovering reality: Feminist perspectives on epistemology, metaphysics, methodology, and philosophy of science.* New York: Dordrecht & Reidel.

Jaggar, Alison. (1983). *Feminist politics and human nature.* New Jersey: Rowman & Allanheld.

Lugones, María. (1987). Playfulness, "world"-travelling and loving perception. *Hypatia, 2*(2).

Lugones, María. (in press a). The logic of pluralist feminism. In Claudia Card (Ed.), *Feminist Ethics.* Lawrence: University Press of Kansas.

Lugones, María. (in press b). *Pilgrimages/peregrinajes: Essays in pluralist feminism.* Albany, NY: State University of New York Press.

Lugones, María, & Spelman, Elizabeth. (1983). Have we got a theory for you! *Hypatia, 1,* [Special Issue] *Women's Studies International Forum, 6,* 573–81.

Morgan, Robin. (1970). *Sisterhood is powerful: An anthology of writings from the women's liberation movement.* New York: Random House.

Narayan, Uma. (1988, Summer). Working together across difference. *Hypatia, 3*(2).

Raymond, Janice. (1986). *A passion for friends.* Boston: Beacon Press.

Reagon, Bernice Johnson. (1983). Coalition politics: Turning the century. In Barbara Smith (Ed.), *Home girls: A Black feminist anthology.* New York: Kitchen Table/Women of Color Press.

Rich, Adrienne. (1979). Disloyal to Civilization. In *Lies, secrets and silences.* New York: W W Norton.

Spelman, Elizabeth. (1988). *Inessential woman.* Boston: Beacon Press.

Chapter 38

Agency—Who Is to Blame?

Barbara Pope

When we first confront the fact of female oppression, the question of origin or blame almost inevitably arises. Who or what is responsible for something so universal and overwhelming? Answering this question seems urgent for both psychological and strategical reasons: It feels good to know and name our enemy. Moreover, a "correct" formulation of the answer could lead us to effective strategies for changing the situation. Fifteen years ago a strongly held position about the origins of women's condition almost seemed to define the different political tendencies within feminism.

In the 1980s, however, most feminists involved in the daily struggle of maintaining and building institutions and writing were giving increasingly complex and tentative answers to grand theoretical questions. Yet basic assumptions about who or what we should blame often remain silently embedded in mature formulations. These assumptions, whether stated or not, continued to divide feminists. Increasingly they divided us most passionately "where we live," at the level of what seem like mutual assault on one's most personal choices. This is why pornography became such a controversial issue. [See Susanne Kappeler, this volume.]

I have divided this survey into three kinds of theories about the origins of women's oppression. My categorization corresponds roughly to the self-conscious political divisions of new wave feminists: The first and third ("Men are to Blame" and "Sex is the Hard Core") are more likely to be held by women who think of themselves as radical feminists, while women of color and socialist-feminists tend to look to complex "Systems." Although no one can predict why people will favor one view over another, it is obvious that personal histories, ideological and community loyalties, and intellectual temperament and training are part of what goes into our theory-making, blaming, and sense of moral agency.

MEN ARE TO BLAME: VARIATIONS AND EMENDATIONS ON A THEME

On July 7, 1969, a group of young radical women in New York City opened the current debate by issuing the Redstocking Manifesto (1969). They put the answer to the question of blame quite succinctly:

> We identify the agents of our oppression as men. . . . Men have controlled all political, economic, and cultural institutions and backed up this control with physical force. They have used their power to keep women in an inferior position. *All men* receive economic, sexual and psychological benefits from male supremacy. *All men* have oppressed women. (p. 109)

It would be difficult to overestimate the revolutionary nature of this statement within the context of the flourishing social movements of the late 1960s. After all, the Redstockings were saying that it was not "the system" (as new Leftists were wont to say) nor historically unequal "social relationships" (as the existentialist-Marxist Simone de Beauvoir had asserted in 1949) nor American "society," "culture," or "institutions" (dissected by Betty Friedan in 1963), that could and should be held accountable for the exploitation and victimization of women. It was our fathers, brothers, husbands, sons, lovers, friends, and, most particularly in 1969, our political comrades.

The Redstockings belonged to that fortunate, post–World War II generation that had been taught that the American dream meant equality and justice for all. They were the beneficiaries of a greatly expanded higher education system; veterans of the idealistic and communitarian politics of the Civil Rights movement, New Left and anti-war movements; and the first consumers of the birth control pill. But by the late 1960s many radical women realized that they were not included in the promise of equality for which they had fought so fervently. This realization sparked an anger that enabled them to turn against their male comrades. This clarifying anger allowed them to put aside the "sophisticated analysis" of the New Left and to say something simple, bold and true: men oppressed women. At the same time they also discovered a strategy for getting at the truth: consciousness-raising.

> We regard our personal experience, and our feelings about that experience, as the basis for the analysis of our common situation. We cannot relay on existing ideologies as they are the products of male supremacist culture. (Redstockings Manifesto, 1969, p. 110)

The searing honesty wrought by experience and the sharing of experience, and a continued faith in radical goals and life styles gave this brand of feminism a unique and revolutionary power. Theirs was an ethos that questioned everything at the root while still believing that all things were possible, for while being uncompromisingly prowomen they still held the door open for the men who were willing "to give up their male privileges and support women's liberation in the interest of our humanity and their own" (p. 111).

Few older, liberal feminists noted this opened door. Instead they tended to dismiss such manifestos as ideological, immature and dangerous (Betty Friedan, 1976), for they were very sensitive to charges of radicalism and man-hating. They believed the enemies were rigid sex roles; sexist attitudes; the media image of women; discriminatory legal, educational, and employment practices; and some selected intellectuals (like Freud, Talcott Parsons, and Dr. Spock). Few liberals were interested in finding the ultimate causes of women's ills, for theirs was not the politics of the "correct line." Rather they were interested in effecting practical reforms and in persuading "middle America" of the justice of their cause. Thus the debate about agency and blaming was left largely to the women of the Redstocking generation.

In 1970, with the publication of Shulamith Firestone's *The Dialectic of Sex* and Kate Millet's *Sexual Politics*, radical feminism evolved from manifesto to full-blown theory, albeit in two slightly different directions. Firestone, a founder of the Redstockings, claimed that the first form of human domination was not economic, as Engels and other Marxists had posited, but sexual. She insisted that women were a "sex class" and tried to develop a "dialectical materialism" of sex. The "material" of her materialism is human biology itself, which, when overlaid with politics, psychology, and culture, becomes the source of women's and children's oppression within the family. Although most of Firestone's readers rejected her solution, artificial reproduction, many reacted positively to her depiction of women as *victims* of their bodies and of love.

For Kate Millett, our primary oppressor is the patriarchal culture which forces men and women into the false sex roles of aggressor and victim. By layering her analysis with political theory and current findings on psychological development, and by using the writings of homosexual Jean Genet as an alternative perspective, Millett did much to establish the notion that gender is socially constructed. This idea, now almost a truism of feminist theory, supports the optimistic view that men *and* women may recognize their distorted behaviors and want to change them. But *Sexual Politics* purveyed an even more powerful subtext: That what had passed as "sexually liberating" in the writings of men like Henry Miller, Norman Mailer and D. H. Lawrence was only a new and more violent form of contempt. Millett illustrated so conclusively how the penis functioned as a weapon in the works of these shapers of modern culture, that it was hard to believe that men would ever want to give up this exhilarating power.

Although Kate Millett did not biologize male aggressiveness and contempt as a mechanism of women's oppression, five years later Susan Brownmiller would in her book, *Against Our Will* (1975). She developed the theme Susan Griffin (1971) had set forth in an earlier essay, that men used rape as a means of keeping women in their place. But what had been for Griffin an "All-American Crime," became for Susan Brownmiller the transhistorical and cross-cultural human condition. She defined rape, not as a sex act, but as a criminal and political exertion of male domination. Although Susan Brownmiller concluded by inviting men to cooperate in the struggle against rape, again it was her world history of male violence against women that most impressed the readers. [See also Jane Caputi, this volume.]

Mary Daly also devoted a major portion of *Gyn/Ecology* (1978) to cataloguing misogynist horrors, but her ultimate goal was quite different: In her book men emerge as so irremediable that the only way to escape victimhood is by women spinning their own spiritual journey away from male cruelty, myth, and control. Daly did this not only by exposing what male reality has meant for women, but by breaking down, reconstructing and reclaiming the language. Language also figured prominently in Susan Griffin's *Women and Nature* (1978). She emphasized the inherent nurturance as well as wildness of women, attributing both to their closer identification with nature. Like Mary Daly, she wanted women to discover the free inner space which will reveal who we really are. Thus, self-discovery, a journey of spinning out (Mary Daly) or diving in (Susan Griffin), was the key to female moral agency and genuine liberation.

Since Mary Daly and Susan Griffin, variations on the theme of the difference between men and women have proliferated in the women's spirituality, peace and ecology movements. The point is often made that men have dealt death and destruction, while women are more peaceful and nurturant. These female characteristics are usually attributed to the mothering role which leads women to be more attentive to the need to take care of people and to preserve our planet and all its life forms. This line of thinking suggests three different solutions: We must change individual men. Or we must separate from them. Or we must get women in a position to realize their particular moral values in an endangered world.

Other feminists rejected any universalizing as false. Chief among these were women of color who pointed out that their oppressions and oppressors were the multiples of sexism, racism, and capitalism. As early as 1970, Frances Beal described this condition as "Double Jeopardy." That same year, Pauli Murray wrote an article in much the same vein. Although

Frances Beal and Pauli Murray criticized the male supremacist attitudes of the militant Black nationalists of their day, they insisted that "all human rights are indivisible" (Pauli Murray, 1970, p. 102). So, of course, are women of color who could not choose between necessary struggles and who did not see themselves in much of the overwhelmingly Euro-American feminist theorizing.

Several strong themes about blaming and moral agency emerged in the writings of women of color. Although cognizant of the sexism and homophobia within their own communities, both lesbians and straight women of color have been very wary of separating themselves from the men who are their partners in the fight against racism and class exploitation (e.g., The Combahee River Collective, 1977). They have also blamed white feminists for their own ignorance and racism. Angela Davis' *Women, Race and Class* (1981) demonstrated how social and racial prejudices had shaped the first American feminist movement and continued to permeate the second. In particular, she criticized the radical feminist analysis of male violence for unthinkingly perpetuating the myth of "the black rapist of the white woman." That people of color are disproportionately the victims of crime and imprisonment is seldom acknowledged in white feminist writing (Gloria Joseph & Jill Lewis, 1981).

Chicana feminists were among the first to point out that the family was not the locus of *their* discontent. Given the specific conditions of their communities (internal colonization), the family is crucial as a refuge from a racist society, a place to maintain a distinct culture, and a resource for future struggles. (Elizabeth Sutherland, 1970; Longauex y Vasquez, 1970). Later Native American and African-American feminists like Paula Gunn Allen (1986) and Patricia Hill Collins (1986) asserted that their communities may have different visions of what the relationship between women and men has been, should be, and could be. Finally, as bell hooks (1984) wrote, women of color who have always worked and survived against enormous odds could not identify with a movement of victims; rather she urged women to unite on the basis of strength to overcome the *systems* of domination.

IT'S A SYSTEM

Many young, white feminists also began to look at systems. In its earliest manifestations the brand of analysis known as socialist feminism was less personal and more abstract than any of the works listed above (although many women of color, like Angela Davis, are committed socialists). Because socialist feminists in the 1970s focused on economic conditions, relatively less attention was given to the sexual, psychological, and violent aspects of women's lives. Therefore they seldom "named" men as oppressors who make direct gains from specific acts. They attributed blame to "structures," "systems," or "arrangements" rather than to human beings. As feminists they were increasingly aware that existing socialist states had not solved the problem of women's oppression (Juliet Mitchell, 1966). But as Marxists they believed that unless women and men had a "correct" understanding of their historical situation, they would be doomed to maintain a world not of their own making.

I divide these "abstract" accounts into two categories: the "dual systems" theories based on analyses of *both* capitalism and patriarchy and those which describe "gender arrangements." The work of many English feminists falls somewhere in between. Because England had a stronger socialist tradition and a less diverse and massive youth movement, socialist feminism emerged there before its radical counterpart. English feminists were much less defensive about using "male" theories and defined the problem not so much in terms of finding the origins of women's oppression as how and to what extent one should synthesize

Marxist and psychoanalytical insights. Juliet Mitchell has been the most prominent socialist advocate of psychoanalysis (1974). Others, like Michelle Barrett (1980), have proved less enthusiastic.

At first many American theorists tried to blame capitalism for women's oppression. A few even imagined a "golden age" before industrialization when women enjoyed a "rough and ready" equality with men because of their complementary roles in the precapitalist family economy. But new women's historians and anthropologists (often the comrades of the theorists) soon revealed the naiveté of this view and the longevity and adaptability of patriarchy (e.g., Joan Kelly-Gadol, 1976). In the feminist journal *Quest*, Linda Phelps showed how "Patriarchy and Capitalism" (1975) were two distinct systems of social relationships which have their own history and principles of authority. [See also Cheris Kramarae, this volume.]

In *Capitalist Patriarchy and the Case for Socialist Feminism* (1979, p. 6) editor Zillah Eisenstein optimistically contended that if one "used Marxist class analysis as the thesis" and "radical feminist patriarchal analysis as the antithesis, the synthesis of socialist feminism" would evolve. Just a year later, however, Heidi Hartmann (one of the contributors to Eisenstein's book) was writing about the "Unhappy Marriage of Marxism and Feminism" (1980) and Iris Young was pointing out "The Limits of the Dual Systems Theory" (1980). In an effort to make this marriage of convenience a more perfect union, Ann Foreman (1977) and Alison Jaggar (1983) hypothesized that the Marxist concept of "alienation" provided the needed link. Just as workers under capitalism were alienated from their labor, so women were alienated from a socially constructed "femininity" which presumed male control of their work and sexuality.

All feminists who identified themselves as socialist stressed that capitalism perverts our agency as much as male dominance does by permeating our lives, limiting our vision, and dividing us from our "real" selves and from each other. They insisted that liberation will not come about by creating new visions, or ideas, or cultures alone, but requires changing everyone's "material" conditions: how we work, how our ability to work is determined and divided by capitalists (into racial and sexually segregated markets), our different access to the things that we need, and who makes these decisions (that is, who owns the means of production and controls the state). They also believe that changes in our material conditions will help us to create better and more effective visions for our common future. This means confrontation with the dominant and dominating culture, and it means working with men. These theorists also insist that women and men can be both victims and oppressors. This does not deny that men dominate women; it does recognize that women, too, can be oppressors because of their class, race, or heterosexual privileges.

The "gender arrangements" arguments may be the least "blaming" of all new theories, because they locate the cause of women's oppression deep in history, culture, traditions, and the human psyche. The most notable work on "gender arrangements" comes from the disciplines of anthropology and psychology. In an influential essay, Michelle Zimbalist Rosaldo (1974) suggested that women were oppressed because of their confinement to the domestic sphere and that the way to produce an egalitarian society was not only to urge women's participation in the public culture-creating world, but by getting men to value and participate in the work of the household.

Dorothy Dinnerstein and Nancy Chodorow wrote very different psychoanalytical accounts which seemed to support the Rosaldo hypothesis. Dorothy Dinnerstein's *The Mermaid and the Minotaur* (1976) was a passionate exposition of deformed gender development based on original infant rage against the all-powerful mother. In *The Reproduction of Mothering* (1978), Nancy Chodorow analyzed the processes by which girls develop a propensity to mother and connect with others, while boys learn to be separate and autonomous. [See Mary Roth Walsh, this volume.] Both books concluded that the way to overcome the distortions of gender formation was for men to take equal responsibility for parenting. Later Michelle Zimbalist Rosaldo (1980) criticized her earlier work because she had not taken into account how women's power and authority might vary under different kinship systems. The same ethnocentric critique could be leveled against the works of Nancy Chodorow and Dorothy Dinnerstein. Just as importantly all three interpretations take heterosexuality for granted.

Gayle Rubin's pathbreaking article, "The 'Traffic in Women': Notes on the 'Political Economy' of Sex" (1975) expanded the notion of gender development and arrangements specifically to include sexuality in her "sex/gender system" a concept derived from her own synthesis of Levi-Strauss, Freud, Marx, and Lacan. Gayle Rubin hypothesized that what we know as human society (and its necessary component kinship) developed on the basis of the exchange of women (Levi-Strauss) which later reflected and supported male dominant property relationships and the sexual division of labor (Marx). The way this (now long dysfunctional) kinship system is transmitted to us is through the process which psychoanalytic theory tries to describe (Freud). It permeates not only our emotional formation, but also the language and symbols which determine how we think and feel (Lacan). Because kinship rests upon marriage, Rubin explained, it always enforced the need to have two "complementary" genders; it also always enforced a sexual order based upon heterosexuality.

Like the socialist-feminist theorists described above, those who have put forth theories based upon gender arrangements call on us to understand the depth and complexity of our culturally and societally determined emotions and behaviors and then to make conscious efforts to overcome them. In the problem outlined by Dorothy Dinnerstein and Nancy Chodorow women and men are held to be victims of psychological forces beyond their control; their prescription of co-parenting makes both women and men the agents of a future liberation from gender deformation. Gayle Rubin goes beyond this limited heterosexual view of how family and kinship shape our lives and asks us to liberate our sexuality as well. In this she is as much an ally with gay men as she is with other women. [See also Jacqueline Zita, this volume.]

THE HARD CORE IS SEX

Gayle Rubin was certainly not the first feminist who perceived that to be liberated women must free themselves from the current "sexual order." In the early 1970s a variety of feminists had condemned the norm of heterosexuality because it privileged male sexual pleasure, stigmatized nonheterosexuals, shaped people to fit false sex roles, and separated women from each other by giving men primacy in women's lives (Alison Jaggar, 1983, pp. 266, 271–273; Koedt, 1970; Radicalesbians, 1970). By 1975, Charlotte Bunch could assert that heterosexuality "as an institution and an ideology is a cornerstone of male supremacy" (Charlotte Bunch, 1987, p. 176). In 1979 the Leeds Revolutionary Feminist Group issued "Political Lesbians: The Case Against Heterosexuality," an indication of the development of radical feminist and separatist politics in England (David Bouchier, 1984, p. 133–4).

Adrienne Rich delivered the most famous analysis of the sexual order. In "Compulsory Heterosexuality and Lesbian Existence" (1980), she laid out the many compelling reasons why women "chose" heterosexuality. Among them were physical violence, constraint, and compulsion; economic dependency; socialization and acculturation; and the cramping of female creativity. Rich convincingly demonstrated that no matter what our biological or psychological propensities may be we are very early on driven to accept an ideology which helps to oppress women and which has erased and will continue to erase the existence of lesbians.

For Charlotte Bunch and Adrienne Rich heterosexuality was *one* dominant or compulsory ideology or institution, the sexually repressive component of an interlocking system which oppresses women. For Monique Wittig, Catharine MacKinnon and Andrea Dworkin heterosexuality itself is *the* key to understanding women's oppression. In their analysis it is sex between male and female that generates gender, that divides humans into the categories of men and women.

Monique Wittig first formulated this idea in "One is Not Born a Woman" (1979). For Wittig humans are products of history (i.e., social relationships) and not biology. One of her projects is to resist the feminists in both her native France and in America who make the claim, "woman is wonderful." This she contends "biologizes" or "naturalizes" the category woman, by accepting "this best features which oppression has granted us" (Monique Wittig, 1979, p. 150). She wants to abolish not men, but the "class" or category men and to do away with the political system heterosexuality which "produces the body of thought of the difference between sexes to explain women's oppression" (p. 152). Lesbians can lead the way to the creation of a genderless society, she wrote, because they alone are not tainted by oppressive and distorting social relationships.

Monique Wittig tried always to speak from a point of view that does not take history as nature and which does not accept the sexes as given. Andrea Dworkin and Catharine MacKinnon's projects are quite different—a full-scale critique of heterosexuality from *a gendered point of view*. Although they, too, strive for a society in which gender would not signify, they quite intentionally write and act in the world *as it is*, rampant with sexism. What is exhilarating about their writing is their ability to shift the lens of perception to a place where it discloses what women, untainted by loyalties to men or the establishment, might see. Indeed, one of Catharine MacKinnon's expressed goals is epistemological. For her objectivity is a stance that must be male in a world where the male is both the universal standard and ubiquitous authority.

Catharine MacKinnon's pathbreaking work on sexual harassment (1979) and trenchant dissection of the legal definition of rape (1983) give us a glimpse of what laws conceived by and for women could be. Susan Brownmiller analyzed rape as a political act, Catharine MacKinnon insists that it is sexual as well. She has also pointed out that we should not be lulled into talking about *differences* between men and women when we are really dealing with *dominance*.

More controversial are her attempts, with Andrea Dworkin, to outlaw pornography in a number of U.S. cities. These efforts have made them prominent adversaries in the most bitter debate of the 1980s, discussed elsewhere in this volume. At first glance, it is difficult to understand why the stakes in this particular controversy are so high. I believe it is because the "sex wars" have brought the issue of blame home to feminists themselves at a more personal level than ever before. [See also Susanne Kappeler, this volume.]

Catharine MacKinnon (1983, 1987) and Andrea Dworkin (1985, 1987) stress that males rule by a sexualized power which we must do everything we can to thwart. Despite the complexity of their analysis, they seem to locate the primary source of women's oppression in heterosexual intercourse. For many feminists, it also seems like they are reallocating the blame: The perpetuators of female oppression are not only men, but the women who sleep with them.

420 Barbara Pope

BLAMING AND THE DISCIPLINES

The response of male academics to this debate falls mainly into three categories: Ignorance, some new theorizing about the origins of sex oppression, and involvement in men's studies. The vast majority of academic men are completely unaware of the full range of the debate because it is, after all, usually framed as a women's issue and because the terms in which the arguments unfold are likely to make most men uncomfortable. They have the luxury of either dismissing the arguments unread or dealing with them only at the most abstract and nonthreatening level, where they look like "real" theory—impersonal, often abstruse, and ultimately based upon the works of important men.

A second reaction has been to "correct" feminist ideas (mostly as they have been presented in the popular media) about the possibility of equality by coming up with updated theories about the biological origins of female oppression, and the inevitability of male domination—at least in the past (Steven Goldberg, 1973; Marvin Harris, 1977; E. O. Wilson, 1975).

Finally, some men who heeded early feminist critiques of sex roles reacted by finding that "men are oppressed too." These were the pioneers of men's studies. Now more sophisticated scholars like Harry Brod still continue to study various social-constructed "masculinities" while they acknowledge that men are not merely different or "differently oppressed" from women, but also, in our society, more powerful. As the plural masculinities implies, they recognize race, class, and heterosexual privilege as well. The systemic approach (socialist feminism and the psychological studies) has the most influence on this field (Harry Brod, 1987, pp. 1–17). [See also Lillian Robinson, this volume.]

CONCLUSION

It is unlikely that all feminists will ever agree upon a single causal explanation, vision of liberation, or strategy for getting there. At a time when white feminists have become acutely aware of the need to integrate the different perspectives of women of color, it would be very ironic if we tried to come up with one account of how to live our lives as feminists. What we have to be most wary of is closing off debate. If we do this, how will we ever find out (as the Redstockings urged in 1969) "what is good for women" (p. 111) or, better, what is good for all women in all their class, ethnic, and sexual diversity.

BIBLIOGRAPHY

Allen, Paula Gunn. (1986). *The sacred hoop: Recovering the feminine in American Indian traditions.* Boston: Beacon Press.
Beal, Frances M. (1970). Double jeopardy: To be black and female. In Robin Morgan (Ed.), *Sisterhood is powerful* (pp. 382–396). New York: Vintage.
Barrett, Michelle. (1980). *Women's oppression today: Problems in Marxist feminist analysis.* London: Verso.
Bouchier, David. (1984). *The feminist challenge. The movement for women's liberation in Britain and the USA.* New York: Schocken Books.
Brod, Harry (Ed.). (1987). *The making of masculinities: The new men's studies.* Boston: Allen & Unwin.
Brownmiller, Susan. (1975). *Against our will: men, women and rape.* New York: Simon & Schuster.
Bunch, Charlotte. (1987). Not for lesbians only. In *Passionate politics.* New York: St. Martin's Press.
Chodorow, Nancy. (1978). *The reproduction of mothering: Psychoanalysis and the sociology of gender.* Berkeley: University of California Press.

Collins, Patricia Hill. (1986, Spring). The emerging theory and pedagogy of Black women's studies *Feminist Issues, 6*, 1.

Combahee River Collective. (1974). A Black feminist statement. In Gloria Hull, Patricia Bell Scott, & Barbara Smith (Eds.), (1982). *But some of us are brave: Black women's studies* (pp. 13–22). Old Westbury, NY: Feminist Press.

Daly, Mary. (1978). *Gyn/Ecology: The metaethics of radical feminism.* Boston: Beacon Press.

Davis, Angela. (1981). *Women, race and class.* New York: Random House.

de Beauvoir, Simone. (1953). *The second sex.* (H. M. Parshley, Trans.) New York: Alfred A Knopf.

Dinnerstein, Dorothy. (1976). *The mermaid and the minotaur: Sexual arrangements and human malaise.* New York: Harper & Row.

Dworkin, Andrea. (1985, Summer). Against the male flood: Censorship, pornography, and equality. *Trivia, 7.*

Dworkin, Andrea. (1987). *Intercourse.* New York: The Free Press.

Eisenstein, Zillah. (1979). Developing a theory of capitalist patriarchy. In Eisenstein (Ed.), *Capitalist patriarchy and the case for socialist feminism.* New York: Monthly Review Press.

Firestone, Shulamith. (1970). *The dialectic of sex: The case for feminist revolution.* New York: William Morrow.

Foreman, Ann. (1977). *Feminity as alienation: Women and the family in psychoanalysis.* London: Pluto Press.

Friedan, Betty. (1963). *The feminine mystique.* New York: Dell.

Friedan, Betty. (1976). *It changed my life: Writings on the women's movement.* New York: Random House.

Goldberg, Steven. (1973). *The inevitability of patriarchy.* New York: William Morrow.

Griffin, Susan. (1971, September). Rape: The all-American crime. *Ramparts, 10*, 3.

Griffin, Susan. (1978). *Woman and nature: The roaring inside her.* New York: Harper & Row.

Harris, Marvin. (1977, November 13). Why men dominate women. *New York Times Magazine.*

Hartmann, Heidi. (1980). The unhappy marriage of Marxism and feminism: Towards a more progressive union. In Lydia Sargent, (Ed.), *Women and revolution.* Boston: South End Press.

hooks, bell. (1984). *Feminist theory: From margin to center.* Boston: South End Press.

Jaggar, Alison. (1983). *Feminist politics and human nature.* Totowa, NJ: Rowman & Allanhead.

Joseph, Gloria & Lewis, Jill. (1981). *Common differences: Conflicts in Black and white feminist perspectives.* Garden City, NY: Anchor Books.

Kelly-Gadol, Joan. (1976). The social relation of the sexes: Methodological implications of women's history. *Signs, 1*, 4.

Koedt, Anne. (1970). The myth of the vaginal orgasm. In Anne Koedt, Ellen Levine, & Anita Rapone (Eds.), *Radical feminism* (pp. 198–207). New York: Quadrangle/The New York Times Book Co. (1973).

Longauex y Vasquez. (1970). The Mexican-American woman. In Robin Morgan (Ed.), *Sisterhood is powerful* (pp. 426–32). New York: Random House.

MacKinnon, Catharine. (1979). *Sexual harassment of working women: A case of sex discrimination.* New Haven: Yale University Press.

MacKinnon, Catharine. (1982). Feminism, Marxism, method, and the state: An agenda for theory. *Signs, 7*, 3.

MacKinnon, Catharine. (1983). Feminism, Marxism, method, and the state: Toward feminist jurisprudence. *Signs, 8*, 4.

MacKinnon, Catharine. (1987). *Feminism unmodified.* Cambridge: Harvard University Press.

Millett, Kate. (1970). *Sexual politics.* Garden City, NY: Doubleday.

Mitchell, Juliet. (1966). *The longest revolution.* New England: The Boston Free Press.

Mitchell, Juliet. (1974). *Psychoanalysis and feminism: Freud, Reich, Laing and women.* New York: Vintage.

Murray, Pauli. (1970). The liberation of Black women. In Mary Lou Thompson (Ed.), *Voices of the new feminism* (pp. 87–102). Boston: Beacon Press.

Phelps, Linda. (1975, Fall). Patriarchy and capitalism. *Quest 2*, 2.

Radicalesbians. (1970). The woman identified woman. In Anne Koedt, Ellen Levine, & Anita Rapone (Eds.), *Radical feminism* (pp. 240–45). New York: Quadrangle/The New York Times Book Co.

Redstocking Manifesto. (1969). In Leslie Tanner (Ed.). *Voices from women's liberation* (pp. 108–111). New York: New American Library.

Rich, Adrienne. (1980). Compulsory heterosexuality and lesbian existence. *Signs, 5*, 4.

Rosaldo, Michelle Zimbalist. (1974). A theoretical overview. In Michelle Rosaldo & Louise Lamphere (Eds.), *Woman, culture & society* (pp. 17–42). Stanford: Stanford University Press.

Rosaldo, Michelle Zimbalist. (1980). The use and abuse of anthropology: Reflections on feminism and cross-cultural understanding. *Signs, 5*, 3.

Rubin, Gayle. (1975). The traffic in women: Notes on the political economy of sex. In Rayna Rapp Reiter (Ed.), *Toward an anthropology of women* (pp. 157–210). New York: Monthly Review Press.

Sutherland, Elizabeth. (1970). Colonized women: The chicana. An introduction. In Robin Morgan (Ed.). *Sisterhood is powerful: An anthology of writings from the women's liberation movement* (pp. 423–26). New York: Random House.

Wilson, E. O. (1975). *Sociobiology: The new synthesis.* Cambridge: Harvard University Press.

Wittig, Monique. (1979). One is not born a woman. In Alison Jaggar & Paula Rothenberg (Eds.), *Feminist frameworks* (2nd ed.), (pp. 148–152). New York: McGraw-Hill.

Young, Iris. (1980, March-June). Socialist feminism and the limits of dual system theory. *Socialist review 10*(2/3).

Chapter 39

The Principles of Feminist Research
A Matter of Debate

Shulamit Reinharz

The debates over Feminist Research Principles concern the ways in which a feminist perspective could improve scientific research and research could be done in ways that reflect feminist views. As Ruth Bleier put it, the debate is about how to create a science that is "different, better, feminist, and emancipating" (1986, p. vii).

About 20 years ago this debate was in an embryonic stage, having been conceived from the joining of two disparate phenomena. The first was the social and behavioral sciences' crisis about positivism. Alvin Gouldner (1970), Ken Gergen (1973), William McGuire (1973), Howard Gadlin and Grant Ingle (1975), and Shulamit Reinharz (1979/1984) are a few of the many people who wrote about this crisis. Psychologist Alan Elms wrote:

> [There are] widespread self-doubts about goals, methods, and accomplishments . . . [in] social psychology. Similar doubts have been expressed recently within many other areas of psychology, particularly . . . personality research, developmental psychology, and clinical psychology. Serious self-questioning has developed simultaneously in the other social sciences, including sociology, anthropology and economics. (1975, p. 968)

Those who challenged positivism argued that facts had no meaning outside their context (Elliot Mishler, 1979). The idea of contexts, however, defied the positivist assumption that variables can be isolated. Ideas such as Mishler's led to a paradox about the relation between science and society:

> Science means knowledge about the objective world that is true because that is the way things are, not just because we have imagined it. Yet this science is now asserted to be socially based, determined by the society in which social scientists live. (Randall Collins, 1985, p. 3)

The second phenomenon was the massive social upheavals unfolding in the 1960s such as the rise of the New Left, the anti-war movement, and the liberation movements of Blacks, students and women. The connection between the crisis in science and the crisis in society was apparent, leading M. Brewster Smith, president of the American Psychological Association (APA), to write:

> . . . Much work in experimental social psychology . . . ran afoul of the tide of social concern and discontent that was sweeping the campuses with its call for "relevance." (1974, p. 28)

In response to these twin crises, some researchers developed alternative research paradigms. These were intended to renew social science, address social concerns and rehumanize researchers (Peter Reason & John Rowan, 1981; Shulamit Reinharz, 1981). Some of these efforts took the form of grounded theory (Barney Glaser & Anselm Strauss, 1967), conscientization (Paolo Freire, 1970), participatory research (Brinton Lykes, 1989), and phenomenology (Shulamit Reinharz, 1983a). Others attempted to transcend disciplinary boundaries. These new ways of doing research were later integrated with feminism and called "feminist research methods." [See also Claudia Salazar, and Liz Stanley, this volume.]

THE BACKGROUND FOR THE DEBATE

The epistemological crisis and the emerging women's liberation movement paved the way for a new consciousness among female students, scholars and scientists. Their insight that all aspects of social life were shaped by patriarchy led to the belief that all theory and research methods were patriarchal as well. In contrast to the positivist assumption that science liberated society, feminists claimed that science allowed some groups to oppress others. Science was oppressive, in part, because it was primarily a male endeavor informed by the needs and images of Western masculinity. I later labeled this interpretation of science "feminist distrust" (Shulamit Reinharz, 1985).

Betty Friedan's *The Feminine Mystique* (1963), Kate Millett's *Sexual Politics* (1970), and Naomi Weisstein's "Psychology Constructs the Female" (1971) launched "feminist distrust." Although they worked in different areas, their writings overlapped on three levels: criticism about women's actual lives; attacks on "scientific" theories about women; and dismay about the relative lack of information about women. Their shots from outside ricocheted in the halls of academe.

New works soon appeared showing that the patriarchal bias in nearly every academic discipline actually reproduced gender-based oppression (e.g., Marcia Millman & Rosabeth Moss Kanter, 1975; Julia Sherman & Evelyn Beck, 1979; Dale Spender, 1981). With titles such as Carolyn Sherif's, "Bias in Psychology" (in Julia Sherman & Evelyn Beck, 1979), these writings protested what social science had done to women. By demonstrating that disciplines were political in all their aspects—hiring, theory, methods, and teaching practices—including their so-called objective methods (Irene Frieze, Jacquelynne Talcott Parsons, Paula Johnson, Diane Ruble & Gail M. Zellman, 1978, pp. 14–27)—this critique was part of women's general attack on social conventions, particularly medical practice (Boston Women's Health Book Collective, 1973) and language (Cheris Kramer, Barrie Thorne, & Nancy Henley, 1978; Casey Miller & Kate Swift, 1980; Dale Spender, 1980; Barnie Thorne, Cheris Kramarae & Nancy Henley, 1983). Just as women accused society of sexism and discrimination, they accused social science of distortion, bias, myopia, ethnocentrism, heterosexism, and androcentrism. Both science and society used knowledge as a form of violence to silence women and make them invisible.

Feminist scholars began to postulate that new methods were required to do the missing research (Carol Ehrlich, 1976), especially research that reflected women's actual experiences. New concepts, theories, and approaches stemming from our experience in a patriarchal world were needed as an antidote to the erroneous studies based on men's assumptions about women. Canadian sociologist Dorothy Smith (1974) emphasized the necessity of doing research from women's standpoint, which she defined as a radical critique of sociology.

Acutely aware of the fact that women had few opportunities to do research because of employment discrimination (Evelyn Fox Keller, 1974; Alice Rossi, 1965), the goals of feminist researchers became to enable more women to do research and to release research from its massive patriarchal distortion. Feminists began calling for alternatives to standard methods. What these actually consisted of became a matter for debate.

UNDOING OF "SOCIAL TRUTHS"

The social truth that prevailed when the debate emerged was that researchers' disinterest rendered social science objective. By contrast, people's experiences were value-laden, "soft," worthless, "subjective," and anecdotal. Scales, measures, and tests were "hard" and meaningful. Researchers believed that studies of males applied to all people, but studies of women were not generalized to men. Females, when studied, were compared to men or asked questions of interest to men. Class and race were largely ignored or presented in a way that assumed anyone other than a white, middle-class male was deviant.

Another set of social truths held that women had no aptitude for science because they were not intellectual, logical, or committed to careers. They were "happiest" at home raising children and keeping house. They were ruled by biology and thus should help men, not compete with them. These ideas were sustained by Freudian theory in psychology and structural functionalist theory in sociology. Talcott Parsons, originator of the latter, claimed that the survival of the family and society rested on the sexual division of labor. Because these theories did not allow women to be seen as autonomous beings, studies which derived from them could not overcome this assumption. Thus, stratification studies assigned the status of the husband to wives (Ann Oakley, 1974). Similarly, the assumption that the personalities of men and women differed, led to sex differences research which obscured similarities.

Because of these assumptions, science studied some phenomena and not others. Certain phenomena could not even be seen, because males perceived everything female as Other, alien, and mysterious (Simone de Beauvoir, 1949). This blindness distorted the ability of social science to see social reality. For example, just as women's housework was not recognized as work by husbands, so too it was not recognized as work by male social scientists. Just as women's complaints against violent partners were not heard by their abusers or by the police, so too intimate violence was outside the vision of family sociologists. Conventional wisdom obscured the fact that women's lack of educational achievement reflected their socialization (Lenore Weitzman, 1979). The mythology of social science blurred the fact that social science had a material base available only to privileged groups, and that dominant groups had a vested interest in protecting that material base from usurpers.

"Social truths" about the sexes have eroded somewhat although belief in biological or genetic determinism remains strong (Ethel Tobach & Betty Rosoff, 1978). Today people may recognize that women vary just as men do, that females are capable of learning given the appropriate socialization and opportunities, and that women are autonomous beings with rights. Structural functionalist theory is challenged by models of conflict, "social constructionism," and theories of social change.

Many "social truths" were undone by feminist challenges in research and in the courts. Founding mothers who repudiated Freud include Nancy Chodorow, Dorothy Dinnerstein, Jean Baker Miller, and Hannah Lerman; those who challenged Parsons include Mirra Komarosky (Shulamit Reinharz, 1989b), Dorothy Smith (1974), and Heidi Hartmann (1981). In addition, women willing to discuss their experiences of rape, abortion, and battering challenged the definitions of crime and family. Speak-outs led to new ways of doing research on uncovered, redefined phenomena. Concepts such as "the family" were understood to serve white men's interests rather than reflect women's experiences. New concepts and methods had emerged. [See Rose Brewer, this volume.]

RESEARCH WITH WOMEN

We began by recognizing the need to study women and to reevaluate theories that were based on men (e.g., Carol Gilligan, 1982). We saw the need for methods to study women's strengths, not only their victimization (Shulamit Reinharz, 1984b). Ways were needed to approach women as actors-in-the-world rather than objects of other people's actions. Ways of listening to and hearing female language and recognizing the damaging way men speak of them (Shulamit Reinharz, 1986a) were called for. It was necessary to locate issues of actual concern to women (e.g., Shulamit Reinharz, 1987, 1988a, 1988b) rather than to use women as a comparison group for issues of concern to men. It was necessary for researchers to state their premises rather than hide them.

These goals led to the study of rape, lesbianism, voluntarism, divorce, sexism, mothering, interrupting, abortion, single parenting, "the empty nest," pornography, fear of success, miscarriage, housework, beautyism, the double standard of age, job ads, advertising, dual-career marriages, childlessness, sexual harassment, wife battering, incest, marital rape, date rape, displaced homemakers, neighborhood organizations, food obsessions, and more. These were not simply "social problems," they were the "female world." Whereas traditional research had trivialized women's concerns, feminist research saw the phenomena of everyday life as politics.

But it was not just the subject matter that had changed. These new foci required a new way of relating to people. Sometimes it required studying others as human beings whose social reality the researcher shared. Sometimes it required enabling those studied to define the research. In a sense, the women's movement's slogan—"the personal is political"—was transformed by researchers into "the personal is researchable" or "research can be personal."

As a result of the debate, new research principles were articulated: doing research with people rather than on them; having women do research; doing research in ways that empower people; valuing experiential knowledge; honoring female intelligence; and seeking the causes of oppression.

An example from Pauline Bart and Patricia O'Brien's rape avoidance research can serve as illustration:

> The women were paid $25 for their time; moreover, all their expenses, including travel from outside Chicago and babysitting, were reimbursed. . . . During the initial telephone call, we asked them for their own definition of the situation. Specifically, we asked them to tell us whether they had been raped or had been attacked but avoided being raped. In this way, the women defined themselves into parts of the sample: rape avoiders versus raped women. . . .
>
> Women need and want to know what to do if they are assaulted. Since we are feminists as well as sociologists, we believe in using our skills and resources to demystify the world for women, to answer questions women want answered. Therefore, we felt compelled to search for the answer to that age-old problem. . . . We hope other people will continue where we left off so that women everywhere will not only be able to take back the night . . . but take back the control of our lives which has been relinquished to men in our quest for survival (1985, pp. 7, 14)

METHODOLOGICAL ISSUES

Academic feminists continued to critique the disciplines in which they had been trained (see Marcia Westkott, 1979, and disciplinary review articles in *Signs*) and the methods they had been taught to use. But they also developed strategies for rectifying the problems they uncovered. First, they created the new "interdiscipline" of women's studies. They developed journals, publishing houses, and book series to communicate their scholarship, in addition to publishing in conventional outlets.

Book-length treatments of feminist methods appeared (Liz Stanley & Sue Wise, 1983; Helen Roberts, 1981; Gloria Bowles & Renata Duelli-Klein, 1983). These books frequently eliminated the distinction between the private life of the researcher and the subject matter on which she worked (Evelyn Fox Keller, 1985). They also tried to free themselves from "scientific methodolatry" (Mary Daly, 1978) and reexamined how old methods could be salvaged (Toby Jayaratne, 1983).

Jurist Catharine MacKinnon (1983) argued that the only truly feminist method was the method of the women's movement—consciousness raising. Similarly, the only context which could enhance feminist research was a feminist research support group (Shulamit Reinharz, 1984a) or other forms of feminist support. This was particularly necessary when the research had frightening components, as in the cases of obscene phone calls (Liz Stanley & Sue Wise, 1979) or rape.

This outpouring of statements about new ways of doing research was accompanied by cries of alarm on the part of some feminists who felt that the "new" methods were neither new nor beneficial. Florence Denmark (1985) warned that these approaches could ghettoize research on and for women because they distanced themselves from the mainstream. Others accused those who were abandoning old methods as "throwing the baby out with the bath water." They warned, too, that it would be difficult to obtain funding for feminist research unless it proceeded according to standard methodology. Some outsiders claimed that feminist research was ideological in contrast to their own, which they defined as objective. Thus, some feminists feared that attempts to formulate a feminist methodology would actually disempower women (Evelyn Fox Keller, 1980) or reinforce women's disempowered position. This latter idea has been suggested by Mirra Komarovsky:

> If women indeed possess a distinctive epistemology enabling them to reformulate the paradigms of our discipline, then their advantages over men, I believe, derive paradoxically from women's inferior status, whether it be the intuition the weak must develop in order to manipulate the powerful or the women's mothering of young children with so little participation of fathers. (1988, p. 592)

Ironically, this very argument against claiming superior insight for women because it justified continuing their oppression, was made long ago by George Eliot (Nicholas McGuinn, 1978).

MALESTREAM RESPONSE

Many feminist researchers are interested in the question of how malestream institutions have responded to their critique, but it may be too early to make the assessment. It may also be too difficult to answer this question because an assessment of feminism is frequently confounded with an assessment of the employment status of women. By this I mean that to study feminism's impact on an academic department, one might count the number of women employed. Yet, some of those women could adopt an antifeminist or nonfeminist perspective in their work. Thus, a much closer study of the position of women, the attitudes of men and women, and a broad examination of scholarship is needed.

The actual methods used to answer this question usually rely on journal publications. Ellen DuBois and her colleagues (1985), assessed the amount of feminist research in journals of 5 disciplines and found it to be surprisingly low. Others have found that in comparison with the past, more women are being published, more women are listed as editors, women's work is more likely to be cited, women are more likely to be studied, and methods are more likely to be used in which people can speak to their researchers in their own voice.

On the other hand, some feminists conclude that the impact has been modest if we use the criterion of understanding the relation between power and gender, or the relations between class, race, ethnicity, age, disability, sexual orientation, and gender. The criterion of women expressing their own meaning, or the criterion of the research being con-textualized also leads to a more modest assessment. True, more women are published than in the past, and some men are interested in studying issues of relevance to women, but, in general:

> The discipline of psychology, like marriage, work and parenting practices, has basically retained its shape, its boundaries and its resistance to disruption in the eye of the feminist storm (Michelle Fine & Susan Gordon, 1989, p. 4) [See also Mary Roth Walsh, this volume.]

I would say the same has been true of the "new anthropology" which claims it is responding to a crisis in social science, yet also ignores feminism's response to the same crisis (see *Inscriptions, 3/4,* 1988). Judith Stacey and Barrie Thorne (1985) argue that feminism's impact on sociology, too, has been inadequate. [See also Liz Stanley, this volume.] If social science can be said to ignore feminism to a certain extent, it certainly can be said to ignore the debate about research method within feminism. Ruth Bleier used an apt metaphor:

> While, over the past 10–12 years, feminists within science and without have been dissenting from and criticizing the many damaging and self-defeating features of science (the absolutism, authoritarianism, determinist thinking, cause–effect simplifications, androcentrism, ethno-centrism, pretensions to objectivity and neutrality), the elephant has not even flicked its trunk or noticeably glanced in our direction, let alone rolled over and given up. (Ruth Bleier, 1986, p. 1)

Like all generalizations, this one is only partially true. Some men have understood the critique that feminists developed and are using it to critically evaluate and guide their own work (David Morgan, 1981). Feminists, on the other hand, are divided as to whether any man can call himself a feminist. For this reason, there is no call among feminists that men do "feminist research." [See Lillian Robinson, this volume.]

PROTECTION OF POWER BASE?

Men have expressed little interest in feminist research methods or in the debate. Some feminists believe that out of respect for women, men should not write about feminism, and some question the appropriateness of men writing about women. After all, if women argue that they alone can study women, then men could exclude women from studying men. We would have a social science in which people would only study "their own kind." Aside from this epistemological question, men generally dismiss the idea that feminists consider nonfeminist research to be ideological. Their lack of interest probably reflects a lack of threat. When feminists severely criticize sexist work, those criticized attack, in turn, the methods used by their feminist critics (see special issue of *Transaction/SOCIETY,* 1986). Only when the feminist research principles debate is defined more broadly as an attempt to have everyone change their research method, does it become relevant to ask if the malestream has protected its powerbase. Protecting the powerbase would then be evident in academic gatekeeping. In part, these interactions conform to typical academic behavior, regardless of gender.

When they have not ignored the debate, men have applauded without understanding how feminist research requires a revision of malestream work. Thus Rosabeth Kanter received the prestigious C. Wright Mills award for her book, *Men and Women of the Corporation* (1977), in which she documented the key role (female) secretaries and wives play in a corporation. Yet, subsequent textbooks have not revised standard organization charts to include secretaries and wives. This applauding-without-utilizing attitude has not yet been fully recognized and exposed by feminists.

Some feminists, such as Shere Hite, author of three books concerning gender and sexuality, have sought male approval of their work as "science" despite the fact that they have used unconventional methods that violate standard social science procedures. In general, however, feminists have not sought male participation in the methods debate. Books on the topic typically do not have contributions by male authors (but see Arnold S. Kahn & William P. Gaeddert, 1985).

Many male scholars adopt a liberal approach that someone should "do" feminism, but feel they have no personal responsibility for it. As Biblical scholar, Carol Meyers wrote of her own field: "Many male scholars support and even applaud research with a feminist perspective; relatively few engage in such research" (1988, p. 20). [See also Carol Christ, this volume.] A kind of division of labor has resulted. The tolerant response is typically unaccompanied by the recognition that men or conventional disciplines must change. Because of the strength of this liberal reaction, feminist research proceeds less in an environment of resistance than in one of "two cultures," arranged hierarchically. There are still many feminist (untenured) academics who are afraid to discuss feminism or do feminist research, lest they suffer academic punishment.

That feminist and mainstream scholars inhabit different worlds (Jessie Bernard, 1981) can be seen in studies of citation patterns. Articles in mainstream psychology journals have a very low rate of citing articles from feminist journals, whereas articles in feminist journals are likely to be cited in other feminist journals (Michelle Fine & Susan Gordon, 1989). The flourishing of two cultures depends on an adequate market. At the moment, there is room to market both worlds. New feminist journals are being founded; social concern about "sexism" allows some feminist articles to find their ways into mainstream journals; and some feminist scholars are getting tenure.

The "two cultures" idea should not disguise the fact that women are still trained in and internalize male-dominated paradigms. Feminists must learn to speak malestream language while inventing their own language (e.g., methodolatry, gynopia [Shulamit Reinharz, 1985], ltmdt, i.e., low threshold for male dominance theorizing [Shulamit Reinharz, 1986a]). Not surprisingly, women must work to sustain two cultures, whereas men are rewarded for work in one.

STRATEGIES OF FEMINISTS

At the same time that feminists were criticizing the disciplines, they were agitating to have access to them. The desire for a job (or promotion) compelled many feminist academics to take a stand in the research methods debate. True, one could always do research outside the academy. But to survive in a world whose motto was "publish or perish," one had to both publish and evaluate the publication of others.

Getting or keeping an academic position typically meant demonstrating that one had conventional skills. Adopting a nonconventional research stance could jeopardize academic opportunities. Some women feared that doing feminist research would be perceived as not being "serious." Some feminists may have criticized those developing new methods so as to disassociate themselves and demonstrate commitment to conventional methods. The possibility that feminists would start "trashing" each other's work from a "lefter than thou" or "more scientific than thou" stance was great. Gaining visibility may have motivated "harsh reviews of feminist writings—sometimes by feminists" (Dale Spender, 1985, p. 3).

My *personal* response was to write a synopsis of the debate and argue for pluralism. I was concerned that a backlash would squelch the creativity that the search for feminist methods could foment. I also tried to address outsiders by linking the goals of feminist research with conventional social science methods, particularly qualitative research (Shulamit Reinharz, 1983b). I also used my role as editor of a quarterly sociological journal (*Qualitative Sociology*) to help feminist scholars. At the same time, I tried to clarify the issues by publishing a bibliography (Shulamit Reinharz, Marti Bombyk, & Jan Wright, 1983) that catalogued and honored the various emerging ideas. And each time I published an article or book, I specified how my work was an *example* of feminist research methods as I saw them. For example:

> Reconstructing a phenomenon such as miscarriage in terms of the way women experience it and examining how such experiences reflect the definition of women as a group, is, in my view, essentially a feminist undertaking. (Shulamit Reinharz, 1988b, p. 5)

The debate about feminist research principles has been conducted primarily among feminists and shows no signs of abating. New methods (e.g., interviewing women in groups) are being developed, while old accusations (concerning class and ethnocentrism) originally hurled at mainstream disciplines are now applied to feminist research. For example, Lynn Cannon, Elizabeth Higginbotham, and Marianne Leung (1988) argue that because whites are more likely to volunteer to be studied than Blacks, recruiting Blacks is more labor intensive. Studies with small samples are thus likely to exclude Blacks. In some cases, however, the process is reversed and race consciousness leads to feminism:

> I owe the motivation for this anthology to my sisters in West Africa whose unrewarded patience with patriarchy and inequality made me challenge my own assumptions and perspectives about white women and women of color in the United States and led me to ardent feminism (Joyce Penfield, 1987, acknowledgments)

In general, however, attention to race in social research, including feminist research, is inadequate (Angela Davis, 1983).

ENRICHING OUR LIVES

The debate has enriched the lives of female academics in two ways. First, any debate strengthens a community by creating a forum for the expression of ideas. Second, it has provided some feminists with the opportunity to improve their methods, and has created job opportunities as feminists are hired to teach courses on this topic. Because the debate has not been resolved, I predict that writing on this topic will continue to flourish. For example, Judith Lorber, founding editor of *Gender & Society*, addressed this topic in two ways:

> The question I want to raise is whether a special way of doing research—feminist methodology—is the only way women's realities can be tapped and understood. The second, related question, is whether feminist methodologies are unique to feminists. (1987, p. 5)

She then reviewed a session of the 1987 American Sociological Society, Sex and Gender Section, on "Feminist Theory and Methods." Persistent interest in this topic led me to write the book, *Social Research Methods, Feminist Perspectives* (Shulamit Reinharz, 1991).

The debate has also enriched the lives of women nonacademics in the short run and long run. In the short run, women who participate in research in which they can express their true feelings have reported an experience of catharsis. This catharsis can lead to action as a woman clarifies what is wrong and what needs to be done. In the long run, researchers who bring women's issues to the attention of the public in effective ways may also have an impact on public policy. Feminist researchers have testified as expert witnesses and have helped formulate laws concerning mandatory child support, murder as self-defense in domestic violence cases, sexual abuse by therapists, sexual harassment and more. There are feminist scholars in many different disciplines who now feel confident that their knowledge base concerning feminist research principles is strong enough to create conferences whose purpose is to educate nonfeminist scholars. (A recent example is a conference organized by Linda Smircich and Marta Callas of the School of Management, University of Massachusetts, Amherst, to educate people in the field of organization science who did not identify themselves as feminist).

THE FUTURE

In my view at least three blindspots remain in the development of feminist research practices. First, we have not challenged the assumption that research is always conducted in a political context that is safe, and that researchers can expect to be trusted. Second, we have yet to discuss the impact of our work practices on the health of the earth and the survival of animals. [See Irene Diamond, this volume.] Third, we have not yet examined the financing of our research.

Although an assessment of the current situation may rest on the question—have we settled the debate or not?—I think this is a misguided question. The point is not to settle the debate but to be dialectically engaged in it. I think a more fruitful way of assessing the situation is to consider a range of questions:

1. Is there a lot of discussion about the debate?
2. Is the quality of the discussion stimulating?
3. Do people respect different points of view?
4. Have we already covered a lot of ground?

In my opinion, the answer to all of these questions is "yes"—there is a lot of high quality, primarily respectful discussion in highly visible places (Sandra Harding, 1987).

Feminist challenges to conventional research methods have raised our consciousness in many ways. First, we are now more aware of additional biases, especially those concerning race (bell hooks, 1984), class, sexual orientation, ethnocentrism, and age. For example, we are becoming aware that youth and middle-age have conventionally been defined as the norm, with childhood and old age defined as "other" (Barrie Thorne, 1987; Shulamit Reinharz, 1989c). As feminists have begun to apply a radical consciousness to issues of age, positivist methods are again seen as inadequate (Emily Abel, 1988; Shulamit Reinharz, 1986b; Shulamit Reinharz & Graham Rowles, 1987).

Second, feminist methods now actively incorporate history. History is recognized as one of the many missing contexts of academic research (Mary Jo Deegan, 1988; Evelyn Glenn, 1986), one that is "essential and indispensable to the emancipation of women" (Gerda Lerner, 1986, p. 3). Feminist scholars in all the disciplines are engaged in a search for their foremothers, another version of the search for sisters (Ute Gacs, Alsha Khan, Jerrie McIntyre, & Ruth Weiberg, 1988; Shulamit Reinharz, 1989a).

My personal search for foremothers in sociology led me to the white British woman, Harriet Martineau (Michael Hill, 1988) and the Black American woman, Ida Wells-Barnett (1892/1987). It also led me to the woman—Manya Wilbushewitz Shohat—who conceived of the first kibbutz (Reinharz, 1984c) and to an exploration of the contributions of one of my teachers, Mirra Komarovsky (Reinharz, 1989b). It seems quite clear that feminist biography is emerging as a methodological offshoot of feminist history (Judy Long, in press a & b; Joan Mark, 1988; Shulamit Reinharz, 1988c; Liz Stanley, 1984). A debate exists among those interested in adding a historical dimension to understanding women. It concerns the propriety of "adding women" to existing frameworks versus the necessity of transforming patriarchal frameworks, including periodization.

Feminist research concerns have led some women beyond the question of the relation between feminism and method to the larger question of whether or not women have a distinctive way of knowing (Mary Belenky, Blythe Clinchy, Nancy Goldberger, & Jill Tarule, 1986; Sara Ruddick, 1980). For example, Nadya Aisenberg and Mona Harrington studied women academics and found that:

> The most general characteristic of women's intellectual work consists of placing subject matter in a cultural context, in the real and complicated life of the relevant time and place. (1988, p. 90)

Such studies typically analyze the way women talk about themselves in in-depth interviews and thus take an implicit stand on feminist method. There is no escape from the dilemma that every search for understanding starts with a premise about the way one should search for understanding.

A third emerging debate concerns the desirable level of clarity and sophistication on which research findings should be presented. Is it valuable for researchers to translate their work into language that is comprehensible to others, or does this represent a violation of its intellectual integrity? Even the most "empowering" study can be mystifying to people who do not understand the language in which the study results are communicated.

Because sufficient time has passed, we are now beginning to see surveys and assessments of methodological approaches of feminist researchers (Linda Grant, Kathryn B. Ward, & Xue Lan Rong, 1987). These follow assessments of the impact of feminism on the disciplines (Judith Cook & Mary M. Fonow, 1986; Kathryn B. Ward & Linda Grant, 1985).

By virtue of the feminist critique, research methods have not yet been entirely transformed, nor have they remained unchanged. There are some who want to get power in the mainstream so that they can make room for feminist research; still others want to forge their own streams. As feminists now write the disciplinary textbooks, we are beginning to shape the way knowledge is passed to future generations (Margaret Andersen, 1983; Beth Hess, Elizabeth Markson & Peter Stein, 1988). Yet the debate about how one should do feminist research continues because feminism means constant criticism, restlessness, and dissatisfaction with the status quo and a commitment to work for change.

BIBLIOGRAPHY

Inscriptions, 3/4. (1988). *Feminism and the Critique of Colonial Discourse.* pp. 1–154.

"Patriarchy and Power" (1986). A group of essays by various authors in *Transaction/SOCIETY, 23* (6), 4–39.

Abel, Emily K. (1988). *Informal care of the frail elderly: A critique of recent literature.* Unpublished manuscript, UCLA School of Public Health. Los Angeles, CA.

Aisenberg, Nadya & Harrington, Mona. (1988). *Women of academe: Outsiders in the sacred grove.* Amherst, MA: University of Massachusetts Press.

Andersen, Margaret. (1983). *Thinking about women: Sociological and feminist perspectives.* New York: Macmillan.

Bart, Pauline & O'Brien, Patricia. (1985). *Stopping rape: Successful survival strategies.* Elmsford, NY: Pergamon Press.

Belenky, Mary, Clinchy, Blythe, Goldberger, Nancy, & Tarule, Jill. (1986). *Women's ways of knowing: The development of self, voice, and mind.* New York: Basic Books.

Bernard, Jessie. (1981). *The female world.* New York: Free Press.

Bleier, Ruth (Ed.). (1986). *Feminist approaches to science.* Elmsford, NY: Pergamon Press.

Boston Women's Health Book Collective. (1973). *Our bodies, ourselves.* New York: Simon & Schuster.

Bowles, Gloria & Duelli-Klein, Renate. (Eds.). (1983). *Theories of women's studies.* Boston: Routledge & Kegan Paul.

Cannon, Lynn Weber, Higginbotham, Elizabeth, & Leung, Marianne. (1988). Race and class bias in qualitative research on women. *Gender & Society, 2*(4), 449–462.

Collins, Randall. (1985). *Three sociological traditions.* New York: Oxford University Press.

Cook, Judith A. & Fonow, Mary M. (1986). Knowledge and women's interests: Issues of feminist epistemology and methodology in feminist sociological research. *Sociological Inquiry, 56,* 2–29.

Daly, Mary. (1978). *Gyn/Ecology: The metaethics of radical feminism.* Boston: Beacon Press.

Davis, Angela. (1983). *Women, race & class.* New York: Vintage.

de Beauvoir, Simone. (1949). *The Second Sex.* New York: Knopf.

Deegan, Mary Jo. (1988). *Jane Addams and the men of the Chicago School, 1892–1918.* New Brunswick, NJ: Transaction Books.

Denmark, Florence. (1985). Women's worlds: Ghetto: Refuge, or power base? In Marilyn Safir, Martha Mednick, Dafne Israeli, & Jessie Bernard (Eds.), *Women's worlds: From the new scholarship* (pp. 38–48). New York: Praeger.

DuBois, Ellen, Kelly, Gail, Kennedy, Elizabeth, Korsmeyer, Carolyn, & Robinson, Lillian. (1985). *Feminist scholarship: Kindling in the groves of academe.* Chicago: University of Illinois Press.

Ehrlich, Carol. (1976). *The conditions of feminist research.* Baltimore, MD: Research Group One.

Elms, Alan. (1975). The crisis of confidence in social psychology. *American Psychologist, 30* (10), 967–976.

Fine, Michelle & Gordon, Susan. (1989). Feminist transformations of/despite psychology. In M. Crawford & M. Gentry (Eds.), *Gender and thought: Psychological perspectives* (pp. 146–174). New York: Springer-Verlag.

Freire, Paolo. (1970). *Pedagogy of the oppressed.* New York: Herder & Herder.

Friedan, Betty. (1963). *The feminine mystique.* New York: W W Norton.

Frieze, Irene, Parsons, Jacquelynne, Johnson, Paula, Ruble, Diane, & Zellman, Gail. (1978). *Women and sex roles: A social psychological perspective.* New York: W W Norton.

Gacs, Ute, Khan, Aisha, McIntyre, Jerrie, & Weiberg, Ruth. (Eds.). (1988). *Women anthropologists: A biographical dictionary.* New York: Greenwood Press.

Gadlin, Howard & Ingle, Grant. (1975). Through the one-way mirror. *American Psychologist, 30*(10), 1003–1009.

Gergen, Ken. (1973). Social psychology as history. *Journal of Personality and Social Psychology, 26*, 309–320.

Glenn, Evelyn. (1986). *Issei, Nisei, war bride: Three generations of Japanese American women in domestic service.* Philadelphia, PA: Temple University Press.

Gilligan, Carol. (1982). *In a different voice: Psychological theory and women's development.* Cambridge: MA: Harvard University Press.

Glaser, Barney & Strauss, Anselm. (1967). *The discovery of grounded theory.* Chicago: Aldine.

Gouldner, Alvin W. (1970). *The coming crisis of western sociology.* New York: Avon Books.

Grant, Linda, Ward, Kathryn B., & Rong, Xue Lan. (1987). Is there an association between gender and methods in sociological research? *American Sociological Review, 52*, 856–62.

Harding, Sandra (Ed.). (1987). *Feminism & methodology.* Bloomington, IN: Indiana University Press.

Hartmann, Heidi. (1981). The family as the locus of gender, class, and political struggle: The example of housework. *Signs, 6*(3), 366–394.

Hess, Beth, Markson, Elizabeth, & Stein, Peter. (1988). *Sociology* (3rd ed.). New York: Macmillan.

Hite, Shere. (1988). *Women and love: A cultural revolution in progress.* New York: Alfred A Knopf.

Hill, Michael (Ed.). (1989). Harriet Martineau's *How to observe morals and manners.* New Brunswick, NJ: Transaction Books. (Original work published 1838.)

hooks, bell. (1984). *Feminist theory: From margin to center.* Boston: South End Press.

Jayaratne, Toby Epstein. (1983). The value of quantitative methodology for feminist research. In G. Bowles & R. Duelli-Klein (Eds.), *Theories of women's studies* (pp. 140–161). Boston: Routledge & Kegan Paul.

Kahn, Arnold S. & Gaeddert, William P. (1985). From theories of equity to theories of justice: The liberating consequences of studying women. In Virginia O'Leary, Rhoda Unger, & Barbara Wallston (Eds.), *Women, gender and social psychology.* Hillsdale, NJ: Lawrence Erlbaum Associates.

Kanter, Rosabeth Moss. (1977). *Men and women of the corporation.* New York: Basic Books.

Keller, Evelyn Fox. (1974). Women in science: An analysis of a social problem. *Harvard Magazine,* 14–19.

Keller, Evelyn Fox. (1980). Feminist critique of science: A forward or backward move? *Fundamenta Scientiae, 1*, 341–349.

Keller, Evelyn Fox. (1985). *Reflections on gender and science.* New Haven, CT: Yale University Press.

Komarovsky, Mirra. (1988). The new feminist scholarship: Some precursors and polemics. *Journal of Marriage and the Family, 50*, 585–593.

Kramer, Cheris, Thorne, Barrie, & Henley, Nancy. (1978). Perspectives on language and communication. *Signs, 3*(3), 638–651.

Lerman, Hannah. (1986). *A mote in Freud's eye: From psychoanalysis to the psychology of women.* New York: Springer.

Lerner, Gerda. (1986). *The creation of patriarchy.* New York: Oxford University Press.

Long, Judy. (in press a). *Telling women's lives.* New Haven, CT: Yale University Press.

Long, Judy (Ed.). (in press b). *The new sociobiography.* New Brunswick, NJ: Rutgers University Press.

Lorber, Judith. (1987). From the editor. *Gender & Society, 2* (1), 5–7.

Lykes, M. Brinton. (1989). Dialogue with Guatemalan Indian women: Critical perspectives on constructing collaborative research. In Rhoda Unger (Ed.), *Representations: Social constructions of gender* (pp. 167–185) Amityville, NY: Baywood.

MacKinnon, Catharine A. (1983). Feminism, Marxism, method and the state: Toward feminist jurisprudence. *Signs: Journal of Women in Culture and Society, 8* (4).

McGuinn, Nicholas. (1978). George Eliot and Mary Wollstonecraft. In Sara Delamont & Lorna Duffin (Eds.), *The nineteenth century woman: Her cultural and physical world* (pp. 188–205). London: Croom Helm.

McGuire, William J. (1973). The yin and yang of progress in social psychology: Seven Koan. *Journal of Personality and Social Psychology, 26,* 446–456.

Mark, Joan. (1988). *Stranger in her native land: Alice Fletcher and the American Indian.* Lincoln, NE: University of Nebraska Press.

Meyers, Carol. (1988). *Discovering eve: Ancient Israelite women in context.* New York: Oxford University Press.

Miller, Casey & Swift, Kate. (1980). *The handbook of nonsexist writing: For writers, editors and speakers.* New York: J B Lippincott.

Miller, Jean Baker. (1976). *Toward a new psychology of women.* Boston: Beacon Press.

Millet, Kate. (1970). *Sexual politics.* Garden City, NY: Doubleday.

Millman, Marcia & Kanter, Rosabeth. (Eds.). (1975). *Another voice: Feminist perspectives on social life and social science.* Garden City, NY: Anchor Press, Doubleday.

Mishler, Elliot. (1979). Meaning in context: Is there any other kind? *Harvard Educational Review, 49* (1), 1–19.

Morgan, David. (1981). Men, masculinity, and the process of sociological enquiry. In Helen Roberts (Ed.), *Doing feminist research.* Boston: Routledge & Kegan Paul.

Oakley, Ann. (1974). *The sociology of housework.* New York: Pantheon Books.

Parsons, Talcott. (1955). *Family, socialization and interaction process.* Glencoe, IL: Free Press.

Penfield, Joyce (Ed.). (1987). *Women & language in transition.* Albany, NY: State University of New York Press.

Reason, Peter & Rowan, J. (Eds.). (1981). *Human inquiry: A sourcebook of new paradigm research.* New York: John Wiley.

Reinharz, Shulamit. (1979, 1984). *On becoming a social scientist: From survey research and participant observation to experiential analysis.* San Francisco: Jossey-Bass, 1979; and New Brunswick, NJ: Transaction Books, 1984.

Reinharz, Shulamit. (1981). Implementing new paradigm research: A model for training and practice. In P. Reason & J. Rowan (Eds.), *Human inquiry: A sourcebook of new paradigm research* (pp. 415–436). New York: John Wiley.

Reinharz, Shulamit. (1983a). Phenomenology as a dynamic process. *Pedagogy and Phenomenology, 1*(1), 77–79.

Reinharz, Shulamit. (1983b). Experiential analysis: A contribution to feminist research methodology. In G. Bowles & R. Duelli-Klein (Eds.), *Theories of women's studies* (pp. 162–191). Boston: Routledge & Kegan Paul.

Reinharz, Shulamit. (1984a). Feminist research methodology groups: Origins, forms and functions. In Louise Tilly and Vivian Petraka (Eds.), *Feminist visions and revisions* (pp. 197–228). Ann Arbor, MI: University of Michigan Press.

Reinharz, Shulamit. (1984b). Women as competent community builders: The other side of the coin. In A. Rickel, M. Gerrard and I. Iscoe (Eds.), *Social and psychological problems of women* (pp. 19–43). New York: Macmillan.

Reinharz, Shulamit. (1984c). Toward a model of female political action: The case of Manya Wilbushewitz Shohat, founder of the first kibbutz. *Women's Studies International Forum, 7*(4), 275–287.

Reinharz, Shulamit. (1985). Feminist distrust: Problems of context and content in sociological work. In David Berg & Ken Smith (Eds.), *The self in social inquiry* (pp. 153–172). Beverly Hills: CA, Sage Publications.

Reinharz, Shulamit. (1986a). Patriarchal pontifications *Transaction/SOCIETY, 23*(6), 23–39.

Reinharz, Shulamit. (1986b). Friends or foes: Feminist and gerontological theory. *Women's Studies International Forum, 9*(4), 39–50.

Reinharz, Shulamit. (1988a). What's missing in miscarriage? *Journal of Community Psychology, 16*(1), 84–103.

Reinharz, Shulamit. (1988b). Controlling women's lives: A cross-cultural interpretation of miscarriage accounts. In Dorothy Wertz (Ed.), *Research in the Sociology of Health Care.* Greenwich, CT: JAI Press, 7, 3–37.

Reinharz, Shulamit. (1988c, December). *The sociological value of feminist biographies of women scientists.* Paper presented at the annual meeting of the History of Science Society, Cincinnati, Ohio.

Reinharz, Shulamit. (1989a). Teaching the history of women in sociology: Or Dorothy Swaine Thomas, wasn't she the one who was married to W.I.? *The American Sociologist, 20* (1), 87–94.

Reinharz, Shulamit. (1989b). Finding her sociological voice: The work of Mirra Komarovsky. *Sociological Inquiry, 59* (4), 374–395.

Reinharz, Shulamit. (1989c). Feminism and anti-ageism: Emergent connections. In Regula Herzog, Karen Holden & Mildred Seltzer (Eds.), *Older women: Research issues and data sources.* Farmingdale, NY: Baywood Press.

Reinharz, Shulamit, with the assistance of Lynn Davidman. (1991). *Feminist methods in social research.* Oxford: Oxford University Press.

Reinharz, Shulamit, Bombyk, Marti, & Wright, Jan. (1983). Methodological issues in feminist research: A bibliography of literature in women's studies, sociology and psychology. *Women's Studies International Forum 6*(4), 437–454.

Reinharz, Shulamit & Rowles, Graham. (Eds.). (1987). *Qualitiative Gerontology.* New York: Springer.

Roberts, Helen. (1981). *Doing feminist research.* Boston: Routledge & Kegan Paul.

Rossi, Alice. (1965). Women in science: Why so few? *Science, 148,* 1196–1202.

Ruddick, Sara. (1980). Maternal Thinking. *Feminist Studies, 6,* 342–367.

Segal, Marcia Texler. (1984, November 22). Feminism and the self-conscious sociologist: An essay on the sociology of knowledge, Unpublished manuscript prepared for the Sociology Departmental Seminar. University of Malawi. Available from Dept. of Sociology, Indiana University Southeast, New Albany, Indiana 47150.

Sherif, Carolyn. (1979). Bias in psychology. In Julia Sherman, & Evelyn Beck (Eds.), *The prism of sex: Essays in the sociology of knowledge* (pp. 93–134). Madison, WI: University of Wisconsin Press.

Sherman, Julia & Beck, Evelyn. (Eds.). (1979). *The prism of sex: Essays in the sociology of knowledge.* Madison, WI: University of Wisconsin Press.

Smith, Dorothy. (1974). Women's perspective as a radical critique of sociology. *Sociological Enquiry, 44*(1), 7–13.

Smith, M. Brewster. (1974). *Humanizing social psychology.* San Francisco, CA: Jossey-Bass.

Spender, Dale. (1985). *For the record.* London: The Women's Press.

Spender, Dale. (1980). *Man made language.* London: Routledge & Kegan Paul.

Spender, Dale. (1981). *Men's studies modified: The impact of feminism on the academic disciplines.* Oxford: Pergamon Press.

Stacey, Judith & Thorne, Barrie. (1985). The missing revolution in sociology. *Social Problems, 32,* 301–316.

Stanley, Liz (Ed.). (1984). *The diaries of Hannah Cullwick: Victorian maidservant.* New Brunswick, NJ: Rutgers University Press.

Stanley, Liz & Wise, Sue. (1979). Feminist research, feminist consciousness and experiences of sexism. *Women's Studies International Quarterly, 2*(3), 359–374.

Stanley, Liz & Wise, Sue. (1983). *Breaking out: Feminist consciousness and feminist research.* Boston: Routledge & Kegan Paul.

Thorne, Barrie. (1987). Re-visioning women and social change: Where are the children? *Gender & Society, 1*(1), 85–109.

Thorne, Barrie, Kramarae, Cheris, & Henley, Nancy. (Eds.). (1983). *Language, gender and society.* New York: Newbury House.

Tobach, Ethel & Rosoff, Betty. (Eds.). (1978). *Genes & gender.* New York: Gordian Press.

Ward, Kathryn B. & Grant, Linda. (1985). The feminist critique and a decade of published research in sociology journals. *Sociological Quarterly, 26,* 139–57.

Weisstein, Naomi. (1971). Psychology constructs the female. In Vivian Gornick & Barbara K. Moran (Eds.), *Woman in sexist society* (pp. 207–224). New York: New American Library.

Weitzman, Lenore. (1979). *Sex role socialization.* Palo Alto, CA: Mayfield Publishing Company.

Wells-Barnett, Ida B. (1987). *On lynchings.* Salem, NY: Ayer Company. (Original work published 1892)

Westkott, Marcia. (1979). Feminist criticism of the social sciences. *Harvard Educational Review, 49*, 422–430.

Chapter 40

A Good Man Is Hard to Find
Reflections on Men's Studies

Lillian S. Robinson

Women's studies? they used to ask us, great quotation marks appearing in the air around their words. *Then what about men's studies?* And our reply, after a time, became almost reflexive: "Men's studies is what the *rest* of the University, the *rest* of the intellectual tradition is about." This was the spirit in which Dale Spender (1981) entitled a book about feminist scholarship *Men's Studies Modified.* And that use of the term is by no means obsolete, because women's studies remains subject to assault on the grounds of this "narrow focus" on only just over half of human-kind. ("I'm not for women's liberation, I'm for *human* liberation," some people still say, pointing self-righteously to the egregious bias of feminism and ignoring the fact that they themselves have never lifted a finger, written a word, or marched a foot, or contributed a penny to the liberation of anyone at all.)

In recent years, however, "men's studies" has acquired a new and less surely rhetorical meaning, as scholars have applied the insights of feminism to the category of gender and to male experience, social, historical, and sexual. The result has been an increasing body of material about the operations of gender itself, as well as the specifics of men's lives considered as *male* lives. Institutionally, several American research facilities have assumed names that reflect this new focus: A Center for the Study of Women and Men in Society at the University of Southern California, Institutes for Research on Women and Gender at both Stanford and Columbia Universities. And journal articles, special issues, entire new periodicals, anthologies, monographs, and scholarly series proliferate. At best, all this activity provides both a complement and a support to feminist thought; at worst, it has been little more than a continuation of pedestrian social science research on sex roles. Especially problematic is the introduction of "gender" into the discourse. For this word, which one might expect to be especially clear and explicit, in fact serves every function in the register of signification from code word to force for equality to obfuscator of oppression.

The general organizing questions sent to all contributors by the editors of this volume did much to clarify my thinking. But the impossibility of turning around the categories in which they are couched—of substituting, say, "men" for "women," "men's movement" for "women's movement," "founding fathers" (heaven forbid!) for "founding mothers," and so on—reflects the special nature of this particular debate. Precisely to the extent that it cannot be forced into an intellectual framework that appears quite flexible as long as it is being applied to women' studies within a given discipline or across disciplinary lines, men's studies reveals some of its characteristic strengths and weaknesses. Although my responses follow the numbered questions, the frequent incongruity between the assumptions and underlying those questions, on the other hand, and the men's studies debate, on the other, say something important about the debate itself.

The men's studies movement is as much a phenomenon of the 1980s as the Women's Studies movement is of the 1970s. (Among the similarities are the roots that each of them has in social and intellectual movements of the *previous* decade, those roots, for men's studies, actually being in feminism and feminist scholarship.) [See also Pat Cramer and Ann Russo, this volume.] Twenty years ago, which happens to be when I wrote my own first contribution to what was not yet called *women's* studies, academic disciplines were essentially divided into two sorts: those that accommodated some recognition of gender as an analytic category and those that did not. (For a discussion of this division see Ellen Carol DuBois et al. 1985).

Generally speaking, the humanities and the "hard" social sciences (economics and political science) were alike in a gender-blind approach to their subject matter, whereas the social sciences that deal directly with human society or personality—anthropology, sociology, psychology, and the theoretical areas of education—frequently made use of gender when they counted things and, sometimes, when they attempted to understand them. (Legal studies were a special case, and the natural sciences, of course, were commonly understood as having no relation to social forces, including those defining male and female identity, status, or interactions.)

To say all this is not necessarily to say anything in praise of those fields in which gender did feature. Although anthropologists and sociologists did notice issues of gender—principally sex roles themselves and socialization into them—their own expectations often led them to misinterpret the evidence presented to them and hence to describe it from a position informed by bias. The tendency in anthropology is critiqued in such revisionist commentaries as Sally (Linton) Slocum (1975), Betty Chinas (1973), Michelle Zimbalist Rosaldo and Louise Lamphere (1974) and Ruby Rohrlich-Leavitt, Sykes, & Weatherford (1975). Psychologists and education specialists tended to be even more normative, convinced that they already knew right from wrong on the question of sex roles and providing essentially prescriptive studies based on this conviction. (See, for example, Patricia Cayo Sexton [1969].) [See also Mary Roth Walsh, and Dale Spender, this volume.] Sex–role socialization tended to be studied with respect to both boys and girls, but in other areas where gender was an issue, female experience was the marked category, the variant. And dominant assumptions about male and female were rarely called into question, except in so far as observing cultural differences in these matters at least implicitly challenged the notion that contemporary Euro-American societies fostered the only natural or imaginable patterns of sex role attribution (For example, Margaret Mead, 1974, 1953).

Unsurprisingly, in those fields where gender was not problematized, there was almost no attention to such issues as sex roles or stereotypes. Far from analyzing such stereotypes, in fact, some literary scholars made uncritical use of female stereotypes like the repressed virgin or the man-eating bitch as if they were reflections of a universally accepted reality (for a discussion—and a *reductio ad absurdum*—see Mary Ellmann, 1968). By contrast, male characters in literature might be stereotyped as fools or villains, but these failings were not attributed to their sex, nor was the traditional male role considered open to serious debate.

PROFEMINIST MOVEMENT

The early history of feminist scholarship is marked by a strong overlap between works that are part of the academic tradition and those that come out the women's movement to address an audience wider than either academe or feminism can provide. (Kate Millett's [1970] *Sexual Politics* is an influential example of this kind of work.) Occasionally, reference was made in books of this sort to the ways in which women's oppression also limited or even oppressed men, and academic interest in androgyny as a literary and political theme may have its roots in feminist recognition of the male half of the dilemma.

But it was not until the formation of what is now called the "profeminist" (or simply the "feminist") men's movement that books like Warren Farrell's (1974) *The Liberated Man* and Marc Feigen-Fasteau's (1974) *The Male Machine*—books that, like the earlier feminist ones, addressed both scholarly and popular audiences—began to appear. These books point out the damage that is done to men by the expectations attendant on their traditional role. Both as breadwinner and as authority figure, the unliberated man, they argue, has to bear a burden rendered all the heavier by his alienation from emotional expression. Their vision of a better society is based on an essentially liberal version of feminism: egalitarian attitudes informing relationships within heterosexual couples. The mid-1970s also saw the publication of an anthology, *Unbecoming Men* (1971), compiled by a men's consciousness-raising group, whose countercultural contributors acknowledged and identified with some of the more radical analyses and goals of the feminist movement.

In the previous paragraph, I used the phrase, "What is now called the 'profeminist men's movement'" advisedly. At the movements's inception, "men's movement," "men's" or "male liberation" referred unambiguously to men who were joining feminists in challenging traditional roles and power relations. But today *anti*-feminist sentiment is also expressed by groups that make use of the word "liberation" in their names, as if it is feminism from which men need liberation, and the assertion of those traditional roles and power relations were an act of the downtrodden. Arguing that the pro- and antifeminist men's organizations are not left and right wings of the same movement, but are ideological and strategic opposites, what used to be called simply "the men's movement" now distinguishes itself by the adoption of the label "feminist." Challenging the imputed brotherhood of the two movements are essays like Robert Brannon (1981–1982). Despite this protestation, it does appear, from the outside looking in, that certain forces link the two as poles of a continuum: for instance, "fathers' rights" groups organized around child custody issues and hence challenging traditional roles, or the men's spiritual movement, with the values it attaches to the "wild man" over the "soft man."

At any rate, some of the anti-feminist books produced in the past fifteen years have explicitly identified themselves with "men's rights" causes, where these are understood as opposed to the movement for women's rights. Works like George Gilder's *Sexual Suicide* (1986) also associated with neoconservative economic and social philosophies, are meant to bear the same sort of relation to what their authors consider an emerging current in American thought that the feminist and "male liberation" books did to those movements. It is by no means clear, however, what impact, intellectual or societal, these books have had, because the "backlash" against feminism where it exists, is animated by different principles than the ones the books lay out. Similarly, although the Farrell and Feigne-Fasteau books may have been included in the syllabi of women's studies courses hungry for complementary material about men, they did not have much to contribute to the global analysis feminists were developing.

CHALLENGES BY BOTH MOVEMENTS

The prevailing "social truths" about masculinity prior to the challenges posed by both women's and men's movements have been admirably summarized in Kate Stimpson's introduction to one of the major men's studies anthologies:

> To be "masculine" is to have a particular psychological identity, social role, cultural script, place in the labor force, and sense of the sacred. In secular, modern industrial cultures, "real men" should define themselves in at least three ways. First, they earn money in the public labor force and support their families through that effort. Next, they have formal power over women and children. Finally, they are heterosexual. They sleep with the women whom they dominate and bully the homosexuals whose desires openly surge elsewhere. (Harry Brod, 1987a, p. xii).

In their own lives, beings, and relationships, many academics of both sexes implicitly challenged this definition of masculinity. But there was no systematic intellectual challenge, no analysis of the ways the several disciplines actually contributed to perpetuate it. Some of the contributors to Harry Brod's men's studies collection do constitute "what may be the beginnings of a trend to claim certain texts as precursors of men's studies (p. 11), identifying William F. Whyte's *The Organization Man* (1956) and C. Wright Mills's *White Collar* (1951) as probably the most important of these. If these writers are to be considered in some measure the male equivalents of founding mothers (for founding fathers I will not say), it is because their critique of late industrial society and its impact on the work and inner lives of the men who staff it stresses that such a society is *dehumanizing,* not, as others may have done, that it is *emasculating.* Like Herbert Marcuse, whose *One-Dimensional Man* (1964) cites these critiques, they look forward to a breakdown in the system that inhibits individual freedom, rather than a return to more rigid sex role traditions.

Nonetheless, the first works in men's studies challenged not only a discrete set of "male authorities," but the entire received wisdom on the subject. Men's studies began and still flourishes in sociology, with contributions from other disciplines like psychology, political theory, and literature [see Liz Stanley, this volume]. Among the early books that belong more to a men's studies model than to the general sort of social criticism engaged in by Farrell and Feigen-Fasteau are such studies as Peter Filene (1975), Joseph H. Pleck (1976), Deborah S. David and Robert Brannon (1976), and Eli Zaretsky (1975).

NEW RESEARCH PRIORITIES

As men's studies developed, its establishment of new research priorities chiefly involved acknowledging as problematic much that had been accepted as entirely appropriate but *un*problematic areas of intellectual inquiry. Thus, in addition to considering male sex roles as much of an issue as female ones, men's studies reconsiders the male experience of work or war, from a perspective that does not accept or assume men's relations to the given structure. War, for example, is so much the subject of traditional historical studies that conventional periodization often uses wars as its milestones. Feminist historians have been eloquent in calling this attitude toward history into question, underlining the ways it may not be adequate to the description of women's experience. Harry Brod (1987a, pp. 54 ff.) points out, further, that it does not do justice to men's experience, either, suggesting that a "men's studies" approach to this most typically masculine subject would be more intellectually and politically fruitful. Such an approach to the issue rejects the formulations of masculinist scholarship, relying for its framework on feminist revisions of the standard disciplinary thinking about war and the politics that underlie it.

But so far, such reconsiderations of intellectual tradition remain at the level of suggestions. As I observed in a review of several of the new books about men (1988):

> Their present concern is fundamentally and exclusively about examining, challenging, and modifying the traditional male sex role.
> Well, of course it is. What else did I expect?. . . . But, after all, women's studies, far from restricting itself to or even being principally concerned with female sex roles, evolves from immediate and particular experience to a re-examination of everything—everything we have been taught and the system into which that received wisdom fits. [By contrast, these volume's] contributors stick closer to the specific problems they address and offer little that could be called political—in terms of either analysis of the larger forces that constitute our society or the operation of dominance and power in our individual lives. (p. 3)

METHODS AND PARADIGMS

New methods and paradigms have emerged most clearly when sex roles have not only been studied and called into question, but when the sex-roles *formulation* has also been challenged. Sociologists like Tim Carrigan, Bob Connell, and John Lee (1985) and Michael Kimmel (1987) suggest that the sex-roles model lets men off the hook by omitting issues of power from the discourse. They therefore propose a "gender relations" model, which has built into it a greater possibility for understanding the "roles" of one with respect to their impact on the roles and status of the other.

Kimmel's essay makes an interesting use of historical material, focusing as it does on England from 1688 to 1714 and the United States from 1880 to 1914 as "precursor" moments in which the male role was also experienced, as it is today, as being in crisis. It is the historical perspective that allows Kimmel to adopt the power centered "gender relations" alternative to the dominant "sex role socialization" model of describing what is wrong between women and men. This enables him to underline the politics built into contemporary presentations of the masculinity crisis, for, in minimizing the historicity of those roles, social scientists also obscure the possibility of changing them.

"Gender relations" as an analytic category places equal emphasis on both words. Because feminist questions are invariably questions about power—power relations—the "answers" generated by means of this approach are likely to appeal to a feminist as at least occurring within the right discursive and conceptual framework. The notion, that is, of inequality, of *unequal* relations, is inherent in the term "gender relations." But "gender" by itself is an even more commonly invoked category, these days, and one of the reasons I characterized it as problematic in my introduction is precisely the neutrality, real or apparent, in the term itself. "Race" is another such externally neutral category, implying a simple description of an existing difference. It is also clear, however, that race is a category or factor to consider because of the operations of ra*cism*. Whereas for "gender" we have the operation of—what? [See also Rose Brewer, this volume.]

On the one hand, "gender" offers feminists freedom from the limits imposed when it is woman that is marked or variant (even the deviant) category. "Gender" is not only grammatically neuter and affectively neutral, it is objective, universal, and dialectical. That is why it is sometimes used as a code word or euphemism for women's studies in contexts where the latter represents a threat. Moreover, it is often useful to think of particular issues as assuming the form they do, not because of what happens to "women," but because "gender" functions in all our lives and consciousnesses. On the other hand, women know all too well that, in so far as it determines what happens to women, gender is far from neutral. There is reason to be suspicious of a term that also has the capacity to identify differences in essence and hence perhaps homogenize references to differences in status. To the extent that it is possible to talk about gender without talking about dominance or oppression, popularization of the term can entail a loss of the political edge so vital to feminism.

Moreover, although reconsiderations of homosexuality are a basic element in men's studies emphasis on "gender" or even "gender *relations*," can have heterosexist overtones, as the specific oppression of lesbians and even the lesbians themselves become obscured by a framework in which they are at best a subgroup within the category "women." It is because sexual behavior itself constitutes a motive for discrimination and oppression that Gayle Rubin who, in the 1970s, posited a "sex–gender system" of women's oppression, called in 1982 for a separation of the terms that would recognize sexual marginality as a category in itself (Gayle Rubin 1975, 1984). Similarly, "gender" provides a descriptive concept parallel to "class" and "race," but those who use it often ignore the intersections between and among the social forces that these terms represent. [See also Jacqueline Zita, this volume.]

RESPONSE OF THE ACADEMY

Men's studies has not been the object of the same amount or intensity of opprobrium as women's studies. (Nor, of course, has the quantity of work in the field been sufficient, as yet, to invite a similar level of attack.) In sociology, where the "sex role" paradigms were already in place, it is a recognized approach, but not to the point that it is one of the specialties any department *must* include to provide appropriate "coverage" of the discipline as it currently perceives *itself*. Elsewhere— which is to say, everywhere else—the situation is one of neglect, sometimes benign, sometimes malign, but always neglect, on the part of the male dominated tradition.

And yet, although macho voices from the intellectual center may call men's studies a wimp's approach, when they notice it at all, there is nothing so interesting to the malestream as itself, the male. If a feminist gives a guest lecture or is interviewed for an academic post, she may speak (as I myself have, in that situation, often spoken) nonstop for an hour about women-this and female-that and feminist-the-other, only to hear, as the first question, *but what about men?* From this perspective, sharing our newly (and often hard) won intellectual or institutional space with men's studies can create at least as many problems for feminists as it resolves. For, even when it makes use of the insights and results of feminist scholarship, men's studies lacks the urgency of women's studies. What is more, should it assume that urgency, it would be a false intensity, unless we are all to redefine the crisis of our movement as one that asks primarily *what about men?*

IN RELATIONSHIP TO WOMEN'S STUDIES

Although the men engaged in men's studies seem to experience no difficulty in describing themselves as feminists, it is a term that only some (female feminists?) are comfortable with, while some feel they have to qualify it and some consider it an oxymoron. Men's studies is problematic within feminism only to the extent that it arouses fear in certain quarters that it could distract interest from concerns—women's concerns—that are only now being brought from the margins of intellectual debate to the center.

Because the contributions of men's studies remain the object of widespread neglect, the debates within it, its congruencies and occasional conflicts with women's studies and its potential as a resource are all equally unexplored territory to academe as a whole. As I indicated earlier, sociology is the discipline that has been the site of most men's studies research, but the principal preoccupations of sociology are certainly elsewhere. [See Liz Stanley, this volume.] Men's studies books and articles are beginning to appear on bibliographies and course syllabi, so the resource is slowly beginning to be tapped and to influence the way certain issues are perceived. Indeed, as I began this essay, I had to ask a colleague to return two books in men's studies I'd lent her some months earlier, when she was designing a new course on "Adult Development" for graduate students of education. This is precisely the sort of case where it is clearly desirable, from a feminist point of view, that the human norm not be taken as male, but that both male and female specificity be considered and considered problematic.

I find this kind and this level of attention a progressive step, one that is potentially beneficial to women and to feminist studies. Many of the men engaged in this field consider themselves not only feminists but individuals committed to a larger social change. The revolutionary vision is less readily grasped from their work, however, than from work in women's studies. Lip service is often paid in men's studies collections to interracial and cross-class perspectives, but there is comparatively little energy devoted to working-class men or men of color, to the different meanings of masculinity for such men, or to whether upper middle-class white males have anything to learn from those different experiences of power and powerlessness.

Similarly, almost all of the new scholarship and theory about sexuality itself has come from women—straight, lesbian, and bisexual—or from gay men. A men' studies approach to sexual theory from the perspective of the heterosexual male would be a needed complement to work the rest of us are already doing, as well as adding a vital counterweight to the straight male authorities who have hitherto drowned us out on the subject of our own desires and their ties to our own liberation.

CONCLUSION

Like many feminist scholars, I welcome the extension of our concerns to gender and to male specificity. But I fear the contradictions inherent in a system's becoming an object of study to those who are the beneficiaries of that system itself and also of the very institutions through which knowledge is organized, generated, and diffused. I think Douglas Michael Massing's (1982) poem, "Men's Needs," about the men's movement, as represented by the Men's Needs Center, also says something about the men's *studies* that have arisen from that movement:

Three browning blossoms
  droop in the window
    of the Men's Needs Center.

Stems disintegrate
  in a wine-bottle swamp
    overlooking a rust-ringed sink.

I hear Miriam mutter
  What these men need
    is to learn to throw the flowers out
      before they start to stink.

(Copyright © 1982 Douglas Michael Massing. Printed with permission of the author.)

I may be keeping my tongue at least as far in cheek as Miriam herself, a wry recurrent voice of feminist realism in a series of Massing's poems, but I do see potential for some interesting flowerings, as well, in the development(s) of the men's studies movement, as I keep an eye out for noxious growths.

BIBLIOGRAPHY

Abbot, Franklin. (1987). *New men, new minds, breaking the male tradition: How today's men are changing the traditional role of masculinity.* Freedom, CA: Crossroad Press.

Abbott, Franklin (Ed.). (1990). *Men and intimacy: Personal accounts exploring the dilemmas of modern male sexuality.* Freedom, CA: Crossroad Press.

Astrachan, Anthony. (1986). *How men feel: Their responses to women's demands for equality and power.* Garden City, NY: Anchor-Doubleday.

August, Eugene P. (1985). *Men's studies: A selected and annotated interdisciplinary bibliography.* Littleton, CO: Libraries Unlimited.

Baumli, Francis (Ed.). (1985). *Men freeing men.* Jersey City, NJ: New Alchemists Press.

Beere, Carole A. (1990). *Gender roles: A handbook of tests and measures.* New York: Greenwood Press.

Bell, Donald H. (1982). *Being a man: The paradox of masculinity.* Lexington, MA: Lewis.

Bradley, Harriet. (1989). *Men's work, women's work.* Minneapolis: University of Minnesota Press.

Brannon, Robert. (1981–1982, Winter). Are the "free men" a fraction of our movement? *M: Gentle Men for Gender Justice.*

Brod, Harry (Ed.). (1987a). *The making of masculinities: The new men's studies.* Boston: Allen and Unwin.

Brod, Harry. (1987, Winter). The new men's studies: From feminist theory to gender scholarship. *Hypatia: A Journal of Feminist Philosophy, 2*(1).

Carrigan, Tim, Connell, Bob, & Lee, John. (1985). Toward a new sociology of masculinity. *Theory and Society, 5*(14), 551–604.

Chesler, Phyllis. (1978). *About Men* New York: Harcourt Brace Jovanovich.

Chinas, Betty. (1973). *The Isthmus Zapotecs: Women's role in cultural context.* New York: Holt, Rinehart & Winston.

Cockburn, Cynthia. (1983). *Brothers: Male dominance and technological change.* London: Pluto Press.

Cockburn, Cynthia. (1985). *Machinery of dominance: Women, men, and technical know-how.* London: Pluto Press.

David, Deborah & Brannon, Robert (Eds.). (1976). *The forty-nine percent majority.* Reading, MA: Addison-Wesley.

Dubbert, Joe L. (1979). *A man's place: Masculinity in transition:* Englewood Cliffs, NJ: Prentice-Hall.

DuBois, Ellen Carol, Kelly, Gail Paradise, Kennedy, Elizabeth Lapovsky, Korsmeyer, Carolyn W., & Robinson, Lillian S. (1985). *Feminist scholarship: Kindling in the groves of academe.* Urbana, IL: University of Illinois Press.

Ehrenreich, Barbara. (1983). *The hearts of men: American dreams and the flight from commitment.* New York: Anchor-Doubleday.

Ellmann, Mary. (1968). *Thinking about women.* New York: Harcourt Brace Jovanovich.

Farrell, Warren. (1974). *The liberated man.* New York: Random House.

Feigen-Fasteau, Marc. (1974). *The male machine.* New York: McGraw-Hill.

Filene, Peter. (1975). *Him/her/self: Sex roles in modern America.* New York: Harcourt Brace Jovanovich.

Franklin, Clyde W. II. (1984a). Black male-black female conflict: Individually caused and culturally nurtured. *Journal of Black Studies, 15*(2), 139-154.

Franklin, Clyde W. II. (1984b). *The changing definition of masculinity.* New York: Plenum Press.

Gary, Lawrence E. (Ed.). (1981). *Black men.* Beverly Hills, CA: Sage.

Gilder, George. (1986). *Sexual suicide.* Gretna, LA: Pelican.

Hoch, Paul. (1979). *White hero, black beast: Racism, sexism and the mark of masculinity.* London: Pluto Press.

hooks, bell. (1984). Men: Comrades in struggle. In bell hooks (Ed.), *Feminist theory: From margin to center.* Boston: South End Press.

Jardine, Alice & Smith, Paul (Eds.). (1987). *Men in feminism.* New York: Routledge, Chapman & Hall.

Jeffords, Susan. (1989). *The remasculinization of America: Gender and the Vietnam War.* Bloomington, IN: Indiana University Press.

Kessler, S.J. & McKenna, W. (1978). *Gender: An ethnomethodological approach.* New York: John Wiley & Sons.

Kimmel, Michael S. (Ed.). (1987). *Changing men: New directions in research on men and masculinity.* Newbury Park, CA: Sage Publications.

Klein, Ethel. (1984). *Gender politics.* Cambridge, MA: Harvard University Press.

Kroker, Arthur & Kroker, Marilouise (Eds.). (1991). *The hysterical male: New feminist theory.* New York: St. Martin's.

Lewis, Robert (Ed.). (1981). *Men in difficult times: Masculinity today and tomorrow.* New York: Haworth Press.

Lewis, Robert (Ed.). (1986). *Men's changing roles.* New York: Haworth Press.

Marcuse, Herbert. (1964). *One-dimensional man: Studies in the ideology of advanced industrial society.* Boston: Beacon Press.

Massing, Douglas Michael. (1982). *Men's Needs.* Unpublished poem.

Mead, Margaret. (1953). *Male and female.* New York: Morrow.

Mills, C. Wright. (1951). *White collar: The American middle classes.* New York: Oxford University Press.

Millett, Kate. (1970). *Sexual politics.* New York: Avon Books.

Minow, Martha. (1987). The Supreme Court, 1986 term, foreword: Justice engendered. *Harvard Law Review, 101*(1), 10–95

Morgan, David. (1981). Men, masculinity and the process of sociological enquiry. In Helen Roberts, (Ed.), *Doing feminist research.* London: Routledge & Kegan Paul.

Pitkin, Hanna Femichel. (1984). *Fortune is a woman: Gender and politics in the thought of Niccolo Machiavelli.* Berkeley, CA: University of California Press.

Pleck, Joseph H. (1976). The male sex role: Definitions, problems and sources of change. *Journal of Social Issues, 32,* 155–164.

Reiter, Rayna (Ed.). (1975). *Toward an anthropology of women.* New York: Monthly Review Press.

Robinson, Lillian S. (1988). The man question. *Women's Review of Books, 5*(5), 1, 3–4.

Rohrlich-Leavitt, Ruby, Sykes, Barbara, & Weatherford, Elizabeth. (1975). Aboriginal women: Male and female anthropological perspectives. In Rayna Reiter (Ed.), *Toward an anthropology of women.* New York: Monthly Review Press.

Rosaldo, Michelle Zimbalist, & Lamphere, Louise (Eds.). (1974). *Women, culture, & society.* Stanford: Stanford University Press.

Rubin, Gayle. (1975). The traffic in women. In Rayna Reiter (Ed.), *Toward an anthropology of women.* New York: Monthly Review Press.

Rubin, Gayle. (1984). Thinking sex: Notes for a radical theory of the politics of sexuality. In Carole S. Vance (Ed.), *Pleasure and danger: Exploring female sexuality.* Boston: Routledge & Kegan Paul.

Seidler, Victor J. (1989). *Rediscovering masculinity: Reason, language, and sexuality.* New York: Routledge, Chapman & Hall.

Sexton, Patricia Cayo. (1969). *The feminized male: Classroom, white collar, and the decline of manliness.* New York: Random House.

Slocum, Sally. (Linton). (1975). Woman the gatherer: Male bias in anthropology. In Rayna Reiter (Ed.), *Toward an anthropology of women.* New York: Monthly Review Press.

Spender, Dale (Ed.). (1981). *Men's studies modified: The impact of feminism on the academic disciplines.* Elmsford, NY: Pergamon Press.

Unbecoming men: A men's consciousness-raising group writes on oppression and themselves. (1971). New York: Times Change Press.

Whitney, Catherine. (1990). *Uncommon lives: Gay men and straight women.* New York: New American Library.

Whyte, William. (1956). *The organization man.* New York: Simon & Schuster.

Yoydanoff, Patricia (Ed.). (1984). *Work and family: Changing roles of men and women.* Palo Alto, CA: Mayfield.

Zaretsky, Eli. (1975). Male supremacy and the unconscious. *Socialist Revolution, 4,*7–53.

Chapter 41

Unruly Women
Deconstructing Development Practices

Claudia Salazar

It has become very difficult nowadays to talk about the field of "Development studies" without invoking a history of dominance and oppression that often characterizes the relationship between social scientists in the "first" world and the majority of poor women in the periphery. In this paper, I want to retrace that history and analyze the radical and emancipatory changes that feminist scholarship has had on both the field of Development studies and on the practices of "development" institutions. To accomplish this, I examine the position of women both as "recipients" and as "practitioners" of development from before the current surge of the feminist movement to the first feminists' critiques of the discriminatory practices of the development apparatus; the institutionalization (and further "colonization") of Women in Development, and the present moment when women (both in the "first" as well as "third" worlds and working in and against "development") are constructing oppositional discourses and practices that seek to empower the poorest and most oppressed sections of people.

As Irene Gendzier (1985) claims, since its institutionalization after the second world war and in articulation with other international bodies such as "development" agencies, Development studies have served a justificatory function "in providing a theoretical mask for the support of authoritarian views of social and political change in the third world." I conclude by arguing that feminist scholarship, because of its theoretical and political orientation to the emancipation and empowerment of women, has become a major force in redressing the balance of power not only between men and women, but also between the "first" and "third" worlds.[1]

INTERNATIONAL DEVELOPMENT:
WOMEN DID NOT COUNT

Before the 1970s, women were not only left to the fringes of development processes in the third world but also were discriminated against within the development apparatuses in the first world. The ways in which this double exclusion became articulated within global economic and political structures of power has had devastating effects for those women living and struggling in the margins of developing societies.

In analyzing the discrimination of women inside the development establishment in the past two decades, Barbara Rogers (1980) argues that because development institutions usually share a heritage of colonial rule and administration, like their colonial counterparts, they have also been (and still are) structured around a male hierarchy and a patriarchal ideology of domination in which the problems of capitalist Development are located in the third world and their solutions are located in the first world (Adele Mueller, 1988). In fact, given its male-dominated character, Barbara Rogers claims that

> of all the professional employment opportunities available to women [both in the "first" and "third" worlds], perhaps the greatest difficulties and the most severe forms of discrimination are to be found in the international sphere, including development planning for the Third World. (p. 48)

Third world women were not only absent from managerial positions in development agencies but were also marginalized in the development models themselves. The androcentric assumptions underlying these models contributed to the widespread view that women's subsistence activities in developing societies were not important to development and that their gains as wage workers, farmers, and traders were only complementary, not primary, to the family income. Thus excluded from the mainstream of economic analysis, in the eyes of development planners, women simply did not count. A consequence of such erasure was that women and children were the ones mostly negatively affected by inherently unequal economic and political processes implemented by development policies and programs. However, as Lourdes Beneria and Gita Sen (1982) and Beneria and Martha Roldan (1987) have alerted us, to blame development planners' own blindness to women's work in the third world for women's oppressive condition is, by implication, to accept the view that women need to be "integrated" into the development process. The danger of this approach is that it assumes that development projects are usually beneficial to poor women (Gita Sen and Caren Grown, 1987)—an assumption which demands investigation. In fact, Ester Boserup (1970) was one of the first women working in the field who, after analyzing the impact of development on men and women across societies, concluded that development had worsened the condition of women. Her study became the first of its kind to articulate a feminist critique of the development apparatus.

BRINGING THE MARGINAL TO THE CENTER?

Ester Boserup's book *Women's Role in Economic Development*, represented a first comprehensive and systematic analysis of the marginalization of women in the development processes. Despite recent critiques of Boserup's theoretical framework (like other social scientists at the time, Boserup was still working within a modernization paradigm of development), her work continues to be regarded by many feminists in the field as "a pioneering effort to provide an overview of women's role in the development process" (Lourdes Beneria and Gita Sen, 1986).

As Lourdes Beneria and Gita Sen (1986) discuss, Boserup found when doing a comparative analysis of the division of labor by gender across cultures, that contrary to the dominant beliefs among development planners and social scientists,

1. women, not only men, have been food providers in many parts of the third world, thus playing a fundamental role in agricultural production;
2. the penetration of capitalism into subsistence economies, by means of modern technol-

ogy and cash crops, pushed women out of farming (which was considered by development planners to be more properly men's work) into the traditional subsistence sector of food production, hence increasing the productivity gap between men and women and entrenching women's dependence on men's income;

3. subsistence activities such as family labor, performed mostly by women, had not been adequately represented in official statistics, hence making women's important and active participation in economic life nearly invisible.

Ester Boserup concluded her study by making what became at the time a shocking statement: Economic development in the third world affected men and women differentially and that its impact on women had been negative. Unfortunately, the solution she called for to correct such inequality was to allow women an equal share in the development process. What was left unquestioned was the (modernization) assumption that development, whenever well-administered, would be beneficial to poor women. In fact, as pointed out by Lourdes Beneria and Gita Sen (1986), Ester Boserup's study, with its focus only on the sphere of production, failed to articulate a feminist analysis of the subordination of women taking place inside the household and in other spheres of social life. [See also Patricia Thompson, this volume.]

In retrospect, however, we can say that perhaps one of the most damaging theoretical practices of social scientists working in the area of international development was the equation of men's labor with primary/economically significant/productive work and of women's labor as complementary/unproductive, that is, subsistence (unpaid family) work. Starting from such conceptual distortions based on the status of sex rather than the status of work, development models were devised and development programs were implemented that actually worsened the situation for a large number of poor women in the third world.[2]

Besides recommending and implementing policies that were clearly detrimental to women, social scientists used language and abstract concepts in a way that resulted in the construction of a reality in which "the method of speaking itself [became] a means *not* to know and *not* to see the lived reality, in this case of women who experience oppression" (Sylvia Hale, 1988). As denounced by Barbara Rogers (1980), the androcentric (and ethnocentric) bias underlying conceptual models and statistical categories devalued women's experiences and work in myriad of ways:

• Subsistence food production by women in the third world, because "unpaid" (read: noneconomic), have been unvalued by statisticians and omitted from the Gross National Product estimates.

• In labor statistics, women who are not paid for their work are defined as nonproductive. The implication of such a measure is that women in third world countries (who usually work in the fields all day) have appeared in national data collections as the least "economically active"!

• In many writings on third world agriculture, terms such as "farmer," "peasant," and "husbandman" are reserved only for men. Women, regardless of their role in agricultural production, appear as "farmers' wives."

• The arbitrary identification of the "household head" with one individual (usually taken to be male and seen as the financial supporter of the household) in developing societies resulted in the classification of all other family members as "dependents." Such statistical moves dumped working-age women "in a miscellaneous category with children, old people, and the sick and handicapped" (Barbara Rogers, 1980, p. 65).

According to Lourdes Beneria and Martha Roldan (1987), a number of theoretical and empirical studies on the third world followed Ester Boserup's scholarship since 1970.[3] Third World Women were not only "discovered," but became "institutionalized:" The U.S. Congress passed the Percy Amendment requiring that government development agencies pay attention to women (Adele Mueller, 1988). However, as pointed out by Lourdes Beneria and Gita Sen (1986), much of this interest showed by development officials did not necessarily derive from any inherent concern with gender-based inequities, but rather from a need

> to make Third World women more efficient as food producers, water carriers, cooks and nutritionists, and as childbearers. . . . It neither question[ed] the existing sexual division of labor nor call[ed] for its elimination. Indeed, the agencies' emphasis on poor women may be seen as largely instrumentalist, premised on the existing sexual division of labor. Its goal [has not been] necessarily the elimination of women's subordination. (p. 159)

It became clear to many feminists by then that far from being corrective, the institutionalization of Women in Development brought along other dangers and abuses. However, before examining the negative consequences of such institutionalization, it would be good to point out some of the positive changes that emerged in research priorities and directions as a result of a focus on women.

FOCUSING ON WOMEN

The Impact of Feminist Research

Although the discovery of women in the field of International Development studies took place in the 1970s, Nora Ceboratev (1982) argues that it was only very much later that modest amounts of research funds were assigned for projects analyzing the multifaceted participation of Third world women in social development. Lack of resources, however, did not prevent the generation of provocative and high-quality research results. As Nora Ceboratev explains,

> The remarkable quality of this research is that much of it was able to transcend the ideological straitjackets of Western culture and of the male-defined social sciences, as well as the more narrowly conceived interests of the sponsoring institutions. The significance of these findings go beyond the context of research on the nature of women, because they raise fundamental questions that point to the need to reassess the very foundations of development theory and practice: the notions of development as modernization, with Western science and technology in central roles and their concomitant structural requirements; the conceptual and methodological tools and ideological limitations of the social sciences; and the prevalent notions of "appropriate" sexual division of labor and power positions of men and women, which form a great deal of "development" work. (p. 28)

When assessing the impact of feminist scholarship in this field, different authors place different emphases according to their own research agendas. For example, among the major theoretical contributions by feminist scholars identified by Nora Ceboratev (1982), I would like to emphasize two:

1. the conceptualization of women's status as their control over resources, which has allowed researchers both to theorize women's socioeconomic status as independent from the male members of the women's family and to focus studies more explicitly on women;

2. the reconceptualization of work categories, such as agricultural production, which has
    enabled researchers to make women's contribution to agricultural work more visible,
    thereby making possible its inclusion in the official statistics.

In terms of research practices, a focus on women expanded the boundaries of what was
taken to be legitimate themes and areas of concern as well. For instance, Lourdes Beneria
and Martha Roldan (1987, p. 5) point out that the emphasis women researchers placed on
household and family relations encouraged studies focusing on: the household and wom-
en's paid and unpaid work (therefore making their participation in economic activities more
visible)[4]; survival strategies of families at different income levels, including female-headed
households; fertility studies, analysis of social reproduction, population policies, migration,
and processes of proletarianization. Placing women in the center of the agenda also allowed
researchers to study the significant impact that the international division of labor has had
on women's work. For example, studies by Helen Safa (1981), June Nash and Patricia
Fernandez-Kelly (1983), Annette Fuentes and Barbara Ehrenreich (1983), Maria Mies
(1986), and Aihwa Ong (1987) all document how national and multinational capital use
third world women as sources of cheap labor.

These advances, however, were not necessarily unproblematic. In an overview of the
literature, Lourdes Beneria and Martha Roldan (1987) argue that because of researchers'
diverse theoretical affiliations and political commitments, many studies contained serious
shortcomings. Some of the assumptions researchers brought to the field in their theoretical
baggage include: a tendency to view growth-oriented models of development; a tendency
only to *describe*, not to *explain*, the location of women in the development process; a
tendency to theorize processes occurring in the third world by using models prevalent in
industrialized countries (e.g., using the model of the Western nuclear family to study family
relations in developing societies); a tendency to view women as victims of the development
process and passive recipients of change; and a tendency to study issues confronting women
in the third world in isolation from issues confronting women in industrialized societies.[5]

These shortcomings, however, do not overshadow the radical impact that a focus on
women has made in studies of development processes. Many feminists presently working
in the field are engaged in criticizing past conceptualizations of, and research approaches
to, Women in Development in attempts to make scholarship in this area less damaging to
poor women in the third world. As Nora Ceboratev (1982) once put it,

> They [women] bring with them a fresh perspective; they are less conditioned by the predom-
> inant frameworks, and are therefore better able to shed new light on these phenomena. Many
> of these female researchers also appear more willing than their male counterparts to view
> development work and their own research in a broader political context. Less prone to hide
> behind notions of disciplinary specializations and scientific/technological neutrality, they
> acknowledge more readily the political significance of these works. (p. 28)

Because most feminist work in any field usually takes place within institutional boundaries, bureaucratic structures and discursive practices necessarily delimit and regulate what
can be said and done. However, the next section discusses how feminist scholarship,
despite the enormous constraints imposed by the Development apparatus, has been struggling to rupture the boundaries of such apparatus in an attempt to clear the ground for
innovative, politically committed and emancipatory research on and *for* women in the third
world.

Unruly Practices

The feminist "explosion" of knowledge taking place in the Women in Development field has been contained most effectively and systematically by the bureaucratic and discursive procedures that organize the production knowledge in the Development apparatus. Adele Mueller (1987) argues that because much of the work done by scholars and professionals in this field is appropriated for the Development apparatus, the work becomes transformed into projects, that is, the work becomes part of the information systems for planning, managing, and administering development to the third world. Thus codified into the bureaucratic language of the ruling institutions and formal organizations (a language that is integral to these institutions' methods of domination), knowledge about third world women acquires a factual, objective, and scientific character and is used by Western Development agencies "to ensure their continuing control over the uses of the money they extend, and thus exert a strong force in shaping the economic and political directions of Third World countries" (p. 11).

Such violence done to feminist knowledge by the Development apparatus, however, is not taking place without active resistance from many feminist academics and professionals. They, as both Adele Mueller (1988) and Sylvia Hale (1988) show, are learning the language and ruling practices of bureaucratic organizations such as development agencies in order to construct oppositional discourse that seeks to empower women both in the first and third worlds (e.g., see Kathleen Staudt, 1985; Cornelia Butler Flora, 1983; and Barbara Rogers, 1980). Like double-agents, these professionals are also infiltrating the development apparatus to undermine it from within, not asking "how can we integrate women in development?" but "how can we go about getting the Development institution out of women's business?" (Adele Mueller, 1988, p. 37). Concomitantly, indigenous women in the third world are developing their own critiques of the Development institution on the one hand (Zenbworke Tadesse, 1984; Marjorie Mbilinyi, 1984; Achola Pala, 1977) and of Western feminist discourses on the other (Marnia Lazreg, 1988; Valerie Amos and Pratibha Parmar, 1984; Maria Lugones and Elizabeth Spelman, 1983; Hazel Carby, 1983). They are reclaiming a space from which to speak about their oppression and their visions of feminism.

In terms of research practices, the world is witnessing the emergence of *participatory action research*—which, by combining techniques of adult education (Paulo Freire's dialogical method), social science research, and political activism—attempts both to reject the object/subject dichotomy and to generate popular counterpower for social transformation (Gerrit Huizer, 1986; Arturo Escobar, 1984; Maria Mies, 1983).

Along with participatory research, there is also an increase in detailed, historically specific, sophisticated analyses and ethnographies that, using concepts such as subject positions and discursive practices, attempt to grasp the multiple ways in which women resist dominant discourses and practices. To illustrate this point, Aihwa Ong's (1987) study of factory women in Malaysia stands as a fine example of an approach that, in seeking to assess the effects of capitalist development on Malay peasant society, focuses on women's subjective experiences and locates gender construction and sexuality within the larger context of capitalist production and complex discursive practices. In this context, eruptions of spirit possession among Malay factory women (or "mass hysteria," according to Western medical vocabulary) are interpreted by Aihwa Ong as resistance against capitalist discipline. For her, these "nomadic tactics" constitute both an idiom of protest against the demands of the modern industrial system and a means of launching attacks on male staff members and, occasionally, on factory equipment (e.g., here damaged microchips become the site for the inscription of microprotests).

The final set of resistance practices discussed here is the recent proliferation in the West of illiterate peasant women's testimonies. Collecting these women's narratives and publishing them, feminists in the West are opening a discursive space for subjected knowledge (i.e., poor women in the third world "write" their own autobiographies.) As pointed out by Barbara Harlow (1987), third world women's personal narratives are playing an important role in inscribing in the historical record the political–cultural trajectories and collective memories of erased/silenced ethnic groups. These resistance narratives, by subverting the dominant systems of representation, are articulating a new historical awareness and beginning to mount a counter hegemonic strategy of intervention in the political imaginary of dominant cultures.

Alongside the collection of women's personal narratives, in an equal attempt to make women's voices heard, feminist scholars are also studying third world women's informal communication networks (e.g., Cheris Kramarae, 1988). For instance, the careful and contextually sensitive study of Kay B. Warren and Susan C. Bourque (1985), which focuses on gender and the politics of communication in a Peruvian village, shows how village women, otherwise taken to be muted and passive, are, in fact, actively challenging dominant structures of communication by articulating alternative and creative forms of expression to gain access to the public arena of discourse.[6]

Taken together, these new research strategies, focuses, and practices speak not only to the theoretical sophistication of feminist scholarship in the field of Women in Development but also to the political commitment of feminist scholars, here and abroad, to use their research findings "to serve and empower the subjects of the research" (Gita Sen and Caren Grown, 1987). As Elvia Alvarado, a Honduran peasant organizer, advises Medea Benjamin (who was collecting her life history for publication in the United States):

> I hate to offend you, but we won't get anywhere by just writing and reading books. I know that books are important, and I hope this book will be important for the people who read it. But we can't just read it and say, "Those poor campesinos. What a miserable life they have." Or others might say, "What a nice book. That Elvia sounds like a nice woman." The important thing is not what you think of me; the important thing is for you to do something. We're not asking for food or clothing or money. We want you with us in the struggle. We want you to educate your people. We want you to organize your people. We want you to denounce what your government is doing in Central America. From those of you who feel the pain of the poor, who feel the pain of the murdered, the disappeared, the tortured, we need more than sympathy. We need you to join the struggle. Don't be afraid, gringos. Keep your spirits high. And remember, we're right there with you! (Medea Benjamin, 1987, p. 146)

CONCLUSION: METHODOLOGICAL PRECAUTIONS OR HOW TO UN-DEVELOP THE WOMEN IN DEVELOPMENT DISCOURSE

Nora Ceboratev (1982), reviewing past research on rural women, claimed that we already have too many studies documenting the effects of the expansion of the modern capitalist system on the structural aspects of women's lives in the third world; on their changing status; and on their social and economic contribution to the family, community, and by extension, to the development process. All these studies, in one way or another, are assessing the gender-specific effects of structural transformation by showing "how complex and fraught with contradictions the 'development' process is." However, missing from this large body of mostly quantitative literature are women's perceptions—that is, the perspectives from which they see and experience their own worlds. To put it metaphorically, aerial photographs or rural villages in process of change need to be superimposed by in-depth views from below which document the ways in which particular people in particular places and at particular historical conjunctures experience and interpret these changes. As Gita Sen and Caren Grown (1987) point out, feminist scholarship on Women in Development, beginning its analysis from the vantage point of the *lived reality* of poor women in the third world, not only represents a challenge to traditional, masculinist, ethnocentric research methods and concepts but perhaps also provides researchers with the means "to evaluate the extent to which development strategies benefit or harm the poorest and most oppressed sections of people" (p. 24).

To accomplish these objectives, however, a methodological caution is in order. As Chandra Mohanty (1984) remarks, because gender and other concepts such as patriarchy, the family, and the sexual division of labor, are manifested and contested in multiple ways in different historical conjunctures and in particular (im)balances of power, the analytical categories (e.g., women's subordination) that are used in our theoretical constructs must come "from within the situation and context being analyzed" (p. 345). As she warns us,

> If such concepts are assumed to be universally applicable, the resultant homogenization of class, race, religious, cultural and historical specificities of the lives of women in the third world can create a false sense of the commonality of oppressions, interests and struggles between and amongst women globally. Beyond sisterhood there is still racism, colonialism, and imperialism! (p. 348)

Sensitivity for the contexts (geographical, structural, discursive, historical, etc.) in which women are simultaneously positioned combined with a respect for women's different voices and a political commitment to the empowerment of women are the major methodological prerequisites for a truly emancipatory feminist scholarship in the Women in Development field.

What the empowerment of women could bring cannot be better expressed than by these words of a courageous Honduran woman:

> When you come to think of it, campesina women are terrific administrators. With the measly dollar a day the men give us, we buy corn, beans, sugar, salt, rice, oil, and coffee. If we can run our homes on a dollar a day, we'd surely do a better job running our country than these rich guys can. What do they know about being thrifty? What do they know about "making do"? What do they know about sharing? Nothing. Wait till you see what a good job we do when we get a chance to run the country! We'll spread the wealth. We'll distribute the land, we'll get the banana companies in line, we'll take good care of our minerals and forests. And we won't depend on the United States or anyone else. We women like our independence. (Elvia Alvarado, 1987, p. 105–106)

NOTES

I would like to thank Linda Baughman for suggesting my subtitle.

1. For an incisive analysis of the construction of the "first" world/"third" world terminologies, see Trinh Minh-ha (1989; 1988). According to this author, "third world" has become a signifier that tells more about the power of linguistic exclusion in the articulation of hegemonic relations between national blocks than it refers to actual "geographically and economically determined nations of the 'South' (versus 'North') divide." I, too, have reservations about these terms, but for convenience I shall use them, without quotation marks, hereafter.

2. As an illustration we have the case of land reforms: policies and laws were passed in many areas of developing nations to insure a more equitable distribution of land among their rural population. In doing so, however, the land titles were allocated to the 'head of the household,' that is, to men. In many areas of the world such reforms not only violated women's traditional use-rights to the land, but, because land titles provide the criterion for assistance, they also prevented them access to labor, technology, and credit. Landless, women found themselves pushed out of the cash economy into subsistence agriculture and, if necessity demanded, into seasonal and temporary labor at very low wages (Sen & Grown, 1987). Besides concentrating cash and property in the hands of men, land reforms projects ultimately resulted in the suppression of bilateral or matrilineal systems of inheritance and its substitution by a patrilineal system (Rogers, 1980). In the name of progress, men were effectively allocated more resources.

3. See, for instance, Youssef, 1974; Safa & Nash, 1976; Wellesly Editorial Committee, 1977; Young, Wolkowitz, & McCullagh, 1981; Nash & Fernandez-Kelly, 1983; and Buvinic, Lycette, & McGreevey, 1983.

4. Maria Mies' (1982) study of the lace-makers of Narsapur, India, stands out as an excellent example of how definitions of women as "non-working housewives" actually hide both women's crucial contribution to the economy and the exploitative conditions under which much of their work is carried out.

5. A failure to make such linkages leads Western feminists to ignore the fact that many times the improvement of social conditions for women in the West has resulted in the further impoverishment and oppression of women in the 'third' world. As an example, Gayatri Spivak (1987) has pointed out that, because most United States universities have dubious investments in the third world, the hiring of more tenured women in these institutions might contribute to the increasing proletarianization of the women of less developed countries.

6. For further illustrations of women's creativity in articulating new metaphors and symbols to express their voices, see Marjorie Agosin (1987).

BIBLIOGRAPHY

Amos, Valerie and Parmar, Pratibha (1984). "Challenging Imperial Feminism." *Feminist Review* 17: 3–19.

Agosin, Marjorie (1987). "Metaphors of Female Political Ideology: The Cases of Chile and Argentina." *Women's Studies International Forum* 10(6): 571–77.

Beneria, Lourdes and Roldan, Martha (1987). *The Crossroads of Class and Gender: Industrial Homework, Subcontracting, and Household Dynamics in Mexico City*. Chicago: The University of Chicago Press.

Beneria, Lourdes and Sen, Gita (1986). "Accumulation, Reproduction, and Women's Role in Economic Development: Boserup Revisited." In Leacock, Eleanor and Safa, Helen I. (eds.). *Women's Work: Development and the Division of Labor by Gender*. South Hadley, Mass.: Bergin & Garvey Publishers, pp. 141–57.

Beneria, Lourdes and Sen, Gita (1981). "Class and Gender Inequalities and Women's Role in Economic Development: Theoretical and Practical Implications." *Feminist Studies* 8(1): 157–76.

Benjamin, Medea (ed.) (1987). *Don't Be Afraid, Gringo: A Honduran Woman Speaks from the Heart* (trans. Medea Benjamin). San Francisco: Institute for Food and Development Policy (Food First).

Boserup, Ester (1970). *Women's Role in Economic Development*. New York: St. Martins Press.

Buvinic, Mayra, Lycette, Margaret A., and McGreevey, William Paul (Eds.) (1983). *Women and Poverty in the Third World*. Baltimore: Johns Hopkins Press.

Carby, Hazel V. (1983). "White Woman Listen! Black Feminism and the Boundaries of Sisterhood." In Centre for Contemporary Cultural Studies (ed.). *The Empire Strikes Back*. London: Hutchinson, pp. 212–35.

Ceboratev, E. A. (Nora) (1982). "Research on Rural Women: An International Perspective." *Resources for Feminist Research* 11(1): 28–32.

Escobar, Arturo (1984). "Discourse and Power in Development: Michel Foucalt and the Relevance of his Work to the Third World." *Alternatives* 10: 377–400.

Flora, Cornelia Butler (1983). "Incorporating Women into International Development Programs: The Political Phenomenology of a Private Foundation. In Staudt, Kathleen and Jaquette, J. S. (eds.). *Women in Developing Countries: A Policy Focus*. New York: Haworth Press, pp. 89–106.

Fuentes, Annette and Ehrenreich, Barbara (1983). *Women in the Global Factory*. Boston: South End Press.

Gendzier, Irene (1985). *Managing Political Change: Social Scientists and the Third World*. Boulder, Colo.: Westview Press.

Hale, Sylvia (1988). "Using the Oppressor's Language in the Study of Women in Development." *Women and Language* 11(2): 38–43.

Harlow, Barbara (1987). *Resistance Literature*. London: Methuen.

Huizer, Gerrit (1986). "Women in Resistance and Research: Potential Against Power?" In Dube, Leila, Leacock, Eleanor, and Ardener, Shirley (eds.). *Visibility and Power*. New Delhi: Oxford University Press, pp. 235–51.

Kramarae, Cheris (1988). "Informal Communication Networks: Who is Listening to Women." *Women and Language* 11(2): 46–50.

Lazreg, Marnia (1988). "Feminism and Difference: The Perils of Writing as a Woman on Women in Algeria." *Feminist Studies* 14(1): 81–107.

Lugones, Maria C., and Spelman, Elizabeth V. (1983). "Have We Got a Theory for You! Feminist Theory, Cultural Imperialism and the Demand for 'The Women's Voice.'" *Women's Studies International Forum* 6(6): 573–81.

Mbilinyi, Marjorie (1984). "Research Priorities in Women's Studies in Eastern Africa." *Women's Studies International Forum* 7(4): 289–300.

Mies, Maria (1986). *Patriarchy and Accumulation on a World Scale: Women in the International Division of Labour*. London: Zed Books Ltd.

Mies, Maria (1983). "Towards a Methodology for Feminist Research." In Bowles, Gloria and Klein, Renate Duelli (eds.). *Theories of Women's Studies*. London: Routledge & Kegan Paul, pp. 117–39.

Mies, Maria (1982). *The Lacemakers of Narsapur: Indiana Housewives Produce for the Worldmarket*. London: Zed Books.

Minh-Ha, Trinh T. (1989). *Woman, Native, Other: Writings on Postcolonialism and Feminism*. Bloomington: Indiana University Press.

Minh-Ha, Trinh T. (1988). "Wo/Man/Third/World." *Women and Language* 11(2): 6–7.

Mohanty, Chandra Talpade (1984). "Under Western Eyes: Feminist Scholarship and Colonial Discourses." *Boundary 2* 12–13(3): 333–58.

Mueller, Adele (1988). "In and Against Development: Feminists Confront Development on Its Own Ground." *Women and Language* 11(2): 35–37.

Mueller, Adele (1987). "Peasants and Professionals: The Production of Knowledge about Women in the Third World." Paper presented to the Meeting of the Association for Women in Development, April 15–17, Washington, DC.

Nash, June and Fernandez-Kelly, Patricia (eds.) (1983). *Women, Men, and the International Division of Labor*. Albany, N.Y.: State University of New York Press.

Ong, Aihwa (1987). *Spirits of Resistance and Capitalist Discipline: Factory Women in Malaysia*. Albany, N.Y.: State University of New York Press.

Overholt, Catherine, Anderson, Mary B., Cloud, Kathleen, and Austin, James E. (eds.) (1985). *Gender Roles in Development Projects: A Case Book*. West Hartford, CT: Kumarian.

Pala, Achola O. (1977). "Definitions of Women and Development: An African Perspective." *Signs: Journal of Women in Culture and Society* 3(1).

Pletsch, Carl E. (1981). "The Three Worlds, or the Division of Social Scientific Labor, circa 1950–1975." *Comparative Studies in Society and History*.

Rogers, Barbara (1980). *The Domestication of Women: Discrimination in Developing Societies*. London: Tavistock Publications.

Safa, Helen (1981). "Runaway Shops and Female Employment: The Search for Cheap Labor." *Signs: Journal of Women in Culture and Society* 7(2): 418–33.

Safa, Helen and Nash, June (eds.) (1976). *Sex and Class in Latin America*. New York: Praeger Publishers.

Sen, Gita and Grown, Caren (1987). *Development, Crises, and Alternative Visions*. New York: Monthly Review Press.

Spivak, Gayatri C. (1987). *In Other Worlds: Essays in Cultural Politics*. New York: Methuen.

Staudt, Kathleen (1985). *Women, Foreign Assistance and Advocacy Administration*. New York: Praeger Publishers.

Tadesse, Zenbworke (1984). "Bringing Research Home." *Development: Seeds of Change* 4: 50–4.

Young, Kate, Wolkowitz, Carol, and McCullagh, Roslyn (eds.) (1981). *Of Marriage and the Market: Women's Subordination in International Perspective*. London: CSE Press.

Youssef, Nadia H. (1974). *Women and Work in Developing Societies*. Westport, Conn.: Greenwood Press.

Warren, Kay Barbara and Bourque, Susan C. (1985). "Gender, Power, and Communication: Women's Responses to Political Muting in the Andes." In Bourque, S. C., and Divine, Donna R. (eds.). *Women Living Change*. Philadelphia: Temple University Press, pp. 255–86.

Wellesly Editorial Committee (1977). *Women and National Development: The Complexities of Change*. Chicago: University of Chicago Press.

Chapter 42

Do Mothers Invent?
The Feminist Debate in History of Technology

Autumn Stanley

Twenty years ago the feminist debate in history of technology did not exist. The discipline itself was only about ten years old, the Society for the History of Technology (SHOT) having been founded in 1958 and its journal *Technology and Culture (T&C)* in 1959. The question arose in 1976, with the founding of Women in Technological History (WITH) inside SHOT and the appearance of Ruth Cowan's article "The 'Industrial Revolution' in the Home" in *T&C*.

DELAYED DEBATE IN HISTORY OF TECHNOLOGY

On one level, it could be argued that the debate has still scarcely begun. I see three main streams in feminist scholarship on technology—the achievement perspective (What have women done in technology?), the effects perspective (What has technology done to women?),[1] and the analytical perspective (What is this thing called technology, and what is its role in society?).[2] Many males in the field, like the general public, are still blissfully unaware of the challenge of the first, tend to denigrate the most critical aspects of the last as Luddism[3] or a threat to national security, or both, and seem concerned with the second only if it affects their own daughters. According to Joan Rothschild, as of 1983 (Joan Rothschild, 1983, p. xiv), in 24 years of publication *T&C* had printed *only four articles* and 23 book reviews on women's subjects (fewer reviews than generally appear in a single issue)!

In other words, feminists in history of technology are, to some extent, still talking to themselves. Nevertheless, they have already transformed and are continuing to expand knowledge in this still relatively new discipline. Moreover, given the central social importance of technology today, the debate, when fully joined, will be crucial. It may also be explosive. It is no accident that technology is the last major area of human endeavor to receive a substantial compensatory history. I suggest that men have adopted technology—and specifically its creative aspect, invention—as their equivalent for childbearing, have made it taboo for women, and will fight harder, if sometimes unconsciously, than in virtually any other discipline or field of endeavor, to keep it that way.

Historical Perspective

For the historical perspective here see Martha Trescott's introduction to her path breaking *Dynamos & Virgins Revisited* (1979), Ruth Cowan's "From Virginia Dare to Virginia
Slims" (1979), and Joan Rothschild's introduction to *Machina Ex Dea* (1983). As these
scholars show, the institutional context for raising the issues was a professional (mostly
academic) association for research in the history of technology (SHOT) and the time was
the resurgence of the women's movement in the early 1970s.

Nature of the Debate

As for the debate itself— the prevalent social "truths" that denied women's experience,
and the women's challenge to these stereotypes—I can speak only for the achievement
perspective, where I have worked for the past dozen years.[4] The dominant stereotype was,
quite simply, that women do not invent.[5] Or, if they do, they invent nothing significant, and
they certainly do not become professional inventors.

The Suffrage Context

To my knowledge, in the United States, this ridiculous but powerful idea was first
directly challenged in print[6] by Matilda J. Gage about 1870. Gage, a committed suffragist
and feminist, saw women's inventions being credited to men in exhibits proposed for the
American Centennial of 1876—and blew the whistle in a series of letters for the Fayetteville, New York, *Recorder,* later published as a suffragist pamphlet, *Woman as Inventor.*

Gage's work, drawing contemporary as well as ancient examples of women's inventive
achievement, was followed by articles or book chapters by Rev. Ada C. Bowles (1899, after
12 years of study!), Ida Tarbell (1876), Phebe Hanaford (1883), Caroline Romney (1894),
Martha Rayne (1893), and in the early twentieth century, by Minnie J. Reynolds (1908) and
Mary Logan (1912), among others. The context of this first-wave challenge to the stereotype was the campaign for female suffrage: one of the ways of proving women competent
to vote was to show that they had achieved with distinction in many of the same areas as
men. These feminists instinctively realized the central importance of technology and
invention.

Ironically, however, what should have been one of the most effective nineteenth-century
challenges to the stereotype was mounted by a man: Otis T. Mason, one of the few trained
ethnologists[7] of the century. His *Woman's Share in Primitive Culture* (1894) effectively
credits most of early human technology to women.

Second-Wave Challenge

Mason's work is unfortunately little known today, and the suffragists' campaign, though
it eventually won women the vote, never won us recognition as inventors, active participants in and creators of technology. With the second wave of feminism, cresting in the
1970s, arose a second challenge and a second framing of the debate. Here, after the opening
statements already described, have come such startling revisionist works in anthropology
and archaeology as Rayna Reiter's *Toward an Anthropology of Women* (1975), Frances
Dahlberg's *Woman the Gatherer* (1981), Eleanor Leacock's *Myths of Male Dominance*
(1981), Nancy Tanner and Adrienne Zihlman's articles in *Signs* (1976), and Nancy Tanner's book *On Becoming Human* (1981), revealing that women do hunt, that women's

technical and economic roles in proto- and early human society were far greater than we dreamed and perhaps most important of all, that patriarchy was not part of the world order from the beginning. Indeed, the most accurate epithet for the early human female might be Woman the Provider.

Diane Bell's *Daughters of the Dreaming* (1984) has forever transformed our view of Australian aboriginal women: Annette Weiner's *Women of Value, Men of Renown* (1976) has revised Bronislaw Malinowski's view of Trobriander women, particularly their economic role and importance; and Marija Gimbutas (1982), many years of solid work on the Neolithic[8] in Old Europe now call into question the whole idea of male dominance—social, religious, or economic—in that era.

REWRITING THE HISTORY
OF TECHNOLOGY

Here, too, belongs my own work, attempting nothing less, as the subtitle of my forthcoming book indicates, than a revised history of technology, and demonstrating in no uncertain terms that not only do women invent, but they invent in all areas of human endeavor from the most significant to the most trivial, and they sometimes become professional inventors (Stanley, 1987). Indeed, women were probably the first and foremost technologists of the species, with such inventions to their credit as: digging sticks, food- and child-carriers, hunting nets, the taming of fire, food-detoxification and other processing, food preservation, cooking, travel foods, weaning foods, and invalid foods, the needle, fitted clothing in cold climates, tent/yurt/hut/house-building, spinning (spindles, spindle whorls, etc.), weaving (which obviously demands looms) and textiles, cosmetics, dyes, herbal medicine, small-animal domestication, pottery, and horticulture—all before the high Neolithic.

Even later, after what I call the Takeover (a period of technological, economic, and religious change accompanied by professionalization, commercialization, and male usurpation of activities previously done by women as part of their daily work round), which I suggest occurred in the Near East after about 3000 BC (Autumn Stanley, in press), women's contribution to technology has been greater than once imagined. This is especially obvious if *technology* and *significant technology* are defined to include areas of women's work and concerns vital to human welfare, such as food, clothing, and shelter, menstruation, childbirth, nursing (i.e., breastfeeding), contraception, childcare and socialization, healing, and preparation of the dead for burial. However, as my book also shows, women now achieve and always have achieved even in areas already defined as significant by men, such as agriculture, medicine, and machines.

The Gatekeepers

The authorities being challenged are the largely male professors of history of technology in academia, editors and peer reviewers of *T&C*, program committees of SHOT and—most directly—the revered authors and editors of standard histories of technology and invention (Charles Singer, E. J. Holmyard, & A. R. Hall, 1954, 1958, Melvin Kranzberg & Carroll Pursell, 1967, Lewis Mumford, 1966, Lynn White, Jr., 1962, 1968). We must also mention the compilers of more popular histories such as Edward De Bono (1974), Patrick Harpur (1982), Ernest Heyn (1976), Jeremy Hornsby (1977), Walderman Kaempffert (1924), and Trevor Williams (1987). With the exception of Lewis Mumford, these men all seem to agree with Voltaire that women do not invent. Whether they mention not a single woman as inventor (e.g., Charles Singer, E.J. Holmyard, & A.R. Hall, 1954, 1958)—and ignore all or virtually all female-identified technologies—or whether they mention a few token women (e.g. Waldermar Kaempffert, 1924; Ernest V. Heyn, 1976),[9] the message seems to be the same: technology is a male preserve. Even Valerie Giscard d'Estaing's 1985 compilation, though it mentions nearly twenty women, does little to disturb the stereotype.

REDIFINING TECHNOLOGY AND "SIGNIFICANT" TECHNOLOGY

To change this pernicious stereotype, it will not be sufficient to compile lists of women's inventions, though this is an indispensable first step. It will be necessary, as I explain in "Women Hold up Two-Thirds of the Sky" (Autumn Stanley, 1983), to change both the current definition of *technology* (What men do) and the current definition of *significant technology* (the important stuff men do). Thus in my study I needed not so much to devise new research *methods* as to devise new research *attitudes* and underlying assumptions. For example, I needed to assume that women *do* invent, and that gender is an important variable, always to be included in any discussion of technological change.

The Sources for Change

On the other hand, the absence of secondary sources and sometimes even patent records on women inventors means that my bibliography looks rather different from that of the standard history of invention or technology. For the modern period, this absence dictated hard digging in primary sources—nineteenth-century diaries and biographies, exposition catalogues, feminist and suffragist tracts, trade journals, inventors' periodicals, records of invention–development companies and inventors' associations, and popular periodicals, as well as patent and United States Congressional records. For the medieval and early modern periods, and antiquity, it meant looking into the silences—those inventions and technologies not credited to males—and also following the newest of scholarship, such as Marilyn Arthur's work on the Classical period (1987), Susan Stuard's analysis of the rise of gender in the Middle Ages (1987), Barbara Hanawalt's book on women and work in Pre-Industrial Europe (1986), and Daryl Hafter's ongoing work on women and the European guilds (1989).

For prehistory, it dictated close attention to myth (technologies given to humans by first ancestresses, goddesses, etc.), taboo (who is forbidden to work with what and the meanings of such prohibitions), archaeology (what tools are buried with whom, graphic representations of women's and men's work, etc.), and anthropology (gender roles and comparative division-of-labor studies in surviving primitive tribes or groups, etc.), language (origins and travels of words for techniques, devices, and processes; see, e.g. Catharine A. Callaghan, 1986), and primate ethology (modern studies of primate behavior and culture, particularly by women; origins and spread of invention among Japanese monkeys [Lampe, 1988]; gendered patterns of tool use among chimpanzees [Christophe Boesch & Hedwig Boesch, 1982; Frances Dahlberg 1981, Jane van Lawick Goodall 1968; Nancy M. Tanner, 1981; Nancy M. Tanner & Adrienne Zihlman, 1976]). All of this has begun to provide a more balanced picture both of technology in relation to all areas of life, and of economic and power relations between the sexes. Peggy Sanday's (1981) brilliant insights on the relationship between equity in economic contribution and sex equity in society are relevant here.

RECEPTION OF REVISIONIST CHALLENGE

I have encountered unmistakable male-establishment resistance to redefining technology to include women's work. In the early 1980s I participated in a doctoral research project conducted by Gay Bindocci at West Virginia University, using a questionnaire technique and a panel of "experts" to identify "foundational" advances in human invention and technology. Becoming aware that the first-round lists include no women's technologies, such as cooking, the needle and fitted clothing, and menstrual technology–foundational though I knew at least the former two to be—I inserted some of these on the next round. In every case, these were rejected by the male panel members (majority), and one more officially sanctioned, exclusively male-oriented view of significant technology appeared (Bindocci, 1983).

The male establishment in the anthropology, archaeology, and history of technology has also responded by ostracizing and/or criticizing colleagues who report unpopular findings, such as James Mellaart (1965, 1967) and Marija Gimbutas (1982). Ruby Rohrlich points out that the archaeological–anthropological literature is strangely silent on James Mellaart, seemingly avoiding referring to his landmark work on Çatal Hüyük, a Neolithic city with great art and no signs of warfare, a religious center where women were obviously extremely important if not, in fact, in charge (Ruby Rohrlich, personal communication, 1979). Whenever I mention Marija Gimbutas to people in history—or even anthropology or archaeology—they always say, "Oh, but she's very controversial." Gimbutas is controversial because she challenges received ideas of male dominance. She is also extremely solid, with many years of experience directing excavations in an area of the world not well known in the West. In other words, her findings are unimpeachable; only her *interpretations* can be debated, and these will be threatening only to those concerned to defend patriarchy as the eternal order of things. I suggest that you read her *Goddesses and Gods of Old Europe* (1982)—looking carefully at the striking graphic evidence—and make up your own mind.

I am not certain to what extent feminists have succeeded in countering these male strategies of stone-walling and denial. I do know that Ruby Rohrlich, who regards James Mellaart's findings as crucial evidence of the status of women in the Neolithic Near East, and cited him extensively in her article on the period of state formation in the first edition of *Becoming Visible* (Renate Bridenthal & Claudia Koonz, 1977), was dropped from the second edition (Renate Bridenthal, Claudia Koonz, & Susan Stuard, 1987).[10] For my own part, I can only say that I cite both James Mellaart and Marija Gimbutas in my own writings and conversation, calling attention not only to the liberating effect of their views, but to how well their interpretations fit the accumulating evidence.

DEBATES WITHIN FEMINISM

The debate about women as active participants and creators in technology goes on within feminism, as I see it, to whatever extent feminists are still brainwashed by the dominant surrounding culture. A women who on the deepest level feels that males are superior and/or that technology is a male preserve, will have a hard time believing that ancient females invented just as much as—probably more than—ancient males. She may doubt that ancient female inventions dealing with food, clothing, shelter, pottery, herbal medicine, and the like are as important and were as prestigious as the males' hunting technology. She will also have trouble classifying her grandmother's home remedies as medical inventions, be surprised to hear cloth described as a structure (and weaving therefore a form of structural engineering), and be astonished to learn that a woman (Mary Gibbon) collaborated in the prototype heart–lung machine in 1935 (Patrick Harpur, 1982, p. 100; John H. Gibbon, 1970).

Once in the early 1980s, after I gave the Friends of the Fawcett Library in London a whirlwind compensatory history of women and invention, a woman in the audience accused me of doing women a disservice by suggesting they could follow in these Superwomen's footsteps. My reply today is the same as then: collecting the facts about women's past achievement is a first step before any analysis or new knowledge will make sense; women need heroines, role models, and inspiration, just as men do; and finally, yes, many women can and do follow in these high-achievers' footsteps.

Another aspect of the debate that takes place within feminism is the question whether it is better to try to get women placed on the inside of technology, as inventors or other practitioners, and as decision-makers, so that we can change it from within; or to turn our backs on technology as an area of employment, and try to get it stringently regulated by federal, state, and local legislatures and courts.

My Contribution

The contribution I see my work making to the women-and-technology debate—and to women's interests—is threefold. First, it fills a major gap in compensatory history, where a solid book on women inventors is long overdue.

Second, it adds an important missing piece to the knowledge necessary for women's self-esteem. Technology is so highly valued and so crucial in modern society that being excluded from it can almost singlehandedly lower women's opinion of ourselves. It is a little like being excluded from the Christian Church in Medieval Europe.

Third, insofar as it allows women to feel more comfortable dealing with technology, whether as practitioners, inventors, or assessors, my work and our debate should contribute to the desperately needed taming of technology. In a world of chemical weapons, Semtex explosive, and reproductive and genetic engineering techniques that bring us dangerously close to playing God, not only with plants and animals, but with our own germ cells and embryos, the potential exists for evils that will make Hitler look like a lamb in comparison. In the absence of time to transform our whole child-socialization process in the female direction, we need all the females we can get to involve themselves in technology, at minimum, in its assessment and regulation. [See also Irene Diamond, this volume.]

On the individual level, invention is work that can be followed inside or outside the corporate world, and thus can be combined more easily with motherhood than some other careers. Invention is a creative pursuit that provides satisfaction far beyond that of a production-line or secretarial job, can begin in the teens or the mature years and knows no mandatory retirement age, can bring financial rewards from selling or licensing inventions, or can even lead to forming one's own company. This in turn gives the inventor–entrepreneur power to hire other women and offer them such creative benefits as maternity leave, on-site childcare, housecleaning supplements, sick-child leave, profit-sharing, rewards for creativity and suggestions, a health plan that pays for preventive medicine, early vesting in pension plans, educational subsidies—all the things you always wished your company would provide. It enables women, in other words, to do an end run around the job and pay discrimination still plaguing the workplace today, reach financial security for themselves and their children, and possibly help other women at the same time.[11]

NEW DEBATE/NEW STRATEGY

Yet this scenario will not occur to most women, without an image in their head that it's "OK" for a woman to invent. That women—thousands and thousands of them, in fact—in the past have invented, and even been admired in their day for doing so; and that women are still inventing today, with greater or lesser degrees of financial success. Which is why I've spent the last dozen years digging up those thousands of role models for today's would-be women inventors, and why I'd like to see the current debate changed as follows:

1. Let us no longer debate whether women do or do not invent. My book should put that question to rest forever, in any case, if rationality will do the trick. Let us instead (a) complete the inquiry (which my research has begun) into precisely what women *have* invented, and (b) study to see which social, economic, and religious conditions in a society correlate best with female achievement in invention and female participation in technology.

2. Let us devote less energy to the effects perspective (what technology has done to women), at least in so far as it risks casting women as victims once again, and leads mainly to negative results. Equally dangerous, it risks casting technology as the villain, which encourages women in the catastrophic tendency to turn our backs on technology altogether. As I have argued elsewhere, technology is far too dangerous to turn our backs on (Autumn Stanley, 1983).

3. Let us devote more energy to the achievement perspective, for its concrete value to women's self-esteem and willingness to approach technology, both as practitioners (holders of technical jobs, inventors) and as evaluators and regulators.

4. Let us also devote more energy to the analytical perspective, not from a Luddite stance, but starting from the idea that technology should be the servant of society, not its master. That granted, let us see how best to achieve this good end. Necessary to any such project will be further clarity on the gender and power relations of technology. Here, if anywhere, should lie the new debate, and women *must* be involved.

Prospects for Success

Whether or not all of this will happen, I can only say that if it does not, our whole social fabric–even our planet—is at risk. Regarding the relation of the technology debate to the women's liberation movement, I am sad to say that, after raising the debate in the first place, the movement as a whole has not done much to advance it. In 1984–1988, for example, the Institute for Research on Women and Gender at Stanford University (Stanford, CA), had only one of thirty-odd scholars working in technology-related studies; in 1989 it had none and did not seem to find the lack disturbing. Some feminists seem focused on technology-bashing. This is the unfortunate consequence of decades in which women were so thoroughly excluded from science and technology that most of us shy away from both subjects.

The general public, too, still has a blind spot when it comes to women inventors. "Women as inventors" is still not a category librarians use for filing information. And when Gertrude Elion won a Nobel Prize in 1988 for her illustrious career in research on anti-cancer and other drugs, her collaborator's patents were mentioned, but hers—sometimes, indeed, the same as his, for they were often co-patentees—were not mentioned in the newspaper articles (e.g. "3 share," 1988 p. A-14). However, things are changing. More women have recently entered engineering where they will get the training necessary for at least several kinds of inventions—and for feeling comfortable enough with technology to assess it if called upon to do so. [See Pat Hynes, this volume.] The Society for the History of Technology scheduled not just one but several panels dealing with women and technology for its 1989 conference, and generally encourages papers from those who have never presented before (among whom are many women).

At the national Women's Studies Association Conference in Minneapolis, Minnesota, in June 1988, there was an entire panel devoted to women inventors, in addition to the panels devoted to women and technology (see Fred Amram, 1988; Karen Koziara, 1988; Susan A. McDaniel, Helene Cummins, & Rachelle S. Beauchamp, 1988; Autumn Stanley, 1988), a striking change from past conferences, where a lone paper on the achievement perspective might find its way into a lone panel on women and technology. Meanwhile, elsewhere in the city, the first museum-quality exhibit devoted to women inventors and their inventions had just opened (Fred Amram et al., 1988).

In the past 5 or 6 years, two popularized books on women inventors have appeared. Both are superficial treatments. One is in French (Farag Moussa, 1986), and the other is marred by rather shocking errors.[12] Nevertheless, the fact that they have appeared is significant.

Other clear signs of progress are the appearance of works on black women inventors (Autumn Stanley, 1983; Patricia Carter Sluby, 1989) and of bibliographies on women and technology (notably, Kathleen H. Ochs & Cynthia Gay Bindocci, forthcoming). An excellent book on the pedagogy of women and technology has appeared (Joan Rothschild, 1988). At least three women have been voted (U.S.) Inventor of the Year (most recently—1990—Diane Pennica of Genentech in South San Francisco, California, for her role, with two male scientists, in developing the clot-dissolving heart-attack drug t-PA); and the first woman has at last (1990) been inducted into the National Inventors Hall of Fame in Akron, Ohio: Nobel laureate Gertrude Elion, mentioned earlier.

Finally, works have begun to appear on feminist *theory* of technology and invention. Of course, theory has been imbedded in writings dealing centrally or peripherally with women and technology long before now, notably in the works of Corlann Bush (1983), Daryl Hafter (1979), Karen Sacks (1979), Peggy Sanday (1981), Nancy Tanner (1981), Martha Trescott (1977, 1979), Adrienne Zihlman (1978), and, of course, in my own work on the Takeover (Autumn Stanley, in press) to mention only a few. Some recent works have focused entirely on theory (Autumn Stanley, 1988; Judy Wacjman in press). This is an unmistakable sign, in traditional scholarly terms, at least, of a mature field and debate.

NOTES

1.   The "effects" literature is far too large to summarize here, having received a disproportionate share of attention from both feminist and nonfeminist scholars in the past two decades. I can give only the barest idea of the pathbreaking work going on here. Noteworthy among feminists working from the effects perspective are Cynthia Cockburn, with her perceptive work on gender-segregation in the workplace as related to technological change; Heidi Hartmann, also writing about the workplace; and the late Sally Hacker (see bibliography). Daryl Hafter's work on technology and female employees in the textile industry of the 18th-Century France is interesting not only for documenting effects of technological change on women workers, but for its theoretical insights on the impetus for invention and for technological change.

Three women with exciting revisionist work on women and household technology are Joanne Vanek, Ruth Cowan, and Christine Zmroczek.

Also noteworthy here are the many women warning against the dangerous effects of the new reproductive technologies (Jalna Hanmer, Gena Corea, Rita Arditti, Renate Duelli-Klein, Joan Rothschild, and Helen B. "Becky" Holmes, among others).

2. The line between the effects and analytical perspectives can be indistinct. Not content with analyzing the effects of the drastic new reproductive technologies on women—and on society—the critics just mentioned have sometimes generalized to a harsh and sweeping critique of male-dominated and male-oriented technology, which claims to be value-free and demands the right to create anything that can be created (e.g., Sally Gearhart, 1979; Barbara Ehrenreich, 1989). Sally Gearheart call for "An End to Technology," and, if necessary, to the human species that seems addicted to it.

The mainstream of the analytical perspective is producing some of the most creative research in the field. From a preoccupation with technological origins, transmission, and determinism, feminist scholars have forced their colleagues to consider such difficult questions as sexism in traditional definitions of technology and thus in traditional history of technology; the value-laden nature of our culture's body of technology; relationships between gender and technology and power; the nature of technological "progress"; real motivations for invention and technological change; and what is appropriate technology. Some of the earlier voices in the analytical perspective were those calling for identifying and where possible adopting *appropriate technology* and proper concern for the environment and for human beings. Notable here were Judy Smith and Carolyn Merchant.

A moderate view, still feminist and still insisting that technology needs to be carefully evaluated for its social effects, but not usually advocating the abolition or prohibition of particular techniques, is the *technology-assessment* approach, best articulated by Corlann Bush on general grounds and by Becky Holmes in reproductive technology. As closing and keynote speakers, respectively, for the University of Connecticut (Storrs) Conference on Women, Work, and Technology in 1984, Barbara Ehrenreich and I argued—albeit from quite different starting-points—making technology the servant, not the master, of humanity. A recent voice for the close assessment approach, doubly effective because of her science background and career experience with the Environmental Protection Agency, is Patricia Hynes (1989). Her careful revisionist treatment of Rachel Carson's work is important and welcome.

3. Violent, irrational opposition to technological change, especially in the workplace. The name comes from a movement of the early 19th Century that began when stocking-knitters in northern England objected to production practices resulting in a shoddier product. The unrest spread to other areas and other types of work where new machines had displaced skilled workers, and eventually, led by a "General Ludd," progressed to a smashing of the newly introduced machines. Lord Byron spoke on the worker's behalf in Parliament.

4. I have not been working quite alone here, though at times it seemed so. Among other researchers documenting women's inventive contributions to technology are Fred Amram, JoAllyn Archambault, Sue Armitage, Rachelle Beauchamp and colleagues at the Women Inventors Project in Canada, Judith Brody (formerly of the British Science Library), Karen Koziara, Martha Trescott, and Deborah Warner of the Smithsonian.

5. The most famous voice for this sentiment was a man who should have known better, for he was the lover of one of the most brilliant women of his age, Emilie du Châtelet. Said Voltaire, "On a vu des femmes tres savantes, comme en fut des guerrieres, mais il n'y en eut jamais d'inventrices" (*Dictionnaire Philosophique,* s.v. "Femmes").

6. We should note, however, the much earlier (medieval and early modern) indirect challenges by Boccaccio in *Of Famous Women* and by Christine de Pisan in *The Book of the City of Ladies,* both of whom disproved this stereotype.

7. Ethnology, the comparative study and analysis of the races of humankind and their origins, forerunner of modern anthropology.

8. The so-called New Stone Age, varying in actual date from area to area, connected with such economic "advances" in human society as pottery, weaving, animal-domestication, and the deliberate cultivation of plants for food.

9. Kaempffert mentions two, one patronizingly and misleadingly; the other, Mlle Anne Crépin, admiringly but so briefly as to obscure her real contribution which seems to have been nothing more nor less than the invention of the modern bandsaw. Heyn mentions three, all patronizingly.

10. There may, of course, have been other reasons for the change. However, if Rohrlich's theories on once-high female status had anything at all to do with her being dropped, then the most

effective form of male control—whereby oppressed females act to control themselves—is still in place.

11. Any men hired would of course be given the same benefits, where applicable, including paternity leave.

12. To give some flagrant examples, this book (Vare & Ptacek, 1988) credits Marie Curie with discovering radioactivity (rather than Henri Becquerel, who actually did so in 1896, receiving a Nobel Prize for it in 1903, and with inventing the Geiger counter (instead of Hans Geiger and Ernest Rutherford, 1908)! It credits Anna Bissell with inventing the Bissell carpet sweeper (whereas it was actually her husband, Melville). She, however, helped with the physical construction of the first model—and later ran the company and invented a *toy* sweeper that rescued the company from financial doldrums. This book also deliberately conflates discovery and invention, leading to such unfortunate statements as that women "invented" clay; overstates the contributions of some women, and trivializes others. It calls the cotton gin "a device conceived, perfected, and marketed by Mrs. Catherine Littlefield Greene" (p. 15); and on the next page gives Lady Lovelace sole credit for the proto-computer, without even mentioning Charles Babbage (see pp. 15, 16, 21, 37–38)!

BIBLIOGRAPHY

Amram, Fred. (1988, June). *Invention as problem-solving: Special contributions of female inventors.* Paper presented at the National Women's Studies Association Conference, Minneapolis, MN.

Amram, Fred, *et al.* (1988, June–December). *Her works praise her: An exhibition of inventions by women,* Goldstein Gallery, University of Minnesota, Minneapolis, MN.

Archambault, JoAllyn. (1981). Women inventing the wheel. In Jan Zimmerman (Ed.), *Future, technology, and women.* Proceedings of the conference. San Diego: San Diego State University Women's Studies Department.

Arditti, Rita, Duelli-Klein, Renate, & Minden, Shelley. (Eds.). (1984). *Test-tube women.* London: Pandora Books.

Armitage, Sue. (1979). History of women and technology. In Judy Smith (Ed.), *Women and technology: Deciding what's appropriate* (pp. 17–19). Proceedings of a conference on women and technology, April 27–29, 1979, Missoula, MT: Women's Resource Center.

Arthur, Marilyn. (1987). From Medusa to Cleopatra: Women in the ancient world. In Renate Bridenthal, Claudia Koonz, & Susan Stuard (Eds.), *Becoming visible: Women in European history* (2nd ed.) (pp. 79–105). Boston: Houghton Mifflin.

Bell, Diane. (1984). *Daughters of the dreaming.* London: Allen Unwin.

Bindocci, Cynthia Gay Mason. (1983). *Identification of technology content for science and technology centers.* Unpublished doctoral dissertation, West Virginia University, Morgantown.

Boccaccio, Giovanni. (1963) (1355–9). *Of famous women* (Guido A. Guerino, Trans.). New Brunswick, NJ: Rutgers University Press.

Boesch, Christophe, & Boesch, Hedwig. (1982, January). Sex bias between brawn and brain in chimps. *New Scientist,* p. 81.

[Bowles, Ada C.] (1899, March 18). Women as inventors. *The Woman's Journal,* 88.

Bridenthal, Renate, & Koonz, Claudia (Eds.). (1977). *Becoming visible: Women in European history.* Boston: Houghton Mifflin.

Bridenthal, Renate, Koonz, Claudia, & Stuard, Susan. (Eds.). (1987). *Becoming visible: Women in European history* (2nd ed.). Boston: Houghton Mifflin.

Brody, Judit. (1985). *Patterns of patents: Early British inventions by women.* Paper presented at the XVIIth International History of Science Congress, Berkeley, CA, July 31–August 8.

Bush, Corlann Gee. (1982). The barn is his, the house is mine: Agricultural technology and sex roles. In George Daniels and Mark Rose (Eds.), *Energy and Transport.* Beverly Hills, CA: Sage.

Bush, Corlann Gee. (1983). Women and the assessment of technology: To think, to be, to unthink, to free. In Joan Rothschild (Ed.), *Machina ex dea* (pp. 151–170). Elmsford NY: Pergamon Press.

Callaghan, Catherine A. (1977 March). *The wanderings of the goddess: Language and myth in western culture*. Paper presented at the Symposium on Women, Language, and Culture, George-town University, Washington DC. Printed in *Phoenix: New Directions in the Study of Man, 3*(2) (Fall/Winter, 1979), 25–37. Reprinted (1981) in Linda Clark & Marian Roman (Eds.), *Image-Breaking/Image-Building*. New York: Pilgrim.

Callaghan, Catherine A. (1986). Patridominance and Proto-Utian words for 'man,' 'women,' and 'person.' Unpublished manuscript.

Cockburn, Cynthia. (1983). *Brothers*. London: Pluto Press.

Cockburn, Cynthia. (1988). *Machinery of Dominance*. Ithaca, NY: Northeastern University Press. (Original work published 1985.)

Corea, Gena. (1985). *The mother machine: Reproductive technologies from artificial insemination to artificial wombs*. New York: Harper & Row.

Cowan, Ruth S. (1978). The "Industrial Revolution" in the home: Household technology and social change in the 20th century. *Technology and Culture, 17*, 1–22. (Reprinted in Trescott, 1976, 205–32).

Cowan, Ruth S. (1979). From Virginia Dare to Virginia Slims: Women and technology in American life. In Martha Trescott (Ed.), *Dynamos and virgins revisited: Women and technological change in history* (pp. 30–44). Metuchen, NJ: Scarecrow Press.

Cowan, Ruth S. (1982). *More work for mother: The ironies of household technology from the open hearth to the microwave*. New York: Basic Books.

Dahlberg, Francis (Ed.). (1981). *Woman the gatherer*. New Haven, CT: Yale University Press.

DeBono, Edward. (1974). *Eureka: An illustrated history of inventions from the wheel to the computer*. New York: Holt, Rinehart.

Ehrenreich, Barbara. (1984). Closing speech, Conference on Women, Work, and Technology, Storrs, CT, 1984. Revised, abridged as Feminism and Collective Action. *Changing Work,* Spring/Summer, 1985: 41–2.

Ehrenreich, Barbara. (1989, January). A surge of phallic science. *Mother Jones,* 8.

Gage, Matilda Joslyn. (1870). *Woman as inventor*. Fayetteville, NY: New York State Woman Suffrage Association. (Reprinted May, 1883.) *North American Review, 136.*

Gearhart, Sally. (1983). An end to technology: A modest proposal. In Joan Rothschild (Ed.), *Machina ex dea* (pp. 171–182). Elmsford, NY: Pergamon Press.

Gibbon, John H., Jr. (1970, July–August). The development of the heart-lung apparatus. *Review of Surgery, 27*(4), 231–44.

Gimbutas, Marija. (1982). *The goddesses and gods of old Europe, 6500–3500 BC: Myths and cult images*. London: Thames & Hudson.

Giscard d'Estaing, Valerie-Anne. (1985). *The world almanac book of inventions*. New York: Ballantine.

Goodall, Jane van Lawick. (1968). The behavior of free-living chimpanzees in the Gombe Stream Reserve. *Animal Behavior Monographs, 1,* 165–311.

Goodall, Jane van Lawick. (1970). Tool-using in primates and other vertebrates. *Advances in the Study of Behavior*. New York: Academy Press.

Hacker, Sally. (1983). Mathematization of engineering: Limits on women and the field. In Joan Rothschild (Ed.), *Machina ex dea* (pp. 38–58). Elmsford, NY: Pergamon Press.

Hacker, Sally. (1986). Technological development in a patriarchal society. In Mona Dahms, Helle Juncker, Lotte Kjaergaard, Inger Lutje, & Gitte Marling (Eds.), *Kvinder og Teknologi Konference Rapport*. Aalborg, Denmark: University of Aalborg.

Hacker, Sally. (1987). *The eye of the beholder: Feminist debates on technology and pornography*. Paper prepared for the Third International Interdisciplinary Congress on Women, University of Dublin, Ireland.

Hacker, Sally. (1989). *Pleasure, power, and technology: Some tales of gender, engineering, and the cooperative workplace*. Boston: Unwin Hyman.

Hafter, Daryl. (1979). The programmed brocade loom and the decline of the drawgirl. In Martha Trescott (Ed.), *Dynamos and virgins revisited: Women and technological change in history* (pp. 49–66). Metuchen, NJ: Scarecrow Press.

Hafter, Dayrl. (1989). Gender-formation from a working class viewpoint: Guildwomen in eighteenth-century Rouen. *Proceedings of the Western Society for French History, 16,* 415–22.

Hanaford, Phebe A. (1883). *Daughters of America.* Augusta, ME: True & Co.

Hanawalt, Barbara (Ed.). (1986). *Women and work in pre-industrial Europe.* Bloomington, IN: Indiana University Press.

Hanmer, Jalna. (1983). Reproductive technology: The future for women? In Joan Rothschild (Ed.), *Machina ex dea* (pp. 183–197). Elmsford NY: Pergamon Press.

Harpur, Patrick (Ed.). (1982). *The timetable of technology.* New York: Hearst.

Hartmann, Heidi L. (1974). *Capitalism and women's work in the home.* Unpublished doctoral dissertation, Yale University, New Haven.

Hartman, Heidi L. (1976). Capitalism, patriarchy, and job segregation by sex. In Martha Blaxall & Barbara Regan (Eds.), *Women and the workplace: The implications of occupational segregation.* (pp. 137–169). Chicago: University of Chicago Press.

Hartmann, Heidi L., Kraut, Robert E., & Tilly, Louise A. (1988). *Computer chips and paper clips: Technology and women's employment.* Washington, DC: National Academy Press.

Heyn, Ernest V. (1976). *The fire of genius: Inventors of the past century.* New York: Doubleday/Anchor.

Holmes, Helen B. (1980). *Birth control and controlling birth.* Clifton, NJ: Humana Press.

Hornsby, Jeremy. (1977). *The story of inventions.* New York: Crescent.

Hossie, Linda. (1986, March 6). Society a hurdle for women inventors. *Toronto Globe and Mail,* p. A-3.

Howell, Martha. (1989). *Women, production and patriarchy in late medieval cities.* Chicago: University of Chicago Press.

Huws, Ursula. (1982). *Your job in the eighties: A woman's guide to new technology.* London: Pluto Press.

Huws, Ursula. (1984). *The new homeworkers: New technology and the changing location of white-collar work.* London, Low Pay Unit.

Hynes, H. Patricia. (1989). *The recurring silent spring.* Elmsford, NY: Pergamon Press.

Kaempffert, Waldemar (Ed.). (1924). *A popular history of American invention.* New York: Scribner's.

Koziara, Karen. (1988, June). *Women inventors as entrepreneurs.* Paper presented at the National Women's Studies Association Conference, Minneapolis, MN.

Kranzberg, Melvin, & Pursell, Caroll Jr., (Eds.). (1967). *Technology in western civilization,* (Vols. 1–2). New York: Oxford.

Lampe, David. (1988, July). Give me a home, where the snow monkeys roam. *Discover, 9*(7), 36–43.

Leacock, Eleanor. (1981). *Myths of male dominance: Collected articles on women cross-culturally.* New York: Monthly Review Press.

Leacock, Eleanor. (1987). Women in egalitarian societies. In Renate Bridenthal, Claudia Roonz, & Susan Stuard (Eds.). *Becoming visible: Women in European history* (2nd ed.) (pp. 15–38). Boston: Houghton Mifflin.

Liberty, Margot. (1982). Hell came with horses: Plains Indian women in the equestrain era. *The Magazine of Western History* (Montana), *32*(3) 10–19.

Logan, Mary S. (1972). *The part taken by women in American history.* Wilmington, DE: Arno. (original work published 1912, Perry-Nalle).

Mason, Otis T. (1894). *Woman's share in primitive culture.* New York: Appleton.

McDaniel, Susan A., Cummins, Helene, & Beauchamp, Rachelle S. (1988). Mothers of invention? Meshing the roles of inventor, mother, and worker. *Women's Studies International Forum, 11*(1) 1–12.

McGaw, Judith A. (1979). Technological change and women's work: Mechanization in the Berkshire paper industry, 1820–1855. In Martha Trescott (Ed.), *Dynamos and virgins revisited: Women and technological change in history* (pp. 77–99). Metuchen, NJ: Scarecrow Press.

McGaw, Judith A. (1982, Summer). Women and the history of American technology. *Signs* 7, 798–828.

Mellaart, James. (1965). Çatal Hüjük, a Neolithic city in Anatolia. *Proceedings of the British Royal Academy, 51,* pp. 201ff.

Mellaart, James. (1967). *Çatal Hüjük. A neolithic town in Anatolia.* New York: McGraw–Hill.

Merchant, Carolyn. (1980). *The death of nature: Women, ecology, and the scientific revolution.* San Francisco: Harper & Row.

Moussa, Farag. (1986). *Les femmes inventeurs existent—Je les ai rencontrées.* Geneva: Editions Farag Moussa.

Mumford, Lewis. (1970). *The myth of the machine.* New York: Harcourt Brace Jovanovich. (Original work published 1966).

Ochs, Kathleen H., and Bindocci, Cynthia Gay. (forthcoming). *Women and technology, an annotated bibliography.* New York: Garland.

Pisan, Christine de. (1982) *The Book of the City of Ladies.* (Earl Jeffrey Richards, Trans.). New York: Persea Books. (Original work published 1405).

Pursell, Carroll. (1981, July). Women inventors in America. *Technology and Culture, 22*(3), 545–549.

Rayne, Martha. (1893). *What can a woman do: Or, her position in the business and literary world.* Petersburgh, NY: Eagle.

Reiter, Rayna R. (1975). *Toward an anthropology of women.* New York: Monthly Review Press.

Reynolds, Minnie J. (1908). Women as inventors. Interurban Woman Suffrage Series No. 6 (Reprinted in part from New York *Sun,* October, 25, 1908).

Rohrlich, Ruby. (1980, Spring). State formation in Sumer and the subjugation of women. *Feminist Studies, 6*(1), 76–102.

Rohrlich-Leavitt, Ruby, Sykes, Barbara, & Weatherford, Elizabeth. (1979). Aboriginal woman: Male and female anthropological perspectives, in Gerit Hoizer & Bruce Mannheim (Eds.), *Politics of Anthropology* (pp. 117–29). Hawthorne, NY: Mouton.

Rohrlich-Leavitt, Ruby, Sykes, Barbara, & Weatherford, Elizabeth. (1977). Women in transition: Crete and Sumer. In Renate Bridenthal & Claudia Koonz (Eds.), *Becoming visible: Women in European history.* Boston: Houghton Mifflin.

Romney, Caroline. (1894, September). Women as inventors, and the value of their inventions in household economics. *Journal of Industrial Education, 9*(1), 1–11, 22–26.

Rothschild, Joan (Ed.). (1983). *Machina ex dea.* Elmsford, NY: Pergamon Press.

Rothschild, Joan. (1988). *Teaching technology from a feminist perspective: A practical guide.* Elmsford: Pergamon Press.

Rothschild, Joan. (Forthcoming). [*Reproductive Technology and the 'Perfection Ideology'*]. Elmsford, New York: Pergamon.

Sacks, Karen. (1979). *Sisters and wives: The past and future of sexual equality.* Westport, CT: Greenwood Press.

Sanday, Peggy Reeves. (1981). *Female power and male dominance: On the origins of sexual inequality.* Cambridge: Cambridge University Press.

Singer, Charles, Holmyard, E. J., & Hall, A. R. (Eds.). (1954, 1958). *A History of Technology.* Oxford, Eng.: Oxford University Press, 4 vols. (with supplemental vol. 5, 19th century).

Sluby, Patricia Carter. (1989). Black women and inventions. *Sage 6*(2), 33–35.

Smith, Judy. (1978). *Something old, something new, something borrowed, something due: Woman and appropriate technology.* Butte, MT: National Center for Appropriate Technology.

Smith, Judy (Ed.). (1979). *Women and technology: Deciding what's appropriate.* Proceedings of a conference on women and technology, April 27–9, 1979, Missoula, MT: Women's Resource Center.

Smith, Judy, & Balka, Ellen. (1988). Chatting on a feminist computer network. In Cheris Kramarae (Ed.), *Technology and women's voices (pp. 82–97).* New York: Routledge & Kegan Paul.

Stanley, Autumn. (1983a). From Africa to America: Black women inventors. Jan Zimmerman (Ed.), *The technological women.* New York: Praeger.

Stanley, Autumn. (1983b). Women hold up two-thirds of the sky. In Joan Rothschild (Ed.), *Machina ex dea* (pp. 3–22). Elmsford, NY: Pergamon Press.

Stanley, Autumn. (1984). *Women return to technology: From neo-Luddism to brave renewed world in four difficult steps.* Keynote speech at a conference on Women, Work, and Technology, University of Connecticut (Storrs), October. Reprinted, abridged, in *Changing Work,* Spring/Summer 1985: 40ff.

Stanley, Autumn. (1987). The patent office clerk as conjurer: The vanishing lady trick in a nineteenth-century historical source. In Barbara Wright (Ed.), *The history of invention: From stone axes to silicon chips.* London: MacDonald.

Stanley, Autumn. (1987, April). *Professional women inventors of the 19th century.* Paper presented at the Western Association of Women Historians Conference, Davis, CA.

Stanley, Autumn. (1988, June). *Once and future power: Women inventors: The role of play.* Paper presented at the National Women's Studies Association Conference, Minneapolis, MN.

Stanley, Autumn. (in press). *Mothers of invention: Notes for a revised history of technology.* Metuchen, NJ: Scarecrow.

Stuard, Susan. (1987). The dominion of gender: Women's fortunes in the High Middle Ages. In Renate Bridenthal, Claudia Koonz, and Susan Stuard (Eds.), *Becoming visible: Women in European history* (2nd ed.) (pp. 153–176). Boston: Houghton Mifflin.

Tanner, Nancy M. (1981). *On becoming human: A model of the transition from ape to human and the reconstruction of early human social life.* Cambridge: Cambridge University Press.

Tanner, Nancy M. & Zihlman, Adrienne. (1976, spring). Women in evolution, Part I: Innovation and selection in human origins. *Signs, 1*(3) 585–608. (For Part II see Zihlman, 1978).

Tarbell, Ida C. (1987, March). Women as inventors. *The Chatauquan 7*(6), 355–357.

3 share Nobel for medicine. (1988, October 17). San Francisco *Examiner,* pp. A-1f.

Trescott, Martha (1977, January). Julia B. Hall and Aluminum. *Journal of Chemical Education, 54*(1), 24–25.

Trescott, Martha (Ed.). (1979). *Dynamos and virgins revisited: Women and technological change in history.* Metuchen, NJ: Scarecrow Press.

Trescott, Martha. (1990). *New images, new paths: Women engineers in american history in their own words.* In preparation.

United States Patent Office. (1888, 1892, 1895). *Women inventors to whom patents have been granted by the United States Government, 1790 to July 1, 1888.* (with supplements). Washington DC: Government Printing Office.

Vanek, Joann. (1974, November). Time spent on housework. *Scientific American, 23,* 116–20.

Vare, Ethlie Ann & Ptacek, Greg. (1988). *Mothers of invention: From the bra to the bomb: Forgotten women and their unforgettable ideas.* New York: William Morrow.

Wacjman, Judy. (in press). *Feminist theories of gender and technology.* Cambridge: Cambridge University Press.

Warner, Deobrah J. (1979). Women inventors at the centennial. In Martha Trescott (Ed.), *Dynamos and virgins revisited: Women and technological change in history.* Metuchen, NJ: Scarecrow Press.

Weiner, Annette B. (1976). *Women of value, men of renown: New perspectives in Trobriand exchange.* Austin: University of Texas Press.

White, Lynn, Jr. (1962). *Medieval technology and social change.* Oxford: Oxford University Press.

White, Lynn, Jr. (1968). *Dynamo and virgin reconsidered: Essays in the dynamism of Western culture.* Cambridge, MA: MIT Press.

Williams, Trevor I. (1987). *The history of invention: From stone axes to silicon chips.* London: MacDonald.

Wright, Barbara D. (Ed.). (1987). *Women, work, and technology: Transformations.* Ann Arbor, MI: University of Michigan Press.

Zihlman, Adrienne. (1978, Autumn). Women and evolution, Part II: Subsistence and social organization among early hominids. *Signs, 4*(1), 4–20f.

Zihlman, Adrienne. (1981). Women as shapers of the human adaptation. In Frances Dahlberg (Ed.), *Woman the gatherer.* New Haven, CT: Yale University Press.

Zimmerman, Jan (Ed.). (1981). *Future, technology, and women.* Proceedings of the Conference. San Diego: San Diego State University Women's Studies Department.

Zimmerman, Jan. (1983). *The technological woman: Interfacing with tomorrow.* New York: Praeger.

Zmroczek, Christine. (1989, June 14-18). *'New' technologies in the British working class home, 1930s–1950s.* Paper presented at the National Women's Studies Association Conference Towson State University, Towson, MD.

Chapter 43

Reframing the Revisions
Inclusive Thinking for Family Sociology

Maxine Baca Zinn

Family life has occupied a central and often controversial place in the knowledge explosion about women. Most of the feminist thinking about women and the worlds they occupy has rested on rethinking the relationship between the family and the social order. Indeed, our new insights about gender and the family have irrevocably transformed the conventional wisdom about social organization—about what holds society together, what makes social arrangements "work" and how women, men, and children "fit" into various settings within the social order.

In the past two decades, feminist scholarship has produced a flood of studies about the family. This research has produced new descriptions of family experience, conceptualized family processes and structures in revised ways, and identified new topics for investigation (Margaret L. Andersen, in press). Two objectives have driven the development of this work. The first has been a reinterpretation of women's lives by uncovering new information about their past and present family experiences and by analyzing these experiences with a gender perspective. The second, which is an outgrowth of the first has involved correcting social science generalizations about families and ultimately about females, males and social organization.

Stock-taking articles on feminism and the family have appeared frequently in recent scholarship on women (Margaret L. Andersen, in press; Renate Bridenthal, 1982; Myra Marx Ferree, 1990; Evelyn Nakano Glenn, 1987; Mirra Komorovsky, 1988; Rayna Rapp, 1982; Dena Targ, 1989; Barrie Thorne, 1982). These works offer incisive reviews of the new feminist scholarship on the family and the conceptual transformation such scholarship has produced. [See also Patricia Thompson, this volume.] In this essay, I examine the feminist reconstruction of the family. I also raise issues somewhat different from than those typically voiced in reviews of this nature. Along with a brief glance at the family in the social sciences before feminism, I present an account of the changing intellectual currents leading to a gendered perspective. This is followed by a look at the impact of feminist thinking on the mainstream of family studies. Here the essay takes a different turn—that of how racial ethnic families have fared in feminist scholarship. As a feminist of color and a family sociologist, my goal has long been to make the study of the family inclusive.

FEMINIST TRANSFORMATION

Perhaps the most widely acknowledged and accepted axiom in the feminist revision today is the deeply gendered quality of family life that results in different and conflicting experiences for women and men, girls and boys. That axiom is reflected in several themes within this body of scholarship that will be referred to as feminist family studies. The following themes reverberate throught the new scholarship.

1. The family is problematic. Though it is familiar, it requires explanation. Like other aspects of the everyday world (Dorothy Smith, 1987), many family processes are deceptive or invisible.
2. The family is in continous interaction with other social institutions and continually changing as society changes. Rather than being a separate sphere, it is closely inter-connected with the social order.
3. Families are diverse in form and in their operation due to different social and historical circumstances within which families are embedded.
4. Families, like other social institutions require transformation if they are to meet the needs of women, men, and children.

Several key aspects of this new scholarship on families distinguish it from traditional social science. In fact the current themes in feminist family studies have envolved largely as challenges to the central themes within mainstream thought. The tenets of mainstream family sociology have been summarized by Dena Targ:

> The family is a unity of interacting personalities exisiting chiefly for the development and mutual gratification of its members . . . held together by internal cohesion rather than external pressures . . . the roles of husbands and wives are biologically based; these roles are complementary and necessary for the maintenance of society. There is separation of the family and the economic sphere: the family is a "haven in a heartless world." (Dena Targ, 1989, p. 151)

Evelyn Glenn's description of traditional social science underscores similar ideas:

> In whatever guise, the family is writ large as *the* Family, a fixed unchanged and singular entity. This entity is defined as a "bounded set of people" (the nuclear unit), responsible for child rearing (domesticity), sharing residence (home), and tied together by affective bonds.... The concept of a private-public split and the notion of the family as a "haven in a heartless world" cast the family in opposition to the wider society. (Evelyn Nakano Glenn, 1987 pp. 349–350)

In traditional approaches to family, sex roles were the primary unit of analysis. Women's "expressive" roles provided affection and emotional support. They complemented men's "instrumental" roles of providing economic support outside of the family. Such a division of labor was thought to be practical and necessary to insure family stability. With its roots in functionalist social science, the family was simply a system of mutually supportive roles that enchanced family well-being and social efficiency. Sex role division was considered necessary in modern industrial society, and this assumed necessary masked the inequality that is built into these supposedly complementary roles. As Thorne put it (1982, p. 8) the terms "sex roles," "the male role," and "the female role" obscure differences of power between women and men as well as the presence of conflict.

The crucial impact of feminist scholarship has been to reconceptualize the family, to move thinking from family roles, to show that families, like all other social institutions are constructed by a system of gender stratification. We now understand that role theory ignored the power dimension of roles and in this way neglected the political underpinnings of families.

It is interesting that it took so long for socialists to see this, given that power is a primary concern of mainstream sociology. In an essay of family sociology before and after the new feminist scholarship, Mirra Komorovsky (1988) finds that until feminist scholarship, power was missing, missing from family textbooks of the 1960s, and that the word power was nowhere to be found in the index of her own book, *Women in the Modern World* (Mirra Komorovsky, 1953). Even as research on family power did gain momentum in the 1960s, it was a far cry from the popular decision-making studies to the demonstration that marriage is in fact male dominated. And even as studies of power, authority, and decision making accelerated, the mainstream approach to power never made patriarchy explicit. Mirra Komorovsky concludes that in mainstream family research, the concept "power" was powerless. Feminist family studies changed that.

Revisioning the family has been a vital thread in the evolution of feminist social science. As part of an emergent "critical" tradition within the social sciences, the feminist revision gained momentum by challenging both the legitimacy of male dominance and a scholarly tradition that justified it.

INTELLECTUAL ROOTS

Among the many intellectual roots of the radical-critical tradition was Friedrich Engles's *The Origin of the Family, Private Property and the State* (1942). Although not feminist by contemporary standards, this work offered a coherent framework that explained the relationship between women's subordination and the political economy. When I was a graduate student in sociology during the 1970s, this work served as my introduction to an analysis of family relationships in terms of larger material conditions.

It would be foolhardy to try and identify all of the foremothers of feminist family studies. Yet the work of three feminists stands out: (a) Juliet Mitchell's insight that the family is composed of several underlying structures including production, reproduction, sexuality, and socialization (1966); (b) Gayle Rubin's theory of the sex-gender system that shapes all social arrangements including the family (1975); and (c) Jessie Bernard's conclusion that there are two marriages in every marital union... and that "his is better than hers" (1971). These and many other scholars laid the groundwork for moving family studies to a different plane. They began to see through the facades of the family ideal, and to demythologize family life.

Barrie Thorne's review essay "Feminist Rethinking of the Family" (1982) provided an excellent synthesis of the new scholarship as well as a conceptual framework for the ongoing feminist transformation. This continues to be the major conceptual piece in the field.

EFFECT ON THE MAINSTREAM

To what extent have feminist family studies touched the mainstream? Dena Targ addresses this question in a careful analysis of recent sociology. She examines recent book chapters and articles that are prominent summaries of the field, guided by the following questions: "to what extent are the experiences of women actually represented . . . how does this representation compare with the empirical role of women in social life . . . and do the subject categorizations themselves make sense from the perspective of women's situation? (1989, p. 155). This study yields equivocal conclusions:

Feminism has had some impact on mainstream family sociology, especially in the subjects considered and in the addition of empirical knowledge of women's lives. It would be next to impossible to ignore the influence of feminism on the family. (1989, p. 155)

Clearly, feminist knowledge has influenced the treatment of family within the social sciences. Judith Stacey and Barrie Thorne (1985, p. 310) have argued that the *major* achievements of feminist theory have been grounded in analysis of family, kinship, and domestic relationships. Dena Targ finds that although feminism has influenced studies of family and work, and violence within the family, a preponderance of research treats gender as a variable to be measured rather than as a fundamental category for analyzing family experience. Thus, "feminist family sociology has had a substantive influence on the field but has made fewer inroads in the area of theory, methodology and praxis" (Dena Targ, 1989, p. 57). [See also Liz Stanley, this volume.]

Despite these limitations, family research continues to move forward in ways deeply reshaped by feminism. Nevertheless, enormous changes are still required to complete the transformation. Many changes lie outside of feminist thinking and practice, in mainstream scholarship and mainstream institutions. In addition, *inclusive* family theorizing and research still awaits reforms within feminist scholarship itself. The failure to explore fully the interplay of class, race, and gender has cost the field the ability to provide a broad and truly complex analysis of the family in this society.

DEBATES

Issues that are rooted in racial and class differences have always produced debates within feminist scholarship. Racial differences have evoked deeply felt divisions among feminists about the meaning of the family for women. Rayna Rapp's description of a typical feminist meeting about the family captured well the essence of the early debate:

> Many of us have been to an archetypical meeting in which someone stands up and asserts that the nuclear family ought to be abolished because it is degrading and constraining to women. Usually, someone else (often representing a Third World position) follows on her heels, pointing out that the attack on the family represents a white middle-class position and that other women need their families for support and survival. (Rayna Rapp, 1982, p. 168)

This was precisely the setting in which I presented my first "feminist" paper on the family. At a conference entitled "Women on the Move" at the University of Oregon in 1972, I argued (in contrast to the widely accepted view that the family subordinated women), that for Chicanos "the family" meant something different. [See also María Lugones & Pat Alake Rosezelle, this volume.] I speculated about how Chicanos were using their families to forge new kinds of political activism. (Later, I would call this "political familism" and study the ways in which family participation in the Chicano movement was also generating new forms of gender struggle that might foster greater equality between women and men [Maxine Baca Zinn, 1975].) Conference participants listened politely to my early conjectures about the meaning of family life in Mexican-American communities. But they made it clear that they thought I was missing the point.

Feminism eventually resolved the debate, at least as far as minority families were concerned. The resolution had much to do with Minna Davis Caulfield's essay (1974) on how colonized families often use cultural forms to resist imperialist control. Not that the debate as to whether the family is oppressive or has a progressive potential was only about race. Class entered the discussion as well. Some feminists argued that the family empowers working class resistance to capitalism (Libby Bishop, 1983). The debate about the either/or quality of the family has disappeared. Feminists of color now routinely explore the close connections between race and gender hierarchies. Most often, they discover that this interconnection has progressive as well as oppressive consequences for women (Evelyn Nakano Glenn, 1987; Patricia Zavella, 1987). Within mainstream feminism, this debate has given way to the generalization that the meaning of family differs by class and race as well as gender.

NEW DIRECTIONS

Although feminism makes family diversity a central theme, it still marginalizes racial ethnic families as special "cultural" cases. In contrast to the structural perspective adopted for understanding families (what we might call "generic" families), when it comes to racial ethnic families, their differences are treated as elements of group culture not structure. The feminist revision has been reluctant to grapple with race as a power system that affects families throughout society and to apply that understanding to "the family" writ large. Little attention is given to family diversity that is the result of race-specific opportunity structures and the relationship with resource granting institutions. As Evelyn Glenn says, "systematically incorporating hierarchies of race, and class into the feminist reconstruction of the family remains a challenge, a necessary next step into the development of theories of families that are inclusive" (1987, p. 368).

All families are positioned by a variety of structural forces. Socioeconomic, political, and racial stratificiation interact with the gender system to place families differently. This has two important consquences for new directions in feminist revisioning. First, we must abandon the conventional treatment of racial ethnic families as cultural phenomena best understood at the microstructural or group level. We must ask instead how racial stratification as a macrostructural force situates families in ways that require diverse arrangements. Second, we must acknowledge that racial stratification affects people throughout society, not only those who are its victims. Racial formation, a system of social placement and rewards has profound consequences for white families as well as racial ethnic families. Adding the perspective of racial stratification reveals a social order in which some families are privileged and others are not. In a recent essay on family, feminism, and race (Maxine Baca Zinn, 1990), I explore some historical and contemporary consequences of racial formation of all families.

Including racial stratification in our thinking about family life leads to new questions, new topics, and new conclusions that ultimately reshape our ideas about families and social organization. At the same time this poses some troubling issues for feminist thinking. A growing body of research reveals how different connections of race, class, and gender create interdependent forms of privilege and subordination. These conditions demand new explanations of women's experiences in all realms. Judith Rollins' study of Black female domestics and their white employers is aptly titled *Between Women*. This work highlights the relational nature of privilege and inequality as they are reproduced by the interaction of race, class, and gender systems. Judith Rollins uses the relationships between Black domestics and their white employers to show how one class and race of women escapes some of the consequences of patriarchy by using the labor of other women. She shows that the systems of race, class, and gender affect the status and experiences of privileged women as well as those who are the victims.

The relational themes of privilege and subordination appear frequently in studies of informal work and housework. Victoria Byerly (1986) found that white women who worked in the southern textile mills in the United States hired African-Americans as domestic workers. The labor of these domestics enabled the white women to engage in formal work. Vicki Ruiz (1988) describes how Mexican-American women factory workers in Texas have eased their housework burdens by hiring Mexican domestic workers (Kathryn Ward, 1990, pp. 10–11). Such intricate connections between women of different races and classes have profound consequences for family life.

The feminist reconceptualization of the family must now become inclusive. The racial ethnic composition of the United States is shifting dramatically. Along with other structural changes in society, this shift has implications for families throughout the social order. It is time to sharpen our understanding of how gender, class, and race are interrelated in family life.

BIBLIOGRAPHY

Andersen, Margaret L. (in press). Feminism and the American family ideal. *Journal of Comparative Family Studies.*

Baca Zinn, Maxine. (1975). "Political familism: Toward sex role equality in Chicano families" *Aztlan, International Journal of Chicano Studies Research, 6*(1), 13–26.

Baca Zinn, Maxine. (1990, March). "Family, feminism, and race in America." *Gender & Society, 4*(19), 68–82.

Bishop, Libby. (1983). "The family: Prison, haven, or vanguard?" *Berkeley Journal of Sociology, 28,* 19–38.

Bernard, Jessie (1972). *The future of marriage.* New York: Bantam.

Bridenthal, Renate. (1982). "The Family: The View from a Room of Her Own." In Barrie Thorne & Marilyn Yalom (Eds.). *Rethinking the family: Some feminist questions.* New York, Longman.

Byerly, Victoria. (1986). *Hard times cotton mill girls.* Ithaca, NY: ILR Press.

Caulfield, Minna Davis. (1974). "Imperialism, the family and cultures of resistance." *Socialist Revolution, 20,* 67–85.

Engles, Friedrich. (1942). *The origin of the family, private property, and the state.* New York: International Publishers. (Original work published 1884).

Ferree, Myra Marx. (1990). "Beyond separate spheres: Feminism and family research." *Journal of Marriage and the Family, 52*(4), 866–884.

Glenn, Evelyn Nakano. (1986). *Issei, Nisei, war bride: Three generations of Japanese American women in domestic service.* Philadelphia: Temple University Press.

Glenn, Evelyn Nakano. (1987). "Gender and the family." In Beth B. Hess & Myra Marx Ferree (Eds.), *Analyzing gender.* Newbury Park, CA: Sage Publications.

Komorovsky, Mirra. (1953). *Women in the modern world: Their education and their dilemmas.* Boston: Little Brown.

Komorovsky, Mirra. (1988). "The new feminist scholarship: Some precursors and polemics. *Journal of Marriage and the Family, 50,* 585–593.

Mitchell, Juliet. (1966, November/December). Women: The Longest Revolution. *New Left Review,* 44.

Rapp, Rayna. (1982). Family and class in contemporary America: Notes toward and understanding of ideology. In Barrie Thorne & Marilyn Yalom (Eds.), *Rethinking the family: Some feminist questions.* New York: Longman.

Rollins, Judith. (1985). *Between women.* Philadelphia: Temple University Press.

Rubin, Gayle. (1975). The traffic in women: Notes on the "political economy" of sex. In Rayna R. Reiter (Ed.), *Toward an anthropology of women.* New York: Monthly Review Press.

Ruiz, Vickie. (1988). By the day or the week: Mexican domestic workers in El Paso. In Vickie Ruiz & Susan Tiano (Eds.), *Women on the U.S. Mexico border.* Boston: Allen & Unwin.

Smith, Dorothy. (1987). *The everday world as problematic.* Boston: Northeastern University Press.

Stacey, Judith & Thorne Barrie. (1985). The missing feminist revolution in sociology. *Social Problems, 32,* 301–315.

Targ, Dena. (1989). Feminist family sociology: Some reflections. *Sociological Focus, 22*(3), 151–160.

Thorne, Barrie. (1982). Feminist thinking on the family: An overview. In Barrie Thorne & Marilyn Yalom (Eds.), *Rethinking the family: Some feminist questions.* New York: Longman.

Ward, Kathryn. (1990). *Women workers and global restructuring.* Ithaca, NY: ILR Press.

Zavella, Patrica. (1987). *Women's work and Chicano families.* Ithaca, NY: Cornell University Press.

Chapter 44

The Future of Feminist Sex Inquiry

Jacquelyn N. Zita

Many historians of turn-of-the-century feminism have focused on white Western women's struggle to win the vote and access to higher education. Yet, there always persisted in that era, a wider agenda which targeted sexual issues (Ellen Dubois & Linda Gordon, 1983; Estelle B. Freedman, 1982; Sheila S. Jeffreys, 1982;). Nineteenth-century Western women politicized sexual double standards, woman-to-woman romance, clitoral masturbation, invasive obstetrical and gynecological procedures, birth control, abortion, prostitution, domestic violence, and sexual abuse—all areas related to modern feminist concerns about women's bodily integrity and sexual freedom (Margaret Jackson, 1987). In the nineteenth century, debate over these issues polarized social purity advocates, who fought to end prostitution and curb male sexual excesses, and sexual libertarians, who advocated sexual liberation. While social purity activists disparaged the separation of sexuality from reproduction (Judith Walkowitz, 1980), pro-sex women promoted nonprocreative sexuality, use of birth control for that purpose, and women's rightful claim to sexual pleasure. What was at times missing from this pro-sex theorizing, as in its modern counterpart, was a more sophisticated understanding of how male supremacy and other forms of domination affected women's personal experiences of sex and gender, as well as an understanding of how crude, repressive means of controlling sexuality were being supplanted by new "productive technologies of sex" in market economies and human sciences (Michel Foucault, 1978). With these historical changes, sex inquiry became secular and discursive as sexuality itself was transformed into a means of individual self-expression, identity-construction, and medical surveillance.

Post–World War II feminism in the United States continued to pursue the relationship between sexuality, gender division, and social inequalities. Through the sloganized lens of "the personal is political," radical feminists of the 1970s, such as Shulamith Firestone (1970), Ann Koedt (1973), Ti-Grace Atkinson (1974), Kate Millet (1977), Susan Griffin (1979), Andrea Dworkin (1974), Adrienne Rich (1976), and Mary Daly (1978), expanded the limits of legitimate political discourse to include analyses of female sexual pleasure, sexual abuse in domestic and romantic relationships, gender dynamics in heterosexual love and friendships, and the special challenges of lesbian eroticism. This expanded meaning of "politics"—a definition best captured by Kate Millet as "power-structured relationships" or "arrangements whereby one group of persons is controlled by another" (1977, p. 23)—

made sex not only more visible in the writings of feminists but also essentially political in content. If "the political" can exist wherever power as social domination can exist, then sexuality and sexual practice become political in their power disposing aspects, especially those played out across the registers of gender, age, race, and class.

In viewing sex itself as political, feminists of 1970s made significant advances in deconstructing hegemonic heterosexual practices and in challenging the "normalization" of sexual violence and gender oppression, which were obscured by the ideologies of male libido, romantic love, and conjugal duty. As progressive as it was this feminist strategy often became totalizing and rhetorical (Linda Alcoff, 1988), giving space to a late twentieth-century "pro-sex" revolt which called for liberating sex from the stranglehold of feminism's political categories. Libertarian ethics, the rights of sexual minorities, and a flouting of conservative sexual norms constitute a move towards the reprivatization of sex in the name of pleasure, danger, and personal preference (Susie Bright, 1990). The traditionally liberal "pro-sex" movement, unlike radical feminism which locates women's subordination in certain sexual practices regardless of consent, gave privacy to individual self-determination and impermeable privacy of consenting adults.

The tension between this new "pro-sex" movement and radical feminist analysis provides a framework for my overview of feminist theorizing about sexuality and its implications for future feminist inquiry. By way of organizing this vast terrain of discourse, I find it helpful to construct three axes which generate central questions in feminist theorizing about sex: the Explanatory Axis (where does sex come from?), the Topographic Axis (where is sex?), and the Normative Axis (is sex political?). These axes provide a framework for understanding feminist theorizing on sexuality, while allowing various viewpoints on the relationship between sexual practices and women's subordination.

The nature and extent of this relationship is at the heart of feminist controversy (cf. Kate Ellis, Nan Hunter, Beth Juker, Barbara O'Pair, & Abby Tallmer, 1986, Ann Ferguson, 1984, Laura Lederer, 1981, Robin Linden, Darlene Pagno, Diana Russell & Susan Leigh Starr, 1982, Ann Snitow, 1983, Carole S. Vance, 1984). Described at one extreme, if sex is oppressive in some ways and if women's subordination is instated in certain sex practices, feminist theorizing inbreeds a curious Victorian closure. Such "politicized sex" makes its own forbidden oddly political, if not daring. Hence, we find new personages, such as sadomasochist practitioners, pedophiles, leather lesbians, drag queens, transsexuals, using public platform, to decry the limits of feminist moralism. In an age of increasingly conservative sex politics in the dominant culture (Linda Gordon & Allen Hunter, 1978; Rosalind Petchesky, 1981), one has to wonder if this preoccupation with sexual polyphony functions primarily to confine rebellious progressive consciousness to an endless pursuit of body pleasure and gonadal infractions against tradition. Or is it the case, as Queer Theory and sexual minority rights activists suggest, that such developments incite a new radical possibility for social change and personal liberation (Judith Butler, 1990; Sue-Ellen Case, 1988–1989; Cindy Patton, 1985; Guy Hocquenghem, 1978)?

AXES OF NEW FEMINIST DISCOURSE ON SEXUALITY

The Explanatory Axis—Where Does Sex Come From?

Sexual activity has long been considered private, intimate, personal, and subject to natural laws. According to conservative ideologies the contiguity of sex with bodies, coital mating, and animality marks sex as a zone outside of culture and as the naturally endowed domain of heterosexuality, where an overpowering force of nature draws the sexes together, across their bestowed differences. This naturalistic view holds that sex is a biological drive carried by its own directive and apocalyptic force which culture must either repress and control or seek to nurture and enhance.

Feminists have successfully analyzed how this way of thinking about sex has been used to legitimate the imbalance of power between the sexes (Ruth Bleier, 1984; Anne Fausto-Sterling, 1985; Janet Sayers, 1982), especially in Western culture where "libido" is defined as primarily masculine (Kathleen Barry 1979; Rosalind Coward, 1985), "sex" as whatever causes male arousal (Catharine MacKinnon, 1987b), "sex acts" as penile penetration of vaginas (Marilyn Frye, 1988; Angela Hamblin, 1983; Audre Lorde, 1984), "female nudity" as provocation for male aggression and sexual violence (Andrea Dworkin, 1981), and "sex competency" as time-delayed penile ejaculation into an ever-ready female vagina (Margaret Jackson, 1987). Instead of viewing such representations of sexuality as divinations of natural law, feminist theorizing, with few exceptions, has promoted a social constructionist view of sexuality, in which sexual meaning exists never as a prelinguistic event, but only through its *social* form and organization, constituted through cultural and personal categories of meaning and generated within personal sex encounters and institutional structures involved in the dispersion of pleasure and desire across a multitude of sexually ordained or tabooed phenomena (Rosalind Coward, 1985). According to this view, the body's biology sets a limit on what is possible, but does not effectively predetermine the meanings and organization of a sexual practice. The social constructionist questions whether or not anything is intrinsically sexual or only so named (Kenneth Plummer, 1981), and, if only so named, then to what extent sexual preferences, styles, and fetishes can be unlearned or expanded upon? This tension between the fluidity of sexual desire and its stabilization in relationships or preference patterns raises anew the question of how the "sexuated individual" is constructed.

Clearly individuals are "sexed" and "gendered" in a dispersion of power favoring the subordination of women. Whereas conservatives often reify this inequality as a natural ordering imprinted in sex itself, social constructionists view subordinating sexual practices as an indication of "the intricate and multiple ways our emotions, desires, relationships, experiences of pleasure are shaped by society" (Jeffrey Weeks, 1986). Sex is something that we "make up" as we make love. Making women subordinate through sex is a particular social use of sex. If sex is only so named (Kenneth Plummer, 1981) and held in place by an apparatus of coercion, compulsion, and fear, as well as desire and pleasure (Adrienne Rich, 1980), then social change activism must locate the source of sex negativity in this construction and alter its conditions and limits.

As Irene Diamond and Lee Quinby (1984) have pointed out in their analysis, feminist sex rhetoric makes recurrent reference made to control, as in such phrases as "taking back our bodies," "seizing control of our sexuality," "reclaiming what was robbed from us"—or as Catharine MacKinnon has put is "what is most ours has been most taken away." Such locutions imply that something has been lost, and the point is to get it back. Irene Diamond and Lee Quinby suggest that such appeals incur some political problems: "We are asked to seize power, yet power is no longer held by a clearly identifiable and coherent group . . . Our physical cultural world is largely an indeterminate one; the epistemological certainty requisite for control is unavailable" (1984, p. 119).

In addition, the rhetoric of control slips readily into an appeal for something essentially female or feminine to be retrieved in and through sex, an essence which requires political and personal struggle for its reclamation. At times this appeal simply makes the loss itself visible, as in Ann Koedt's (1973) pioneering work on the mislocation of female orgasm, Mary Jane Sherfey's (1970) speculation on repressed female orgasmic potential or Shere Hite's (1976) empirical study of the frequently "phantomed" female orgasm. At other times, theorists attempt to name what is absent in terms of a lost essence or authenticity. This can be seen in a widely divergent set of projects, in the the-body-lost writings of the French feminists (Luce Irigaray, 1985a,b; Julia Kristeva, 1980; Monique Wittig, 1986), in the magical significance sometimes ascribed to lesbian sexuality (Mary Daly, 1978; Katie King, 1985), in recent attempts to reclaim an authentic female heterosexuality as an expression that "springs from and expresses our own female nature" (Angela Hamblin, 1983) and in the claim to an authentically unrepressed female libido in lesbian sadomasochism literature (Pat Califia, 1981; Gayle Rubin, 1984).

As others have pointed out, this retreat into a new feminist essentialism, whether it appeals to nature, truth, or authenticity, ironically mirrors the very conservatism against which feminism revolted (Alison Jaggar, 1983), even though it opposes reactionary male-centered sexual practices. When such reactionary practices are construed as "false" and "oppressive," then the antithesis would appear to be "true," "more natural or authentic," "more liberating" and hopefully more pleasureful. However, Laura Brown (1988), Margaret Nichols (1987) and Jo Ann Loulan (1984) have argued that the notion of an authentic female sexuality, which prioritizes communication, emotional intimacy, low-risk venture, and less emphasis on physical performance, may reflect the one-sidedness of female socialization, and among lesbians, a peculiar eroto-homophobia. With no claim to an authentic female sexuality, it becomes more difficult to rank sex practices in essentialist ways. What is called for is a reconsideration of the myriad of particular circumstances that contribute to a sex-positive or sex-negative experience for the individual. Sexual morality is not equivalent to essentialist moralism.

Essentialism versus social constructionism is thus one axis of feminist theorizing about sexuality. At one extreme, feminist essentialists seek to rescue an authentic female sexuality from male domination, through a polymorphic search for the missing body or a language for naming its desires. At the other extreme, construing desire and sexed-subjectivity as a fragile point of cultural stabilization leaves social constructionists with the problem of attaching such lability to the fabric of history (Juliet Mitchell & Jacqueline Rose, 1982), to the materialism of women's needs (Grimshaw, 1988), and even to bodies (Jacquelyn Zita, 1989, 1990). Using the "language of control" raises questions of what needs to be controlled, who is in control, and what is being controlled. Oddly we find such rhetoric referring to ecstacies often best experienced in losing control and letting go. In the end what individuals are capable of "reclaiming" is absolutely personal, perishable, and at times rather small compared to its meaning. Essentialist language, however, adds magnitude to the catch.

The Topographic Axis—Where Is Sex

Western liberalism enhanced the cause of sexual diversity by promoting individual self-expression and sexual privacy. In condensed urban settings, where anonymity and private space are more protected from coercive community moral controls, "free spaces" for sexual exploration and alternative rhetorical possibilities became available (Vivienne Cass, 1983–1984; Ann Ferguson, 1981). This concept of "privacy", however, has been

double-edged for feminist analysis: while it frees women from conservative sexual moralism, it closes off domestic spaces, where violence against women and children is rampant.
What has clearly marked modern feminist sex politics is the politicization of this space—a
sustained and remarkable effort to disclose and mobilize against domestic violence and
sexual abuse in the family home and in personal relationships.

As the "private" is made "public," however, there is often an accompanying plea for
State intervention, especially in cases of incest, domestic abuse, marital rape, and abortion.
Such interventions raise new questions about the relationship between the State and social
controls on sexuality. To what extent are the State and its related institutions involved in
policing human desire: in constituting that desire, scripting "sex behaviors" which bespeak
that desire, and interrogating the "epistemic behaviors" of such desire? Under what conditions should the State intervene into an individual's sexual privacy? Should the State
deregulate pornographic representations of sexuality and decriminalize prostitution and
sodomy? To what extent do capitalist motives affect the loss of rights to abortion, sex
education, effective and safe contraception, and sex literacy and capitalist ideologies of
body shame and corporeal perfection promote the work of repression? (Wendy Chapkis,
1986; Kim Chernin, 1981.)

Such issues raise a deeper question about the location of sex within our culture. On one
level, sex seems a very private event, located in and between bodies, but on another level
sex is dispersed in domains beyond the body, as advertising annexes it to cars, sinks, camel
snouts, and many other objects. The work of advertising "sexuates" objects. It produces
meaning. According to Michel Foucault (1978), the State and its related institutions create
"sexuality" and its multiple articulations. While feminists have berated Foucault's gender
omissions (Irene Diamond & Lee Quinby, 1988), more recent post-Foucauldian feminist
work (Rosalind Coward, 1985; Teresa de Lauretis, 1987; Catharine MacKinnon 1982,
1987b; Eve Kosofsky Sedgwick, 1985) suggests how modern representations and technologies of sex actually constitute our desire, pleasure, and *gendered* identities. According
to this view, we make ourselves up into "men" and "women" in our daily transactions,
sexual encounters, and self-presentations, a labor not done in isolation from institutions and
social controls which conspire toward this achievement. Sexuality and its uses are important
in the dispersion of power both in and outside of bodies, just as power is productive of
sexual meaning (John Stoltenberg, 1990).

The question of the origin of sex—whether innately within the individual or socially
imposed—finds no easy consensus in feminist theorizing, although most feminists favor a
social constructionist point of view. Likewise, the location of sex appears to be dispersed
over bodies and other spaces: wherever sex is named, used, and expressed (Rosalind
Coward, 1985). The loss of a clear boundary between private and public spheres in the area
of sexuality has made theorizing about sexuality and sexual desire extremely problematic,
more especially in feminist theorizing where sexual practice is considered to be linked to
female subordination. Compare, for example, Catharine MacKinnon's "Pleasure Under
Patriarchy" (1987b), where the desiring female subject is almost wholly constituted by her
subjection to patriarchy, with Nancy Friday's (1983) or Pat Califia's (1988) positivistic
accounts, where female desire constitutes pristine points of self-origination. In these
conflicting views on the origin and location of desire and satisfaction, new questions disturb
the picture. It becomes necessary to re-examine the pleasures offered, the desires experienced, and the interests served. Controversially, such questions, when taken seriously,
can take away from the "sum of fun," a sacrilege in Western capitalism where pleasure is
sacrosanct and sexual adventure a method of commodification.

The Normative Axis—Is Sex Political?

Modern feminist theorizing often claims that sex is political, not only in terms of an individual's right to sexual self-determination, but also in content, in what happens when sex occurs. Controversy exists over how the content of sex—of who does what to whom and how and where and when—can be construed as moral and political. If sexual activity in itself is morally neutral, with the exception of certain heinous sex crimes such as rape and sex murder, then the politics and moralism of sex can be rewritten into a discourse of rights, privileging personal rights to sexual freedom and sexual pluralism.

Within feminist theory, questions have been raised concerning the relationship between socially shaped sexual practices and the social construction of gender. This controversy is clearly fleshed out in the work of Gayle Rubin, whose early writing supported the radical feminist notion of heterosexual practice as a mainstay for male oppression of women. In her 1975 essay, "Traffic in Women: Notes on the 'Political Economy' of Sex," Rubin collapses the social construction of sexual practice and gender division into one system, the sex–gender system, thus allowing for an overlapping analysis of both sexuality and gender:

> Every society also has a sex/gender system—a set of arrangements by which the biological raw material of human sex and procreation is shaped by human, social intervention and satisfied in a conventional manner, no matter how bizarre some of the conventions may be. (Gayle Rubin, 1975, p. 165).

> A sex/gender system is not simply the reproductive moment of a "mode of production." The formation of gender identity is an example of production in the realm of the sexual system. And a sex/gender system involves more than the "relations of procreation," reproduction in the biological sense. (Gayle Rubin, 1975 p. 167).

In 1984 when Rubin's controversial essay "Thinking Sex: Notes for a Radical Theory of the Politics of Sexuality" appeared, she had clearly changed her mind. As a newly emergent "sex radical" and practicing sadomasochist (1982), Rubin called for the separation of sexual theorizing from feminist analyses of gender and male oppression. According to Rubin, the history and social practices of sexuality are best understood as functions of a relatively autonomous sex system which has its own mechanism of oppression, exclusion, and normalization. This conceptual separation marks the edge of a new theoretical terrain, "Queer Theory":

> In contrast to my perspective in "The Traffic in Women," I am now arguing that it is essential to separate gender and sexuality analytically to more accurately reflect their separate social existence. . . . For instance, lesbian feminist ideology has mostly analyzed the oppression of lesbians in terms of the oppression of women. However, lesbians are also oppressed as queers and perverts, by the operation of sexual, not gender, stratification. (Gayle Rubin, 1984, p. 308).

According to this position, what is wrong with modern sexual practice is not its assimilation into masculinist norms or complicity with male dominance, but its privileging of a narrowly prescribed norm of heterosexuality which marginalizes other forms of sexual expression, thus making perversions of oppositional practices. According to Rubin and other sadomasochists (Pat Califia, 1980, 1981), power transactions in sex acts are not necessarily gendered, unless so scripted by the intentions of the participants. Power exchanges in sexual acts, stripped of gender essentialism, acquire a new apolitical surface upon which the fantasies of practitioners can be innocuously inscribed and acted out.

This contrasts with the views of Andrea Dworkin (1981, 1987) and Catharine Mac-Kinnon (1982, 1987b) who argue that sex is political because sex inequality is largely constituted in and through sex, that in "having sex" or "re-presenting it" in certain ways, we are creating the conditions of sex inequality, whatever else we may think we are doing. Power in such transactions is essentially gendered and gender-constituting. As MacKinnon has stated:

> A theory of sexuality becomes feminist to the extent it treats sexuality as a construct of male power—defined by men, forced on women, and constitutive in the meaning of gender. Such an approach centers feminism on the perspective of the subordination of women to men as it identifies sex, that is, the sexuality of dominance and submission, as crucial, as a fundamental, as on some level definitive, in that process. (1987b, pp. 68–69).

The legacy of this perspective can be seen not only in women's growing criticism of the institution of heterosexuality (Andrea Dworkin, 1987; Shulamith Firestone, 1970; Angela Hamblin, 1983; Shere Hite, 1976; Adrienne Rich, 1980) but also in the feminist discourse on rape. Important breakthroughs in the clinical and male-dominated research on rape began to appear in the 1970s (Susan Brownmiller, 1976; Susan Griffin, 1979; Kate Millet, 1977), when attention was turned to the female victim's experience and the way in which family, community, courts, and the State habitually regarded nonconsensual and coercive sex as unremarkable and undeserving of social concern (Linda Bourque, 1989). In the 1970s feminist analysis attempted to show the similarities between rape and other violent crimes, revealing the unjustified violence of sexual abuse. However problematic, woman-as-victim emerged as a new figure in feminist writing, a figure given the right to speak, to tell her story and to be believed (Diana Russell, 1975).

Gradually this strategy developed into a much broader analysis in which rape was linked to other structures of male domination (Susan Griffin, 1979; Florence Rush, 1980; Diana Russell, 1984). Fear of rape, rape myths, gendered sexual socialization, and a heterosexual practice in which the line between "pressure" and "force" is at times difficult to determine not only stationed the sexes in different locations with respect to hetero-sex but also ascribed to men and women different sexualities (Steven Seidman, 1989). As sex became gendered in feminist theory, the rapist or the male aggressor emerged as an arbitrator of women's reality (Andrea Dworkin, 1987). Socially learned male sex behavior became suspect and its relationship to male dominance more disturbing (Kathleen Barry, 1979; Andrea Dworkin, 1981; Susan Griffin, 1981; Robin Linden, Darlene Pagano, Diana Russell, & Susan Leigh Starr, 1982; Catharine MacKinnon, 1982).

Through such theorizing, sex becomes political as a site of women's oppression and as a place where the work of culture on the body and psyche materially constitutes "men" and "women," where sexuality is "substantially what makes the gender division be what it is, which is male dominant, wherever it is, which is nearly everywhere" (Catharine MacKinnon, 1987 p. 69). Andrea Dworkin in her book *Intercourse* (1987) analyzes how women's inferiority originates in intercourse, a physiological means of making "women," through the culturally encoded meanings of "entry," "possession," "occupation," and other serial violations of female physical integrity. According to Dworkin, in eroticizing self-annihilation, one becomes "woman." According to Catharine MacKinnon (1987b) a forcible violation of women's bodily integrity is definitive of male-engendered sexuality.

The validity of these views depends on the degree to which the content of sex is gendered and how much this contributes to male domination over women. If, for example, the use of power in sex acts favors male dominance in heterosexual practice and reinforces masculinist meanings in other social practices, then feminist analyses of sex inequality can be transferred to the meanings of sex acts. Given such maneuvers, what is wrong with current sexual practices is what is wrong with sex inequality: women's loss of power, dignity, and authenticity, women's sufferance of unnecessary harm, and women's lack of self-determination and control over their bodies. This helps explain why unexamined sexual behaviors have been particularly harmful and life-threatening for women and children.

PROBLEMATIZED AND CONTESTED ZONES

Feminist theorizing has done much to dislodge traditional assumptions about sexuality. Deconstruction of naturalistic views about human sexuality has seriously challenged heterosexual hegemony, even to the point of questioning its very possibility as a feminist practice (Shulamith Firestone, 1970; Angela Hamblin, 1983). Understanding sexual practice as a relationship between sexed- and gendered-bodies, rather than bodies in general or libido in the abstract, further differentiates feminist sex theory from that of male progressives, such as Reich (1972), Marcuse (1962), and Foucault (1978). Finally, the three axes of new feminist theorizing have allowed historically new questions to emerge, concerning the social construction of sexual practice and its relationship to gender division and women's subordination. [See also Renate Klein, this volume.]

In addition to the axial controversies I have outlined above, one finds a number of other debates in the contested zone of feminist theorizing that take up the social practices of prostitution, cross-generational sex, fetishism, butch–femme roles in lesbian relationships, sadomasochism, the use of sex paraphernalia and pornography, and the like. Although it is beyond the scope of this essay to review the intricacies of all these debates, my analysis of the three axes of feminist theorizing and the polarization between radical feminists and sex radicals provides a general framework for understanding how these subsidiary debates are shaped. [See Susan Kappeler, this volume.] For example, radical feminists, such as Andrea Dworkin (1981), who view sexuality as gendered and as such, political, see in pornography a representation of *what women are,* in the existence of sexual violence against women an indication of *what women are for,* and in prostitution evidence of *what women do.* According to Dworkin, pornography eroticizes sexual domination over women, a code that holds regardless of the participant's biological sex, and defines in a fundamental way women's social position under male power. Pornography's handmaiden, prostitution, further "entraps" a reserve population of women, keeping them readily available for men, while circumscribing the roles of all women through the norms of proper and illicit sex. [See Jane Caputi, this volume.] Allied with these views, one finds strenuous political organizing against pornography and prostitution, including several attempts to use the legal and municipal systems to regulate these practices (Catharine MacKinnon & Andrea Dworkin, 1988; Lisa Duggan, Nan Hunter, & Carole Vance, 1985).

Sex radicals, who lean towards seeing sex as a private matter between individuals, protected by the right to sexual self-determination and the right to sex work, have fought passionately against the radical feminists. Together with sex workers, prostitutes, sadomasochists, fetishists, and others from the sexual fringe, sex radicals have politicized the limitations placed on "free sexual expression" (Laurie Bell, 1987; Pat Califia, 1981; Frederique Delacoste & Priscilla Alexander, 1987; Gail Pheterson, 1989; Gayle Rubin, 1984). For example, the exchange of sex for money, according to Margo St. James (1987), is not inherently dangerous or disgusting, unless the circumstances and meaning contextualizing such encounters make such exchange dangerous and devalued. Both Andrea

Dworkin (1981) and Margo St. James (1987) are concerned about the abuse of women in prostitution, yet each places its extent, location, and evidence differently.

A similar analysis could be given for the other debates involving controversial sex practices. The construction of sexual meaning within this contested zone is a matter of disagreement, as are the presence and significance of power, agency, consent, harm, risk, pleasure, and even anatomical parts. It is unfortunate that sex radicals have cast radical feminists as "sex police" and as "sex puritans," as radical feminism pushes inquiry beyond contractual terms and towards an examination of how the content of sex acts might relate to erotic division and women's subordination. It is also unfortunate that radical feminists have, in informal conversations, dismissed sex radicals as "uncle toms" "milkweed liberals," and "bewildered sex addicts," because the force of the sex radical critique raises important questions about the authority and contradiction in women's sexual experience, repressions stemming from eroto-homophobia and the material conditions of women's sex work.

This contested zone, it should be noted, is hemmed in by two outer limits—at one end, a new normative view of sexuality involving caring, intimacy, mutuality, and equality in power, and at the other end, by acts defined as largely unethical and violent, such as incest, rape, sexual abuse, and sex murder. Controversy ensues over the boundaries between acts, between those which seem legitimate and sanctionable, those that incur risk but no agreed on proscription, and unconscionable acts, hate crimes, and abuse. However the lines are drawn, Millet's definition of "politics," as "power-structured relationships" or "arrangements whereby one group of persons is controlled by another" (1971, p. 23), remains a central problem. If sex is political, its politic is about the use and abuse of power and how that relates to women's subordination. Stretching between the soft cuddles of "vanilla" couples and hard-core Snuff films, the conceptual territory gets a little too murky and difficult for simplistic solutions. The extreme polarization and moralism in the feminist sex debates (Ann Ferguson, 1984) avoids what is necessary: yet more thinking about sex.

IMPLICATIONS FOR FUTURE RESEARCH AND INQUIRY

The future of feminist sex inquiry is not easy to grasp because it has consequences for nearly all the disciplines. By way of summary, it would be helpful to survey various disciplinary interests in sexuality and explore how disciplines are shaped by unexamined heterosexual–gendered assumptions (Sandra Harding, 1986), a task largely exceeding the limits of this essay. Given my three axes of feminist theorizing, one way to think about the future of feminist sex inquiry is to focus on basic questions which define each axis and which persistently reemerge in more specialized disciplinary and interdisciplinary projects. These questions include the following:

1. The **Explanatory Axis** focuses on how sexuality comes to be what it is. Feminists of the 1970s began asking these questions which still today direct our inquiry and research: How is sexuality—a practice of social meaning and behavior—socially constructed? Are there any biological limits? Are there any cultural limits? Is the distinction between body and culture culturally specific? Is anything intrinsically sexual? Along with these general questions, feminists bring a specific focus on gender, race, and class to bear: In foregrounding gender division, how is the social construction of gender complicit in the shaping of sexual practices and norms? How is sex–gender construction contextualized by and contributive to differences in race, class, and age?

2. The **Topographic Axis** problematizes the location of sexuality: What is the rela-

tionship between sexuality conceived as a private interaction between bodies and "sex policing" in the public sphere? How do these two spheres interface and reinforce one another on the level of meaning, norms, desire, power, and pleasure? What should be the relationship between the State and the individual in the area of sexual, erotic, and reproductive freedoms? Feminist inquiry in foregrounding gender specifically asks how the construction of gender division and gendered sexual practices is related to the maintenance of and resistance to State power. How is this further contextualized by and contributive to differences in class, race, and age?

3. The **Normative Axis** interrogates the politics of sex: What is the relationship between a sexual practice and the social construction of gender division and sex inequality? If the former is implicated in the latter, does the analysis of sex inequality provide a basis for understanding the oppressive construction of sex practices? Can a political or ethical discourse be used to interpret the content of sex acts? Is sexuality best understood as separate from gender, as belonging to a system that is analytically and socially autonomous in its controlling interests in the body? What aspects of sex are politically related to the mechanism of women's subordination?

Regardless of how these questions reemerge in debates in the contested zone or in disciplinary-specific projects, they are inevitable tools of feminist sex inquiry. What makes this form of inquiry *feminist* is a shared set of research and scholarship strategies: (1) an attention to women's actual experiences of sexuality, (2) a persistent examination of the relationship between sexual practice and women's subordination, across the registers of race, class, and other differences, (3) an effort to "denaturalize" those orthodoxies of sexual practice, which are abusive to women and children, and other human beings, and (4) an effort to maximize a social practice of sexual pluralism and erotic freedom for the individual.

Given the social constructionist leaning of most feminist sex inquiry, explaining the mechanism of socially constructed gender division and sexual practice seems imperative. To avoid the omission in past theories of women's sexuality, this must be done with special regard for women's sexual experiences and the meanings that women subjects give to those experiences (Dorothy Smith, 1979). Special attention to women's experiences should not replace understanding with the authority of subjectivism, but provide a port of entry for social constructionist questions—why these meanings, these behaviors, in this time, place, or situation? Such historicized and socially contextualized strategies of investigation guard against the excesses of wrongful prejudgment and naive subjectivism.

THROWING CAUTION TO SEX

In closing, I propose the creation of a buffer zone against modes of assimilation that undermine the radical challenge of feminist sex inquiry. These modes of assimilation engage the very technologies of modernist sex discourse which have been oppressive to women and supportive of the conservative orthodoxies of heterosexual practice. If feminist sex inquiry is to be a "catalystic" challenge to the edifice of modern sex practice and discourse, I offer the following areas of concern:

1. *Deconstruction of monolithic categories of sexuality.* Feminist inquiry must place emphasis on the diversity and complexity of human sexual experience, often swept under wide-ranging categories such as "heterosexual," "lesbian," "pervert," and "sex addicted." Monolithic categories encourage stereotyping and oversimplified views on sexuality, lending advantage to a power structure which remains invulnerable to critical reflection upon itself and its categories of specialization.

2. *Contextualization of sexual practices.* Another tactic which renders sex impervious to critical analysis is its isolation from other forms of social practice, making "sex" appear to be part of nature rather than one of many assorted social practices. In feminist analysis, interconnection and annexation should be emphasized, especially the interconnections between sex, race, and class and the annexation of sexuality into the service of other social oppressions such as racism, classism, ageism, and physicalism (Sarah Hoagland, 1988; Cheríe Moraga & Amber Hollibaugh, 1983; Minnie Bruce Pratt, 1984).

Likewise, sexual practices should not be viewed in isolation from one another. For example, homophobia is operative in a variety of antagonisms towards nonprocreative sexual practices. This can be seen in the threatened loss of abortion rights and the lack of safe and effective contraception which profoundly affect heterosexual women's access to nonprocreative sex, especially when norms of sexual practice heavily proscribe oral and anal pleasure or any sexual format that challenges the supremacy of compulsory coitus. Connections between procreative and nonprocreative sex bring into view a wide range of issues, such as abortion rights, compulsory heterosexual coitus, homophobia, birth control, sex education, and women's subordination.

3. *Deconstruction of lesbianism as a magical sign.* In 1970s feminist sex theorizing, lesbianism was sometimes treated as a magical solution (Katie King, 1985) to the gendered injustice of heterosexual practices, the only possible way "to stop loving the enemy" and "affirm one's woman-identified sexuality." Although lesbian feminism was articulated through the rituals of coming-out stories, the development of lesbian cultures, and tirades against heterosexism and its practices, on another level lesbianism held its own opacity, refusing to examine the diversity, complexities, and negative "closets" of its politically correct identity construction. Such denial reproduces the hypocrisy and opacity of hierarchical sex categories.

4. *Re-evaluation of "gay-positive" research.* Against the homophobia and homohatred in research on lesbian and gay people, efforts have been made to show that homosexuals are really no different than heterosexuals. Although such research supports identity affirmation politics of the 1980s, its effect erases the reality of counter-hegemonic sexualities as oppositional practices (Ceclia Kitzinger, 1987). The project of "denaturalizing" heterosexual orthodoxy is not successfully achieved through an ideology of sameness across the homo/hetero divide or across the lesbian/gay divide in our communities. Such sameness distills the threat of oppositional practices and encourages an easy toleration of "nothing new." What is required here is a more careful inquiry into the homophobic and somatophobic behaviors anchoring sexual practice, heterosexual privilege, gender division, and the construction of difference in sex (Suzanne Pharr, 1988).

5. *Partial essentialism.* According to Foucault (1978), sex at the end of the nineteenth century was subjected to a new epistemic pressure. It acquired a truth value, as it became the truth of the individual. In subscribing to the modernist assumptions, that sex establishes a fundamental personal identity and resides within the body as an open frontier for deep personal interrogation, we also come to see sex as a truth for the individual. Strategies are easily available to recast this truth as an essence: what I do is who I am and what I am is my essential being.

In contrast to this, the other grand narrative of our time—postmodernism—rails against these modernist assumptions and its totebag of essentialisms. However, sex discourse under the siege of postmodernism loses its grounding, as anybody can come to inhabit the interstices of discourse where speaking sex occurs. In speaking, I become one who speaks like that—*one of them* by the power of word. Discourse ontologizes (Susan Bordo, 1990).

I would encourage us to rethink the issue of essentialism that locks these metatheoretical debates. Perhaps in the end a little essentialism is a good thing: to speak the truth about sex as a personal truth and an identity is not to speak with a universal voice but with a voice connected to a real material body. A postmodernist male cannot become a lesbian by talking like one. I encourage us to stay in touch with out bodies however culturally embodied we are. The future of feminist sex inquiry needs to carefully examine the presumptions of postmodernist theorizing before giving up the margins to the agency of discourse.

6. *More Plain Talk.* Finally, we need to talk more about what is done—to whom, by whom, when, why, and how—in sex acts and practices. Typically, academic discourse on sexuality sublimates action into wordiness as a proper conduct for the body. By making explicit what we actually do in sex—more plain talk about it—the mystification regarding sexual categories and sex differences based on sex acts can be more openly scrutinized. However, in a culture where personal sex repertoires are locked away in private, public discourse couched in abstract sexual theory incurs the risk of professing nothing. There is room here for more empirical research, as well as more honesty and/or "bad taste." Feminist theoretical discourse on sex needs to make explicit its investment in hauteur or suspend it and get plain.

BIBLIOGRAPHY

Alcoff, Linda. (1988). Cultural feminism versus poststructuralism: The identity crisis in feminist theory. *Signs, 13*(3), 405–436.

Atkinson, Ti-Grace. (1974). *Amazon odyssey: The first collection of writing by the political pioneer of the women's movement.* New York: Links Books.

Barry, Kathleen. (1979). *Female sexual slavery.* Englewood Cliffs, NJ: Prentice-Hall.

Bell, Laurie (Ed.). (1987). *Good girls/bad girls: Feminist and sex trade workers face to face.* Seattle, WA: Seal Press.

Bleier, Ruth. (1984). *Science and gender: A critique of biology and its theories of women.* Elmsford, NY: Pergamon Press.

Bordo, Susan. (1990). Feminism, postmodernism and gender-skepticism. In Linda Nicholson (Ed.), *Feminism/postmodernism* (pp. 133–156). New York: Routledge.

Bourque, Linda. (1989). *Defining rape.* Durham, NC: Duke University.

Bright, Susie. (1990). *Susie sexpert's lesbian sex world.* Pittsburgh, PA: Cleis Press.

Brown, Jan. (1990, Winter). Sex, Lies, and Penetration. *Outlook,* 30–34.

Brown, Laura S. (1988). Beyond thou shalt not: Thinking about ethics in the lesbian community. *Women and Therapy, 1,* 13–25.

Brownmiller, Susan. (1976). *Against our will: Men, women, and rape.* New York: Simon and Schuster.

Butler, Judith. (1990). *Gender trouble: Feminism and the subversion of identity.* New York: Routledge, Chapman, & Hall.

Califia, Pat. (1979). Lesbian sexuality. *Journal of Homosexuality, 4*(3), 255–266

Califia, Pat. (1980). *Sapphistry: A book of lesbian sexuality.* New York: Naiad Press.

Califia, Pat. (1981). Feminism and sadomasochism. *Heresies, 12* (3/4), 30–34.

Califia, Pat. (1988). *Macho sluts.* Boston: Alyson.

Case, Sue-Ellen. (1988–1989). Towards a butch-femme aesthetic *Discourse, 11*(1), 55–73.

Cass, Vivienne. (1983–1984). Homosexuality identity: A concept in need of definition. *Journal of Homosexuality, 9*(2/3), 105–126.

Chapkis, Wendy. (1986). *Beauty secrets.* Boston: Southend Press.

Chernin, Kim. (1981). *The obsession: Reflections on the tyranny of slenderness.* New York: Harper & Row.

Coward, Rosalind. (1985). *Female desires: How they are sought, bought, and packaged.* New York: Grove Press.

Daly, Mary. (1978). *Gyn/Ecology: The metaethics of radical feminism.* Boston: Beacon Press.

Delacoste, Frederique, & Alexander, Priscilla. (1987). *Sex work: Writings by women in the sex industry.* Pittsburgh, PA: Cleis Press.

de Lauretis, Teresa. (1987). *Technologies of gender: Essays on theory, film, and fiction.* Bloomington, IN: Indiana University Press.

Diamond, Irene, & Quinby, Lee. (1988). *Feminism and Foucault: Reflections on resistance.* Boston: Northeastern University Press.

Diamond, Irene, & Quinby, Lee. (1984). American feminism in the age of the body. *Signs, 10*(1), 119–125.

Dubois, Ellen, & Gordon, Linda. (1983). Seeking ecstasy on the battlefield: Danger and pleasure in nineteenth-century feminist sexual thought. *Feminist Studies, 9*(1), 7–25.

Duggan, Lisa, Hunter, Nan, & Vance, Carole. (1985). False promises: Feminist anti-pornography legislation in the U.S. In Vard Burstyn (Ed.), *Women against censorship (pp. 130–151).* Vancouver, British Columbia: Douglas & McIntyre.

Dworkin, Andrea. (1974). *Woman hating.* New York: Dutton.

Dworkin, Andrea. (1981). *Pornography: Men possessing women.* New York: GP Putnam's Sons.

Dworkin, Andrea. (1987). *Intercourse.* New York: Free Press.

Ellis, Kate, Hunter, Nan, Jaker, Beth, O'Pair, Barbara, & Tallmer, Abby. (1986). *Caught looking: Feminism, pornography, and censorship.* New York: Feminist Against Censorship Taskforce (FACT) Book Committee.

Epstein, Steven. (1987). Gay politics, ethnic identity: The limits of social constructionism. *Socialist Review,* 93/94, 9–54.

Fausto-Sterling, Anne. (1985). *Myths of gender: Biological theories about women and men.* New York: Basic Books.

Ferguson, Ann. (1981). Patriarchy, sexual identity, and the sexual revolution. *Signs, 7*(1), 158–172.

Ferguson, Ann. (1984). Sex war: The debate between radical and libertarian feminists. *Signs, 10*(1), 106–135.

Firestone, Shulamith. (1970). *The dialectics of sex: The case for feminist revolution.* New York: Bantam.

Foucault, Michel. (1978). *The history of sexuality. Vol. I. An introduction.* New York: Random House.

Freedman, Estelle B. (1982, December). Sexuality in nineteenth-century America: Behavior, ideology, and politics. *Reviews in American History,* 196–215.

Friday, Nancy. (1983). *My secret garden.* New York: Simon & Schuster.

Frye, Marilyn. (1988). Lesbian "sex." *Sinister Wisdom, 35,* 46–54.

Frye, Marilyn. (1986). To be and be seen: The politics of reality. *The politics of reality: Essays in feminist theory* (pp. 152–174). Trumansburg, NY: Crossing Press.

Gordon: Linda, & Hunter, Allen. (1978, November). Sex, family, and the new right: Antifeminism as a political force. *Radical America.*

Griffin, Susan. (1981). *Pornography and silence: Culture's revenge against nature.* New York: Harper & Row.

Griffin, Susan. (1979). *Rape: The power of consciousness.* New York: Harper & Row.

Grimshaw, Jean. (1988). Autonomy and identity in feminist thinking. In Morwenna Griffiths & Margaret Whitford (Eds.), *Feminist perspectives in philosophy.* Bloomington, IN: Indiana University Press.

Guber, Susan, & Hoff, Joan (Eds.). *For adults only: The dilemma of violent pornography.* Bloomington, IN: Indiana University Press.

Hamblin, Angela. (1983). Is a feminist heterosexuality possible? In Sue Cartledge & Joanna Ryan (Eds.), *Sex and love: New thoughts on old contradictions* (pp. 105–123). London: The Women's Press.

Harding, Sandra. (1986). *The science question in feminism.* Ithaca, NY: Cornell University Press.

Hoagland, Sarah. (1988). *Lesbian ethics: Toward new value.* Palo Alto, CA: Institute of Lesbian Studies.

Hocquenghem, Guy. (1978). *Homosexual desire.* (Daniella Dangoor, Trans.) London: Allyson & Busby.

Hite, Shere. (1976). *The Hite Report: A nationwide survey of female sexuality.* New York: Dell.

Irigaray, Luce. (1985a). *Speculum of the other woman.* New York: Cornell Press.

Irigaray, Luce. (1985b). *The sex which is not one.* New York: Cornell Press.

Jackson, Margaret. (1987). "Facts of life" or the eroticization of women's oppression? Sexology and the social construction of heterosexuality. In Pat Caplan (Ed.), *The cultural construction of sexuality.* New York: Tavistock Publications.

Jaggar, Alison. (1983). *Feminist politics and human nature.* Totowa, NJ: Rowman & Allanheld.

Jeffreys, Sheila. (1982). Free from all uninvited touch of man: Women's campaigns around sexuality 1880–1914. *Women's Studies International Forum, 5*(6), 629–645.

King, Katie. (1985, Fall). The situation of lesbianism as feminism's magical sign: Contests for meaning and the U.S. Women's Movement, 1968–1972. *Communications, 9*(1), (Fall) 65–91.

Kitzinger, Celia. (1987). *The social construction of lesbianism.* Beverly Hills, CA: Sage.

Koedt, Ann. (1973). The myth of the vaginal orgasm. In Anne Koedt, Ellen Levine & Anita Rapone (Eds.), *Radical feminism.* New York: New York Times Book Company.

Kristeva, Julia. (1980). *Desire in language: A semiotic approach to literature and art.* Oxford: Basil Blackwell.

Lederer, Laura (Ed.). (1981). *Take back the night: Women on pornography.* New York: Dell.

Linden, Robin, Pagano, Darlene, Russell Diana, & Starr, Susan Leigh. (1982). *Against sado masochism.* East Palo Alto, CA: Frog in the Well Press.

Lorde, Audre. (1984). Uses of the erotic: The erotic as power. *Sister outsider* (pp. 53–65). Trumansburg, NY: Crossing Press.

Loulan, Jo Ann. (1984). *Lesbian sex.* San Francisco: Spinsters Ink.

MacKinnon, Catharine. (1982). Feminism, marxism, method, and the state: An agenda for theory. *Signs, 7*(3), 515–544.

MacKinnon, Catharine. (1987a). *Feminism unmodified: Discourses on life and law.* Cambridge, MA: Harvard University Press.

MacKinnon, Catharine. (1987b). Pleasure under patriarchy. In James H. Geer & William O'Donohue (Eds.), *Theories of human sexuality* (pp. 65–90). New York: Plenum Publishing.

MacKinnon, Catharine, & Dworkin, Andrea. (1988). *Pornography and civil rights: A new day for women's equality.* Minneapolis: Organizing Against Pornography.

MacKinnon, Catharine. (1989). *Toward a feminist theory of the state.* Cambridge, MA: Harvard University Press.

Marcuse, Herbert. (1962). *Eros and civilization.* New York: Random House, Vintage Books.

Millet, Kate. (1971). *Sexual politics.* London: Virago.

Mitchell, Juliet, & Rose, Jacqueline (Eds.). (1982). *Feminine sexuality: Jacque Lacan and the ecole freudienne.* New York: Pantheon Books.

Moraga, Cheríe & Hollibaugh, Amber. (1983). What we're rollin around in bed with. In Ann Snitow, Christine Stansell, & Sharon Thompson (Eds.), *Powers of desire: The politics of sexuality.* New York: Monthly Review.

Nestle, Joan. (1987). *A restricted country.* Ithaca, NY: Firebrand Books.

Nichols, Margaret. (1987). Lesbian sexuality: Issues and developing theory. In Boston Lesbian Psychologies Collective (Eds.), *Lesbian psychologies* (97–125). Chicago: University of Illinois Press.

Patton, Cindy. (1985). *Sex and germs: The politics of AIDS.* Boston: Southend Press.

Petchesky, Rosalind. (1981). Antiabortion, antifeminism, and the rise of the new right. *Feminist Studies, 7,* 206–246.

Pharr, Suzanne. (1988). *Homophobia: A weapon of sexism.* Little Rock, AR: Chardon Press.

Pheterson, Gail (Ed.). (1989). *A vindication of the rights of whores.* Seattle, WA: Seal Press.

Plummer, Kenneth. (1981). Homosexual categories: Some research problems in the labelling perspective of homosexuality. In Kenneth Plummer (Ed.), *The making of the modern homosexual.* Totawa, NJ: Barnes & Noble.

Pratt, Minnie Bruce. (1984). Identity: Skin blood heart. In Elly Bulkin, Minnie Bruce Pratt, & Barbara Smith (Eds.), *Yours in struggle: Three feminist perspectives on anti-semitism and racism*. New York: Long Haul Press.

Reich, Wilhelm. (1972). *Sex-pol: Essays, 1929–1934*. New York: Vintage Books.

Rich, Adrienne. (1976). *Of woman born: Motherhood as experience and institution*. New York: W W Norton.

Rich, Adrienne. (1980). Compulsory heterosexuality and lesbian existence. *Signs, 5*(4), 631–660.

Rubin, Gayle. (1975). The traffic in women: Notes on the 'political economy' of sex. In Rayna Reiter (Ed.), *Toward an anthropology of women* (pp. 157–210). New York: Monthly Review.

Rubin, Gayle. (1982). The leather menace: Comments on politics and s/m. In Pat Califia (Ed.), *Coming to power: Writings and graphics on lesbian s/m*. Boston: Alyson.

Rubin, Gayle. (1984). Thinking sex: Notes for a radical theory of the politics of sexuality. In Carole S. Vance (Ed.), *Pleasure and danger: Exploring female sexuality*. Boston, MA: Routledge & Kegan Paul.

Rush, Florence. (1980). *The best kept secret: Sexual abuse of children*. New York: McGraw-Hill.

Russell, Diana. (1975). *The politics of rape: The victim's perspective*. New York: Stein & Day.

Russell, Diana. (1984). *Sexual exploitation*. New York: Russell Sage.

Sayers, Janet. (1982). *Biological politics*. New York: Tavistock Publications.

Scheper-Hughes, Nancy. (1988). The madness of hunger: Sickness, delirium, and human needs. *Culture, Medicine and Psychiatry, 12*, 429–458.

Sedgwick, Eve Kosofsky. (1985). *Between men: English literature and male homosexual desire*. New York: Columbia University Press.

Sherfey, Mary Jane. (1970). A theory on female sexuality. In Robin Morgan (Ed.), *Sisterhood is powerful: Writings from the women's liberation movement*. New York: Vintage.

Seidman, Steven. (1989). Constructing sex as a domain of pleasure and self expression. *Theory, Culture, and Society, 6*, 293–315.

Smith, Dorothy. (1979). A sociology for women. In J. Sherman and E.T. Beck (Eds.), *Prism of sex: Essays in the sociology of knowledge*. Madison: University of Wisconsin.

Snitow, Ann, Stansell, Christine, & Thompson, Sharon (Eds.). (1983). *Powers of desire: The politics of sexuality*. New York: Monthly Review of Books.

Stein, Arlene. (1989, Winter). All dressed up, but no place to go? *Outlook, 34–42*.

St. James, Margo. (1987). The reclamation of whores. In Laurie Bell (Ed.), *Good girls/bad girls: Feminists and sex trade workers face to face*. Seattle: Seal Press.

Stoltenberg, John. (1989). *Refusing to be a man: Essays on sex and justice*. New York: Penguin.

Vance, Carole S. (Ed.). (1984). *Pleasure and danger: Exploring female sexuality*. Boston: Routledge & Kegan Paul.

Vicinus, M. (1982). Sexuality and power: A review of current work in the history of sexuality. *Feminist Studies, 8*, 133–155.

Walkowitz, Judith. (1980). The politics of prostitution. *Signs, 6*, 123–35.

Weeks, Jeffrey. (1985). *Sexuality and its discontents: Meaning, myths, and modern sexuality*. New York: Beacon.

Weeks, Jeffrey. (1986). *Sexuality*. New York: Routledge, Chapman, & Hall.

Wittig, Monique. (1986). *The lesbian body*. Boston: Routledge, Chapman, & Hall.

Zita, Jacquelyn. (1989). *Medical essentialism, erotic speciation, and the problem of theorizing difference and lesbian identity or How to speak as a pervert*. Paper presented at the Center for Advanced Feminist Studies, University of Minnesota.

Zita, Jacquelyn. (1990). Lesbian body journeys: Desire making difference. In Jeffner Allen (Ed.), *Lesbian Philosophies and Cultures* (pp. 327–345). New York: State University of New York Press.

About the Editors and Contributors

ABOUT THE EDITORS

Cheris Kramarae is professor of Speech Communication and Sociology at the University of Illinois at Urbana–Champaign, Illinois, USA. She is the author of *Women and Men Speaking;* editor of *Voices and Words of Women and Men* and *Technology and Women's Voices;* and co-author of *Language, Gender and Society, For Alma Mater, Language and Power: A Feminist Dictionary, Radical Women of the 1850s,* and *The Revolution in Words.* Part of the editing work on *The Knowledge Explosion: Generations of Feminist Scholarship* was done while she was acting director of the Center for the Study of Women in Society at the University of Oregon. Her current research deals with the labels people use to designate differences involving such social classes as race, gender, class, appearance, religion, sexual orientation, and ethnicity.

Dale Spender is the author/editor of 30 books. Her publications include *Man Made Language; Women of Ideas - and what men have done to them; Mothers of the Novel; The Pandora Anthology of British Women Writers* (with Janet Todd); *The Writing or the Sex? or why you don't have to read women's writing to know it's no good; The Diary of Elizabeth Pepys;* and *The Knowledge Explosion: Generations of Feminist Scholarship* (with Cheris Kramarae). She has also written about Australian women writers and is the editor of the Penguin Australian Women's Library and other series. She is currently working on *Talking Comfort: Women's Language;* is researching and writing in the area of the relationship between computers and the literary tradition; and is concerned with the nature of knowledge requirements for the twenty-first century. She would like to live in one place but with her constant companion, her laptop computer.

ABOUT THE CONTRIBUTORS

Joan M. Altekruse, M.D., M.P.H., Dr. P.H. is professor of Preventive Medicine at the University of South Carolina School of Medicine and a fellow of the American College of Preventive Medicine. An active participant in academic, professional, and community medicine organizations, Dr. Altekruse has served as Departmental Chair of Preventive Medicine, Trustee of the American Board of Preventive Medicine, consultant to the National Board of Medical Examiners, president of the Association of Teachers of Preventive Medicine, and President of the American Heart Association South Carolina Affiliate. She works with local and national groups concerned with the advancement of women in higher education and in medicine. Her special interests in research, policy setting, and health care delivery focus on the area of maternal and child health.

Robyn Arianrhod is an Australian, feminist, tarot-reading scientist with a Celtic heritage, a love of the Australian landscape, and an international outlook. She is currently working toward her Ph.D. in the area of General Relativity, and is teaching undergraduate university students in applied mathematics. In the past, she has taught bridging mathematics classes for mature-age women and Aboriginal Australian children, and has taught conventional math classes to both tertiary and secondary students. Robyn has worked (as an assistant social worker) at trying to help economically and socially disadvantaged women take more control of their lives. She has also worked (as a Project Officer) with youth, with whom she founded the alternative magazine Maggie's Farm, which has been in publication over 10 years. She has explored first-hand the tenents of feminism: cooperation rather than competition, creativity rather than consumerism. She is now trying to synthesize these experiences with those to be found in mainstream science in a way that will be mutually beneficial to feminists and scientists.

Susan S. Arpad is a professor in the Women's Studies Program at California State University, Fresno, California, USA. She is a historian with major interests in oral history, regional history, and women's material culture. Susan and her husband Joseph, a folklorist and writer, write books and articles and produce television documentaries about regional history and culture and about the maintenance and changing of cultural and personal consciousness. She is currently in Hungary, where she is working on an oral history project about Hungarian women's lives.

Elise Boulding is professor emerita of Sociology at Dartmouth College and past secretary general of the International Peace Research Association, which she helped to found in the early 1960s. She was also involved in founding the North American Consortium for Peace Education and Development in 1970 and in establishing the section on War and Peace in the American Sociology Association; she was instrumental in the formation of the Research Committee on Women in the society of the International Sociological Association. The International Chairperson of the Women's International League for Peace and Freedom in the late 1960s, she has been a researcher and writer in the fields of women's studies, peace studies, future studies and development studies. She began professional life as a family sociologist and is the mother of five children; the grandmother of fifteen. Elise Boulding received her Ph.D. in sociology from the University of Michigan at the age of 49; her most recent book is *One Small Plot of Heaven: Reflections on Family Life by a Quaker Sociologist.*

Rose Brewer is an associate professor of Afro-American and African Studies at the University of Minnesota. She also has appointments in the Department of Sociology and the Department of Women's Studies. Her research and writings are in race, class, gender, the Black family, social stratification, and Black feminism. She is co-editor with Lisa Albrecht of *Bridges of Power: Women's Multicultural Alliances* and is currently completing a book manuscript entitled *Race, Gender, and Political Economy: The American Case Since the New Deal.*

Mary Ellen S. Capek is a founding officer and currently executive director of the National Council for Research on Women, a 10 year old coalition of research and policy centers in the United States. She is the editor of *A Women's Thesaurus: An Index of Language Used to Describe and Locate Information By and About Women* (1987). She is the former director of the Program in Continuing Education at Princeton University and as the first New Jersey coordinator of the American Council on Education's National Identification Program for the Advancement of Women in Higher Education Administration, she has been active in building women's research and education networks since the early 1970s. Her research and publications have focused on women in higher education administration and governance; linguistics, technology, and writing; and contemporary women's poetry.

Jane Caputi teaches Women's Studies and popular culture in the American Studies department at the University of New Mexico. She is the author of *The Age of Sex Crime,* an analysis of the contemporary atrocity of serial sex murder which won the Emily Toth Award for 1988. She also collaborated with Mary Daly on *Webster's First New Intergalactic Wickedary of the English Language* (1987). Currently, she is writing a book on a female power and the nuclear age.

Berenice A. Carroll is director of Women's Studies and professor of Political Science at Purdue University, where she teaches courses on women and politics, political theory and feminist theory. She served as director of the Women's Studies Program at the University of Illinois at Urbana–Champaign from 1983 to 1987. She has also been an activist for more than 25 years in the peace movement and the women's movement. She is author and editor of many books, articles, journal volumes, and other publications, and is currently completing work on a book entitled *Minerva in the Shadows: The Political and Social Thought of Women.*

Carol P. Christ was the founder of the Women's Caucus—Religious Studies and one of its original co-chairs, the co-chair of the Women and Religion Section, and a member of the American Academy of Religion's National Program Committee. She is author of *Laughter of Aphrodite* and *Diving Deep and Surfacing* and co-editor of *Womanspirit Rising* and *Weaving the Visions.* In 1987, despairing of finding a suitable position in Religious Studies, tired of teaching introductory feminism, and in love with Greece, she resigned a tenured professorship in Women's Studies at San Jose State University and moved to Lesbos where she wrote *A Year of Seasons,* the story of her life in a Greek village. She currently lives in Athens.

Jennifer Craik teaches Media and Cultural Studies in the Division of Humanities, Griffith University, in Brisbane, Australia. She is currently Deputy Director of the Institute for Cultural Policy Studies at Griffith University. She studied Social and Political Sciences at the Australian National University and the University of Cambridge. Her research interests include aspects of cultural policy, including media and politics, fashion and sexuality, and tourism.

Patricia Cramer teaches English and is the coordinator of the Women's Studies Program at the University of Connecticut at Stamford. She is currently working on a book on Virginia Woolf.

Suzanne K. Damarin teaches in the Department of Educational Policy and Leadership at Ohio State University. Her current work focuses on the articulation of feminist ideas and theories with education in mathematics, sciences, and technology. She is especially interested in the implications of computer and information technologies for feminist features.

Irene Diamond teaches political science at the University of Oregon in Eugene, Oregon, USA where she lives with three generations of her family and is active in Green Politics. Her most recent books are *Feminism and Foucault: Reflections on Resistance* (1988), co-edited with Lee Quinby, and *Reweaving the World: The Emergence of Ecofeminism* (1990) co-edited with Gloria Orenstein. She is currently working on a book entitled, *Resisting the Logic of Control: Feminism, Fertility and the Living Earth.*

Micaela di Leonardo teaches in the Department of Anthropology and the Women's Studies Program at Northwestern University. She has written *The Varieties of Ethnic Experience: Kinship, Class, and Gender among California Italian-Americans* and is editor of *Gender at the Crossroads of Knowledge: Feminist Anthropology in the Postmodern Era.* She is currently completing a book on gender, class, and race in the American past and present and is working (with Adolph Reed) on field research on race, gender, and class in New Haven, Connecticut.

Marilyn Frye teaches Philosophy and Women's Studies at Michigan State University, and is actively involved in local lesbian community work. She is the author of *The Politics of Reality: Essays in Feminist Theory* (1983). A recent work is a talk "Do you have to be a lesbian to be a feminist?" prepared for a plenary session of the National Women's Studies Association conference in 1990, and published in the *off our backs* August/September issue.

H. Patricia Hynes is professor of environmental policy at M.I.T. and director of the Institute on Women and Technology. An environmental engineer, she was section chief in the Hazardous Waste Division of the U.S. Environmental Protection Agency and chief of Environmental Management at the Massachusetts Port Authority. She is author of *The Recurring Silent Spring* (Pergamon, 1989); *Reconstructing Babylon: Women and Technology* (Indiana University, 1990); and *Earth Right* (Prima/St. Martin's, 1990).

Jane S. Jaquette is professor of Political Science at Occidental College, Los Angeles, California, USA. In 1974 she edited *Women in Politics,* the first comparative anthology on the subject, and has since published extensively on international feminist issues. Her most recent book is *The Women's Movement in Latin America: Feminism and the Transition to Democracy,* which includes articles by Latin American as well as North American scholars. She is currently serving as president of the U.S.-based Association for Women in Development (AWID), and writing a feminist analysis of the concept of power in Western political thought.

Susanne Kappeler teaches feminist theory and literary studies in England. She is also a member of the editorial collective of the British radical feminist magazine *Trouble & Strife.* Relevant publications include *The Pornography of Representation* (1986) as well as articles on pornography and related issues in feminist and other publications. She is also a feminist activist.

Renate Klein has a biology degree from Zurich University and degress in Women's Studies and education from the University of California at Berkeley and London University. She is co-editor with Maresi Nerad and Sigrid Metz-Gockel of *Feministische Wissenschaft und Frauenstudium* (1982) and with Gloria Bowles of *Theories of Women's Studies* (1983). With Rita Arditti and Shelley Minden, she co-edited *Test-Tube Women: What Future for Motherhood?* (1984/89) and with Gena Corea and colleagues *Man Made Women* (1985). She is a co-founding member of the Feminist International Network of Resistance to Reproductive and Genetic Engineering (FINNRAGE) and an editor of *Issues in Reproductive and Genetic Engineering: Journal of International Feminist Analysis.* She edited *Infertility: Women Speak Out About Their Experiences of Reproductive Medicine* (1989). She has served as the Post-Doctoral Research Fellow in Women's Studies at Deakin University in Australia and as a Distinguished Visiting Professor in Women's Studies at San Diego State University, USA. Her new research projects are feminist investigations into menopause specifically with regard to the administration of hormone replacement therapy, and her latest book is *RU486: Misconceptions, Myths, and Morals* (1991), with Janice Raymond and Lynette Dumble.

Jane Lewis is a professor of Social Policy at the London School of Economics. Her research interests are in the history of social policy and in women and social policy. She is the author of *The Politics of Motherhood* (1980), *Women in England, 1870–1950* (1984). *What Price Community Medicine?* (1986), and *Daughters Who Care* (1988) with Barbara Meredith. She is currently working on a study of marriage guidance in the post-war period and on the work of late nineteenth- and early twentieth-century women social reformers.

Marian Lowe was for many years a member of the Chemistry Department and of the Women's Studies faculty at Boston University. She has long been interested in the social implications of scientific research, particularly the role science plays in shaping ideas about women and women's roles in society. Her current interests are in the interactions of science and gender and with the social and environmental consequences of these. She is presently living in Seattle and working on a book about science, gender, and power.

María C. Lugones is an Argentinian feminist philosopher, grass-roots organizer, and educator. She is developing a nonracist feminism which she calls "pluralist feminism." Maria is the author of *Playfulness, World-Travelling and Loving Perception* and co-author with Elizabeth Spelman of the essay *Have we got a theory for you?* She teaches at Carleton College in Minnesota, and at La Escuela Popular Nortena, a grass-roots center for radical political education in northern New Mexico.

Joan E. Mulligan is emeritus professor, School of Nursing, and emeritus professor (affiliate), Program in Women's Studies at the University of Wisconsin-Madison, Wisconsin, USA. She received her Bachelor of Arts from Queens University in Kingston, Ontario, Canada, her Masters in Nursing from Yale University, her Master of Science and Master of Public Health from the University of California San Francisco and Berkeley, California, USA, and her Ph.D. from the University of Michigan, Ann Arbor, Michigan, USA. She works as a consultant to Women's Health Graduate Programs and has published in *Nursing Outlook, American Journal of Public Health, Women and Health, Journal of Nursing Administration,* and other journals.

Carole A. Oglesby is a professor of physical education at Temple University, Philadelphia, Pennsylvania, and is completing a second doctorate in counseling psychology. Dr. Oglesby received her Ph.D. from Purdue University in 1969 and has worked for over 20 years in the area of gender identity and sport. She has authored a text in this area, published in English and French. She is a fellow of the Association for the Advancement of Applied Sport Psychology and a former president of the NASPE Sport Psychology Academy. She has served as an educational sport psychology consultant with numerous teams and has presented workshops extensively both nationally and internationally. She is a member of the USOC Board of Directors and a trustee of the Women's Sports Foundation.

Barbara Pope is a historian, and associate professor and director of the Honors Program at the University of Oregon. Most of her previous work has dealt with the history of women and of religion in modern France, although she recently co-scripted a documentary film on a Sicilian procession and has headed a campus-wide project to integrate materials about women of color into humanities and social science survey courses that deal with the United States.

Lana F. Rakow is an assistant professor of communications at the University of Wisconsin at Parkside, Wisconsin, USA. She is the co-editor with Cheris Kramarae of *The Revolution in Words: Righting Women 1868-1871* (1990) and has conducted an ethnographic study of women's relationship to the telephone, *Gender on the Line: Women, the Telephone, and Community Life,* University of Illinois Press. Her most recent book is *Women Making Meaning.* She has spent the past few years trying to be a feminist thorn in the side of the field of communication research.

Shulamit Reinharz was born in Amsterdam and raised in the United States. She is associate professor of Sociology at Brandeis University in Waltham, Massachusetts, USA. Currently she teaches courses in gerontology, group dynamics, qualitative research methods, and the history of women in sociology. She is married to a historian and is the mother of two daughters. Her fifth book, *Feminist Methods in Social Research,* written with the assistance of Lynn Davidman, will be published in 1991 by Oxford University Press. She has been actively involved in the debate about feminist research for many years.

Lillian S. Robinson is visiting professor of English and American Studies at the University of Texas, Austin, and affiliated scholar at the Institute for Research on Women and Gender, Stanford University. She has held chairs at the University of Hawaii, San Diego State University, Scripps College, Albright College, and the University of Paris, and has also held appointments at the Tulsa Center for the Study of Women's Literature, the Wellesley College Center for Research on Women, the State University of New York at Buffalo, the Massachusetts Institute of Technology, and Columbia University. Her books include, *Sex, Class, and Culture* (1978, reissued 1986), *Monstrous Regiment* (1985) and, as co-author, *Feminist Scholarship: Kindling in the Groves of Academe* (1985). Her articles have appeared in many journals, and she is a frequent contributor to *The Nation* and *The Women's Review of Books.*

Pat Alake Rosezelle is a feminist, activist, and teacher. She taught at the A.C.M. Urban

Studies Program in Chicago, Illinois, USA, for the last 15 years. She is currently engaged in establishing an institute of political theory and practice for academics and organizers in New Orleans, Louisiana, USA.

Sue V. Rosser, Ph.D., is director of Women's Studies at the University of South Carolina at Columbia, and also holds an appointment as Professor of Preventive Medicine and Community Health in the USC Medical School. She has authored several publications dealing with theoretical and applied problems of women and science and authored the books *Teaching Science and Health from a Feminist Perspective: A Practical Guide* (1986), *Feminism Within the Science and Health Care Professions: Overcoming Resistance* (1988), *Female-Friendly Science: Applying Women's Studies Methods and Theories to Attract Students* (1990), and *Feminism and Biology* (in press). She has worked with faculty at many institutions that are attempting to include the new scholarship on women in the science curriculum.

Ann Russo teaches "Violence Against Women: A Social and Cultural Heritage" at the Massachusetts Institute of Technology. Her major political and research interests include creating feminist courses, programs, actions, and analyses around sexual violence against women, and addressing the intersections and complexities of sex, race, ethnicity, class, and sexuality. She is working on a book on the feminist debates over pornography and the civil rights antipornography legislation proposed by Andrea Dworkin and Catharine MacKinnon. She was an assistant on *A Feminist Dictionary* and co-editor with Cheris Kramarae of *The Radical Women's Presses of the 1850s* (1990) and co-editor with Chandra Talpade Mohanty and Lourdes Torres of *Third World Women and Feminist Perspectives* (1991).

Claudia Salazar is a graduate student in the Department of Speech Communication at the University of Illinois, Urbana–Champaign. Her dissertation work involves the collection and analysis of life-history narratives of Latin American women in order to understand the ways in which they construct their identities and places in light of broader political, economic, and cultural discourses.

Jocelynne A. Scutt graduated from the University of Western Australia in 1969 and did postgraduate studies in law at the Universities of Sydney, Michigan, and Cambridge. She also spent a year in West Germany at the Max Plank Institute for Criminal Law. She has been research criminologist with the Australian Institute of Criminology, director of research with the Victorian Parliamentary Legal and Constitutional Committee, and commissioner and deputy chairperson of the Law Reform Commission, Victoria. From 1982 to 1983 she was associate to his Honor Justice Lionel Murphy of the High Court of Australia. Her many books include *Rape Law Reform* (1980), *Violence in the Family* (1980), *For Richer, For Poorer—Money, Marriage, and Property Rights* (1984, with Di Graham), *Growing Up Feminist—The New Generation of Australian Women* (1985), *The Baby Machine—The Commercialisation of Motherhood* (1988) and *Women and the Law* (1990). Jocelynne Scutt has long been active in the Women's Movement in Sydney and Canberra, and more recently in Melbourne.

Joni Seager isa Canadian, now living in Boston, Massachusetts. She is a feminist geographer, and focuses on urban design and issues of housing and homelessness for women. She is currently writing a book on feminism and environmental politics, *Earth Follies:*

Making Feminist Sense of Environmental Issues (1992). She is the author of an international environmental atlas *(The State of the Earth: An International Atlas of Environmental Concerns,* (1991). She is co-author of *Women in the World: An International Atlas* (1986). She teaches in the Women's Studies program at the Massachusetts Institute of Technology, where she was previously the Coordinator, and is also a member of the New Words Bookstore Collective, the largest and one of the oldest feminist bookstores in the United States.

Susan E. Searing is the Acting Deputy Director of the General Library System, University of Wisconsin—Madison. She previously served as Women's Studies Librarian for the fourteen universities that comprise the University of Wisconsin System. Ms. Searing is the author of *Introduction to Library Research in Women's Studies* (1985) and co-author of *Women's Studies: A Recommended Core Bibliography, 1980–1985* (1987), along with many articles on library services in women's studies.

Christine M. Shelton is an assistant professor in the Department of Exercise Science and Sport at Smith College in Northampton, Massachusetts, USA. A graduate of James Madison University for both the baccalaureate and master's degree, Ms. Shelton has been named to that University's Athletic Hall of Fame and the 1988 Alumni of the Year. Ms. Shelton was a Peace Corps volunteer in Venezuela for 2 years and then served as a trainer for the Peace Corps. Upon returning to the United States, she was named the head of the National Association for Girls and Women in Sport (NAGWS) Latin American Project, founded in 1979 and still continuing. Christine also served as President and acting executive director of NAGWS. In addition to her full time positions and volunteer efforts, Christine has spent the last 10 years both writing and facilitating workshops in the area of race and sex equity in sports. She has coached at all levels including women's and men's collegiate teams, and is currently developing a specialized coaching and Women's Studies master's degree program at Smith College.

Autumn Stanley is an independent scholar in the history of technology, particularly interested in gender roles and women's contributions to invention and innovation. For the past 12 years, she has been researching and writing a book on women inventors, and publishing articles on the same and related subjects. She is currently researching a biography of a nineteenth-century magazine editor, labor leader, and reformer named Charlotte Smith—who was an advocate for women inventors and wanted to write a book about them 100 years ago—and planning a biographical dictionary of nineteenth-century American women inventors. From 1984 to 1988 she was an affiliated scholar with the Institute for Research on Women and Gender at Stanford University. She is a member of the Institute for Historical Study.

Liz Stanley has taught in the Sociology Department at the University of Manchester since 1977. She is working class by birth, a northerner in England by choice and a lesbian by luck. Most recently, her research and writing interests have focused on feminist auto/biography and on historical topics, and she's currently researching some aspects of the Mass-Observation presence in Bolton, England, in the 1930s. Her central feminist and sociological interest is with the diverse processes by which "knowledge" is produced and contested. Publications include *Breaking Out: Feminist Consciousness and Feminist Research* (1983,

2nd Edition, 1992 with Sue Wise), *The Diaries of Hannah Cullwick, Georgie Porgie: Sexual Harassment in Everyday Life* (1987, with Sue Wise), *The Life and Death of Emily Wilding Davision* (1988), *Feminist Praxis: Theory, Research & Epistemology in Feminist Sociology* (1990), and the *The Auto/Biographical I* (1992).

Patricia J. Thompson, born in New York City, is professor of Women's Studies and Family and Consumer Studies (Home Economics) at Lehman College of the City University of New York. She graduated from Barnard College and attended Columbia's Graduate School of Public Law and Government. She later received Master of Arts, Master of Education, and Doctor of Education degrees from Teachers College, Columbia University, and a Master of Science degree in Home Economics Education from Lehman College in New York City, New York, USA. Co-author of *Self, Space, and Shelter* and *Nutrition Issues for the 1980s,* she is senior author of the textbook trilogy *Teens in Action, Resources for Living,* and *Lifeplans.* The first life member of NWSA (National Women's Studies Association), Pat is active in both Women's Studies and Home Economics professional organizations. Her latest book is *Home Economics and Feminism: The Hestian Synthesis.* Her research interests emphasize equity, ethics, epistemology, and women's educational needs, and she has lectured internationally on Hestian feminism and on Home Economics as a Hestian discipline of everyday life.

Lourdes Torres teaches linguistics and Spanish at the University of Kentucky. Her research interests include sociolinguistics, Spanish varieties, and women and language. Her articles have appeared in the *International Journal of the Sociology of Language, World Englishes,* and in books on U.S. Spanish. She is co-editor (with Chandra Talpade Mohanty and Ann Russo) of the *Third World Women and Feminist Perspectives.*

Mary Roth Walsh is University Professor of Psychology at the University of Massachusetts in Lowell, Massachusetts, USA. She has published two books on women, *Doctors Wanted: No Women Need Apply* (1977) and *The Psychology of Women: Ongoing Debates* (1987). An instructor's manual, which includes an annotated bibliography on teaching the psychology of women course and a guide to the 14 debates in the field is also available: *Study Guide to the Debates* (1988). The chapter in this book is part of her larger project of advancing the field of the psychology of women and this includes workshops on teaching which she has been organizing and chairing for the past several years. A new research area she is developing is gender and conflict management and she has a special research interest in women's anger, and academic women's negotiation of conflict.

Marilyn J. Waring is a farmer and writer. Her Ph.D. is in Political Economy and she is a senior lecturer in Politics at the University of Waikato, New Zealand. She served three terms as a member of the New Zealand Parliament (1975–1984) and is an international consultant; her "statistical strategy" has been adopted by women's organizations in Australia, Brazil, Canada, Egypt, New Zealand, the Phillipines, and the United States. Her recent book is *If Women Counted: A New Feminist Economics* (1989).

Leslie Kanes Weisman is associate professor and past associate dean of the School of Architecture at the New Jersey Institute of Technology. Her latest book is *Discrimination by Design: A Feminist Critique of the Man Made Environment.* She is among the founding coordinators of Sheltering Ourselves: A Women's Learning Exchange, an international education forum on women's housing issues, ongoing since 1987.

Elizabeth Wood is a musicologist and novelist who teaches Lesbian and Gay Studies at Sarah Lawrence College. She has published essays and reviews of nineteenth and twentieth century women's music and autobiography, British and Australian music and opera, and musical representations of gender and sexuality. She is completing a study of the English composer Ethel Smyth for Bloomsbury Publishing of London.

Maxine Baca Zinn is professor of Sociology at Michigan State University where she is also senior research associate in the Julian Samora Research Institute. She is the co-author of *Diversity in Families* (1990) a textbook that demythologizes the family and shows how public issues shape the private lives of a population varied in class, race, and gender, and co-editor of *The Reshaping of America* (1989), a volume examining the social consequences of the changing economy (both with D. Stanley Eitzen). With Bonnie Thornton Dill, she is co-editing a collection of social science works on women of color (in press).

Jacquelyn N. Zita is an associate professor of Women's Studies at the University of Minnesota. She is coordinating editor of the newsletter "Matrices: a Lesbian Feminist Resource and Research Network" and currently Executive Secretary of the Midwest Society for Women in Philosophy. She is finishing a collection of essays on theorizing the body as it travels through the tunnels of postmodernism, history, ideology, and the joys of sex and gender.

Index

medical investigation, 29
division of labor, 4
international, 452
between women and men, 450
divisions within feminism, 145,
148
divorce, no-fault, 148
Dix, Linda, 162
Dizinno, Gerard, 344
Dobash, R. Emerson, 340
doctoral programs, nursing, 176
documentation, 4
dogmas, 5–6
Doing Feminist Research, 260
domestic architecture, 93
domestic labor debate, 156
domestic sphere, 121
domestic workers, 345
domesticity, 93
dominance, 2
difference as, 419
English feminist analysis, 416
sex as, 418
domination
as characteristic of science, 166
male, 397–405
Marxist analysis of, 416
Donnerstein, Edward, 345
Donovan, Josephine, 78, 293
double consciousness, 286
double-edged success, 2
double standard, 137, 236, 343,
358
in knowledge making, 8
in science achievements, 41
Douglas, Ann, 93
Dowell, David R., 227
Downing, Christine, 84
dowry murders, 340
Draine, Betsy, 79
Dreyfus, Hubert L., 362
Dreyfus, Stuart E., 362
Drinker, Sophie, 325
drugs, 10
Dryden, Sherre H., 230
d'Souza, Corinne Kumar, 57, 375
dual systems of capitalism and
patriarchy, 416
dualism, 358
and western thought, 43
dualistic structure of the academy,
181
DuBois, Ellen Carol, 75, 428,
439, 480
du Chatelet, Emile, 467n
Duchen, Claire, 146, 149
duelling as intellectual rigor, 129
Duggan, Lisa, 346, 487
DuMont, Paul, 228

DuMont, Rosemary Ruhig, 227,
228
Duquin, M., 185
Durkheim, Emile, 258
Dworkin, Andrea, 122, 193, 203,
340, 344, 345, 346, 380,
419, 480, 482, 486, 487
Dworsky, Nancy, 163
Dyer, K., 185
Dyer, Richard, 94
Dyhouse, Carol, 235
Dynamos & Virgins Revisited,
460
dysmenorrhea, 34

Eagleton, Mary, 79
Easlea, Brian, 166
East, Catherine, 193
East, Marjorie, 270
Eastern Africa, 99
eclipse of women's meanings, 19
ecofeminism, 6, 10, 14, 371–378
and ambiguities, 377
and essentialism, 375
global concerns, 373–374
and human agency, 375
and language, 375
origins of, 372
and postmodernism, 375
as reconstruction, 373
theory of, 376
as transformation of feminism,
374–375
ecological crisis, 57
ecological movement, 373–374
ecological world view, 241
ecology, 5, 136, 272–273
economic activity, definition of,
306
economic analysis, 307, 308
economic dependency, 142
economic policies, impact on
women, 307–308
economic statistics, 10
economic theory, 303
economic values, 306–307
Economics, 303–309
defining the discipline, 304
feminists in, 305
future research directions,
307–308
and mathematics, 303
political, 303
economy, women's experience of,
304
editorial experiences, 18
editorial guidelines used in this
book, 19–20
editorial limitations, 16

education
as cohesive discipline, 235
definition of, 235
erasure of women's history
within, 238
medical, resistance to for
women, 155
for men, 12
and miseducation of physicists,
41
traditional, 13
women's entry into, 235–253
educational achievement, 425
educational campaigns, 235
educational computing, 366
educational hierarchy and inverse
influence of women, 236
Edwards, Anne, 341, 342, 343
Edwards, Susan S. M., 203, 259
Eggleton, Richard, 227
Ehrenreich, Barbara, 165, 399,
452, 467n
Ehrlich, Carol, 424
Eicher, Joanne, 273
Eichler, Margrit, 257, 259, 263,
263
Einsiedel, Edna F., 192
Einstein and objectivity, 43
Eisenberg, Sue E., 202
Eisenstein, Hester, 296
Eisenstein, Zillah, 145, 148, 398,
417
Eisler, Riane, 57
Elbers, Doris, 59
El Dareer, Asma, 340
Elder, Ruth, 175
electronic media, 7
electronic literature searches, 183
Elion, Gertrude, 465, 466
Eliot, George, 427
elite-only level bias in sport
research, 186
Elliott, Rogers, 298
Ellis, Kate, 481
Ellman, R. Amy, 346
Ellmann, Mary, 72, 439
Elms, Alan, 423
El Saadawi, Nawal, 340
Elshtain, Jean Bethke, 145, 276
emancipation of women, 22
embryo biopsy, 388
Emma Sonderband, 385
emotional response of men, 10
empiricism, 144
employment of feminists, in
journalism and mass
communication, 196
empowerment of women, 13
through body knowledge, 29